POLITICS, POWER AND

AN INTRODUCTION TO POLITICAL SCIENCE

THE COMMON GOOD

POLITICS, POWER AND

AN INTRODUCTION TO POLITICAL SCIENCE

THE COMMON GOOD

Eric Mintz   Sir Wilfred Grenfell College, Memorial University of Newfoundland

David Close   Memorial University of Newfoundland

Osvaldo Croci   Memorial University of Newfoundland

PEARSON

Prentice
Hall

Toronto

Library and Archives Canada Cataloguing in Publication

Mintz, Eric
   Politics, power and the common good : an introduction to political
science / Eric Mintz, David Close, Osvaldo Croci.

Includes bibliographical references and index.
ISBN 0-13-121218-4

1. Political science. I. Close, David, 1945– II. Croci, Osvaldo III. Title.

JA66.M55 2005   320   C2004-906817-2

Copyright © 2006 Pearson Education Canada Inc., Toronto, Ontario

ISBN 0-13-121218-4

Vice-President, Editorial Director: Michael J. Young
Executive Editor: Christine Cozens
Marketing Manager: Cynthia Smith
Senior Developmental Editor: Lise Dupont
Production Editor: Charlotte Morrison-Reed
Substantive Editor: Cheryl Cohen
Copy Editor: Lesley Mann
Proofreader: Laurel Sparrow
Senior Production Coordinator: Peggy Brown
Manufacturing Coordinator: Susan Johnson
Page Layout: Phyllis Seto
Photo Research: Sandy Cooke
Art Director: Mary Opper
Cover and Interior Design: Michelle Bellemare
Cover Image: Masterfile

Statistics Canada information is used with the permission of the Minister of Industry, as Minister responsible for Statistics Canada. Information on the availability of the wide range of data from Statistics Canada can be obtained from Statistics Canada's Regional Offices, its World Wide Web site at http://www.statcan.ca, and its toll-free access number 1-800-263-1136.

2 3 4 5   10 09 08 07 06

Printed and bound in the USA.

To my parents, Sidney and Sally Mintz

E.M.

To family, friends, and those who use this book

D.C.

To Livianna

O.C.

BRIEF CONTENTS

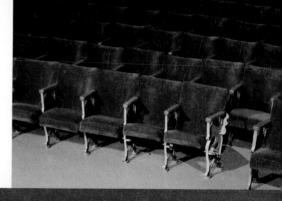

CONTENTS

PREFACE

In our many years of teaching introductory courses in political science, we have found that some students come to our classes with considerable knowledge and interest in politics. They are excited about developing a solid framework for their understanding of political issues and enthused about the knowledge not just of Canada but of other countries and cultures that they acquire in their introductory course. Other students, however, have a limited level of interest, and their knowledge about politics—even the basics of how their own country is governed—is very sketchy before they take a political science course. Similarly, while some young people are actively engaged in political life, many others feel that politics is something that does not really concern them—at least until a seemingly inexplicable terrorist attack occurs, or a large increase in university tuition fees motivates their desire to take some kind of action.

Politics is a fascinating subject and one that affects all of our lives. We decided to write this textbook in order to provide students with an interesting, easy-to-read, and straightforward introduction to politics. Our goal has been to offer a clear explanation of the basics of politics for those with little or no background, while at the same time raising challenging questions that will encourage all students to think deeply about the contemporary political world. Although it is important to understand the politics and governing of our own country, globalization is making it equally important to understand what is happening in the world at large and how this affects our lives in Canada.

Some students are turned off by politics because they see it as an activity involving people who seek personal benefits or glory. The overblown rhetoric, distortions, and lies of government leaders, the exaggerations and unfulfilled promises of the politicians who seek our votes, and the violence and wars that have been justified with political ideals are certainly sufficient to lead us to a skeptical view of politics.

However, there is another side to the story. Politics can and should also be about how we might best achieve what is good for our communities and the world as a whole. Humanity faces many important challenges—for example, how to establish and expand human rights, protect the environment, reduce poverty, and create a more peaceful world. Political actions and decisions are very important in dealing with such challenges. In order to act effectively in political life, it is essential to understand how the political world works. We need to examine different views about how political communities should be organized and the values they should pursue.

In this book, we provide the basic knowledge that every citizen should have—from understanding the political parties that seek our votes to the way that Canada's parliamentary system works. But politics is about more than the institutions of governing. As you read this text, you will learn about the contending perspectives that are used to understand the world, different economic systems, the problems of the five-sixths of the world that lives in poverty, the global political system of the twenty-first century, and much more.

The authors of this book do not claim to have all of the answers to political problems. Nor do we want to promote a particular political perspective. Instead, our goal is to introduce our readers to the analysis of politics and government and raise important political questions to ponder and discuss.

The pedagogy of this text has been carefully developed. For example:

- A unique feature of this book is the *vignettes* that open each chapter, with an interesting and often provocative story that relates to the content of the chapter. Among the vignettes are the 1960s "bra-burning" at the Miss America pageant, the strange election that made Arnold Schwarzenegger governor of California, and Canada's turbot war with Spain.
- *Boxes* in each chapter offer special focus on key theoretical issues and provide global and Canadian examples. These boxes deal with such topics as the conflict between Israel and the Palestinians, media coverage of the invasion of Iraq, and Canada's health care system.
- To help students effectively structure their reading, we have provided *Chapter Objectives* at the start and a *Summary and Conclusion* at the end of each chapter.
- *Key terms* are printed in bold in the text, defined in the margin for instant reference, and compiled in the end-of-book Glossary.
- The *Discussion Questions* at the end of each chapter are designed to spark critical thought and discussion.
- The *Further Reading* section, also at the end of each chapter, steers students towards references that will expand their understanding of the chapter's topics. *Web links* in the margins provide additional research resources.
- The text's *graphics*—photos, figures, tables, and cartoons—are sure to illuminate concepts discussed in the text and capture students' interest.

This book originated as a course manual for an introduction to politics class taught by Eric Mintz. David Close and Osvaldo Croci generously agreed to add their expertise to the book's development by drafting Chapters 12, 18, and 19 (Close) and Chapter 20 (Croci) and also contributing to other aspects of the book. Although this textbook is the product of three different authors, we have tried to maintain a consistent tone and style throughout and attempted to avoid the overlap and inconsistencies that can sometimes occur in multi-authored books.

ACKNOWLEDGEMENTS

Writing a textbook is somewhat of a parasitic activity. We have ransacked the books and articles of our esteemed colleagues for ideas that we hope we have explained in an interesting and accessible way to readers unfamiliar with the theories and jargon of the discipline. We have attempted to cite what we have borrowed from the extensive literature of political science and related disciplines. If we have overlooked someone's contributions, we extend our apologies and ask that we be informed so that proper acknowledgement can be made in the next edition.

We would like to thank the many political science professors who provided detailed and helpful suggestions in reviewing draft chapters for Pearson Education Canada. Among these reviewers were the following individuals (in alphabetical order):

Cameron D. Bodnar,
Mount Allison University

Duanne Bratt,
Mount Royal College

Bruce Foster,
Mount Royal College

Joan Grace,
University of Winnipeg

Malcolm Grieve,
Acadia University

Ann Griffiths,
Dalhousie University

Karl A. Henriques,
University of Regina

Harold Jansen,
University of Lethbridge

Doug Long,
University of Western Ontario

Chaldeans Mensah,
Grant MacEwan College

Hugh Mellon,
University of Western Ontario

Nigmendra Narain,
University of Western Ontario

Mark Neufeld,
Trent University

Tracy Summerville,
University of Northern British Columbia

John Sutcliffe,
University of Windsor

Cam Sylvester,
Capilano College

Philip Resnick, University of British Columbia

Jonathan Rose, Queen's University

Alan Whitehorn, Royal Military College

E. Lori Williams, Mount Royal College.

We would also like to thank the many people at Pearson Education Canada whose professional expertise and enthusiasm have been essential in developing this text. In particular, we would like to thank Lori Will, Sponsoring Editor; Lise Dupont, Senior Developmental Editor; Christine Cozens, Executive Editor; Charlotte Morrison-Reed, Production Editor; Michelle Bellemare, Senior Designer; substantive editor Cheryl Cohen; and copy editor Lesley Mann. Finally, we would like to thank Tami Thirlwell, whose original cartoons were specially designed for this book.

Eric Mintz would like to thank student assistants Dale Haynes, Lisa Cullihall, Natalie Payne, and Stephanie Balsom. Special thanks go to Dr. Nick Novakowski. who provided comments on a number of draft chapters. Most importantly, Diane Mintz carefully read and suggested improvements for each of the drafts of this book. She also provided a greatly appreciated and comfortable home environment during the lengthy writing process. His daughter Kaila and son Aaron, both of whom have a keen interest in politics, provided much inspiration and encouragement. Beethoven provided much-needed relief from the stresses of writing.

David Close would like to thank Sherrill Pike for reading and commenting on the chapters that he drafted. He also appreciates the support of the Political Science Department at Memorial University of Newfoundland for his work.

Osvaldo Croci would like to thank his colleagues at Memorial University for making the atmosphere in the Political Science Department enjoyable, professional, and ideal for research.

We look forward to receiving comments and suggestions from students, teaching assistants, professors, and other readers to help us in writing the next edition. Please send comments to emintz@swgc.ca with the subject line "politics text."

INTRODUCTION

Chapter 1

UNDERSTANDING POLITICS

PHOTO ABOVE: Tens of thousands of protesters demonstrated at the Third Summit of the Americas in Quebec City, 2001. Protesters argued that the free trade pact would give private corporations the right to provide key public services.

CHAPTER OBJECTIVES

After reading this chapter you should be able to:

1. discuss the importance of politics
2. explain why conflict is a major feature of politics
3. define the concepts of power, authority, and legitimacy
4. discuss whether seeking the common good is a meaningful goal of political life
5. describe political science, its subfields, and types of analysis

Tens of thousands of protesters demonstrated in Quebec City in April 2001 as government leaders and officials from thirty-four countries met to discuss the establishment of a free-trade area that would include almost all of North and South America. Generally, the protestors were peaceful. However, some of the youthful protestors hurled teddy bears, rocks, and other objects across the 3.8-kilometre-long chain-link fence that had been erected to keep protestors out of the centre of Quebec City, where the Summit of the Americas was being held. Police responded with tear gas, pepper spray, plastic bullets, and stun guns. About four hundred protesters were arrested. Fifty-seven protesters and forty-five police officers were hurt—none seriously, fortunately.

The protest was part of the anti-globalization movement that had shut down meetings of the World Trade Organization in Seattle in 1999 and continues to demonstrate at the meetings of various international organizations committed to developing a global free market capitalist economy. The Quebec City protesters—including students, environmentalists, trade unionists, social activists, and nationalists from many countries, but especially from across Canada— argued that the proposed Free Trade Area of the Americas (FTAA) agreement would give private, profit-oriented corporations the right to provide such public services as education and health care and reduce governments' power to protect the environment and workers.

The events at Quebec City illustrate some important features of the nature of politics. For example, exaggeration is commonplace as interested parties struggle to affect public opinion. Members of the general public who tried to make sense of the Quebec City events received very different interpretations from government, protesters, and the media. The Canadian government claimed that the summit was a major step toward ensuring democracy throughout the Americas. On the other hand, many protesters asserted that the terms of a free-trade agreement would subvert democracy in the interests of big corporations. The mass media highlighted the clashes between protestors and police, but generally devoted little attention to the arguments for and against the proposed free-trade agreement.

Clearly, politics involves not only governments, legislatures, and politicians, but a wide range of groups and individuals. There are almost always differences of opinion, values, and perspective, as we discuss in this chapter.

POLITICS AND CONFLICT

Conflict and disagreement are basic features of politics, as exhibited, for example, in the dispute over the FTAA. Politics is concerned with making policies for a political community. There are three major reasons why it is often characterized by conflict:

- people have different interests
- people embrace different values
- people struggle for power in the political arena

Different Interests

The policies that are adopted for a political community often benefit (or harm) some members of the political community more than others. For example, the business community generally supports free trade because it expects to benefit by having better access to larger markets for its goods and services. Business executives like the fact that free-trade agreements can limit governments' ability to pass laws and regulations that restrict trade and investment. In general, the business community sees free-trade agreements as desirable because they reduce the ability of government to "interfere" in business decision making.

Unions, on the other hand, worry that free-trade agreements will make it easier for business to relocate to low-wage countries. The workers that unions represent may face the loss of their jobs or pressure to accept lower wages and poorer working conditions. And student organizations are concerned when they see proposals for free trade in services because they fear that this will lead to the erosion of publicly funded education by making it easier for profit-seeking corporations to provide educational services.

The cynical view that politics involves some people trying to enrich themselves at the expense of the community undoubtedly has some degree of validity. However, human beings are not just competitive individuals concerned with promoting our own interests. We are also social beings concerned with the well-being of the communities with which we identify and, potentially, with the well-being of humanity.

Different Values

The values that people seek to achieve through political action are undoubtedly affected by their interests. We are not surprised when we hear business people praise the free-enterprise economic system and seek to reduce government regulation of business. Nor are we surprised when students demand lower tuition fees and criticize policies that might undermine publicly funded education. In fact, people often refer to general values that have widespread support to try to justify political actions designed to advance their own personal interests. For example, business people asking for a government subsidy argue that it will be good for job creation, regional development, or Canada's technological advancement—not that it will make them richer.

Nevertheless, the values that people seek to obtain through politics are not only a product of their own interests and circumstances. Consider students who are active in the nongovernmental organization Oxfam because of a concern about poverty in Africa, or who participate in the letter-writing campaigns of Amnesty International because they want to promote human rights around the world. They are not seeking benefits for themselves, but rather are acting to pursue their values. These values reflect their view of what is good for humanity.

The pursuit of values, like the pursuit of one's own interests, can be a source of political conflict. For example, the disputes between pro-life and pro-choice activists over the issue of abortion reflect differences in deeply held values. Although differences concerning interests can often be settled by compromise, it can sometimes be difficult or impossible to find an acceptable compromise when opposing values are at stake. Neither pro-life nor pro-choice groups would likely be satisfied with a compromise in which abortion was legal in certain but limited circumstances.

Fortunately, there are often a variety of general values that are widely shared within a political community. For example, most Canadians would agree that freedom, equality, justice, order, prosperity, and peace are desirable values. However, this does not mean that we all think about these values in the same way. Some people think of equality as existing when all persons have the same rights and are treated in the same way by the law. Others argue that equality exists only if each individual has the same opportunity to get ahead in life. Still others define equality in terms of an equal sharing of the wealth of the country. Thus, we may agree that equality is desirable, but disagree about what policies are desirable to achieve greater equality.

Furthermore, different people often place a different priority on the values that they share with others. For example, even though many people value both freedom and order, these values sometimes conflict. For those who place a higher value on freedom, police attempts to limit protest activity in the name of maintaining order may be viewed as unjustified. Those who place a higher value on order may expect the police to curtail protest demonstrations because of the risk of unruly behaviour.

The existence of shared values, therefore, does not eliminate conflict over the policies that a political community should adopt. However, it can help to reduce the intensity of disagreements and encourage discussion about how best to achieve the shared values.

The Competitive Struggle for Power

When we think about politics, our attention is often drawn to the struggle for political power. High-profile political events such as election campaigns, the selection of the leader of a political party, and question period in the House of Commons can be easily understood as part of an ongoing struggle for power.

Most politicians enjoy being in positions of political power and vigorously compete to gain and maintain their positions. The desire to have power to affect or control decision making for the community and the longing for the status of high political office can be strong motivating factors for political competition. As well, some people engage in political activity because they enjoy the competition that it often involves. To work hard for a candidate or party and see them win an election can be as exciting as being on a winning hockey team.

Most political activity, however, is motivated primarily by a desire to affect the direction and policies of the political community in order to promote one's interests and values. Power is usually a means to an end rather than a goal in itself (Easton, 1953). Even on the international level where the pursuit of power is often most evident, power is often sought to achieve particular objectives, such as protecting the security of a country, rather than for its own sake.

"Don't they understand that politics is about power?"

The extent to which the interests and values of a particular group are taken into account in decision making is strongly affected by the power that a group is able to bring to bear in affecting that decision. The demonstrators protesting in Quebec City were trying to show that they were not just powerless individuals who could be ignored: rather, they were a group that needed to be reckoned with. By mobilizing a substantial number of determined supporters and attracting media attention, they were able to raise concerns that might otherwise have gone unnoticed. In particular, the members of general public were largely unaware of the Summit of the Americas and issues involved in negotiating the FTAA until the public spectacle of the demonstrations brought it to their attention.

Raising public awareness is one way in which a group can try to affect government politics, particularly in the long run. In the short run, however, the Quebec City demonstration had little effect on the free-trade negotiations, other than encouraging government spokespersons to emphasize the democracy principles agreed to at the Summit of the Americas. Other powerful forces, such as the business representatives who were directly involved in consultations about free-trade negotiations and had good access to top government officials, likely have had a greater impact on the positions taken by the Canadian government. Power is often exercised behind closed doors and is thus not visible to the casual observer.

POLITICS AND CONFLICT RESOLUTION

Politics is not only about engaging in conflict. Nevertheless, war and other extreme forms of political conflict are a significant part of the reality of politics, indicating that some conflicts may only be resolved by brute force and intimidation. Approximately 100 million people were killed in the wars of the twentieth century, and various forms of political violence continue to occur in the first decade of the twenty-first century.

Fortunately, most conflicts are settled in a more peaceful fashion. Indeed, much political activity is directed at the resolution of conflicts. Governments and political parties often attempt to find compromises to try to keep different groups reasonably satisfied. In the view of British political scientist Bernard Crick (1963), politics in democratic countries involves listening to discordant interests, conciliating them, and bringing them together so that each contributes positively to the process of governing. When decisions are made after considerable discussion, consultation with groups that have differing interests and values, and efforts to find acceptable compromises, the intensity of political conflict can be reduced. As well, the use of fair and widely accepted procedures for making decisions will generally assist in the resolution of conflicts.

BASIC CONCEPTS

In learning about a new subject, it is normal to begin with a clear definition of the subject and the key concepts that are essential to understanding that subject. Open an introductory textbook in psychology, economics, or chemistry, and you will quickly learn what the discipline is about. In political science, however, many of the basic concepts are contested. There are major disputes as to how they should be thought about, defined, and used. Even politics, the subject matter of political science, is often defined in different ways. These differences are not just trivial quibbles about how best to define a term. Rather, they often reflect different perspectives on the world. For example, those who analyze politics from a liberal, conservative, Marxist, or feminist perspective (as discussed in Chapters 5 and 6) will often define the basic concepts of the discipline in quite different ways.

Choosing one definition over another can affect how we understand politics. Because there is no consensus about which one of these perspectives is most fruitful for understanding the political world, there is no "correct" definition of the basic concepts of the discipline. In the following section, we will look in more detail at some of the concepts that arise from our introductory comments about the nature of politics. Other important concepts will be introduced in subsequent chapters.

Politics

The *Oxford Concise Dictionary of Politics* tells us that politics is the "art and science of government" (McLean, 2003, p. 423). However, while government is an important focus of political activity, studying government provides only a very limited perspective on politics. Jean Blondel provides a broader understanding by defining politics as "the activity by which decisions are arrived at and implemented in and for a community" (1991, p. 482). Viewing politics as an activity draws our attention to the wide variety of groups and individuals that attempt to affect the decisions that are taken for the community.

David Easton's definition of politics as the "authoritative allocation of values for a society" (1953, p. 129) is probably the definition most widely used by political scientists. The "allocation of values" refers to how the limited resources of a society (more generally, those things that are desired or valued) are allocated (distributed). By referring to the *authoritative* allocation of values, Easton suggests that what is distinctive about the allocation of values through political institutions is that this allocation is generally accepted as binding on all persons in the community. People feel that they should accept or obey the policies of government that affect them (Easton, 1953). Politics, in this view, "concerns all those varieties of activity that influence significantly the kind of authoritative policy adopted for a society and the way it is put into practice" (Easton, 1953, p. 128).

In a general sense, politics is a feature of all organized human activity (Leftwich, 1983). Conflicts over what should be done and relationships of power and authority exist within families, business enterprises, religious organizations, universities, and other social and economic organizations. Nevertheless, political scientists usually study politics in terms of public issues and problems and the struggle to affect **public policies**. The way that society and the economy are organized and function is very important as background to understanding politics in this more limited sense. The distinction between what are matters of public concern and what is private, however, is often contentious. For example, relationships of power and the use of some forms of violence within a family are considered by some people to be basically private matters, while others see this as an important public problem that should be of general concern to the community as a whole.

For the purposes of this book, we define **politics** as activity related to making and implementing policies and decisions to deal with what are generally considered to be public problems. Influencing or controlling governments and the policies that they adopt is a major focus of political activity. However, as Box 1-1, A Broader View of Politics, discusses, political activity can also be directed at affecting important social and economic organizations on matters of public concern.

PUBLIC POLICY
A course of action or inaction chosen by public authorities to address a given problem or interrelated set of problems.

POLITICS
Activity related to making and implementing policies and decisions to deal with what are generally considered to be public problems.

BOX 1-1
A Broader View of Politics

We usually think of political activity as directed at trying to affect the policies or composition of government. But this may be too limited a focus. Consider the following example.

Various environmental groups have sought to end the clear-cutting practices of forest companies in British Columbia. Having had limited success in persuading the B.C. government to pass stricter logging regulations, they turned to other methods to achieve their objective. Europeans were encouraged to participate in a boycott of products made with B.C. lumber and pressure was put on retail businesses such as Home Depot to sell only lumber produced in an environmentally friendly manner. These activities had considerable success and a number of B.C. forest companies began to change their logging practices.

In many ways, these activities by environmental groups are similar to what we normally consider as political. People were mobilized to try to achieve an objective that was viewed as being in the public interest. Rather than influencing government to adopt a policy that might change the actions of logging companies, environmental groups were able to directly pressure some of the companies to change their actions to deal with a public problem. The activities of environmental groups could therefore be considered political, even though the groups did not affect the making of public policy.

Power and Influence

Discussion and analysis of politics often focuses on power. Statements such as "the prime minister is very powerful," "big business is more powerful than ordinary citizens," "the mass media have the power to make and unmake governments," and "the United States is the most powerful country in the world" are very frequently made. Determining the validity of such statements, however, can be difficult and controversial.

The terms *power* and *influence* are sometimes used interchangeably in political science. However, we prefer to think of **influence** as a general term referring to a relationship where one political actor is able to affect the behaviour of other political actors (Lawson, 1997; Dahl, 1984). Within this general category, we can distinguish among three basic types or means of influence: rational persuasion, power, and authority.

Persuasion is a very important aspect of political life as people are often involved in trying to persuade other people to think and act in particular ways. A useful distinction can be made between **rational persuasion** and manipulation (a form of power). Rational persuasion involves the use of truthful information to encourage people to act in accordance with their own interests or values For example, if a friend persuades you to stop smoking by informing you of the health problems caused by cigarettes, we would not ordinarily say that your friend has exerted power because your friend has not persuaded you to act against your own interests. In practice, however, it is often hard to distinguish between rational persuasion and manipulation. If a political party wins an election by raising fears about the consequences of electing an opposing party, was the persuasion rational or manipulative if the party used exaggeration or selectivity to make its case?

Power involves getting people to act against their own desires or interests through coercion, inducements, or manipulation.[1] **Coercion** involves using fear or threats of harmful consequences to achieve an outcome (Dickerson & Flanigan, 2002). For example, Nazi Germany's threat to invade Czechoslovakia in 1938 was successful in convincing the Czech government to allow Germany to annex part of its territory. If your employer threatens to fire you unless you work on behalf of a certain candidate in an election, coercive power has been used to intimidate you.

Inducements (rewards or bribes) are a softer form of power. For example, if your employer promises to give you a promotion should you decide to support a particular candidate, power has been exercised in the form of an inducement.

---

[1] Power can be significant even when there is no intentional exercise of power. Political actors may change their behaviour because they *anticipate* that there will be negative consequences from those with greater power if they act in a particular way, even if no direct threat has been made. For example, knowing that the United States has imposed severe economic sanctions on Cuba, other Caribbean countries may be reluctant to act in ways that could result in similar consequences.

INFLUENCE
A relationship in which one political actor is able to affect the behaviour of other political actors.

RATIONAL PERSUASION
A form of influence involving use of true information to encourage people to act in accordance with their own interests or values.

POWER
The ability to get people, groups, or states to act against their own desires or interests through coercion, inducements, or manipulation.

COERCION
A form of power that involves using fear or threats of harmful consequences to achieve an outcome.

INDUCEMENT
A form of power that involves using rewards or bribes.

Political power can also be exerted by persuasive **manipulation**. Manipulation involves getting people to act in ways that the powerful would prefer, through such techniques as providing misleading information. For example, some would argue that American and British government leaders manipulated their publics and legislators into supporting the 2003 Iraq War through misleading claims that Iraq possessed weapons of mass destruction and had links to al-Qaeda terrorists.

The use of power is often viewed negatively because it involves getting people to act against their own will. Those who are powerful tend to be reluctant to admit the extent of their power so as to avoid criticism. Thus the powerful and their supporters are more likely to define the concept of power narrowly, while the critics of the powerful are more likely to define it broadly (Connolly, 1974).

THE DISTRIBUTION OF POWER AND INFLUENCE In any society, the resources that give individuals and groups the potential to exercise power and, more generally, to influence what gets done, are unequally distributed. Wealth, control of important aspects of the economy, social status and prestige, official position, control of information and expertise, ability to mobilize supporters, control of the means of force, and the ability to influence people are some of the resources that can be used for advantage in politics. Although all citizens in a democracy have some potential influence through their ability to vote, other resources are less equally distributed.

Understanding the distribution of power or influence involves more than adding up the resources available to different groups. To understand power and its effectiveness, we need to examine the means and strategies by which different groups and organizations try to influence or control the making of decisions. For example, we should analyze how groups mobilize the potential interests of different elements of society, the alliances they form with other groups, and how they appeal to the values and beliefs of the community to achieve their objectives (see Box 1-2, People Power).

Analysts often disagree about how concentrated or dispersed power is in particular political communities. In part, these disagreements are a result of different perspectives about power, which can lead to different conclusions about the distribution of power and about who is powerful. Disagreements about how to analyze and measure the distribution of power are summarized as the **three faces of power** (see Table 1-1).

THE THREE FACES OF POWER One way to assess the distribution of power is to examine which groups or individuals are most successful in

MANIPULATION
A form of power that involves getting people to act in ways that the powerful would prefer, through providing misleading information and other techniques.

THREE FACES OF POWER
The argument that looking at who affects particular decisions is insufficient to analyze power. Power can also involve the ability to keep issues off the political agenda and the ability to affect the dominant values of society.

FIRST FACE	Ability to affect decisions
SECOND FACE	Ability to ensure that issues are not raised
THIRD FACE	Ability to affect the dominant ideas of society

TABLE 1-1.
THE THREE FACES OF POWER

BOX 1-2

People Power

Those who control large corporations, occupy top government positions, or head major social organizations clearly have many resources that can be used to affect what the political community does. Occasionally, however, groups and individuals with seemingly few resources are able to bring about major changes.

The dictatorial Philippine government of Ferdinand Marcos was successfully challenged when people, including praying nuns, sat down in front of the army's tanks and refused to move. In Eastern Europe, peaceful demonstrations by ever-larger numbers of people helped to bring down communist regimes in 1989. Black South Africans, by engaging in a determined struggle against the White-minority-controlled government and organizing international support for their cause, were eventually successful in challenging the system of apartheid that had suppressed them. Canadian Aboriginals, who in the past were ignored in the political system, have been able to make their voices heard through successful legal cases in the courts, occasional armed confrontation with Canadian authorities, and building a strong moral case that they have been treated unjustly. In each case, ordinary or disadvantaged people were able to challenge the powerful through determined and skillful action, even though serious personal risks and sacrifices were involved.

Of course, "people power" is not always successful. For example, in the People's Republic of China, student-led actions to support demands for democracy were brutally suppressed by the army on orders from the Communist party leadership in 1989. Despite the outrage in many parts of the world when news coverage revealed the suppression of peaceful protest, the Chinese government did not back off from its hard-line stance.

People power. Citizens of Prague, Czechoslovakia, turned out by the hundreds of thousands in November 1989 to protest the Communist regime led by General Secretary Milos Jakes. Just one month later, the regime toppled peacefully, and the formerly Communist Assembly elected Vaclav Havel as the country's forst democratic president.

affecting a variety of decisions (the "first face" of power). If, for example, one group is usually successful in getting its way, then we would conclude that political power was highly concentrated. If, on the other hand, a variety of groups representing different interests had a significant influence on decisions, or if different groups influenced different decisions, we would conclude that political power was dispersed rather than concentrated.

However, some have argued that measuring political power in terms of who influenced particular decisions does not tell us the complete story.

Bachrach and Baratz (1962) point out that power can be manifested not only by winning contentious issues, but also by ensuring that certain issues are not raised in the first place. They term this deliberate avoidance of an important problem a "non-decision." For example, the owner of a polluting factory may be said to be powerful if discussion of the pollution problem is deliberately avoided by the political leaders or the media in the community. In other words, this "second face" of power involves exercising control over the **political agenda**, that is, the issues that are considered important and are given priority in political deliberations.

Steven Lukes (1974) argues there is a third face of power that is ignored when we focus on who influences specific decisions and "non-decisions." Those who are able to shape the dominant ideas in a society will have a general effect on the politics of that society and the decisions that are made. If those dominant ideas work against the interests of the weaker groups in society, and result in the weaker groups' acting against their own "true" interests, then power has been exercised.

Take, for example, societies where women are expected to confine themselves to domestic responsibilities such as cooking, cleaning, and raising children, while men are involved in public activities, including politics. Ideas that these "separate spheres" are "natural" or that women do not have the qualities to participate in public life might lead many women to believe that the proper role of women is different from that of men and thus not to challenge that system. Power, in this case, has been exerted through the dominant ideas that favour the interests of men, rather than through coercion or particular political decisions.

A problem with Lukes' analysis is that it is often difficult and controversial to determine what a person or group's true interests are. For example, are workers who vote for a party that is oriented toward the interests of business acting against their true interests? The assumption that the leading ideas in a society necessarily reflect and serve the interests of the dominant groups in society can also be controversial. Do the leading ideas in Canada reflect the interests of big business, or are some of these ideas critical of business interests?

PLURALIST AND ELITIST PERSPECTIVES Studies of the distribution of power in terms of who influences the making of decisions in some American communities have suggested that power is not highly concentrated in a small number of hands (Dahl, 1961). In this **pluralist perspective**, a wide variety of groups have an ability to influence the decisions of government in democratic systems that allow groups the freedom to organize and take action. Some groups may have a good ability to influence particular types of decisions, but no one group or set of groups is influential on most or all decisions.

Others, however, have tried to show that power in all communities is concentrated in a small number of hands, particularly in the elites that hold the top positions in the major institutions of the economy, society, and politics (Panitch,

POLITICAL AGENDA
The issues that are considered important and given priority in political deliberations.

PLURALISM/PLURALIST PERSPECTIVE
Individuals' freedom to establish and join groups that are not controlled by the government results in a wide variety of groups having an ability to influence the decisions of government, with no group dominant.

1995). Those who take this **elitist perspective** often focus on examining the interconnections among elite groups, their common backgrounds, and the degree to which they have a shared outlook that would bias their key decisions (Scott, 2001). For example, C. Wright Mills (1956) argued that a power elite, consisting of the top government, business, and military leaders, was crucial in setting the direction for the United States. In Canada, John Porter (1965) found that the economic elite were drawn primarily from upper class Anglo-Saxon, Anglican families. The political elite interacted with the economic elite and shared their conservative values. Power was, in Porter's view, largely concentrated in the hands of various connected elites. There was, however, conflict from time to time, particularly between the economic and political elites.

Generally, the pluralist view (discussed further in Chapter 11) sees democratic politics as working to satisfy (though not necessarily perfectly) the wishes of a wide variety of interests in society. The elitist view is more critical, suggesting that democratic procedures hide the reality that the "true" interests of much of society are not properly served. Elites are able not only to influence government decisions and "non-decisions," but also to influence the leading ideas of the society as a whole in ways that serve their own interests.

Authority and Legitimacy

Authority, the right to make decisions, is of special importance in understanding politics. Those who are in positions of political authority have been *authorized* (that is, given permission) in some way to make decisions on behalf of the political community. Authority, like power, involves getting people to do something that they might not otherwise do. In the case of authority, influence is not achieved by rewards, sanctions, or persuasive arguments. Rather, those being influenced accept the general right of those in authority to make decisions on their behalf. In practice, authority is usually accompanied by power. Those in governing positions may have not only the authority to govern, but also the tools of power (such as the police) and persuasion (such as access to the media) that are usually needed to implement and enforce their decisions.

What gives those in governing positions the authority to govern? Why do most Canadians accept the right of some people to make decisions for the political community, even though they may not agree with the decisions that are being made? When the members of the political community accept that those in positions of authority have a right to govern, we can say that the governing authorities have **legitimacy**, or that the government is a legitimate authority. Where the governing authorities have legitimacy, their decisions are more likely to be accepted, and they will not have to use as much power to put their decisions into effect. Because the exercise of power is often resented and can lead to challenges, those in governing positions will always try to establish the legitimacy of their authority (see Box 1-3, Establishing Legitimate Authority).

Establishing Legitimate Authority

After the successful invasion of Iraq by the United States, Britain, and some of their allies in 2003, a key problem was to establish a legitimate government for Iraq. Although the dictatorial regime of Saddam Hussein had been feared and hated by many Iraqis, the Governing Council created by the occupying powers had trouble establishing its legitimacy. It was seen as closely linked to the United States, which had selected its members, and was subordinate to the American officials in Iraq. Because the Governing Council's legitimacy was limited, it had difficulty in establishing order. The large numbers of foreign troops remaining in Iraq created the view that Iraq was dominated by the United States and its allies, rather than being liberated from a dictatorial ruler. Various forces critical of the occupation mounted attacks on foreign troops, other foreigners involved in the reconstruction effort, and those Iraqis who were seen as collaborating with the Americans and their allies. The American government opposed the use of elections to choose an Iraqi government for fear that the Shiite majority would dominate the government, leading to conflict with the Sunni and Kurdish minorities. Instead, the occupying authorities designed an indirect process of selecting a transitional Iraqi government that took office in June 2004. But despite a formal handover of sovereign authority by the occupying power to the new Iraqi government, large numbers of foreign troops were still needed to maintain that government in power.

Defeating Iraq's military on the battlefield and overthrowing the Iraqi government were far easier than establishing a new legitimate government. Power may come from the barrel of a gun, but gaining legitimacy requires winning the hearts and minds of the people.

ESTABLISHING AND MAINTAINING LEGITIMACY How is the legitimacy of governing authorities established? German sociologist Max Weber (1864–1920) described three basic types of authority, each of which could try to establish its legitimacy in its own way:

- charismatic authority
- traditional authority
- legal–rational authority

Charismatic authority is based on the extraordinary or supernatural qualities of a leader that might be established through such means as performing miracles, issuing prophecies, or leading a military victory. The legitimacy of charismatic authority "rests upon the belief in magical powers, revelations and hero worship" by the followers (Weber, 1958, p. 296). Charismatic leaders, such as Mao Zedong, leader of the Chinese Communist revolution, inspire intense devotion in their followers.

CHARISMATIC AUTHORITY
Authority based on the extraordinary or supernatural qualities of a leader.

Traditional authority, whether exercised through the elders of a tribe or a ruling family, is based on customs that establish the right of certain persons to rule. The traditional authority of monarchs who inherited their position was often buttressed with the idea that rulers had a divinely created right to rule that was sanctified by religious authorities. Japanese emperors, for

TRADITIONAL AUTHORITY
Authority based on customs that establish the right of certain persons to rule.

▶ Charismatic leaders, such as Mao Zedong, leader of the Chinese Communist revolution, inspire intense devotion in their followers. Charismatic authority rests upon the belief of followers in magical powers, revelations, and hero worship. The Chinese media depicted an elderly Mao supposedly performing the heroic feat of swimming across the Yangtze River to maintain his charismatic image.

example, claimed to be descended from the sun goddess. The legitimacy of traditional authority can be based on beliefs that a certain family has always ruled and that customs are sacred practices that will bring evil consequences if violated (Weber, 1958).

Modern societies, in Weber's view, are characterized by efficient management and bureaucratic organization (see Chapter 16). The **legal–rational authority** of modern societies is based on legal rules and procedures rather than on the personal qualities or characteristics of the rulers. Authority is impersonal in the sense that it rests in official positions such as prime minister or president, rather than in the individuals holding such positions. The right of those in governing positions to rule is based on being chosen by a set of established and accepted legal procedures. Those holding official positions are expected to act in accordance with legal rules and procedures. Thus, their authority is limited. The legitimacy of the system of governing is based on a belief in the legality of the procedures for selecting those who have official duties and the legal "correctness" of the procedures that are used in governing (Weber, 1958).

Holding free and fair elections involving all adult citizens to designate those authorized to make governing decisions is often considered to be the most effective way of establishing the legitimacy of government. Nevertheless, a "legitimacy crisis" can occur even in democratic systems

LEGAL–RATIONAL AUTHORITY The right to rule based on legal rules and procedures rather than on the personal qualities or characteristics of the rulers.

(Habermas, 1975). Although an unpopular government in a democracy can be voted out, if governments are persistently ineffective in dealing with serious problems, citizens might question the legitimacy of the democratic institutions and processes in their country. For example, if the policies of successive governments lead to widespread poverty and unemployment or to a collapse in the value of the currency, then the legitimacy of the system of governing may be challenged. Legitimacy can also be reduced if some groups feel that there is a long-term pattern of mistreatment by the government. In other words, legitimacy may be based not only on the acceptance of government's claim to authority (for example, by being chosen through an accepted set of procedures), but also on the perceived rightfulness of how government generally exercises its authority (Barnard, 2001).

In addition, a system of rule that is imposed on a country or on a part of the population without its consent might be viewed by the population as illegitimate, even if it establishes democratic procedures. For example, when a democratic system of governing was established in Germany after World War I, some Germans doubted its legitimacy, partly because they viewed it as being imposed on the country by the victors in that war. The problem of legitimacy eventually contributed to the demise of the democratic system and the takeover by Adolf Hitler and the Nazi party.

THE SIGNIFICANCE OF LEGITIMACY Effective governing depends not only on governing institutions having the power to force people to act in certain ways, but also on their establishing and maintaining legitimate authority. A government that is not accepted as legitimate by a significant proportion of the population will have to devote much of its energy and resources to persuading or coercing the population to obey its laws and to maintain order. All governments rely on coercion to some extent, but generally people feel an obligation to obey a legitimate government. Thus, a government whose rule is considered legitimate can rely more on authority than on coercion to get people to obey the laws it adopts.

Having legitimate authority gives government a powerful resource to achieve its goals. People usually obey laws, even when they find those laws against their interests or values, because they view the source of those laws as legitimate. This can potentially allow the government to act for the good of the community as a whole, even when some may object to the policies adopted. However, even though most people would agree that political authority is a necessary and desirable feature of an orderly society, questions can arise concerning whether there are circumstances in which authority should be resisted or disobeyed. What would you do if you were drafted to fight in a war that you considered unjust? Would you resist the authority of a democratically elected government that was persecuting an unpopular minority, even if that persecution were done in a legal manner?

The Common Good

Political philosophers have often viewed politics as different from other activities in that it is concerned with what is common to the community as a whole. Ensuring the good functioning of the basic activities of governing—such as maintaining order and security, providing for a just settlement of disputes, and regulating the economy—benefits all members of the political community (Wolin, 1960). Politics, in other words, is ideally about seeking the **common good** of a political community.

But what exactly is meant by "the common good"? There is no standard definition because different people think about the common good in different ways. We will define the common good as what is good for the political community as a whole, as well as for the general welfare of the members of the political community. In the **collectivist perspective**, the common good should be thought of in terms of the interests and well-being of the political community *as a whole*. This may seem uncontroversial, but in its strongest form it suggests that the well-being of the community is more important than the well-being of the individual members of the community. It raises such questions as whether, and under what circumstances, we should be expected to sacrifice our own interests or even our lives for the greater good of our country.

For those who have an **individualist perspective** on politics, it is the well-being of individuals that matters. The community is seen only as the sum of the individuals who happen to live in that community. The good of individuals is the only proper measure of the quality of the political community. Further, those who hold the individualist perspective typically argue that individuals know what is best for themselves, and thus regulation of the activities of individuals by government or other collective institutions is generally undesirable. The common good is best achieved by allowing individuals to be free to live their own lives and pursue what is good for themselves.

Should we be concerned only with our own good? If individuals pursue their own good, will the good of the community be served? Are the communities that we live in no more than a collection of independent individuals? Critics of the individualist perspective argue that humans are social beings who flourish through harmonious interaction with others. Connected to our social nature is the capability to care about others. This capability initially develops within our own family, but can extend to the citizens of our country and potentially to the world as a whole. Further, the communities to which we belong—including political communities—help to shape our sense of ourselves, that is, our identity. A sense of belonging to and participating in a community (or a set of communities) could be considered an important part of a fulfilling and meaningful life. People do not only have an interest in their own material well-being, but also an interest in the quality of their community and the social relations that are a part of that community (Lutz, 1999).

COMMON GOOD
What is good for the political community as a whole, as well as for the general welfare of the members of the political community.

COLLECTIVIST PERSPECTIVE
A perspective that focuses on the interests and well-being of the political community as a whole.

INDIVIDUALIST PERSPECTIVE
A perspective that focuses on the well-being of individuals rather than the community as a whole. The community is seen as only the sum of the individuals who live in that community.

As described here, the collectivist and individualist perspectives provide sharply opposing views on the common good. Is there some middle ground? The common good might be thought of in terms of finding the appropriate balance between the good of individuals and the good of the community as a whole. Most people would probably agree that concern for the general good of the community and respect for individual rights and freedoms are both highly desirable. The question of what is an "appropriate balance" can, however, be controversial (see Box 1-4, Language Policy and the Common Good in Quebec).

A QUESTION OF COMMUNITIES The common good is often thought of in terms of the country that we live in. But the common good of the country may not necessarily be the same as the common good of the other communities to which we belong. If we view Canada as a "community of communities," as former Prime Minister Joe Clark once suggested, then it might be argued that the good of our provincial community should not be subordinated to the good of the country as a whole. Although the good of

BOX 1-4

Language Policy and the Common Good in Quebec

French-speaking Quebeckers have a long history of being concerned about the survival of the French language and culture. Faced with the predominance of the English language in the rest of Canada and the United States and the assimilation of many French-Canadians outside Quebec into the dominant culture, since the early 1960s the Québécois have looked to collective action to ensure that their language and culture is not eroded in Quebec. In particular, Bill 101, passed by the Quebec National Assembly in 1977, declared French the official language of Quebec and required many businesses to convert their language of work from English to French. In addition, the children of people who had immigrated to Quebec were restricted in their ability to attend English-language public schools, and French was required to be the sole language of public signs. Bill 101 created considerable controversy inside and outside Quebec.

The Quebec situation raises several questions: Should the collective good of the large majority of Quebeckers take precedence over the language rights of individuals? What is the appropriate balance between protecting the French character of Quebec and respecting the individual rights of all Quebeckers? Does the protection of the French language by the Quebec government undermine the efforts by the Canadian government to protect the rights of French-speaking minorities throughout Canada and the English-speaking minority in Quebec?

our province or other communities may coincide with the good of the country, this will not always be the case. For example, putting price controls on energy might be good for Canada as a whole in some circumstances, but not for provinces whose economies are dependent on the sale of oil and natural gas.

Furthermore, should we be concerned about the common good of humanity? The processes of globalization (Chapter 2) are creating increased interaction and interdependence among the peoples of the world. However, despite greater awareness of and concern about what happens in other parts of the world, for most of us our sense of being part of a global political community is much weaker than our sense of being Canadian. As well, major differences among the peoples of the world in culture and circumstances mean that there are fewer shared values upon which a consensus about the common good of humanity could be based.

Some environmentalists suggest that the common good should include not only humanity, but the earth as a whole, including plants, animals, and the ecosystems upon which life is based (Daly & Cobb, 1994). Protecting the environment is ultimately essential for humanity as well as for plants and animals. But, when faced with the issue of protecting the jobs of loggers or protecting the habitat of an endangered animal or plant, should the good of human beings be given greater priority than the good of other life forms? Or as parts of an interrelated whole, are all life forms, including humans, of equal inherent worth? (See Devall & Sessions, 1998.)

Thus, what is in the common good varies, depending on which community or communities we consider important. Although in politics the common good is usually thought of in terms of the country in which we live, that may be viewed as too narrow a focus. The good of humanity (both current and future generations) and of the planet are also of importance.

ACHIEVING THE COMMON GOOD? The idea of the common good is based on the notion that some common interests and values exist within a political community. However, because people give different priorities to these values or interpret these values in their own way, it can be difficult to reach a consensus on what is needed to achieve the common good. As well, even if people could reach a consensus about an action that is for the common good, will each individual act voluntarily to achieve that goal? Is the coercive power of government really needed to achieve the common good?

Power is often necessary to induce people to cooperate in order to achieve objectives that benefit themselves and their community. This can be illustrated by what is known as the **free rider problem**. Imagine that all persons in a community agreed that a road that would benefit everyone should be built. One miserly individual might decide not to contribute to the cost of building the road, knowing that the road would still be built with the contributions of

FREE RIDER PROBLEM
A problem with voluntary collective action that results because an individual can enjoy the benefits of group action without contributing.

others. However, if enough people followed this self-interested logic, the road would never be built and everyone would suffer. The use of the power of government (for example, to enforce the payment of taxes) is often necessary to achieve the common good.

How can we be assured that government will act to try to achieve the common good rather than pursuing the particular interests of those in government? In *The Republic*, the ancient Greek philosopher Plato (c. 429–c. 347 BCE) sketched out an ideal of how the common good might be achieved if government were placed in the hands of a wise philosopher–king who had been thoroughly educated in the art of governing. To ensure that such a leader would rule for the common good rather than out of personal interest, leaders would be prevented from having a family or owning property.

What might this suggest for governments and their citizens operating in the real world and not a great thinker's utopia? The common good could be viewed as an objective that should be continually pursued, although it will never be fully attained.

We should expect governments to try to act in the common good and hold them accountable if they do fail to do so. There is, however, a danger that the notion of the common good can be used to justify evil. Ruthless leaders have tried to justify brutal actions in the name of the long-term good of the political community. For example, the Soviet leader Joseph Stalin tried to justify his actions, which resulted in the starvation of millions of peasants, in terms of the ideal of creating a "classless society." Fascist leaders such as Adolf Hitler and Benito Mussolini used the appeal of the good of the nation to suppress dissent and justify wars of aggression.

In the contemporary world, democracy is often seen as the best form of government and the one most likely to actually pursue the common good. Ideally, through discussion among citizens, an informed consensus can be reached about the policies that are desirable for the common good. However, meaningful discussion is often difficult to achieve outside of small groups and small communities. Instead, there is an expectation that decisions in a democracy will tend to reflect the opinions of the majority of the population. Even if this is the case, this does not ensure that the common good of the community will be achieved. The majority is not necessarily oriented towards the common good of all members of the community. Indeed, majorities have at various times supported policies that oppress minorities.

Generally, in politics as in life, words can be used to deceive as well as inform. Although pursuing the common good is a desirable political objective, we have to be careful to examine how fine-sounding terms such as "the common good," "freedom," "equality," and "justice" are actually used in practice. Ideals and values are important if politics is to be more than the pursuit of power for its own sake. However, power struggles and oppressive policies are often cloaked in the rhetorical use of ideals and values.

WHAT IS POLITICAL SCIENCE?

POLITICAL SCIENCE
The systematic study of politics.

The term **political science** may sound confusing, as politics and science seem to be very different. Indeed, some universities and colleges prefer to use terms such as "political studies," "politics," or "government" rather than political science. However, keeping in mind that the word "science" is derived from a Latin word meaning knowledge, we could define political science simply as the systematic study of politics.

EMPIRICAL ANALYSIS
Analysis that involves explaining various aspects of politics particularly by using careful observation and comparison to develop generalizations and testable theories.

NORMATIVE ANALYSIS
Analysis that involves examining ideas about how the community should be governed and what values should be pursued through politics.

A distinction is often made between empirical analysis and normative analysis (see Table 1-2). **Empirical analysis** involves explaining various aspects of politics particularly by using careful observation and comparison to develop generalizations. The goal of empirical analysis is not simply to describe various features of politics and government, but to develop testable theories that will help us to understand how politics works. **Normative analysis** involves examining ideas about how the community should be governed and what values should be pursued through politics. Normative analysis builds on a rich tradition of political philosophy that goes back almost 2400 years.

POLICY ANALYSIS
Analysis that involves evaluating existing policies and suggesting what policies should be adopted to deal with particular problems.

In practice, the distinction between empirical and normative analysis is not as clear-cut as it sounds. Political scientists are part of the world they study and inevitably the empirical questions they choose to study and the way they go about researching those questions will be affected by their values and perspectives. Likewise, normative analyses are based on understandings of human nature and how the political world works. The combination of empirical and normative analysis is particularly evident in **policy analysis,** which involves evaluating existing policies and suggesting what policies should be adopted to deal with particular problems. In providing practical advice, policy analysts have to consider what is feasible rather than ideal, which calls for an understanding of political realities. They need to consider how best to achieve desired values under particular circumstances.

COMPARATIVE POLITICS
The branch of political science that examines the similarities and differences in the politics and governing of different countries.

INTERNATIONAL RELATIONS
The branch of political science that studies politics at the international level.

POLITICAL PHILOSOPHY
The branch of political science that examines ideas about how the community should be governed and what values should be pursued through politics.

Political science is quite a diverse discipline with a number of different subfields. Some political science courses focus on understanding the politics and governing of a particular political community such as Canada. Courses in **comparative politics** examine the similarities and differences in the politics and governing of different countries. **International relations** looks at the interactions among different countries. **Political philosophy** (sometimes termed political theory) examines ideas about how the community should be governed and what values should be pursued through politics. Other sub-

TABLE 1-2
EMPIRICAL, NORMATIVE, AND POLICY ANALYSIS: AN EXAMPLE

EMPIRICAL ANALYSIS	Why are women less likely than men to run for Parliament?
NORMATIVE ANALYSIS	Should legislatures be a microcosm of society?
POLICY ANALYSIS	What is the best way of increasing the proportion of women in Parliament?

fields include public administration, public policy, political behaviour, and empirical theory and methodology. As well, some areas of study, such as political economy and political sociology, involve combinations with related social sciences.

Why Study Politics?

The most basic answer to the question "Why study politics?" is simply that politics is important and that knowing about it is an essential aspect of understanding the world we live in. The politically motivated terrorist attack on the United States on September 11, 2001, illustrates how political actions can affect the world. Less dramatically, but no less importantly, decisions taken by government can affect our material well-being, the accessibility of health care, the quality of the air we breathe, and the degree of freedom we enjoy.

Understanding politics is also essential in order to take effective action to achieve our goals and ideals. Imagine that you are concerned about global climate change and would like governments to take actions to reduce the use of fossil fuels. Or perhaps you think that university tuition fees are too high and should be lowered to allow greater accessibility to higher education. Or you heard that a friend has been killed by someone who was drinking and driving and you decide that stricter laws are needed. How would you go about trying to achieve your goals? Would you write a letter to the prime minister, your member of Parliament, your member of the provincial legislature, or your local municipal council? Join a group that is taking up your cause? Organize a protest demonstration? Vote for a party that appears sympathetic to your concerns? Sit back and hope that decision-makers in government make the right decision?

Understanding politics can help you think about the issues that arise in politics, how to achieve what is best for yourself and your community, and how to recognize some of the obstacles that hinder the achievement of your goals.

CAREER TIES Students often ask how taking political science courses or getting a degree in political science will help them in finding employment and pursuing a career. Political science would obviously be useful for anyone contemplating a career in politics, but most of those who study politics are not budding politicians. Nevertheless, about one-fifth of Canadians work for government or its agencies. Those who work for business or non-profit organizations often interact with government and government agencies. Knowledge of government policies and regulations is useful in almost every field of endeavour. And, in an increasingly globalized world, knowledge of foreign political systems and international political organizations and agreements is very important for doing business globally.

As in most fields of study in the arts and sciences, students receiving a degree in political science often do not end up in a career that is directly related to their

Canadian Political Science Association
www.cpsa-acsp.ca

Political Science: A Net Station
www.library.ubc.ca/poli/welcome.html

Political Science Resources
www.psr.keele.ac.uk

studies. Rather, an undergraduate degree in political science provides a good background to a wide variety of career choices. Many students pursuing careers in such fields as law, journalism, and public administration take political science before entering a professional program. Those planning to pursue a career in the business world will find political science useful because of the importance of the relationships between business and government. Those pursuing careers in the armed forces and law enforcement agencies also find political science courses useful. At the university where the authors of this textbook teach, nursing students are required to take a political science course because of the importance of public policy and political action in the health care field.

Political science courses can be also be helpful in developing general intellectual skills that are useful in one's personal development and eventual career. Such skills include developing the ability to communicate effectively, read carefully, do good research, and think critically. Political science contains a great diversity of perspectives and approaches. This diversity helps to make political science interesting, challenging, and useful in the development of general intellectual skills.

Summary and Conclusion

Politics plays a vital role in our lives and our communities. Whether or not we are interested in politics, we are affected by political decisions. A basic characteristic of politics is conflict, and political activity often involves trying to resolve conflicts. To understand politics, we need to examine the different interests, values, and ideas that individuals and groups bring to political life, the distribution of power, and the operations of political organizations, including political parties, interest groups, and the institutions of government.

People often have a negative view of politics. When a job or a promotion goes to a person because of their contacts and family connections, or because they have flattered their employer, others often grumble that the decision was "political." Likewise, if a politician makes a decision based on trying to gain power or a personal benefit, win re-election, or reward supporters, rather than on a careful analysis of what is best for the country, the decision is often criticized for being "political." Politics, in other words, is often thought of as involving the selfish or competitive pursuit of one's own interests, without concern for others or the community as a whole.

Politics is also often viewed negatively because many people distrust governments and politicians (see Chapter 7). Governments are often criticized for being inefficient, wasteful, and prone to corruption. Some governments have supported or acquiesced in the domination and exploitation of the weak within the society that they govern. The laws and policies adopted by governments may reflect the interests and values of the dominant groups in society, resulting in the harassment, persecution, or neglect of the less powerful. As well, some governments have pursued the conquest, control, and exploitation of other countries.

There is, however, also a positive side to politics. Many people engage in political activity not only to advance their own interests or to pursue power for its own sake, but also with the hope of advancing the common good of the political community (that is, what is good for the community as a whole, as well as for the general welfare of the members of the community). Governments have usually been able to establish peace and order within society by establishing and enforcing rules of conduct. The power and authority of government is often needed to achieve various collective goals of the political community. Governments can potentially help to regulate and check the power wielded by various social and economic institutions, and thus help to protect and assist the weaker elements of society.

A key political problem is how to ensure that the power and authority of governments are used for the common good. As the famous saying of nineteenth-century British historian Lord Acton warns, "Power tends to corrupt and absolute power corrupts absolutely." Because power and authority are easily abused, it is important to ensure that those in governing positions are held accountable for their actions. Excessive concentrations of power, whether in the hands of governing authorities, police and military forces, private business, the media, or religious organizations, can be dangerous.

Political science, the systematic study of politics, has its roots in thousands of years of discussion and analysis about what is good for the communities we live in and how this good can best be achieved (Strauss, 1945). Through empirical analysis, political science is building a systematic, theoretically based understanding of politics; through normative analysis, fundamental questions about the values upon which our communities should be based are examined; and through policy analysis, practical advice about what should be done is provided to the members and decision-makers of the political community.

Key Terms

Discussion Questions

1. What are the major political issues in your local, provincial, or national community? What about the global community? Do the most talked-about issues reflect the most serious problems that each of these communities faces? Are any important issues ignored?

2. Should we be concerned if power is highly concentrated?

3. Is it meaningful to talk about the common good in a diverse society?

4. How important is the study of politics? Is it an essential component of a good education?

5. Do all citizens have a responsibility to keep themselves informed about politics?

Further Reading

A number of novels provide interesting and provocative descriptions of politics in the past, present, and possible future:

Achebe, C. *A man of the people.* London: William Heinemann, 1966.

Allende, I. *Eva Luna.* New York: Bantam Press, 1987.

Anonymous. *Primary colors.* New York: Warner Books, 1996.

Atwood, M. *The handmaid's tale.* Toronto: McClelland and Stewart, 1985.

Atwood, M. *Oryx and Crake.* Toronto: McClelland and Stewart, 2003.

Gordimer, N. *July's people.* New York: Viking Press, 1981.

LeGuin, U.K. *The dispossessed.* New York: Avon Books, 1974.

Lessing, D. *The good terrorist.* London: Jonathan Cape, 1985.

Orwell, G. *1984.* New York: New American Library, 1948.

Warren, R.P. *All the king's men.* New York: Bantam, 1959.

NATION-STATES, NATIONALISM, AND GLOBALIZATION

PHOTO ABOVE: When Thailand's exports declined, the Thai government was unable to continue supporting the high value of the baht. The currencies of most of Thailand's Asian trading partners spiralled downwards, with widespread global repercussions.

1. explain the difference between a nation and a state
2. discuss the nature of the modern state
3. consider the meaning of citizenship

4. explain the nature and significance of nationalism
5. outline the nature and significance of globalization
6. discuss the controversies surrounding globalization

In December 1997, the government of Thailand temporarily closed most banks. The value of its currency plummeted, its stock market crashed, unemployment soared, and some rich Thais whose companies had gone bankrupt were forced to eke out a living on the street.

In previous decades, Thailand, like many other Asian countries, had experienced a tremendous economic boom. Foreign investors poured money into the country, attracted by high interest rates and a currency (the baht) whose value was tied to that of the American dollar. However, when Thailand's exports declined, the Thai government was unable to keep spending large amounts of money to maintain the high value of the baht and allowed it to float. The value of the baht and the currencies of most of Thailand's Asian trading partners began a downward spiral. Speculators and jittery investors sold Asian currencies, fearing further declines in value. The currency panic became a self-fulfilling prophecy (MacLean, Bowles, & Croci, 1999). By the end of the crisis in May 1998, the Indonesian rupiah had shed more than three-quarters of its value and the Korean won was worth just two-fifths of its value a year earlier.

Although Thailand's currency crisis had its strongest effects in Asia, it also had global repercussions. Investors and banks became reluctant to invest in emerging markets such as Latin America and Russia, contributing to the temporary inability of Russia to make payments on its debts. To prevent the crisis from worsening, the International Monetary Fund (IMF) mobilized nearly US$120 billion in loans to various countries, which had to meet conditions laid down by the IMF. Stock markets around the world suffered substantial declines, and the American government bailed out a major fund that owed investors US$125 billion to prevent a collapse in global stock and bond markets (Friedman, 2000).

The Asian currency crisis shows how economic globalization links countries together so that an event in one of them has inevitable repercussions on a number of others. It also provides an example of how globalization hampers the ability of national governments to steer their own economies. Globalization is making countries increasingly interdependent and limiting the policy options of national governments in the management of the economy and other fields.

We begin this chapter by examining the nature of the modern state. Then we look at the concept of nation, which is often viewed as the basis of the modern state, and the idea of nationalism, which has had an important impact on how the world is organized. Finally, we discuss the processes of globalization, which many observers believe is altering human existence and eroding the significance of modern states.

THE STATE

A **state** is an independent, self-governing political unit that acts through various governing institutions to make rules that are binding on the population within a particular country (Shively, 2005). The state can be viewed as a more extensive and permanent expression of the political community than the **government**, the set of institutions that make decisions and oversee the implementation of decisions on behalf of the state for a particular period of time (Heywood, 2002). The Canadian state, for example, includes not only the Canadian government and the governments of the provinces, but also the court system, the military and police forces, the employees of government, and publicly owned corporations (termed Crown corporations in Canada).[1]

The term *state* is confusing in some situations (see Box 2-1, The State and the United States). It may also create an unrealistic image of a powerful, unified body. In reality, the various institutions that make up a state often do not work cooperatively in pursuit of a common interest or goal.

STATE

An independent, self-governing political unit that acts through various governing institutions to make rules that are binding on the population within a particular country.

GOVERNMENT

The set of institutions that make decisions and oversee the implementation of decisions on behalf of the state.

BOX 2-1

The State and the United States

The term *state* is often confusing because a state in the United States is the equivalent of a province in Canada. But if we consider the origins of the United States, the term becomes more understandable.

By the mid-1770s, thirteen British colonies had been established in North America. They waged the American War of Independence from 1775 to 1783 to end their subservience to Britain. Upon becoming independent, each of the former colonies became self-governing, with only a modest amount of cooperation among the states. Within a few years, however, there was widespread agreement that it would be a good idea to unite the separate states. The constitution establishing the United States of America came into effect in 1788. Each of the formerly independent states retained some degree of self-government, and they continued to call themselves states. However, it is the American government, rather than the governments of the individual states, that is most likely to act on behalf the American state, particularly in relations with other countries.

---

[1] Usually the state is defined in terms of all of the institutions that relate to governing a country. Sometimes, however, the people of a country, in their role as citizens, are also considered part of the state.

SOVEREIGNTY AND THE STATE

Modern states are often depicted as having a monopoly on the *legitimate* use of force within their boundaries, such that the state can enforce the rules it adopts within the territory it controls. The territory of a state involves borders that are recognized by other states, or at least borders that can be defended by force if necessary. Most modern states have **jurisdiction** (exclusive governing and law-making authority) over sizable geographic areas and substantial permanent populations.

States are often described as being sovereign, meaning that they are the highest authority for their population and their territory. The idea of **sovereignty** developed in the sixteenth century as various European monarchs strove to establish themselves as the highest authority in the territory that they controlled. Conflicts between the monarchs, religious leaders, and feudal lords, each of whom had considerable governing powers, led to the idea that there should be a single highest authority in each territory in order to maintain peace and avoid civil war. In particular, the Treaty of Westphalia (1648), which ended the devastating Thirty Years War (based, in part, on conflicts between Protestants and Catholics), established the supreme authority of states and their monarchs, including the ability of monarchs to determine the official religion of their state.

In various countries, legislatures and/or the people challenged the absolute power claimed by monarchs. In Britain, the "Glorious Revolution" (1688) resulted in Parliament's removal and replacement of the monarch and established the idea that Parliament is the supreme authority. The leaders of the French Revolution (1789) proclaimed that sovereignty rested with the people. Regardless of whether sovereignty is viewed as resting in the hands of a single individual (such as a monarch), a particular organization, several sets of organizations (for example, the Canadian Parliament and provincial legislatures), the people as a whole, or some combination, the modern state itself is viewed as sovereign.

The concept of the **sovereign state** is particularly important when we look at the relationship among states. A central principle of international law is that the states of the world are the legal equals of one another, and thus states should not interfere in the affairs of other states, unless invited to do so. In other words, states are expected to respect each other's sovereignty. States, whether large or small, powerful or weak, rich or poor, are viewed as being self-governing.

TODAY'S STATES Most of the contemporary world's people and land mass (and some of the adjoining ocean) is divided among the individual states of the world. The empires that ruled over conquered territories and peoples have been dissolved and the number of sovereign states has increased substantially (see Figure 2-1). There are, however, some anomalies.

JURISDICTION
The state's governing and law-making authority over a particular geographic area and population.

SOVEREIGNTY
The principle that states have the right to govern their population and territory without outside interference.

SOVEREIGN STATE
A state that has the ability to govern its population and territory without outside interference.

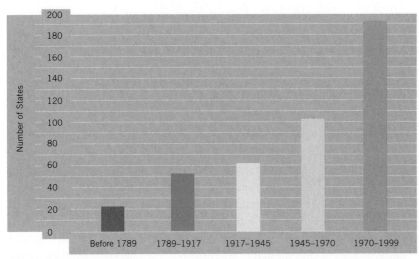

SOURCE: From R. J. Jackson and D. Jackson, *An Introduction to Political Science: Comparative and World Politics,* Fourth Edition, Pearson Education Canada, 2003, p. 48. Reprinted with permission by Pearson Education Canada Inc.

Civil wars have occasionally shattered states, resulting in no real authority in a particular area. For example, in Somalia and Afghanistan (as of 2004), competing warlords have control over much of each country and the state is largely ineffective. These cases are sometimes referred to as **failed states,** in which governments cannot enforce laws, maintain order, or protect the lives of citizens. A few areas, such as some small Caribbean and Pacific islands, are still controlled by foreign countries. In other areas, control of some territory is contested or its future uncertain. For example, Israel occupies territories that it captured in wars with neighbouring countries, India and Pakistan have clashed over control of Kashmir for decades, and the People's Republic of China (mainland China) claims jurisdiction over the island of Taiwan (known as the Republic of China).

FAILED STATE
A state that no longer has the capacity to maintain order.

◄ Afghanistan, 2004: a failed state. Competing warlords have control over much of the country, and the state is largely ineffective. The government cannot enforce laws, maintain order, or protect the lives of citizens.

FIGURE 2-1
THE INCREASING NUMBER OF SOVEREIGN STATES

In reality, the sovereignty of states is not absolute. Because of the great disparities in power among the states of the world, it is not surprising that weaker countries have found their sovereignty limited at times. The United States, for example, has a long history of involving itself in the affairs of Caribbean and Latin American countries, including invading and overthrowing the governments of Grenada (1983) and Panama (1989). The former Soviet Union exercised tight control over the countries of Eastern Europe.

As well, various elements of the international community have taken actions to persuade states to protect human rights or to avoid potentially aggressive policies. For example, the North Atlantic Treaty Organization, including Canada, bombed Yugoslavia in 1999 to force it to end its mistreatment of the Albanian minority in the province of Kosovo. Often such actions are controversial (for example, the invasion and occupation of Iraq by the United States and some of its allies in 2003) because of differences of opinion about whether the action was justified and whether it would have the desired effects.

Citizenship and the State

CITIZENSHIP
The idea that the permanent residents of a particular country should have legal status as members of the state and should have various rights and responsibilities.

Connected to the development of the modern state is the idea of **citizenship**. We expect that those who reside in a particular country should not only be subject to the laws passed by the governing institutions of that state, but also should be treated as citizens with various rights and responsibilities. As citizens, individuals share in the power of the sovereign state (Rousseau, 1762/1968). Those who are born in a particular country are usually considered to be citizens of that country, as are those whose parents are citizens. Those who immigrate to a new country can usually apply for citizenship after a certain period of time. They may have to pass an exam testing their knowledge of their new country, including its political system, and take an oath of allegiance before becoming citizens.

Some countries, however, connect citizenship to particular characteristics. Germany and Israel, for example, allow persons from other countries the right to become citizens based on their ancestry. A number of European countries have been reluctant to grant citizenship to "guest workers" from North Africa and the Middle East, even when they have resided in the country for a lengthy period of time.

The concept of citizenship implies that each citizen has an equal status and thus an equal set of rights and responsibilities. This concept, however, has only been fully applied in relatively recent times when citizenship rights were extended to women, minority groups, and those without significant property. Indeed, some argue that less visible barriers still inhibit persons from such groups from participating in the political community as equal citizens (Pierson, 1996).

In a classic analysis, T.H. Marshall (1950) portrayed the concept of citizenship as expanding, often as a result of considerable political struggle, from civil rights (such as freedom of speech and religion) to political rights (such as the right to vote) to social rights (such as the right to free education, health care, and the right to work).[2] The social rights to which citizens are entitled are, however, often a matter of controversy, as will be discussed in Chapter 3. Further, questions arise as to whether citizenship carries obligations to the state and to other citizens. Citizens may, for example, be expected to defend their country in times of war. Governments have used this argument to justify compulsory military service and to draft men (and likely women in the future) to fight in wars, even those that are not strictly defensive in nature. As well, since citizenship is associated with being a member of the political community, some have argued that citizens have an obligation to become informed participants in politics. Indeed, some argue that citizens should put aside their personal interests and act in political life for the common good of their country (Pierson, 1996).

THE NATION-STATE

Modern states are often referred to as **nation-states**: states based on people who share a sense of being a member of a particular nation. However, not all states are based on a single nation. A **nation** is a group of people who share a sense of common identity. This sense of identity may result from living in a particular country, but it is also often a result of sharing characteristics such as ethnicity, language, culture, religion, and a common history (Leach, 2002). Because a nation can be thought of as basically an identity that exists in the minds of its members, nations have been described as "imagined communities" (Anderson, 1983).

Until modern times, people tended to view themselves mainly in terms of their clan, tribe, or local community. European monarchs typically had little in common with the people they ruled, and territories changed hands as a result of dynastic marriages and conquest. In many parts of the world, clan, tribal, and local identities continue to be stronger than broader national identities.

Although elements of national identity can be found before modern times, historians generally view the French Revolution of 1789 as sparking the development of a sense of nationhood among the general public. The French Revolution was based on the idea that the state is an instrument of the people (the nation), with the people having the right to overthrow rulers who do not reflect the will of the people. The subsequent Napoleonic Wars helped to create a sense of unity and pride in the French nation and its citizen army, which replaced reliance on mercenaries. In reaction to the French conquest of

NATION-STATE
A sovereign state based on people who share a sense of being a member of a particular nation or nationality.

NATION
A group of people who share a sense of common identity.

---

[2] In practice, social rights are often provided to all permanent residents of a country, not just those who are citizens.

much of continental Europe, other European peoples developed their own sense of national identity.

Creating National Identities

To some extent, the process of developing national identities has involved building upon existing ethnic identities and cultural characteristics. However, states have often made deliberate efforts to replace local and regional dialects, cultures, and identities with a national culture. For example, the government of France created a French identity in the rural areas of the country in the latter part of the nineteenth century by instilling patriotism through the educational system and encouraging the use of Parisian French throughout the country instead of the very distinct dialects that were spoken in various parts of France (Weber, 1976). In the United States, where persons from a variety of countries settled, American governments devoted considerable effort to the creation of a common sense of citizenship, although Blacks and Native Americans were largely excluded from the American "melting pot."

We often think of states as being based on nations, but states have often tried to create a sense of national identity that did not exist before the states themselves were formed. As Italian writer and politician Massimo D'Azeglio is supposed to have said in 1861 after the creation of the Kingdom of Italy, "Italy has been made. Now Italians need to be made." Nearly a century and a half later, however, many people in Italy retain local and regional identities that pre-date the formation of the Italian state.

Modern means of transportation, such as railways, and new forms of communication, such as mass circulation newspapers, helped to create a sense of national identity in many countries. Smaller communities were now linked to the major cities, reducing the distinctiveness of local dialects and cultures, and ideas about the larger community could be transmitted to the population throughout the country. Likewise, the development of a national economy made local communities less insular and encouraged the flow of labour, products, and capital. By creating independence "martyrs," national heroes, flags, and national anthems, and by subsidizing national culture and Olympic teams, governments continue to try to promote a sense of common national identity and national pride.

Sovereign states usually view themselves as representing a particular nationality. These days, we no longer have the British, French, Austrian, Belgian, Dutch, Spanish, Portuguese, Russian, and Ottoman empires that existed in the past. The principle of national self-determination (that each nation should be able to choose to govern itself as a sovereign state) became widely accepted after World War I and was the basis for the establishment of a number of new European states, such as Poland, Czechoslovakia, and Lithuania.

If we think of a nation as based on some shared characteristics such as language, culture, and ethnicity, many countries do not fit the model of a nation-state or do not fit it neatly. There are only a few countries (for example, Japan, Norway, and Iceland) in which the vast majority of people share a common ancestry, language, and culture. In many countries, such as Spain and the United Kingdom, there are minority groups that view themselves as substantially different from the dominant nationality. In other countries (such as Belgium and Nigeria), there is no dominant nationality, either because there are two or more important nationalities, or because identities are based on a large number of tribes. In still other countries, such as Switzerland, local or regional identities may be as important as, or more important than, the overall national identity.

Difficulties in Creating Nation-States

It is hard to divide the world into nation-states. Persons sharing a particular national identity do not always live in well-defined geographical areas. In many parts of Eastern Europe and the Balkans, for example, different nationalities are so highly interspersed it is difficult to draw boundaries that will include particular nationalities within particular states.

The attempt to create a single national identity within a diverse country has not been very successful in many parts of the world. The countries of Africa, for example, retain the boundaries that resulted from conquest by various European empires. These political boundaries often bear little relationship to the geographical location of peoples, languages, cultures, and religions. In other words, the boundaries are artificial, often combining very dissimilar cultures into the same country. Despite efforts by the leaders of independence movements and post-independence governments to create new political identities, severe tensions often exist among peoples sharing the same country. This has helped to fuel the civil wars that have plagued a number of African countries.

Is Canada a Nation-State?

Although the nation-state is generally considered to be the basic type of political community in the modern world, many countries can be better described as **binational** or **multinational states,** that is, states in which there are two or more significant nationalities. The depiction of a country as a nation-state, a binational state, or a multinational state can be controversial, as the case of Canada illustrates.

Canada was largely built on the foundations laid by three peoples: Aboriginals (who are themselves very diverse in language and culture), the French colonists of the sixteenth and seventeenth centuries, and persons of British Isles ancestry (English, Scottish, Irish, and Welsh), many of whom

BINATIONAL AND MULTINATIONAL STATES
States in which there are two or more significant nationalities.

came to Canada from the United States after the American War of Independence. Added to this diverse foundation were large numbers of persons from various countries in Europe, Asia, and other parts of the world, particularly since the latter part of the nineteenth century.

In the past, Canadian governments tried to marginalize or eliminate Aboriginal identities by moving Aboriginals off lands that were being opened for European settlement and by trying to discourage or prevent Aboriginals from practising their cultural traditions. However, unlike many European immigrants who gradually assimilated to the dominant culture of English-speaking Canada, Aboriginals have generally retained their separate identities. Many Aboriginals view themselves as part of a particular Aboriginal nation, based on their tribal ancestry, and Aboriginal leaders often suggest Canada should be viewed as a partnership between Aboriginal First Nations and the communities of subsequent settlers.

Descendants of the French settlers can be found in most parts of Canada, although it is in Quebec and northern New Brunswick that the French language has flourished and the French-speaking community is most vibrant. In the past, the French-Canadian minority retained its identity because of a sense of a religious mission to retain its culture in a hostile environment. In recent decades, a Québécois identity has been asserted based on the distinct French-speaking Quebec nationality. Almost one-half of Quebeckers supported the idea of a sovereign Quebec in a referendum in 1995. However, the majority of Quebeckers view themselves not only as Québécois, but also as Canadians.

THE CANADIAN IDENTITY In the past, many English-speaking Canadians held the view that Canada was basically British. A strong sense of being Canadian did not fully develop until the second half of the twentieth century. Indeed, until a few decades ago, Canada lacked specifically Canadian symbols of nationhood such as a flag, national anthem, or even citizenship. Most English-speaking Canadians now consider themselves to be basically Canadian—although many Newfoundlanders retain a strong sense of Newfoundland identity. Many English-speaking Canadians have been critical of proposals that Quebec should be officially recognized in the Constitution as a "distinct society," or that Canada be thought of as consisting of two or more "nations." For many Canadians, Canada is one nation, even though individuals have different languages, cultures, and origins. Indeed, modern Canada is often described as **multicultural**. In recent decades Canadian governments have recognized the diverse cultural heritage of Canadians and have provided encouragement for different groups to retain their cultures.

Thus, there are different views of nationality in Canada. English-speaking Canadians, in particular, generally view Canada as a nation-state, based on each permanent resident of Canada having the same rights. Many French Quebeckers think of Canada in terms of a partnership between English- and

MULTICULTURALISM
The idea that the diverse cultural heritage of a country should be officially recognized and that different groups should be encouraged to retain their language and culture.

French-speaking communities or between Quebec and the rest of Canada, with a significant minority favouring the establishment of a Quebec nation-state. Aboriginal Canadians resent the privileging of those of British and French ancestry in such ideas as "two founding peoples" and "two nations." Instead, many Aboriginals would like to establish a sense of partnership and sharing between Aboriginal First Nations and the descendants of subsequent settlers. Thus, Canada can be considered a multicultural nation-state, a binational state, or a multinational state, depending upon one's perspective. The complexity of the concept of *nation* is illustrated by the fact that many Quebeckers view themselves as both Québécois and Canadian without necessarily seeing one identity as subordinate to the other.

Is the Nation-State the Most Desirable Form of Political Community?

In a nation-state, people have a bond with each other, and thus will feel a commitment to advancing the good of the political community. A sense of trust in government and other institutions may be easier to develop. Political compromises that are acceptable to different social groups may be easier to achieve because an appeal can be made to a common national interest (Keating, 1996). In a nation-state, rule is by members of the nation who can claim to have the interests of the nation at heart and to share the basic values of the other members of the nation. The legitimacy of the state is less likely to be questioned when the state is based on a single nationality.

However, the nation-state is not the only successful model for organizing the political community. The founders of modern Canada (Robert Baldwin and Louis-Hippolyte Lafontaine; John A. Macdonald and George-Étienne Cartier) believed that a partnership between two peoples, based on trust and mutual respect, could provide a secure foundation for the new country (Saul, 1997). Canada has survived and flourished as a bilingual and multicultural country despite its differences and occasional national unity crises. Likewise, Switzerland successfully unites four different language groups located in different cantons (provinces).

As immigration brings large numbers of persons of diverse backgrounds to countries such as France that have viewed themselves as nation-states, perspectives about the proper basis for the state (for example, nationalism) may have to change. The multicultural model that has been developing in Canada may be preferable to the traditional concept of the nation-state based on a common language, culture, and ancestry.

NATIONALISM

Nationalism is based on the idea that "humanity is naturally divided into nations" (Kedourie, 1994), each of which has certain distinctive characteris-

NATIONALISM
The idea that humanity is naturally divided into nations, each of which has certain distinctive characteristics.

▶ Nationalism is a powerful force in the modern world, and it has played an important role in the struggle of various peoples for liberation from foreign rule. For instance, Basque nationalists, whose homeland has been divided by the international border between France and Spain, have resisted outside domination since the tenth century.

Internet Modern History Sourcebook: Nationalism
www.fordham.edu/halsall/mod/ modsbook17.html

tics. Nationalists believe that each nation should be as independent as possible: thus, the nation-state is the ideal form of political organization. Nationalists seek to promote the interests and values of their particular nation, and typically argue that people's loyalty to their nation should take precedence over their other loyalties, such as to their family, tribe, clan, local community, or religion.

Nationalism has been, and continues to be, a powerful force in the modern world. For example, in the nineteenth century nationalism was an important stimulus for movements to create Germany and Italy out of a variety of small states. Nationalism has played an important role in the struggle of various peoples for liberation from foreign rule. Many nationalists today—for example, the Kurds and Basques—continue to try to create independent nation-states based on their nationality. The break-up of the multinational Soviet Union and Yugoslavia has resulted in a number of bitter nationalist conflicts among peoples who were formerly part of those multinational states. As discussed in Box 2-2, Conflicting Nationalisms in the Mideast, the clash of nationalisms is a major source of tension in the Middle East.

Types of Nationalism

A distinction is often made between ethnic nationalism and civic nationalism. **Ethnic nationalism** views ancestry and the historic cultural traditions associated with a particular ethnic group as the basis for a nation. **Civic nationalism** views shared political values and political history as the basis for nationhood. In practice, it is often hard to separate the two types of nationalism. For example, contemporary Quebec nationalists often claim that their nationalism includes all residents of Quebec. However, occasional comments implying that only those descended from the original French settlers are "true" Quebeckers

ETHNIC NATIONALISM
Nationalism based on ancestry and the historic cultural traditions associated with a particular ethnic group.

CIVIC NATIONALISM
Nationalism based on the shared political values and political history of those who are citizens of a country.

BOX 2-2

Conflicting Nationalisms in the Mideast

Creating nation-states can bring different nationalities into conflict over the same territory, as has long been the case in the Middle East.

The Jewish people were largely dispersed from their ancient homeland in Israel after the Roman Empire suppressed Jewish uprisings about 2000 years ago. A Zionist (Jewish nationalist) movement seeking to re-establish a homeland for the Jewish people developed in the late nineteenth century. Jews, particularly from Eastern Europe, started to move to Palestine (the name given by the Romans to what the Jews called the land of Israel), then part of the Ottoman Empire. After defeating the Ottomans in World War I, the British government issued the Balfour Declaration (1917) supporting the establishment in Palestine of a national home for the Jewish people. This was formalized in the British Mandate for governing Palestine approved by the League of Nations (the predecessor of the United Nations) in 1922.

Increased Jewish migration to Palestine resulted in conflict between Jewish settlers and the Palestinian (Arab) population. As well, there was conflict between various Zionist groups and the British administration in Palestine that turned away European Jews seeking refuge during and after the Nazi Holocaust. In 1947, Britain decided to end its control of Palestine, and the United Nations proposed partitioning Palestine into Jewish and Palestinian states. In 1948, Israel declared its independence and succeeded in defending itself from an attack by neighbouring Arab countries. Many Palestinians fled Israel, and the Kingdom of Jordan occupied the West Bank territory that had been set aside for the Palestinian state.

A war between Israel and its neighbours in 1967 resulted in Israeli occupation of the West Bank and the Gaza Strip, which had been under Egyptian control. Peace treaties were eventually negotiated with Egypt and Jordan, but agreements between Israel and the Palestinians to create self-government for a Palestinian state on the West Bank and Gaza Strip proved unsuccessful. Palestinians rebelled against Israeli occupation of the West Bank and the establishment of Israeli settlements on occupied territory. Suicide bombings by Palestinian militants (termed martyrs by many Palestinians and terrorists by many Israelis) have been directed primarily at Israeli civilians; in response, the Israeli military has countered with forceful retaliation.

For many Israelis, whether secular or religious, the biblical lands of Israel, including the West Bank, are their homeland and inspire a proud assertion of their identity after many centuries of persecution. The statements of Arab leaders that Israel should be driven into the sea have made Israelis determined to build up their military strength and allow few concessions. Many Palestinians view Israelis as colonizers who are backed by the military assistance of Western powers, particularly the United States, and settle on land that the Palestinians have lived on for centuries. The development of a distinctive Palestinian identity is relatively new, but the resentment of Palestinians, many of whom still live in refugee camps in Arab countries, is deep.

There is a general acceptance that some sort of Palestinian state will eventually be created on the West Bank. However, Israeli concerns about security, as well as nationalist pressure to retain the West Bank settlements, make it unlikely that Israel will give up complete control of the West Bank. And Palestinian militants, supported by several countries in the region, are determined to prevent concessions to Israel. As a result, negotiations between the Palestinian Authority (the "official" representatives of the Palestinians) and Israel will continue to be hindered by the clash of conflicting nationalisms.

(for example, former Premier Jacques Parizeau's remark that the 1995 referendum was lost because of "money and the ethnic vote") suggest that there is also an element of ethnic nationalism.

Ethnic nationalism is typically viewed as a more negative form of nationalism. Persons who do not have the characteristics of the ethnic group on which the nation is based may be shunned, excluded, and harassed. Civic nationalism is more inclusive because it potentially includes all persons within a particular territory. Civic nationalism can, however, be intolerant of those who do not share the political principles associated with the nation or are deemed to be insufficiently loyal and patriotic. For example, the civic nationalism that was associated with the French Revolution was intolerant of those who did not share the revolutionary principles. Ethnic nationalism tends to be more disruptive than civic nationalism because ethnic nationalism can challenge the legitimacy of existing states.

A distinction can also be made between aggressive and non-aggressive forms of nationalism. Aggressive forms of nationalism, including imperialism, are often based on the view that some nations are better than others, and that stronger nations should dominate and control weaker ones. For example, in the late nineteenth century and early twentieth centuries, various European powers justified their imperialist conquest and control of much of Africa, Asia, and the Middle East by arguing that they were bringing the superior government, economy, religion, and culture of their country (and of European civilization generally) to "backward" peoples. In what we now regard as racist language, the British writer Rudyard Kipling called imperialism "the White Man's burden." However, by imposing imperial control and Western values, powerful nation-states such as Britain, France, and the United States were denying the right to national self-determination to other peoples.

Nationalism also differs considerably in its objectives, depending on circumstances. In some cases, nationalists seek to unify people of a similar cultural background by uniting existing states. Other nationalists seek to gain independence for a particular nationality by separating from an existing state. As well, nationalists in many parts of the world have struggled to liberate their people from the control of imperial powers.

Nationalism is not always directed at the establishment of a new nation-state. Nationalists may seek to enhance the independence of an existing state. For example, Canadian nationalists have been concerned about the extent of American economic and cultural influence on Canada. Thus, they advocate measures to limit that influence—for example, by putting restrictions on foreign investment and ownership of Canadian businesses. As well, minority nationalities within a state do not always seek to establish their own nation-state. Instead, their nationalism may be expressed by seeking greater self-government and autonomy within the state, or by advocating measures to protect their distinctive cultural identity. For example, many Quebec nationalists would like to see enhanced powers for the Quebec government without Quebec necessarily becoming a sovereign state. Likewise, most Aboriginal nationalists favour self-government within Canada rather than establishing sovereign Aboriginal states.

Evaluating Nationalism

Nationalism has played a major role in encouraging people to unite against foreign domination. Throughout Africa, Asia, and Latin America, the development of nationalism was useful in challenging the domination and exploitation by European imperial powers. Contemporary nationalists suggest that nationalism can be useful in maintaining diversity in the world against the pressures for a homogeneous or American-dominated world.

The Nationalism Project
www.nationalismproject.org

Nationalism is often viewed negatively because it has been the cause of many wars and conflicts in the past two centuries or so. Some nation-states have been created in a peaceful manner. For example, Norway peacefully separated from Sweden in 1905 and Czechoslovakia split into the Czech and Slovak Republics in 1993 without violence. In a number of other cases, however, attempts to create new nation-states have involved serious conflicts. Efforts in the 1990s to create nation-states within the former Yugoslavia involved wars between Serbs, Croats, and Muslims, as well as **ethnic cleansing**, the forcible removal and in some cases massacre of people whose ethnic group differed from that of the group claiming and controlling an area. Likewise, attempts by nation-states to expand their existing borders to include territory or people that they believed to be part of their nation have been a major cause of war.

ETHNIC CLEANSING
The forcible removal and in some cases massacre of people whose ethnic group differed from that of the group claiming and controlling an area.

Nationalism has been criticized for being narrow and limiting. It may encourage uniformity within countries and the adoption of a single identity. Extreme forms of nationalism can encourage xenophobia—fear or hatred of other nationalities. A vibrant civilization may be more likely to flourish in heterogeneous, cosmopolitan communities than in ones in which a particular culture is defended and promoted (Calhoun, 1997). And although nationalism can encourage people to consider the common good of their own political community, it does not encourage people to think of the good of humanity as a whole. In the pursuit of national interests, the interests of other nations may be harmed.

The glorification of a national culture may result in people isolating themselves from enjoying poets, artists, writers, and musicians from the rest of the world. Likewise, in political life, nationalistic feelings may reduce the likelihood that successful policies and practices from elsewhere will be seriously considered. For example, Canadians who are generally convinced (based on comparisons with the United States) that our health care system is the best often do not look seriously at the experiences of other countries that may offer more effective models of delivery or cost control. On the other hand, a sense of nationality can allow people to orient themselves in a complex world and develop a sense of solidarity with others. Is it realistic, defenders of the nation-state argue, to expect people to identify with and be loyal to the people of the world as a whole?

Finally, questions have been raised as to whether states based on small nations are viable. Certainly, there are advantages to larger states in terms of having large internal markets and increased military strength. However, small states such as Iceland, the Republic of Ireland, Singapore, and Luxembourg have been successful economically and able to maintain their sovereignty. The development of economic agreements and military alliances that are composed of a number of countries has helped to offset some of the problems that might otherwise face small nation-states. Nevertheless, there are some nations so small and lacking in economic capabilities (such as the many Aboriginal First Nations in Canada) that establishing a sovereign state for each nation is unrealistic.

Overall, the diversity of nationalism makes it difficult to assess. Nationalism can be used to defend the values and traditions of the past (as, for example, Mahatma Gandhi's version of Indian nationalism) or it can be an instrument of modernization when countries seek to overcome the past in order to strengthen the nation-state (examples include Japan and Turkey) (Leach, 2002). Nationalism can help to create and sustain democratic political systems. Democracy, like the nation-state, is based on the idea of the people governing themselves. The existence of a common language, culture, and history facilitates democratic dialogue among the people. On the other hand, extreme forms of nationalism, such as fascism, stress the importance of national interests and loyalties and seek to suppress the expression of various other interests and loyalties. Thus, they are incompatible with a meaningful democracy. An exclusive focus on the interests of the nation can provide a justification for the authoritarian (non-democratic) rule of those who claim to speak on behalf of the nation.

GLOBALIZATION

The Globalization Website
www.emory.edu/SOC/globalization

A significant number of analysts have argued recently that the modern state is declining in significance. Globalization is making the boundaries of states less relevant, eroding state sovereignty, and reducing the ability of governments to determine the direction of their country. Indeed, one author predicts that by 2025 we will see the end of the nation-state, to be replaced by small units subordinate to a global economy (Ohmae, 1995).

GLOBALIZATION
The processes that are increasing the interconnectedness of the world.

Globalization is often described in terms of the processes that are, in effect, shrinking the world. The obstacles of space and time are being rapidly overcome by contemporary technology, such as high-speed, low-cost communications. This is increasing the interconnectedness of the world and creating a greater awareness of the world as a whole. American journalist Tom Friedman (2000, p. 9) describes globalization as *the inexorable integration of markets, nation-states and technologies to a degree never witnessed before—in a way that is enabling individuals, corporations and nation-states to reach around the world farther, faster, deeper and cheaper than ever before, and in a way that is enabling the world to reach into individuals, corporations and nations farther, faster, deeper, and cheaper than ever before.*

A key aspect of globalization is the development of a global economic system. Such a development concerns manufacturing, trade, and finance. Many business corporations are becoming multinational; they move or contract out their production facilities to wherever goods and services can be produced at the lowest cost and sell their products and services in a variety of countries. Global trade has increased greatly (see Figure 2-2). The process of globalization has been most pronounced in the financial markets that provide a substantial proportion of the money and credit needed by business and government. Approximately US$1.2 trillion is traded daily on the currency markets, much of it for speculative purposes (Held, McGrew, Goldblatt, & Perraton, 2000). This means that currency trading is not generally linked to the international trade of goods or services or to tourism, but is done in the expectation of the gains that can be derived from changes in exchange rates.

Globalization also involves the spreading of cultural products and values around the world. Advances in communications, such as the Internet, have greatly increased the interaction of people, businesses, and other organizations worldwide. Leading brands such as Coke, Pepsi, McDonald's, Taco Bell, and Nike have become familiar to people across the globe. American movies, television shows, and music videos are leading sources of entertainment in many parts of the world.

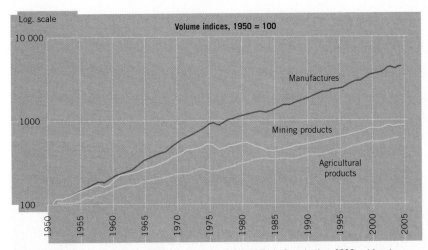

FIGURE 2-2

THE INCREASE IN GLOBAL TRADE, 1950 TO 2002

SOURCE: From *International Trade Statistics, 2003*, by the World Trade Organization, 2003, retrieved July 14, 2004 from www.wto.org/.

There is little doubt that we live in an era of rapid change, and that the interconnectedness of the world's population is increasing. However, as discussed in Box 2-3, Is Globalization Overhyped?, some critics argue that the extent and consequences of globalization have been exaggerated.

BOX 2-3

Is Globalization Overhyped?

Is globalization a novel feature of human existence that is rapidly transforming the world? Or is the widespread discussion of globalization since the early 1990s largely an intellectual fad? The technological changes that have brought the world much closer together in the past few decades are truly amazing. But for a substantial part of the world's population, computers and the Internet are unaffordable; for some, even telephones and televisions are beyond their financial reach.

Globalization is not entirely a new phenomenon. Trading is a very ancient occupation. Two thousand years ago, the Romans built a large empire, as did the Han dynasty in East Asia. Spanish, Portuguese, and Dutch explorers set up a global system of trading posts in the sixteenth century. A massive slave trade bringing Africans to the Americas developed in the seventeenth century. Britain built a global empire ("where the sun never sets") in the nineteenth century. Similarly, long before modern communications and transportation, religions spread across large areas of the earth. Christianity spread throughout the Roman Empire and continued to expand its geographical reach after the empire fell. And in a relatively short time after the death of its founder Mohammed (632 CE), Islam spread from its home in Saudi Arabia as far as Spain and India.

Countries vary in the extent to which they are connected to global markets. Canada has always relied quite heavily on foreign exports and imports and has always had a high level of dependence upon foreign investment. The U.S. economy is still primarily based on production for its large domestic market, although it has become quite dependent upon imports of oil and some other natural resources.

Although world trade has been increasing, much of the trade occurs within regions of the world rather than truly on a global basis. For example, a large majority of the goods and services imported and exported by European countries is traded among the countries of the European Union. Likewise, a very high proportion of Canada's trade is with the United States.

Questions have arisen as to whether a global "monoculture"—that is, a single global culture based on the cultural values of the Western world, particularly the United States—is developing. Certainly cultural diversity is diminishing as many traditional languages and cultures are endangered. American cultural products are widely distributed throughout much of the world. However, there are substantial cultural differences among various regions of the world that American movies, television shows, music, fast foods, and brand labels will not easily erase. Indeed, contemporary communications media, such as the Internet and satellite television, can help minority cultures that are spread across a variety of countries to maintain and develop their cultural values (Elkins, 1995).

We should keep in mind that globalization is a process rather than a finished product. There may be trends towards a global economy and a global culture, but the policies adopted by various governments can accelerate, slow down, or even reverse the trends.

Globalization and Politics

Although globalization is often described as an inevitable process, governments have played a role in the encouragement of a global economic system. After World War II, leaders of Western countries worked towards reducing the barriers to trade because of their negative experiences with nationalism and economic protectionism in the 1930s. These political decisions set the framework in which economic globalization could develop. The development of the massive currency market was a product of many countries' decisions to adopt floating (market-determined) exchange rates for their currency instead of fixed rates, and to remove restrictions on the flow of capital. The trend of governments since the early 1980s to reduce the regulation of their economies, privatize publicly owned enterprises, and reduce government spending and taxes has contributed to the acceleration of the growth of a global free-market capitalist economy.

Global Policy Forum
www.globalpolicy.org

A global political system exists to some extent, but it is not very well developed. A substantial number of international agreements have been reached. The United Nations includes almost all sovereign states, although it has not functioned as a global government. The World Trade Organization has established detailed trade rules that affect the economic policies of its member countries, now a large majority of the countries of the world. The rules of the World Trade Organization also indirectly affect policies in other areas, such as environment and health, by allowing such policies to be challenged if they are deemed to be disguised restrictions of trade. The International Monetary Fund and the World Bank require that countries seeking loans and development assistance adopt free market policies, such as removing barriers to the entry of foreign products and investments.

International Forum on Globalization
www.ifg.org

In addition to institutions and agreements that involve most of the world's states, there are various regional arrangements that reduce the sovereignty of member states. Most countries in Europe are now members of the European Union (EU), which has an increasing ability to regulate what is done in the Union and attempts to develop common European policies. The North American Free Trade Agreement (NAFTA), involving Canada, the United States, and Mexico, does not integrate its member countries as tightly as does the EU, but nevertheless limits what each country can do in terms of trade, regulation of investment, energy exports, and other economic matters.

There are also a large number of groups that engage in political action on a global level. Greenpeace, for example, has grown from a small Vancouver organization concerned with nuclear testing in Alaska to a large international organization involved in environmental causes around the world. A concerned American, Jody Williams, made extensive use of e-mail to mobilize a wide variety of groups and individuals around the world who successfully pressed for an international treaty banning anti-personnel landmines. Growing networks of non-governmental organizations operate in a variety of countries, seeking to influence the policies of states and sometimes corporations in such areas as human rights, the environment, the status of women, and peace. International business, labour, and religious groups are also important actors on the global political stage.

Globalization: A Contentious Issue

Globalization can bring many benefits:

- *Efficiency.* The economic principle of **comparative advantage** holds that economic wealth is maximized when countries focus on those activities at which they are most efficient, and then trade with other countries for those products and services that they cannot produce as efficiently.
- *Access to money.* Easier access to global financial markets can help countries that are developing their economies to obtain the loans and investment capital they need.
- *Consumer prices.* Consumers benefit from the lower prices that can result from shifting the production of goods and services to areas where the costs of production are the lowest.
- *Democratic ideas.* Freer flows of communication have helped to undermine authoritarian regimes and spread democratic ideas.
- *Understanding.* Increased communication has also helped to give us a better understanding of global problems such as environmental degradation and poverty. The Internet has been of great assistance to groups organizing to advance a variety of global causes.

Globalization has, however, come under considerable criticism, for several reasons:

- *The poor stay poor.* The increased wealth associated with economic globalization has not done much to help the poorest members of the global community. Although shifting production to poor countries has created jobs, competition to attract those jobs has typically resulted in extremely low wages. The benefits of the globalized economy have largely gone to wealthier persons in the rich countries. As well, the ease with which large amounts of money can be instantaneously transferred has resulted in wealthy individuals and corporations shifting their money to tax havens (jurisdictions that do not levy taxes) such as the Cayman Islands.
- *Concentration of power.* Globalization has substantially increased the power of the largest corporations. By threatening to shift production to other countries, they have been able to secure a variety of profitable concessions from governments, such as lower taxes. Large global corporations are difficult for governments to regulate or control.
- *Westernization.* Because of the great power of the United States, whether in economic, military, or cultural terms, globalization has often meant the spread of American (and, more generally, Western) products and values.

COMPARATIVE ADVANTAGE
The economic principle that wealth is maximized when countries focus on those activities at which they are most efficient, and then trade with other countries for those products and services that they cannot produce as efficiently.

McDonald's has come to symbolize globalization. While American or Western products have found ready acceptance throughout the world, there is often a reaction among those who feel that local customs, traditions, and products are threatened. Globalization is viewed by many as a form of cultural imperialism that erodes diversity. Fears about the character of globalization can heighten international political tensions.

- *Economic crises snowball.* Globalization may increase the risk of serious global economic crises. As we saw in the chapter opening, economic problems in one country can now quickly spread to other parts of the world because of the interdependence of economies, the instantaneous nature of contemporary communication, and the high level of speculation in financial markets.

- *Other risks.* Similarly, high levels of international trade and travel can bring increased health and environmental risks. And the interconnectedness of global communications systems makes them vulnerable to computer viruses that can cause billions of dollars in damages. In general, the interconnectedness of the world can increase our vulnerability to disruptions, whether through malfunctioning equipment, human error, or terrorist attacks.

Some of the problems of globalization have been brought to public attention by the anti-globalization movement that developed in the late 1990s. The term *anti-globalization* is a rather imprecise description of this diverse international movement. As Canadian author Naomi Klein has pointed out, this movement has focused its protests on the "dismal human rights, labour, and ecological records" of large multinational corporations, and the concentration of power in the hands of large corporations generated by the unregulated processes of globalization (Klein, 2002, p. 4). Thus, the movement might be better described as "anti-corporate" rather than "anti-globalization" (Klein, 2002, p. 4) or as a global social justice movement. The protests of the anti-globalization movement have been primarily directed at meetings of international bodies such as the World Trade Organization, International Monetary Fund, World Bank, and the G-8 (heads of government of countries with the largest economies), based on the view that these organizations are serving the interests of global capitalism rather than the common good of humanity.

Globalization and the Nation-State

Is globalization seriously eroding the power of nation-states? The heightened pressures of economic competition may encourage countries to adopt policies that focus on removing barriers to the global free market, reducing the role of government in regulating the economy, and cutting the taxes that are needed to provide social benefits. The rules of trade that are adopted by bodies such as the World Trade Organization are aimed at trying to establish a "level playing field" in which government policies that give preferential treatment to domestic businesses are expected to be eliminated.

Nevertheless, there is still a wide diversity among the policies adopted by different countries. The relatively prosperous countries of Western Europe, for example, have continued to maintain a wide range of social benefits for their populations, as well as high environmental and health standards. The governments of the newly industrialized countries of East Asia are heavily involved in directing their industries. Generally, countries have tended to adapt to globalization in different ways, and have chosen to integrate into the global economy to differing extents (Garrett, 1998).

Globalization may be eroding the power of the nation-state not only by shifting power upwards to global institutions, global markets, and global corporations, but also by indirectly challenging the nation-state from below (see Box 2-4, Jihad Versus McWorld). The assertion of ethnic and regional identities (for example, the development of separatist movements) may be a result of the decreasing importance of states in providing for the well-being of their people. The development of organizations such as the European Union and the North American Free Trade Agreement makes it possible for some people in smaller areas, such as Scotland and Quebec, to think that belonging to such organizations will offset the disadvantages that they would face by separating from a large country. The growth of religious fundamentalism (for example, in Islamic countries) may also be a reaction to globalization among those who feel that their traditions are threatened by the changing world (Giddens, 2000).

BOX 2-4

Jihad Versus McWorld

American political scientist Benjamin Barber describes the key forces in the contemporary world as "McWorld" (globalization) and "Jihad" (a term referring to Islamic holy war that he uses more generally to describe the "retribalization" of different peoples opposed to global interdependence and homogenization).

These forces "operate with equal strength in opposite directions, the one driven by parochial hatreds, the other by universalizing markets, the one recreating ancient sub-national and ethnic borders from within, the other making national borders porous from without" (Barber, 1995, p. 6). In Barber's view, the success of either of these trends would lead to a bleak and undemocratic political future. McWorld involves imposing an unnatural uniformity, while Jihad involves intolerance.

As an alternative, Barber advocates working towards a loose democratic union ("confederation") of semi-autonomous communities, smaller than nation-states. In such communities, citizens might enjoy a high level of participation in decisions affecting all aspects of their lives—a far cry from McWorld and Jihad.

Summary and Conclusion

The nation-state is often considered to be the primary basis for the way the modern world is organized. States claim to be the highest authority within a particular, well-defined territory. State sovereignty is a legal principle implying that states have the right to govern their population and territory without outside interference, and that they should be treated as equals on the world stage. The rationale often given for state sovereignty is that states are the political expression of a nation, and that nations should have the right to govern themselves. The determination of what nation people belong to is, however, often controversial. Nations are sometimes thought of in terms of the common ancestry and other characteristics of a people, but governments, along with intellectuals and artists, have often created or developed myths of nationhood to unify the people of their country and create a common culture.

The political doctrine of nationalism—with its goals of trying to achieve a self-governing state for nations and promoting the interests and values of nation-states—has been and continues to be a powerful force in the modern world. From a nationalist perspective, the state should look after the common good of the nation upon which it is based. In reality, however, many states are not based on a people with a single, common identity or set of characteristics. Although such states can be stable and successful, the determination of the common good in a binational or multinational state can be difficult because the good of each nation has to be taken into account.

The contemporary state faces challenges from globalization as well as from regions and groups within the state that would like to gain greater autonomy or independence. Ethnic nationalism and the continuing relevance of subnational identities threaten the existence and legitimacy of some states. However, claims that the state is becoming irrelevant seem to be exaggerated. The state is still the most important political community. Nevertheless, politics and governing are becoming more complex as a variety of organizations beyond the state are assuming increased importance. Politics and governing are no longer as strongly focused on the state as they were in the nineteenth and twentieth centuries.

Globalization presents important political challenges; in particular, how to regulate global forces so that they work to the advantage of the world's population as a whole, rather than concentrating unaccountable power in the hands of large multinational corporations or certain powerful states. Effective forms of governing at the global level are needed to direct economic and technological globalization for the common good of humanity (Valaskakis, 2001). "Civilizing globalization"—in other words, trying to make globalization more equitable, environmentally sustainable, democratic, controllable, and less threatening to cultural diversity—is a key political challenge for the twenty-first century (Sandbrook, 2003). To make progress towards achieving the common good of humanity, the development of a consciousness of being part of a global community may be necessary.

Key Terms

Discussion Questions

1. What should be the rights and obligations of citizens? How should citizenship be determined? Should a person be allowed to be a citizen of more than one country?

2. Should each nation be self-governing?

3. Is Canada a nation-state?

4. Will globalization make the state irrelevant?

5. Is globalization a threat to cultural values? Is economic globalization undesirable?

Further Reading

Barber, B. *Jihad vs. McWorld: How globalization and tribalism are reshaping the world.* New York: Ballantine, 1995.

Brawley, M.R. *The politics of globalization: Gaining perspective, assessing consequences.* Peterborough, ON: Broadview, 2003.

Calhoun, C. *Nationalism.* Buckingham, UK: Open University Press, 1997.

Friedman, T. *The Lexus and the olive tree.* New York: Anchor Books, 2000.

Geider, W. *One world, ready or not: The manic logic of global capitalism.* New York: Simon and Schuster, 1997.

Giddens, A. *Runaway world: How globalization is reshaping our lives.* New York: Routledge, 2000.

Guibernau, M.G., & Hutchinson, J. (Eds.). *Understanding nationalism.* Cambridge, UK: Polity Press, 2001.

Held, D., McGrew, A., Goldblatt, D., & Perraton, J. *Global transformations: Politics, economics and culture.* Cambridge: Polity Press, 1999.

Hirst, P., & Thompson, G. *Globalization in question: The international economy and the possibilities of governance,* 2nd ed. Cambridge: Polity Press, 1999.

Keating, M. *Nations against the state: The new politics of nationalism in Quebec, Catalonia and Scotland.* Basingstoke, UK: Macmillan, 1996.

Martin, H.-P., & Schumann, H. (P. Camiller, Trans.) *The global trap: Globalization and the assault on democracy and prosperity.* Montreal: Black Rose Books, 1997.

McQuaig, L. *The cult of impotence: Selling the myth of powerlessness in the global economy.* Toronto: Viking 1998.

Saul, J.R. *Reflections of a Siamese twin: Canada at the end of the twentieth century.* Toronto: Penguin, 1997.

Stiglitz, J.E. *Globalization and its discontents.* New York: W.W. Norton, 2002.

Weiss, L. *The myth of the powerless state.* Ithaca: Cornell University Press, 1998.

Woodward, S.L. *Balkan tragedy: Chaos and dissolution after the Cold War.* Washington, DC: The Brookings Institution, 1995.

Chapter 3

POLITICS AND THE ECONOMY

PHOTO ABOVE: Mikhail Khodorkovsky, former chief executive of Yukos, Russia's second-largest oil producer, is well-known for his political opposition to President Vladimir Putin. Now he faces up to ten years in jail if convicted of fraud and tax-evasion charges. Should Yukos collapse, the ramifications for the Russian economy would be unpredictable.

After reading this chapter you should be able to:

1. outline the strengths and weaknesses of the free-market capitalist system
2. examine the ways in which the free-market capitalist system has been modified by modern governments
3. evaluate the controversies concerning the welfare state
4. discuss the alternatives to a free-market capitalist system
5. explain how economic issues relate to political conflicts

In October 2003, Mikhail Khodorkovsky was on his private jet at a remote airport in Siberia. With assets of over US$16 billion, surely he had every reason to relax. Suddenly, his plane was stormed by dozens of armed security men who took him off to jail, charged with fraud, embezzlement, and tax evasion. How did Russia's richest man become an accused criminal?

Khodorkovsky had been raised in a typical two-room communal apartment and was a leader in the Communist Youth League. But as restrictions on private enterprise began to ease in the 1980s, he opened a café, established an import business, and soon emerged as an owner of Russia's first privately-owned bank, Bank Menatep. When the Soviet Union disbanded in 1991 and the state-owned economy was dismantled, Bank Menatep was hired to auction off Yukos, the leading oil company. In a dubious transaction, the bank bought the company for a tiny fraction of its worth. Like a small number of so-called "oligarchs," Khodorkovsky accumulated great wealth—in part through his political connections.

Khodorkovsky, however, made the mistake of being a political opponent of Vladimir Putin, the former head of the security service elected president of Russia in 2000. Khodorkovsky's arrest occurred shortly after he had purchased a newspaper and hired a journalist known to be highly critical of Putin, who has taken actions to ensure that the mass media are supportive of his rule. Many Russians support Putin's arrest of Khodorkovsky—they suffered great hardships during the transition to capitalism and blame the oligarchs for plundering Russia's wealth.

Politics and economics are closely related. Political decisions have important effects on the distribution of wealth and people's well-being. Those with economic power often use their wealth to try to affect politics. High levels of inequality can lead to tensions between the wealthy and the rest of the population. The clash of communism and capitalism that was characteristic of much of the twentieth century has faded—most countries are now part of the global capitalist system. However, there continue to be substantial variations among countries regarding the role of the state in managing the economy and in providing for the well-being of the population.

The Russian example also indicates that, contrary to popular belief, a capitalist system is not necessarily associated with freedom and democracy. Capitalism has flourished not only in free, democratic countries, but also in strict dictatorships such as contemporary China and military-ruled Chile of the 1970s and '80s. This chapter examines the variations and contradictions at work in the interaction of politics and the economy.

THE RELATIONSHIP BETWEEN POLITICS AND THE ECONOMY

American political scientist Harold Lasswell described politics as "who gets what, when, how" (Lasswell, 1936). Usually we think of the economic system as determining how wealth and income is distributed, but political decisions often have a substantial effect on "who gets what." In a fundamental sense, an economic system depends on the laws and regulations established by government. Without laws, no substantial economic system could exist. Those with the means of force would simply plunder the goods of those who are weaker.

Political decisions also determine the basic nature of the economic system. The business corporations operating at the centre of the economic system in countries such as Canada are a product of laws providing for the limited liability of shareholders (that is, shareholders can lose no more than they have invested). Indeed, corporations have been granted similar rights to those of individuals. In contrast, some countries place the state at the centre of the economic system, with the state owning or directing most economic activities.

Inequality

Inequality in the distribution of goods and services is a feature of all economic systems, except for communal systems where all goods are shared equally. Nevertheless, government spending and taxing policies can have significant effects on the distribution of wealth and income. In fact, as Table 3-1 illustrates, there is considerable variation in inequalities from country to country, in part because of governmental actions.

Political controversy often centres on questions related to the distribution of wealth and income, such as:

- whether government should redistribute income and wealth from the rich to the poor
- whether government should ensure that all persons have a reasonable standard of living
- whether various services (such as health care and education) should be available free of charge to all members of the political community

Political life, then, often revolves around issues related to material well-being and the regulation of economic activity. This is especially true when physical security is not seriously threatened by war or violence. Those in different economic positions (such as business owners and workers) and those in different economic circumstances (such as the rich and the poor) often have conflicting views about many government policies. Government policies affect the extent to which different groups of people are able to retain their wealth, have the basic necessities, feel secure against the hardships that may

TABLE 3-1
THE DISTRIBUTION OF INCOME, SELECTED COUNTRIES

Notes: The Gini Index measures the extent to which the distribution differs from a perfectly equal distribution. A figure of 0.0 indicates perfect equality. A figure of 100.0 would result if all income were in the hands of one person. The data are based on different years for different countries. The figures for different countries are not strictly comparable. Some are based on distribution of income while others are based on distribution of consumption.

COUNTRY	GINI INDEX	POOREST 10%	RICHEST 10%	COUNTRY	GINI INDEX	POOREST 10%	RICHEST 10%
Slovak Republic	19.5	5.1%	18.2%	India	37.8	3.5%	33.5%
Japan	24.9	4.8%	24.7%	China	40.3	2.4%	30.4%
Sweden	25.0	3.7%	20.1%	United States	40.8	1.8%	30.5%
Czech Republic	25.4	4.3%	22.4%	Turkey	41.5	2.3%	32.3%
Italy	27.3	3.5%	21.8%	Russia	48.7	1.7%	36.7%
Germany	30.0	3.3%	23.7%	Nigeria	50.6	1.6%	40.8%
Pakistan	31.2	4.1%	27.6%	Mexico	53.1	1.3%	41.7%
Canada	31.5	2.8%	23.8%	Chile	56.7	1.3%	45.6%
South Korea	31.6	2.9%	24.3%	South Africa	59.3	1.1%	45.9%
France	32.7	2.8%	25.1%	Nicaragua	60.3	0.7%	48.8%
Australia	35.2	2.0%	25.4%	Brazil	60.7	0.7%	48.0%
United Kingdom	36.8	2.3%	27.7%	Sierra Leone	62.9	0.5%	43.6%

SOURCE: *Adapted from* World Development Report, 2002: World Development Indicators, Distribution of Income or Consumption, *by the World Bank, 2002, retrieved August 5, 2004 from www.worldbank.org/poverty/data/2_8wdi2002.pdf.*

be caused by unemployment, disability, or old age, and find opportunities to develop themselves.

Not only can political decisions affect the impact of the economic system on people's lives, but the economic system can affect the nature of political decisions. Those with economic power often translate that power into political power. Thus, the policies and laws of the political community may be strongly influenced by those who control the economic system.

THE FREE-MARKET CAPITALIST SYSTEM

The basic economic system that was developed in the nineteenth century in countries such as Britain, the United States, and Canada can be labelled as a **free-market capitalist economic system** (also often referred to as a free enterprise system). This system involves private ownership and control of most businesses. Economic activity is coordinated mainly through market transactions, rather than by the commands of government or other authorities (Lindblom, 2001).

Key features of the free-market capitalist economic system include:

- businesses produce for the marketplace in search of profits
- consumers choose among competing products at prices determined by the marketplace
- workers supply their labour for wages determined by the marketplace

Although the use of markets to buy and sell goods is thousands of years old, markets generally played only a limited role in economic life before the

FREE-MARKET CAPITALIST ECONOMIC SYSTEM
An economic system involving private ownership and control of most businesses. Economic activity is coordinated primarily through market transactions, rather than by the commands of government or other authorities.

modern era. Households produced food and other products primarily for their own use. In feudal societies, there was often no free labour market, and competition among businesses was severely restricted. The Industrial Revolution resulted in economies that were based on the production of goods and services for sale in the marketplace. Setting up large-scale production required both a large labour force available for hire and large amounts of money (capital) to be invested in the expectation of profit. In other words, the Industrial Revolution resulted in a great increase in the markets for goods and services and the development of labour and capital markets.

Free-market capitalist systems can be very effective in matching the demands of consumers with the supply of products by business (see Box 3-1, Adam Smith and the Efficiency of Free Markets). In fact, the establishment

BOX 3-1
Adam Smith and the Efficiency of Free Markets

Scottish philosopher Adam Smith (1723–1790) provided the classic argument for a free-market system in 1776 with the publication of his book *The Wealth of Nations*.

Smith's basic argument was that a free, competitive economy is the most efficient way of producing goods. It is desirable because it maximizes the total wealth of the community. Individuals pursuing their own economic interests will be guided by the "invisible hand" of the marketplace to act in a fashion that is in the interests of the community as a whole. Smith wrote, "It is not from the benevolence of the butcher, the brewer, or the baker that we expect our dinner, but from their regard to their self-interest" (Smith, 1776/2004, p. 105). Competition among producers leads to the production of goods at the lowest possible price. The signals of the marketplace lead to a balance between what goods are produced and what goods consumers desire. The marketplace, in other words, is self-regulating. Intervention by government lowers the overall level of wealth and creates special privileges for those who are able to influence govern-

ment at the expense of the society as a whole. The common good is best achieved by allowing individuals to pursue their own economic self-interest.

Smith also advocated the removal of barriers to international free trade. Tariffs (taxes) on imports designed to protect domestic industries result in higher prices for consumers and special privileges for protected industries. In Smith's view, pursuing the interests of the nation-state through protectionist policies, the granting of monopolies to particular merchants, and the extraction of wealth from colonies (the **mercantilist policies** common in the seventeenth and eighteenth centuries) hindered the creation of a prosperous and peaceful world.

For Smith, the proper role of government was to provide protection from foreign invasion and to protect property and maintain order through a system of laws. Involvement in the economy should be limited to providing certain "collective goods," such as roads, canals, education, and street lighting, that are unlikely to be provided by private business (Ball & Dagger, 2004).

MERCANTILIST POLICIES
Pursuit of the interests of the
nation-state through protectionist policies, the granting of
monopolies to particular merchants, and the extraction of
wealth from colonies.

The Capitalism Site
www.capitalism.org

of the free-market capitalist system (replacing **mercantilist policies**) in the nineteenth century, combined with new techniques of production, was revolutionary, resulting in the mass production of consumer goods. Large-scale industrial production contributed to the growth of cities and the decline of traditional, rural ways of life.

On the surface, the free-market capitalist system does not appear very efficient. Businesses regularly go bankrupt, different companies produce the same product, and major miscalculations by business executives are common. However, if competition and entrepreneurship are strong and capital is easily available for new enterprises, the free-market capitalist system can be highly flexible. Entrepreneurs seeking new sources of profit will quickly seek financing for new endeavours, while enterprises that are not competitive, efficient, or sufficiently profitable will be shut down in favour of newer, more efficient, technologically advanced, and profitable ones. In the view of Austrian economist Joseph Schumpeter (1943), the essence of capitalism is the process of "creative destruction"—the perpetual cycle of rejecting older and less efficient products and services and replacing them with newer, more efficient ones. A drawback is that workers suffer insecurity because the company that they work for may collapse. Likewise, communities, particularly smaller communities, may be harmed if a major employer becomes bankrupt.

Innovation and Profits

The Center for the Advancement of
Capitalism
www.moraldefense.com

The free-market capitalist system is often praised for its innovative capabilities. It has a built-in incentive to innovate as those who take risks with new products or processes can reap large rewards. Businesses will want to adopt new technologies in order to stay ahead of their competitors. This point should be qualified, however, by noting that a variety of technological advances have also resulted from government- and military-sponsored research—including nuclear fission, rockets, jet engines, radar, computers, the Internet, plastics, and a variety of synthetic materials (Hedley, 2002).

Problems can arise if a business or a group of businesses gains control over a sector of the economy because it can then charge exorbitant prices without the need to focus on efficiency. The highly competitive marketplace that Adam Smith envisioned has been replaced, to a considerable extent, by a system in which several hundred large and powerful corporations control a substantial proportion of the global economy. Some have expressed concerns that the rise of large business corporations will eventually result in a decline in the dynamic element of entrepreneurship (Schumpeter, 1943).

Adam Smith was aware that business could be a powerful force; for example, businesses would be tempted to collude to limit competition, or seek privileges from government. However, in his influential model of a free-market economy, individual businesses have no significant power; rather, they compete with each other to produce the goods that consumers want at

"The Wal-Stores are coming! The Wal-Stores are coming!"

the lowest possible price. In reality, large corporations have the ability to affect the economic well-being and employment opportunities of the communities and countries in which they operate. This gives them substantial potential political power. To attract or retain businesses, governments often offer special incentives such as tax exemptions, grants, and free serviced land. Because governments are concerned with maintaining a favourable investment climate, they may tailor their policies to meet the demands of the leading business interests and will try to ensure the profitability of business.

The Environment

A free-market capitalist system can create problems for the environment. The massive increase in production and consumption that has accompanied the growth of the free-market capitalist system has resulted in a greatly increased use of the world's limited resources. There has also been a major increase in the emission of wastes into the atmosphere, soil, and water as a by-product of production and consumption. The competitive pursuit of profit typically does not encourage business to spend money on pollution abatement equipment or on sustainable resource management unless required by government legislation or encouraged by the pressure of consumer boycotts. In other words, the efficiency of the free-market capitalist system in producing goods for the marketplace is not necessarily matched by efficiency in minimizing negative effects on the environment.

In the long run, protection of the natural environment and conservation of natural resources are important for business as well as the public. However, individual businesses may be reluctant to take costly measures to limit their negative impact on the environment unless they can be assured that their competitors will take similar actions. Thus, government action is often needed to protect the environment.

The Longer Term

Corp Watch: Holding corporations accountable
www.corpwatch.org

Individual businesses are often focused on maintaining and enhancing their profitability in the short term. Corporations whose shares trade on the stock market are often particularly concerned with ensuring that each of their quarterly reports shows a positive performance. This may mean that insufficient attention is given to long-term planning.

Concern has also been expressed about the distribution of the wealth created by the free-market capitalist system. This system tends to generate considerable disparities in income and wealth. For example, top corporate officers typically earn many times as much as the workers in their company (see Box 3-2, Business Reward$: Nortel and Enron). In a pure free-market system, individuals who are unable to find employment or lack skills for which there is a strong demand may find themselves dependent upon charity to survive.

SOCIALIST ECONOMIC SYSTEMS

A socialist economic system involves social (public) ownership and control of the major economic institutions. Communist-led governments in the former Soviet Union, China, Eastern Europe, North Korea, Cuba, and Vietnam established **centrally planned state socialist economic systems** in the twentieth century. These systems featured state ownership of almost all enterprises and centralized planning by state officials. As they tried to carry out five-year plans, state officials made decisions as to what goods would be produced, the quantities to be produced, and where and how they would be produced, along with decisions about how consumer goods would be priced.

CENTRALLY PLANNED STATE SOCIALIST ECONOMIC SYSTEM
An economic system involving state ownership of almost all enterprises and centralized planning by state officials.

Communist-led governments were often successful in mobilizing their countries to industrialize and in achieving key objectives set by the political leadership—for example, the Soviet Union was the first country to put a satellite into orbit. As well, the communist-led countries generally provided a wide variety of social services to their population, including childcare, education, subsidized housing, health care, and pensions. Unemployment was almost unknown, and workers were essentially guaranteed their jobs for life.

Business Reward$: Nortel and Enron

During the 1990s, the top executives of large North American corporations were not only able to obtain very large increases in annual salaries, but also received options to buy shares in their companies at discounted prices. Stock options, the argument went, were needed to ensure that top executives had a stake in the companies they were running; executives should share in the profits their efforts generated. However, when the high-technology stock market bubble of the 1990s burst, the huge amount of wealth garnered by top executives began to be questioned.

Consider John Roth, the former head of Canadian-based Nortel Networks, North America's largest telecommunications manufacturer. Roth cashed in $135 million worth of stock options in 2000. Soon afterwards, shareholders, including pension funds, saw Nortel shares plummet from a peak of over $120 to less than a dollar a share. Tens of thousands of workers were laid off and Nortel lost US$27.3 billion in 2001. Despite his very poor business decisions, Roth, who was pushed out of his position in 2001, had been very generously compensated.

Interestingly, the problems at Nortel continued under his successor, Frank Dunn. Although Dunn and other senior executives received huge bonuses when Nortel returned to profitability in 2003, it was subsequently discovered that profits had been greatly overstated by the company. Dunn and other executives were fired in 2004 amid investigations of Nortel's accounting practices, lawsuits, and criminal probes.

The corruption that can exist in the business world was highlighted by the scandal at Enron, the seventh-largest company in the United States. With the assistance of senior personnel at one of the world's largest accounting firms, top executive officers were able to make their company appear to be highly profitable. These dishonest accounting practices boosted the price of the company's stock so that top executive officers could sell their stock options at highly inflated prices. Enron subsequently went bankrupt in 2001, leaving its shareholders, including its workers, with huge losses. Enron's top executives had secretly sold their shares before the collapse of the company even as they were encouraging their employees to buy more shares.

Nortel and Enron are not isolated cases. Similar accusations of greed and corruption have been made concerning a number of major corporations. Although the pursuit of profit can result in efficiency and innovation, it can also lead to unproductive forms of greed and exploitation.

Problems

The centrally planned state socialist economies had serious difficulties, however. It is very difficult to plan all the details of a complex economy. Making the task more difficult was inadequate information. Information that reflected negatively on the government and the performance of the economy was routinely suppressed. Thus, planners did not have the data needed to direct the economy. The outcome was that the centrally planned economies were inefficient. Planners were often unable to match supply and demand, resulting in a surplus of some goods and shortages of others. Heavily subsidized prices for

▶ Heavily subsidized prices for basic necessities, such as bread, sometimes result in shortages as demand exceeds supply.

basic necessities like bread resulted in shortages as demand exceeded supply. Consumers often had to wait in long lines to obtain the limited amount of goods available. Because factory managers were generally expected to meet quotas based on the quantity of goods to be produced, low-quality goods were often produced. With strict bureaucratic controls in place, there was not much of an incentive to innovate and take risks. As well, in their efforts to achieve rapid industrial growth, the communist-led countries typically ignored environmental concerns, and thus suffered severe pollution problems.

The communist-led countries were committed to creating a classless society. However, those with political power, such as the Communist Party elite, often were, in effect, a privileged class. For example, many goods were frequently only available at special stores for the party elite. Likewise, certain holiday resorts were only open to a privileged few.

With the collapse of communism in the Soviet Union and Eastern Europe at the end of the 1980s and in the early 1990s, only North Korea and Cuba, to some extent, continue to have state socialist economies. The People's Republic of China, although still governed by the Communist Party, has been gradually moving away from state ownership and central planning.

Alternatives

A state-owned, centrally planned economy is not the only possible model of a socialist economy. Socialist economies can involve cooperative rather than state ownership and control of enterprises. The communist-led government of the former Yugoslavia, for example, established a system of market socialism, in which industries controlled by their workers produced goods and services that were sold in a basically free marketplace. Likewise, some cooperative enterprises run by workers on a democratic basis exist in numerous countries.

In the Basque region of Spain, for example, the Mondragon network of 150 cooperatives, with about 23 000 workers, produces a wide variety of goods and services. However, the Mondragon network is only a small part of the overall Spanish economy.

MIXED ECONOMIES

Virtually all contemporary economic systems contain a mixture of government and private business involvement in the economy. In Canada, for example, the generation and distribution of electricity is in the hands of a Crown (state-owned) corporation in many provinces. Most cities run public transit systems and the Canadian government owns VIA Rail, the national passenger rail service. Nevertheless, a large majority of business enterprises are in private hands and governments play only a minor role in planning and directing the economy. Other countries in which government owns and controls a substantial proportion of business activity or plays a major role in planning and directing the economy can be described as having **mixed economies** (see Box 3-3, Mixed Economies). In other words, mixed economies are a mixture of socialist and capitalist economic systems.

Since the early 1980s, a number of countries with mixed economies have been moving, to varying extents, in the direction of a more free-market capitalist economic system. Advocates of free-market policies have successfully argued that state-owned enterprises are less efficient than their private sector counterparts and that state planning and direction of the economy is often unsuccessful. The pressure of economic globalization had contributed to the tendency to privatize (sell to private investors) many state-owned enterprises and to reduce direct government involvement in economic planning in a number of countries.

MIXED ECONOMY
An economic system in which the government owns and controls a substantial proportion of business activity or plays a major role in planning and directing the economy; in other words, a mixture of socialist and capitalist economic systems.

GOVERNMENT INVOLVEMENT IN THE ECONOMY

Few countries today have socialist economies, and a number of countries have reduced the amount of state ownership and planning of their economies. However, governments in all modern countries play a significant role in the economy.

Governments are major economic actors, collecting a sizable proportion of a country's income through taxation to spend on government operations and services and to transfer to individuals for various purposes. As Table 3-2 indicates, government expenditure relative to the size of the economy tends to be higher in the richer countries than in the poorer countries.

Protecting Consumers

Why are governments, even in countries with free-market capitalist economies, active in the economy? One reason is that various sectors of the

BOX 3-3

Mixed Economies

Many countries, both Western and non-Western, have economies in which both government and privately owned businesses play a major role in managing the economy (Wade, 1990).

In rebuilding and modernizing France's economy in the decades after World War II, the French government established national plans for economic development through a system of voluntary cooperation with business and labour. The French government had considerable power to persuade business to follow its economic plans as many important sectors of the economy—including banking, insurance, energy, transportation and communications, and automobile production—were at least in part state-owned. As well, the French government used its controls over prices, lending rates, and investment funds to influence business to follow its economic plans (Roth, Warwick, & Paul, 1989). Through investments in large projects, such as high-speed trains, France became a world leader in some technologies. From 1958 to 1973, state direction of the economy was successful in creating a modern, prosperous economy. Since then, however, the French economy has suffered from weak economic growth and high unemployment (Hauss & Smith, 2000).

Similarly, as will be discussed in Chapter 18, substantial government economic involvement in collaboration with major business interests has been successful in pursuing rapid economic development in newly industrialized countries such as South Korea and Taiwan. On the other hand, there are a number of poorer countries with substantial state economic involvement that have not succeeded in developing their economies.

Although leading economic theories suggest that a free-market economy maximizes economic efficiency and prosperity, the experience of several countries indicates that, properly done and under the right conditions, active government involvement in the economy can also promote successful economic development.

economy do not feature a substantial level of competition. Governments have at times taken action to try to restore competition and to protect consumers. For example, American and European governments have taken legal action against Microsoft Corporation, alleging that it engages in anti-competitive practices that allow it to dominate the Internet browser and software markets. Some Canadian provinces regulate the price of gasoline and some other petroleum products because of concerns that limited competition may result in price gouging.

Governments also have adopted a variety of business regulations to protect consumers and to try to ensure that they have the information that they need to make informed choices in the marketplace. For example, government inspection and regulation of food products is important in protecting the health of consumers. Likewise, requiring that food products be labelled with information about ingredients and nutritional values is essential for persons with allergies and other medical conditions, as well as for those who wish to pursue a healthy lifestyle. Before such regulations, few businesses voluntarily provided such information and many products were unsafe.

TABLE 3-2
GOVERNMENT SPENDING IN SELECTED COUNTRIES

COUNTRY	GOVERNMENT EXPENDITURE AS % OF GDP	GOVERNMENT CONSUMPTION AS % OF GDP	COUNTRY	GOVERNMENT EXPENDITURE AS % OF GDP	GOVERNMENT CONSUMPTION AS % OF GDP
Sweden	58.3%	28.0%	Australia	36.0%	18.0%
Denmark	55.3%	26.1%	United States	35.6%	15.5%
France	54.0%	23.8%	Russia	34.1%	14.3%
Hungary	52.2%	11.0%	Romania	33.7%	6.3%
Austria	51.9%	19.4%	Egypt	30.0%	11.9%
Belgium	50.2%	22.3%	Nigeria	28.9%	25.2%
Germany	48.6%	19.1%	India	28.2%	13.1%
Italy	47.7%	19.2%	South Africa	26.9%	19.0%
Netherlands	47.3%	24.2%	Argentina	26.6%	12.2%
Norway	46.7%	22.0%	Brazil	26.5%	19.3%
Czech Republic	45.3%	21.4%	South Korea	24.6%	10.6%
Poland	43.2%	15.0%	Indonesia	23.8%	7.4%
United Kingdom	40.9%	20.0%	Chile	23.7%	12.6%
Canada	40.6%	21.3%	Mexico	23.7%	11.6%
Switzerland	39.9%	15.2%	Pakistan	21.8%	10.3%
Spain	39.8%	17.6%	China	20.0%	13.7%
Japan	38.6%	17.9%	Bangladesh	14.5%	4.5%
New Zealand	36.5%	17.8%			

Notes: *GDP* is Gross Domestic Product. *Government consumption* refers to government purchases of goods and services and wages paid to government employees. *Government expenditures* include government consumption and transfers to individuals.

SOURCE: *Compiled from* 2004 Index of Economic Freedom *by The Heritage Foundation, 2004; retrieved May 11, 2004 from www.heritage.org/research/features/index/countries.html.*

Protecting the Environment

Government regulation of business activity can be very useful in protecting the environment. Limitations on discharges of pollutants, the elimination of the use of some highly toxic chemicals, requirements that renewable resources be managed in a sustainable manner, and protection of natural areas and endangered species may "interfere" with economic decision making, but are necessary limitations on economic freedom.

Protecting Workers

Government plays an important role in the relations between business and labour. To prevent workers from being exploited by business, most contemporary governments legislate the minimum wage that workers must receive, set limits on the hours of work, require that vacation time be provided, and establish safety standards for workplaces. As well, to try to avoid the bitter conflicts that often occurred between business and labour in the past, governments provide a legal basis for unions to bargain collectively on behalf of workers, and establish rules and procedures concerning the relationship between unions and management.

Keeping Things Moving

Business activity in a free-market capitalist economy tends to go through cycles of expansion and contraction ("boom" and "bust"). **Keynesian economic policies and monetarism,** as described in Box 3-4, Avoiding the Economic Rollercoaster, provide different perspectives on how to achieve sustained growth without high levels of inflation or unemployment.

Assistance to Business

Most governments provide support for various sectors of the economy. For example, governments often provide subsidies to fledgling industries, to industries that are vital to the country's economy or military capabilities, and to high technology industries that are considered to be the wave of the future. As well, governments often provide various forms of assistance to sectors of the economy that are experiencing decline, such as textile, steel, and ship-building industries, or have very volatile fortunes, such as agriculture. Governments also often provide loans and subsidies to encourage businesses to locate in the less economically developed areas of a country.

The Welfare State

Modern governments have also modified the workings of the free-market system by providing for the well-being of their citizens. The term **welfare state** is used to describe countries in which "government-protected minimum standards of income, nutrition, health, housing, and education [are] assured to every citizen as a political right, not as a 'charity'" (Wilensky, 1975, p. 1).

In the past, societies generally believed that individuals should be self-reliant. The failure to provide for oneself and one's family was seen as a result of personal irresponsibility rather than a general failure of the economy. This view was challenged by the Depression of the 1930s, when millions of people were unable to find work. The Depression also demonstrated the inability of private charities and local governments to deal with the problems faced by the needy. The successful mobilization of society and economy by governments for World War II increased the capabilities of government and created more positive attitudes towards an active role for government. There were expectations that governments should take responsibility for the well-being of returning soldiers and the families of those who had sacrificed their lives. As well, the threat of communism and the growing strength of labour and socialist parties created a political climate favourable to the development of the welfare state as a way of protecting the free-market capitalist system from challenges.

The welfare state has been the subject of considerable debate in recent decades, as discussed in Box 3-5, Criticism of the Welfare State. While some welfare state programs, such as medicare in Canada and old age pensions, are popular among the public at large, support for social assistance (welfare) and

KEYNESIAN ECONOMIC POLICIES
The idea that government can smooth out the ups and downs of the free-market economy by stimulating the economy when private business investment is low, and cooling down the economy when excessive investment is creating inflation.

MONETARISM
An economic perspective based on the view that government's role in the economy should be largely restricted to controlling the supply of money.

WELFARE STATE
A term used to describe countries in which government ensures that all people have a minimum standard of living and are provided some protection from hardships resulting from unemployment, sickness, disability, and old age.

BOX 3-4

Avoiding the Economic Rollercoaster: Keynes and Friedman

British economist John Maynard Keynes (1883–1946) and American economist Milton Friedman (b. 1912) both put forward ideas to keep economies operating on a relatively even keel, but they had different thoughts on the role that government should play.

It was during the 1930s Depression, when business activity collapsed and unemployment rates skyrocketed, that Keynes developed the idea that government could smooth out the ups and downs of the free-market economy. **Keynesian economic policies** involve stimulating the economy (by spending money and/or reducing taxes) when private business investment is low, and cooling down the economy (by reducing spending and/or raising taxes) when excessive investment is creating inflation. As well, because the poor tend to spend rather than save their money, government programs that put money into the hands of the poor can help to ensure that there is sufficient demand for the goods and services that business can supply. This in turn can result in full or nearly full employment. In general, Keynesian economic policies view government as having a positive role in ensuring the smooth functioning of the free-market capitalist system without directly intervening in business decisions.

Keynesian economic policies were adopted by most of the advanced capitalist countries during and after World War II. They were successful in providing for three decades of sustained growth and prosperity. However, Keynesian economic policies fell out of favour among economists and government policymakers in the mid-1970s when economies suffered from a simultaneous combination of inflation and economic stagnation ("stagflation"). In part, government deficits resulting from increased government spending led to growing government debt.

Instead of the Keynesian emphasis on the need for government to manage the economy by maintaining sufficient demand for the products of the economy, traditional ideas that the free-market economy will stabilize itself without government intervention have been influential in recent decades. In particular, the ideas of American economist Milton Friedman have had considerable importance.

Friedman's perspective, known as **monetarism,** is based on the view that government's role in the economy should be largely restricted to that of controlling the supply of money. Keynesian policies led governments to increase the supply of money, which caused inflation, in order to cover the debts caused by the government spending. Friedman argues instead that each year, governments should have a "balanced budget" (that is, spending should not exceed revenues), even though this means that government will reduce its spending in recessionary times as tax revenues decline. As well, in the monetarist view, autonomous central banks such as the Bank of Canada (or in the United States, the Federal Reserve) should fight inflation by limiting the growth of the money supply and keeping interest rates high when inflationary pressures occur. By keeping government out of direct involvement in managing the economy, autonomous central banks could administer the bitter medicine needed to prevent inflation.

Friedman also argues that the role of government in the economy should be substantially reduced. With less regulation and lower taxes, there will be greater incentives for investment and production. Economic problems will be resolved by the free market rather than by government. In practice, however, major tax cuts have often not been matched by significant cuts in government spending, even by governments strongly committed to free-market policies. For example, the substantial tax cuts instituted in the United States after the 2000 election of President George W. Bush led to large government deficits and mounting government debt as government spending rose—due, in part, to increased spending on security and defence.

BOX 3-5

Criticism of the Welfare State

Critics view the welfare state as responsible for expanding the size of government and creating pressures for more government activities. The costs of welfare state programs are viewed as contributing to the tax burden that people face, and to government deficits and the resulting government debt. The increase in government spending and borrowing is seen as crowding out private investment and activity. The welfare state interferes with the "discipline" of the marketplace, particularly by reducing the incentive for people to work if welfare or unemployment benefits are too generous. Instead, the welfare state encourages people to become dependent upon government and less likely to take responsibility for their own lives.

Are these criticisms of the welfare state valid? The provision by the Canadian government of basic health care, education, and various social services has contributed to the high quality of life of Canadians. Furthermore, the welfare state does not necessarily reduce the competitiveness of an economy. It can allow people to take greater risks, such as finding new jobs, knowing that they have security to fall back on. As well, various social programs help people to adjust as economies change in response to globalization (Atkinson, 2000). Welfare state programs contributed to the long period of social peace and economic growth in the decades after World War II by helping to achieve a compromise between the demands of workers and the pursuit of profit by business.

Cutbacks in social assistance and employment insurance have increased the number of people in dire poverty and overburdened charitable organizations like food banks. The lack of political power of the poor has often made them targets for government cutbacks while the rich have benefited from tax cuts. A basic question underlies the debate over the welfare: Do all citizens have the right to a basic standard of living regardless of their circumstances?

employment insurance is often limited. The Canadian government has substantially reduced the proportion of unemployed persons who are eligible to collect employment insurance, and most provincial governments have reduced social assistance payments (Dyck, 2004). In addition, some provinces have required that the able-bodied work for their social assistance payments. For example, Ontario requires some welfare recipients to take basic education and receive addictions treatment, if needed. British Columbia limits, with some exceptions, social assistance for the employable to two years within any five-year period.

Government and the Economy: Involvement or Interference?

Government involvement in the economy is sometimes described as interference with the free market. Excessive regulation can reduce the flexibility of the free-market system. High taxes can reduce the competitiveness of business in the global marketplace and result in the emigration of persons with specialized skills (the "brain drain"). Price controls can lead to shortages and insufficient investment for future demand to be met.

Government involvement in the economy, however, is not necessarily harmful to the free market and the interests of business. Government restrictions on monopolies can help to encourage a competitive market. Government provision or funding of research and development (R&D) can be of major assistance to business in a technological age. The provision of some public services by government, such as education, hospitals, and parks, does remove some activities from the market. However, the interests of business, as well as the population as a whole, are served by providing a healthy and educated workforce and by ensuring a higher quality of life. Likewise, health, safety, and environmental regulations may limit some business activities, but are for the common good of all parts of society in the long run. Welfare state policies may help to legitimate the free-market capitalist system in the eyes of the public by removing some of the harshness of an economic system that would otherwise lead to challenges and criticisms.

POLITICAL CONFLICT

Many of the conflicts that occur in political life concern the distribution of the products of the economy and the extent to which government should be involved in providing for the well-being of the population. Not surprisingly, those with different economic positions tend to differ substantially in their views on economic and welfare policy.

Class Divisions

Many theorists have postulated that as societies modernize and industrialize, class divisions would become the most important basis of political conflict. A **social class** is a grouping of people who have a similar position in terms of their position in the economy and related social status. As will be discussed in Chapter 5, Marxists see modern societies as fundamentally divided between the working class, who sell their labour power, and the capitalist class, who own the means of production. In the middle are groups such as small business owners and professionals. Others theorists view social class in terms of a combination of differences based on income, occupation, and social status, and thus see a more complex pattern of class divisions.

Class divisions are not as rigid as the social and economic divisions in pre-modern times, such as the division between lords and serfs in feudal times or the caste system that still exists in some rural areas of India. There is some mobility between classes, and some very wealthy individuals come from ordinary backgrounds. However, there is a tendency for people to stay in the same social class for life and, to some extent, for class positions to be passed on to the next generation. The growth of middle-class occupations and the

SOCIAL CLASS
A grouping of people who have a similar position in terms of their position in the economy or a combination of income, education, and social status.

availability of higher education to middle- and working-class families have reduced the sharpness of class divisions. Although inequalities in income and wealth have not significantly decreased in the richer countries, and in some cases have increased, the development of the welfare state has served to blunt the conflict between social classes. Nevertheless, even in richer countries there is an underclass of persons who struggle to make ends meet, working in low-wage and part-time positions or unemployed.

CLASS CONSCIOUSNESS
The extent to which people see themselves as members of a particular social class.

The political significance of social class depends, to a considerable extent, on the level of **class consciousness**—that is, the extent to which people see themselves as members of a particular social class. Where unions and working-class-oriented political parties are strong, workers are more likely to view themselves as members of the working class and act politically in solidarity with their social class. In countries where other divisions are strong, such as those based on ethnicity, religion, or region, people are less likely to identify with a particular social class and less likely to act in accordance with their class interests.

United Students Against Sweatshops
www.studentsagainstsweatshops.org

A number of analysts argue that class divisions are declining in importance in post-industrial societies, where a high proportion of the workforce is engaged in information and technology-based enterprises and in service occupations, rather than in manufacturing or resource-based industries. The increasing availability of post-secondary education to a substantial proportion of the population may have also reduced the significance of education-based differences in the perspectives of different classes. Other analysts argue that economic globalization will result in new forms of class differences. The movement of manufacturing and information technology jobs from wealthier countries to low-wage countries may result in a heightened division in post-industrial countries between a minority with high-paying jobs and the majority with low-paying, insecure service jobs.

Geographical Divisions

Conflict concerning the distribution of income and role of government in the economy does not only involve social classes. Economic development in many countries has occurred in an uneven fashion, and prosperity often varies considerably from one part of a country to another. Areas with high unemployment, lower incomes, and a weak economic base may feel that they have been treated unfairly by government and by businesses in the economically powerful regions. Furthermore, as societies modernize, there is typically a large migration of people from rural areas and smaller communities to large urban centres. This creates practical problems for those remaining in rural areas as institutions such as schools and hospitals become less viable and subject to closure. People living in poorer regions and rural areas will often demand special assistance from the central government.

Women and Minorities

Women and ethnic or racial minority groups tend to face discrimination in seeking employment and have lower-paying jobs and fewer opportunities for promotion. In Canada, for example, there are exceptionally high rates of poverty and unemployment among Aboriginals, and many recent immigrants have difficulty finding employment that matches their qualifications. In some countries, the situation is reversed, with many wealthy business people being members of a minority group. This can cause resentment among the members of the majority ethnic group. In Uganda, for example, the East Indian minority (many of whom had been brought by the British as indentured servants to build a railway) played a major role in business life until their expulsion in 1972. Similarly, many French Quebeckers have been resentful of the wealth and economic power traditionally concentrated in the hands of some members of the English-speaking minority in Quebec.

The entry of a large proportion of women into the paid workforce has highlighted issues related to gender-based economic inequalities in recent decades. Although laws in Canada and many other countries require that employers pay women and men equally for work that is substantially the same, women on average earn significantly less than men, even when calculated on a per-hour basis.

To a considerable degree, this gap is a result of women tending to work in different and lower-paying occupations than men. As well, women are more likely to interrupt their careers for child-raising and other family responsibilities that can reduce their income earning capacity. Although younger women are now more likely than younger men to obtain a higher education in countries like Canada and the United States, women in the workforce generally have less education than men because of the greater opportunities for males in the past. Finally, despite laws prohibiting discrimination against women, many women do undoubtedly face obstacles in obtaining promotions (the "glass ceiling") or working in non-traditional occupations.

Rectifying inequalities often requires more than laws forbidding discrimination. Despite laws prohibiting discrimination in employment, women's groups and groups representing various minorities argue that substantial inequities persist and that government needs to take stronger measures to ensure a fairer distribution of income and employment opportunities. In particular, women's groups have advocated the adoption of affirmative action policies, pay equity legislation, and subsidized childcare.

Affirmative action (also known as employment equity) involves the adoption of programs designed to result in the hiring and promotion of a higher proportion of women and disadvantaged minorities. Such programs are designed to create a more representative and diverse workforce and to overcome subtle forms of discrimination that persons in disadvantaged groups

AFFIRMATIVE ACTION
The adoption of programs designed to make the workplace, universities, legislatures, or other institutions more representative of disadvantaged groups and groups that have suffered from discrimination.

often face. Critics argue that affirmative action programs constitute reverse discrimination against white males and lead to an undesirable emphasis in hiring and promotion on one's personal characteristics rather than qualifications and performance. Affirmative action programs have been established in the Canadian public service with targets for increasing the proportion of women, Aboriginals, persons with disabilities, and visible minorities in each occupational category. Employers with sizable federal government contracts are also required to establish affirmative action programs. Some universities have adopted affirmative action programs to increase the proportion of women preparing for careers in such fields as engineering and medicine. Special efforts have also been made to encourage Aboriginals to attend university.

Pay equity legislation requires that employers provide equal pay for work of equal value. In particular, this involves raising the pay of persons in occupations that are largely staffed by females to the same pay as persons in comparable occupations (in terms of a combination of skill, effort, responsibility, and working conditions) that are largely staffed by males. For example, an employer might be required to bring the pay of secretaries up to the level of pay of janitors after an assessment of the two occupations. Pay equity legislation applies to public servants at the national and provincial levels in Canada and in some cases to workers in the broader public sector such as schools and hospitals. It also applies to most private sector employees in Quebec and Ontario and to nationally incorporated companies. Governments have often been reluctant, however, to implement the large salary increases that pay equity commissions have awarded. The business community has generally been opposed to pay equity legislation, believing that the market should determine salaries. As well, since pay equity involves raising salaries, it is an additional cost to business.

Finally, the provision of government subsidized, quality childcare would help to overcome the obstacles that working women with young children often face. A number of continental European countries provide comprehensive childcare programs. In most of Canada, inadequate numbers of subsidized childcare spaces are available. Thus far, only Quebec has implemented a comprehensive subsidized childcare program.

Identity Politics

Political conflict is not only a result of competition over the limited economic resources in any political community. Different groups often have different values, leading to conflicts over the policies that should be adopted. As well, a variety of groups that have traditionally been ignored or suffered discrimination—including women, gays and lesbians, minority ethnic groups, and Aboriginals—seek recognition and respect for their particular identities. **Identity politics** is not just about achieving an equitable distribution of income and opportunities for each individual in the political community, but

PAY EQUITY
A policy that employers provide equal pay for work of equal value; for example, by raising the pay of persons in occupations that are largely staffed by females to the same pay as persons in comparable occupations that are largely staffed by males.

IDENTITY POLITICS
A perspective in which groups seek recognition and respect for their particular identity. This may include trying to gain particular rights, political power, and autonomy for a particular group.

◀ Identity politics is not just about achieving an equitable distribution of income and opportunities for each individual in the political community, but also about gaining particular rights, political power, and autonomy for specific groups. In the United States in the 1960s and early 1970s, Americans demonstrated for the rights of African Americans.

also often about gaining particular rights, political power, and autonomy for the specific groups (Heard, 2002; Whitaker, 1997). Thus, achieving an equitable distribution of goods, services, and employment opportunities for all members of the political community would not eliminate all group-based political conflicts.

Summary and Conclusion

Politics often revolves around questions related to how the wealth of society should be produced and distributed. A major topic of political controversy is the extent to which government should involve itself in the economy. The free-market capitalist economy is typically viewed by economists as the most efficient way to produce goods and services. Government involvement beyond the minimum needed for the capitalist system to function reduces the overall wealth of society. The common good is achieved through the pursuit of individual interests in the free marketplace. This results in the maximization of the total wealth of the community.

Others argue that more substantial government activity is needed to achieve the common good. In the pursuit of profit, business may exploit its workers, mislead consumers, and despoil the environment. Government action is needed to regulate business activity to direct it towards the common good. The highly uneven distribution of wealth created by the free-market capitalist system should be modified through government action so as to reduce inequalities and ensure that the needs of all persons are met.

Supporters of the free-market system point out that competition in the marketplace determines what is produced and how wealth is distributed. This, they argue, avoids the arbitrary use of power, which leads to privileges for some and discrimination for others. People are rewarded according to their contribution to the wealth of society regardless of their personal characteristics. Critics of the free-market capitalist system argue that in reality it is often characterized by a concentration of power in the hands of business interests. This gives the business community considerable ability to influence or control government and the thinking of society. The result is that governments may be more interested in promoting the interests of business than in seeking the common good of society as a whole.

Placing ownership and control of the economy in the hands of the state may eliminate the power of business, but does not necessarily result in the common good. Socialist economic systems are generally more egalitarian than capitalist ones. State socialist economic systems, however, concentrate economic power in the hands of state officials who may lack the information and flexibility needed to effectively make the large number of decisions involved in a planned economy. Thus, a socialist economy may have difficulty producing a good standard of living for the population. As well, the interests of the state (and state officials) are likely to override the wishes of the people in making decisions. Combining great economic as well as political power in the hands of the state can create a domineering government that will be insensitive to the needs and wishes of the people and result in privileges for an elite.

The prosperity of countries with basically free-market capitalist economies and the failures of countries with state socialist economies have encouraged many countries to move in the direction of a free-market system. This direction has been encouraged by important international agencies (such as the International Monetary Fund, World Bank, and World Trade Organization), by pressure from the forces of economic globalization, and by the influence of powerful countries with free-market capitalist systems. Nevertheless, many countries continue to have mixed economies in which the state has an important role in owning and managing major elements of the economy. Further, even in countries committed to a free-market capitalist economy, governments have an important influence on the economy. Politics and the economy are thus closely related.

The development of the welfare state has become a focal point for much political controversy. Critics of the welfare state argue that it discourages hard work and initiative. Reducing or eliminating the welfare state will encourage people to take greater responsibility for their own well-being, reduce the unhealthy dependence of people on the state, and allow taxes to be reduced, which will stimulate economic growth. Supporters of the welfare state argue that many individuals and families are unable to protect themselves from circumstances beyond their control. Unemployment and poverty are often not the product of laziness or lack of initiative, but may be the result of economic or social forces over which the individual has no control. Wealthy societies can afford to ensure that all persons have the means to live with dignity and to have some security against potential hardships. The common good, it is argued, is best achieved by ensuring that all persons have an adequate standard of living even if this results in a reduction of the total wealth of the society.

Class divisions related to the organization of the economy and its effects in creating inequalities in income, wealth, status, and power typically play a major role in the politics of modern societies. Those in different class positions often have different views as to whether, and to what extent, government should be involved in redistributing wealth from rich to poor, protecting people from the hardships of unemployment, poverty, sickness, and old age, and regulating or directing the activities of private business.

Inequalities can be thought of not only in terms in class position but also in terms of one's geographical location, gender, ethnicity, race, language, religion, and age. For example, the economic hardships faced by a female Aboriginal worker living in a northern community could be attributable to the exploitation of the working class, the subordinate position of women, the unfair treatment of her region, or discrimination against Aboriginals. Perceptions of inequalities and their significance in politics are affected by ideas, ideologies, and the ways in which various political organizations seek to mobilize support. The feminist ideology and women's movement, for example, have helped to focus attention on gender inequalities that were often not seen as politically relevant in the past. The focus of the major political parties on ethnic, linguistic, and regional divisions may have reduced the political significance of class divisions in Canada (Brodie & Jenson, 1988).

Overall, politics is often about "who gets what." The exercise of power is often directed at gaining a larger share of the economic pie for particular groups.

Appeals to justice, fairness, efficiency, maximizing wealth, rights, equality, or the common good may be used to persuade people to support a particular pattern of distribution. Politics is, however, not only about the production and distribution of wealth. Other values and identities also play an important role in political life. Political conflicts based on religious and cultural differences, for example, can be very intense.

Key Terms

Affirmative action 69

Centrally planned state socialist economic system 58

Class consciousness 68

Free-market capitalist economic system 54

Identity politics 70

Keynesian economic policies 64

Mercantilist policies 56

Mixed economy 61

Monetarism 64

Pay equity 70

Social class 67

Welfare state 64

Discussion Questions

1. Should Canada move toward a purer free-market capitalist economic system?

2. Are business corporations too powerful in Canada? Should corporations be accountable for their actions?

3. Should the welfare state be reduced or expanded? Should welfare recipients be required to work for welfare? Should a maximum time limit be placed on one's right to collect welfare payments?

4. How important are class divisions in Canada? Do you think that class divisions will have a greater or lesser impact on politics in the future?

5. Are affirmative action programs desirable? As a student about to enter the workforce, do you believe pay equity legislation should be applied to private business?

Further Reading

Brown, M.B. *Models in political economy: A guide to the arguments* (2nd ed.). London: Penguin, 1995.

Friedman, M. *Capitalism and freedom.* Chicago: University of Chicago Press, 1981.

Korten, D.C. *When corporations rule the world.* West Hartford, CT: Kumarian Press, 1996.

Lindblom, C.E. *The market system: What it is, how it works and what to make of it.* New Haven, CT: Yale University Press, 2001.

Pierson, C., & Castles, F.G. (Eds.). *The welfare state: A reader.* Cambridge, UK: Polity Press, 2000.

Rae, B. *The three questions: Prosperity and the public good.* Toronto: Viking, 1998.

Richards, J. *Retooling the welfare state: What's right, what's wrong, what's to be done.* Toronto: C.D. Howe Institute, 1997.

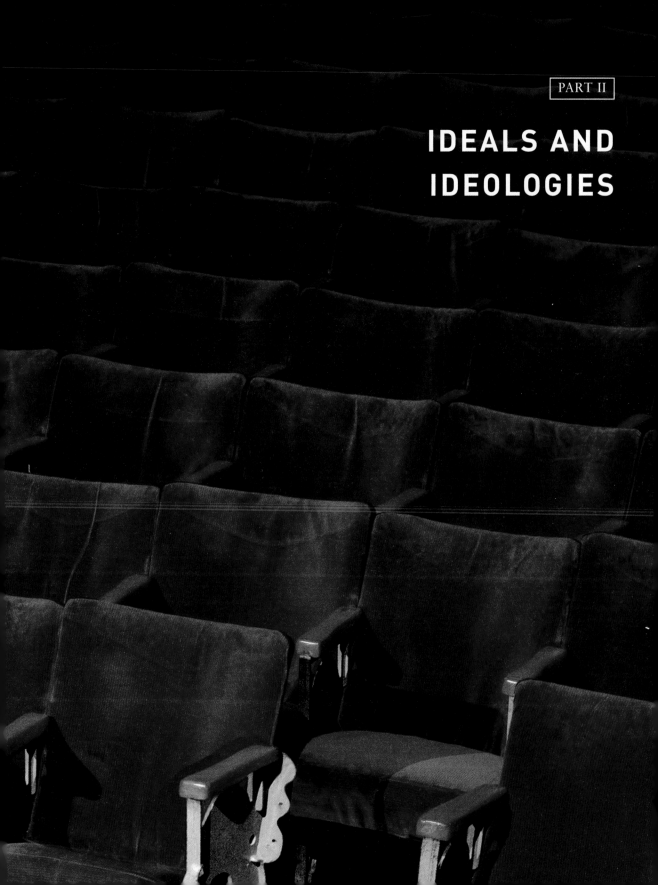

PART II

IDEALS AND IDEOLOGIES

THE DEMOCRATIC IDEAL

PHOTO ABOVE: Arnold Schwarzenegger, former bodybuilder and Hollywood icon, drew international attention when he was sworn in as governor of California in November 2003.

Chapter 4

1. discuss the advantages and disadvantages of democracy

2. distinguish between direct democracy and representative democracy

3. explain liberal democracy and discuss the possible tensions between liberal and democratic ideals

4. evaluate the desirability of referendums, initiatives, and recall

5. discuss the concept of deliberative democracy

6. explain the problems that globalization may create for democracy

Arnold Schwarzenegger drew international attention when he was sworn in as governor of California in November 2003. Thousands watched live and millions more were able to tune in to the televised version as the former bodybuilder and star of such films as *The Terminator* and *Total Recall* took political control of the most populous American state. Exercising their right to recall elected politicians, voters had sacked Governor Gray Davis—who had been re-elected governor just a year earlier—and put their political futures in the hands of a Hollywood icon.

The right to recall politicians before their term is up is allowed in only a few democratic systems. Some American states and municipalities provide for the recall of state and local politicians, voters in Venezuela can recall any elected politician including the president, and British Columbia in 1994 adopted procedures for the recall of members of the provincial legislature.

In the case of California, elected public officials can be recalled if signatures equal to at least 12 percent of the votes cast for the position in the previous election are obtained. This results in a recall election in which a question placed on the ballot asks whether the official should be immediately recalled. A second question on the same ballot asks voters who should replace that official if the first question passes. In 2003, a Republican congressman spent over US$1 million of his own money hiring a professional petition-gathering company to launch a recall campaign against the Democratic governor, who was blamed for the large state deficit and a proposal to raise taxes. After more than a million signatures were obtained in the allotted time, a recall election was held. Fifty-five percent voted to recall Governor Davis. Schwarzenegger was elected by just under 50 percent of those answering the second ballot question, which had a list of 135 candidates for the governor's position. Gray Davis was the first California governor recalled since the recall legislation was adopted in 1911.

No representatives in British Columbia have thus far been recalled, as the requirement that 40 percent of eligible voters sign a petition makes recall more difficult than in California. However, one member of the provincial legislature who had engaged in unscrupulous behaviour, including writing letters to the editor praising his own accomplishments using phony names, resigned rather than face a recall election.

Some people argue that simply electing a representative every few years is insufficient to make a political system truly democratic. Through mechanisms such as recall elections, people can have more control over the decisions for their political community. In particular, representatives who do not act on the wishes of their constituents or who engage in corrupt practices can be removed from office. Others argue that recall elections can make it difficult for representatives to act for the common good because they make it easier for particular interests to pressure elected representatives and give added power to those with the money or organization needed to mount a recall campaign.

A POPULAR IDEAL

Democracy, meaning rule by the people, is one of the most popular political ideals in contemporary societies. Almost all contemporary government leaders proclaim their belief in democracy, and claim that their country is democratic or on the path to democracy. Wars have been fought in the name of democracy. The democratic ideal that all adult citizens should have an equal and effective voice in the running of their country is a powerful force in the contemporary world. Democracy has ancient roots. Nevertheless, it drew criticism and skepticism from most political thinkers until about a century and a half ago. It was only in the past century that a significant number of countries became democratic.

Despite the popularity of democracy, the ideal of rule by the people is difficult to fully implement. Even though we normally think of countries like Canada, the United States, Britain, and Germany as democratic, the question can be raised as to whether the people really rule in these countries. As we will examine in this chapter, there are different views as to what makes a political system democratic.

IS DEMOCRACY DESIRABLE?

Democracy has often been subject to criticism and ridicule, as some of the quotations in Box 4-1, Some Views of Democracy, indicate. Even some of those who support democracy have often been less than enthusiastic.

BOX 4-1

Some Views of Democracy

What is democracy? Many writers, politicians, and thinkers have offered their thoughts on the topic:

- "The art and science of running the circus from the monkey cage." (American journalist H. L. Mencken)
- "The bludgeoning of the people, by the people, for the people." (Irish writer Oscar Wilde)
- "It substitutes election by the incompetent many for appointment by the corrupt few." (Irish playwright George Bernard Shaw)
- "The worst form of government except all those others that have been tried from time to time." (British Prime Minister Sir Winston Churchill)

- "Democracy means choosing your dictators, after they've told you what it is you want to hear." (American writer Alan Coren)
- "Democracy is not perfect, but it is the only form of government that respects the dignity of the individual and protects the individual's human rights." (American political scientist James David Barber)
- "Man's capacity for justice makes democracy possible, but man's inclination to injustice makes democracy necessary." (German theologian Reinhold Niebuhr)

Arguments in Favour

Those who promote the democratic ideal argue that it is the best way to achieve the common good. By involving the population as a whole in governing, the interests and values of different parts of the population are more likely to be reflected in decisions than if control of decision making is in the hands of a single individual or a particular group. As well, by encouraging people to be freely involved in making governing decisions, those decisions can potentially benefit from the discussion and deliberation of persons with a wide variety of different viewpoints. Even if the public as a whole is not directly involved in governing, democratic procedures such as elections can help to ensure that those holding governing positions are held accountable to the people and serve the interests of the population as a whole.

Governments that have been chosen by the people are more likely to be accepted as legitimate by their populations. Because the people have a role in the governing process, they are more likely to accept what government does, even if they happen to disagree with particular decisions. Democratic governments thus may be more effective than non-democratic ones, even if the processes of democratic decision making are often complex. As well, democracies have the positive feature of allowing for a peaceful transition of power. Citizens can remove a government with which they are dissatisfied without resorting to violence. Democracy may also encourage people to be more civic minded. Through involvement in governing, people may feel a greater attachment to the political community and be more likely to assume a sense of responsibility to their fellow citizens. As well, citizens may derive a sense of fulfilment and meaning through sharing in the governing of their community.

Finally, democracy is often associated with the value of equality. Although the adoption of democratic procedures does not necessarily result in greater social or economic equality, democracy does have the potential to give some influence to those who would otherwise be powerless. This influence may result in policies designed to aid the disadvantaged.

Arguments Against

Critics of democracy often question whether ordinary citizens have the time and knowledge to make intelligent decisions concerning the governing of their society. Classic political philosophers such as Plato (c. 428–347 BCE) and Aristotle (384–322 BCE) argued that demagogues (persuasive speakers) would sway the citizenry, leading to decisions that were not for the common good. Modern critics worry about the masses being swayed by emotional appeals in the mass media. Similarly, critics of democracy argue that undesirable policies result from politicians pandering to the wishes and prejudices of the mass public. For example, politicians often offer "goodies" to the public in order to gain its support in an election—and frequently the public fails to pay due attention to the costs of what is being promised.

Although democracy is often promoted as an alternative to the tyranny of dictators, some political thinkers have worried about whether democracy can degenerate into the "tyranny of the majority." The majority, particularly if aroused by a sensational issue, may be inclined to demand that the rights and freedoms of unpopular minorities or individuals be removed. A democratic system may result in decisions that reflect the wishes of the majority, but there is a danger that minorities could be consistently ignored.

Democracy is also sometimes criticized for being "all talk, no action," involving endless debate and rules that often seem designed to prevent government from acting. Because a variety of interests and viewpoints are taken into account, the democratic decision-making process can be slow. To satisfy different interests, democratic decisions often involve compromises rather than adherence to principles. Non-democratic systems, it is argued, are better able to take the strong measures that may be needed to deal with serious problems.

Finally, there are those who argue that democracy is an impossible ideal to achieve. Power will always be in the hands of a few people. In this view, democracy is a sham—window-dressing to hide the realities of politics and add a facade of legitimacy to those who really hold power. Elections are exercises in manipulation, and those in positions of power, even if elected, serve their own interests, rather than the interests of the population.

Lingering Concerns

While the democratic ideal appears very popular in the contemporary world, many political thinkers over the centuries have had serious concerns about democracy. Even if, in general, democratic countries seem to function better than non-democratic ones, this does not mean that every democracy functions well, nor does it mean that every non-democratic country is corrupt or tyrannical. Although we think that is an exaggeration to term democracy in countries like Canada a sham, it would be naive to assume that governing decisions always reflect the interests and values of the citizenry as a whole, or even the majority of citizens.

THE MANY VERSIONS OF DEMOCRACY

Direct Democracy

DIRECT DEMOCRACY
A system in which citizens make the governing decisions.

About 2500 years ago, the important Greek city-state of Athens adopted a system of **direct democracy**, that is, a system in which citizens make the governing decisions. The citizens of Athens met in an open assembly about ten times a year and, after discussion in which all citizens could participate, the decisions governing this powerful state were made by a vote of those present. The ideal of the citizenry involved in actively discussing and deliberating about public issues was defended by the fourth century BCE Athenian states-man Pericles, who argued that "instead of looking on discussion as a stumbling-block in the way of action, we think it an indispensable prelimi-nary to any wise action at all" (Thucydides, *The Peloponnesian War*, II, 40; quoted in Warren, 2002, p. 174).

By today's standards, ancient Athens would not be considered highly democratic: only a minority of Athenians had the rights of citizens. Women, slaves, and those not born in Athens were excluded from political life. In other ways, however, ancient Athens was highly democratic. Not only were citizens directly involved in deliberating about and deciding on the major issues for their state, but many of the officials who administered the decisions of the Assembly were chosen by lottery. Because administrators held their positions for only a relatively short period of office, many citizens, at some point in their life, would serve as state officials. By keeping terms of offices short, the democrats of ancient Athens hoped to prevent powerful individu-als or groups from controlling the political system and exercising tyrannical power.

The influential Greek philosophers Plato and Aristotle criticized Athenian democracy, arguing that the common people ruled in their own selfish inter-ests. In particular, they argued that the majority of people, being poor, would use their political power to take the wealth of the rich, rather than acting for the common good of all.

Better than democracy, in Aristotle's view, was a system he called polity, which involved a mixture of rule by the few and rule by the many. This ideal of mixed rule has been put into practice in various countries, including the ancient Roman Republic (where a few consuls implemented laws passed by the Senate, composed of aristocrats, and the Assembly, composed of ordinary citizens); Britain after 1689 (where in theory the monarch, the House of Lords, and the House of Commons prevent one another from abusing their power); and the United States (where the constitution separates the powers of the executive, legislative, and judicial branches of government so that each checks the power of the others).

The direct democracy of ancient Athens lasted only about 250 years, but the idea of direct democracy has not completely disappeared. Citizen meet-ings make decisions in a few New England towns and small Swiss cantons (provinces). As well, the random selection of citizens to serve on juries bears a resemblance to the practices of ancient Athens. However, the idea of citi-zens assembling to make governing decisions became impractical as larger states developed. Thus, democracy in the modern era is generally associated with the concept of elected representation of the citizenry. However, some have suggested that contemporary technology, such as interactive television and the Internet, could be used to recreate the decision making by citizens' forums that is characteristic of direct democracy.

Canadians for Direct Democracy
www.npsnet.com/cdd

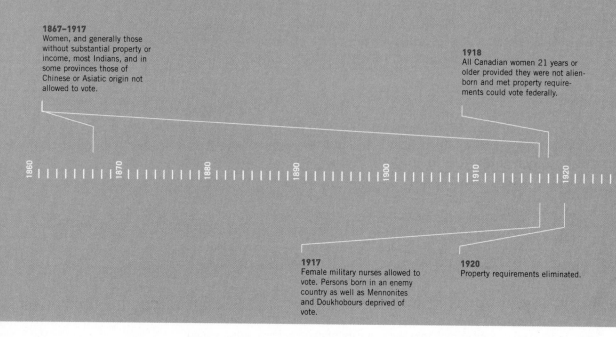

SOURCES: From Electoral Facts by W. Brown, 1999, *Electoral Insight*, *1*(2), pp. 28–36; and *A History of the Vote in Canada* by Elections Canada (1997), Ottawa: Minister of Public Works and Government Services.

Representative Democracy

REPRESENTATIVE DEMOCRACY
A form of democracy in which citizens elect representatives to the legislature to make decisions on their behalf.

LEGISLATURE
A body that is responsible for the formal approval of legislation.

Representative democracy involves the citizens electing representatives to the **legislature,** a body that is responsible for the formal approval of legislation. As well, in parliamentary systems like Canada's (see Chapter 15), elected legislatures are the source of political authority for government. The prime minister and cabinet (the political executive that oversees the government) are usually members of the elected legislative body and must retain the support of the majority of elected representatives. Representatives must seek re-election after a limited period of time. In presidential systems, such as the United States, the president is also an elected representative of the people. Representative democracy is an indirect form of democracy in the sense that the people do not directly make the governing decisions, but rather through an election determine who makes such decisions on their behalf.

Representative legislatures originated in meetings called by monarchs when they needed to gain the support of persons from different parts of their realm for new taxes. Eventually in Britain and elsewhere, legislatures challenged the power of the monarch and gained control of governing. Later still (generally in the early twentieth century), pressure from various sections of the public that did not have the right to vote resulted in representative

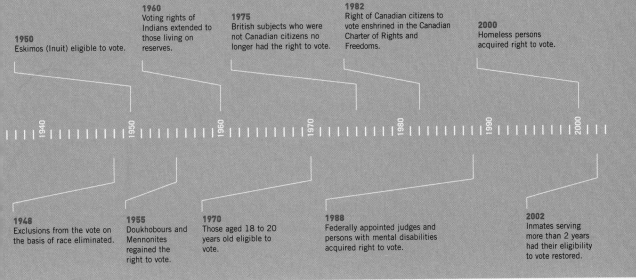

1950
Eskimos (Inuit) eligible to vote.

1960
Voting rights of Indians extended to those living on reserves.

1975
British subjects who were not Canadian citizens no longer had the right to vote.

1982
Right of Canadian citizens to vote enshrined in the Canadian Charter of Rights and Freedoms.

2000
Homeless persons acquired right to vote.

1948
Exclusions from the vote on the basis of race eliminated.

1955
Doukhobours and Mennonites regained the right to vote.

1970
Those aged 18 to 20 years old eligible to vote.

1988
Federally appointed judges and persons with mental disabilities acquired right to vote.

2002
Inmates serving more than 2 years had their eligibility to vote restored.

bodies becoming democratic in the sense that all citizens could participate in the election of representatives. As Figure 4-1 illustrates, it took nearly a century for the right to vote to be extended to almost all adult citizens.

Extending the right to vote and hold office to all citizens does not, however, ensure that legislatures will be representative in the sense of accurately reflecting the characteristics of the population. For example, women are underrepresented to varying extents in all legislatures, as Table 4-1 indicates.

In most contemporary democracies, elected representatives, other than those who are in the cabinet, have a limited involvement in developing governing decisions. (The United States is an important exception.) It is the executive (in Canada, the prime minister and cabinet), along with public servants, who have a key role in the development of laws and policies. The general role of Parliament is to debate and approve proposed laws that are presented to it by the prime minister and cabinet. Representatives are almost always members of a political party and elections focus on the competition among political parties to determine which party (or parties) will form the government. Elected representatives are generally expected to vote along party lines, which means that they do not necessarily vote in accordance with the views of those whom they represent. Representation, then, is more by party than by individual representatives.

Democracy Watch
www.dwatch.ca

▶ Elections Canada has recently made it possible for the homeless to vote.

TABLE 4-1
WOMEN IN NATIONAL LEGISLATURES

Note: Figures are for the lower house (such as the Canadian House of Commons) in countries with two legislative chambers.

COUNTRY	% WOMEN IN LEGISLATURE	COUNTRY	% WOMEN IN LEGISLATURE
Rwanda	48.8%	United Kingdom	17.9%
Sweden	45.3%	United States	14.3%
Denmark	38.0%	Italy	11.5%
Netherlands	36.7%	Indonesia	11.1%
Cuba	36.0%	Russia	9.8%
Spain	36.0%	Brazil	8.6%
Argentina	34.0%	India	8.3%
Germany	32.2%	Japan	7.1%
Australia	25.3%	Egypt	2.4%
Mexico	22.6%	Bangladesh	2.0%
Canada	21.1%	Saudi Arabia	0.0%
Poland	20.2%	**World Average**	**15.6%**

SOURCE: *Adapted from* Women in National Parliaments *by Inter-Parliamentary Union (IPU) (2004). Retrieved June 30, 2004 from www.ipu.org/wne-e/classif.htm.*

Liberal Democracy

The version of democracy that developed in modern Western societies is also often described as **liberal democracy**. Liberal democracy, as the term suggests, combines the ideology of **liberalism**, which advocates a high level of individual freedom, with the ideal of democracy. The power and scope of government should be limited and the rights of the people protected in order to ensure there is a vibrant **civil society** in which free discussion can take place.

Liberal democracy is generally accepted not only by liberals, but also (sometimes with qualifications) by contemporary conservatives and democratic socialists.

Liberal democracy is based on the belief that power, even the power of a government that is supported by the majority of the people, is liable to be abused. Liberal democracy includes the following principles:

- Limits should be placed on what governments can do. Those in positions of political authority should not be able to rule in an arbitrary manner; rather, decisions should be taken according to established laws and procedures.
- All persons should have the freedom to express their views, including the freedom to criticize government, and the freedom to organize themselves for political action.
- The communications media should be free of government control so that diverse sources of information and ideas are easily available to the public.
- Political parties should be able to freely compete for political power.

To some extent, the liberal ideal of individual freedom fits nicely with the democratic ideal of rule by the people. If government is overbearing and exercises too much control over society and individuals, the ideal of rule by the people will be undermined. On the other hand, some view liberal democracy as a combination of two different and potentially inconsistent ideas. The democratic ideal is based on the view that the political equality of all citizens is desirable. Each citizen should count equally in making the governing decisions for the political community. However, the liberal ideal, particularly in its classic form of favouring the free marketplace, does not necessarily challenge the concentration of economic and social power in the hands of a few. The wealthy, and those who control large business corporations, have the potential to use their economic power to gain a much larger voice in affecting political decisions than the ordinary citizen. Thus, socialists often argue that liberal democracy is a limited form of democracy. In their view, a substantial degree of social and economic equality is needed for a meaningful democracy (Macpherson, 1965).

LIBERAL DEMOCRACY
A political system that combines the liberal ideas of limited government, individual freedom, and the rule of law with the democratic idea of rule by the people.

LIBERALISM
An ideological perspective advocating a high level of individual freedom, based on a belief in the inherent dignity and worth of each individual.

CIVIL SOCIETY
The independent groups and organizations that are not controlled by the state.

Plebiscitary Democracy

PLEBISCITARY DEMOCRACY
A form of democracy in which citizens have more control of decisions than in representative democracy through the use of such devices as referendums, initiatives, and recall elections.

POPULISM
A perspective that advocates putting power in the hands of the people rather than the elites who control politics and society.

REFERENDUM
A vote by citizens on a particular issue or proposed law.

Plebiscitary democracy involves giving citizens more control of decisions through the use of such devices as referendums, initiatives, and recall elections. This version of democracy is often associated with the perspective of **populism**,[1] which is based on the idea that fundamental differences exist between ordinary people and the elites who control politics and society (Laycock, 2002). Ordinary people, in the populist perspective, possess common sense. Politicians, government bureaucrats, political parties, intellectuals and leading cultural figures, the wealthy, and owners of big business are often viewed by populists as immoral, corrupt, or out of touch with common people. Elites and "special interests" control the community and take advantage of the hard-working majority.[2] Representative democracy, populists argue, places power in the hands of politicians who may be more interested in their own political careers, in acting in accordance with the views of their party, and in promoting special interests than in taking direction from the people whom they are supposed to represent.

REFERENDUMS Referendums give people the opportunity to vote on particular issues or proposed laws.[3] Many American states and municipalities make frequent use of referendums, although there has never been a national referendum in the United States. In other countries, including Canada (as discussed in Box 4-2, The Use of Referendums in Canada) referendums have been used occasionally, particularly on fundamental issues such as constitutional changes.

Although referendums involve a vote by the people, the decision to hold a referendum and the wording of a referendum are set by those in control of the government or the legislature. Thus, there is a possibility that a referendum can be used to manipulate the people through misleading wording. Indeed, non-democratic governments have used referendums at times to try to legitimate their rule. For example, some dictators, such as Saddam

---

[1] Populism had considerable influence in the United States in the late nineteenth and early twentieth centuries, resulting in the modification of representative democracy in some states. Populism has also had an influence on Canadian politics, particularly on the Prairies, both in the early twentieth century and, more recently, through the Reform party, which was established in 1987 and subsequently became the basis for the Canadian Alliance, which merged with the Progressive Conservative party in 2003.

[2] The populist movements of the late nineteenth and early twentieth centuries, generally based in the farming community, were critical of the power wielded by such interests as the banks, railway companies, and industrialists, and of the politicians and political parties that protected these interests. Some contemporary right-wing populists view feminists, environmentalists, and those promoting the rights of minorities as "special interests" that are supported by intellectuals, the media, and government bureaucrats, but, it is claimed, are not reflective of the views of the majority.

[3] A distinction can be made between referendums whose results are binding on government and those that are only advisory (the latter sometimes referred to as plebiscites). However, even if a referendum is not legally binding, governments will often accept its results.

The Use of Referendums in Canada

There have been only three referendums at the national level in Canada. They concerned the prohibition of liquor (1898), conscription during World War II, and the package of constitutional changes known as the Charlottetown Accord (1992).

Referendums have been somewhat more common at the provincial and local levels. The Quebec government has held two referendums concerning independence. In 1980, 40.5 percent of Quebeckers voted in favour of giving the Quebec government a mandate to negotiate "sovereignty-association" (a politically independent Quebec in an economic association with Canada) with the Canadian government. In 1995, 49.3 percent of Quebec voters supported giving the Quebec government a mandate to negotiate Quebec sovereignty. In response to a challenge to the 1995 referendum, the Supreme Court of Canada provided an opinion in 1998 that only if there were a clear majority on a clear question could a province negotiate its independence with the other Canadian governments. The Canadian Parliament reinforced this ruling by passing the *Clarity Act* (2000). This Act states that the Canadian government will only enter into negotiations regarding the secession (separation) of a province if the Canadian House of Commons determines that a clear majority of the population of that province has voted in favour of

secession on the basis of a clear question.

The *Clarity Act* raises important issues. Should referendums on important questions require the approval of more than 50 percent of those voting to be passed? How can we ensure that a referendum question is clear? If a referendum is necessary to allow a province to secede, does this suggest that referendums should be required for other important issues?

Although referendums involve a vote by the people, the decision to hold a referendum and the wording of a referendum are set by those in control of the government or the legislature, as was the case in Canada in 1995. Debate raged over whether the wording was misleading.

Hussein, have held referendums asking for approval of their continued rule without allowing a choice among alternative candidates and without providing an opportunity for public criticism of the leader.

INITIATIVES A stronger means of giving the public a direct voice in decision making is the **initiative**. This procedure gives citizens the right, by obtaining a sizable number of signatures on a petition, to have a proposition that they have drafted put to a vote by the electorate for approval (see

INITIATIVE
A procedure that gives citizens the right, by obtaining a sizable number of signatures on a petition, to have a proposition that they have drafted put to a vote by the electorate for approval.

The Initiative and Stockwell Day

One of the policy positions of the Canadian Alliance, which merged with the Progressive Conservative party in 2003, was a proposal to allow citizen initiatives at the national level if signatures were obtained from 3 percent of voters. Stockwell Day, the Alliance's leader at the time of the 2000 Canadian election, was ambiguous during the campaign about his position on this proposal. Rick Mercer of the comedy show *This Hour Has 22 Minutes* satirized the issue by conducting a mock initiative campaign. His proposed law to force Stockwell Day to change his name to Doris Day was supported by millions of e-mail votes!

Although there is a possibility that initiatives could be used for frivolous purposes, as Mercer demonstrated, setting a high threshold for petitions can limit the number of initiatives that come to a general vote. For example, no initiatives in British Columbia have thus far gained enough support to come to a vote. The requirement that at least 10 percent of eligible voters in each provincial electoral district must sign the initiative petition within a ninety-day period has discouraged initiative efforts.

Box 4-3, The Initiative and Stockwell Day). This right for laws to be proposed and approved by the people has been established in Switzerland, Italy, many American states, and British Columbia. For example, in 1978, a California initiative (Proposition 13) requiring major tax cuts was passed. This led to major cutbacks in government programs because of the reduced tax revenues.

RECALL

A procedure that allows citizens to remove representatives from office. By gaining a sufficient number of signatures on a petition, citizens can require that their representative be required to seek re-election before the representative's term is over.

RECALL As discussed in the opening vignette, **recall** procedures allow citizens to remove representatives from office. Although California includes the choice of a new representative on the same ballot as the question about whether the current representative should be recalled, other jurisdictions that allow the recall of representatives will only hold an election to choose a new representative after a majority has voted to recall their representative. The adoption of recall elections is often viewed as incompatible with a parliamentary system of government, since the recall of representatives from a small number of constituencies could result in the defeat of the governing party.

PROBLEMS WITH PLEBISCITARY DEMOCRACY There are some practical problems with referendums, initiatives, and recall. Citizens are not always prepared to vote on long and difficult proposals. When faced with a number of complex referendum and initiative questions on the ballot, voters may find it difficult to make informed decisions. This is particularly the case if referendums or initiatives are worded in a manipulative fashion. Concerns have been expressed that voters may be swayed by the expensive advertising efforts of interest groups that present the issues simplistically or unfairly, or by businesses that may stand to profit by the vote. For example, various businesses spent

$700 000 in order to obtain a "yes" vote in a 2001 New Brunswick referendum regarding the establishment of video lottery terminals in that province. As in regular elections, it takes money and organization to win votes.

Referendums, initiatives, and recall may stimulate some public discussion of important issues, encourage representatives to be more responsive to voters, and result in laws that reflect the wishes of the majority. However, like regular elections, there are possibilities for manipulation and the exertion of one-sided influence. Voting is not necessarily the product of informed discussion and deliberation. As well, although some referendums have had a high rate of turnout, such as when 93.5 percent of Quebeckers voted in the 1995 referendum, frequent use of referendums, initiatives, and recall may result in low turnout rates.

Deliberative Democracy

In recent years, there has been considerable discussion among political theorists about the possibility of a **deliberative democracy** in which decisions are made based on discussion by free and equal citizens (Elster, 1998). Through involvement in deliberative processes, it is hoped that people will become better informed, more active citizens. Through dialogue, people will come to understand the viewpoints of others and then, ideally, work together constructively to find solutions to problems. Unlike representative and plebiscitary versions of democracy, deliberative democracy brings citizens into decision making through discussion, rather than just through voting.

In theory, representative democracy involves thorough discussion and deliberation about political issues by the elected representatives of the people who have the time, knowledge, and experience to devote to this important task. However, the reality is that thorough discussion and deliberation rarely occurs in bodies such as the Canadian House of Commons that consist of elected representatives. Instead, it is behind the closed doors of cabinet and among senior government officials and advisors to the cabinet that almost all laws and policies are formulated. Debate in the Canadian House of Commons typically involves the governing party defending its actions and proposals and the opposition parties criticizing the government. Thus, debate is related more to the struggle among parties for power than to an effort to seek the common good through discussion and compromise. In other words, representative democracy is adversarial in nature, particularly in countries like Canada, the United States, and the United Kingdom.

To some extent, contemporary governments have been encouraging increased public participation in the decision-making process through various forms of public consultation, such as public hearings and forums on various issues. Although this is useful in allowing a variety of viewpoints to be heard, there is a tendency for public hearings to be dominated by spokespersons for

DELIBERATIVE DEMOCRACY
A political system in which decisions are made based on discussion by citizens rather than by elected representatives alone.

Deliberative Democracy Consortium
www.deliberative-democracy.net

▶ In theory, representative democracy involves thorough discussion and deliberation about political issues by the elected representatives of the people who have the time, knowledge, and experience to devote to this important task. In practice, however, debate is related more to the struggle among parties for power than an effort to seek the common good through discussion and compromise.

CITIZENS' JURIES
Groups of randomly selected persons that deliberate about and make recommendations concerning particular issues.

particular interests. Further, governments often do not feel obliged to explain and justify why they are not following the advice given to them.

Advocates of deliberative democracy often envision it as operating primarily among citizens at the local level, where face-to-face dialogue is possible and the issues being discussed may have direct relevance for the lives of those involved. Giving people in local communities responsibility for the management of their resources, such as rivers, forests, or coastal fisheries, or by establishing community Parliaments (Resnick, 1997) may encourage deliberative decision making. **Citizens' juries,** as discussed in Box 4-4, The Citizens' Jury, are another way to involve ordinary citizens in deliberation and decision making.

Although the ideal of deliberative democracy is to encourage an understanding of a variety of different viewpoints, there is a danger that the outcomes of deliberation will reflect the views of more educated, articulate, and dynamic persons. Those who are disadvantaged may be less willing or able to participate effectively. Thus, many advocates of deliberative democracy see it as complementing representative democracy, rather than as an alternative to representative democracy. Deliberative democracy may help to bridge the gap that often exists between citizens and politicians by encouraging dialogue that includes both representatives and citizens. However, the "one person, one vote" principle of representative democracy is still needed to maintain the democratic principle of equality.

BOX 4-4

The Citizens' Jury

The citizens' jury brings together a group of randomly selected citizens. Like the juries used to determine the outcome of some court trials, citizens' juries are composed of persons without any special knowledge of the topic under consideration. Trained facilitators are used to guide the deliberation, jurors are provided with information, and witnesses are called to explain and justify different viewpoints. The jurors then make recommendations that are passed on to a governmental body for possible action. For such a process to be meaningful, the recommendations of the citizens' jury must have some significance in the policy-making process (Smith & Wales, 2002).

Citizens' juries only directly involve a tiny proportion of the public in deliberation. However, if combined with public hearings or referendums, they may stimulate broader public discussion of particular issues. Problems may exist in ensuring that the jury is representative of the diversity of the population, particularly if the jury is small or if many people are unwilling to sit on the jury. It is also not easy to ensure that the questions asked, the information supplied, and the guidance provided are unbiased.

Until recently, citizens' juries have been used only occasionally on an experimental, unofficial basis. However, in 2003 British Columbia's government introduced what it termed a Citizens' Assembly to make a recommendation as to whether a new system should be used to elect provincial legislators. Two citizens were randomly selected from each provincial district to form, along with an appointed chair (a former university president), an assembly of 159 members. The random selection procedure was adjusted to ensure that equal numbers of males and females were chosen and that the assembly reflected the age distribution of the population. Service on the assembly is voluntary and members receive $150 a day. In addition to obtaining expert advice on different electoral systems, the assembly is required to hold public hearings across the province before making its recommendations. If the assembly recommends that a new electoral system be adopted, that option will go to a referendum at the time of the next provincial election (May 17, 2005). If approved by 60 percent of voters and in 60 percent of the province's electoral districts, the new system will be adopted for the 2009 British Columbia election.

DEMOCRACY AND THE NATION-STATE

Democracy is often thought to work best in a political community where there is a common identity, common culture, and common ideals. When one has a sense of partnership with one's fellow citizens, it is easier for one to consider the common good of the community. It is not surprising, therefore, that modern democracy developed alongside the development of the nation-state.

In countries that are divided by language, it may be difficult to include all of the people in a common dialogue about political issues. In countries with sharp cultural, regional, class, or other divisions, there may be insufficient trust and respect to sustain a dialogue about the good of the community as a whole. Nevertheless, viable democracies have been built in countries such as Canada, Belgium, and Switzerland despite the challenges posed by linguistic, cultural, and regional divisions. Indeed, diversity may help to create a more vibrant democracy because a variety of different perspectives can be brought into political discussion.

One way that democracy can be sustained in countries with sharp divisions is by avoiding a strict application of the principle of majority rule. By trying to ensure that there is a broad consensus among different groups about major issues, and by trying to ensure that different groups are represented in government, minority groups may be less likely to feel dominated by the majority. Indeed, politics in many continental European democracies leans in the direction of finding a consensus rather than majority rule (Lijphart, 1999). Another way to try to accommodate different cultural groups that are geographically concentrated is to adopt a **federal system** in which some important decisions are made at the provincial level (see Chapter 14). In this way, different groups can have a degree of democratic self-government.

FEDERAL SYSTEM
A system of governing in which sovereign authority is divided or shared between the central government and regional governments, with each deriving its authority from the constitution.

GLOBALIZATION AND DEMOCRACY

Democracy is based on the idea that the members of a political community should make the decisions that determine the direction and well-being of their community. Of course, there are always limits to the ability of even a small community to control its own destiny. Our understanding of the consequences of our actions is often limited, such that we may have trouble determining what actions are in our community's best interests. Unexpected events—whether a crop failure, a severe storm, an environmental disaster, or the discovery of a new source of wealth—can throw plans off course.

For several reasons, globalization is sometimes seen as a threat to democracy. It tends to increase the extent to which countries are affected by events that are beyond their direct control. As a country's economy becomes more and more intertwined with those of other countries and the rest of the world, its government is less able to independently manage the national economy. Our well-being as individuals and as a community becomes increasingly affected by what is happening beyond our borders. Global markets, financial institutions, and business corporations become increasingly important.

Globalization also tends to foster multiple identities. As the globalization of culture develops, there may be increased tendencies for identification with the nation-state to decline in intensity while other identities develop. For example, citizens of France and Germany may be slowly developing a European identity while at the same time increasing their identification with their particular region as the nation-state declines in significance. Feminists, environmentalists, and executives of multinational corporations may develop some degree of identification with their counterparts around the world.

Ethnic minorities may develop increasing ties with those of similar ancestry in other parts of the world. Although these multiple identities are very positive in some ways, they have the potential to reduce the feeling of being involved in a common endeavour for the good of the national community.

Globalization also tends to create multiple sources of governing to deal with the growing number of problems, such as climate change, the AIDS epidemic, global financial problems, and international terrorism, that require international action. In addition to being governed by several levels of government within the state, globalization involves new regional and global organizations beyond the state that also have an effect on our lives. International organizations such as the World Bank, International Monetary Fund, World Trade Organization, and the United Nations are not particularly democratic. Such organizations, although directed by representatives of member governments, are not generally accountable to the people affected by their actions. The decisions of many international organizations are made behind closed doors with little public input. The principle of political equality does not generally apply to international organizations, and their rules and decisions often seem to be based more on power than on fairness (Coleman, 2002).

A sense of common citizenship among the members of a political community is often thought to be a necessary basis for a stable democracy. As discussed in Box 4-5, "cosmopolitan citizenship" may need to grow among the people of the world if the democratic ideal is to be meaningful in an era of globalization. Dialogue among ordinary people in different countries about the common good of the world is currently very limited. Nevertheless, recent years have seen the development of various global political movements (for example, feminist, environmentalist, and human rights movements) that previously would not have been heard but that now seek to raise various issues and demands at the international level.

Cosmopolitan Citizenship

David Held, a professor of political science and sociology at Britain's Open University, argues that the concept of citizenship needs to be broadened to include cosmopolitan citizenship if the increasingly important systems of power that exist beyond the level of the state are to be democratically controlled:

"If many contemporary forms of power are to become accountable and if many of the complex issues that affect us all—locally, nationally, regionally and globally—are to be democratically regulated, people must have access to, and membership in, diverse political communities.... democracy for the new millennium should describe a world where citizens enjoy multiple citizenships. They should be citizens of their own communities, of the wider regions in which they live, and of a cosmopolitan, transnational community (Held, 2000, p. 57).

Several questions arise when we consider just how realistic Held's ideal of cosmopolitan citizenship is:

- Can people put aside, at least to some extent, the interests of their nation-state to consider the good of the world as a whole?
- Can fundamental cultural differences, "the clash of civilizations" (Huntington, 1996), be overcome to create a cosmopolitan citizenship?
- Are the divisions between the rich and poor countries so great as to prevent the development of trust among the peoples of the world?

Nevertheless, as systems of power beyond the state become increasingly important, people may need to develop a sense of cosmopolitan citizenship if democracy is to remain meaningful.

Summary and Conclusion

The democratic ideal is that of rule by the people. By placing political power in the hands of the people, those who hold the democratic ideal believe that the common good is more likely to be achieved than in non-democratic systems, in which decisions are made by rulers who are not held accountable to the people they govern. Representative democracy has generally been the system used to implement the democratic ideal. Through the competitive election of representatives and political parties, it allows citizens the opportunity to hold government accountable for its actions. Representatives and governing parties, it is assumed,

will be sensitive to the interests and wishes of voters because of their desire to be re-elected.

Representative democracy could, however, be considered a limited version of democracy, as the people elect others to make decisions on their behalf rather than directly participating in decision making. As well, questions often arise as to whether the decisions of elected representatives really reflect the interests, values, and opinions of the citizenry. There has, therefore, been a continuing interest in supplementing representative democracy with aspects of direct democracy. Plebiscitary democracy involves making greater use of voting, in the forms of referendums, initiatives, and recall elections, to determine issues by a majority vote and to try to ensure that representatives act in accordance with the wishes of those who elected them. Deliberative democracy seeks to involve citizens in the discussion and resolution of problems.

Supporters of representative democracy argue that politicians are best suited to seek the common good by using their experience, knowledge, and judgment to make decisions subject to being held accountable periodically to the electorate. Those who advocate plebiscitary democracy associate the common good with the common sense of the majority of citizens expressed through greater use of voting mechanisms. Advocates of deliberative democracy assume that dialogue among citizens having a variety of perspectives will lead to a search for the common good, or will make possible acceptable compromises among different views of the common good (Warren, 2002).

Associated with the democratic ideal are the values of freedom and equality. Liberal democracy focuses on the necessity of individual freedom for democracy to be meaningful. Freedom of expression, association, and opinion are needed to ensure that the voice of the people is heard and that elections are meaningful. On the other hand, socialist or social democratic views of democracy focus more on egalitarian values. Establishing equal political rights for citizens to vote is useful, but insufficient for a meaningful democracy. Powerful groups, such as large corporations, are able to exercise a dominant influence on government. Inequalities in the distribution of social and economic power need to be reduced in order to allow all citizens to have an equal voice in the decisions taken by the political community.

Although the ideal of democracy has gained widespread acceptance in the modern world, it faces difficult challenges. In states with substantial divisions, the mechanisms of majority rule can result in the heightening of tensions among different groups. Further, democracy may become less meaningful as international and global institutions become more important. Developing a reasonable level of democracy is more difficult in international and global political communities than in those states where a common sense of citizenship exists.

Key Terms

Discussion Questions

1. Is democracy the best form of government?
2. Should Canada move in the direction of becoming more democratic? If so, how could this best be achieved?
3. Should representative bodies reflect the characteristics of the population?
4. Should governments try to do what they think is best for the people or what the people want them to do?
5. Is democracy possible for governing organizations beyond the state?

Further Reading

Barber, B. *Strong democracy: Participatory democracy for a new age.* Berkeley, CA: University of California Press, 1984.

Carter, A., & Stokes, G. (Eds.). *Democratic theory today: Challenges for the 21st century.* Cambridge, UK: Polity Press, 2002.

Cronin, T. *Direct democracy: The politics of initiative, referendum, and recall.* Cambridge, MA: Harvard University Press, 1989.

Dahl, R.A. *On democracy.* New Haven, CT: Yale University Press, 1998.

Held, D. *Models of democracy* (2nd ed.). Stanford, CA.: Stanford University Press, 1996.

LeDuc, L. *The politics of direct democracy: Referendums in global perspective.* Peterborough, ON: Broadview Press, 2003.

Mansbridge, J. *Beyond adversary democracy.* New York: Basic Books, 1980.

Resnick, P. *Twenty-first century democracy.* Montreal: McGill–Queen's University Press, 1997.

Weale, A. *Democracy.* New York: St. Martin's Press, 1999.

Chapter 5

LIBERALISM, CONSERVATISM, SOCIALISM, AND FASCISM

PHOTO ABOVE: Vladimir Lenin's brother was arrested and then hanged for plotting to assassinate Tsar Alexander III. On learning of the execution, Vladimir promised to "make them pay for this!" Soon thereafter, he began studying the works of revolutionary thinkers Karl Marx and Frederick Engels and later, as the leader of the Bolsheviks, advocated revolutionary action.

CHAPTER OBJECTIVES

After reading this chapter you should be able to:

1. explain the meaning and significance of political ideology

2. discuss the ideas of liberalism, conservatism, socialism, and fascism

3. outline the development and major variations of each ideology

4. apply the terms "left" and "right"

After his brother was arrested for concealing a bomb in a medical encyclopedia, Vladimir Ilych Ulyanov—and ultimately world politics—underwent a profound change. Vladimir was still a teenager when his older brother Alexander was hanged for planning to assassinate Russia's Tsar Alexander III. On learning of the execution, Vladimir proclaimed, "I'll make them pay for this! I swear it!" (Shub, 1966, p. 16).

Expelled from university for supporting student demands, Vladimir began studying the works of revolutionary thinkers Karl Marx and Frederick Engels and passed examinations needed to become a lawyer. Later, in exile in Switzerland, he adopted the name Lenin. He became the leader of the Bolshevik party (later known as the Communist party), which advocated revolutionary action.

With Russia suffering extreme hardships and military defeats in the First World War, Tsar Nicholas II was forced to abdicate in March 1917. A provisional government continued the devastating war and did little to alleviate the dire circumstances faced by much of the population. Using the slogan "peace, bread, land," the Bolsheviks led a successful attack on the seat of government in Petrograd (now St. Petersburg). After a bitter civil war, Lenin was able to gain control of Russia, which was renamed the Union of Soviet Socialist Republics.

In many ways, the communist regimes of Lenin and his successor Stalin were even more oppressive than the tsarist governments that had ruled Russia for centuries. Dissent of any kind was brutally repressed. Forced labour camps were set up in remote regions of Russia. Whole populations were exiled from their homelands. And millions of peasants died of starvation as a result of the policies adopted by the Communist government.

Strongly held ideas and beliefs, whether religious or political, can have a profound effect on the world and on our lives. They can, for example, shape the way that we understand the world. In this chapter and the next chapter, we will examine various basic perspectives on the world, termed political ideologies.

POLITICAL IDEOLOGIES

A **political ideology** is a package of interrelated ideas and beliefs about government, society, the economy, and human nature that inspire and affect political action. Each ideology provides a different perspective that is used to understand and evaluate how the world actually works (Sunderlin, 2003). Marxism, for example, looks at the world through the lens of class conflict; feminism, as will be discussed in Chapter 6, sees the world in terms of male dominance; and liberalism views historical development as involving the struggle for individual liberty.

Most political ideologies also provide a vision of what the world should be like and how it should work. Usually, ideologies propose a means of political action to achieve their objectives. Some ideologies challenge and seek to transform the existing basic power arrangements; other ideologies provide justifications for the existing order.

The development of political ideologies is associated with the ideas of the European **Enlightenment** and with the economic and social upheavals associated with the development of capitalism and the Industrial Revolution. The mid-eighteenth-century Enlightenment involved a major shift from traditional religious beliefs towards an optimistic belief in the power of human reason to make the world better. Setting the tone for the modern world, Enlightenment thinkers argued that through reason and science, people could understand the world. Progress could be achieved by consciously shaping the world and its institutions. Human beings could create a better society on earth, rather than waiting for the life after death promised by religion. The French Revolution of 1789, influenced in part by Enlightenment ideas, involved a fundamental challenge to the traditional bases of authority—the monarchy, the aristocracy, and the Catholic Church. New and competing sets of ideas developed about how society and the state should be organized and run. Likewise, the rise of capitalism and the Industrial Revolution disrupted previous patterns of economic and social life, leading to intense disputes over the desirability of the capitalist system.

Ideological conflict has been at the centre of political life for the past two centuries. Intellectuals, politicians, journalists, and political activists often have a particular ideological perspective. Controversies over a variety of specific public policy issues are often based on the "hidden agenda" of those who have a particular ideological perspective. Many people do not consciously hold an ideological perspective, but nonetheless are affected in their thinking by elements of one or more ideologies. Whether in a subtle or explicit manner, ideological perspectives are often conveyed to the public by governments, various political and social groups, the educational system, and the mass media.

POLITICAL IDEOLOGY
A package of interrelated ideas and beliefs about government, society, the economy, and human nature that affect political action. Each ideology provides a different perspective that is used to understand and evaluate how the world actually works.

ENLIGHTENMENT
An intellectual movement that developed in the mid-eighteenth century, emphasizing the power of human reason to understand and improve the world.

The Negative Side of Ideology

The term *ideology* is sometimes used in a negative sense to describe viewpoints that are inflexible, designed to persuade the public in a deceptive manner, and extreme. There is some truth to this negative characterization. There are those who treat the leading texts of their ideology as if they were the word of God. Some adherents of an ideology are closed-minded persons who refuse to seriously consider any criticisms of their perspective. Ideological thinking can be simplistic, and ideological adherents may provide distorted depictions of reality to fit their mental model of the world. More importantly, ideologies have been used to justify the unjustifiable, such as the mass starvation of peasants by the Soviet Union and the extermination of the European Jewish population by the Nazis.

However, ideologies are not only the belief systems of fanatics, extremists, and simplistic thinkers. An ideology can provide some coherence, consistency, and direction to a person's political thinking and actions. Even those who consider themselves pragmatic or practical are often influenced by an ideological perspective. As Boris DeWeil argues, the ongoing debate among different ideologies is an inherent and desirable aspect of democratic politics, resulting from the fact that people have different value priorities (for example, whether equality or freedom is more important). Ideologies provide us with different ideas about the common good and how it may be achieved. "Without ideology, politics becomes the pursuit of power as its own reward" (DeWeil, 2000, p. 5).

▶ Ideologies have been used to justify the unjustifiable, such as the death of about one-fifth of the population of Cambodia from 1975 to 1979. In an attempt to create an agrarian communist utopia, Pol Pot's Khmer Rouge regime evacuated the cities and undertook a deliberate campaign of destroying the educated part of the population through starvation, slave labour, and executions. Some Western intellectuals, blinded by the regime's ideology, tried to deny the reality of the Cambodian "killing fields."

Examining Ideologies

In examining ideologies, we should keep in mind that each ideology is a broad perspective containing many variations and changing over time. It is not always easy to clearly distinguish between one ideology and another because differences between them may be subtle. However, each of the major ideologies does have some distinguishing themes (see Table 5-1).

Political parties with ideological names, such as the Liberal or Conservative parties, do not *necessarily* reflect the ideology corresponding to their name. Political parties are often, but not always, founded on a set of ideological principles. However, in the pursuit of electoral success, they may find it desirable to modify or ignore those principles.

LIBERALISM

The ideology of liberalism emphasizes the desirability of a high level of individual freedom, based on a belief in the inherent dignity and worth of each individual. Individuals are assumed to be capable of using reason and taking rational actions in pursuit of their interests. Thus, individuals should take responsibility for their own lives with as little interference from others as possible (see Box 5-1, John Stuart Mill: A Liberal Perspective, for a classic statement of this point of view). Because liberals have an optimistic view about the potential capabilities of the individual, liberals believe that human institutions can be improved. The progress of humanity can be achieved by using the power of individual reason to reform society and government.

TABLE 5-1
IDEOLOGIES: KEY THEMES

LIBERALISM	CONSERVATISM	SOCIALISM	FASCISM
Progress based on human reason	Human imperfection and capacity for evil	Humans cooperative and social	People motivated by emotion rather than reason
Individual freedom	Order, stability, social harmony	Equality	Loyalty to nation-state
Limited government	Respect for authority	Social ownership of major means of production	Subordination of individual to state
Rule of law	Respect wisdom of ages	Capitalism exploitative	Inequality natural
Government based on consent of people	Property, marriage, family and religion	Collective action desirable	Heroic leader
Protection of rights	Maintain traditional moral values	Move towards equality of condition	Democracy undesirable
Oppose special privileges	Government should not impose equality	Plannning to meet the needs of all	Anti-communist

BOX 5-1

John Stuart Mill: A Liberal Perspective

In his influential essay *On Liberty* (1859), the prominent English liberal thinker John Stuart Mill (1806–1873) made the case that individuals should be free to pursue their own good in their own way:

The only purpose for which power can be rightfully exercised over any member of a civilised community, against his will, is to prevent harm to others. His own good, either physical or moral, is not a sufficient warrant. He cannot rightfully be compelled to do or forbear because it will be better for him to do so, because it will make him happier, because, in the opinions of others, to do so would be wise, or even right. These are good reasons for remonstrating with him, or reasoning with him, or persuading him, or entreating him, but not for compelling him, or visiting him with any evil in case he do otherwise.... Over himself, over his own body and mind, the individual is sovereign" (Mill, 1859/1912, p. 15).

Although Mill was a passionate advocate of individual liberty and *On Liberty* is regarded as a definitive defence of individual human liberty, Mill, like other liberals and conservatives of his time, did not believe that the conquered peoples who were ruled by the British Empire were ready for self-rule. Liberty, it seems, was suitable for the British. Like children, people in India and elsewhere needed paternalistic guidance and control.

Historically, liberalism developed out of the struggles against the arbitrary power of absolute monarchs, restrictions on free business activity, the imposition of one set of religious values on the population of a country, and the granting of special privileges to particular groups—whether churches, aristocrats, or business monopolies.

Although liberals see a need for government, they are concerned that government will abuse its power. Thus, a central goal of liberalism is to ensure that the rights of individuals are firmly protected so they cannot be taken away by government. Liberals strongly advocate the **rule of law**. Government should act only in accordance with established laws rather than in an arbitrary fashion, and all persons should be equally subject to the law.

Liberals also want to limit the scope of government activity. This involves distinguishing a substantial area of private activity, where government should not be involved, from matters of public concern, in which government may be involved. As former Canadian Liberal Prime Minister Pierre Trudeau argued, "The state has no place in the nation's bedrooms." What goes on between consenting adults, in this perspective, should be left to their own moral judgment.

Religion, in the liberal view, is a private matter based on the conscience of the individual. A policy of tolerance should be adopted concerning those holding different beliefs. Government should not require or promote adherence to any particular religion, and laws should not be based on any one particular religious perspective. Government, in the view of most liberals, is not

RULE OF LAW
The idea that we should be subject to known, predictable, and impartial rules of conduct, rather than to the arbitrary orders of particular individuals. Both the rulers and the ruled are subject to the law.

a creation of God to promote moral values, but rather a human creation for more limited purposes.

Classical Liberalism

A distinction is often made between classical and reform versions of liberalism. Classical liberalism places great importance on limited government and the free marketplace. Reform liberalism, by contrast, favours a somewhat greater role for government

John Locke (1632–1704) was a key figure in the development of **classical liberalism**. Individuals, he argued, had been free and equal in the state of nature (that is, before the establishment of government), but lacked the means to settle disputes fairly. Therefore, through what he termed the "social contract," people agreed to establish government for limited purposes—namely, the protection of life, liberty, and property. Government should be limited in its powers, acting as a trustee to protect the rights of the people, and removable by the people, by force if necessary, if it infringes on the liberties that it is supposed to protect.

Classical liberals also advocate the adoption of a **laissez-faire system** in which workers, consumers, and privately owned businesses freely interact in the marketplace without government interference. Economic freedom, including the freedom to produce and trade, to sell one's labour, and to own and enjoy one's property, is seen as a basic human freedom. Individual property rights are also viewed as important in protecting liberty against the power of the state by dispersing power and resources among the population. The proper role for government in economic matters is only to protect property, prevent fraud, and impartially settle disputes.

Although classical liberals promote the idea that all individuals should have the equal right to enjoy life, liberty, and property, in the past they were reluctant to extend the right to vote to all citizens. They feared those without property would use their votes to undermine property rights and the free-market economy in order to redistribute wealth from the rich to the poor. In addition, classical liberals of the past viewed the uneducated masses as not sufficiently committed to the value of individual liberty. Thus, despite the idea that government should rest on the consent of the people, many classical liberals prior to the twentieth century argued that the right to vote could not be entrusted to the entire adult population.

Reform Liberalism

Reform liberalism (sometimes referred to as welfare liberalism, social liberalism, or modern liberalism) developed in the latter part of the nineteenth century as many liberals became concerned that the laissez-faire system established in countries such as Britain seemed to offer little to develop the

CLASSICAL LIBERALISM
A form of liberalism that emphasizes the desirability of limited government and the free marketplace.

LAISSEZ-FAIRE SYSTEM
A system in which privately owned businesses, workers, and consumers freely interact in the marketplace without government interference. The role of government is limited to such activities as maintaining order and enforcing contracts.

REFORM LIBERALISM
A version of liberalism that argues government should play a role in assisting the disadvantaged.

capabilities of workers and disadvantaged sectors of society. Life was harsh for the majority of the population, who worked long hours in unsafe conditions to eke out a living with no protection against sickness, disability, unemployment, or old age. Freedom was of little benefit for those who had to worry about where their next meal was coming from.

English philosopher T.H. Green (1836–1882) laid some of the foundation for reform liberalism by arguing that government action is not necessarily the enemy of freedom, but can provide the basis for people to be free to develop their individuality. The absence of physical and legal restraints on our actions ("negative freedom") does not necessarily make us free. If we think of freedom as a "positive power or capacity of doing something worth doing or enjoying," then individuals in a primitive society with little or no government are less free than modern citizens, who are subject to the many laws and regulations of governments (quoted in Qualter, 1986, p. 98). Although modern society presents greater opportunities to be free, in Green's positive sense, there are many obstacles that can prevent people from fully developing themselves, such as poverty, ill health, a deadening environment, and long hours of work. Government, by helping to ensure that individuals have the means to live a life of dignity and self-respect, can help to make freedom meaningful for all rather than a special privilege for a few.

Thus, Green argued, government has a responsibility to remove the social and economic obstacles that can hinder individual development in order to establish a meaningful right to freedom. A somewhat active government is needed in order to establish the conditions in which individuals can freely develop their capabilities. While individuals should be responsible for their own development, government, by helping to ensure that individuals have the means to live a life of dignity and self-respect, can aid individuals in the pursuit of freedom. Fighting poverty, protecting the health and safety of workers, improving the quality of the cities, and ensuring that everyone has adequate housing are, therefore, proper activities of government.

Reform liberals argue that government should play a role in assisting the disadvantaged through such measures as unemployment insurance, old age pensions, health care, and subsidized education. This creates a more meaningful freedom for the less fortunate members of society by ensuring that a minimum standard of living is available to all.

Reform liberals generally share with classical liberals a belief in the virtues of a free-enterprise system. However, reform liberals argue that property rights may need to be limited, to some extent, in order to advance the rights and freedoms of others. For example, the freedom of a factory owner may need to be limited by government regulations in order to ensure that the health and safety of factory workers is protected, consumers are protected from harmful products, and the environment is protected from the discharge of pollutants.

Reform liberals also generally accept the view of British economist John Maynard Keynes that laissez-faire policies based on the pursuit of self-interest do not necessarily lead to the common good. Government needs to use its powers to make the economy run more smoothly, particularly in pursuing policies that foster full employment, while leaving private businesses unhindered in their individual operations. Reform liberals also favour a role for government in regulating business activities so that large business corporations do not stifle competition.

Although both classical and reform liberals believe that individuals are naturally equal, classical liberals focus on *equal rights*—the right of all individuals to be treated the same in terms of the law. Reform liberals go beyond equal legal rights to advocate government policies that are designed to create *equal opportunities*. For example, reform liberals argue that government should ensure that young persons, whether their parents are rich or poor, should have the opportunity to receive a good education. This might also involve providing special assistance in obtaining education and employment to members of groups that have suffered from discrimination.

With their more positive view of the role of government in aiding the disadvantaged, it is not surprising that reform liberals supported the expansion of the right to vote to the entire adult population. Nevertheless, many liberals prefer representative democracy to more direct and participatory forms of democracy, which they see as having a greater potential to limit individual rights and freedoms.

Liberal International
www.liberal-international.org

Contemporary liberalism, particularly in North America, is sometimes associated with reform liberalism. However, classical liberalism continues to be important, particularly in the form of neo-liberalism discussed in Chapter 6. Many liberal parties, including the Liberal party of Canada, are influenced by both the classical and reform liberal perspectives.

CONSERVATISM

Conservatism emphasizes the values of order and stability in the community. Conservatives are usually critical of those who advocate rapid and fundamental change. Although societies were generally conservative in nature and thought before the modern era, the *ideology* of conservatism developed in response to liberal and radical ideas promoting major changes. In particular, the development of conservatism is often associated with the reaction to the French Revolution (1789).

CONSERVATISM
An ideology that emphasizes the values of order, stability, respect for authority, and tradition, based on a view that humans are inherently imperfect, with a limited capacity to reason.

The French Revolution swept away the "old order," replacing the authority and privileges enjoyed by kings, nobles, and clergy with the *Declaration of the Rights of Man*. The revolutionaries attempted to rationally reorganize society and institute the principle of popular sovereignty. However, the revolution degenerated into terror directed at the opponents of the new regime, and eventually Napoleon seized power and crowned himself as Emperor. Although the ideas of the French Revolution were spread by Napoleon's conquest of much of continental Europe, his defeat resulted in efforts to restore the old order in Europe.

REACTIONARY

A conservative who favours a return to the values and institutions of the past.

Some conservatives (labelled **reactionaries**) responded to the failures of the French Revolution by advocating a return to the values and institutions of the old order. Other conservatives, such as Edmund Burke, took a more moderate position arguing that change, when necessary, should be slow, gradual, and consistent with the particular traditions of a country (see Box 5-2, Edmund Burke: Traditional Conservatism).

Conservative thinkers view humans as inherently imperfect, with a great potential for evil and a limited capacity to use their reasoning abilities. To

BOX 5-2

Edmund Burke: Traditional Conservatism

Edmund Burke (1729–1797), an Irish member of the British Parliament best known for his condemnation of the French Revolution, is often considered the founder of conservatism in the English-speaking world.

In his *Reflections on the Revolution in France* (1790), Burke argued that the attempt to create a new society in France based on the application of abstract, universal principles would fail. The French revolutionary ideology, if imported to Britain, would destroy the constitutional traditions that had served Britain well. Human beings, Burke argued, are naturally flawed in their character and limited in their reasoning abilities. Governing decisions should be based on the circumstances surrounding a particular issue, rather than on abstract principles based on reason. Civilized institutions have been built up over a long period of time and those institutions reflect the accumulated wisdom of many generations. Change, although necessary, should proceed slowly, building on the past, rather than pursuing innovations that are disruptive of the gifts of the past.

The radical liberals who supported the French Revolution viewed society as a collection of independent individuals, each with a set of rights. For

Burke, in contrast, society should be viewed as a living organism in which the well-being of the individual is dependent on the well-being of the whole, or as a fabric composed of interwoven threads. Society and the state are not simply based on a temporary contract among individuals, but rather are a permanent partnership "between those who are living, those who are dead, and those who are to be born" (Burke 1790/1955, p. 110). Government, along with an official, established religion, are necessary and important features of human society, needed to restrain the passions of individuals. Instead of proclaiming the universal rights of all humanity, Burke argued that the traditional liberties of particular countries should be defended. Government should not be viewed as an obstacle to freedom, as freedom is dependent on the order created by government. Political power should be in the hands of the "natural aristocracy" found largely among the nobility and gentry, men of law, science, and the arts, and some businessmen who had the virtues needed to represent the people as a whole. Rather than acting according to the opinions of voters, who may be uninformed, legislators should use their own judgment about the good of society.

maintain civilized values against the ever-present tendencies of evil, laws need to be respected and vigorously enforced by government, and respect for those in positions of authority must be maintained. Thus, conservatives have generally favoured a strong government able to protect order and stability and to pursue national interests. As well, conservatives often argue that traditional, religious-based moral values need to be maintained in order to prevent the collapse of civilized society.

Because of the individual's limited capabilities to reason and because of the complexity of society, conservatives argue that we should respect the wisdom that has been slowly built up over the ages. This wisdom, they argue, is reflected in traditional customs and practices. Reactionary conservatives favoured a counter-revolution to restore the old order, but other conservatives accepted moderate changes in the direction of a more modern society, provided that necessary changes were achieved slowly, without being perceived as breaking with tradition. Conservatives tend to be very skeptical of attempts to improve society by deliberate political effort.

Conservatives are strong defenders of property. Property, along with religious institutions, marriage, and family, is viewed as a bulwark of the social order. Conservatives typically oppose government policies designed to move society in the direction of greater equality (for example, by redistributing income, wealth, and property from the rich to the poor). In the conservative perspective, people are naturally unequal. Attempts to impose equality are disruptive and undermine the natural leadership of elite groups.

The Canadian Conservative Forum
www.conservativeforum.org

Conservatives often have mixed feelings about the free-market capitalist system. In the past, some conservatives looked back fondly to the feudal order, where a land-owning hereditary aristocracy preserved civilized values. The relentless pursuit of profit by entrepreneurs was often viewed with disdain. Although most contemporary conservatives are strong supporters of the free-market capitalist system, some traditional conservatives continue to be concerned that an unrestricted free-market capitalist system creates social divisions that can threaten national unity and social order. Further, some traditional conservatives have worried that the revolutionary impact of the modern free-market economy and associated global free trade could undermine the local values and particularisms that conservatives cherish. The individualistic and materialistic values associated with the capitalist system do not fit easily with the more organic and community oriented values of many traditional conservatives.

Tensions often exist within contemporary conservative parties between the enthusiastic supporters of a laissez-faire capitalist system and traditional conservatives, who see more fundamental importance in such values as order, stability, and social harmony. Other differences among contemporary conservatives exist between those who believe that laws should reflect traditional moral and religious values on such issues as abortion, divorce, and same-sex marriage, and those who take more tolerant and secular positions on moral issues. Contemporary versions of conservatism, known as the New Right, will be explored further in Chapter 6.

SOCIALISM

SOCIALISM

An ideological perspective based on the view that human beings are basically social in nature and that the capitalist system undermines the cooperative and community-oriented nature of humanity. Socialism advocates the establishment of an egalitarian society.

Modern versions of **socialism**, like reform liberalism, developed in reaction to the harshness of the early capitalist system, which was reinforced by the laissez-faire approach of governments. However, unlike liberalism, socialism views human beings as basically social in nature. Socialists often criticize the capitalist system not only for its oppressive nature, but also for its emphasis on competition, which is seen as undermining the cooperative and community-oriented nature of humanity.

Within the socialist ideology, there are a variety of views as to what an ideal society would be like and how such a society could be achieved. Some have envisaged the establishment of small, self-sufficient communes in which property would be collectively owned, all would work cooperatively, and material goods would be shared equally (see Box 5-3, Utopian Socialism). Others have looked to the state to own the major means of production and operate them for the good of society as a whole. Still others envision a system of worker-run enterprises.

BOX 5-3

Utopian Socialism

In his classic book *Utopia*, English writer Thomas More (1478–1535) condemned the evils of pride, envy, and greed that result "wherever men have private property and money is the measure of everything" (1516/2004, p. 198).

In existing societies, More asserted, the rich "serve their own interests under the name of the common good" while in reality looking after only their private good. Instead of only a few being prosperous and happy "while all the rest live in misery and wretchedness," he imagined a society in which all things are owned in common, money is no longer used, and everyone is free to take from the common storehouses all the necessities that are needed to live a meaningful life. In such a society, people would be concerned with the "common affairs" of the society, rather than worrying about earning a livelihood (More, 1516/2004, pp. 198–202).

More did not intend Utopia, which literally means "nowhere," to be a blueprint for society. However, a number of socialists, particularly in the nineteenth century, developed elaborate models of an ideal communal society. These "utopian socialists" were criticized by other socialists, including Marx and Engels, for having the naive view that fundamental changes could occur by developing visionary schemes or establishing model communities.

Nevertheless, a number of small-scale communes of a religious or secular nature have been established at various times. One of the few long-lasting communal societies is Israel's *kibbutzim*, which, although successful, involve only a very small proportion of the Israeli population.

Generally, socialists favour some form of social rather than private ownership of the major means of production so that many of the decisions that affect the life of the community are no longer in the hands of the owners of business. In their view, the capitalist system encourages and promotes the selfish and competitive side of human nature. Ending the exploitation and inequality of an economy based on private ownership and competition would, socialists hope, allow the cooperative and social side of human nature to be fostered. Greater equality in income, wealth, and power would help to create a more just society.

Socialists have a positive view of collective action. Organizations based on the participation of ordinary people, along with the creation of a more egalitarian society, are seen as essential to achieving the common good. Although socialism is often associated with the expansion of the state, some versions of socialism favour a highly decentralized state, or even the elimination of the state.

Marxism and Communism

The writings of Karl Marx (1818–1883) and Frederick Engels (1820–1895), often termed Marxism, are of great importance, particularly in the development of **communism**. Their analysis, termed **historical materialism**, starts with the assumption that to understand historical development, we must examine the way society is organized to produce essential material goods such as food, clothing, and shelter. In every society except the most primitive, Marx and Engels argued, production involves the exploitation of a subordinate class by a smaller, dominant class. The leading ideas, beliefs, and morals of a society serve the interests of the dominant class, and thus help it in its struggle against challenges by the exploited subordinate class. However, each of the basic systems of production—slave-owning, feudal, and capitalist—has internal tensions ("contradictions") that eventually become irresolvable. This leads to an overthrow of that system and its replacement by a new system of production.

In their examination of the capitalist system of production, Marx and Engels argued that the profits obtained by the owners of capital (the bourgeoisie) were based on the exploitation of the workers (the proletariat). The capitalist system appeared to be free, as goods and labour could be freely bought and sold in the marketplace. It was, however, only the appearance of freedom. Workers, in reality, had little choice but to sell their labour power to survive. In addition, the emphasis on competition, profit, and selfishness in the capitalist free-market system violated what Marx and Engels viewed as the essentially social and creative nature of humanity.

The capitalist system was an important, but not the final, stage of historical development. Conflict between the working class and the bourgeoisie will intensify because the two groups have incompatible interests. The large

Socialist International
www.socialistinternational.org

COMMUNISM
A system in which private property has been replaced by collective or communal ownership and in which everyone would be free to take from society what they need.

HISTORICAL MATERIALISM
The view that historical development can be understood in terms of the way society is organized to produce material goods.

working class developing as a result of industrialization will eventually organize itself into a revolutionary force. Workers will come to see the need to overturn the capitalist system and replace it with a system based on social, rather than private, ownership of the means of production.

Because the state generally acts in the interests of the capitalist class, the working class will have to take control of the state and then use the state apparatus to transform the capitalist system into a socialist system. This will likely necessitate a revolution, as capitalists will be unlikely to give up their control voluntarily or peacefully. However, as workers in Europe began to gain the right to vote in the late nineteenth century, Marx and Engels saw a possibility that in some countries, working class control of state power *might* be achieved through the election of socialist political parties provided that police and military forces were not used to suppress the socialist movement.

In the perspective of Marx and Engels, the capitalist system faces inherent contradictions that will contribute to its eventual demise. Competition among capitalists will result in weaker capitalists being forced out of business. The remaining capitalists will then have monopoly control of the marketplace, undermining free competition. Marx and Engels also argued that the capitalist system was prone to ever-increasing crises of severe unemployment and depression because of the chaotic nature of capitalism.

Marx and Engels were more concerned with analyzing the dynamics of the capitalist system than with setting blueprints for the socialist future. But they did suggest that after the revolution, the workers would control the state in the interests of the working class ("the dictatorship of the proletariat"), and would use the state to expropriate the property of the capitalists. *Eventually*, they argued, the selfishness that is characteristic of economic systems based on private ownership would disappear. The increased production of an economy devoted to human needs would lead to material abundance that could fulfill the basic needs of everyone. A further transition from a socialist to a communist society would then occur. In a communist society, everyone would be free to take from society what he or she needed. Although production would be highly organized, the need for a coercive state would diminish or disappear because, in the view of Marx and Engels, the need for a coercive state arises out of the need to use coercion to maintain private property and the inequality that it entails.

MANIFESTO OF THE COMMUNIST PARTY Marx and Engels wrote the *Manifesto of the Communist Party* (1848) for a small group known as the Communist League. It eventually became one of the most widely read works in the world. Among its most famous passages are the following statements:

> The history of all hitherto existing society is the history of class struggles.... The modern bourgeois society that has sprouted from the ruins of feudal society has not done away with class antagonisms. It has but

established new classes, new conditions of oppression, new forms of struggle in place of the old ones.... Society as a whole is more and more splitting up into two great hostile camps, into two great classes directly facing each other: Bourgeoisie [owners of capital] and Proletariat [workers].... Political power, properly so called, is merely the organised power of one class for oppressing another. If the proletariat during its contest with the bourgeoisie is compelled, by the force of circumstances, to organise itself as a class, if, by means of a revolution, it makes itself the ruling class and, as such, sweeps away by force the old conditions of productions, then it will, along with these conditions, have swept away the conditions for the existence of class antagonisms and of classes, and will thereby have abolished its own supremacy as a class. In place of the old bourgeois society, with its classes and class antagonisms, we shall have an association, in which the free development of each is the condition for the free development of all. Let the ruling classes tremble at a Communist revolution. The proletarians have nothing to lose but their chains. They have a world to win. Workingmen of all countries, unite! (Marx & Engels, 1848/1955, pp. 9, 10, 32, 46)

The Communist Manifesto, with its dramatic portrayal of history in terms of class struggle and its confident assertion that a successful proletarian revolution is inevitable, had a profound effect on the politics and thinking of the late nineteenth and much of the twentieth centuries.

LENINISM   As Russian Communist party leader, Vladimir Lenin (1870–1924) modified the ideas of Marx and Engels. In Lenin's view, the capitalist system could only be overthrown by force—but the workers themselves could not spontaneously overthrow the system. What was needed was a tightly disciplined party firmly controlled by an ideologically oriented leadership. These ideas have come to be known as **Leninism**.

Because nineteenth-century Russia was a largely peasant society with a relatively small working class, the role of the party that was in the vanguard of the proletariat (that is, the Communist party) was particularly important in leading the revolution and directing the subsequent course of revolutionary change. Instead of putting power in the hands of councils of workers and peasants, as many of those involved in the Russian Revolution had hoped, Lenin, and even more so his successor Joseph Stalin (1877–1953), established a tight grip on Soviet society and established a **totalitarian** regime dedicated to rapidly building an industrialized economy. Similarly, tight party control has been characteristic of government in China, where the Communist party under Mao Zedong (1893–1976) was successful in capturing power in 1949 after a lengthy guerrilla war.

THE COMMUNIST SYSTEM COLLAPSES   Communist party control of the Soviet Union and Eastern Europe collapsed at the end of the 1980s. A

LENINISM
The version of Marxism that includes the belief that the capitalist system can only be overthrown through force by means of a tightly disciplined party controlled by an ideologically oriented leadership.

TOTALITARIANISM
The idea that the state should control all aspects of life within a country. Examples of totalitarian regimes include Mussolini's Italy, Hitler's Germany, Stalin's Russia, and Mao Zedong's China.

loosening of the tight control exercised by Communist leaders allowed the people to overthrow their governments with a minimum of violence. Although China is still controlled by the Communist party, it has abandoned efforts to create a communist society, as we saw in Chapter 3. Various versions of Marxism continue to provide important perspectives on the world. However, communism, as developed and implemented by Lenin, Stalin, and Mao, is no longer a powerful force in the contemporary world.

Democratic Socialism and Social Democracy

DEMOCRATIC SOCIALISM
A version of socialism that argues socialism should be achieved by democratic rather than revolutionary means, and that a socialist society should be democratic in nature.

A key difference between **democratic socialism** and communism is that democratic socialists believe that only democratic methods should be used to work towards a socialist society. Democratic socialists reject the notion of the dictatorship of the proletariat, arguing instead that political rights and freedoms should be respected. Likewise, although they believe that an active government is needed to provide for the well-being of the citizenry, they share the view of liberals and conservatives that governments should abide by the rule of law and not act in an arbitrary manner.

Rather than complete state ownership of the means of production, democratic socialists propose various methods to achieve democratic control of the economy. These include:

- public ownership of some key industries
- encouragement for cooperative enterprises
- requirements that workers have a voice in business decisions
- increased government regulation and planning of the economy

To achieve greater equality, democratic socialists advocate government provision and subsidization of a variety of services, along with the redistribution of income and wealth from the rich to the poor through the tax system.

Over time, democratic socialist parties have watered down or dropped their commitment to fundamentally transforming the economic system. For example, British Labour Prime Minister Tony Blair has promoted a "Third Way" (a mixture of conservatism, liberalism, and social democracy) that has come under strong criticism from those Labour party members who hold traditional socialist views. (See Box 5-4, Democratic Socialism in Canada, for a look at issues in contemporary Canada).

Ideas about nationalizing (having the government take over) the "commanding heights" of the economy, or about replacing the capitalist system, have generally moved to the fringes of democratic socialist parties. Indeed, many leading figures within democratic socialist parties prefer to call themselves social democrats to indicate that they no longer believe in a socialist economic system (that is, one with a substantial level of state ownership). Instead, social democrats support government regulation of the free market and seek to provide greater equality through government assistance to the

BOX 5-4
Democratic Socialism in Canada

Contemporary democratic socialists and social democrats have debated at length whether socialism, particularly in the sense of the replacement of a capitalist by a basically socialist economy, is still relevant. In Canada, there have been important divisions within the democratic socialist New Democratic Party (NDP) concerning the ideological direction of the party.

Bob Rae, the former NDP premier of Ontario, argues that the policies his party has often advocated, such as government ownership and intervention in the economy and big, centralized government, are no longer acceptable means of governing. Such policies are not the essence of social democracy, which he views in terms of the equal right of every person to enjoy the good things of life, freedom, and the solidarity of "ordinary people" working together to improve their lives. The pursuit of self-interest is natural and the competition of the marketplace is healthy, but they need to be balanced by the need for generosity, the well-being of the whole community, and a shared responsibility for the public good (Rae, 1998).

Others within the NDP, who are more likely to refer to themselves as democratic socialists, view the "moderation" of leading figures like Rae as capitulation to the forces of global capitalism. For example, James Laxer, a professor of political science at York University who has been active in the NDP, argues that the power of global capitalism needs to be challenged. Class divisions have become increasingly sharp as the working class has been battered by the power of global capitalism. Laxer sees hope for a revitalized Canadian democratic socialism not only in the trade union movement, but also in various progressive social movements, including the feminist, environmentalist, and gay and lesbian movements (Laxer, 1996).

disadvantaged, maintaining the welfare state, and placing a greater burden of taxation on the rich or on large corporations.

Anarchism

Anarchism, which literally means "without rule," seeks to eliminate the state, which it views as a key source of oppression. Anarchism comes in some very different versions. On the far right, libertarian anarchists take the classical liberal idea of a laissez-faire system to what they see as its logical conclusion: the provision of all government services by a free marketplace, the right to use one's private property with restriction, and the elimination of taxes. On the far left, socialist anarchism (or anarcho-communism) advocates the elimination of both the state and private property. In its place, socialist anarchists advocate a cooperative or communal society based on what they see as the natural principle of mutual assistance. Instead of large and powerful states, they envision a world based on voluntary cooperation among a network of local communities.

ANARCHISM
An ideology that views the state as the key source of oppression and seeks to replace the state with a system based on voluntary cooperation.

Anarchy Archives
www.anarchyarchives.org

Although various forms of socialist anarchism were important in the international socialist movement in the latter part of the nineteenth century, anarchism has generally been overshadowed by communism and democratic socialism in the past century. Nevertheless, anarchism continues to exist—for example, as an element of the anti-globalization movement.

FASCISM

FASCISM
An ideology that combines an aggressive form of nationalism with a strong belief in the naturalness of inequality and opposition to both liberal democracy and communism.

The ideology of **fascism** developed in the period between the First and Second World Wars. It was based, in part, on the views of various thinkers who were critical of the ideas of the Enlightenment. Fascism combines an aggressive form of nationalism with a strong belief in the naturalness of inequality and opposition to both liberal democracy and communism.

Nationalism and Racism

Loyalty to the nation-state is extremely important in fascist thought. In the fascist view, the well-being of the individual is based on the well-being of the nation-state to which the individual belongs. Individuals owe absolute loyalty to the state, and the state has the right to control all activities in order to promote its interests. Further, the state is seen by fascists as a cohesive or organic whole that is based on the bonds of a common culture or ancestry. Foreigners and those of minority cultures are typically viewed as a hindrance to the creation of a homogenous society based on the dominant nationality.

Related to the extreme nationalism of fascist ideology is a belief in the superiority of particular nationalities and races. This superiority is exhibited not only in cultural achievements, but also in such characteristics as bravery and heroism. War allows that superiority to be realized, and the conquest and subordination of "inferior" nations and races is justified.

NAZISM
A version of fascism associated with Adolf Hitler, emphasizing racial conflict and the superiority of the "Aryan race."

HOLOCAUST
The systematic extermination of six million European Jews by the Nazis during World War II.

NAZISM The idea of racial superiority and racial conflict was particularly evident in **Nazism**, a German version of fascism. Building on some nineteenth= century theories that viewed racial differences as profound, the Nazis proclaimed their belief that the Germans and some related Nordic peoples were the heirs of an "Aryan master race" that could be restored through careful breeding. As a "culture-creating" master race, a revived Aryan race would exert dominance over other "inferior" races. The Nazis viewed the Jews as their key racial enemy and sought to rid Europe of the Jews through the systematic genocide known as the **Holocaust** (see Box 5-5, The Holocaust).

Belief in a Natural Inequality

Not only do fascists believe that the inequality of nations and races is natural and inevitable, they also believe that there is a natural inequality within society between the masses (ordinary people) and their natural leaders. The masses

The Holocaust

The potential of ideological thought to lead to horrific consequences is clearly demonstrated by the outcome of the racist ideology of the Nazis.

Anti-Semitism (that is, hatred and persecution of Jews) has a very lengthy history throughout Europe. In the 1920s and '30s, stirring up anti-Semitic prejudices was an important part of the Nazi appeal. After gaining power, the Nazis began taking away the rights of Jewish citizens and encouraged attacks on Jewish businesses and individuals. As the German armies conquered Eastern Europe, they began rounding up Jews and shooting them in mass pits or gassing them in mobile gas chambers. Eventually, Adolf Hitler and his top officials decided on what they termed the "final solution" to the "Jewish problem" (that is, the total elimination of the Jewish people). Persons of Jewish ancestry were transported to massive concentration camps for slave labour and systematic, industrial-style extermination.

In all, the Nazis organized the deliberate murder of about six million persons of Jewish ancestry, including about one and a half million children. In addition, about five million other persons were killed, deemed "unfit" because of their nationality, disabilities, sexual orientation, or political views. The **Holocaust** is particularly horrifying because of the systematic, determined, and state-directed nature of the "extermination." Further, it occurred in modern and so-called civilized societies, often with the acquiescence and involvement of people throughout Europe, despite some heroic exceptions.

---

are typically portrayed by fascists as a herd that can be mobilized by skillful leaders through the use of slogans and symbols. Democratic leaders are seen as weak because they pander to the masses to gain their support. Instead, fascists often argue that a heroic leader with a creative "will to power" will arise above the masses in exceptional circumstances. Such an exceptional leader, fascists believe, embodies the will of the people. Thus, fascism favours authoritarian leadership, arguing that natural leaders should be allowed free rein to rule in the interests of the nation-state enhancing its unity, culture, and power.

Fascism
www.brookes.ac.uk/schools/
humanities/Roger/fascrev.htm

Rejection of Enlightenment

Underlying the fascist ideology is a rejection of much of Enlightenment thought. Human beings, fascism assumes, are basically motivated by emotion rather than reason. People are rooted in their past and their territory, and can be mobilized into action through myths and propaganda. The liberal and socialist ideologies that are based on Enlightenment ideas about human progress are thus rejected. As well, fascism rejects the modern, Enlightenment-based idea that we are all part of a common humanity (Eatwell, 1995). Instead of the liberal and socialist belief that a peaceful world can be created, fascism sees struggle and the use of force as inevitable.

Because fascists see the world as based on a struggle for dominance, they argue that constant preparation for war is necessary. The strength of one's nation-state must be developed to ensure its dominance. Divisions or disagreements within the nation-state cannot be tolerated because they might lead to weakness. Fascists believe that it is right and natural that the strong should dominate and subjugate the weak, and that humanitarian policies directed to aiding the disadvantaged lead to weakness. Adapting the **Social Darwinist** ideas of English social theorist Herbert Spencer (1820–1903), fascists see war and conflict as a natural process allowing humanity to evolve through the "survival of the fittest."

SOCIAL DARWINISM
The use of Darwin's theory of evolution to argue that competition and conflict allow humanity to evolve through the "survival of the fittest."

Economic Views

Fascism is also critical of liberal and socialist systems of thought for their focus on achieving material well-being. Not surprisingly, then, the fascist ideology tends to be unclear about the economic organization of society other than seeking an alternative to both capitalism and communism. Benito Mussolini's Italian fascist regime adopted the idea of the **corporate state**, in which business and labour would be closely tied to the state and directed to goals established by the state. In practice, this involved the subordination of labour and business to the fascist regime and the suppression of the labour movement.

CORPORATE STATE
A system associated with fascist Italy in which business and labour are closely tied to the state and directed to goals established by the state.

A New Order

Fascism is often depicted as a reactionary ideology. To some extent this is valid, as fascism rejects many aspects of modern society and politics, including individualism and materialism, which fascism views as a cause of moral decay. Instead of the modern ideal of democracy, fascism seeks to create a totalitarian order. However, fascism embraces only selected myths from the past—such the ideal of the heroic Teutonic warrior or the glories of the Roman Empire. Unlike the reactionary conservatives of the nineteenth century, fascists do not want to restore the old order, but rather view themselves as revolutionaries creating a new order. Indeed, fascism tends to both glorify the feudal past of ethnically homogenous rural communities and to celebrate modern technology and envision a technological future (Neocleous, 1997).

The Continuing Significance of Fascism

Fascism is often associated with the dictatorial regimes of the Italian fascist leader Benito Mussolini (1883–1945) and the German Nazi leader Adolf Hitler (1889–1945). However, fascist movements also had substantial followings in a variety of countries in the 1930s, and some leading non-fascist figures expressed admiration for Mussolini and Hitler. The decisive defeat of the militarist fascist regimes in World War II and the revelation of the horrors they perpetrated resulted in the discrediting of the fascist ideology.

Nevertheless, there has been a revival of fascism, to some extent, in various countries in recent years.

NEO-FASCISM Contemporary fascism (**neo-fascism**) often tries to cultivate a more respectable and democratic image than the fascist movements of the interwar period. The second-place finish—albeit with only 18 percent of the vote—of French neo-fascist National Front leader Jean-Marie Le Pen in the 2002 presidential election shocked many persons. (Le Pen is notorious for his dismissal of the Holocaust as "a detail of history.") Likewise, the Austrian Freedom Party, which has been a part of the governing coalition since 1999, is often viewed as leaning in a fascist direction, although it denies that it is fascist. The Italian National Alliance, originally a neo-fascist party, calls itself "post-fascist" and is a member of a governing conservative coalition. Although neo-fascist political parties avoid the thoroughly racist doctrines of Hitler's Nazi party, they often appeal to nationalist values and express animosity towards immigrants, particularly darker-skinned immigrants.

NEO-FASCISM
A revival of fascism in contemporary times.

NEO-NAZISM AND OTHER EXTREMIST GROUPS More extreme than the neo-fascist parties are various neo-Nazi groups in Germany that have terrorized members of minority groups and immigrants. In the United States, groups like the Aryan Nation promote racism and the ideal of an all-White America. As well, there are various militia groups that train for armed resistance to what they believe is a world government conspiracy to take over the United States. Individuals influenced by these groups carried out the bombing that killed one hundred and sixty-eight people at the U.S. government building in Oklahoma City in 1995.

LEFT AND RIGHT

The terms **left** and **right** are often used to provide a simple depiction of the relative positioning of different political perspectives. Political parties, movements, governments, and individuals involved in politics are frequently described and analyzed in terms of their position on the left–right dimension (see Figure 5-1). The terms left and right originated in the seating arrangements of the French National Assembly established after the French Revolution of 1789. Those who favoured the old order sat to the right of the chairman of the Assembly. Those who opposed the absolute authority of the monarch, demanded that the power and privileges of the Catholic Church be reduced or eliminated, and favoured redistributing the property and wealth of the nobility sat on the left (Needler, 1996).

LEFT
The general ideological position associated with criticism of the capitalist system, advocacy of greater social and economic equality, and liberation from traditional institutions and practices.

RIGHT
The general ideological position associated with defending the free-market capitalist system, property rights, and traditional moral values.

Over time, the left has become associated with criticism of the capitalist system, advocacy of greater social and economic equality, and liberation from traditional institutions and practices. The right has become associated with defending the free-market capitalist system, property rights, and traditional moral values. Communism is viewed as being on the far left because of its commitment to

FIGURE 5-1
POLITICAL IDEOLOGIES ON THE LEFT–RIGHT DIMENSION

equality of condition (an equal sharing of material wealth) and to revolutionary change. However, the depiction of fascism on the left–right dimension is somewhat problematic. Fascism is normally depicted as being on the extreme right because of its strong belief in inequality and certain values of the past. A key basis of the appeal of fascism was its vigorous opposition to communism. However, fascists often argue that they favour a middle road between capitalism and communism, and view themselves as creating a revolutionary new order. Nevertheless, fascism bears a closer resemblance to the counter-revolutionary reactionaries of the far right than to the ideologies of the centre and left.

Although the left–right dimension is useful, it has its limitations. For example, the depiction of communism as extreme left and fascism as extreme right ignores the fact that there are some similarities between these two perspectives, particularly in the totalitarian practices of communist and fascist regimes. As well, other perspectives, such as nationalism, feminism, and environmentalism, do not fit neatly on the left–right dimension. Thus, some prefer to depict political perspectives along two (or more) separate dimensions. For example, an authoritarian–libertarian dimension focusing on the proper relationship of the individual to the state or other authorities can be distinguished from the left–right dimension that focuses on the proper role of government in the economy and in pursuing equality.

Your ideological position: an easy, anonymous five-minute quiz
www.politicalcompass.org

Summary and Conclusion

Political ideologies have had a major impact on politics in the modern era. Most ideologies have a vision of a better world and some ideas about the political action needed to achieve that objective. Political ideologies provide not only basic sets of values and goals to those who engage in political activity, but also differing ways of analyzing and understanding the world.

Liberalism focuses on the ideal of individual liberty. The coercion of individuals, even to promote the

values of the groups and communities to which the individual belongs, should be minimized. In the perspective of liberalism, the common good of society is best achieved by allowing individuals to pursue their own interests, develop their own capabilities and morality, and act on their own values. Those with power are likely to use that power for their own interests. Thus, limiting power, protecting individual rights and freedoms, and establishing the rule of law are important means to achieve the objectives of liberalism. A peaceful and prosperous world can be developed through the promotion of tolerance, adherence to laws, and facilitating global interactions through free trade and the free interaction of ideas. For classical liberals, the free market, equal legal rights, and limited government ensure that individuals are not subject to the arbitrary and oppressive power of government and other institutions. Reform liberals are concerned with achieving meaningful freedom for all; thus, government can play a useful role in removing the obstacles to individual development, even if that means that some limitations may have to be placed on the free market.

Conservatism, because of its pessimistic view of human capabilities, does not generally present an ideal of a better world that can be achieved through conscious political action. The common good is best obtained in an orderly community in which traditional moral values and institutions are maintained. Traditional practices are seen as containing accumulated wisdom. The limitations of human reason suggest that change should be gradual in nature. Individuals should accept their place in society and be encouraged to work for the good of the community as a whole. Respect for those in positions of authority should be promoted, and those with wealth and privilege should be encouraged to look after the well-being of society as a whole. Because of human frailties and the human capacity for evil, restraints on individual actions are necessary to ensure the common good of the community.

Socialism promotes the ideal of a society based on cooperation and equality. The focus of the capitalist system on the pursuit of profit and individual wealth hinders the achievement of the common good. Eliminating oppression and inequalities and ensuring that the needs of all are fulfilled will allow humans, as social and cooperative beings, to pursue the common good of humanity. For communists, a revolution led by the working class is needed to destroy the oppressive power of capitalism and the capitalist-based state. This will allow for the creation of a classless socialist— and eventually communist—society. Democratic socialists, on the other hand, argue that socialism can be achieved through the election of a socialist party and the gradual evolution of society towards socialism. Many contemporary democratic socialists (social democrats) suggest that the major ideals of socialism can be achieved by humanizing capitalism through the appropriate government policies, rather than replacing the capitalist system with a socialist economic system.

Fascism seeks to build a powerful, united, militaristic nation-state that will provide strong leadership and direction to the masses. Order, leadership, and discipline are needed to be strong in a world characterized by conflict and the struggle for dominance. Fascists view the idea of the common good of humanity as a whole as unrealistic. Instead, the collective good of the state, nation, or race is emphasized in fascist thought.

Key Terms

Discussion Questions

1. How important are political ideologies in contemporary political life?

2. Is there a particular ideological perspective that is prevalent at your university or college?

3. Is J.S. Mill's argument that individuals are the best judges of what is in their own interest valid? Are contemporary laws that require the use of seat belts and ban the use of "recreational" drugs unjustified?

4. Are socialism and communism still relevant in the contemporary world? Is fascism likely to become a significant political perspective again?

5. Which one of the ideologies has the best perspective on how the common good can be achieved?

Further Reading

Berlin, I. *Liberty*. Oxford: Oxford University Press, 2002.

Eatwell, R. *Fascism: A history*. New York: Penguin Books, 1995.

Gaus, G.F. *Contemporary theories of liberalism: Public reason as a post-Enlightenment project*. London: Sage, 2003.

Gray, J. *Liberalism*. Milton Keynes, UK: Open University Press, 1986.

Griffin, R. *The nature of fascism*. London: Routledge, 1993.

Harrington, M. *Socialism*. New York: Penguin Books, 1989.

King, P. (Ed.). *Socialism and the common good: New Fabian essays*. London: Frank Cass, 1996.

Laqueur, W. *Fascism: Past, present, future*. New York: Oxford University Press, 1996.

Manning, D.J. *Liberalism*. New York: St. Martin's Press, 1976.

McLellan, D. *Marxism after Marx*. London: Macmillan, 1983.

McMurtry, J. *The structure of Marx's world-view*. Princeton, NJ: Princeton University Press, 1978.

Nisbet, R. *Conservatism: Dream and reality*. Milton Keynes, UK: Open University Press, 1986.

Roussopoulos, D. (Ed.). *The anarchist papers* (rev. ed.). Montreal: Black Rose, 2002.

Scruton, R. *The meaning of conservatism* (2nd ed.). London: Macmillan, 1984.

Singer, P. *Marx*. Oxford: Oxford University Press, 1980.

Woodcock, G. *Anarchism*. Harmondsworth, UK: Penguin, 1963.

Chapter 6

FEMINISM, ENVIRONMENTALISM, AND THE "NEW RIGHT"

PHOTO ABOVE: During a highly publicized demonstration by feminists against the 1968 Miss America contest, protesters, who criticized the long-standing beauty contest for exploiting women's bodies for the satisfaction of men, nominated a sheep as the new Miss America. Women threw their high heels, girdles, and false eyelashes—but no bras—into a freedom trash can.

CHAPTER OBJECTIVES

After reading this chapter you should be able to:

1. discuss the feminist perspective
2. describe and analyze the distinctive features of environmentalism
3. explain the perspective of the New Right
4. analyze the similarities and differences between the New Right and traditional conservatism
5. discuss the significance of culture wars in contemporary politics

The year is 1968. A sheep has just been nominated for the title of Miss America, and women are throwing their high heels, girdles, false eyelashes, and other symbols of oppression into a "freedom trash can." This is all part of a much-publicized demonstration against the Miss America Pageant by feminists who attack it as a beauty contest that exploits women. A young female reporter, seeking to link the Miss America demonstration to Vietnam War protests where draft cards and the American flag had been burned, describes the women as burning their bras. Although no bras are actually burned, militant feminists will thenceforward be ridiculed by their critics as "bra burners."

The Miss America contest was one of the early targets of the women's liberation movement because it was viewed as a manifestation of how a male-dominated society dehumanizes women by treating them as sexual objects. Some of those involved in this movement developed the radical feminist perspective that holds that the oppression of women is the most basic feature of all societies. A fundamental transformation of society is needed to liberate women and achieve true equality.

Over the years, feminism has developed challenging new political perspectives and visions of what the world should be like. The same is true for environ-mentalism. Likewise, the New Right has provided a vigorous new form of conservatism based on values that are very different than those of feminism and environmentalism. Yet some prominent political commentators have argued that the age of ideologies has ended (Bell, 1988; Fukuyama, 1992). Now that communism has collapsed and the differences between liberals, conservatives, and social democrats are diminishing, they say, political controversy will involve the details of policy rather than the clash of sharply different perspectives.

In this chapter we focus on the highly contentious issues raised by these newer ideological perspectives.

FEMINISM

Feminism is often thought of in terms of achieving equality for women. This involves not only establishing equal rights and opportunities for women and eliminating discriminatory practices, but also challenging the traditional views about women that have had the effect of confining women to domestic life and restricting their freedom. Beyond seeking to achieve equality with men, many feminists also want to affirm the different experiences and values of women. For example, they argue that political decision making reflects male values and gives insufficient attention to female values.

In the view of most contemporary feminists, all societies are, to varying extents, characterized by **patriarchy**. As explained by Lorraine Code, "patriarchal societies are those in which men have more power than women, readier access than women to what is valued in the society and, in consequence, are in control over many, if not most aspects of women's lives" (1988, p. 18). Changing the patriarchal nature of society is a basic goal of feminism.

The *Declaration of the Rights of Man,* a product of the French Revolution of 1789, inspired one of the first statements of feminist ideas. In *A Vindication of the Rights of Woman* (1792), Mary Wollstonecraft (1759–1797) rejected the common notion that women's natural role was to please men and to bear and raise children. Wollstonecraft argued that women are human beings with the same capacity for rational thinking as men and should therefore have the same rights as men. If women appeared more emotional and less concerned about the good of the political community, it was a result of being deprived of adequate education and the opportunities to develop themselves, rather than being an inevitable product of their nature (Adams, 2001). Likewise, John Stuart Mill argued in *The Subjection of Women* (1869) that freeing women from being subordinate to men, providing equal educational opportunities, and establishing a full set of civil and political rights for women were justified because women had the same capacity for rational thought and action as men.

Although both Wollstonecraft and Mill advocated full equality for women, they assumed that women were more likely to choose domestic life rather than paid employment. By being educated and equal, women would be better equipped to raise their children, and marriages would be happier if wives could interact intelligently with their husbands. By contrast, some other early feminists, particularly those involved in the revolutionary politics of Marxism and anarchism of the late nineteenth and early twentieth centuries, advocated the liberation of women from their domestic roles as well as advocating liberation from traditional sexual constraints.

As with other ideological perspectives, there is a variety of different versions of feminism. This diversity is often discussed in terms of three basic categories:

1. liberal feminism
2. socialist feminism
3. radical feminism

FEMINISM
A perspective that views society as patriarchal and seeks to achieve full independence and equality for women.

PATRIARCHY
A system in which power is in the hands of men and in which many aspects of women's lives are controlled by men.

Feminist Collection
www.library.wisc.edu/libraries/
WomensStudies/fcmain.htm

We focus particularly on radical feminism in this chapter, as it is the most distinctive version of feminism. It should be noted, however, that both liberal and socialist versions of feminism are important in Canada and elsewhere.

Liberal Feminism

LIBERAL FEMINISM
A version of feminism that advocates equal legal and political rights and equal opportunities for women.

Liberal feminism extends the struggle of many early feminists for equal legal and political rights to the advocacy of equal opportunities for women in such areas as education and employment. As the influential American feminist Betty Friedan put it, "My definition of feminism is simply that women are people in the fullest sense of the word, who must be free to move in society with all the privileges and opportunities and responsibilities that are their human and American right" (Friedan, 1998, p. 317). In particular, she discussed the problems of women in American suburbs in the early 1960s and concluded that women suffered by being confined to the role of housewife. Pursuing a career and gaining economic independence would allow women to lead more fulfilling lives (Friedan, 1963).

For liberal feminists, the key problem is the discrimination against women that limits their opportunities. Ending unjust laws and adopting affirmative action programs will allow women to participate fully in the mainstream of society. Liberal feminism thus focuses on ensuring that women have the freedom and opportunity to engage in politics, business, careers, and employment on the same basis as men.

Socialist Feminism

SOCIALIST FEMINISM
A version of feminism that views women as oppressed by both the male-dominated character of society and the capitalist system, and argues that the liberation of women is connected to the transformation of capitalism into a more cooperative and egalitarian socialist system.

Socialist feminism views women as oppressed both by the male-dominated character of society and by the capitalist system. Women's housework and childcare are unpaid labour that is essential for the profitability of capitalism and for ensuring that there is a supply of labour for the future. Women also provide the capitalist system with a "reserve army" of low-cost labour that can be mobilized when needed to maintain the profitability of capitalist enterprises. Socialist feminists argue that male–female relations reflect the exploitative relationships of capitalists to workers. Just as the capitalist boss dominates and exploits workers, so too husbands are dominant in the home and exploit the labour of their wives.

Socialist feminists argue that the liberation of women is connected to the transformation of capitalism into a more cooperative and egalitarian socialist society. The free, public provision of childcare and possibly other domestic services, for example, would help to create the conditions for the liberation of women. Overcoming the sexual division of labour, in which women have primary responsibility for most domestic duties, along with transforming the division of labour in the capitalist system, it would also enable humans to live more creative, fulfilling lives.

In more recent times, socialist feminism has broadened its analysis from a focus on class and capitalism to viewing race, ethnicity, disability, age, and other forms of discrimination as also connected to the struggle of women for equality. Challenging the capitalist system, in other words, is not sufficient to create a society that ensures equality for all groups of women—and men.

Both liberal and socialist feminism involve the application of classic ideologies to the situation of women. Liberal feminism views the achievement of equal opportunities and participation of women in the workforce and politics, particularly in the higher positions traditionally occupied by men, as the major way to change the patriarchal nature of society. A fundamental transformation of the organization of society is not needed to achieve the objectives of liberal feminism. Socialist feminism generally sees the capitalist system as a major obstacle to equality for women. A society in which women and men are truly equal would be organized on the principle of cooperation rather than competition. For those influenced by the Marxist perspective, the struggle of working-class women and men to overturn capitalism is the fundamental strategy needed to achieve women's liberation. However, most socialist feminists today do not accept the idea that the struggle of women should be subordinated to the struggle of the working class. In their view, a working-class revolution would not necessarily liberate women and end the sexual division of labour.

Radical Feminism

In the late 1960s, the women's liberation movement developed among women who had been involved in the various political movements that were seeking major changes, such as the American civil rights movements, the peace movement, and the student movement. Associated with these movements was the **New Left** ideology, which sees the marginalized in society as oppressed and emphasizes the need for liberation, promotion of different identities, and the creation of an egalitarian, participatory society. However, many women involved in the movements of the 1960s found that these movements were male-dominated in practice, and often did not treat women and issues concerning women with equal respect. This led to the development of the women's liberation movement and the associated perspective of **radical feminism**.

In the radical feminist perspective, patriarchal values are deeply embedded in culture and affect the way that women, as well as men, see themselves (Millett, 1985). Institutions such as the state, the family, and schools are designed to perpetuate male dominance and the subjugation of women. Male supremacy is maintained through the dominant values, ideas, and practices of society, which encourage women to be dependent upon and subservient to

NEW LEFT
A perspective that sees the marginalized in societies (such as ethnic and racial minorities, students, youth, women, the poor, and the unemployed) as oppressed and the potential source of radical change; it emphasizes the need for liberation, promotion of different identities, and the creation of an egalitarian, participatory society.

RADICAL FEMINISM
A version of feminism that views society as based fundamentally on the oppression of women, and seeks to liberate women through the fundamental transformation of social institutions, values, and personal relationships.

men. Beauty contests, feminists argue, are just one example of how women are treated as sexual objects whose role is to satisfy men. Male supremacy is also maintained, according to radical feminists, by the use of force in the form of violence against women, including the threat of rape, to keep women under control and subordinate (Brownmiller, 1975).

Radical feminism views the oppression of women as the oldest, most pervasive, and most deeply entrenched form of oppression responsible for the ills of society. As Robin Morgan, a leading feminist writer and organizer of the Miss America protest, argued, "Sexism is the root oppression, the one which, until and unless we uproot it, will continue to put forth the branches of racism, class hatred, ageism, competition, ecological disaster, and economic exploitation" (Morgan, 1977, p. 9). The implication is that the struggle of women against oppression is fundamentally revolutionary because it has the potential to end various forms of domination and subordination.

Feminist Theory Website
www.cddc.vt.edu/feminism/enin.html

LIBERATION

Freeing the human potential that has been stifled by the organization and values of society.

LIBERATION   The goal of radical feminism is **liberation**. Liberation, whether used in feminist theory, the New Left ideology, Marxism, or the theories developed by those challenging imperialist power, goes beyond the concept of freedom that is at the core of the liberal ideology. Liberation involves freeing the human potential that has been stifled by the organization and values of society. Oppression warps the personality of the oppressed, particularly by forcing them to adopt the values of the oppressor. As well, those in the oppressor groups are also deprived of an authentic human existence by being expected to take the dominant role.

In other words, radical feminists argue that the way that society defines what it is to be female and male is restrictive to both women and men. Patriarchal values are not only oppressive to women, but also force men to adopt socially defined masculine values and behaviours, rather than developing a fully rounded character. For radical feminists, women as an oppressed class are the revolutionary force needed to bring about liberation by struggling against male dominance and the ideology of male supremacy. Liberation will ultimately be for the good of all.

Liberation, thus, is not simply a matter of ending male domination of positions of governing authority or of limiting the power of the state over women. Rather, radical feminism seeks a fundamental transformation of social institutions, values, and personal relationships. Because male power is exhibited in all aspects of life, radical feminists view their task as one of challenging male dominance in all of its manifestations. Thus, they are critical of those who define politics only in terms of activity concerning government and the state. Instead, radical feminists argue that "the personal is political," suggesting that conventional personal and sexual relationships between women and men need to be challenged as part of their struggle against a patriarchal society. Indeed, many radical feminists view male dominance in the family as the root of male social, political, and economic domination. By making the personal political, radical feminists hope to expose and challenge what they view as a major basis of male power (Bryson, 2003).

Many radical feminists argue that women must organize separately from men in order to free themselves from oppression. Even though there are some men who are sympathetic to the cause of women's liberation, men who join women's organizations are likely to take a dominant position, and women will tend to be passive and subordinate. The prevalence of male power and values makes it necessary for women as an oppressed class to organize themselves collectively as women. Further, because those who are oppressed often do not realize that they are oppressed and have internalized the values of the male-dominated society, radical feminism argues that a key task is to raise women's consciousness (awareness) of their oppression and to encourage women to take pride in their identity as women.

Feminism and Male–Female Differences

From the feminist viewpoint, gender roles, such as the expectation that males will be breadwinners and women will look after domestic duties, are socially created and imposed, rather than reflecting inherent biological differences between males and females. Liberation involves being free of such socially created roles and thus able to adopt or experiment with different roles.

Nevertheless, many feminists believe that women tend to have different values and ways of thinking than men, based on their experiences as women (see Box 6-1, Do Women Think About Moral Values Differently Than Men?). Female values such as nurturing, caring, cooperation, emotion, and spirituality are undervalued in male-dominated societies based on such values as competition, aggression, and rationality. Society, particularly in the radical feminist view, needs to be transformed so that female values are given greater importance, either because they are superior to male values (for example, more likely to lead to a peaceful and harmonious world), or because female and male values are complementary if given equal weight. As Barbara Ehrenreich and Deidre English argue (1979, p. 292),

> The human values that women were assigned to preserve [must] expand out of the confines of private life and become the organizing principle of society. The market... must be pushed back to the margins. And the "womanly" values of community and caring must rise to the centre as the only human principle.

Thus, the experiences and values of women should be affirmed and celebrated (Code, 1988).

Traditionally, women were often viewed as more "natural" than men because of their role in reproduction. This was used to justify their confinement to domestic activities and their exclusion from the public sphere, where the "higher" human qualities, such as the ability to reason, are desirable.

Do Women Think About Moral Values Differently Than Men?

Some classic thinkers (including Aristotle, Rousseau, and Freud) argued that women have a less developed sense of morality than men. However, based on studies of the moral development of men and women, American psychologist Carol Gilligan concluded in her book *In a Different Voice* (1982) that men and women tend to have a different, but equally valid, sense of morality.

Because women think of themselves more in terms of their relationships with others, they are more likely to base their moral judgments on an ethic of care and on the specific context and circumstances in which moral issues arise. In contrast, men tend to think of themselves in more individualistic terms, which leads them to base their moral judgments more on abstract, universally applicable principles of "right" and "wrong."

In Gilligan's view, male conceptions of morality have been the standard by which morality has been judged. The "different voice" of women has not been heard (Freedman, 2001).

Most feminists reject the idea that biological characteristics result in differences between women and men in values and behaviour. Instead, feminists typically argue that women's values are based primarily on the roles that society has prescribed for them, such as raising children and caring for sick and elderly family members.

The argument that male–female differences are a product of society rather than nature is sometimes questioned. Despite the best efforts of some parents to engage in gender-neutral child raising, many young girls seem to prefer to play with dolls and young boys are more likely to want to play with guns. We are left without a definitive answer as to whether female tendencies to be caring and nurturing and male tendencies to be competitive and aggressive are socially created or a product of biological differences.

Promoting Women's Identity

Connected to the emphasis on women's values, feminists have sought to promote the identity of women. By celebrating women and their characteristics, feminists hope to encourage women to be more independent and politically active. The development of a distinctive identity and culture of women is seen, particularly by radical feminists, as an important element in encouraging women to have the confidence to collectively liberate themselves from oppression. Instead of the view that all individuals should be treated the same regardless of their particular characteristics, many feminists, particularly radical feminists, hold the view that women *as a group* should be treated equally to men and their distinctive identity be recognized and fostered.

Some feminists, however, have been critical of the notion that women share a common identity arising out of their common experiences as women. Black feminists, for example, have argued that women of colour suffer double oppression based on their gender and their race. The characteristics of sisterhood proclaimed by the largely White, middle-class, educated, heterosexual spokespersons for the feminist movement do not, some feminists argue, adequately reflect the diversity of women's experiences (Code, 1988).

Is Feminism Still Relevant?

The feminist ideology and the women's movement have raised a variety of issues that were previously largely ignored in politics. Feminist scholars have challenged traditional ways of understanding the world in areas of study such as political science, history, and literature. There is, however, considerable disagreement about the extent to which the women's movement has succeeded in changing the position of women in countries such as Canada (see Box 6-2, "You've Come a Long Way, Baby"?). Table 6-1 gives an indication of the current circumstances of women in Canada.

TABLE 6-1

THE CIRCUMSTANCES OF CANADIAN WOMEN

	FEMALE-TO-MALE RATIO
Total income after tax (1997)	0.63
Total workload (1998)	1.04
- Paid work	0.62
- Unpaid work	1.56
University graduates working in higher-level jobs (1998)	0.78
Average hourly wage (2004)	0.82
Full-time university enrollment (2004)	1.28
Part-time university enrollment (2004)	1.51

Note: A ratio of 1.0 indicates female–male equality. A value below 1.0 indicates that women have or do less than men, while a value above 1.0 indicates that women have or do more than men.

SOURCE: *Adapted from* Economic gender equality indicators 2000, *by W. Clark, 2001, retrieved July 15, 2004 from www.swc-cfc.gc.ca/pubs/egei2000/egei2000_e.html;* Average hourly wages of employees by selected characteristics, profession, and by province, *by Statistics Canada, 2004, retrieved July 15, 2004 from www.statcan.ca/english/Pgdb/labour69g.htm; and Statistics Canada data cited in* CAUT Almanac of post-secondary education in Canada, *by Canadian Association of University Teachers (2004), CAUT: Ottawa. Some calculations by author.*

BOX 6-2

"You've Come a Long Way, Baby"?

Some years ago, commercials for a brand of cigarette designed for women celebrated the advances made by women. It featured, in language that could be deemed sexist, the slogan "You've come a long way, baby." But there is still debate about whether feminism has achieved its objectives and whether contemporary Western societies like Canada's are patriarchal and oppressive.

There is little doubt that women continue to suffer from brutal and oppressive treatment in many parts of the world. In a number of countries, women continue to be deprived of adequate education, limited in their employment opportunities, restricted in their personal life, treated as inferior in law, and subject to such cruelties as genital mutilation. However, in Western and many non-Western societies, there have been some major changes in the position of women, particularly in the past few decades:

- Discriminatory laws have generally been abolished.
- Women have entered the paid workforce in large numbers and mothers with young children are often employed outside the home.
- Females now form the majority of university students in North America, and even high-status professional programs such as law, medicine, and business administration have, or will soon have, more female than male students.
- The tendency for the mass media to portray women in negative terms has diminished. Instead of "dumb blondes" and *Father Knows Best*, some television shows treat males as a subject of ridicule.
- Publishers carefully vet textbooks to eliminate sexist language, many universities have established women's studies programs, affirmative actions programs have been created

to encourage the hiring and promotion of women, and sexual harassment officers have been hired by universities and some businesses to try to protect women from being abused by those in positions of power.
- Rights to divorce, contraception, and abortion have allowed women to free themselves from abusive relationships and to gain control over their bodies.

However, feminists argue that progress towards equality and liberation is still limited, even in Western societies. Women still hold only a small proportion of political power. For example, in Canada only about one-fifth of legislators at the national and provincial levels are female. Likewise, the proportion of women in top positions in the business world is still small. Women tend to be employed in jobs that are perceived as "women's work" (secretary, nurse, and primary school teacher), with the employment earnings of women still substantially below that of men. Women continue to have primary responsibility for raising children in most households, and also often have the task of caring for sick and elderly family members. Women are still often judged in terms of their physical attractiveness, and negative stereotypes of women are still quite prevalent.

Do women still have a long way to go to be fully equal? Will the current generation, which includes many highly educated and motivated young women, complete the feminist revolution, or are obstacles still in their way? Even though the position of women in Western societies has changed considerably in recent decades, the underrepresentation of women in positions of power will undoubtedly continue to be an issue in politics and the working world.

ENVIRONMENTALISM

The world faces numerous serious environmental problems. These include:

- Increasing emission of greenhouse gases, such as carbon dioxide and methane, resulting from fossil fuel burning, deforestation, and increased agricultural production. The resulting global climate changes could have profound consequences for all life forms.

- Thinning of the protective ozone layer of the atmosphere by the release of chlorofluorocarbons (used in aerosols and refrigerators), which has resulted in increased harmful ultraviolet radiation. This problem will persist long after the use of chlorofluorocarbons has been phased out.

- Depletion of many natural resources.

- Contamination and misuse of water supplies. A substantial proportion of the world's population lacks access to clean water, and water shortages may reduce food production in the future.

- Devastation of tropical rain forests, which contain much of the earth's biological diversity, and the extinction of an unprecedented number of species of animals and plants. The decline in biodiversity may hamper the search for new medicines and hinder our capability to maintain agricultural production.

- Pollution of various forms, which is degrading the environment and harming the health of humans and other species.

In 1962, American biologist Rachel Carson's *Silent Spring* eloquently made the case that synthetic pesticides were silencing the voices of birds that heralded the coming of spring. More generally, Carson pointed out that the fragile ecology of the earth was threatened by the large-scale production and use of dangerous chemicals. A series of environmental disasters, including massive oil spills, further increased concern about environmental problems and led to the development of a large environmental movement. In conjunction with this movement, the ideology of **environmentalism** (also known as ecologism[1] or green political thought) developed.

Although the term *environmentalism* is sometimes applied to any concerns about environmental degradation, we will focus on the stronger versions of environmentalism that are based on the idea that humanity needs to fundamentally change its relationship with nature. Influenced by the science of ecology, which emphasizes the complex interrelatedness of the natu-

ENVIRONMENTALISM
A perspective based on the idea that humanity needs to change its relationship to nature. Environmentalism emphasizes the need to create a sustainable society because there are environmental limits to growth.

---

[1] A distinction is sometimes made between ecologism, a distinctive political ideology seeking to transform humanity's relationship with the environment, and environmentalism, which seeks technical and managerial solutions to environmental problems (Dobson, 2000). We will, however, use the more familiar term *environmentalism* to refer to the perspective that sees a need for substantial changes to deal with environmental problems.

▶ Environmentalists raise basic questions about the relationship between human beings and the environment that have been largely ignored by other political ideologues. Environmentalists advocate a fundamental transformation of society and politics, as well as basic changes to our ways of thinking.

Green Information
**www.greeninformation.com/
TABLECONTENTS.htm**

ral world, environmentalism argues that humanity needs to view itself as part of the intricate and fragile web of nature, and to understand our dependence on nature so as to live in harmony with it.

As Petra Kelly (1947–1992), a founder and key spokesperson for the German Green (environmentalist) party, stated:

> *We must learn to think and act from our hearts, to recognize the interconnectedness of all living creatures, and to respect the value of each thread in the vast web of life.... We have borrowed the Earth from our children. Green politics is about having just "enough" and not "more," and this runs counter to all of the economic assumptions of industrial society.... The industrialized countries must move from growth-oriented to sustainable economies, with conservation replacing consumption as the driving force (quoted in Ball & Dagger, 2004, pp. 442, 445).*

Foundation for Deep Ecology
www.deepecology.org

Some who hold the environmentalist perspective view human arrogance and our focus on human well-being as a basic cause of environmental problems. Because we tend to think of humans as fundamentally different from the rest of nature, we think that we can control nature and use it for human benefit without concern for the disruptive consequences of our actions for other species or the earth as a whole. In the view of Dave Foreman, a founder of the radical environmental group Earth First!:

> *Human beings must adjust to the planet; it is supreme arrogance to expect the planet and all it contains to adjust to the demands of humans. In everything human society does, the primary consideration should be for the long-term health and biological diversity of Earth (Foreman, 1991, p. 26).*

Institute for Social Ecology Online Library
www.social-ecology.org

Others who hold an environmentalist perspective see environmental problems as basically resulting from the patterns of hierarchy and domination that have developed in human society (Bookchin, 1990). The "rape of the earth" is seen as an extension of dominance of men over women and of the exploitation of the weak by the powerful.

The Limits to Growth: A Famous Bet

In 1972, a group of industrialists, politicians, and academics known as the Club of Rome predicted that within one hundred years, there would be an uncontrollable and disastrous collapse of society when the limits to growth were exceeded (Meadows, Meadows, Randers, & Behrens, 1972).

The scenario appeared in a Club of Rome report called *The Limits to Growth,* which was based on a global computer model that attempted to project a variety of current trends into the future. The growth of the world's population and the accelerating use of non-renewable natural resources, particularly oil, caused by an expanding global economy would mean that the resources needed to provide materials and energy would become very costly and scarce.

The doomsday scenario of the Club of Rome has come under considerable criticism. Their computer model simplistically projected current trends into the future, assuming that the accelerating rate of increase in resources and population would continue indefinitely. In reality, the rate of increase in population growth and resource usage has slowed down. In 1980, economist Julian Simon publicly bet Paul Ehrlich, a biologist well known for his doomsday scenarios, a thousand dollars that the real price of any set of natural resources Ehrlich chose would be lower in the future. Ehrlich chose the prices of copper, chrome, nickel, tin, and tungsten as of 1990. As it turned out, the price of each of these minerals *was* lower in 1990, and Simon won the bet (Dryzek, 1997).

Simon argues that there are no limits to growth. Human ingenuity and the competitive marketplace will result in more resources being found, substitutes invented, and pollution problems resolved. The resourcefulness of humanity and the vast resources of the world will allow for indefinite economic growth, provided that governments do not take actions to restrict growth. However, some of the optimistic predictions Simon made in 1984—that by the year 2000 fish catches would increase, there would be no scarcity of water, no climate change, cheap nuclear power, a decline in soil erosion, and no serious air or water pollution (Simon & Kahn, 1984)—were inaccurate. For example, one study estimated that the world's oceans contain only about one-tenth of the amount of large predatory fish such as cod that existed before the adoption of large-scale industrial fishing. The collapse of various fish stocks due to overfishing may in turn have significant but unknown impacts on ocean and planetary ecosystems (Myers & Worm, 2003).

Raising fears about the survival of humanity and life on earth has helped to increase awareness of environmental problems, although exaggerated claims of impending doom can also damage the credibility of environmentalists. On the other hand, the view that human use of the environment can continue to grow and human ingenuity can deal with any problems that might arise ignores the ever-growing strain on the earth's ecosystems created by increased production, consumption, and population.

Limits to Growth

A basic assumption of environmentalism is that there are **limits to growth** (see Box 6-3, The Limits to Growth: A Famous Bet). As one study put it, "The earth is finite.... Growth of anything physical, including the human population and its cars and buildings and smokestacks, cannot continue forever" (Meadows, Meadows, & Rander, 1992, p. 7). The increasing production and consumption of goods, along with the increasing human population,

LIMITS TO GROWTH
The environmentalist view that there are limits to the ability of the earth to sustain the growth of production and consumption of goods and to support the growth of the size of the human population.

are placing the earth under excessive strains. The carrying capacity of the earth (that is, its ability to sustain life) is limited. Continuing growth in human use of the earth's resources cannot go on endlessly. At some point, the earth will reach the end of its ability to absorb our effluents and provide the resources for our ever-increasing consumption.

The argument that there are limits to growth provides a profound challenge to conventional thinking. In analyzing the state of the economy, it is normally assumed that the economy is healthy only if growth, as measured by the gross national product (GNP, or the total value of goods and services produced in a country) is increasing. The degradation of the environment is not included in most calculations of economic progress, even though the health of the economy is ultimately dependent upon the state of the environment. Likewise, increased extraction of natural resources is seen as contributing to economic growth, without taking into account that economic wealth in the form of accessible natural resources may be reduced as a result.

SUSTAINABILITY

Maintaining the integrity of ecosystems by ensuring that renewable resources are not being used at a rate that exceeds the ability of ecosystems to regenerate them, developing renewable substitutes to replace the consumption of nonrenewable resources, and ensuring that the emission of pollutants does not exceed the ability of the ecosystem to handle them without damage.

A central theme of environmentalism is that of **sustainability**, particularly in terms of maintaining the integrity of ecosystems. Specifically, renewable resources should not be used at a rate that exceeds the ability of ecosystems to regenerate them. Renewable substitutes should be developed to replace the consumption of nonrenewable resources. The emission of pollutants should not exceed the ability of the ecosystem to handle them without damage (Korten, 1996). Instead of continual growth of production and consumption, those who hold the environmentalist perspective often favour a steady-state (no growth) economy so as to live within the capacities of the earth. This would ensure that future generations have the same enjoyment and benefit of the environment that we do. Further, a sustainable society would not squeeze out other life forms by increasing the already large share of the earth's resources that are used for human benefit.

SUSTAINABLE DEVELOPMENT A basic problem with a no-growth philosophy is that a substantial proportion of the world's population lives in poverty. Limiting economic growth on a global basis might deprive persons in the poorer countries of the opportunity to try to catch up to the richer countries, or even to ensure that their basic needs are satisfied. Poorer countries are unlikely to accept environmental policies that restrict their economic development. Discussions of environmental problems have, therefore, often focused on the concept of sustainable development.

SUSTAINABLE DEVELOPMENT

Meeting the needs of the present without compromising the ability of future generations to meet their own needs; it involves development to ensure that the needs of the poor are fulfilled and protecting the environment for the well-being of future generations.

The World Commission on Environment and Development (1987), which popularized this concept, defined **sustainable development** as "meeting the needs of the present without compromising the ability of future generations to meet their own needs." There are two elements to this definition:

- First, development is needed to ensure that the needs of the poor are fulfilled.

- Second, the sustainability of the environment needs to be protected for the well-being of future generations.

It is, however, not easy to achieve the development that is needed by the poorer countries without damaging the long-term sustainability of the earth's ecosystems. Although the commission's report highlighted a number of serious environmental challenges and noted the necessity of maintaining the carrying capacity of the earth, it did not accept the limits-to-growth argument. Instead, the commission noted that economic growth was needed for much of the world to overcome poverty. Hope was placed on reorienting technology to deal with environmental problems, integrating environmental and economic objectives in political decision making, and increasing public participation in the decisions that affect the community.

Although the concept of sustainable development has become popular not only among environmentalists, but also government and business leaders, some of those who hold a strong environmentalist perspective are critical of the approach of the World Commission on Environment and Development. Environmentalist thinking often focuses on the need to reduce consumption, particularly in the richer countries. In our consumer-oriented society, advertising creates artificial and wasteful consumer wants. Reducing consumption, it is argued, would lead to more fulfilling lives than we experience in a society based on material acquisition and consumption. A simpler lifestyle would lead to an enhanced quality of life.

Beyond Attitudes

Environmentalism is not only about encouraging people to change their attitudes concerning nature and adopting an environmental ethic ("reduce, reuse, recycle") in their personal lives. In its stronger versions, environmentalism argues that major social, economic, and political changes are also needed to achieve a sustainable society. In the view of British environmentalists Jonathon Porritt and Nicholas Winner, environmentalism seeks "nothing less than a nonviolent revolution to overthrow our whole polluting, plundering and materialistic industrial society and, in its place, to create a new economic and social order which will allow human beings to live in harmony with the planet" (quoted in Dobson, 2000, p. 9).

For some environmentalists, the ideal economic and social order would be based on local communities that are largely self-sufficient and self-governing. Greater self-sufficiency would reduce the damaging effects of transportation on the environment and encourage communities to live within the ecological capabilities of their local area. Large global corporations would no longer be the basis of the economy. Smaller locally based enterprises, cooperatives, and communes geared to local needs rather than the global marketplace might be the basis of production. Instead of remote, bureaucratic governing bodies, members of the local community would make decisions on a participatory basis. Their decisions would be sensitive to environmental concerns, it is assumed, because residents of the local community can see the direct effects of their decisions on the local environment. Generally, the local community, with its possibilities for face-to-face interaction, is seen as a more natural community. Large states, governing organizations above the state (for example, the European Union), and global corporations are viewed as based on relationships of power, domination, and hierarchy. Of course, there would be a need for coordination among local communities. For those who hold a decentralizing vision, this could be achieved by a loose association of communities in a peaceful, global network.

Disagreement

Although the vision of a sustainable world is attractive, questions concerning whether it is realistic can be raised. Can local communities become largely self-sufficient without a sharp decline in the quality of life? Does the ideal of local participatory decision making make sense in the contemporary highly urbanized world? Is a loose network of communities capable of handling environmental problems?

Not surprisingly, there is disagreement among environmentalists concerning the best way to organize society, the economy, and politics. While some view a highly decentralized world as ideal, others see a continuing need for a strong state and even a world government with the power to develop and implement plans to deal with large-scale and global environmental problems (Dobson, 2000).

More generally, radical versions of environmentalism involve a fundamental critique of the nature of modern societies and advocate a major transformation of society, economy, politics, and thinking about the world. By contrast, reformist versions of environmentalism view the solution to environmental problems primarily in terms of better science, technology, and management. Instead of fundamentally changing our ways of organizing and thinking about the world, reformist environmentalists believe that developing and utilizing better pollution control technology, encouraging more recycling efforts, promoting measures to assess and mitigate the negative potential effects of new developments, and taking more care to conserve natural resources will result in environmental improvement. Reformist environmentalism does not view economic development and environmental protection as incompatible. Industry, it is argued, can become more efficient and profitable by incorporating environmental considerations into the production process and adopting more sophisticated, less polluting technologies (Weale, 1992). Indeed, considerable progress has been made since the 1970s in reducing pol-

BOX 6-4

Are We All Green Now?

British Prime Minister Margaret Thatcher once declared, "We're all green now." Politicians, government officials, and business leaders regularly proclaim their commitment to protecting the environment. But despite the passage of environmental laws, signing of international environmental agreements, and establishment of plans for sustainable development, many environmentalists claim that we are still headed toward environmental disaster. For example, although the drastic reduction in the use of ozone-depleting chlorofluorocarbons counts as a major success story, reduction in greenhouse gas (GHG) emissions continues to be an elusive goal.

Building on a commitment of one hundred and fifty-five states at the 1992 Earth Summit to prevent an increase in GHG emissions, representatives of one hundred and sixty countries reached an agreement in 1997 (the Kyoto Protocol) to deal with the climate change problem. The Kyoto Protocol would require most of the wealthier industrialized countries to reduce their emission of the greenhouse gases that are responsible for climate change to a level below their 1990 levels (6 percent below for Canada) by 2008 to 2012. Developing countries would not be subject to the same requirements, but would be encouraged to voluntarily limit emissions.

Although the United States government signed the Kyoto Protocol, it has refused to ratify it.

President Bush and the American Senate claimed that studies concerning climate change are not definitive. Further, they argue that because developing countries are not required to reduce their emissions, the Kyoto Protocol could make American industries uncompetitive.

The Canadian government ratified the protocol in 2002 despite objections from the Alberta government and the petroleum industry in particular. However, as Figure 6-1 indicates, emissions of greenhouse gases have been substantially increasing in Canada, and if this trend were to continue, we would be very far from meeting the Kyoto commitment. At the time this book went to press, the Canadian government had not developed a plan that would lead to a substantial reduction in emissions.

Despite mounting evidence that greenhouse gas emissions carry serious long-term risks to humanity, governments have often preferred talk to action. Many petroleum companies have tried to discredit the evidence of global climate change, and business think-tanks raise fears about the costs of reducing emissions, ignoring the eventual costs of climate change. Meanwhile, people continue to buy gas-guzzling vehicles that contribute to the emissions. Environmentalists may have been successful in raising our environmental consciousness, but this does not mean that we always act in a green fashion.

lution and using energy more efficiently. However, as Box 6-4, Are We All Green Now?, indicates, we continue to face serious environmental challenges

THE NEW RIGHT

The ideas of reform liberalism and social democracy were influential throughout much of the Western world from the end of the Second World

FIGURE 6-1

CANADA'S GREENHOUSE GAS EMISSIONS

Actual and projected emissions of six greenhouse gases (CO_2, CH_4, N_2O, HFCs, PFCs, SF_6)

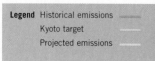

| Legend | Historical emissions |
| Kyoto target |
| Projected emissions |

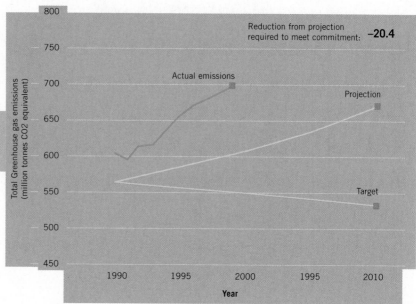

SOURCE: *Greenhouse Gas Emission Graphics*, by the United Nations Environment Program (n.d.), retrieved July 15, 2004 from the UNEP GRID-Arendal website, www.grida.no/db/maps/collection/climate6/canada.htm.

War in 1945 until about the mid-1970s. During that period, the role of the state expanded substantially, governments became more activist (for example, in promoting a more egalitarian society and increasing government regulation of business), and welfare state policies were adopted. In addition, the New Left and the various movements that developed out of the New Left raised criticisms about some of the values and practices of Western societies. The **New Right** arose in response to these challenges, combining, in various ways, a vigorous promotion of free-market capitalism and traditional moral and cultural conservative values.

Neo-liberalism

One component of the New Right is **neo-liberalism,**[2] a perspective based on a strong belief in the free marketplace and opposition to government intervention in the economy. Neo-liberalism is, to a considerable extent, a modern version of classical liberalism, focusing on the virtues of a laissez-faire system and

NEW RIGHT

A perspective that combines, in various ways, a vigorous promotion of free-market capitalism and traditional moral and cultural conservative values.

NEO-LIBERALISM

A modern version of classical liberalism, focusing on the virtues of a laissez-faire system and the problems caused by government action.

---

[2] The terms *neo-liberalism* and *neo-conservatism* are often used interchangeably. However, neo-conservatives, although usually favouring neo-liberal economic policies, are often more concerned with conservative cultural and moral values. Neo-liberalism also overlaps with libertarianism, but where neo-liberalism is concerned primarily with the free market, libertarians advocate a very minimal role for government in all aspects of society.

◄ The New Right attributes contemporary problems to the expansion of government and the undermining of traditional Western values. It generally favours a purer free-market system and seeks to reduce or eliminate social welfare, which, it argues, creates dependency upon government and illegitimately infringes upon fundamental property rights.

the problems caused by government action. Neo-liberals have often favoured policies that can be described as **fiscal conservatism**, including reducing government spending, paying off government debt, and establishing requirements that government spending should not exceed government revenues.

For advocates of neo-liberalism, the marketplace provides a just system of incentives for hard work and initiative. Government economic planning, business regulation, redistributive taxes, and social welfare are seen as illegitimate infringements on fundamental property rights. Human beings are motivated by self-interest, particularly material self-interest. The competitive marketplace responds to the wishes of consumers and ensures that the economy operates at maximum efficiency.

Government and its agencies, being in a monopolistic position, are inevitably inefficient and concerned with advancing the power and privileges of bureaucrats and politicians. State-run services, such as health, education, and welfare, lack the efficiency created by competition and restrict the ability of consumers to choose the kinds of services that they want. Welfare, neo-liberals argue, takes away the incentive to work and creates dependency upon government. High taxes to support government services reduce the incentives for entrepreneurs to invest and create jobs. Subsidies to business, assistance to help the development of poorer regions, marketing boards for agricultural products, and other government projects serve to distort the marketplace, reducing efficiency and disrupting the natural processes of economic adjustment.

Neo-conservatism

A second major component of the New Right is **neo-conservatism**, sometimes referred to as "social conservatism." This term originated with a group of

FISCAL CONSERVATISM
The view that government spending should be reduced, that government debt should be reduced or eliminated, and that government spending should not exceed government revenues.

NEO-CONSERVATISM
A version of the New Right, based on the view that the West faces a cultural crisis because of the decline of traditional values. Neo-conservatives argue that the United States should exercise global leadership and use its strength to promote the values of democracy, freedom, and the free-market capitalist system worldwide.

American intellectuals in the 1960s who were critical of the New Left and what they viewed as its challenge to Western values. As well, they felt that governments in the 1960s had gone too far in developing a welfare state and adopting affirmative action policies. Neo-conservatives were also strongly anti-communist, arguing that the West should strive to overthrow communist regimes and criticizing those who downplayed the horrors perpetuated by these regimes.

Understanding Neo-conservatism
www.publiceye.org/conservative/
neocons/neocon.html

In the neo-conservative view, the West faces a cultural crisis because of the decline of traditional moral values. Neo-conservatives defend the capitalist system, which they view as the basis of the prosperity and freedom of Western societies. However, in their view, capitalism cannot rely on an appeal to self-interest and hedonistic consumerism to ensure its long-term survival. Instead, a moral vision is needed to defend capitalism from its opponents (Kristol, 1978).

Although neo-conservatives initially favoured a limited welfare state and some government regulation of business, over time they have moved toward the neo-liberal view on government and the free market. However, as discussed in Box 6-5, David Frum: A Neo-Conservative Critique of "Big Government," their opposition to big government is generally based more on moral grounds than on economic efficiency. The traditional moral views of neo-conservatives and the New Right generally can be also be seen in their views on crime. Unlike the liberally minded, who often blame societal injustices for crime and seek to rehabilitate criminals, neo-conservatives argue that criminals need to take full responsibility for their crimes. They favour harsh punitive measures to deter criminal behaviour.

Neo-conservatives have also been strongly critical of the pursuit of equality of outcomes. Affirmative action programs that involve giving special preference in hiring or education to women, minorities, and other disadvantaged groups are criticized as undesirable "social engineering." Preserving legal equality and preventing discrimination is sufficient, they argue, to provide for equal opportunities for all. Attempting to ensure equal outcomes creates unrealistic expectations and an overly activist, coercive government (Medcalf & Dolbeare, 1985).

Neo-conservatives are often critical of the identity politics that focuses on promoting and gaining recognition for the specific identities of groups, particularly those who feel that they are the victims of discrimination and inadequate representation, including women, Aboriginals, and ethnic and racial minorities. Many neo-conservatives criticize government encouragement for groups to develop their distinctive cultures and identities (for example, multiculturalism programs). They argue that such programs weaken the nation-state by undermining the common interests and common values of the nation (Whitaker, 1997).

BOX 6-5

David Frum: A Neo-Conservative Critique of "Big Government"

Canadian-born David Frum, a former speechwriter for U.S. President George W. Bush, argues for limited government based on neo-conservative principles rather than on individualistic, neo-liberal ideas.

Frum argues that by providing services that used to be the responsibility of communities and families, "big government" has undermined community and family bonds and thus led to moral and cultural decline:

Conservatives want to roll back the state not because they envision human beings as selfish individualists who must be left alone to make as much money as they can, but because they see the functions of real communities being usurped by overweening governments—a usurpation that ends with the citizens ultimately unable to do anything for themselves without the aid of the central authorities.... Having arrogated to itself the functions of real communities, modern Canadian government has proceeded to attack the very preconditions of communities' existence: the moral norms that they enforce on their members (Frum, 1996, pp. 5–6.).

Frum argues that big government discourages individual responsibility. But could it be argued that his view that the community should be able to enforce moral values on its members contradicts his emphasis on individual responsibility?

Neo-conservatives advocate a strong military to defend and promote national interests and national values. American President Ronald Reagan, who reflected neo-conservative thinking, fought what he termed "the evil empire" (the Soviet Union). Although the collapse of communism removed a key challenger to the West, neo-conservatives have argued that non-Western civilizations, particularly Islamic countries, continue to be important enemies of Western values (Huntington, 1996). Thus, even before the terrorist attacks of September 11, 2001, neo-conservatives were calling for the United States to build up a strong military to deal with any potential challenges. In the neo-conservative view, the United States, because of its superior moral values, should exercise global leadership and use its strength to promote the values of democracy, freedom, and the free-market capitalist system worldwide.

The terrorist attacks on the United States gave political credibility to the neo-conservative perspective. President George W. Bush, influenced by neo-conservatives, expressed a determination to fight what he called "the axis of evil" (Iraq, Iran, and North Korea). His administration invaded and occupied Iraq to install a more pro-Western regime, and pursued the development of new weapons to ensure American global military superiority.

The Christian Right

CHRISTIAN RIGHT

A perspective that seeks to
apply conservative or fundamentalist Christian values to
politics. The Christian Right
focuses on the promotion of
traditional family values, which
it views as threatened by abortion, homosexuality, divorce,
feminism, and a permissive
society.

A third element of the New Right is the **Christian Right**,[3] which is particularly significant in the United States, where organizations such as the
Christian Coalition have been active and influential in the Republican party.
The Christian Right has also had some significance for Canadian politics,
particularly through the Reform and Canadian Alliance parties (now part of
the Conservative party, as discussed in Chapter 9), the Christian Heritage
party, and Ontario's Family Coalition party.

Based on many Protestant fundamentalist and evangelical religious
groups, as well as appealing to traditionalist Catholics, the Christian Right is
critical of liberal social values, which it says have fostered a permissive society in which "anything goes." Intellectuals, educators, the media, and government, they argue, have promoted "secular humanism," which denies the
absolute truths and moral principles provided by religion.[4]

Christian Coalition of America
www.cc.org

FAMILY VALUES   The Christian Right has focused on the promotion of
traditional family values, which it contends are threatened by abortion,
homosexuality, premarital sex, divorce, and sexually explicit television,
movies, and music. It argues that religious private schools should receive the
same funding as public schools in order to give parents the right to provide a
religious education for their children. Religion should not be simply a private
matter; rather, prayer and religious observances should be allowed in schools
and public places. The decline of the traditional family and the decay of
morality are seen as responsible for the increase in crime (although, in fact,
crime rates have been declining in North America).

As with other elements of the New Right, the Christian Right generally
favours reducing the scope of government activity and lowering taxes. The
welfare state is viewed as discouraging hard work and thrift. Responsibility
for welfare should be shifted, as much as possible, from government to faith-
based charities and other voluntary organizations. Tax credits should be used
to provide the opportunity for women to stay at home and raise their family
(Reed, 1984). The Christian Right generally favours the free-enterprise system. However, some leading figures in the Christian right—including Pat

---

[3] The Christian Right is also often termed the Religious Right, as many of the values and issue positions of the Christian Right are also shared by orthodox believers of other religions. In particular,
fundamentalists of different religions typically believe that laws should be based on a strict adherence to the divine injunctions contained in classic scriptural texts. In this they differ sharply from
progressive religious believers, who favour interpreting scripture in light of evolving realities, and
from religious or non-religious persons who do not see religious beliefs as the highest authority in
determining the direction of the political community (Hunter, 1991). We use the term Christian
Right because the leading groups and spokespersons for this perspective often express the view that
their country should be based on Christian values.

[4] The following description of the Christian Right is based, in part, on *Politically Incorrect* by Ralph
Reed (1994), the president of the Christian Coalition.

Buchanan, who has sought the American presidency several times—oppose free trade and instead advocate more nationalistic policies of protecting American industry and jobs from foreign competition.

The Christian Right has been strongly critical of feminism, which it views as undermining family values. For example, in the United States, the Christian Right and other groups associated with the New Right were successful in preventing the Equal Rights Amendment, which would have entrenched male–female equality in the constitution, from gaining the necessary approval by state legislatures. Likewise, Christian Right groups in Canada and the United States are strongly critical of efforts to establish rights for gays and lesbians, as they view homosexual activities as an evil that should be suppressed.

The challenge of the Christian Right to liberal social values, feminism, and the "identity politics"[5] of various minority groups has generated what some describe as **culture wars** over issues such as abortion, gay and lesbian rights, multiculturalism, school prayers, and the promotion of safe sex (Hunter, 1991). Underlying such hot-button issues are sharp differences between those who believe that the unchanging higher authority of the word of God should guide our lives and that of the political community, and those who view themselves as progressive, believing that moral traditions need to be re-evaluated in light of the realities of modern times.

It should be noted that many Christian religious groups and activists do not share the perspective of the Christian Right. Many Catholics and Protestants, as well as those of other religious faiths, believe that it is a highly important duty to strive to achieve social justice, which typically includes eliminating poverty and discrimination and pursuing equality. **Liberation theology** has had considerable influence, particularly among Catholics in Latin America. It argues that the poor should not accept their fate, but rather should actively struggle to liberate themselves from oppression of dominant social, political, and economic institutions and ideologies.

Tensions Within the New Right

There are important tensions within the New Right perspective. The individualist perspective characteristic of neo-liberalism clashes with neo-conservatives' and the Christian Right's criticism of the individualism and materialism of modern society and with their desire for a moral community. Although the New Right favours limited government, the goal of "getting government off of the backs of the people" seems inconsistent with the strict policies concerning law, order, and morality often advocated by

CULTURE WARS
Controversy between those who hold liberal and conservative (religious) values over issues such as abortion, gay and lesbian rights, multiculturalism, school prayers, and the promotion of safe sex.

LIBERATION THEOLOGY
A theological perspective that argues that the poor should not accept their fate, but rather should actively struggle to liberate themselves from oppression of dominant social, political, and economic institutions and ideologies.

---

[5] The Christian Right might be considered to be engaging in its own form of identity politics by trying to create a Christian identity and claiming that the rights of the Christians are being ignored by secular elites (Isaac, Filner, & Bivins, 1999).

neo-conservatives and the Christian Right. Likewise, the nationalism and tendencies to be intolerant of diversity (as exemplified by opposition to multiculturalism) characteristic of some elements of the New Right seem inconsistent with the emphasis on individual freedom expressed by neo-liberals.

In general, the New Right has been described as advocating a free economy in a strong state (Gamble, 1984). Leading political figures associated with the New Right, such as British Prime Minister Margaret Thatcher and American President Ronald Reagan, combined a vigorous advocacy of a laissez-faire economic system with an emphasis on building up the strength of their country.

NOT ALL NEW   In some ways, the New Right is not entirely new. Conservatives in the past (for example, Edmund Burke) and in the present have defended property rights, often favoured a free-market capitalist economy, and supported the idea of limited government. However, conservatives often have been willing to modify free-market policies, if necessary, to moderate class conflict and pursue national interests. For example, in the nineteenth century Conservative Prime Minister Sir John A. Macdonald provided large public subsidies to build a national railway, protected Canada's fledgling industries from foreign competition, and adopted some policies to improve the position of workers. Traditional conservatives (other than reactionary conservatives) preached the virtues of moderation and gradual change. The New Right, however, has tended to pursue its convictions with ideological zeal.

Traditional conservatism emphasizes the need to respect authority and favours, at most, fairly limited forms of democracy. In contrast, the New Right has a substantial element of populism that is critical of authority, and believes that the common people should be in more direct control of decision making through such devices as referendums, initiatives, and recall (as discussed in Chapter 4). New Right populists claim that politicians, government officials, and judges have undermined traditional values, catered to what it considers to be "special interests" (such as feminists, environmentalists, groups representing ethnic and racial minorities, and gay and lesbian groups), and do not reflect the views of the majority. Plebiscitary democracy is viewed as a way of ensuring that political decisions reflect the views of the "silent majority" that holds traditional or conventional moral values.

Summary and Conclusion

Feminism and environmentalism raise basic questions that have been largely ignored by other political ideologies.

The goal of feminism is to achieve a society in which women enjoy independence and equality, with full control over their own lives and bodies. In addition to working towards removing obstacles in the way of the full and equal participation of women in social, economic, and political life, many feminists have sought to affirm the distinct identity of women. Achieving equality and giving greater significance to female values are seen as being not only desirable for women, but for the common good of humanity.

The ideology of environmentalism raises important questions about the relationship between human beings and the environment. Environmentalism views human dominance and exploitation of nature as leading to disastrous consequences for the world. Humans need to recognize that they are a part of nature and should learn to live in harmony with nature. This involves treading lightly on the earth and ending the exponential growth in production, consumption, population, and waste. From an environmentalist point of view, the common good should refer not only to the good of human beings, but of the world as a whole of which we are an integral part. An important challenge facing environmentalism is the question of how to achieve sustainability while addressing the need to eliminate global poverty.

The New Right attributes contemporary problems to the expansion of government and the undermining of traditional Western values. It generally favours a purer free-market system and seeks to reduce or eliminate the welfare state. The New Right also advocates a tough-minded approach to preserve law and order and to defend and promote national interests and values.

The New Right believes the common good is advanced by restoring the traditional values and morals of Western societies. Having a common set of values and morals is needed for a well-functioning community. The expanding role of government in pursuit of equality and the promotion of the rights of various groups have challenged institutions such as the traditional family, religious organizations, and private property, which are, in the perspective of the New Right, the bases of good community life.

In general, feminism and environmentalism, particularly in their stronger versions, seek a substantial transformation of the institutions and values of the political community. The New Right seeks to transform the political community in a different way by restoring traditional values and practices. The New Right has been strongly critical of feminism, which it accuses of undermining family values. It has also often been critical of environmentalism, which it sees as restricting growth and increasing government regulation of the economy and private property.

Feminism, environmentalism, and the New Right provide fundamentally different perspectives and raise highly contentious issues. The intensity of the political conflicts generated by the perspectives discussed in this chapter suggests that ideological conflict has not ended, although its focus has shifted to some extent towards social, moral, and cultural issues.

Key Terms

Christian Right 142

Culture wars 143

Environmentalism 131

Feminism 123

Fiscal conservatism 139

Liberal feminism 124

Liberation 126

Liberation theology 143

Limits to growth 132

Neo-conservatism 139

Neo-liberalism 138

New Left 125

New Right 138

Radical feminism 125

Patriarchy 123

Socialist feminism 124

Sustainability 134

Sustainable development 134

Discussion Questions

1. Why do some feminists view women as oppressed? Is this a valid depiction of the position of women in Canada? Are fundamental changes needed to improve the position of women?

2. Would a government that had female majority and female leadership act differently than governments dominated by men?

3. How can a sustainable society best be achieved?

4. Do you agree or disagree with the neo-conservative view of the proper global role of the United States?

5. Should countries where most people identify with a particular religion base their laws on the sacred texts of that religion? Should government try to protect the moral basis of the community?

Further Reading

Dobson, A. *Green political thought* (3rd ed.). New York: Routledge, 2000.

Donovan, J. *Feminist theory: The intellectual traditions* (3rd ed.). New York: Continuum, 2000.

Dryzek, J.S. *The politics of the earth: Environmental discourses.* Oxford: Oxford University Press, 1997.

Freedman, J. *Feminism.* Buckingham, U.K.: Open University Press, 2001.

Kristol, I. *Neoconservatism: The autobiography of an idea.* New York: Free Press, 1995.

Laycock, D. *The New Right and democracy in Canada: Understanding Reform and the Canadian Alliance.* Don Mills, ON: Oxford University Press, 2002.

Segal, H. *Beyond greed: A traditional conservative confronts neo-conservative excess.* Toronto: Stoddard, 1997.

Tong, R. *Feminist thought: A comprehensive introduction* (2nd ed.). Boulder, CO: Westview Press, 1998.

PART III

POLITICAL ORGANIZATION, PERSUASION, AND ACTION

Chapter 7

POLITICAL CULTURE AND POLITICAL PARTICIPATION

PHOTO ABOVE: Clash of civilizations? Daniel Pearl, the Asia bureau chief for the *Wall Street Journal*, was murdered in 2002 in Karachi, Pakistan by a terrorist Islamic group. The group charged that Pearl was a CIA agent and complained about the American government's treatment of Pakistanis captured in the Afghan war and later held at Guantanamo Bay in Cuba.

CHAPTER OBJECTIVES

After reading this chapter you should be able to:

1. explain the meaning and significance of political culture
2. examine the differences between the Canadian and American political cultures
3. outline the level of political interest, knowledge, and participation in Western democracies
4. examine the decline of confidence and trust in politicians and governments
5. discuss the low level of voting by young people
6. define political socialization and discuss the agents of political socialization
7. explain the postmaterialist theory of change in political culture

The image of the twin towers of New York's World Trade Center collapsing after they were struck by jets hijacked by al-Qaeda terrorists is one that few people will forget.

The horrific events of September 11, 2001, seemed to confirm the argument of Harvard University political scientist Samuel P. Huntington (1993, 1996) that a "clash of civilizations," such as the clash between Islam and the West, will become the leading source of international conflict. Cultural conflicts, he suggests, have replaced the ideological conflict between communism and capitalism as the major potential source of world war. Huntington (1993) views the world as increasingly divided into seven or eight major civilizations—broad cultural groupings based on differences in history, language, traditions, and particularly religion. In contrast to those who see globalization and modernization as resulting in increased homogenization or Westernization of the cultures of the world, Huntington argues that non-Western peoples are rejecting Western values and building on their own indigenous cultures. "The Western ideas of individualism, liberalism, constitutionalism, human rights, equality, liberty, the rule of law, free markets, the separation of church and state," he writes, "have little resonance in other cultures" (Huntington, 1993, p. 40).

Huntington's analysis has been criticized on a number of grounds. Although there are major differences between Western and non-Western societies on social and moral issues (such as divorce, abortion, gender equality, and homosexual rights), the adoption of tolerant liberal values by Western societies on

such issues is a relatively recent phenomenon. As well, although authoritarian political institutions are firmly entrenched in some non-Western countries, such as most Arab countries, surveys have found that the majority of the population in some of these countries sees democracy as desirable (Inglehart & Norris, 2003; Tessler, 2002). In a number of cases, the problems of developing a democratic political culture can attributed, in part, to the artificial boundaries imposed by Western powers, the support for dictatorial regimes that has been provided by some Western countries, and the vigorous suppression of democratic movements by some regimes (Bellini, 2004; Stephan & Robertson, 2003).

Huntington has also been criticized for exaggerating the similarities among the cultures of different countries within each broad civilization. The extreme zealots who support terrorism are not representative of the diversity of the Islamic world. Likewise, although there are broad similarities among the peoples of the Western world, important differences in national political cultures continue to exist.

As we explore political culture and participation, consider whether liberal democratic values are potentially universal values that will become increasingly important throughout the world—or are they characteristic only of the countries of the West that are the focus of this chapter?

BASIC POLITICAL VALUES AND ORIENTATIONS

The general political values, attitudes, and beliefs that are widely held within a political community are often referred to as its **political culture**.[1] There is usually some relationship between political culture and the policies and decisions of governments, particularly in democratic countries. Through participation in various forms of political activity (such as voting, working on a political campaign, joining a group seeking to influence government, or participating in a protest march), citizens may express their views to those in governing positions as well as try to elect to office those persons and parties who appear to share their political values, attitudes, and beliefs.

It is often assumed that each country has a particular political culture based on such factors as the characteristics of the population, its history, and political experiences. However, in many countries there are different subcultures based on particular class, ethnic, linguistic, regional, gender, or generational groupings. In Canada, for example, not only are there differences between the political culture of the French-speaking people of Quebec and that of the rest of the country, but also such seemingly similar provinces as Saskatchewan and Alberta have somewhat different political cultures (Wiseman, 2001).

Ideological Characteristics

One way of describing the political culture of a political community is in terms of the ideological perspectives that affect the thinking and the policies of that political community. Louis Hartz (1964) developed an interesting theory to account for the ideological differences between European societies and the countries colonized by the European powers. Hartz argued that as the societies of Western Europe developed from feudalism to capitalism, traditional conservative perspectives clashed with the liberal perspectives that arose among those seeking a freer society and a free-market economy. This clash between conservative and liberal views led to a synthesis in the form of socialism. The outcome, Hartz concluded, is that Western European political cultures are diverse, with conservative, liberal, and socialist perspectives all important elements of their political cultures. In countries colonized by European settlers, however, only part of the mother country's political culture was carried to the new lands. In Hartz's view, the United States and Canada are basically liberal "fragments" where such values as individual freedom are predominant.

---

[1] Political scientists often examine political culture through surveys that reveal what proportion of the public has various attitudes. However, political culture can also be thought of as something more than the aggregate of individual views, that is, as a "collectivity's orientations and assumptions about politics" (Stewart, 2002, p. 24).

There has been considerable controversy about the application of Hartz's theory to Canada. Some point out that it ignores French Canada, which historically had a political culture that was very conservative in nature. Others argue that the United Empire Loyalists (Americans who left the United States after its War of Independence because of their loyalty to the British Crown) brought to Canada some traditional conservative values (sometimes referred to as a "Tory touch") along with the liberal values characteristic of the American political culture.[2] This in turn made possible the later development and acceptance of an element of socialist values, which, in Hartz's theory, require the presence of both liberal and conservative orientations (Horowitz, 1966). Thus, even though the individualistic values of liberalism are important in both Canada and the United States, liberalism is not the only significant ideological perspective in Canada. Needless to say, the idea that Canada has a "richer" political culture than the United States is popular among Canadian nationalists!

ANOTHER VIEW Seymour Martin Lipset (1990) has a slightly different explanation for what he argues is a persistent pattern of differences between the Canadian and American political cultures: the two societies were fundamentally shaped by their historical experiences. The United States was founded through revolution, while Canada's historical experience was counter-revolutionary. Canadians did not join Americans in overthrowing British rule, which resulted in a more conservative political culture in Canada.

Canadians, Lipset argues, are more concerned than Americans about maintaining law and order and are more deferential towards those in positions of authority. Canadians are also less individualistic than Americans and more willing to support collective action for the common good. Thus, he argues, Canadians are more willing to look to government to resolve problems and more willing to trust those in government. Canadian political culture also is characterized by a greater willingness to accept and tolerate differences in society than American political culture.

Although some aspects of Lipset's depiction of the differences between the two political cultures are valid, it is questionable whether Canadians are still more conservative than Americans. Survey research has found that Canadians, on the whole, have become less deferential to authority than Americans (Nevitte, 1996). As well, Canadians are now more likely than Americans to be liberal in their views on social and moral issues such as abortion, homosexual rights, and decriminalization of marijuana. Lipset attributes this to the growing strength of conservative fundamentalist religious

---

[2] The majority of Americans today do not consider themselves "liberal." However, Hartz and others consider the American political culture as liberal, particularly in the classical liberal sense of emphasizing individual rights and freedoms and favouring a free-market economy with a limited role for government.

► Although both the Canadian and American political cultures have changed substantially in recent decades, significant differences remain, especially where social and moral issues are concerned. For instance, Canada recently made international headlines by legalizing marijuana for medicinal purposes.

groups in the United States as compared to the more liberal direction taken by the major Canadian religions. Canadians have also become generally more willing to support egalitarian policies than Americans (Lipset, 1990).

As this discussion indicates, political cultures do change over time. This has led to concerns that American influence, particularly through the mass media, will eventually erase the distinctiveness of Canadian political culture. However, an analysis of changes in social and political attitudes between 1981 and 1990 found little evidence of the Americanization of Canadian values. While Canadians and Americans became somewhat more similar in their economic orientations, differences increased in their social values, and there was no overall pattern of convergence or divergence in political values. (Nevitte, 1996). The gap between Canadians and Americans on social values appears to be continuing to widen. For example, the proportion of Americans agreeing with the statement that the "father of the family must be master in his own house" increased from 42 percent in 1992 to 49 percent in 2000, while the proportion of Canadians agreeing with this traditional value decreased from 26 percent to 18 percent over the same period (Adams, 2003, p. 51).

Democratic Political Culture

While a democratic system requires democratic political institutions such as elections, political parties, and governments that are responsive to the people, it is most likely to be sustained if the country has a democratic political culture. Countries where democratic values are not widely held risk reverting to a nondemocratic system.

At a minimum, there should be support for the basic principles of democracy. Stability will be enhanced if the population has a high level of trust in government and other political institutions (Almond & Verba, 1963). A reasonable level of political interest and political knowledge could also be regarded as necessary so that citizens can participate meaningfully in political life and hold government accountable for its actions. If a stronger version of democracy, such as the deliberative democracy discussed in Chapter 4, is to be successful, a higher level of interest and knowledge is needed than in a more limited representative democracy.

DEMOCRATIC VALUES   A high proportion of the population of the advanced countries has a favourable view of democracy. For example, well over 90 percent of citizens in various Western democracies say that they approve of the idea of democracy; on average, about 82 percent agree that "democracy is the best form of government" (Dalton, 2002). However, satisfaction with the way that democracy works in practice varies considerably.

In one survey, over 80 percent of those interviewed in Norway and Denmark in 1995 reported being very or fairly satisfied with the way democracy works in their country; in contrast, only 50 percent in Great Britain, 48 percent in France, and 20 percent in Italy reported being satisfied. A survey using slightly different wording found that 62 percent of Canadians and 64 percent of Americans were satisfied with the way that democracy works (Nadeau, 2002).

Like other developed Western countries, Canada's political culture is based to a considerable extent on liberal democratic values. Most Canadians share a belief in the desirability of democracy, political freedom, individual rights, political equality, and government based on the rule of law. A consensus about general political values is, however, not always matched by a high level of support for the application of these values in practice. For example, although most Canadians support the principle of protecting civil liberties, the majority of people favour suspending civil liberties if there is a national emergency (Sniderman, Fletcher, Russell, & Tetlock, 1996). Likewise, despite a political culture based on individual rights and freedoms, few Americans opposed the stricter measures limiting rights and freedoms that were adopted after the 2001 terrorist attacks on the United States.

VIEWS OF GOVERNMENT AND POLITICIANS Public confidence in government and political leaders has declined in most advanced democratic countries (Pharr, Putnam, & Dalton, 2000). For example, the proportion of Canadians saying that you can trust the government in Ottawa to do what is right "most of the time" or "just about always" declined from 58 percent in 1965 to 33 percent in 1993 (Roese, 2002). More recently, a 2004 poll conducted by the Environics Research Group found that 58 percent of Canadians had little or no confidence in their political leaders. Similarly, 59 percent of those polled by the CBC said that they thought that most politicians are mainly in politics "because they want to advance their own ambitions" rather than "because they want to do something good for the country" (Canadian Broadcasting Corporation, 2004). About three-quarters of Canadians give political leaders a low or very low rating on ethics and honesty, with a similar proportion feeling that political leaders do not tell the truth or keep their promises (Centre for Research and Information on Canada, 2002).

The low levels of trust and confidence in government are matched by feelings that governments and politicians are not particularly responsive to the people. For example, about two-thirds of Canadians agreed with the statement that "government doesn't care what people like me think," with a similar proportion feeling they had "no say" in what government does (Clarke, Jenson, LeDuc, & Pammett, 1996; Marzolini, 2002). Nearly three-quarters of Canadians agreed that "those elected to Parliament soon lose touch with the people" (Marzolini, 2002). Somewhat similar results have been found for other Western democracies (Dalton, 2002).[3]

What explains the general distrust of government and politicians? In some cases political scandals and broken promises have created suspicion. However, the fact that increasing distrust is a feature of most advanced democracies suggests that other factors are also involved. Citizens have become better informed about the failures of government through the mass media. A more educated public has higher expectations of government, which leads to disappointment when those expectations are not fulfilled. It has also been suggested that dissatisfaction is a result of the declining capacity of governments to satisfy the needs and desires of the citizenry because of the impact of globalization (Pharr, Putnam, & Dalton, 2000).

POLITICAL INTEREST AND KNOWLEDGE Most citizens do not have a high level of interest in politics, although they pay some attention to politics particularly during election campaigns. For example, only about one-fifth of Canadians say that they are very interested in politics or follow politics very closely (Mishler & Clarke, 1995). However, about four-fifths of Canadians say that they often or sometimes discuss politics with others, read about elections in newspapers, watch television election programs, and are very or fairly interested in elections (Clarke et al., 1996). Interest in politics has generally been increasing in Canada and other Western countries (Nevitte, 1996; Dalton, 2002)—though as we shall see, this doesn't necessarily mean that more people are exercising their right to vote.

As an example of how knowledgeable people are about politics, consider that 84 percent of Canadians polled in 2004 could name Canada's prime minister. (Interestingly, 97 percent of Canadians knew who was president of

[3] However, the decline in Americans' confidence in their government was temporarily reversed after the September 11, 2001 terrorist attacks as Americans rallied behind their government and were reluctant to show disloyalty.

the United States.) However, only 33 percent knew who was the leader of the official opposition and only 10 percent could name the minister of finance (Canadian Broadcasting Corporation, 2004). Nearly one-half of Canadians would fail the test of basic knowledge about Canada that new citizens are required to take (Milner, 2001). The majority of Canadian voters do not know which party had taken a particular stand on most of the important issues during election campaigns (Fournier, 2002). Likewise, only one-third of Americans knew who was their representative in the House of Representatives and slightly over one-half knew which of the two major parties was more conservative (Milner, 2002).

Although the general level of political knowledge (and sophistication in understanding politics) tends to be low, most people are knowledgeable (and have a reasonably sophisticated understanding) about those political issues that they consider important to themselves personally (Elkins, 1993). Many citizens are not knowledgeable about the major political issues as defined by politicians, journalists, or academics, but rather focus on understanding the particular issues that interest or concern them. Parents, for example, may be more knowledgeable about the education issues that affect their children than about constitutional issues.

POLITICAL SOCIALIZATION AND CHANGING VALUES

Opinions about specific political issues and personalities can often change quickly. However, it is generally thought that a person's basic political values and beliefs are resistant to change. Therefore, **political socialization**, the processes by which the values, attitudes, and beliefs of the political culture are transmitted to members of the political community, is important. Socialization can provide for continuity as the values and beliefs of older generations are passed on to newer generations. As well, immigrants may want, or be encouraged, to adopt some of the values and beliefs that are prevalent in their new country.

POLITICAL SOCIALIZATION
The processes by which the values, attitudes, and beliefs of the political culture are transmitted to members of the political community.

Political socialization, however, is not always a process than ensures continuity in political thinking. Revolutionary regimes often attempt to change traditional values and beliefs by socializing young people with new values and resocializing older people. Even in non-revolutionary political systems, governments or other powerful forces may attempt to modify the political culture through deliberate socialization efforts so as to promote the legitimacy of government and other social and political institutions, develop a sense of national pride, or achieve other objectives.

Political socialization does not only involve deliberate efforts to indoctrinate people with particular values and beliefs. It often occurs in a more haphazard fashion—for example, when young people observe the discussions and actions of adults.

There are a variety of different agents of political socialization, including the family, peer groups, the educational system, the mass media, and religious organizations. Although socialization is a lifelong process, it is generally assumed that many basic values and orientations are acquired at an early age. Thus, the family is likely to be a major agent of political socialization. In particular, parents are very important in shaping the religious, ethnic, and other group identities of their children. American studies in the 1950s and 1960s found that children and young adults have a strong tendency to adopt the party identification of their parents (Jennings & Niemi, 1968). Later studies, however, found only a moderate degree of correspondence between parents and young adults in party identification (Jennings and Niemi, 1981). The correspondence between parents and young adults in other political attitudes—such as political trust, **political efficacy** (the belief that individuals can have an impact on politics and that government is responsive to what people want), orientations toward political participation, and opinions on public policy issues—is generally not particularly strong (Jennings, 1984; Jennings & Niemi, 1981; Mintz, 1993).

POLITICAL EFFICACY
The attitude that individuals can have an impact on politics and that government is responsive to what people want.

State-Directed Socialization

Countries vary in the extent to which state institutions make deliberate and vigorous efforts to promote particular political values. Likewise, there is considerable variation in the extent to which they encourage young people to become informed and active citizens. Schools in most Canadian provinces provide only a limited amount of political education. Provincial education ministries are more concerned about increasing students' mathematical and literacy skills than in preparing young people to be informed citizens. In the United States, civics courses, which often provided an uncritical perspective on the American political system, used to be required in many schools. American schools still often include patriotic rituals such as reciting the pledge of allegiance. The former Soviet Union, People's Republic of China, and other communist regimes devoted great efforts to socializing the young. The educational system, mass media, and youth groups were systematically used to convey the communist message.

The success of government-directed socialization efforts in many countries should not be exaggerated, however. Teachers do not necessarily follow the government-prescribed curriculum. Religious groups and the Western media brought Eastern Europeans messages that contradicted the socializing messages conveyed by the Communist party. As well, young people do not simply passively accept what they are told. When different socializing agencies provide different perspectives, young people may develop their values, attitudes, and beliefs in their own way. Thus, new generations are neither copies of older generations in their political thinking, nor do their ideas necessarily reflect the ideas of the dominant ruling groups.

Changing Value Priorities

Ronald Inglehart (1977, 1990) has provided considerable evidence that modern societies are undergoing a fundamental change in value priorities. According to his **postmaterialist theory**, political socialization is affected by the conditions present when a person is young. The generations that grew up in the relative security and affluence of the Western world since the Second World War are more likely to give priority to **postmaterialist values** such as freedom of expression, participation, concern about the quality of life, and appreciation of a more beautiful environment. Earlier generations are more likely to have materialistic values such as a concern for economic growth, order, and physical security (see Box 7-1, Are You Materialist or Postmaterialist?). This is not simply a matter of being more concerned with material and security needs as one grows older. Rather, studies conducted by Inglehart and his associates have found that the increased tendency to give priority to postmaterialist values has persisted among recent generations as they age.

POSTMATERIALIST THEORY
A theory that modern societies are undergoing a fundamental change in value priorities because generations that grew up in the relative security and affluence of the Western world since the Second World War are more likely to give priority to postmaterialist values than to materialist values.

POSTMATERIALIST VALUES
Non-materialist values such as freedom of expression, participation, concern about the quality of life, and appreciation of a more beautiful environment.

BOX 7-1

Are You Materialist or Postmaterialist?

Read the following statement and answer the two questions to see if you would be considered materialist or postmaterialist:

There is a lot of talk these days about what the aims of this country should be for the next ten years. Listed below are some of the goals to which different people would give top priority. If you had to choose, which one of these things would you say is the most important? Which would be the next most important?[*]

1. Maintaining order in the nation.
2. Giving people more say in important government decisions.
3. Fighting rising prices.
4. Protecting freedom of speech.

If you chose items 1 and 3, you would be considered materialist; if you chose items 2 and 4, you would be considered postmaterialist; and if you chose a different combination, you would be categorized as mixed.

The four items on this quiz do not fully reflect the all of the values associated with materialism and postmaterialism. Nevertheless, Ronald Inglehart and his associates have found that scores on these four items closely match scores on a fuller list of values; thus, these four items are often used to measure postmaterialism.

Adapted from the World Values Survey.

Postmaterialism, in combination with the development of a post-industrial, knowledge-based economy, greater access to higher education, and more effective means of mass communications, may be creating major changes in the political culture of the advanced democracies. These changes, argues Russell Dalton (2002), have resulted in a **new style of citizen politics**. This includes greater citizen activism, the questioning of authority, the development of new political parties and new social movements, the raising of new types of issues (such as issues related to the environment and gender equality), and the development of more liberal social values (for example, greater acceptance of homosexual rights). As well, the significance of traditional political divisions based on class, religion, and strength of attachments to political parties has been declining.

The extent of value change should not be exaggerated. The majority of the population has a mixture of materialist and postmaterialist values, as indicated in Table 7-1. Materialist concerns about unemployment, economic prosperity, and taxes are still usually the leading political issues. Postmaterialist issues have been added to the political agenda, but have not replaced materialistic concerns, nor have they thoroughly transformed the conflicts and social divisions that affect political life.

NEW STYLE OF CITIZEN POLITICS
Changes in political culture related to postmaterialism, the development of a post-industrial, knowledge-based economy, greater access to higher education, and more effective means of mass communications. This new style includes greater activism, the questioning of authority, the development of new political parties and new social movements, the raising of new types of issues, and the development of more liberal social values.

World Values Survey
www.worldvaluessurvey.org/news/index.html

POLITICAL PARTICIPATION

A substantial proportion of the population participates in the political process by voting in elections. However, as Table 7-2 indicates, there is considerable variation among democratic countries in turnout for elections. The variation in turnout rates can be explained in part by differences in the rules governing elections and by the nature of political parties in particular countries.

Some countries, including Australia, Belgium, and Italy, require that all citizens vote. Where such rules are enforced through fines or other penalties, voter turnout is, not surprisingly, substantially higher than in other countries (Blais, Massicotte, & Dobrzynska, 2003). The amount of time and effort that it takes to vote can also affect the turnout rate. For example, only about one-half of those of voting age cast their ballots in presidential elections in the United States; about one-quarter of potentially eligible voters were unable to

TABLE 7-1
MATERIALIST AND POSTMATERIALIST VALUES

	CANADA 1981	CANADA 1990
MATERIALIST	21.8%	11.9%
MIXED	62.1	62.5
POSTMATERIALIST	16.1	25.6

SOURCE: *Inglehart, Ronald et. al. World Values Surveys 1981 and 1990 [Computer file]. ICPSR version. Ann Arbor, MI: Institute for Social Research [producer], 1999. Ann Arbor, MI: Inter-university Consortium for Political and Social Research [distributor], 2003.*

TABLE 7-2
TURNOUT IN RECENT ELECTIONS, SELECTED COUNTRIES

COUNTRY	YEAR	% VOTER TURNOUT	COUNTRY	YEAR	% VOTER TURNOUT
Belgium	2003	96.3	Greece	2000	75.0
Australia	2001	94.9	Norway	2001	75.0
Chile*	1999	90.6	Hungary	2002	73.5
South Africa	1999	89.3	Spain	2000	68.7
Denmark	2001	87.2	Russia*	2000	68.6
Indonesia	1999	85.7	United States*	2000	67.4
Nigeria	1999	84.8	Mexico*	2000	64.0
Italy	2001	81.4	Ireland	2002	62.6
Austria	1999	80.4	Canada	2004	61.2
Sweden	2002	80.1	Poland*	2000	61.1
Netherlands	2003	80.0	Japan	2000	60.6
France*	2002	79.7	India	1999	59.7
Brazil*	2002	79.5	United Kingdom	2001	59.4
Argentina*	1999	78.6	Czech Republic	2002	58.0
New Zealand	2002	77.0	Switzerland	2003	45.3
Turkey	2002	76.9	Pakistan	2002	41.8

Notes: Turnout is in parliamentary elections, except for countries marked with an asterisk (*), where turnout is for presidential elections. Australia, Belgium, and Italy have compulsory voting. Turnout is calculated in terms of the proportion of registered voters. Turnout in terms of the proportion of the voting age population is 49.3 percent in the United States and 54.6 percent in Canada.

SOURCE: *From International Institute for Democracy and Electoral Assistance. Retrieved February 22, 2004 from www.idea.int/vt/index.cfm. Data for Canada based on a preliminary unofficial figure from Elections Canada.*

vote because they did not take the time to register. Other factors affecting voter turnout in American elections include the fact that the United States holds elections more frequently than many other countries, and voters are often faced with a long, complex ballot that includes candidates for a variety of national, state, and local offices, as well as various referendums and initiatives. Accessiblity also affects voting rates: countries that make voting possible by mail and provide alternatives for those who will be absent on election day have substantially higher voter turnout (Blais et al., 2003).

International Institute for Democracy and Electoral Assistance
www.idea.int

Countries using proportional representation systems of election (see Chapter 10) tend to have higher voter turnout because every vote counts in terms of determining how many representatives each party has in the legislature. In countries that use a single-member plurality system, such as Canada, many votes could be considered irrelevant, as it does not matter whether a candidate wins by one vote or 20 000 votes. Thus, some people may not bother to vote if they think that their preferred candidate is well ahead of the other candidates or, alternatively, if they think that the candidate they support has no chance of winning.

Countries with well-organized political parties that can mobilize people to vote are also more likely to have high turnout rates. Being contacted by a party worker and persuaded to vote on election day by the party that you support increases the likelihood that you will cast a ballot. Likewise, countries where a high proportion of people have a strong attachment to a political party are more likely to have high turnout rates. The nature of party competition can also affect the level of voter turnout. If the major parties differ significantly in ideological terms or on major policy issues, a higher proportion of citizens will likely vote. Voter turnout tends to be higher in countries that feature a larger number of significant political parties because more voters may feel that there is a party that represents their particular interests or ideas. As well, voter turnout tends to be higher in elections that feature a close race among the leading parties or candidates.

Decline in Turnout

Election turnouts have been declining to varying extents in most democratic countries since peaking in the 1960s (Dalton, 2002). For example, turnout in the United Kingdom dropped from 71 percent in the 1997 election to 59 percent in the 2001 election, the lowest turnout since 1918. Turnout has also been declining in recent Canadian elections (see Figure 7-1)—turnout in the 2004 election was the lowest in Canadian history.

The decline in voting participation has been generally matched by a decline in the proportion of people working for a party or candidate during an election campaign and the proportion of people who are members of a political party (Dalton, 2002). Only 7 percent of Canadians say that they sometimes or often work for a party or candidate during election campaigns and less than 5 percent are members of a political party (Mishler & Clarke, 1995). Three percent of Americans and 2 percent of Britons worked for a party or candidate in recent elections (Dalton, 2002).

FIGURE 7-1

TURNOUT IN RECENT CANADIAN NATIONAL ELECTIONS

Notes: Turnout figures represent the total ballots cast as a percentage of electors on the voters' list. Changes in the way the voters' list is prepared and the conduct of elections make comparisons imperfect.

*The final adjusted turnout for 2000 was 64.1 percent, after normal maintenance of the National Register of Electors to remove the names of electors who died and duplicates resulting from people who had moved.

**The turnout figure for the 2004 election is preliminary and unofficial.

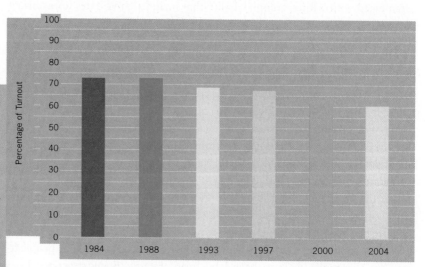

SOURCE: Adapted from data in *Voter Turnout at Federal Elections and Referendums 1867–2000* (2004) by Elections Canada. Retrieved July 12, 2004, from www.elections.ca.

Despite the decline in voting turnout and activity related to elections and political parties, involvement in other forms of political activity is generally increasing. Citizen involvement in a wide variety of groups, ranging in focus from improving the local community to global problems of the environment, human rights, and war, has increased substantially in recent decades (Dalton, 2002), contributing to the creation of a vital *civil society*. Participation in such groups tends to be less sporadic than participation in election campaigns. As well, such participation may involve citizens more directly in trying to affect government policies and to achieve social change. To some extent, involvement in political action groups is replacing involvement in non-political social organizations (see Box 7-2, Bowling Alone?).

BOX 7-2

Bowling Alone?

Political scientists have been concerned about the implications of an apparent decline of citizens in the organizational life of their communities, but the trends are open to debate.

In his travels in the United States in the 1830s, French aristocrat Alexis de Tocqueville (1805–1859) found a high level of involvement of ordinary citizens in the direction of their communities. This, he concluded, provided a firm basis for American democracy (Tocqueville, 1835/2000). Likewise, contemporary political scientists often suggest that a vibrant *civil society*, in which citizens are involved in organizations that are not directly connected to the state, is an important part of a democratic political culture. The development of civil society is often viewed as essential if a country is to move from an authoritarian system to a stable democratic political system.

In a study of the contemporary United States, Robert Putnam found that involvement in a variety of social organizations was declining. For example, membership in bowling leagues had declined sharply; instead, people were bowling with friends or family. Putnam attributed the decline in the membership of social organizations, in part, to the individualizing effects of television viewing. Spending much of our free time watching television reduces the time available for involvement in social organizations. Declining involvement in social organizations, he argued, is leading to a decline in the vitality of democracy (Putnam, 2000).

However, there has been some dispute about whether or not civic involvement has declined. Even though involvement in organizations such as Scouts, Parent–Teacher Associations, and bowling leagues has declined, membership in other organizations, such as conservation and environmental groups, has increased substantially (Ladd, 1999). Likewise, a study of membership in a variety of organizations in fifteen democratic countries found no substantial decline from the 1980s to the 1990s. In the case of Canada, membership in most types of voluntary organizations increased (Baer, Curtis, & Grabb, 2001)

Various forms of protest activity have also become more common in contemporary political life. The majority of citizens in a number of countries, including 77 percent of Canadians, say that they have signed a petition. Beyond the rather passive act of signing a petition, a substantial minority of citizens, including 32 percent of Canadians, report having engaged in stronger forms of protest such as a demonstration, boycott, or occupation of a building (Dalton, 2002).

Who Participates?

Age is strongly related to political participation, with younger people less likely to vote or engage in some other forms of conventional political activity. For example, one estimate is that only 22.4 percent of 18- to 20-year-olds and 27.5 percent of 21- to 24-year-olds voted in the 2000 Canadian election (Pammett & LeDuc, 2003).[4] As explained in Box 7-3, Why Do So Few Young People Vote?, the **life cycle effect** and **generational effect** both contribute to this low level of voting. However, younger people are more likely than older people to engage in protest activities (Dalton, 2002).

LIFE CYCLE EFFECT
The effect on attitudes and behaviour of one's age. As a person grows older, his or her attitudes and behaviours may change due to changing circumstances (such as education, marriage, employment, and retirement) related to age.

GENERATIONAL EFFECT
The effect on attitudes and behaviour of the views of different generations that persist throughout the life cycle.

Political participation is also related to education and other indicators of social class such as income. That is, those with higher levels of education, higher incomes, and professional or managerial occupations are more likely to engage in various forms of political participation, including both electoral and protest activity (Dalton, 2002). However, in countries where there is a major party that represents the working class, differences in voting participation among those in different class positions are small (Verba, Nie, & Kim, 1978). One might expect that the large increase in post-secondary education enrollment in recent decades would have the effect of increasing the turnout in elections. In fact, the rate of voting participation among university graduates has declined only slightly in recent elections. Voting by those with less education has, however, declined sharply, thus offsetting the increase that could be expected from the growth in post-secondary education (Blais et al., 2004).

Although politics has traditionally been thought of as a male activity, studies in Canada and other advanced democracies have found that differences between women and men in some forms of participation are quite small or non-existent (Dalton, 2002; Mishler & Clarke, 1995). For example, in both Canada and the United States, women have been very slightly more likely to vote than men in recent elections. It is in higher-level political activities, such as seeking and holding national or provincial political office (see

---

[4] Because surveys find that a higher proportion of people claim to vote than actually vote, estimation procedures were used to try to determine the actual proportion who voted.

BOX 7-3

Why Do So Few Young People Vote?

Studies of voting behaviour in a variety of countries have found that younger people are less likely to vote than older people.

Surveys conducted at the time of the 2000 Canadian election indicated that while most middle-aged and older people felt that they had a moral obligation to vote, this sense of duty was somewhat weaker among younger voters. Also, younger people pay less attention to elections, have less interest in politics, and less political knowledge (Blais, Gidengil, Nadeau, & Nevitte, 2002, 2004; Pammett and LeDuc, 2003). However, the lower level of voting among the young was *not* a result of a more cynical outlook on politics or negative feelings concerning all the political parties. In fact, younger people were not more cynical than the rest of the population, and only a very small proportion of younger (and older) people had negative views about all the parties (Blais et al., 2002).

To some extent, there is a tendency for people to be more likely to vote as they get older. Termed a **life-cycle effect**, this could be a result of becoming more connected to one's community through work, involvement in community organizations, and raising a family, as well as a result of increased interest and knowledge of politics. However, it has been found that each new group of young people reaching voting age has a lower rate of voting than did the previous group when they reached voting age. It is, in other words, not just the young who are less likely to vote, but also recent generations. This **generational effect** suggests that as they grow older, today's younger people will still be less likely to vote than their parents and grandparents. Indeed, the generational effect is the leading factor in explaining why overall turnout rates have dropped in Canada and are likely to continue to decline (Blais et al., 2004).

Considerable concern has been expressed about the low level of voting among young people. Elections Canada has undertaken a variety of activities to inform young people about the process of elections and to encourage them to participate. Although the rules governing elections have been changed to make it easier for people to vote, many young people do not realize that they can vote on election day even if they are not on the official voters' list. There have also been suggestions that the schools should provide more (and better) political education to encourage young people to engage in political activity and ensure that their viewpoints and interests are represented and respected in the political process.

Chapter 4, especially Table 4.1) or a top position in a political party or interest group, that women are much less likely to be involved than men.

Political participation is also affected by various individual political attitudes. Those with a strong sense of attachment to a political party are more likely to vote and participate in other conventional political activities, including activities not directly related to partisan politics (Dalton, 2002). Those with a high level of political efficacy are more likely to be active participants in politics. In addition, those with higher levels of political interest and political knowledge are more likely to be active participants.

Summary and Conclusion

Understanding the political culture of a country can be helpful in comprehending the politics and governing of a country. The dominant political values in a country will likely affect how its political institutions operate and what kinds of policies its governments tend to adopt. The level of political participation by citizens may affect the degree to which governments are responsive to the wishes of the people. In particular, government policies are more likely to reflect the values and demands of those elements of society that are most politically active.

The ideology of liberalism is a major feature of the Canadian political culture. However, the Canadian political culture is less individualistic than the American political culture, and, reflecting the presence of traditional conservative and socialist ideas, has a greater concern for the collective well-being of society. Although both the Canadian and American political cultures have changed substantially in recent decades, there continue to be significant differences between these political cultures.

Researchers have found that the democratic ideal of an interested, active, and well-informed citizenry is far from realization even in countries where democratic values and institutions are solidly entrenched. Although there has been increasing interest in politics, a relatively small proportion of the population is highly interested in politics and follows politics closely. Despite increased education, the level of political knowledge of much of the population appears to be low. Voting participation has declined in some recent elections, although participation in activities not related to elections and political parties has been increasing. Younger people, in particular, have a low and declining level of voting, which may mean that their viewpoints and interests are not given great attention in the process of political decision-making. Although being active in politics does not necessarily mean that a group is influential, not being involved makes the group invisible and politically irrelevant.

A classic study of political culture argued that a public that generally trusts its political leaders to govern is necessary for the stability of democratic political systems (Almond & Verba, 1963). Although a high proportion of citizens in Western democracies say that they support democracy, the levels of trust and confidence in government and politicians have declined substantially over the past few decades. Some analysts have argued that this indicates that there is a "crisis in democracy." Increasing demands from citizens have "overloaded" governments, in the sense that governments do not have the resources to meet all of the demands being placed on them by citizens. Dissatisfaction with government has grown, creating a potential problem of legitimacy for democratic governments (Crozier, Huntington, & Watanuki, 1975). Others argue that a more educated, postmaterialist citizenry has higher expectations of government. With increased information, citizens are more aware of what goes on in government. Citizens have become dissatisfied because of the slowness of governments to respond to their desire for more effective participation. As well, citizen dissatisfaction has resulted from the broken promises of politicians and government scandals (Dalton, 2002).

Research concerning political culture and political participation raises some important issues concerning the ability of democratic countries to pursue the common good. On the one hand, the development of a more critical citizenry can be helpful in holding government accountable for its actions. The increase in active participation, particularly in groups that seek the common good (or at least their version of the common good) can be viewed as a positive feature of modern, democratic politics. On the other hand, the low level of political knowledge among the citizenry raises questions about whether the common good can be effectively pursued through active citizen participation in politics. The decline of voting participation in recent elections increases the likelihood that governments will be based on the support of a minority of citizens. This may encourage politicians to be concerned with the good of only a limited part of society rather than all of the community. The decline in voting among young people is particularly troubling. If newer generations continue to find politics "boring" and pay little attention to politics (Blais et al., 2002), there may well be long-term implications for the pursuit of the common good and the quality of democracy.

Key Terms

Generational effect 162

Life-cycle effect 162

New style of citizen politics 158

Political culture 150

Political efficacy 156

Political socialization 155

Postmaterialist theory 157

Postmaterialist values 157

Discussion Questions

1. Do you think that a "clash of civilizations" is inevitable?

2. Does Canada have a distinctive political culture? Are differences from the American political culture likely to persist?

3. Why did you vote or not vote in the last election? Why do you think that younger voters are less likely to vote than older voters? Is voting a civic duty that all citizens have a responsibility to perform?

4. Do you have the same basic political values and beliefs as your parents, other family members, or your friends? How would you explain the similarities and differences?

5. Is a postmaterialist political culture developing? What are its implications for political life?

Further Reading

Adams, M. *Fire and ice: The United States, Canada and the myth of converging values.* Toronto: Penguin, 2003

Dalton, R.J. *Citizen politics: Public opinion and political parties in advanced industrial democracies* (3rd ed.). New York: Chatham House, 2002.

Lipset, S.M. *Continental divide.* New York: Routledge, 1990.

Milner, H. *Civic literacy: How informed citizens make democracy work.* Hanover, NH: University Press of New England, 2002.

Putnam, R. *Bowling alone: The collapse and revival of American community.* New York: Simon & Schuster, 2000.

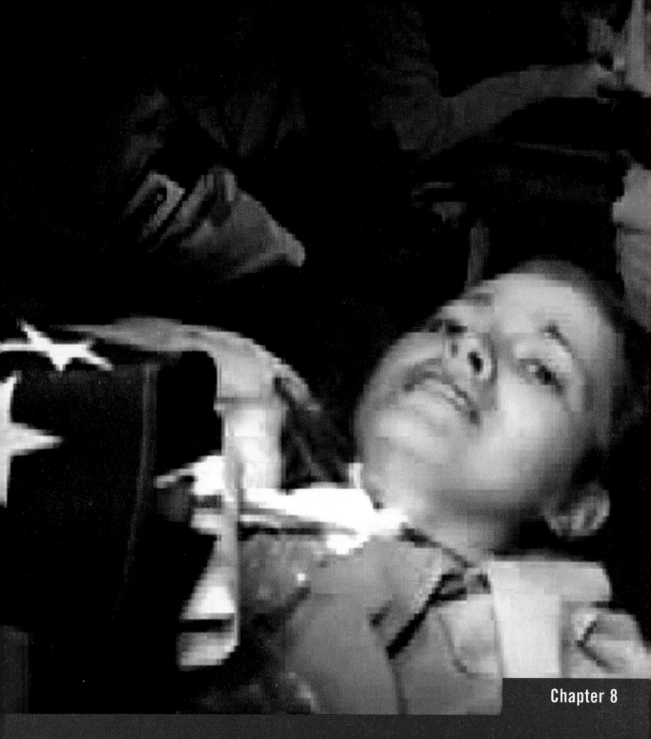

Chapter 8

POLITICS AND THE MEDIA

PHOTO ABOVE: Teenage American army supply clerk Jessica Lynch, pictured here in a video released by the Department of Defense, became a celebrity overnight when the American media set their sights on her in 2003.

CHAPTER OBJECTIVES

After reading this chapter you should be able to:

1. describe the patterns of ownership and regulation of the mass media
2. assess the libertarian, social responsibility, and dominant ideology perspectives on the mass media
3. discuss the treatment of politics by the mass media
4. examine the relationship between the media and government
5. discuss how effective the mass media are in facilitating the achievement of democratic ideals
6. outline the effects of the mass media on the general public

Teenage American army supply clerk Jessica Lynch became a celebrity overnight when the U.S. media set their sights on her in 2003. According to reports, Lynch had resisted capture after being ambushed by Iraqi troops, survived mistreatment in an Iraqi hospital, and then been freed in a daring rescue by American soldiers. The media showed dramatic film of the nighttime rescue, courtesy of the U.S. military. Massive media coverage turned Lynch into a heroine and reinforced the positive image of the American military. Apparently, however, there was considerable exaggeration in the story. Lynch had suffered her injuries in a vehicle accident rather than at the hands of Iraqis. She had been unable to fire at Iraqi soldiers because her rifle had jammed and was treated well in hospital. Iraqi soldiers had left the hospital before her "rescue" (Kampfner, 2003).

That was one of the highlights of media coverage during the American-led invasion of Iraq. From the initial "shock and awe" missile attacks on Baghdad to the toppling of Saddam Hussein's statue in that city twenty days later, the media provided extensive coverage of the invasion. Journalists embedded with military units reported live from the front lines. Retired military officers provided lengthy discussions of the strategies and weapons being used. The sights and sounds of war—although very little of the blood and gore—were broadcast to homes around the world.

There is an old saying that "truth is the first casualty of war." To mobilize the public to support the sacrifices of war, governments typically mount large-scale propaganda efforts trying to depict the enemy as evil. Controls are often placed on the media, not only to prevent the release of strategic details that could help the opposing forces militarily, but also to try to maintain enthusiasm at home for the war effort.

After the invasion of Iraq was officially declared to be over, the American and British media began to take a more critical stance, raising questions regarding whether they had been misled about the justification for the war. In April 2004, investigative reporter Seymour Hersh[1] published articles in the *New Yorker* magazine documenting the abuse and torture of Iraqi prisoners by American soldiers. Although stories of abuse had been circulating for some time, they had been largely ignored by the mainstream media.

With graphic photos available and sentiment turning against continued involvement in Iraq, Hersh's story received widespread publicity. Thus, although most of the American and British mass media initially gave very little attention to critics of the invasion of Iraq and instead provided uncritical support for their governments' actions, the media did eventually adopt a more critical perspective.

In this chapter, we will examine whether the media provide us with an objective or biased view of politics. We'll look at how effective the media are in providing the citizens with an understanding of political events, and whether the media have a major effect on the way that the public thinks about politics.

---

[1] Thirty years previously Hersh had reported the story of an American massacre, covered up by the military, of five hundred and four civilians at the village of My Lai during the Vietnam War.

THE POLITICAL ROLE OF THE MASS MEDIA

Index on Censorship
www.indexonline.org

In most non-democratic countries, the media are generally expected to support the ruling group. Publishers may be required to submit what they propose to print to government censors. Media outlets that are critical of government or spread "dangerous" ideas may be shut down and those responsible for "sedition" punished. The broadcast signals of foreign media may be jammed, Internet sites blocked, the sale of satellite dishes and short-wave radios prohibited, and those caught tuning in to foreign stations even arrested. In totalitarian systems (see Chapter 19), the media are instruments of propaganda that are used systematically to promote the ideological perspective of those in control of the government and encourage the population to actively pursue ideological goals.

Ideally, in liberal democracies the media should play a major role in encouraging the free discussion of ideas, providing the information citizens need to make an informed choice in elections, and preventing abuses of power. There are three prominent lines of thought about how the mass media actually function.

LIBERTARIAN PERSPECTIVE ON THE MASS MEDIA
The idea that the mass media should be free from government control and regulation.

In the **libertarian perspective** (Siebert, Peterson, & Schramm 1956), ensuring that the media are free from government control allows the development of a free marketplace of ideas. With ideas freely competing in the media, citizens can use their own judgment as to which ideas are good and which are bad. Indeed, as John Stuart Mill argued, the suppression of false ideas is undesirable as we gain a "clearer perception and livelier impression of truth" through the "collision" of truth with error (Mill 1859/1912, p. 24).

SOCIAL RESPONSIBILITY PERSPECTIVE ON THE MASS MEDIA
The view that the media have a responsibility to serve the public interest by providing fair and objective reporting of politics.

The **social responsibility perspective** argues that a system of free media will not necessarily result in the public interest being served. In the free competition of the marketplace, the media may resort to sensationalism rather than living up to its responsibility to be "truthful, accurate, fair, objective and relevant" and to provide a "forum for the exchange of comment and criticism" by the public (McQuail, 1994, p. 124). Although the media should be a "public trust," their obligations to the public can generally be served through self-regulation. This can involve the adoption of codes of journalistic ethics, encouraging professionalism among journalists, and establishing press councils to hear citizen complaints about the media (McQuail, 1994).

DOMINANT IDEOLOGY PERSPECTIVE ON THE MASS MEDIA
The view that the major media convey the values of the powerful and serve the interests of those who benefit from the status quo.

The **dominant ideology perspective**, a more radical perspective on the mass media, argues that the major media in liberal democracies convey the values of the powerful and serve the interests of those who benefit from the status quo (see Box 8-1, Herman and Chomsky's Propaganda Model.) Private ownership of the mass media is used to promote capitalist values and the global dominance of capitalist countries rather than to facilitate the free exchange of ideas. From the dominant ideology perspective, public ownership of the mass media, guaranteed access of community groups to the media, or the development of alternative media are some possible ways in which the dominance of capitalist values might be challenged.

Herman and Chomsky's Propaganda Model

A widely discussed version of the dominant ideology perspective is provided by Edward Herman and Noam Chomsky. They argue that "the media serve, and propagandize on behalf of, the powerful societal interests that control and finance them" (Herman and Chomsky, 2002, p. 5) Specifically, in their "propaganda model" of the mass media, they outline five filters that limit what American audiences receive (Herman and Chomsky, 2002):

- the ownership of the mass media by large media corporations
- the dependence of the mass media on advertisers
- the reliance of the mass media on government, business, and conservative think-tanks for information and analysis
- the flak (negative responses or pressure) that the media receive if their presentations are received negatively by powerful groups and individuals
- the expectation that media take a strong stance against those deemed to be enemies of the United States and the American way of life

Although some of the specifics of Herman and Chomsky's analysis apply particularly to the United States, their general argument that the mass media do not challenge dominant ideological values has often been applied to discussions of the media in other liberal democracies. The mass media's emphasis on conventional politics, including elections, party leadership races, and parliamentary debate, means that dissenting voices are often marginalized. Although some social movements, such as the feminist and environmental movements, have been skillful in obtaining media coverage, they do not receive the regular attention given to more conventional political organizations. As well, by focusing their attention on specific events (whether a murder, a hurricane, or the resignation of a cabinet minister), the media often give little attention to ongoing problems such as poverty or the weak enforcement of environmental laws. The problems that the political community faces are portrayed more as a matter of individual defects or unusual circumstances, rather than as a result of the dominant values and structures of society.

THE COMMUNICATIONS MEDIA

Television, radio, and widely circulated newspapers are often referred to as the **mass media**. The mass media tend to reach a large audience that is not strongly differentiated by social characteristics such as class, education, gender, culture, and age. With its ability to attract even the young and the illiterate, television—particularly when there was little choice of programs—most fully exemplifies this aspect of the mass media. However, the proliferation of television channels made possible by cable and satellite television has meant that television viewership has become fragmented as new specialty channels erode the dominance of the major networks, which appeal to a general audience.

MASS MEDIA
Television, radio, and widely circulated newspapers that tend to reach a large audience that is not strongly differentiated by social characteristics.

Television news is the leading source of political information for the public as a whole. For example, 52 percent of Canadians said that television was their main source of information about the 2000 election, compared to 23 percent who cited newspapers and 11 percent who mentioned radio (Blais, Gidengil, Nadeau, & Nevitte, 2002). Surveys have also found that the majority of the public rate television news as the most credible source of information (Ranney, 2001). Although television news reaches a larger proportion of the population than the print media, the quantity of information supplied by television news is very small. A transcript of an hour-long news broadcast would fit easily on a single page of a newspaper.

A distinction can be made between the **elite media** and the mass media. The elite media consist primarily of the newspapers and magazines that are read by decision-makers in government, business, and leading social institutions as well as by those highly interested in public affairs. For example, the *Globe and Mail* and *Le Devoir* in Canada, the *New York Times* and the *Wall Street Journal* in the United States, *The Times* and the *Guardian* in Britain, and *Le Monde* in France could be considered elite media. The elite media are serious in tone, attempt to provide a comprehensive record of political and business news, and generally view themselves as speaking to a national (or occasionally an international) audience. They are more likely to influence political decision-makers than the mass media. Many newspapers imitate the authoritative tone of the elite media and are influenced by their coverage of politics, while giving more attention to the entertainment, sports, and lifestyle news needed to attract a mass audience. Tabloid newspapers and magazines like the *Toronto Sun* and the *National Enquirer* appeal particularly to the less informed and less politically interested segment of mass population, focusing on crime, sports, celebrity gossip, and sexual titillation.

In addition to providing news of current events, the media, to varying extents, provide in-depth treatment of selected topics. Magazines, in particular, provide feature articles that can explore the background and context of a topic. Television newsmagazine shows (for example, *60 Minutes, Dateline,* and *W5*) provide a lengthier presentation of selected topics than do news broadcasts. Newspaper columnists provide commentary on public affairs, and opinion ("op-ed") articles provide a forum for experts and advocates to state their views and proposals.

Although there are a variety of different media and media outlets, the sources of news are often quite limited. Much of what constitutes news comes from news services that collect and disseminate news stories largely from official sources such as government and police. Some newspapers and radio stations simply copy the story intact from the news service, which leads to uniformity of coverage. Canadian Press, a news service that is co-operatively owned by various media outlets, is a prime source for news in Canada, with most of its international news coming from American-based Associated Press.

ELITE MEDIA
The newspapers and magazines that are read by decision-makers in government, business, and leading social institutions, as well as by those highly interested in public affairs.

Center for Media and Public Affairs
www.cmpa.com

Impact of the Internet

The development of the Internet has resulted in a major change in political communications. Through the Internet we are able to easily access a wide diversity of perspectives on politics and, through chat groups, discuss matters that interest us with people around the world. Nongovernmental organizations have been able to mobilize large numbers of people for political actions through their web sites and e-mail messages. Governments and political parties are able to provide information to interested persons without having their message filtered through the critical lens of the mass media. The Internet has not, however, displaced the traditional media as a major source of political news—in fact, many people use their Internet connection to visit the web sites of traditional media. Nevertheless, instead of the traditional pattern of reading a single newspaper or watching a particular news broadcast, those using the Internet will often access a variety of newspapers, magazines, and other media sources.

Although access to the Internet has grown rapidly, concerns have been expressed about the digital divide separating those with access from those without (Norris, 2001). People in poorer countries often have little or no access to the Internet, and the poor within richer countries generally have limited access opportunities (see Table 8-1). As well, most of the content of the Internet is in English, making the Internet of limited usefulness to much of the world's population. In addition, although the Internet provides access to a wealth of political information and ideas, there are indications that it tends to be used more by those who are already politically interested and knowledgeable than by those who are not, thus reinforcing the gap between those who are "information-rich" and the "information-poor" (Norris, 2000).

The Internet provides unregulated access to a wide diversity of perspectives. However, the Internet is used not only to inform, but also to spread lies and hatred. Good journalistic practices such as checking facts and avoiding reliance on a single unverified source do not apply to the Internet. Indeed, in an attempt to stay on top of events, the mass media have sometimes reported Internet-based rumours. For example, during the American presidential primaries in 2004, the mass media gave considerable attention to the false story originating from the sleazy, Internet-based Drudge Report that Democratic candidate John Kerry had had an affair with an intern.

OWNERSHIP AND REGULATION

In liberal democracies, newspapers and other print media have usually been privately owned and free of government regulation, except for censorship related to wartime and national security. Early newspapers were often connected to a particular political party; today, a number of European newspapers continue

TABLE 8-1

INTERNET, TV, AND NEWSPAPER USE, SELECTED COUNTRIES

COUNTRY	INTERNET USERS / 1000 PERSONS (2001)	TELEVISION RECEIVERS/ 1000 PERSONS (2000)	NEWSPAPER CIRCULATION/ 1000 PERSONS (2000)
South Korea	521	348	394
Sweden	516	519	445
United States	502	806	212
Canada	467	710	158
Japan	384	686	578
Germany	374	567	311
United Kingdom	330	521	331
Italy	269	528	104
France	264	595	218
Czech Republic	147	531	254
Poland	98	337	113
Turkey	60	330	110
Brazil	47	223	40
Mexico	36	272	97
Russia	29	410	105
China	26	321	42
Indonesia	19	68	23
Saudi Arabia	13	262	59
India	7	65	26
Pakistan	3	22	21
Nigeria	1	66	27
Bangladesh	1	6	9
Ethiopia	0.4	6	2

SOURCE: *Adapted from* Human Development Report 2003, *by United Nations Development Programme, 2003, retrieved July 11, 2004 from http://hdr.undp.org/reports/global/2003; and United Nations Global Teaching and Learning Project, retrieved July 11, 2004 from http://cyberschoolbus.un.org/infonation/index.asp.*

▶ The Internet is a communications medium that has, to a considerable extent, avoided both corporate and governmental control. Unfortunately, however, in comparison to the mainstream media, it falls short of the democratic ideal of informed discussion.

to be associated with a party or with the Catholic Church. North American newspapers are commercially oriented operations that seek to appeal to a mass audience, although many do support a particular candidate or party on their editorial page.

In many liberal democracies, there is a mixture of private and public ownership of the broadcast media (radio and television). Fears that privately owned American broadcast networks would move into Canada led to the establishment of the Canadian Broadcasting Corporation (CBC) in 1936. Although the CBC is a government-owned Crown corporation and the recipient of substantial funding from Parliament, this network is expected to be non-partisan and independent of government control. In the United States, government ownership has been avoided; television and radio are almost entirely privately owned and profit-oriented. However, in 1967 the American Congress established the non-profit, non-governmental Corporation for Public Broadcasting that is responsible for the Public Broadcasting Service (PBS) and National Public Radio (NPR). These small networks rely primarily on private and corporate donations rather than government for their funding.

Until the early 1980s, almost all television broadcasting systems in Europe were publicly owned. Since then, many countries have opened up their airwaves to privately owned stations (see Box 8-2, Italy: Television and Political Power, for one example). Nevertheless, public broadcasting is still important in almost all European countries. Generally, an independent board appointed by government controls public broadcasting. In several countries, including Germany, Sweden, and the Netherlands, broadcasting is controlled by boards representing different parties and business, labour, religious, women's, and other organizations (Norris, 2000).

Publicly owned broadcasting outlets tend to devote substantially more attention to public affairs than the privately owned media that focus on profitable mass entertainment (Gunther & Mughan, 2000). Although in some countries the state-owned media are instruments of government propaganda, in other countries public broadcasters are not afraid to criticize government actions. By placing control of publicly owned media in the hands of more or less non-partisan boards, democratic countries generally avoid the heavy-handed government control of the mass media that is characteristic of most non-democratic countries.

KEEPING WATCH ON THE MEDIA The broadcast media are regulated, to varying extents in different countries, by government or a government-appointed agency. The initiation of regulation of radio and television was necessitated by technical considerations. Limited bandwidth meant that regulation was needed to allocate valuable licences and prevent stations from attempting to drown out their competitors. As well, governments wanted to ensure that the news media would act in the public interest, and thus typically

BOX 8-2

Italy: Television and Political Power

The Italian government used to have monopoly control of television. However, each of the three public networks was, in effect, under the control of different political parties. Oversight boards helped to ensure that the public networks were generally impartial.

A 1976 ruling by the country's Constitutional Court changed all that by opening the way for private broadcasters. By the end of the 1980s, billionaire Silvio Berlusconi had gained control of private television, with his holding company Fininvest owning the three major private networks. In 1994, as traditional Italian parties collapsed as the result of a major corruption scandal, Berlusconi led his newly formed Forza Italia party to electoral victory. While the public networks were more balanced in their coverage, Berlusconi's television networks devoted much of their campaign coverage to his party's candidates, thus contributing to the victory of Forza Italia and its allies.

Subsequently, the management of the public networks was purged and replaced by Berlusconi supporters (Marletti & Roncarolo, 2000). This did not, however, result in a consolidation of Berlusconi's power. In 1996, his centre–right coalition lost an election to a centre–left coalition. In 2001, Berlusconi returned to power and resumed efforts to influence the direction of the public television networks—while continuing to own and control the major private television networks.

Control of private television, along with expertise in media politics, undoubtedly helped Berlusconi's successful and rapid entry into politics. As well, it suggests that television may help to create a personality-oriented politics in which traditional party allegiances are of diminishing importance. However, control of the media and success in creating a popular image do not necessarily result in success in governing.

required that broadcasting stations allot a certain amount of time to news and public affairs programming. The broadcast media have usually been required to be non-partisan and to provide balanced coverage of politics.

Despite being independent of government, the decisions of regulatory agencies can be controversial. In 2004, the decision of the Canadian Radio-television and Telecommunication Commission (CRTC) not to renew the licence of the most popular Quebec City radio station, CHOI-FM, led to a storm of protest, including a massive demonstration in Quebec City. The CRTC decision was prompted by complaints about the offensive comments of the morning show host concerning women, the mentally ill, and African students. At the same time, the CRTC made a controversial decision to allow cable companies to carry al-Jazeera, the Arab-language television news network well known for broadcasting messages from al-Qaeda, while requiring cable companies to modify or delete anything that could be considered abusive. Jewish organizations criticized al-Jazeera as propagating hatred against Jews; others worried about the precedent of requiring cable companies to act as censors.

There has been a trend towards reducing government regulation of the broadcast media. For example, the "Fairness Doctrine" in the United States, a policy that required that broadcast outlets devote time to important public issues and provide a "reasonable opportunity" for opposing positions to be aired, was repealed in 1987. Then-President Ronald Reagan argued that with the large number of channels available on cable, regulation was no longer needed (Patterson, 2000).

The Internet has thus far generally avoided regulation. With an immense number of different sources of information and ideas and a highly decentralized structure, it could be viewed as the libertarian ideal. As well, the Internet is highly democratic in the sense that it is easy for any person to express and circulate his or her views. It is not clear, however, whether the use of the Internet has increased the quality of political discussion.

An important feature of the privately owned mass media is corporate ownership. Large corporations now own the vast majority of media outlets. There is also a trend towards cross-media ownership, in which large corporations own a variety of different media and related industries (see Box 8-3, The Media: Who Owns What?).

IDEOLOGICAL BIAS

The ownership of much of the mass media by large corporations and the reliance of the media on advertising revenue may result in a bias towards defending and promoting the interests of big business and the values of the capitalist system. Media owners tend to be conservative and oriented to the dominant interests in society. Their choice of executives to run their media outlets will likely reflect, at least to some extent, their ideological orientation. On the other hand, as profit-oriented enterprises, media corporations will normally want to attract as large an audience as possible. This may involve avoiding taking political stances that offend segments of the public or allowing the voices of different elements of the public to be heard.

Nevertheless, a number of prominent newspaper owners have used their position to promote their political views. For example, one of the reasons that Conrad Black established the *National Post* and purchased the largest chain of newspapers in Canada was to give voice to his strongly conservative views. (Under financial pressure, he later sold most of his Canadian interests.) CanWest Global has required that its newspapers cover some news stories in a manner consistent with the views of its owners, the Asper family. As well, local newspapers were required to carry some editorials prepared by the head office until the company backed off after considerable criticism of this directive.

Journalists in general and reporters in particular are, on the whole, less likely to be conservative than the owners and managers of the mass media, although the question of whether they lean in a leftist or socially progressive

Campaign for Press and Broadcasting Freedom
www.presscampaign.org

The Media: Who Owns What?

The details of media ownership often change as corporations merge or divest some of their assets. At the time this textbook was written, for example:

- Bell Canada Enterprises (BCE) was not only the dominant provider of telephone services in Canada, it also owned, through its subsidiary Bell GlobeMedia, the nationally distributed *Globe and Mail*, the CTV network, and the Internet provider Sympatico.

- CanWest Global owned thirteen daily newspapers (including the *National Post*, the *Montreal Gazette*, and the *Ottawa Citizen*); the Global Television network; television networks in Australia, New Zealand, and Ireland; two specialty television channels, radio stations, and the Internet portal canada.com.

- Quebecor, the world's largest commercial printer, owned fifteen daily French and English language newspapers (including the *Toronto Sun*), 180 weekly newspapers, the TVA television network in Quebec, cable TV outlets, the Canoe Internet portal, magazines, book publishers, and video rental stores.

- In the United States, Time Warner, a major movie producer, owned the CNN and HBO cable television outlets, magazines (including *Time*, *People*, and *Sports Illustrated*), record companies, book publishing companies, comic books, and the Internet portal America Online.

- The Disney Corporation, a major movie producer, owned the ABC television network, as well as individual television stations, newspapers, magazines, theme parks, and professional sports teams.

- Viacom owned the CBS television network, Blockbuster Video, Paramount Pictures, a number of specialty channels (including MTV), book publishers, and theme parks.

- General Electric, one of the world's largest corporations, owned the NBC television network and, together with Microsoft Corporation, MSNBC cable news and Internet news sites.

- Australian Rupert Murdoch's News Corporation owned 20th Century Fox movie studios; Fox Broadcasting; the Family Channel; major book publishers; television stations in the major American cities and Australia; satellite TV in Europe, Asia, and Latin America; a high proportion of cable TV franchises in Britain; the world's largest large newspaper chain; a number of magazines; and a major magazine distributing company.

Media outlets that are part of large corporate empires may be less likely to report on problems occurring with other firms in the corporation. As well, there may be expectations that the media will promote other products of their corporate owners. Ownership of different types of media by the same corporation reduces the diversity of the media and may result in a reduction in the number of journalists if resources are shared among the different media owned by the same corporation.

direction is contentious (Alterman, 2003; Croteau, 1998; Miljan & Cooper, 2003). However, editors and producers review and sometimes change the material that journalists submit, choose what stories are to be followed, and decide what stories will appear. For example Arthur Kent, the Canadian-born journalist who reported on the 1991 Gulf War for the American television network NBC, asserted that working journalists have a declining influence on the decisions concerning which stories are selected for the news. In particular, he was critical of NBC and other networks for refusing to run serious stories about foreign affairs. Kent was fired as a result his outspoken criticisms, but during his successful lawsuit against NBC, network executives testified that news coverage was affected by a concern to broadcast entertaining stories (Kent, 1996).

Another potential source of bias stems from the fact that the most prominent journalists, such as TV news anchors, earn high salaries and are treated like celebrities. They hobnob with the rich and powerful, and are often invited to high-paying speaking engagements arranged by business leaders. This raises questions as to whether leading journalists lose their detachment from power and wealth and are therefore less likely to raise the concerns of ordinary people or criticisms of the powerful.

Overall, the mass media do not speak with a uniform political voice. Even if Canadian newspapers tend to be somewhat conservative ideologically and the *Sun* tabloids are strongly right-wing, the *Toronto Star,* with the largest daily circulation in the country, is well known for its liberal and nationalist orientation. Likewise, the CBC tends to provide a somewhat more liberal perspective than the privately owned media (Cooper, 1994).

Advertising Influence

The extent to which the mass media are affected by their dependence upon advertising revenue is not easy to determine. Certainly, there have been cases in which advertisers have attempted to pressure the media, particularly to avoid negative publicity. Indeed, governments may use their large advertising budgets to try to stifle negative coverage. For example, in the 1980s the Newfoundland government withdrew its advertising from an independent weekly newspaper that had been strongly critical of the government's involvement in a costly, unsuccessful effort to make the foggy capital of the province a major producer of greenhouse cucumbers.

To their credit, various media outlets have, on occasion, refused to submit to advertising pressure. However, it is possible that the power of major advertisers is relevant in a more indirect way. A media outlet may think twice before investigating a story that portrays a major advertiser in a negative way. As well, television stations may shy away from producing or carrying controversial programs with which advertisers would not want to be associated. For example, in 2003 the CBS network backed off from its plan to air the docudrama *The Reagans* amid concerns that conservative groups would pressure corporations to withdraw their advertisements.

OBJECTIVITY

When an independent commercial press that appealed to the mass public developed in North America in the late nineteenth century, journalists began

Fairness and Accuracy in Reporting
www.fair.org

Project Censored
www.projectcensored.org

Freedom Forum
www.freedomforum.org

to view themselves as professionals conveying the objective truth to the public. Editors expected writers to report only the facts without exaggeration, interpretation, or opinion (Hackett & Zhao, 1998). A sharp distinction was made between fact and opinion, with opinions relegated to the editorial page.

However, the "facts" do not necessarily speak for themselves. Without background and interpretation, the facts may be largely meaningless for much of the public. Indeed, since the "facts" often come from official sources, the attempt to appear objective has been viewed by some analysts as reflecting a bias in favour of the dominant political forces (Hackett & Zhao, 1998). As well, since reporting inevitably involves selectivity in deciding what to report, objectivity may be impossible to fully achieve.

The New Objectivity

Columbia Journalism Review
www.cjr.org

The ideal of objectivity has not disappeared but, as Robert Hackett and Yuezhi Zhao (1998) point out, it has tended to be treated in the broader sense of allowing background and interpretation, provided that reporters attempt to be impartial, fair, and balanced. For example, to achieve the appearance of fairness, reporters are expected to seek reaction to a statement by a government leader from opposition party spokespersons. When an issue is considered controversial, both sides are often presented. However, this means that complex issues may be simplified into a "pro/con" format, ignoring the reality that there may be more than two sides to an issue. The media may only find it necessary to provide balanced treatment to issues that are matters of dispute among contending political parties. And viewpoints and positions that reflect the leading values of society may go unquestioned.

The media make considerable use of experts to provide comments and some background on issues. However, because most experts come from established institutions and organizations, challenging perspectives are not likely to receive much coverage. In particular, business-supported think-tanks, such as the C.D. Howe Institute and the Fraser Institute in Canada, often supply many of the experts who comment on a variety of topics.

Framing

FRAMING
Selecting and highlighting some facets of events or issues, and making connections among them so as to promote a particular interpretation, evaluation, and/or solution.

Instead of the traditional emphasis on the facts (who said what to whom, when, and why) characteristic of newspaper reporting, television news typically uses a "story" format in order to make the news more interesting. Treating a news item as a story introduces a subtle form of selectivity known as **framing**. Framing involves "selecting and highlighting some facets of events or issues, and making connections among them so as to promote a particular interpretation, evaluation, and/or solution" (Entman, 2004, p. 5). Typically, a problem is defined, the cause of the problem identified, a moral judgment is conveyed or implied, and remedies are suggested or endorsed in order to tell a consistent story (Entman, 2004). For example, during the invasion of Iraq in 2003, the media in the United States framed the story in terms of an effort to liberate Iraqis from an evil dictator who possessed weapons of mass destruction. Alternative interpretations were largely ignored.

Not all news stories carry a complete frame, but the metaphors and images that are chosen to depict a news story affect the way the news is described by journalists and the way it is perceived by the public. For example, election campaigns are often described in terms of a horse race, with great attention being given to public opinion polls (see Box 8-4, Public Opinion Polls). Questions of which party or candidate is ahead or behind and who is gaining or dropping back are often the frame within which specific events—a speech, a debate, or a rally—are discussed. The media tend to analyze the content of a speech or party policy positions in terms of the strategies adopted by a party or candidate for gaining power, instead of examining the feasibility and implications of the party's proposals.

The media typically frame politics in terms of the struggle among party leaders for power. In effect, a choice has been made to explain events and circumstances in terms of the qualities of leaders rather than in terms of broader social, economic, and political forces. This may exaggerate the power of a prime minister or president and create the impression that the leader is personally involved in all decisions. Further, the use of metaphors drawn from warfare and boxing, such as a candidate scoring a "knockout punch" in a debate, may tend to reinforce the image of politics as a male activity (Gidengil & Everitt, 2002).

THE MEDIA AND GOVERNMENT: WATCHDOG OR LAPDOG?

In a liberal democracy, the media are often expected not only to provide the political information needed by the public to choose among the contending parties, but also to play a watchdog role. That is, the media are expected to investigate and bring to public attention abuses of power, which in turn can lead to corrective action. For example:

- The media attention given to the excessive spending of public funds for travel and entertainment expenses by some political office holders, including an Ontario provincial cabinet minister and the federal privacy commissioner in 2003, led to their resignation or dismissal.

- The media played a role in helping to uncover the sponsorship scandal (involving allegations of wasteful and improperly documented payments made to Liberal-connected advertising firms) that rocked the Canadian government in early 2004.

In some cases, the media dig out the abuses themselves; in others, they play the watchdog role by highlighting issues raised by the opposition parties,

BOX 8-4

Public Opinion Polls

"Polls [poles] are for dogs," former Prime Minister John Diefenbaker once said. Many Canadians had similar thoughts after media coverage of the 2004 election heavily featured public opinion polls that wrongly predicted a Conservative party victory.

Properly done, a poll based on a random sample (one in which each individual has an equal probability of being chosen) of one or two thousand people can usually reflect quite accurately the opinions of a large electorate. The statistical laws of probability tell us that random samples of one thousand people, for example, will be accurate within about three percentage points nineteen times out of twenty. In other words, if a poll shows the Liberal party with the support of 40 percent of the population, we can be 95 percent certain that the actual support for the party is between 37 percent and 43 percent. A larger poll will have a smaller margin of error, but there is always a slight possibility that a poll will inaccurately reflect the opinions of the population.

In the 2004 election, several polls, all commissioned by media outlets and conducted near the end of the campaign, found that the Liberal and Conservative parties were virtually tied in popular support. Projections based on these results suggested that the Conservatives would win significantly more seats than the Liberals.[*] The media highlighted this conclusion and speculated about the nature of a Conservative government. Instead, the Liberals beat the Conservatives 36.7 percent to 29.6 percent, winning one hundred and thirty-five seats versus ninety-nine for the Conservatives.

Were the polls wrong? Not necessarily. Polls only reflect opinions at a particular point of time. There are indications that in the several days between the days the polls were conducted and election day there was a shift towards the Liberal party. Indeed, the extensive reporting of the polls could have contributed to this shift: some voters, concerned that the Conservatives might win the election, might have switched their vote to the Liberals. Instead of punishing the Liberals for their perceived misdeeds in office, these voters may have decided that electing a Conservative government was too risky.

Using poll results to predict election outcomes always holds some risks. A significant proportion of survey respondents say that they are undecided or only leaning towards one party. An increasing proportion of people refuse to be interviewed for polls. Many of those who do respond to a poll end up not voting. Finally, although seat projections based on poll results had been very accurate in the previous election, these projections are prone to substantial errors because they are based on a variety of assumptions. Small changes in the popular vote, for example, can result in substantial changes in the number of seats each party wins.

It is important to be aware of the limitations of polls and how they are interpreted. Indeed, political parties have, at times, presented false or misleading reports of the polls that they have conducted. During the 1968 election campaign, for example, PC strategists circulated an imaginary set of poll results showing their party in the lead in a desperate attempt to stem the groundswell of support for the Liberal party. Although the media focus on poll results is often criticized, it has also been argued that the media attention to poll results can provide some useful information to voters. For example, by drawing attention to the possibility of a Conservative victory in 2004, the reporting of poll results may have encouraged voters to consider whether or not they really wanted to elect a Conservative government.

* Polls conducted by four polling firms from June 21 to 24, 2004, found the two leading parties either tied or with only an insignificant difference of 1 percent. A poll conducted by SES Research for the Parliamentary Channel did indicate a Liberal lead of 34 percent to 30 percent for the Conservatives, but little attention was given to this result.

whistleblowers (employees who go public when there has been wrongdoing within their organization), the auditor-general, or anonymous sources within government who leak information.

Early commercial newspapers, particularly in the United States, engaged in some sensationalist exposure of corruption (known as muckraking) in both business and government. The development of the modern watchdog role and associated investigative reporting is often associated with the Watergate scandal of the early 1970s, as discussed in Box 8-5, Watergate: An Investigative Reporting Success. The watchdog role of the media has been aided by the access to information laws passed by many governments in recent decades. Since September 2001, however, concerns about terrorism have tended to reduce access to information.

Center for Investigative Journalism
www.muckraker.org

Attack Dogs

Some critics of the mass media have argued that the contemporary mass media, particularly in the United States, have turned from watchdogs to attack dogs. The media have sometimes mounted sharp personal attacks on politicians and other prominent persons. Political scientist Larry Sabato

BOX 8-5

Watergate: An Investigative Reporting Success

Before the 1972 American election, operatives working for Republican President Richard Nixon's re-election committee broke into the Democratic Party offices in Washington's Watergate complex. Subsequently, the president's senior staff tried to cover up these illegal activities. Investigative reporting by journalists Bob Woodward and Carl Bernstein at the *Washington Post*, aided by an anonymous high-level source nicknamed "Deep Throat," unravelled the story. Eventually Nixon resigned in disgrace rather than face an impeachment trial.

Although the case of Watergate shows the potential significance of the investigative role of the media, questions can be raised as to whether the media take on this role regularly and consistently.

In the case of the Watergate scandal, the publisher of the *Washington Post* was willing to devote considerable resources to allow reporters to pursue the story for a lengthy period of time. President Nixon had never maintained good relations with the press and his administration's failed attempt to prevent the *New York Times* from publishing the Pentagon Papers (a secret study of the decision making that led to the Vietnam War) turned the elite media against Nixon. In other circumstances, such as in the climate of fear that followed the 2001 terrorist attacks on the United States, the media have been more reluctant to conduct investigations that might reflect negatively on government leaders.

(1992) described American journalists as being like sharks, engaging in a "feeding frenzy" when they sense that a politician or a celebrity is in trouble. For example, massive media attention, national and international, was given to the arrest and trial of former football star O.J. Simpson for the alleged murder of his wife, and to musician Michael Jackson for allegedly molesting children. Reporters competed furiously to find juicy bits of information, rumours, and gossip to embellish the stories. Similarly, the media were obsessed with American President Bill Clinton's relationship with Monica Lewinsky in the late 1990s, obscuring important national and international issues. More generally, the media tend to portray politicians and political parties in a negative rather than a positive light, as indicated by a study of newspaper coverage of the 2004 Canadian election (Table 8-2).

The media often scrutinize the words and actions of leading politicians, more to ridicule them than to analyze their ideas. Canadian party leaders have, for example, suffered considerable media ridicule for losing their luggage, dropping a football, wearing a wetsuit to an election campaign kick-off, and wearing a required hairnet while touring a cheese factory. Although these may be harmless diversions from the serious matters of politics (and it may be desirable to know that the high and mighty are just human, after all), when they become the focus of political reporting, the quality of political discussion suffers.

Lapdogs

The prevalence of critical and negative journalism should not be exaggerated. The media can also be seen, to some extent, as lapdogs. There is often a cozy relationship between government and journalists, and much of what constitutes news originates from official sources. In the past, some politicians would hand out cash to journalists in order to encourage them to give favourable treatment to a press release. To this day, some journalists may be influenced by the hope of obtaining employment within government, receiving extra income through speech writing or ghost writing a book for a politician, or gaining access to gather material for a popular biography of a prominent political figure.

TABLE 8-2
PERCENTAGE OF POSITIVE AND NEGATIVE MENTIONS OF PARTIES AND LEADERS, MAJOR NEWSPAPERS, 2004 ELECTION CAMPAIGN

	PARTY POSITIVE	PARTY NEGATIVE	LEADER POSITIVE	LEADER NEGATIVE
Liberal	2%	22%	3%	17%
Conservative	5%	12%	7%	11%
NDP	4%	7%	6%	14%
Bloc	8%	9%	11%	10%

SOURCE: *Adapted from 2004 Federal Election Newspaper Content Analysis: Cumulative Results May 17–June 25, 2004, by Observatory on Media and Public Policy, 2004, retrieved July 10, 2004, from www.ompp.mcgill.ca/pages/election2004.htm#media.*

More importantly, journalists who are seen as sympathetic to the government are more likely to be given the inside story, an exclusive interview with a leading political figure, or a "leak" of an impending government announcement. Even though contemporary journalists generally prefer to avoid too close a relationship with politicians, they still rely on politicians for information to make sense of what is happening within government and to provide anecdotes and gossip for an interesting story.

Sleeping Dogs

Media watchdogs are sometimes asleep or muzzled. For example, the pattern of systematic physical, sexual, and cultural abuse of generations of Aboriginals forced to attend residential schools across Canada did not receive media scrutiny until long after the schools were closed. In the case of physical and sexual abuse of boys by the Christian Brothers at the Mount Cashel Orphanage in St. John's, Newfoundland, the leading provincial newspaper apparently suppressed the story under influence from the hierarchy of the Catholic Church and other community leaders (Harris, 1991). American television networks ignored the use of depleted uranium in U.S. military weaponry in the 2003 Iraq War, despite evidence of long-term, serious potential health consequences both for American soldiers and the Iraqi population.

Walking the Dog: News Management

Governments and politicians often try to manage the news so as to avoid gaining negative treatment. **News management**—controlling and shaping the presentation of information—includes such techniques as providing stories to journalists who are known to be sympathetic to the government and issuing news releases close to news deadlines so that journalists cannot check the facts or obtain critical comments. Information that reflects negatively on government is often released when a more dramatic news event is occurring, or at times like summer or weekends, when many journalists are not working and audiences are small.

Politicians and their media advisors are often concerned with controlling the spin put on what they have said—that is, trying to ensure that a favourable interpretation is placed on information. For example, during a leaders' debate, "spin doctors" for each party will try to persuade journalists that their leader has won the debate and explain away any mistakes that their leader has made.

To avoid unfavourable framing of their proposals and actions, governments spend large sums of money on advertising to carry their message directly to the public. Although some government advertising is designed to increase awareness of government services and programs, governments have also mounted substantial advertising campaigns to promote their perspective

NEWS MANAGEMENT
The controlling and shaping of the presentation of news in order to affect the public's evaluation of news stories.

▶ In April 2004, investigative reporter Seymour Hersh published articles in the *New Yorker* magazine that included pictures illustrating the abuse and torture of Iraqis in the Abu Ghraib prison. This brought to public attention the evidence of abuse that had been largely ignored by the mainstream media.

on particular issues, boast about their accomplishments, and present themselves in a positive light. Similarly, political parties, interest groups, public relations firms, and think-tanks often supply press releases, prepared newspaper articles, and television and radio clips that are distributed to media outlets free of charge. Such stories are sometimes incorporated into the news with little or no editing—particularly by media outlets that have limited resources.

News management by government is most clearly seen in times of war and, more generally, in much of the coverage of international affairs. The mass media often see it as unpatriotic to question their government's decision to go to war and feel obliged to support their country's troops. Government officials and military leaders usually try to tightly control the media during a foreign conflict. In the case of the 2003 invasion of Iraq, discussed at the start of this chapter, only carefully selected embedded journalists were allowed into Iraq and they were restricted in what they could report. During the 1991 Gulf War, journalists were generally confined to the American military's Central Command headquarters in Qatar, a considerable distance from the war, and thus had to rely on military briefings and images supplied by the military.

THE MEDIA AND DEMOCRACY

Debate exists about whether the mass media provide the political information that is needed for people to participate meaningfully in political life, make intelligent choices among parties and candidates, and hold those in public office accountable for their actions. Citizens require not only a set of facts, but also sufficient background and explanations and diverse opinions about what should be done in order to make sense of political issues.

The growth of the mass media in recent decades has greatly increased the amount of political information that is potentially available to the public. Someone addicted to politics could spend every waking hour following politics in the media. However, criticisms are often raised about the quality of information that the ordinary person obtains, particularly through televised news broadcasts.

The mass media need to attract large audiences to be profitable—or, in the case of publicly owned media, to justify the costs of government subsidies. This typically encourages the mass media, particularly television, to focus on providing entertainment to their audiences. Not only may this mean that news and public affairs programming is given limited resources, it can also result in the merging of information with entertainment. This combination, labelled **infotainment**, is particularly evident in television, in part because of the characteristics of the medium (Taras, 1990). Television newscasts often focus on stories that can be portrayed with dramatic images. As the cynical saying about television news puts it, "If it bleeds, it leads."

Stories that can be portrayed in terms of conflict and controversy receive the most attention. News items have become increasingly short to discourage bored viewers from switching to a different channel. Statements and comments by politicians, experts, or ordinary people are edited to a single, snappy sound bite lasting a few seconds. It is obviously difficult, if not impossible, to meaningfully explain an issue in the sixty seconds that may be allotted for a television news story. Television news thus tends to be simplistic, and does not generally provide the context or historical background needed to understand the events that it portrays (Postman, 1985).

Are criticisms of the media exaggerated? There is little doubt that the media emphasize the immediate and the dramatic. Leaders, the competition for power, and public opinion polls are usually given greater attention during election campaigns than the analysis of issues and party platforms. Nevertheless, the media do often play a valuable role by pointing out the inconsistencies in the platforms of political parties and the exaggerations and distortions that are common in the rhetoric of those involved in politics. And by investigating important problems such as poverty, pollution, and the quality of the health care system, the media can draw attention to the need for action.

THE EFFECTS OF THE MEDIA ON THE PUBLIC

Much research and discussion has revolved around the effects of the mass media on the public. Many early researchers viewed the media as having direct and strong effects on the mass public. This **hypodermic model** saw the public as gullible and at the mercy of the communications media. For example, the

INFOTAINMENT
The merging of information and entertainment in news and public affairs programming of the mass media, particularly television.

HYPODERMIC MODEL
The view that the messages conveyed by the mass media have a direct effect on the attitudes and behaviour of the public.

"I'm so glad the media keeps us informed about politics."

German Nazis were thought to have stirred up emotions and expanded their support through dramatic films such as Leni Riefenstahl's documentary of the Nazi rally at Nuremberg, *The Triumph of the Will* (1934).

The first major systematic studies of media effects in the 1940s and 1950s, however, came to the opposite conclusion. Studies of voting behaviour in the United States found that exposure to the election campaigns in the media had little effect on voters. Voters were affected by their social characteristics and long-standing ties to a political party rather than by the mass media or the election campaign. Voters tended to only pay attention to and remember messages that came from the candidate or party that they supported. They also tended to misperceive any messages regarding their favoured party or candidate that were not consistent with their own viewpoints.

Filtering

A **minimal effects model** of media influence was developed to explain the lack of substantial media effects on the public. Through selective attention and selective perception, individuals filtered out messages that might cause them to change their attitudes and behaviour. The effect of messages conveyed

MINIMAL EFFECTS MODEL
Through selective attention and selective perception, individuals filter out messages that might cause them to change their attitudes and behaviour. The effect of messages conveyed through the media is primarily to reinforce existing attitudes.

through the media is primarily to reinforce existing attitudes. Messages carried through the media might have some success in mobilizing those who supported a candidate to vote, but would be unlikely to change a person's mind as to which candidate to support. Persons with little knowledge or interest in politics might be affected by persuasive communications. However, such persons are less likely to make use of the media to follow politics and less likely to vote.

Studies in the past few decades have suggested that the media can in some ways have important effects on the public. Because social characteristics and partisanship have generally been of declining significance in affecting voting behaviour, messages in support of different parties and candidates are more likely to receive attention and potentially have an effect on voters. Likewise, because an increased proportion of citizens make their voting decision during an election campaign, more people may be susceptible to the influence of the media during campaigns than in the past. This may have occurred, for example, at the end of the 2004 Canadian election campaign.

Agenda-Setting

Communications researchers also suggest that the media may not necessarily be able to affect what people think (that is, their attitudes, beliefs, and values), but can affect what they think about (that is, what they consider important). In other words, the media have an important **agenda-setting effect**—they can affect what the public thinks are the key issues or political priorities at a particular point in time. By raising and emphasizing a particular issue, the media can make that issue important in the minds of the public. For example, although famines in Ethiopia are a regular occurrence, the considerable attention given by the mass media to the Ethiopian famine in 1984–85, particularly through pictures of starving children, temporarily made this issue, which few had been aware of, the subject of considerable public interest and concern (Bosso, 1989). Donations poured into relief agencies, and politicians were expected by the public to respond to the crisis. When media attention to the issue faded, famine relief dropped off the political agenda, even though the problem of famine remained.

There are limits to the agenda-setting effect of the media. For example, despite the massive attention the Canadian media gave to the constitutional "crisis" of the 1980s, it did not become a major issue for most Canadians. The agenda-setting effect is strongest when the media raise issues that directly touch the lives of people or are issues that people can relate to.

Although the media sometimes raise issues that would otherwise be ignored, the media often follow the political agenda set by politicians, political parties, and other authoritative sources. During election campaigns, for example, it is the issues and controversies raised by the leading parties that are typically the subject of media attention, even though they may not be the

AGENDA-SETTING EFFECT
The effect of the media on what the public thinks are the key issues or political priorities at a particular point in time.

problems that the public is most concerned about. Those who have a critical perspective on the media point out that there are a variety of important issues that receive little or no attention from the media.

Judgment Criteria

The mass media also have the potential capability to affect the criteria by which people judge political events and personalities (termed **priming**). Topics that are emphasized in television news broadcasts can influence how voters decide which candidate or party to support (Iyengar & Kinder, 1987). If, for example, party A is viewed by most voters as the most competent to handle economic issues while party B is viewed as the most competent to handle social issues, a focus on social issues by the media may encourage people to base their evaluations of the parties more on social issues than economic issues. This may in turn increase the electoral support for party B, even if the evaluations of each of the parties' competence to deal with economic and social issues did not change. Likewise, by drawing attention to particular character traits of political figures, the media can influence perceptions of politicians, particularly new political figures who have not developed a clear image in the minds of the public.

Research Issues

Finally, it should be noted that research supporting the minimal effects model often focuses on the effects of political communication in changing attitudes in the context of an election campaign. During an election campaign, the public is subject to a variety of conflicting messages and people are more likely to be skeptical of what they read, hear, or view. Some studies have suggested that messages not directly related to partisan politics can change the opinions, attitudes, beliefs, and values of the public. For example, an American study found that a specially designed thirty-minute television show was able to change public attitudes in an egalitarian and environmentalist direction (Ball-Rokeach, Rokeach, & Grube, 1984).

The mass media may also have subtle, long-term effects that are not easily detected by researchers. For example, a number of media critics have argued that the tendency of the mass media to treat politics in a negative way has led to cynicism and passivity on the part of citizens, a sense that politics is a nasty business that we can't do anything about. The increasingly negative tone of media coverage of politics in North America in recent decades has resulted, in this view, in the decline of trust in politicians and political parties and in a decline in voting participation (Cappella & Jamieson, 1997; Robinson, 1976). However, researchers have found that those who are heavier users of the political content of the media are more likely to have higher levels of political trust and involve themselves in election campaigns than those who do not use the media to follow politics (Norris, 2000). Indeed, it may be argued that the increased use of investigative reporting and the increased willingness of the media to question the actions of those with political power may have encouraged the public to critically analyze what goes on in political life and to act to try to rectify problems and injustices.

Summary and Conclusion

The communications media play a central role in modern politics. Political activity, whether an election campaign, a debate in the House of Commons, or a protest demonstration, is conducted with a concern for gaining favourable media coverage. Journalists raise or highlight many of the issues that become subjects of political discussion and action. Through their description and definition of political issues, the media may affect thinking about how issues should be resolved. The information and ideas that are used to make sense of politics often come to us from the media. Although empirical research has discounted the idea that the media have a powerful effect in changing political attitudes, it is possible that the media have a subtle, long-term influence on the way people think about politics.

The political information that we receive from the communications media is a result of a complex set of forces. The personal views and corporate interests of the owners of the media, the views and professional values of journalists, the influence of advertisers, the need to attract and maintain an audience, government regulations, the efforts of spin doctors to manage the news, and the characteristics of the different media all affect the presentation of political information.

The libertarian perspective holds that freedom of the communications media from government control is an essential feature of liberal democracy. The common good is promoted by presenting diverse viewpoints and allowing criticisms of government to be aired so that government can be held accountable for its actions.

Critics, however, argue that media freedom does not ensure that citizens are provided with the information needed to hold government accountable for its actions. For example, the profit orientation of the privately owned media often leads to a focus on entertainment and a trivialization of politics. As well, media freedom does not guarantee that all opinions are fully and equally presented. As media commentator A.J. Liebling stated many years ago, "Freedom of the press belongs to the man who owns one."

The dominant ideology perspective provides a very different view of the mass media than the libertarian perspective. This perspective views the mass media as instruments of the powerful used, in liberal democracies, to promote the values of capitalism and defend the status quo against challenges. In this view, the media serve the interests of the privileged and powerful rather than the common good of all.

However, the mass media in the past few decades have tended to become less deferential to persons in positions of authority, and are therefore not simply a vehicle through which the powerful can transmit their views to the mass public. The media have adopted a more critical tone and considerable attention is often given to the failures of government and leading political figures. Depending on the circumstances, the media may frame stories in a way that challenges the interpretation proposed by government leaders (Entman, 2004). Although the mainstream media in Britain and the United States provided uncritical support to their governments during the 2003 invasion of Iraq, a year later they took a more critical stance toward their governments' justifications for the invasion. Generally, there is a diversity of viewpoints presented in the various communications media, although the voices of those in the political mainstream are heard more than voices outside the mainstream.

Disagreement exists as to whether involvement by the government in owning and regulating the media is desirable. Those who hold the libertarian perspective argue that the state should not be involved in owning or regulating the media because of the danger that the media will be used to promote the interests of the governing party, stifle the free flow of discussion, and lead to an authoritarian political system. A free society, in this perspective, requires free communications media. Others argue that state-owned media that are independent of direct government control can be useful in providing more in-depth analysis of politics than the entertainment-oriented private media. The mixture of private and public ownership of the broadcast media in Canada and most other democratic countries has added to the diversity of the mass media. Indeed, the CBC has tended to give more attention to critical voices than the privately owned media. To increase diversity, some have suggested that government should subsidize community operated broadcasting outlets to provide media access to those whose voices are rarely heard in the mass media (Eaman, 1987).

The Internet provides a communications medium that has to a considerable extent avoided both corporate and governmental control. Although access to the Internet is limited in poorer countries, the Internet does allow for interactive communication on a global scale. The Internet provides easy access to an exceptional diversity of sources of information and opinion. However, on the whole, the Internet falls short of the democratic ideal of informed discussion. Rants, rumours, conspiracy theories, hoaxes, and spam clog the Internet, and many Internet sources and groups provide only a one-sided perspective. By contrast, the mainstream mass media, despite the criticisms that have been raised, do generally strive for accuracy and the presentation of informed opinion.

From a social responsibility perspective, the mass media should serve the common good by providing the accurate information and differing opinions that citizens need to be well-informed participants in democratic politics. Because the media do not always live up to their responsibility to the public, those who take the social responsibility perspective typically suggest that media should take the lead in reforming itself by recognizing its obligations to society. This raises the question of whether it is realistic to expect large media corporations to act in a socially responsible way unless there is strong pressure from government to do so. Government regulation of the media may be needed to ensure that the media carries out its democratic responsibilities. However, with regulation comes the danger that the free expression of opinions that is vital to a liberal democracy may be stifled.

Key Terms

Discussion Questions

1. Do the mass media provide you with a good, unbiased understanding of political events?

2. Should there be more or less government ownership and regulation of the mass media?

3. How would you rate the performance of the Canadian mass media in terms of helping to achieve democratic ideals?

4. Does the Internet provide a means to overcome the problems of the mass media?

5. Do you think that the mass media have a greater effect on the way that people think about politics than other influences?

Further Reading

Fox, Bill. *Spinwars: Politics and new media*. Toronto: Key Porter, 1999.

Herman, E.S., & Chomsky, N. *Manufacturing consent* (updated ed.). New York: Pantheon Books, 2002.

Kurtz, H. *Spin cycle: Inside the Clinton propaganda machine*. London, Pan, 1998.

Nesbitt-Larking, P. *Politics, society, and the media: Canadian perspectives*. Peterborough, ON: Broadview, 2001.

Taras, D. *Power and betrayal in the Canadian media*. Peterborough, ON: Broadview, 1999.

POLITICAL PARTIES

PHOTO ABOVE: During the 2003 Progressive Conservative leadership convention, Nova Scotia MP Peter McKay (right) initially emerged as a front-runner, but after the third ballot, he was still short of the votes needed to win. In exchange for a written promise from McKay that the PCs would not merge with the Canadian Alliance, third place candidate David Orchard agreed to ask his followers to vote for McKay, who then easily won the fourth ballot.

CHAPTER OBJECTIVES

After reading this chapter you should be able to:

1. distinguish among different types of parties
2. explain the significance of parties
3. discuss the methods used for choosing party leaders
4. outline the strengths and weaknesses of the major types of party systems
5. discuss the characteristics of the major Canadian parties
6. compare the Canadian party system to the party systems of other democratic countries

The May 2003 leadership convention of the Progressive Conservative (PC) party of Canada would turn out to be its last. Nova Scotia MP Peter McKay was the frontrunner, but after the third ballot he was still short of the 50 percent of the votes needed to win. In exchange for a written promise from McKay that the PCs would not merge with the Canadian Alliance, third-place candidate David Orchard agreed to ask his followers to vote for McKay, who then easily won on the fourth ballot. Several months later, however, McKay, fearing that the PC party would be wiped out in an election, allowed merger talks with the Alliance to proceed. In December 2003, the PC party was dissolved and a new Conservative party—dominated by the Canadian Alliance—was established.

The party that would eventually become known as the PC party has a long-established history—it was founded by Canada's first prime minister, Sir John A. Macdonald. Macdonald's Conservatives dominated Canadian politics in the nineteenth century, but were less successful in the twentieth century, in part because of their difficulty in appealing to Quebeckers. This changed in the 1980s, when PC leader Brian Mulroney achieved remarkable success in reversing the twentieth-century Liberal dominance of Quebec. However, regional tensions resulted in many Quebeckers and Western Canadians switching to new parties (the Bloc Québécois and the Reform Party) that more strongly represented their particular interests and viewpoints. By the end of the 1993 election campaign, the PC party had just two seats in the House of Commons. The Reform party, which represented the New Right ideology as well as the concerns of Western Canada, was the second-largest party in the House by 1997. However, it had little success in gaining representation outside of Western Canada. With the right-wing vote split between the Reformers and PCs, the Liberals regained their domination of national politics. In 2000, an attempt to unite the right under the Canadian Alliance banner foundered. Eventually, though, members of both parties voted in favour of the merger, though a number of prominent members of the PC party refused to join the new Conservative party. Nevertheless, the new party, headed by former Alliance leader Stephen Harper, did win more seats in the 2004 election than the two parties it replaced, though with a smaller percentage of votes. Although David Orchard and some other PC supporters felt betrayed by McKay, the merger created a serious competitor to the governing Liberal party.

In this chapter we examine the development of Canadian parties and the nature of the contemporary Canadian party system. We also look at how parties are organized and operate, and discuss whether they provide a good link between the people and the government.

THE IMPORTANCE OF POLITICAL PARTIES

POLITICAL PARTY

An organization that has a central role in the competition for political power and seeks to occupy positions within the executive and legislative bodies of government.

Organized political parties are a major element of the political systems in democratic and most non-democratic countries. **Political parties** are organizations that have a central role in the competition for political power and seek to occupy positions within the executive and legislative bodies of government.

In democratic countries, political parties play a crucial role in the process of elections: they recruit candidates, organize election campaigns, and present alternatives to the electorate. Political parties often represent the different interests or viewpoints of various groups of voters. As well, parties have a central role in governing, particularly in parliamentary systems where members of one party (or a coalition of parties) comprise the executive (prime minister and cabinet) and control the legislature. Political parties can provide direction for the governing of a political community. By voting for or against the governing party, voters can hold the government accountable. Parties that are not involved in governing, the opposition parties, are important in voicing criticisms of the government, holding the government accountable for its actions, raising public concerns that have not been adequately dealt with by the government, and developing themselves as an alternative to the governing party. However, despite the importance of political parties, questions have been raised as to whether parties are being eclipsed by the growing significance of the interest groups and social movements that are discussed in Chapters 11 and 12 (see Box 9-1 The Decline of Parties?).

THE ORIGINS AND DEVELOPMENT OF POLITICAL PARTIES

Cadre Parties and Mass Parties

A classic study of political parties by Maurice Duverger (1964) made a distinction between two basic party types, cadre parties[1] and mass parties, based on their origins and organizational structure.

CADRE PARTY

A party concerned with the task of electing members of the party to legislative bodies, rather than building a strong, centralized, membership-based organization outside of the legislature.

Cadre parties generally originated as factions within legislative bodies, as individual representatives found it desirable to work together with other members who had similar interests and perspectives. In some cases, the hope of gaining particular benefits for themselves, such as a government position, helped to mould the supporters of the government into a united, disciplined party. In reaction, other legislative members usually organized themselves to challenge and replace the governing party.

---

[1] The term *cadre* is somewhat confusing. As used by Duverger (1964), it refers to the control of the party by an elite group. Unlike a revolutionary cadre, cadre parties are not characterized by a strong ideological commitment. And unlike a military cadre, the leaders of a cadre party do not typically control a highly disciplined and highly centralized organization.

BOX 9-1

The Decline of Parties?

Some political scientists have argued that political parties are in decline (Meisel & Mendelsohn, 2001). The membership of political parties in many countries has been dropping since the 1960s (Scarrow, 2000) and many people no longer have a strong sense of attachment to a particular party. Interest groups and social movements have become more popular vehicles for citizen involvement in political life.

One reason for the apparent decline of political parties is that the public often has a negative view of parties. For example, a survey conducted in eight democratic countries found that only 22 percent of respondents stated that they had a "great deal" or "very much" confidence in political parties, significantly lower than the level of confidence in various other political and governmental institutions (Dalton & Wattenberg, 2000). Likewise, a study found considerable "anti-partyism" in Canada (Gidengil, Blais, Nadeau, & Nevitte, 2002). To some extent, the distrust of parties is understandable. Some political parties have been instruments of corruption—using their political power to gain benefits for their members. As well, there has been considerable criticism of political

parties for their reliance on big business or labour unions for much of their funding. Tendencies to make extravagant promises and ambiguous pronouncements and to wage dirty, unfair campaigns against their opponents also create a negative image for parties.

The growing number of interest groups and the development of social movements have provided citizens with new means to take political action. Unlike working within a political party, where bargaining and compromises are needed to reconcile the interests and values of a diversity of persons and groups, participation in an interest group or social movement may allow a more forthright pursuit of one's goals and interests. However, in the view of Reg Whitaker, the decline of parties, along with the use of legal actions to assert rights and the increasing popularity of the devices of plebiscitary democracy, represent an undesirable "flight from politics" (Whitaker, 2002). Others such as Vaughan Lyon see the central position given to the competition among political parties as providing only a limited version of democracy that is inferior, in his view, to a non-partisan deliberative democracy (Lyon, 1996).

In the latter part of the nineteenth century, as the right to vote expanded in many Western countries to include a large segment of the population, those seeking election to the legislature needed to develop an organization outside of the legislature to gain the support of the substantial number of new voters. This typically involved gaining the support of local notables (prominent or wealthy individuals) who had the influence and financial resources to assist individuals seeking election. A loose network of notables became the basis for the organization of the party outside of Parliament.

Cadre parties are concerned basically with the task of electing members of the party to legislative bodies, rather than building a strong, centralized, membership-based organization outside of the legislature. This leaves the parliamentary grouping of the party and its leadership relatively free to take positions in Parliament and government as they see fit. A cadre party thus provides a limited link between the people and the government.

The **mass party** developed around the end of the nineteenth century and the start of the twentieth century. Socialist and Labour parties were formed as mass parties in many countries to challenge the Liberal and Conservative cadre parties that had developed out of legislative factions. Socialist and Labour parties did not have the support of the wealthy. Instead, they developed a large working-class membership that supported the party by regularly paying a small membership fee.

Collecting fees from large numbers of people required a large organization based on a network of local branches with a central office. The democratic perspective of the socialist movement encouraged the adoption of democratic procedures within the party. This included holding regular meetings of elected delegates of the membership (**party conventions**) to adopt party positions and to choose people for leadership positions in the party. Because socialist parties generally developed outside of the legislature in movements seeking change, there were expectations that members elected to the legislature would follow the wishes of the **extraparliamentary party** (that is, the party organization outside of parliament).

DIFFERENCES AND TENDENCIES   Mass parties generally have a stronger link between citizens and political leaders than cadre parties. Analysts of mass parties have noted, however, that power tends to be concentrated in the hands of party officials (those with paid positions within the party organization) rather than in the ordinary members of the extraparliamentary party. Based on his observation in the early twentieth century of the German Social Democratic party (a classic example of a mass party), Robert Michels (1911/1962) developed what he termed the **iron law of oligarchy**. This generalization claims that all organizations, even those that appear democratic, inevitably become dominated by a small, cohesive group of leaders.

The mass party form of organization is not exclusive to socialist and working-class-based political parties. Parties that developed out of nationalist, farmers, religious, and other movements and interests have tended to adopt, to varying extents, the mass party format. As mass parties in a number of countries were successful in developing large, membership-based organizations, cadre parties eventually found it necessary to respond to this challenge by developing regular membership-based organizations and involving their members on an intermittent basis (Wolinetz, 2002).

In recent decades, the development of modern campaign techniques, such as the use of television advertising and the solicitation of funds through direct mail and the Internet, has reduced the necessity of building and maintaining a large membership organization. In many countries, including Canada, parties are now funded to a considerable extent by the state. Professionals skilled

MASS PARTY
A party that draws its support from a regular dues-paying membership and features a strong extraparliamentary party organization.

PARTY CONVENTION
A meeting of delegates from party constituency associations, the party's legislators, and party officials.

EXTRAPARLIAMENTARY PARTY
A political party organization outside of parliament.

IRON LAW OF OLIGARCHY
A generalization that claims all organizations, even those that appear democratic, inevitably become dominated by a small, cohesive group of leaders.

in the techniques of advertising, public relations, fund-raising, and public opinion research have become increasingly important to parties in their efforts to gain political power.

The differences between cadre and mass parties have generally diminished over time. Cadre parties have developed their extraparliamentary organization and adopted some of the democratic procedures pioneered by the mass parties. Mass parties eventually found it necessary to make use of campaign professionals to supplement door-to-door canvassing of voters by dedicated party members. Most modern political parties can be described as **electoral–professional parties** (Panebianco, 1988). Such parties are electoral in that their dominant concern is winning elections, with ideology and principles of much less importance, and professional in their reliance on professional experts to market their parties.

DIFFERENCES STILL SIGNIFICANT Although differences between cadre and mass parties have diminished, traces of the difference still remain. Parties with cadre origins typically consider the party leadership, rather than the party convention or membership, as the final determinant of party positions. They tend to rely more than other parties on financing from business and the wealthy. In contrast, parties with mass origins tend to involve their members more in policy development and usually have a more active, membership-oriented organization.

Political parties also differ in the types of interests and ideological perspectives that they represent. Party politics in many countries has featured competition between mass parties that appeal particularly to the working class and various cadre parties that appeal particularly to business and middle-class interests. Working-class-oriented mass parties have generally had a socialist ideological perspective, while cadre parties typically have a conservative or liberal ideological perspective. Parties representing farmers have also been established in a number of countries. Many continental European countries and some Latin American countries have important Christian Democratic parties that generally reflect the philosophy of the Catholic Church (although not always exclusively Catholic), or other religious-based parties. Parties defending ethnic and linguistic minorities and parties promoting regional interests or regional autonomy have been significant in several countries.

Otto Kirscheimer (1966) argued that there is a tendency for all of the major political parties to become **catch-all parties** that try to appeal to all segments of the population by downplaying or abandoning their ideology and emphasizing the qualities of their leaders. Researchers have found a tendency for the established parties to become less ideological as time passes and to drift to the centre of the political spectrum (Caul & Gray, 2000). As well, there has been a tendency for parties established to represent particular segments of society to move towards a broader appeal. For example, under the

ELECTORAL–PROFESSIONAL PARTY
A political party whose dominant concern is winning elections and which relies on professional experts to market the party to voters.

CATCH-ALL PARTY
A party that tries to appeal to all segments of the population, particularly by downplaying or abandoning its ideology and emphasizing the qualities of its leaders.

leadership of Tony Blair, the British Labour Party abandoned much of its socialist ideology and moved away from a focus on the interests of the working class.

The Green Factor

Global Greens
www.globalgreens.info

The decline in party ideological differences has been challenged in many countries by the establishment of new parties expressing particular ideological perspectives. For example, in recent decades Green parties have been established in about seventy countries. These parties have a common set of principles combining an environmentalist ideology with commitments to social justice, feminism, grassroots democracy, and peace.

In some countries, these Green parties have only been able to obtain a very low level of support from voters, and thus remain a fringe party without representation in legislative bodies. However, in many Western European countries, Greens have won legislative representation, and in several countries they have gained a voice in government as a junior coalition partner. Germany, for example, has been governed since 1998 by a coalition between the Social Democratic party and the Green party, with members of the Green party obtaining three cabinet posts, including the important position of foreign minister.

Other Distinctive Parties

The Green party is not the only new party with a distinct perspective. Right-wing populist parties favouring major tax cuts and reductions in government have at times been able to gain substantial support in several countries, including Canada, Denmark, and Norway. More extreme right-wing parties have developed significant support in countries such as France, Italy, and Austria.

Even some parties with cadre origins that are considered catch-all parties have at times moved in a strongly ideological direction. For example, the moderate British Conservative party was turned into an ideological vehicle for the New Right under the determined leadership of Prime Minister Margaret Thatcher. Likewise, the Republican party in the United States has tended to move in a strongly conservative direction since the 1980s under the influence of various elements of the New Right. The Ontario and Alberta Progressive Conservative parties under Mike Harris and Ralph Klein, respectively, and the British Columbia Liberals under Gordon Campbell adopted strong neo-conservative or neo-liberal ideological positions.

A focus on winning elections will generally encourage a party's leadership to adopt moderate positions and downplay their ideological orientations. However, many of those active in a political party are concerned not only with winning elections, but also with implementing their views about what is best for the political community. Thus, given the right circumstances, party activists may be able to move their party in a more ideological direction. As well, the inroads made by newer ideological parties may push moderate older parties into taking a firmer ideological stance to offset the threat to their support. In Canada, for example, when faced with the loss of support to the Reform party in the 1990s, the Progressive Conservative party moved to a more right-wing ideological position to try to regain some of its support—a shift that was particularly apparent in the 1997 election.

In general, the tendency for major parties to converge in the centre of the ideological spectrum was the strongest in the decades after World War II, when a general consensus developed about the desirability of moderate welfare state and Keynesian economic policies. The breakdown of this consensus and the development of newer ideological perspectives led to a re-invigoration of ideological debate that in some cases has resulted in parties taking more distinctive ideological stances.

Other Party Types

Different types of parties can be identified even within a particular country. Even if the distinction between mass and cadre parties is not as clear-cut as it once was, some parties are more membership-oriented, while others are more elite controlled. Some parties are more ideological or principled; others are more exclusively focused on winning elections, which makes them more flexible and opportunistic. Some parties are more oriented to a particular interest or segment of society; others attempt to be broadly based. In addition, some parties have been created around a particular popular personality—for example, Charles de Gaulle in France, Juan Péron in Argentina, Pim Fortuyn in the Netherlands, and Silvio Berlusconi in Italy.

CANADIAN POLITICAL PARTIES

The Conservative Party

Canada's first organized political party, the Conservatives, developed out of the coalition of factions that supported the 1867 union of the British North American colonies. The Tory and Quebec *Bleu* factions, associated with business and religious leaders and some moderate reformers, were central elements in the development of the Conservative party. The party added the label Progressive in 1942, when John Bracken, the Liberal-Progressive premier of Manitoba, was selected as the party's leader.[2] As we saw at the start of the chapter, the Progressive Conservative (PC) party merged with the Canadian Alliance in 2003 to form the Conservative party (see Figure 9-1).

Conservative Party of Canada
www.conservative.ca

---

[2] The Progressives, based on a farmers' protest movement, won the second-largest number of seats in the 1921 Canadian election and, under various labels, gained control of the government in several provinces. Many Progressives at the national level switched to the Liberal party, although some were involved in the formation of the CCF.

"I don't think that our tax money should be going to these political parties."

The Liberal Party

The Liberal party developed in the nineteenth century out of a diverse set of factions, including reformers (some known as the "Clear Grits") who favoured greater democracy, the Quebec *Rouges,* who opposed the power of the Catholic Church, and Maritimers who had opposed Confederation.

LIBERALS AND CONSERVATIVES: SIMILARITIES AND DIFFERENCES   Historically, the Conservative Party supported close business–government cooperation to develop a Canadian economy, including tariff protection for fledgling manufacturing industries and subsidies for the railway companies to build transcontinental links. The Liberals tended to favour a more laissez-faire approach, including advocacy of free trade with the United States and increased powers for provincial governments. Over time, the Liberal Party has become associated with support for a somewhat active government, particularly in building the welfare state after World War II. The Liberal party has been more likely than the PC party to favour a strong central government. The PC party tended, in recent decades, to be a strong advocate of reducing government involvement in the economy and developing closer ties with the United States.

Despite some differences between the Liberal and PC parties, these parties generally avoided explicit ideological commitments or exclusive appeals to

FIGURE 9-1

THE DEVELOPMENT OF CANADIAN POLITICAL PARTIES

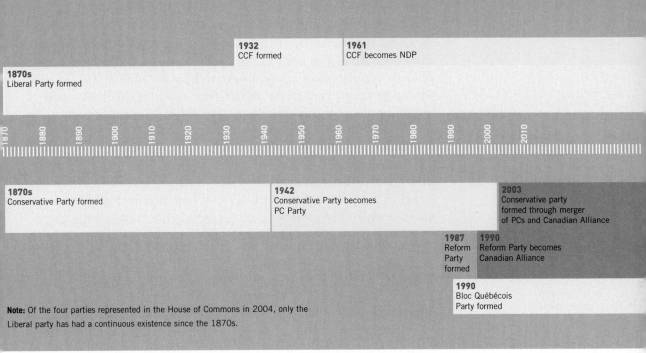

1932
CCF formed

1961
CCF becomes NDP

1870s
Liberal Party formed

1870s
Conservative Party formed

1942
Conservative Party becomes
PC Party

2003
Conservative party
formed through merger
of PCs and Canadian Alliance

1987
Reform
Party
formed

1990
Reform Party becomes
Canadian Alliance

1990
Bloc Québécois
Party formed

Note: Of the four parties represented in the House of Commons in 2004, only the Liberal party has had a continuous existence since the 1870s.

particular interests. Instead, the Liberal and PC parties have often been described as **brokerage parties**. As brokers among a variety of important interests (particularly those of different regions and cultures), the Liberal and PC parties have tried to bridge the differences among different regions and cultures by promising benefits to a variety of different interests.

Differences in policy positions taken in Parliament and in election platforms have often involved posturing for political advantage rather than reflecting long-term principles or ideology. Changes in which party governs the country have not generally led to substantial changes in governing policies. Alternatively, some have suggested that the similarity between the Liberal and PC parties has been a result of the orientation of both parties to the interests of business and the capitalist economic system (Brodie & Jenson, 1988).

The Conservative party that was established in 2003 appears somewhat more ideological than the PC party. Like its predecessors, it favours smaller government, closer economic and military relations with the United States, and increased provincial government power. It also advocates tax cuts and supports the traditional social values that were emphasized by the Reform and Alliance parties.

BROKERAGE PARTY

A party that tries to appeal to a variety of interests and to bridge differences, particularly by promising benefits to a variety of different interests.

The New Democratic Party

The New Democratic Party (NDP) has its roots in the Cooperative Commonwealth Federation (CCF), which was established in 1932 by delegates from various farmer, labour, and socialist groups during the height of the Great Depression. Its limited support at the national level and weak finances led the CCF to join with the Canadian Labour Congress (the largest umbrella organization of labour unions) to form the NDP in 1961. In addition to its formal link to the labour movement, the NDP sees itself as supporting the goals of some of the new social movements such as the environmentalist and feminist movements.

Although the NDP has moderated its democratic socialist ideology, it is distinctive in its advocacy of the welfare state and egalitarian policies. The NDP takes liberal positions on social issues such as support for same-sex marriages. As well, it is distinctive in such nationalist positions as favouring restrictions on free trade and foreign investment, and opposing military involvements with the United States (for example, participation in the national missile defence system).

The Bloc Québécois

The other major party at the national level, the Bloc Québécois, was founded in 1990 by some members of Parliament (mainly PC but also Liberal) who were upset by the opposition that had developed to a proposed constitutional agreement, the Meech Lake Accord, which would have recognized Quebec as a distinct society. The Bloc contests seats only in Quebec and generally has a close relationship with the Parti Québécois, which represents the independence movement at the provincial level. The Bloc is a voice for Quebec nationalism and is primarily concerned with representing Quebec's interests in the Canadian House of Commons. Because the Bloc supports independence for Quebec, it has no interest in running candidates outside of the province.

Other Parties

In Canada there are also various smaller parties that regularly contest elections. These smaller parties receive very little attention and have little chance of electing members. However, by gaining over 4 percent of the vote in the 2004 election, the Green party will qualify for state funding and may receive somewhat more attention in future elections.

PARTY ORGANIZATION

In examining party organization, it is important to distinguish between the **parliamentary party**, composed of the party's representatives in Parliament, and the extraparliamentary party, composed of the membership of the party, including the party's executive, which is generally elected by the membership.

To understand to what extent members of the extraparliamentary party have control or influence over their party, we have to look at the processes that are used to select the party leader and party candidates and to develop the policy positions that the party will take.

Party Leadership

Choosing a party leader is a very important task for political parties. Not only is the leader the chief spokesperson for the party but, more importantly in a parliamentary system, the leader whose party is successful in an election generally becomes the head of government (see Chapter 15). In effect, parties choose the most powerful person in government.

Parties use several different methods to choose their leaders:

- *Selection by parliamentary party.* In the past, parties typically relied on the parliamentary party to select the leader. Such a system, unlike the alternatives discussed below, ensures that leaders have the support of their colleagues so that they can effectively lead their party in Parliament. Leaders chosen by the parliamentary party are likely to have considerable parliamentary experience, and candidates do not need financial backing to seek the leadership. Selection by the parliamentary party, however, does not provide a voice for ordinary citizens who are party members.

- *Selection at party conventions.* Party conventions allow various components of the party to participate in the election of the leader. Typically, delegates elected from each constituency, along with the party's legislators, party officials, and representatives of different associations within the party (for example, women, youth, student, or other groups), choose among leadership candidates at a convention. The standard procedure is to hold successive ballots. The candidate with the least number of votes or any candidate not receiving a certain number of votes is dropped from the ballot until one candidate has a majority of the votes cast.

    While party conventions are more representative of the party as a whole than is the parliamentary party, the choice of the convention will not necessarily reflect the choice of all party members. Delegates will tend to have a higher socio-economic position than the general membership, and the presence of substantial numbers of non-elected delegates may give party elites some ability to influence the results. On the positive side, party conventions allow those choosing the leader to meet the candidates, hear their speeches, and discuss the merits of the candidates with other delegates. Party leadership conventions also attract considerable media attention, which can potentially boost the party's popularity.

- *Selection by membership vote.* In recent times, some parties have decided to choose their leader by a **direct membership vote**. That is, all party members have the opportunity to choose among the leadership

DIRECT MEMBERSHIP VOTE
A system of party leadership selection in which all party members can directly choose among the candidates, rather than selecting delegates to choose the leader.

candidates. In some ways, the direct membership vote is the most democratic way of choosing a leader. Not only does it allow each party member a direct voice in choosing a leader, but also it makes it easier for party members who cannot spend the money or time to attend a leadership convention to participate in the choice. As well, the ability of candidates to perform well in an election campaign can be tested by their campaign for party leadership. On the negative side, direct membership vote systems can place the power to select a leader in the hands of those with little or no involvement or attachment to the party. During leadership campaigns, party membership often multiplies as each candidate's team aggressively tries to recruit large numbers of new party members—many of whom do not renew their membership after voting in the leadership contest. Although these problems are also evident in the choosing of delegates in the convention system, they can be more serious in direct membership vote systems.

COSTS   The choice of leaders by either the convention or membership vote system can be very costly for the candidates. In the case of the 2003 Liberal leadership campaign, Paul Martin spent nearly $10 million. (Because he raised $12.3 million, the surplus was used to pay off the debt of the Liberal

▶ In 2004, the Conservative party required candidates to pay a deposit of $100 000 to enter the leadership race.

party.) Sheila Copps, the only other contender to stay in the race until the end, spent about $900 000. The Conservative party in 2004 required candidates to pay a deposit of $100 000 to enter the leadership race (half was refundable). The high cost of mounting a credible campaign has discouraged a number of potential candidates from contesting the leadership. New rules concerning contributions to leadership contests (discussed later in this chapter) may result in lower spending in the future.

TRENDS Canadian parties adopted the party convention method of choosing a party leader in the first decades of the twentieth century. In recent years, many provincial parties have adopted direct membership vote systems, allowing party members to vote for their choice of leader by mail, telephone, or the Internet. At the national level, recent methods of selecting a leader include the following:

- Jack Layton was chosen as the NDP leader in 2003 through votes that members could cast by mail or the Internet or at a party convention. One-quarter of the votes were reserved for members of affiliated labour unions.
- The Liberal party used a combination of delegate convention and membership vote to choose Paul Martin as its leader in 2003. Party members in each constituency indicated their leadership preference. Based on this, delegates committed to support a particular candidate at the convention were selected, with requirements ensuring selection of an equal number of female and male delegates and a certain number of young people. Delegates were also elected to represent student and women's Liberal clubs and Aboriginal Liberal members. In addition, many persons could vote at the convention because of their position within the party or their role in representing the party in Parliament or as a candidate for election.
- The newly formed Conservative party chose Stephen Harper as leader in 2004 through a membership vote, with each constituency rather than each member having an equal voice in the decision.[3]

The method chosen by the Conservatives and Liberals of giving each constituency an equal weight (either through the election of delegates to a convention or through a direct membership vote system) is intended to ensure that the winning leadership candidate has broad national support. However, in parts of the country where a party is weak, it can mean that a handful of party members in one constituency have the same effect on the outcome as thousands of members in a different constituency.

A study of leadership selection in eighteen established democratic countries found that 44 percent of parties used a party convention to choose their leader, 24 percent used the parliamentary party, 23 percent used a member-

---

[3] For the March 2004 leadership contest, rather than having successive ballots until one candidate obtained a majority, the Conservative party adopted a system of preferential balloting in which the second choices of members would have been counted if no candidate had received a majority of votes.

ship vote, and 10 percent used a national party committee (Scarrow, Webb, & Farrell, 2000). As in Canada, there appears to be a general tendency to include party members in the selection of a leader.

Candidate Selection

Political parties are also important in the selection of candidates for election. Very few candidates are successful unless they represent a political party. In Canada, candidates are normally selected by a vote at a constituency party meeting or by ballot boxes set up in different locations in the constituency. In a few cases, non-members have been allowed to vote, and occasionally in some parts of the country party executives rather than the constituency party members have chosen the candidates. In addition, the Liberal party has given its leader the power to appoint a number of high-profile candidates (see Box 9-2, "Star" Candidates).

BOX 9-2
"Star" Candidates

Liberal leader Paul Martin's preparations for the 2004 election included personally choosing eleven high-profile star candidates who did not have to go through a nomination contest.

On the positive side, this allowed the party leader to attract candidates who would be reluctant to engage in a nomination battle or lacked support among the party's members but might help to boost the party's image among the general public. For example, former British Columbia NDP premier Ujjal Dossanjh would have been unlikely to win a Liberal nomination contest. By appointing him as a candidate in a Vancouver constituency, Martin hoped to broaden the potential support basis for the Liberal party in the general election. (Dossanjh won his seat and became a prominent cabinet member as minister of health.)

On the negative side, the appointment of star candidates by the leader created considerable bitterness within some local party organizations. Potential candidates who spent many months campaigning for the nomination were unhappy when the contest was cancelled in favour of the leader's appointee. In some cases, local party executives resigned in protest.

One of the reasons that the Liberal party gave for allowing its leader to select candidates was that this special power would make it possible to address the inadequate representation of women and minorities. However, the power has not been used systematically to pursue that objective. For example, in another Vancouver constituency, Liberal MP Sophia Leung was encouraged to step aside so that David Emerson, the chief executive of Canfor, a leading forestry corporation, could be anointed as the Liberal candidate.

In the end, what was the outcome of Martin's choice of star candidates to bolster the party's image? Not particularly successful. Only four of the eleven "stars" shone strongly enough to win election.

Canadian election law also gives party leaders the right to reject a candidate from representing the party—a power that has been used occasionally to overturn the choice of an embarrassing candidate by the constituency association. Nevertheless, constituency associations in Canada do generally have control of the process of nominating candidates, giving Canadian parties a more decentralized character than parties in many other countries have (Carty, 2002).

Although members of the constituency association usually play a key role in choosing their party's candidate, they do not generally exercise much influence over the candidate once he or she is elected. In the past, party rules, written or informal, usually ensured the renomination of a sitting member of Parliament. Some Canadian MPs in recent times have been denied renomination by their constituency association, but this is still an infrequent occurrence.

The majority of parties in other advanced democratic countries also involve party members in the selection of candidates, although many parties use local or regional delegate conventions rather than a direct membership vote to select or ratify candidates. Some parties use candidate selection committees to ensure that only suitable candidates are chosen. Most parties allow the party leader or party executive to veto the choice of candidates (Scarrow et al., 2000). Very different is the system of **primary elections** used in the United States to select candidates for political office (as discussed in Box 9-3, Primary Elections).

PRIMARY ELECTION
In the United States, a state-run election in which voters select the candidate they want to represent their party in the general election.

Party Policy

Generally, extraparliamentary party organizations do not have a great deal of power over the policy positions that the party takes. In the past, some cadre parties did not hold regular party policy conventions. For example, until the 1960s, the Liberal and PC parties of Canada usually only held conventions when they needed to choose a new leader. Policy discussion was a sideshow to the main event of the leadership choice, and policy resolutions were not always thoroughly discussed, formally voted upon, carefully recorded, or made accessible. Indeed, after being elected PC leader in 1956, John Diefenbaker ordered the destruction of all copies of the resolutions that had been voted on because they did not reflect the direction in which he wanted to take the party (Dyck, 2004).

In recent times, the Liberal and PC parties have regularly held conventions (usually every second year) at which policy resolutions are discussed. At times, these have been preceded by policy discussions at the local and regional levels. Policy resolutions, however, are not binding on the leader and the party's legislators. Instead, party resolutions adopted at party conventions are simply one source of advice, which leaders may heed or ignore depending on their inclinations and the circumstances.

BOX 9-3

Primary Elections

In the United States, primary elections are held to choose each party's candidates for public office ranging from county sheriff to president. The elections are conducted by state governments and are often held many months before the general election. In the majority of states, only registered supporters of a party may vote in their party's primary, but some states allow voters to participate in whichever party's primary they choose.

The choice of each party's candidate for president involves a combination of primaries and party convention. In most states, delegates to the party's convention are chosen by a primary election in which voters express their preference among potential candidates. This results, through methods that vary from state to state and party to party, in the selection of delegates who support particular candidates. Primary elections for presidential candidates are held over a period of several months as each state decides when to hold its primary election. As the process proceeds, less successful candidates usually drop out of the race, generally because they find it harder to raise money.

In recent decades the choice of the presidential candidates has been clear well before the parties held their conventions. For example, the 2004 Democratic party presidential nomination contest began as a tight contest between a sizable number of candidates, but by the final sets of primaries, John Kerry was the only significant candidate left. George W. Bush did not face a challenge to be the Republican party's candidate.

The primary election system was adopted in order to move away from the sometimes corrupt processes of candidates being selected by party "bosses." The system is more open than the process used in most other countries, as most citizens can vote to determine who the candidates should be. However, the primary system weakens political parties since they do not have much control over the selection of party candidates. The primary election system provides an opportunity for those without a connection to a party to win a party's nomination if they can mount a strong public campaign. The system typically results in potential candidates having to raise large amounts of money to win a nomination, thus making successful candidates dependent on wealthy backers. The adoption of a primary system for choosing candidates, therefore, has not been an entirely positive development.

The importance of party conventions is somewhat different for parties with mass origins. Their constitutions typically state that party convention is the highest authority within the mass party. The party leader and the party's representatives in the legislature are expected to take positions on issues consistent with the resolutions that have been adopted at the party convention.

There is often vigorous debate over policy resolutions at the party conventions of mass parties, providing an opportunity for those active within the extraparliamentary party organization to be involved in the discussion of party policy positions. However, the party leader and key party officials are often able to exercise a considerable degree of control over the process of discussing and adopting resolutions at a party convention. Efforts may be made to modify or avoid a vote on resolutions that could harm a party in its attempts to gain public support. Furthermore, leaders generally feel free to interpret party resolutions or to delay acting on them if in power.

THE LIMITED SIGNIFICANCE OF CONVENTION RESOLUTIONS In the case of both cadre and mass parties, the leaders and their advisors usually oversee the development of the party campaign platform. Therefore, the policy resolutions adopted at a party convention may have only a limited influence on the positions that the party takes in elections. After their party is elected, the prime minister and cabinet typically argue that they have to make decisions that are for the good of the political community as a whole, rather than acting in accordance with their party's policy resolutions. The policy advice that is acted on by the party in power is much more likely to come from the public service and various policy advisors than from the extraparliamentary party organization.

Party Caucus and Party Government

Although extraparliamentary parties are often quite loosely organized, parliamentary parties are generally very tightly organized. In parliamentary systems, there is a strong expectation that each party representative will support the positions that the **party caucus** (a closed-door meeting of the party's parliamentary members) has decided to take. This **party discipline** is not only a product of sharing a particular perspective with other party members. Perhaps more importantly, it results from a desire to avoid giving the appearance of divisiveness, which could hurt the party's electoral fortunes.

Party discipline is also maintained through the party leader's power to impose sanctions on dissident party members. Such sanctions can range from being assigned less desirable office space to being expelled from the party caucus and denied the right to represent the party in the next election. The tightness of party discipline has come under considerable criticism in Canada and party leaders have made promises to loosen it.

Political parties in modern parliamentary systems also play a crucial role in governing. The prime minister and cabinet are almost always members of a particular party or, in the case of coalition governments, members of the parties forming the coalition. The prime minister and cabinet oversee and are responsible for the various departments of government and set the basic direction for the government. Thus, parliamentary systems are often described as systems of **party government.**

Although governments are organized around political parties, we might consider whether it really matters which party governs. People expecting change after the election of a different party are often disappointed when the new government acts similarly to the previous government. In part, this is because the decisions and actions of government are affected by the advice of public servants who remain in their position regardless of which party is in power. As well, any

PARTY CAUCUS
A meeting of the party's parliamentary members.

PARTY DISCIPLINE
The expectation that legislators will vote in accordance with the position that the party has adopted in caucus.

PARTY GOVERNMENT
A government controlled by members of a particular political party.

government is affected by the same circumstances (for example, the financial position of the government and the state of the economy), the same pressures from interest groups and the public, and the same sets of external and global forces. However, keeping in mind these constraints on the ability of governments to change course, some researchers have found that party does make some difference in the policy directions taken by governments.

A study of twenty-one democratic countries, for example, found that governments headed by social democratic parties tended to spend more on health and education that did governments led by parties on the right (Castles, 1982). Parties on the right are more likely to adopt tax-cutting policies. Parties on the left are also more likely to adopt economic policies aimed at reducing unemployment, while parties on the right are more likely to adopt policies aimed at reducing inflation (Hibbs, 1987). However, in many cases, the differences in governing between leftist and rightist parties are not large. The tendencies for ideological differences among the major parties to decline and for parties to appeal to all segments of the electorate has reduced the likelihood that a party in government will favour policies that benefit its core constituency (Caul & Gray, 2000).

PARTY FINANCE

Parties need considerable amounts of money to finance their operations. In particular, modern election campaigns can be very costly. The financing of political parties and candidates in election campaigns has often been considered to be a major political problem. There are risks that donors will be able to buy influence through their financial support. In particular, donations may be made to a party in the hope of, or as a reward for, a government contract or other benefit. Even when such patronage is not involved, politicians may be more concerned about maintaining the support of their financial backers—often large corporations and wealthy individuals—than about acting in the public interest. As well, better-financed parties and candidates may have a strong advantage in attempting to gain the support of the electorate.

Many countries have established limits on election expenses, put restrictions on campaign advertising, provide public subsidies to parties and campaigns, and require public disclosure of significant donations (see Box 9-4, Controlling Election and Party Financing in Canada). Generally, this allows for fairer competition among political parties, reduces the likelihood that undue influence will be placed on politicians, and reduces the taint of scandal and corruption that has often been associated with money in politics. Public financing systems, however, can be used to discriminate against smaller or new political parties and thus maintain the dominance of the larger, established parties. As well, the dependence of parties on public funds may reduce their incentive to maintain strong ties with their supporters (Katz & Mair, 1995).

BOX 9-4

Controlling Election and Party Financing in Canada

Canada has introduced major changes to political party and campaign financing. Until 2004, there were no limits on contributions to political parties and candidates at the national level in Canada. The Liberal and PC parties relied heavily on contributions from business corporations to fund their party and their election campaigns. The NDP derived a significant proportion of its funding from unions.

However, legislation that was passed in 2003 and came into effect on January 1, 2004, bans business and corporate contributions to political parties and leadership contenders, although businesses are allowed to contribute up to $1000 per year to candidates and constituency party associations. Individuals may contribute up to $5000 per year to parties. The restrictions on contributions are offset, to a considerable extent, by payments to parties out of public funds.

Each year, registered political parties, except those that received a very small proportion of votes, now receive $1.75 from the government for each vote they obtained in the previous election. As well, parties are reimbursed for 50 percent of eligible campaign expenses (60 percent in the 2004 election only). Candidates are reimbursed for 60 percent of their expenses if they obtain 10 percent of the vote in their constituency.

Other provisions of the legislation include limits on the spending of candidates and parties in elections and nomination contests; public disclosure of contributors and expenditures, including leadership and nomination contests; and tax credits for those who contribute to parties and candidates.

There was considerable criticism of the strict new regulations by the Canadian Alliance and the PC party as well as by many Liberals. Former Liberal cabinet minister Sheila Copps defended the legislation, arguing that donations from corporations to the Liberal party had unduly influenced the policies of the government. The government's failure for several years to act on the Kyoto Protocol to reduce greenhouse gas emission was, she claimed, "because of the pressure put on by a few corporate interests" (Clark & McCarthy, 2003).

In the past, party and election financing laws have often had limited success because of loopholes in the legislation and lax enforcement of its provisions. It remains to be seen how effective the new legislation will be.

PARTY SYSTEMS

In most consolidated democratic systems, the pattern of competition among the major political parties—the **party system**—is relatively stable over time. What can be significant, however, is the number of *relevant* political parties (Blondel, 1968). Every democratic country has a large number of parties, but many parties (for example, the Communist party of Canada and the Vegetarian party in the United States) have so little support that they have virtually no relevance to the competition among political parties to elect representatives and govern the country.

PARTY SYSTEM
The pattern of competition among political parties.

Determining which parties are relevant is not a simple matter. The Green party, which obtained over 4 percent of the vote in the 2004 Canadian election, has become somewhat relevant in election contests but is still irrelevant in the House of Commons, where it has no representatives. The Bloc Québécois, on the other hand, is irrelevant in the competition for votes outside Quebec. However, by winning fifty-four seats in the House of Commons in the 2004 election, the Bloc gained considerable bargaining power because the Liberal party was twenty seats short of a majority in the House of Commons.

Party systems in democratic countries can be classified into four basic types:

- two-party
- two-plus party
- multiparty
- one-party dominant

TWO-PARTY SYSTEM
A party system in which two major parties contend to control the government. Two-party systems are competitive in the sense that a single party does not govern for a lengthy period of time.

Two-party systems feature two major parties that contend to control the government. Two-party systems are competitive in the sense that a single party does not govern for a lengthy period of time. Normally, one party is able to gain a clear majority of seats in the legislative body and is able to control the government. Parties other than the two major contenders for power are only of minor significance. The United States is a classic example of a two-party system, with the Democratic party, which leans somewhat in a liberal direction, and the Republican party, which leans in a conservative direction, dominating the political scene for the past century and a half. All presidents and almost all members of Congress have been elected as Republicans or Democrats during this lengthy period of time. Other parties such as the U.S. Reform party, founded by Ross Perot, and the Green party have occasionally tried to challenge the dominance of the older parties, but the Democratic and Republican parties have thus far been successful in warding off these challengers.

There are, however, few other countries that currently have a two-party system. Britain is sometimes described as a two-party system, as only the Conservative and Labour parties have formed the government since the 1920s. However, since the 1974 election, the Liberal Democratic Party, which generally positions itself in the centre of the ideological spectrum, has gained the support of about one-sixth of the British electorate. Although its representation in the British House of Commons is relatively small, the Liberal Democratic Party is a significant national party. Thus, Britain could be considered to have a **two-plus party system.**

TWO-PLUS PARTY SYSTEM
A party system in which there are two major contenders for power, but other parties also have a significant amount of support, which may at times prevent either of the larger parties from gaining a majority of legislative seats.

Canada historically has had a two-party system; indeed, only the Liberal and Conservative parties have ever held power at the national level. However, since 1921, various other parties have also been relevant in the competition for political power. In nine of the twenty-five elections from 1921 to 2004, no party was able to win a majority of seats in the House of Commons. Various parties, in addition to the Liberal and Conservative parties, have played an important role in the competition for votes and in minority government situations, thus affecting the governing of the country. The Canadian party system can therefore generally be considered a two-plus party system (see Figure 9-2), although given the significance of the NDP, Bloc, and, from 1993 to 2003, the Reform/Canadian Alliance, the party system in recent decades could also be classified as multiparty (Dyck, 2004)

Multiparty systems feature several parties that are significant actors in the competition for political power. Multiparty systems vary from those with a fairly small number of parties to extreme cases of ten or more significant parties. In the latter case, each party often represents a highly specific interest or viewpoint.

Some simplification of extreme multiparty systems may be obtained where similar parties agree to campaign as a bloc. In Italy, for example, most of the parties, in recent times, have joined either the House of Freedom coalition on the right or the Olive Tree coalition on the left. Multiparty systems typically involve coalition governments in which two or more parties agree to control the government because of the inability of any single party to regularly gain a majority of seats in the legislature. Many of the countries of Western Europe have multiparty systems, as do many of the newer democracies.

MULTIPARTY SYSTEM
A political party system featuring several parties that are significant actors in the competition for political power.

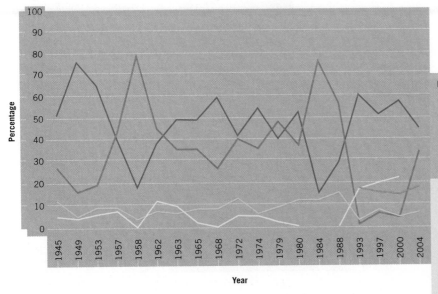

FIGURE 9-2
PARTY REPRESENTATION IN THE HOUSE OF COMMONS, 1945–2004

Legend
— Liberal
— PC and Conservative
— CCF and NDP
— Social Credit and Reform/Alliance
— Bloc Québécois

Notes: PC and Conservative was Progressive Conservative party, 1945–2000; Conservative party, 2004. *CCF and NDP* was CCF, 1945–1958; NDP, 1962–. Social Credit and Reform/Alliance was Social Credit and Ralliement Créditiste, 1945–1980; Reform, 1988–1997; Canadian Alliance, 2000. Independents not shown.

SOURCES: Calculated from *Party Politics in Canada* (8th ed.), by H.G. Thorburn & A. Whitehorn (Eds), 2001, Toronto: Prentice-Hall; and Elections Canada (2004), retrieved July 11, 2004 from www.elections.ca.

ONE-PARTY DOMINANT SYSTEM

A party system in which a single party rules for long periods of time and the opposition parties are not likely to gain the support needed to successfully challenge the dominant party for control of the government.

A **one-party dominant system** is one in which a single party rules for long periods of time and the opposition parties are not likely to gain the support needed to successfully challenge the dominant party for control of the government. For example, the Liberal Democratic Party has governed Japan since the late 1940s, with only a temporary interruption in the 1990s. Typically, one party is able to be dominant in a democratic political system when the opposition to the governing party is divided among a number of parties representing different segments of the electorate. Thus, dominant party systems are usually also multiparty systems, in the sense that there are a number of parties that have significant support. Canada could be considered to have had a one-party dominant system from 1993 to 2003, when opposition to the governing Liberal party was fractured among four parties.[4] Even though the Liberal party obtained only about two-fifths of the popular vote in the three elections in that decade, none of the other parties had the capability to be a serious contender for national power.

Provincial Party Systems

Most Canadian provinces have either two-party or two-plus party systems. Atlantic Canadian provinces have featured two-party competition involving the Liberal and PC parties, although in Nova Scotia the NDP has also become

▶ One-party dominant: Ryutaro Hashimoto is the current leader of Japan's Liberal Democratic Party, which has governed Japan since the late 1940s (except for a temporary interruption in the 1990s). Japan is an example of a one-party dominant system.

[4] The fact that the Liberal party has governed Canada for much of the time since 1896 could be used to argue that Canada has a one-party dominant party system.

a major force in recent years, resulting in a multiparty system. Quebec has usually had a two-party system involving, in recent decades, the Parti Québécois, which favours Quebec sovereignty, and the Quebec Liberal party—though in recent years, the Action démocratique du Quebec (ADQ) has gained a significant proportion of the popular vote. In Ontario, the PC party was dominant in the decades after World War II, but in recent times the province has also had Liberal and NDP governments. It could currently be considered as having a two-plus party system because of the small number of seats held by the NDP. Three of the four Western Canadian provinces feature competition between the NDP on the left and a party on the right (Manitoba's PC party, the Saskatchewan Party, and a conservative Liberal party in British Columbia). In both Manitoba and Saskatchewan, the Liberal party has been able to gain a significant proportion of the vote in recent elections, but few seats in the legislature. Alberta has had a one-party dominant system since the province was established in 1905, with the governing (since 1971) PC party facing generally limited opposition from the Liberal party and, at times, the NDP.

Strengths and Weaknesses of the Different Systems

Two-party systems have the benefit of providing for stable government, as either of the major parties can usually gain a majority of seats in the legislature. This allows the winning party to implement its program and be held accountable for its actions in government. Voters can choose to keep the governing party in office or replace it with the other major party. However, in trying to gain the support of the majority of voters, the two dominant parties may end up becoming so similar that voters are left without a clear choice, and minority viewpoints may be poorly represented.

Two-plus party systems can provide for greater diversity and innovation than two-party systems. Smaller parties can be a source of new ideas and different perspectives. Larger parties may adopt some of their ideas to avoid losing support to a smaller party. For example, in the 1960s and 1970s, the New Democratic Party helped to influence the governing Liberal Party's decisions to adopt various social programs.

Multiparty systems often provide better representation of the various interests and ideologies that exist within a political community than a two-party system. However, if parties only represent various particular interests, there is a danger that the common good of the political community will be ignored. As well, if a multiparty system contains a large number of parties, voters may have difficulty making an informed choice. The coalition governments that are often the product of multiparty systems can have the positive feature of being broadly representative and encouraging greater dialogue and consensus building within government. Coalition governments in countries such as Sweden, Germany, and Switzerland have been stable and effective.

On the other hand, coalition governments in Italy have until recently been unstable, resulting in frequent changes in government. Voters may have difficulty holding a coalition government accountable for its actions if the different parties in the coalition try to blame each other for problems. Since governing coalitions are often formed after an election, voters may not know exactly what governing coalition they are getting with their vote. The choice of a government may be more in the hands of party leaders than in the hands of voters.

A one-party dominant system allows for stability and continuity in government. However, without a strong alternative party that is potentially capable of forming a government, the dominant governing party cannot easily be held accountable for its actions. It may become unresponsive to the public, complacent, or corrupt. Moreover, when one party governs for a lengthy period of time, an overly close relationship between the governing party and public officials may develop (Whitaker, 1977).

Ideological Competition

Analyzing a party system in terms of the number of relevant political parties provides only a limited picture of the nature of the party system. To gain a fuller picture, the ideological positioning of the parties needs to be considered.

As can be seen in Table 9-1, the pattern of party competition in terms of the ideological characteristics of the major competitors differs somewhat from country to country. Outside of North America, competition between social democratic parties and conservative parties has been quite common. Although Canadian party politics has often been viewed as basically

TABLE 9-1
PATTERNS OF PARTY COMPETITION

	COMMUNIST	GREEN	SOCIAL DEMOCRATIC	LIBERAL	CONSERVATIVE	EXTREME RIGHT	NATIONALIST
			IDEOLOGICAL TYPE				
Canada			New Democrats	Liberal	Conservative		Bloc Québécois
U.S.				Democratic	Republican		
U.K.			Labour	Liberal-Democratic	Conservative		
Germany	Democratic Socialist	Green	Social Democrats	Free Democrats	Christian Democrats		
France	Communist	Verts/ Génération Ecologie	Socialist		Rally for the Republic; Union for French Democracy	Front National	

Note: Underlining identifies major current contenders for national power. Parties generally receiving less than 5 percent of the popular vote are excluded. Communist parties might be more accurately described as parties that were formerly communist.

non-ideological, the development of newer political parties has led to a re-examination of the traditional brokerage interpretation of Canadian parties (see Box 9-5, Ideology and the Canadian Party System).

Ideology and the Canadian Party System

The Canadian party system has moved to a more ideological direction in recent years, according to a study by William Cross and Lisa Young (2002).

When the pair surveyed members of five major Canadian parties in 2000, a large majority said that a belief in their party's policies was a very important reason for joining the party. Very few indicated that they joined to get a get job or to help their career.

In examining attitudes concerning social tolerance, the laissez-faire economic approach, the powers of provincial governments, and populism, substantial differences were found among the members of different parties. These ideological differences did not exist only for the members of the newer parties; to some extent, there were ideological differences between the members of the Liberal and PC parties.

Of course, even if parties tend to attract members who have differing perspectives, this does not necessarily mean that parties will differ in the image they present to the public or in their actions if elected to govern (Cross & Young, 2002).

Summary and Conclusion

Political parties play a central role in the competition for political power and in the governing of modern democratic states. Some parties developed as a means to help legislators get elected as the right to vote expanded. Other parties were created by groups outside the legislature to promote a particular ideological perspective or interests that were not adequately represented in the legislature. In pursuit of political power, parties have often moved away from representing particular perspectives or interests. Nevertheless, parties often reflect, sometimes in subtle ways, differing perspectives and interests.

The Canadian party system has undergone dramatic changes in recent times, particularly with the near-collapse of the PC party in the 1993 election, the rapid rise of new political parties, and the creation of a new Conservative party in 2003. Canadian party politics has become less oriented to brokering different interests; instead, the challenge of new parties made party support and representation more regionalized and the competition of parties more ideological. It is unclear whether the merger of the Canadian Alliance and PC party will result eventually in a return to a more brokerage-based, national party system. Although a major competitor to the Liberal party in the rest of Canada, the new Conservative party has almost no support in Quebec.

Political parties have often been thought of as a crucial link between citizens and government. A competitive party system allows voters to choose which set of politicians should be responsible for governing and which party's platform they prefer. However, parties have often been criticized for being elitist organizations. The involvement of people who join political parties is often limited to canvassing on behalf of the party's candidates during an election campaign. In recent decades, political parties have generally become more democratic in the processes they use to select their leaders and candidates and in the holding of regular party policy conventions. Changes in the regulation of party finance in Canada and a number of other countries have helped to reduce the influence on political parties of big business and wealthy donors. Nevertheless, parties still tend to be dominated by the leader and a small number of insiders.

Even though many citizens have negative views of political parties and have turned to other means of political involvement, parties are still crucial elements of modern democracies. By choosing among competing parties, voters may be able to hold the government accountable for its actions or inactions and select which program, direction, and vision for the political community that they prefer. Competition among parties can help to prevent the abuse of power and allow ordinary citizens some ability to influence the direction of the political community.

By raising the concerns of those who might not otherwise be heard and developing policies to gain their support, political parties may also facilitate the development of a more inclusive and egalitarian political community. Where parties are strong, the poor, less educated, and disadvantaged elements of society are more likely to vote and thus, potentially, to be treated as a significant political force. Parties are also important in aggregating (putting together) the interests and perspectives of different sectors of society and trying to develop a coherent programme for governing that will have wide support. Other organizations, such as interest groups, can be effective in articulating particular interests, but are less concerned about aggregating different interests. Thus, it has been argued that parties are essential "to bring interests together for the common good" (Dalton & Wattenburg, 2000, pp. 283–284).

The conflicts generated by parties in their competitive pursuit for power can divert attention from the real problems that a political community faces. Instead of debating about possible solutions to problems, political parties may focus on trivial matters, mislead the public about the positions taken by the contending parties, or turn rational discussion into emotional arguments. On the other hand, by seeking the support of those whose problems would otherwise be ignored in political life and by creating platforms that appeal widely, parties may bridge societal divisions and mobilize those with little political power. Thus, in the pursuit of power, political parties can potentially serve the common good.

Key Terms

Discussion Questions

1. Is there a particular party (or more than one party) that seems to reflect your viewpoints and interests (such as province, social class, gender, or age group), or do you feel that none of the major parties really represent you?

2. Are all the major interests and viewpoints in Canada adequately represented by the major Canadian parties?

3. Is it important for political parties to be democratic in their organization? How should parties choose their leaders?

4. Is the common good better served by two broad catch-all parties, or by a multiparty system in which a variety of different societal interests and ideological perspectives are represented?

5. Are political parties a necessary and desirable aspect of democratic politics?

Further Reading

Bickerton, J., Gagnon, A.-G., & Smith, P.J. *Ties that bind: Parties and voters in Canada*. Don Mills: Oxford University Press, 1999.

Campbell, C., & Christian, W. *Parties, leaders, and ideologies in Canada*. Toronto: McGraw-Hill Ryerson, 1996.

Carty, R.K., Cross, W., & Young, J. *Rebuilding Canadian party politics*. Vancouver: UBC Press, 2000.

Cross, W. *Political parties*. Vancouver: UBC Press, 2004.

Thorburn, H.G., & Whitehorn, A. (Eds.). *Party politics in Canada* (8th ed.). Toronto: Pearson Education Canada, 2001.

Wolinetz, S. (Ed.). *Political parties*. Aldershot, UK: Ashgate, 1997.

Chapter 10

ELECTIONS, ELECTORAL SYSTEMS, AND VOTING BEHAVIOUR

PHOTO ABOVE: During the 2000 U.S. election, Republican George W. Bush beat the Democratic party candidate, Vice-President Al Gore, even though Bush received fewer votes than Gore, and despite irregularities in the Florida ballots and voting procedures. The U.S. Supreme Court rejected Gore's appeal for a recount—thus awarding the presidency to Bush.

CHAPTER OBJECTIVES

After reading this chapter you should be able to:

1. discuss what is needed for elections to be considered free and fair

2. explain and evaluate the different types of electoral systems

3. evaluate the usefulness of election campaigns in helping people decide how to vote

4. outline the different factors that explain voting behaviour

The 2000 U.S. presidential contest was so close that the outcome was in dispute for many weeks. In the end, Republican party candidate George W. Bush, former governor of Texas and the son of former American President George H.W. Bush, beat the Democratic party candidate, Vice-President Al Gore— despite receiving about 500 000 fewer votes.

In the American election system, when members of the public cast their votes for their presidential choice, their votes do not directly result in the election of the president. Instead, the president is selected by members of an electoral college, who are committed to voting for the presidential candidate who has won the most votes in a particular state.* Even if one candidate wins a state by only a tiny margin, that candidate (in almost all states) will receive all the electoral college votes for that state. The votes of the electoral college are, therefore, a distorted reflection of the votes cast by American voters. As a result of the 2000 election, Bush received 271 electoral college votes while Gore received 267. A few hundred votes in the state of Florida made the difference in the choice of Bush as president.

Afterwards, arguments raged concerning irregularities in the Florida vote, where the ballots were not properly designed and inconsistent procedures were used for counting ballots. State Republican politicians, led by Governor Jeb Bush, George Bush's brother, controlled the election procedures but were unwilling to allow a full recount of votes. In the end, the U.S. Supreme Court, in a five to four decision, rejected Gore's appeal for a recount, thus in effect awarding the presidency to George Bush. Gore accepted the Supreme Court decision and encour-

aged Americans to support the president; others, such as filmmaker Michael Moore, viewed Bush as an illegitimate president. An analysis of the Florida vote commissioned by some of the major media later concluded that Gore should have received Florida's electoral college votes and therefore become president.

Elections are a central feature of democracies, providing citizens with the opportunity to choose their representatives and their government. However, as the Bush–Gore case illustrates, questions about the fairness of election procedures may arise. This chapter examines such questions, as well as issues such as whether election campaigns help voters make an informed decision about the governing of their political community, why voters choose particular parties and candidates, and what influences the outcome of elections.

The electoral college does not actually meet and has no function other than selecting the president and vice-president. Members of the electoral college send in their vote. There is no legal commitment for electoral college members, who are generally selected by the political parties, to vote for a particular candidate, but with rare exceptions they always vote for the candidate who won the most votes in their state. A majority of electoral college votes is needed to elect the president. If there is no majority, then the president is chosen by the House of Representatives, the lower chamber of the American Congress. This is highly unlikely, as the U.S. has a two-party system.

DEMOCRATIC ELECTIONS

Nearly all countries now hold elections. However, elections vary greatly, from those that can be considered democratic in terms of ensuring that voters have a free and fair choice to those that coerce or manipulate voters into endorsing a dictatorial ruler (see Box 10-1, An Undemocratic Election). The practice of elections in many countries, particularly newer democracies, falls between these two extremes. Even long-established democracies do not necessarily provide a completely fair election process. We will examine what constitutes a democratic election, and then consider the different electoral systems that translate votes into legislative representation.

The Basic Principles

Freedom House
www.freedomhouse.org

There are several basic features of democratic elections.[1] Voters should be able to choose freely among candidates and parties seeking office. To protect voters from intimidation, democratic countries use a secret ballot. To ensure meaningful competition, all citizens should have the right to run in elections, and all political parties should have the right to nominate candidates and campaign on their behalf. In other words, an election is undemocratic if only those candidates authorized by the state or other institutions are allowed to run, or if some parties are prevented from participating in an election campaign. Sometimes, however, even democratic countries have banned extremist political parties that are viewed as a threat to the democratic system. For example, in the past Canada banned the Communist party, and Germany continues to ban Nazi parties.

Democratic elections are based on the principle of "one person, one vote," with each vote having the same value. Thus, we usually only consider a system of elections fully democratic if there is universal suffrage—that is, all adult citizens have the right to vote regardless of such characteristics as gender, ethnicity, wealth, or education. Further, it should be easy for citizens to exercise their right to vote; for example, provisions should be made for students and others who are away from home on election day to vote, and the use of difficult registration requirements should be avoided. Ensuring that each vote has the same value can be controversial, as persons in rural and remote areas worry that their interests will not be given due attention because of the large numbers of voters in the major cities. As well, elected representatives will have a more difficult task in meeting their constituents in a large, sparsely populated region.

Voters need to be provided with useful information if their vote is to be meaningful. Parties and candidates must have the opportunity to get their

---

[1] This discussion of democratic elections is based in part on the indicators used by Freedom House (n.d.), retrieved May 16, 2004, from www.freedomhouse.org.

message to voters. As noted in Chapter 9, this may involve putting some limits on spending to ensure that one party or candidate does not dominate the campaign, and providing some subsidies to help parties and candidates that do not have the support of wealthy contributors. Extensive government advertising during an election campaign should be avoided, as it could give the governing party an unfair advantage. The media should provide fair and extensive coverage of the contending parties and candidates.

In a number of countries, violence often accompanies elections. For example, as they registered voters in 2004 for Afghanistan's first election, officials faced numerous attacks by Taliban guerrillas seeking to disrupt and delegitimize the election. Likewise, in countries with deep social divisions, where some groups fear serious consequences if a party representing an opposing section of society should win, violence may be used to intimidate candidates from running and voters from casting their ballots.

To ensure that elections are conducted fairly, it is important that the process be overseen by an independent commission. Likewise, the drawing of

Elections Canada
www.elections.ca

BOX 10-1
An Undemocratic Election

In 2002, Iraqis were called on to vote as to whether Saddam Hussein should be given another seven-year term as president. According to an official spokesperson, all 11 445 638 eligible citizens voted and every one of them voted *yes*. Saddam thus succeeded in surpassing the 99.95 percent support that he had received in the 1995 election.

Not surprisingly, outside observers cast doubt on the credibility of the results. There were no booths to provide privacy to voters. Ballots were numbered in such a way that voters' identities could be ascertained by government officials. Banners of Saddam were displayed inside and outside polling stations. People were observed stuffing multiple ballots into ballot boxes. The results of the election were announced before all of the votes had been counted. Although Saddam claimed he had the complete support of the people, there was no way of knowing if that support was genuine.

Saddam's 100% victory? Outside observers cast doubt on the credibility of the results of the 2002 presidential election in Iraq. Although Saddam Hussein was awarded another seven-year term as president, and he claimed he had the complete support of every single voter, the results were highly suspect.

GERRYMANDERING
The manipulation of the division of the country into constituencies so as to benefit a particular party.

Administration and Cost of Elections Project
www.aceproject.org

International Institute for Democracy and Electoral Assistance
www.idea.int

the boundaries of constituencies should be done by an independent body to prevent **gerrymandering**, the manipulation of the division of the country into constituencies so as to benefit a particular party. The contending parties and candidates should be able to observe the casting and counting of votes. Foreign observers have played a role in ascertaining if elections have been properly conducted in newly democratic countries. Losing candidates should have the right to request a recount and to appeal to the courts or an independent body if there is evidence that the election rules have not been properly followed. Interestingly, the adoption of electronic voting systems in some parts of the United States is raising concerns about the possibility of electoral fraud by tampering with ballot software. Without physical ballots, recounts may be impossible and the accuracy of vote tabulations may be questioned.

Elections are only meaningful if those elected have real power. In some countries, elected legislative bodies simply legitimate the decisions of a monarch or dictator. In other countries, the military will step in if it disagrees with decisions taken by elected officials.

A REGULAR VOTE To ensure that those elected to office are held accountable to the people, it is important that elections be held on a fairly regular basis. In most democratic countries, the election of representatives occurs at least once every four or five years, as in Canada. A small number of countries, including Australia and New Zealand, require elections be held within a three-year period.

Most parliamentary systems do not have fixed dates for elections. In Canada, the prime minister can at any time request that the governor general authorize the holding of an election. This flexibility in the timing of elections potentially gives an advantage to the prime minister's party, as an election can be called when public opinion poll results are favourable. It can allow the governing power to call an election to settle a contentious issue— for example, the 1988 Canadian election was called to overcome opposition to the Canada–U.S. Free Trade Agreement. An election will also be called when the governing party is defeated in the elected legislature on a vote of non-confidence or on a crucial aspect of its agenda. In these circumstances, the timing of the election will not necessarily be favourable to the governing party.

A few parliamentary systems, including Norway and Sweden, hold elections at fixed intervals except in unusual circumstances. In Canada, British Columbia and Ontario have adopted legislation setting the dates of elections at four-year intervals; some other provinces are considering following suit. In presidential systems, elections are typically held at fixed intervals; for example, presidential elections in the United States are held every four years. Members of the House of Representatives hold their positions for two years, while senators are elected for a six-year term.

TYPES OF ELECTORAL SYSTEMS

Beyond examining whether elections allow voters a free choice and are conducted fairly and honestly, it is important to understand the **electoral system** that is used to translate the votes that people cast into the composition of the legislature and the selection of the government. The choice of electoral system raises controversial questions about the fairness of elections as well as the effects of elections on politics and governing.

There are four basic types of electoral systems:

- single-member plurality
- majoritarian
- proportional representation
- mixed-member proportional

As Table 10-1 indicates, the single-member plurality (SMP) and the proportional representation (PR) systems are the most common.

Single-Member Plurality

In a **single-member plurality (SMP) system,** people in each geographical constituency elect a single representative to the legislature. The candidate with the most votes is elected, regardless of whether or not that candidate received the majority of votes.

ELECTORAL SYSTEM
The system used to translate the votes that people cast into the composition of the legislature and the selection of the government.

SINGLE-MEMBER PLURALITY (SMP) SYSTEM
An electoral system in which voters in each geographical constituency elect a single representative to the legislature. The candidate with the most votes is elected, regardless of whether or not that candidate received the majority of votes.

TABLE 10-1
ELECTORAL SYSTEMS, SELECTED COUNTRIES

Note: Australia uses a preferential ballot for elections to its House of Representatives and single transferable vote for its Senate elections.

SINGLE-MEMBER PLURALITY	RUNOFF	PREFERENTIAL BALLOT VOTE	SINGLE TRANSFERABLE	MIXED MEMBER PROPORTIONAL	PROPORTIONAL REPRESENTATION
Britain	Egypt	Australia	Australia	Bolivia	Argentina
Bangladesh	France		Ireland	Germany	Austria
Botswana	Iran		Malta	Hungary	Belgium
Canada	Ukraine			Italy	Brazil
Jamaica				Japan	Czech Rep.
India				Mexico	Denmark
Malaysia				New Zealand	Israel
Nigeria				Russia	Greece
Pakistan				South Korea	Netherlands
United States					South Africa
					Sweden
					Turkey
					Spain
					Poland
					Switzerland

SOURCE: *Compiled from International Institute for Democracy and Electoral Assistance, retrieved May 16, 2004, from www.idea.int/.*

Canada, like most countries that have been influenced by Britain, has always used the SMP system.[2] The single-member plurality system (sometimes referred to as a "first-past-the-post" system) provides a simple method for a representative to be chosen from a particular area. Elections, however, involve more than choosing a representative for a legislative body. They are also very important for choosing a party to form a government for the country, and thus involve choices among competing parties. The SMP system has a strong tendency to inaccurately translate the votes a party receives across the country into the seats that it receives in the legislature (see Box 10-2, Distortion in the Single-Member Plurality System). In particular, the SMP system usually gives an added boost in representation to the leading party. In the 1993, 1997, and 2000 elections, for example, the Liberal party received a majority of seats in the House of Commons based on about two-fifths of the votes cast.

In some cases, the effect of the SMP system has been to allow the governing party to completely dominate the legislature, thus hindering the

BOX 10-2

Distortion in the Single-Member Plurality System

Imagine a very small legislature consisting of five seats. The hypothetical results of voting in each of the five constituencies are as follows:

Party A would win all the seats despite having the support of only 40 percent of the voters, while the substantial proportion of the population who voted for parties B or C would be unrepresented.

	CONSTITUENCY #1	CONSTITUENCY #2	CONSTITUENCY #3	CONSTITUENCY #4	CONSTITUENCY #5
Party A	40%	40%	40%	40%	40%
Party B	39%	39%	39%	39%	39%
Party C	21%	21%	21%	21%	21%

[2] Historically in Canada, there were a small number of two-member constituencies at the national level and in some provinces. They were elected in a similar manner to single-member constituencies, with the candidates getting the most votes elected. British Columbia used a preferential voting system for the 1952 provincial election. Some Canadian cities have, in the past, used proportional representation systems.

provision of effective opposition to the governing party. For example, the 1987 New Brunswick provincial election resulted in the Liberal party winning all of the seats based on its 60 percent share of the vote. Similarly, in the 2001 British Columbia provincial election, the Liberals won seventy-seven of the seventy-nine seats based on 57.6 percent of the vote. However, as Table 10-2 indicates, the distorting effects of the SMP were insufficient to give a majority of seats to the Liberal party in the 2004 Canadian election.

Although the SMP system generally favours the most popular party at the expense of smaller parties, parties that have their support concentrated in particular geographical areas tend to do much better than parties with modest support spread across the country. In the 2004 election, for example, the Bloc Québécois benefited from the workings of the SMP system. The NDP, on the other hand, has received a substantially smaller proportion of seats than votes in every national election. Parties with relatively low levels of support are generally unable to gain representation in the legislature. The 580 000 votes that the Green party received in the 2004 Canadian election did not result in its representation in the House of Commons.

The SMP system also tends to exaggerate the regional character of the parties in the legislature. For example, the Conservative party obtained sixty-eight of its ninety-nine seats in the 2004 election from Western Canada, giving the party a strongly Western Canadian character, even though 56 percent of its votes came from other parts of Canada. Likewise, the Liberal party has gained a majority of its seats from Ontario in each election since 1993—but a majority of its votes have come from other provinces.

Occasionally, the distorting effects of the electoral system can result in the most popular party losing the election. The PC party won the 1979 Canadian election with close to a majority of seats based on 36 percent of the vote, even though the Liberal party obtained 40 percent of the vote. Similarly, in several provincial election elections, including British Columbia (1996), Quebec (1998), and Saskatchewan (1999), the party that received the second-highest number of votes won the election. The 2000 American presidential election, discussed at the start of this chapter, illustrates the same basic principle: George W. Bush barely won the presidency, even though Al Gore gained

2000 ELECTION				2004 ELECTION			
PARTY	VOTE	SEATS	DIFFERENCE	PARTY	VOTES	SEATS	DIFFERENCE
Liberal	40.8%	57.1%	+16.3	Liberal	36.7%	43.8%	+7.1
Alliance	25.5%	21.9%	−3.6	Conservative	29.6%	32.1%	+2.5
PC	12.2%	4.0%	−8.2	NDP	15.7%	6.2%	−9.5
Bloc	10.7%	12.6%	+1.9	Bloc	12.4%	17.5%	+5.1
NDP	8.5%	4.3%	−4.2	Green	4.3%	0.0%	−4.3
Others	2.3%	0.0%	−2.3	Others	1.3%	0.3%	−1.0

TABLE 10-2

THE IMPACT OF THE SMP ELECTORAL SYSTEM: CANADA 2000 AND 2004

Note: Results for the 2004 election are based on preliminary unofficial figures.

SOURCE: *Calculated from data at Elections Canada, 2004, retrieved July 11, 2004, from www.elections.ca.*

slightly more of the popular vote, because of the "winner take all" basis of the **electoral college.**

Majoritarian Systems

Majoritarian electoral systems are designed to try to ensure that the winning candidate has the support of the majority of voters. For presidential elections, many countries, including France, Russia, and Chile, use a system of **run-off elections** (also known as two-round elections). If no candidate receives a majority of votes, another election is held in which only the top two candidates appear on the ballot. Run-off elections are also used for the election of representatives to the French Assembly. If no candidate obtains a majority of votes, a second election is held in which candidates who received at least one-eighth of the vote on the first ballot can remain on the second ballot. The candidate with the most votes on the second ballot wins. Usually the winning candidate obtains a majority because parties often make deals so that only two candidates appear on the second ballot.

Another type of majoritarian electoral system is **preferential voting** (also known as the alternative vote). Instead of marking × beside the name of the candidate one prefers, voters can rank candidates in order of preference. If no candidate has a majority of first preferences, the candidate with the least votes is dropped and the second preferences of those who voted for that candidate are added to the votes of other candidates. This process continues until one candidate has a majority.

Proportional Representation

Both the single-member plurality and majoritarian electoral systems typically result in legislatures that do not reflect the overall distribution of support for political parties. To deal with this issue, many countries, including most continental European countries, have adopted some form of **proportional representation** (PR), in which the proportion of seats a party receives in the legislature reflects the proportion of votes it has obtained.[3] Using the example of a hypothetical five-member legislature from Box 10-2, if 40 percent of voters supported party A, 39 percent supported party B, and 21 percent supported party C, this would yield two seats for party A, two for party B, and one for party C.

A PR system requires that several representatives be elected from each electoral district. The larger the number of representatives, the more closely the representation of the parties in the legislature will reflect the support each party has in the electorate. In a few cases—the Netherlands, Israel, and

ELECTORAL COLLEGE
A body that elects the president of the United States based on the votes that the presidential candidates won in each state.

MAJORITARIAN ELECTORAL SYSTEM
An electoral system designed to try to ensure that the winning candidate has the support of the majority of voters.

RUN-OFF ELECTION
An election held if no candidate receives a majority of votes; generally, only the top two candidates appear on the ballot to ensure that the winning candidate has a majority of the votes cast.

PREFERENTIAL VOTING
An electoral system in which voters rank candidates in order of preference. If no candidate has a majority of first preferences, the candidate with the least votes is dropped and the second preferences of those who voted for that candidate are added to the votes of other candidates. This process continues until one candidate has a majority.

PROPORTIONAL REPRESENTATION (PR) SYSTEM
An electoral system in which the proportion of seats a party receives in the legislature reflects the proportion of votes it has obtained.

[3] For a description of the different formulas that are used to calculate how seats are distributed among parties, see Blais and Massicote (2002).

Slovakia—the country as a whole is treated as a single district, such that representatives do not represent a particular geographical area.

In some countries that use PR (for example, Spain, Norway, and South Africa), individual legislators are selected based on the order of their placement on a list of candidates drawn up by each party. In our hypothetical five-member legislature, the top two names on party A's list of five candidates would become legislators. Other PR systems (for example, Sweden, Poland, and Brazil) allow voters to indicate which candidate they prefer in the list of the party that they have chosen to vote for.

A PR system, by quite accurately reflecting the support for parties by voters, almost always results in a situation where no single party has a majority of seats in the legislature. Thus, PR systems typically involve **coalition government,** where two or more parties share in governing. PR systems also often result in a substantial number of parties being represented in the legislature. To try to prevent an overly complex party system in the legislature and keep small extremist parties or parties representing very narrow interests from gaining a voice in legislature, many countries with a PR system require that parties obtain a certain percentage of the popular vote as a prerequisite for gaining legislative seats. For example, the minimum threshold to gain representation is 4 percent in Norway and 3 percent in Greece.

Although a PR system provides for more accurate representation of voter support for political parties than other electoral systems, it may reduce the strength of the link between a legislator and his or her constituency. Multimember constituencies tend to be much larger than single member constituencies, and PR systems tend to focus on representation by party.

Mixed Member Proportional

To try to combine the benefits of a single member representing a particular constituency with an accurate translation of votes into seats, some countries have adopted a mixture of SMP and PR systems, termed a **mixed member proportional system** (MMP). Those who advocate changing Canada's SMP system often propose an MMP system (see Box 10-3, Changing Canada's Electoral System).

In MMP systems, voters cast one vote for the party they prefer and one vote for the candidate they prefer. Some legislators are elected to represent particular constituencies, based on gaining the most votes in that constituency. Others (about one-half of the legislators in the case of Germany) are selected so as to make the overall representation of the parties in the legislature proportional to the votes received by each party in the election. In effect, the selection of representatives by PR in most MMP systems is used to compensate parties that were hurt by the workings of SMP (this is termed a compensatory system). In the MMP systems used in Japan and Russia, however, part of their legislative body is elected by SMP and the other part by PR (this

COALITION GOVERNMENT
A form of government in which two or more parties jointly govern, sharing the cabinet positions.

Fair Vote Canada
www.fairvotecanada.org

MIXED MEMBER PROPORTIONAL (MMP) SYSTEM
An electoral system in which voters cast one vote for the party they prefer and one vote for the candidate they prefer. Some legislators are elected to represent particular constituencies based on gaining the most votes in that constituency, while others are elected based on the popular vote received by their party.

BOX 10-3

Changing Canada's Electoral System

A number of Canadian political scientists and other observers of Canadian politics have advocated modifying or changing Canada's single member plurality (SMP) electoral system. Concerns have often focused on the effects of SMP in heightening regional divisions (Cairns, 1968).

More recently, adopting some form of PR has been seen as a way of encouraging parties to provide for greater representation for women and minority groups. In countries with a PR system, parties are often more likely to make their candidate lists more representative of different social groups than in countries with SMP systems, where constituency party associations are usually responsible for choosing candidates.

The leading political parties have had limited interest in electoral system change because the SMP system works to their political advantage. As well, until recently there was relatively little public pressure for change. However, there has been growing interest in electoral reform. At the time this textbook was written, British Columbia, Saskatchewan, Ontario, Quebec, New Brunswick, and Prince Edward Island were considering electoral system change. The Quebec government, for example, promised to introduce legislation in 2004 to establish an MMP system, while the Prince Edward Island Electoral Reform Commission recommended that an element of proportionality be added through either a mixed member proportional system or a single transferable vote.

At the national level, a report of the Law Commission of Canada (2004) tabled in the House of Commons recommended that an MMP system similar to that of Scotland be adopted.* In this proposal, two-thirds of the seats in the House of Commons would be filled by the candidates who had received the most votes in their single-member constituencies, while votes for the parties would be used to select the other members, who would represent provinces (or regions within Ontario and Quebec) on a compensatory basis. During the 2004 election campaign, NDP leader Jack Layton stated that a commitment to adopting PR would be a condition for the NDP's support of a minority government.

Another Commonwealth country, New Zealand, switched from a single-member plurality system to MMP in 1993 after two consecutive elections in which the party with the most votes did not win the election. Changing the electoral system had major effects on politics and government. Since adopting MMP, New Zealand has had coalition governments and there has been greater diversity in the legislature as more parties have been able to gain representation.

*See the Law Commission of Canada's report on electoral reform at www.lcc.gc.ca/en/themes/gr/er/er_report/er_report_toc.asp.

is referred to as a parallel system). The overall result for party representation in parallel systems is not as proportionate as in compensatory MMP systems.

The **single transferable vote** (STV) used in Ireland and Australian Senate elections could also be viewed as a variation on the proportional representation system. Voters mark their preferences for candidates in a multimember constituency. Candidates receiving a certain proportion of the vote are declared elected. The second preferences of votes that are surplus to what the winning candidates need are then transferred to candidates who have not reached the quota. The process is continued until all seats in the constituency are filled (Blais & Massicotte, 2002). Unlike proportional representation systems, STV focuses on the choice of candidates rather than parties. Indeed, it encourages competition for votes among the candidates of the same party, thus potentially contributing to tensions within a party. However, like PR systems, it generally results in a reasonably accurate translation of the voters' party preferences into party legislative representation.

ELECTION CAMPAIGNS

Parties, leaders, and candidates have many potential ways of appealing to voters for support. Pippa Norris (2002) distinguishes between three types of campaigns:

- premodern campaigns
- modern campaigns
- postmodern campaigns

Premodern Campaigns

Premodern campaigns were characteristic of the democratic countries until the 1960s or 1970s. They involved considerable personal contact with the voters and campaigning was largely localized. Party volunteers canvassed their neighbourhoods, seeking to determine who supported their candidate so that they could ensure that their supporters voted on election day. Leaflets were dropped in mailboxes and supporters were encouraged to put up signs. National leaders traversed the country by train, greeting supporters at the railway station in small communities and holding rallies in the larger centres. National campaign organizations were small, with the leader and a few experienced party advisers establishing the general direction of the campaign.

Modern Election Campaigns

Modern election campaigns are more sophisticated. Extensive public opinion polling is used to provide the basic information needed to develop campaign strategies. Professional consultants, including experts in advertising and marketing, largely determine how the campaign will be conducted and the kinds of appeals that will be made to the voters. Modern campaigns are more centrally coordinated or controlled than premodern campaigns. Creating favourable "photo ops" of the leader that will be picked up by the national television news broadcasts is of great importance. As well, short, attention-getting television advertisements are a central feature of modern election campaigns. Instead of appealing primarily to the party faithful, the goal of the modern campaign is to appeal to a broader, national audience. The more

SINGLE TRANSFERABLE VOTE (STV)
An electoral system in which voters mark their preferences for candidates in a multimember constituency. Candidates receiving a certain proportion of the vote are declared elected. The second preferences of votes that are surplus to what the winning candidates need are then transferred to candidates who have not reached the quota. The process is continued until all seats in the constituency are filled.

localized and personalized techniques of the premodern campaign continue to be used, but they are not of central importance in the modern campaign (Norris, 2002).

Waging a modern election campaign requires substantial amounts of money and access to professional expertise. Particularly in the United States, an industry of professional campaign consultants has developed. American-based campaign professionals have been hired by parties in a number of countries to assist in running their campaigns. However, in some countries, legal regulations prevent the full adoption of modern campaign techniques. For example, a number of countries, including the United Kingdom, France, and Belgium, do not allow paid political advertising on television. Instead, most countries provide longer, free-time television broadcasts to the parties (Norris, 2002).

Postmodern Campaigns

Norris suggests that a new postmodern style of campaigning is currently developing. New forms of communication like the Internet allow a return to more interactive and personalized styles of political communication. Specialized television channels and computerized direct mail allow campaigners to direct specific messages to targeted groups. Norris argues that we are moving towards "the permanent campaign, in which the techniques of electioneering become intertwined with those of governing" (2000, p. 147). The interactive nature of postmodern campaigning may help the public to become more informed and help parties to be more responsive to the public. However, a permanent campaign could result in a more intense and continual manipulation of the public.

ELECTION CAMPAIGNS AND INFORMED CHOICE

Ideally, elections allow people to choose among parties offering different platforms or directions for the country, and thus affect the way the country is governed. Political parties nowadays put their platforms on their web sites and carry their basic message through advertising. Candidates try to meet as many of their constituents as possible during the election campaign. The mass media provide extensive coverage of election campaigns.

Political parties, however, do not always clearly state their views on major issues during election campaigns. Because parties want to appeal to a diverse set of voters, they are often reluctant to take clear positions that might be viewed negatively by a significant group of voters. Instead, vague statements about how they are going to make the political community great are often combined with sharp attacks on their opponents. Much of the 2004 Canadian election campaign, for example, consisted of each party attacking one or more of the other parties rather than explaining what it would do if elected.

◀ Do campaigning politicians tell us what they will really do if elected?

Parties usually make a variety of specific promises during an election campaign. However, voters cannot be certain that the promises will actually be carried out. For example, during the 2003 Ontario election, Liberal leader Dalton McGuinty signed a written promise not to raise taxes. After the party was elected, the Liberals claimed that the provincial government's finances were much worse than had been portrayed by the defeated PC government. The Ontario government's 2004 budget included an increase in taxes in the form of health care premiums.

The short, often thirty-second television advertisements that have become a major feature of modern election campaigns do not provide detailed information. Rather, they often rely on repeating a simple slogan or playing on people's fears (see Box 10-4, Negative Campaign Ads). The emphasis in modern campaigns on the party leaders can mean that consideration of the policy directions proposed by the parties is limited. The televised leaders' debates that have become a regular feature of election campaigns in most countries do potentially provide an opportunity for the voters to compare the arguments of the different parties as well as some of the qualities of the leaders. However, leaders' debates in Canada have sometimes degenerated into shouting matches. Finally,

BOX 10-4

Negative Campaign Ads

Negative advertising plays on voters' fears—but its success is unclear.

In the 1988 American presidential election campaign, television ads for George Bush Sr. featured images of convicted rapist Willie Horton, an African-American who had escaped while on furlough from jail. The ads went on to claim that Bush's opponent, Governor Michael Dukakis of Massachusetts, had furloughed 268 convicts who went on to commit rape and murder. Although the claim was false, its appeal to the fears and racism of voters is often thought to have contributed to Bush's victory.

Negative advertising has also been present in Canadian election campaigns. For example:

- A 1988 Liberal election advertisement depicted the erasing of the border between Canada and the United States as part of strongly negative attacks on the Canada–United States Free Trade Agreement signed by the PC government.
- The PC party ran a television ad in the 1993 election featuring a close-up of Jean Chrétien's face along with highly negative commentary. The ad, however, strongly backfired. Faced with an angry public outcry over the ad's highlighting of Chrétien's physical disability, the PC party quickly withdrew the ad.
- The Reform party in 1997 ran a television ad featuring images of the three national party leaders who were from Quebec and the Quebec premier with a slash through their faces. The vocal component of the ad stated that there should be "a voice for all Canadians, not just Quebec politicians," and that it was time for a prime minister from outside Quebec.
- The 2000 PC campaign featured an imitation K-Tel commercial asking voters to buy Chrétien's *101 Greatest Lies* CD.
- Liberal party ads in 2004 featured strong attacks on Conservative leader Stephen Harper, such as one that quoted Harper saying, "When we're through with Canada, you won't recognize it," against the backdrop of a Canadian flag disintegrating.

Negative advertising is not necessarily more effective in persuading voters than positive ads that focus on the reasons to vote for a particular party or candidate (Lau, Sigelson, Heldman, & Babbitt 1999). However, viewers are more likely to remember an attack ad than a positive advertisement. Researchers have also found that negative attack ads have the effect of reducing voting turnout, while positive ads slightly increase turnout (Ansolabehere, Iyengar, Simon, & Valentino, 1997). The increasing use of negative advertising may be a contributing factor to the decline in voter turnout as well as to the increasing distrust of politicians and political parties.

as discussed in Chapter 8, coverage of election campaigns in the mass media has often been criticized for avoiding serious discussion of the issues, focusing instead on the horse-race aspect of the election.

Gleaning Useful Information

Although election campaigns can be criticized for being exercises in manipulation, obfuscation, and dishonesty, those who follow a campaign carefully can often gain useful information about the parties' positions on specific issues and their general values. In the 2004 Canadian election campaign, for example:

- The Conservative party advocated major tax cuts and major increases in spending for health care and defence. A thoughtful voter would realize that this would likely result in substantial cuts to other government activities. The Conservatives differentiated themselves from the Liberals and the NDP by favouring greater power and financial resources for provincial governments, and differentiated themselves from all parties by favouring withdrawal from the Kyoto Protocol on global climate change. In addition, the Conservatives were less committed to abortion and homosexual rights than were the other parties. Although the Conservative party's official campaign positions were not as extreme as the other parties claimed, there were clear indications that it favoured a more conservative direction for the country.

- The NDP also differed significantly from most of the other parties. For example, it advocated increased taxes on business and high-income earners to finance expanded social services. It also opposed the involvement of Canada in the American national missile defence system.

- Although all parties promised increased health care spending, the Liberal party differed from the Conservatives and the Bloc in emphasizing that it favoured a substantial role for the Canadian government in setting health care policy rather than leaving most of the responsibility to provincial governments. As well, it favoured the creation of subsidized child care spaces rather than providing a general tax benefit to all parents, as the Conservatives proposed.

- The Bloc advocated reducing the Canadian government's "interference" in Quebec's affairs, took liberal positions on various social issues and, like the NDP and Greens, advocated strong measures to protect the environment.

Canadian Broadcasting Corporation
www.cbc.ca/canadavotes/index.html

Of course, we have to be careful in interpreting the meaningfulness of the parties' campaign rhetoric. The Liberals, for example, have often been criticized for leaning to the left in election campaigns by promising a variety of social programs, such as subsidized child care, while leaning to the right in government by being fiscally conservative. Nevertheless, those who follow election campaigns closely and critically examine campaign rhetoric can gaine a sense of what the different parties stand for. Party differences have been expressed somewhat more clearly in recent Canadian election campaigns than was often the case in the past.

VOTING BEHAVIOUR

Why do people vote the way they do? Who tends to vote for which party? What affects the outcome of elections? Political scientists have devoted much research effort to such questions, particularly by using survey research techniques. However, the answers tend to be complex because a large number of factors can affect voting behaviour.[4] These factors can be divided into two categories (Miller & Niemi, 2002):

- long-term predispositions based on the interests, values, and identifications of voters

- short-term factors related to the circumstances of a particular election

Long-Term Predispositions

Canadian Election Study
www.ces-eec.umontreal.ca

Members of a social grouping, whether based on class, religion, ethnicity, region, or gender, may tend to support a particular party that they associate with the interests or the identity of their group. Thus, one or more major social divisions often affect the long-term patterns of support for different political parties.

CLASS In most countries there is a tendency for class divisions (divisions based on position in the economy or a combination of income, education, and social status) to affect voting behaviour. Most democratic countries have one or more socialist parties, allied formally or informally to labour unions, that are able to gain the votes of a substantial proportion of workers. As well, most democratic countries have one or more conservative parties, often informally allied to business interests, that are able to gain the votes of a substantial proportion of the more affluent and business-oriented segments of society. However, there has been a tendency for such differences in voting by class to decline over time as class distinctions have become blurred, the traditional industrial working class has shrunk, and many workers in the richer countries have gained the ability to attain more middle-class lifestyles in times of prosperity.

In the case of Canada, class voting has never been strong at the national level, although class differences are significant in affecting voting behaviour in provincial elections in several provinces. Many Canadians think of themselves more in terms of provincial and ethnic identities than in class terms, and political parties (except, to some extent, the NDP) have not been viewed by the majority of voters as connected to particular classes. Nevertheless, a poll conducted during the 2004 election found that the Conservative party received 39 percent of the votes of those with annual incomes of over one hundred thousand dollars but only 25 percent of those with incomes under twenty thousand dollars. The NDP and Bloc received stronger support from lower- than higher-income voters. Liberal support did not vary substantially across income categories (Ekos, 2004).

---

[4] The discussion of voting behaviour in the following sections is based on the model of Blais, Gidengil, Nadeau, and Nevitte, 2002.

RELIGION In a number of countries, the religious affiliation of voters is somewhat related to their party preferences. For example, in the United States, Catholics are more likely than Protestants to vote for the Democratic party; in Britain, Anglicans are slightly more likely than Catholics to vote Conservative; and in France, those who are not religious are more likely than those who are religious to vote for one of the parties of the left. In Canada, Catholics are generally more likely than Protestants to vote Liberal, although the reverse is true in Newfoundland and Labrador. The continuing significance of religious differences in voting behaviour is a puzzle for some political science researchers, as in most modern democracies political discussion does not often explicitly revolve around religious differences.

CULTURE Ethnic, racial, cultural, and linguistic differences in voting behaviour are apparent in a number of countries that have distinctive groups. For example, a very high proportion of Black Americans vote for the Democratic party. Likewise, a large majority of Canadians of non-European ancestry vote for the Liberal party (Blais, Gidengil, Nadeau, & Nevitte, 2002).

REGIONAL DIFFERENCES In some countries, such as Canada, there are important regional differences in voting behaviour. The support for different parties varies substantially across Canada, reflecting not only differences in culture and the economy in different parts of the country, but also a tendency to evaluate governments and political parties in terms of how good or bad they are for the interests of the province or region one resides in. The development of regional parties in 1987 and 1990 (the Reform party and the Bloc Québécois) increased regional differences in voting behaviour.

GENDER DIFFERENCES The differences in voting behaviour between women and men have attracted considerable interest in recent years. However, gender differences in voting behaviour are generally quite small. In some countries, there is a tendency for women to be more likely than men to vote for conservative (or religious) parties than men. In other countries, women, particularly younger women, are more likely to vote for liberal or moderate leftist parties (Dalton, 2000).

The gender gap (female–male differences in party support) is particularly evident in the United States: since 1980 women have been somewhat more likely to vote for the Democratic party than the Republican party. For example, in the 2000 American presidential election, 54 percent of women voted for Democratic candidate Al Gore, as compared to 42 percent of men (Norris, 2001). In Canada, women have been slightly more likely than men to vote for the Liberal party. In the 1997 and 2000 elections, women were more likely than men to vote for the NDP and considerably less likely than men to vote for the Reform/Alliance parties (Blais et al., 2002). In the 2004 election, the Conservative party did slightly better among men (34 percent in a pre-election poll) than women (28 percent), while the NDP and Liberal parties received slightly more support from women than men (Ipsos-Reid, 2004).

Some analysts have suggested that the gender gap will widen, in part because of the tendency of women to hold different (more liberal or leftist) values on such topics as social programs, free enterprise, military action, and the treatment of criminals (Gidengil, 2003; O'Neill, 2002).

OTHER CHARACTERISTICS AFFECTING VOTING BEHAVIOUR

There are various other social characteristics that are related to differences in voting behaviour in some countries. For example, although age is not usually a major factor in how people vote, Green parties have tended to receive greater support from younger than older voters. In the 2004 Canadian election, senior citizens were more likely than young and middle-aged voters to support the Liberal and Conservative parties. Conversely, the NDP, Bloc, and Green parties drew less support from older voters (Ekos, 2004). Rural voters are often more likely to be supportive of conservative parties than urban voters. In the 2004 Canadian election, the low level of support for the Conservative party in large cities other than Calgary was a major factor in its inability to defeat the Liberal party—only about 20 percent of those voting in Toronto and Vancouver supported the Conservative party (Elections Canada, 2004)

Although social divisions have generally been of declining importance in affecting voting choice in the mature democracies, there are still important differences in the voting patterns of different social groupings. In the case of Canada, region, ethnicity, and religion continue to affect which party people support.

VALUES Studies in a number of countries have found that general values such as equalitarianism and libertarianism, along with how people view themselves in left/right terms, affects their voting choice (Miller & Niemi, 2002). In Canada, a study of voting in the 2000 election found that there was quite a strong relationship between the general values of voters and the party that they supported. Those who voted for the NDP had the greatest tendency to be skeptical of the free-enterprise system, while supporters of the two conservative parties (PC and Alliance) generally had a favourable view of the free-enterprise system. Canadian Alliance voters were also distinctive in their support for traditional moral values. Support for Quebec sovereignty clearly distinguished those who voted for the Bloc Québécois from those who voted for the Liberal party in Quebec (Blais et al., 2002).

Thus, regardless of whether voters consciously evaluate the parties in terms of left and right, views on basic political values affect the choices made by voters. Indeed, although values were not emphasized in the 1997 Canadian election campaign, the basic values of voters tended to affect their vote (Nevitte, Blais, Gidengil, & Nadeau, 2000). Values appear to be a long-term predisposition affecting voting rather than being relevant only in particular elections.

PARTY IDENTIFICATION Political scientists often use party identification as a major explanation for why people vote the way that they do. **Party identification** can be thought of as a long-term psychological attachment to a particular political party. It is not simply an agreement with the positions that a party is currently taking, or a preference for a particular leader or candidate representing the party. Rather, it is a long-term feeling of closeness to a party, often developed at quite an early age, that is similar to one's attachment to a particular religious or cultural group.

Those who identify with a particular political party will tend to develop a positive view of the party's leader and candidates, prefer that party's position on the issues of the day, and believe that their party is most competent to handle the tasks of governing. Thus, even though one's vote may be strongly affected by the leaders, candidates, and issues of a particular election, the long-term influence of party identification may lie behind one's evaluation of the particular features of the election.

The theory of party identification is not meant to suggest that an individual's vote is completely determined by long-term party ties. The minority of voters with weak or non-existent ties to a party will frequently shift their votes from election to election, resulting in changing election outcomes. A particularly unpopular party personality or issue position may alienate or turn off even some strong party supporters. However, the theory suggests that deviations from voting for one's party will be only temporary. Party identifiers may occasionally vote for another party while still retaining their original party identification.

Although the theory of party identification is useful in understanding voting behaviour, party identification has been declining in importance in many countries. Fewer people now view themselves as strong party identifiers, and the proportion of people who view themselves as independent or without a party identification has been increasing in recent decades in the mature democracies (Dalton, 2000).

In the case of Canada, 56 percent of eligible voters at the time of the 2000 election considered themselves as fairly strong or very strong identifiers with a particular party at the national level (Blais et al., 2002). At that time, the Liberal party had a substantial lead in party identification, particularly in Ontario and Atlantic Canada (Blais et al., 2002). However, party identifications are not necessarily stable. For example, a study conducted through the 1974, 1979, and 1980 elections found that at some point within that fairly short length of time, about two-fifths of the electorate changed their party identification, either from one party to another, or to and from no identification (Clarke, Jenson, LeDuc, & Pammett, 1996). This quite high level of flexibility in party identification in Canada may in part be explained by the fact

PARTY IDENTIFICATION
A long-term psychological attachment to a particular political party.

that many Canadians identify with different parties in national and provincial politics. As well, the basic differences between the leading political parties have often not been clear cut, making it easier for voters to switch their identification.

Short-Term Influences

If some long-term influences on the vote are declining in significance, short-term factors such as the personalities and issues of an election campaign could hold increasing significance. A substantial proportion of voters now claim that they make their voting choice during the election campaign, and a significant proportion change their vote intention during the campaign. Surveys conducted during the 2000 Canadian election campaign found that about one-third of the voters could be considered to have been affected by the campaign (Blais et al., 2002). A poll conducted at the end of the 2004 Canadian election found that about one-quarter of respondents said that they made up their minds in the twenty-four hours before they voted (Compas, 2004).

It is not easy to determine the relative importance of such factors as the quality of leaders and candidates, the issue positions of the parties, and general perceptions of the quality and competence of the parties, as each factor will tend to influence the others. For example, those who trust a particular party leader may come to agree with the positions that leader's party takes on certain issues, while those who agree with a party's positions may be more inclined to develop a favourable impression of that party's leader and candidates. As well, the importance of different short-term factors may differ from election to election and from country to country, depending upon how the parties appeal to the voters and what the mass media emphasize in their coverage of a particular election.

On a very simple level, Canadian surveys have asked voters whether the party leaders, the constituency candidates, or the parties as a whole are the most important factors in a person's voting decision. Typically, a majority of voters have cited the parties as a whole, with the remainder fairly evenly divided between leaders and candidates. When asked a follow-up question, those who cited parties as a whole tended to be evenly divided between viewing issues and the general approach of the parties as most important. Those who cited leaders as most important were somewhat more likely to claim that the issue positions of the leader are more important than the personal qualities of the leader (Pammett, 2001).

LEADERS Evaluations of the leaders can have a significant effect on which party a voter chooses to support in an election (Blais et al., 2002). However, the evaluations of different party leaders often do not vary widely, thus limiting their effect on the outcome of an election. As well, having a popular leader will not necessarily overcome other disadvantages a party faces. For example, although Joe Clark was the best-regarded leader by the end of the 2000 election campaign (Turcotte, 2001), his PC party only managed a fifth-place finish in terms of House of Commons seats.

In the case of the 2004 election, the proportion of voters thinking that Martin, Harper, or Layton would make the best prime minister quite closely matched the proportion of votes that each party received (SES Research, 2004). More detailed analysis would be required to determine the extent to which evaluations of the leaders had an effect on how people voted. Interestingly, even though polling indicated found that Harper was generally viewed as having won the English-language televised debate (CTV.ca, 2004), this does not seem to have affected the outcome of the election.

CANDIDATES Constituency candidates tend to be less important than leaders in affecting voting behaviour. However, in a closely contested constituency, a strong candidate may make a difference. In American elections, candidates can have very important effects because candidates often distance themselves from their party. Thus, they gain or lose support based, to a considerable extent, on their own characteristics, campaign, and positions. Incumbent members of the U.S. Congress have a very strong ability to win re-election even if their party has become unpopular. Although incumbency can help Canadian MPs in their fight for re-election, it is insufficient to save them if their party has become unpopular—as almost all PC MPs found in 1993, when the party was reduced to two seats in Parliament.

ISSUES Although many voters cite issues as the most important reason for their vote choice, the leading parties often do not stake out clearly different positions on what should be done about important problems. For example, health care was the leading issue in both the 2000 and 2004 Canadian elections, but differences among the parties were subtle rather than clear. Each party proclaimed its commitment to improve the health care system and to spend more money on health care. Liberal accusations that the Alliance (2000) and the Conservatives (2004) favoured privatization of public health care were met with denials of that claim. Likewise, the economic issues such as unemployment and inflation that have been the focus of many campaigns are often discussed by the competing parties in terms of who should be blamed for problems or be given credit for improvements, rather than in terms of the choice of economic policies.

Do voters hold the governing party accountable for its actions in office? An analysis of the 2000 Canadian election found that voters' evaluations of the Liberal government's performance did generally have a significant effect on their electoral choice. (In Quebec, however, voters made their choice primarily based on their views about Quebec sovereignty.) Interestingly, though, the Liberal party was re-elected despite considerable voter dissatisfaction with its record on such key issues as health, taxes, and corruption. Those who were dissatisfied with the Liberal government's record divided their votes among the various opposition parties, thus limiting the negative impact of their dissatisfaction. A complicating factor was the tendency of many voters to blame their provincial government as well as the federal government for problems with the health care system (Blais et al., 2002).

In the case of the 2004 election, the sponsorship scandal involving unaccounted government spending undoubtedly contributed to the decline in Liberal party support. However, the right-wing positions associated with the Conservative party and the Liberal party's ability to raise fears about the consequences of electing a Harper-led Conservative government appear to have swung support away from the Conservative party late in the election campaign. This example shows that holding a governing party accountable for its actions is difficult if voters are not comfortable with voting for an alternative party.

Summary and Conclusion

Elections are often viewed as the central feature of democratic politics. Elections allow voters to choose who will represent them in the legislature. More importantly, elections can provide an opportunity for voters to maintain or remove a government. If parties take different ideological positions, voters can shift the general direction of the government by their choice of which party to support. Although election campaigns feature manipulation of the voters by the competing parties and politicians, elections also tend to bring politicians into closer contact with voters. In anticipation of an election, parties and politicians ask themselves, "What do voters want?" Appealing to the public may have to be modified, however, to ensure the support of the party's financial backers and party activists.

A basic problem with elections is that we are asked to convey a lot of information by our vote. We may use our vote to express which of the competing platforms we prefer, which candidates and leaders we

think are most competent, which party we think is best, what our evaluation is of the current governing party, and so on. The single x on a ballot in a single-member plurality system cannot really convey our views on a variety of matters.

Voters often express a variety of different attitudes, values, preferences, and judgments when they cast their vote. This can make the interpretation of the result of a particular election difficult and controversial. The messages being sent by voters to politicians through an election are often unclear. Statements by a governing party that it has a mandate to carry out particular policies because it won an election can be misleading.

The electoral system can distort the choices made by voters. The single-member plurality electoral system tends to give a boost to the leading party at the expense of the smaller parties. Thus, the governing party often does not have the support of the majority of the voters for the direction in which it plans to take the political community, even though it has the majority of elected representatives on its side. Representation of diverse viewpoints and interests tends to be inhibited because of the discrimination suffered by smaller parties. Systems of proportional representation, although providing fairer representation, typically result in coalition governments that may be difficult to hold accountable for their actions. Elections often result in only small changes in party representation, and major changes in government are less common than in SMP systems. Furthermore, some PR systems do not give voters the opportunity to get rid of undesirable representatives.

When we consider whether elections serve the common good, we should remember that elections are the culmination of the struggle for political power within a democracy. So it should not be surprising that election campaigns are designed to manipulate rather than to enlighten voters. The contending parties in an election are not engaged in deliberation about what is best for the community, but rather are engaged in a competitive struggle for support. In societies with deep social divisions, election campaigns can inflame those divisions, and thus violence sometimes accompanies elections. This is particularly the case for elections that are conducted on a winner-takes-all basis (for

example, elections using the SMP system or presidential elections) in countries where some groups fear serious consequences if a party representing an opposing section of society wins. Finally, in the competitive struggle for votes, parties may try to outbid each other in making costly promises to voters. Promises hastily made in the heat of an election campaign may not result in the common good.

Despite their limitations, elections are important in enabling voters to hold a government accountable for its actions. In democratic systems, voters do sometimes use the opportunity provided by elections to remove governing parties that have become corrupt, incompetent, unresponsive, or lacking in new ideas. If elections are viewed by citizens as free and fair, those elected to govern will normally be viewed as legitimate authorities. Transitions of political power from one group to another can be accomplished smoothly. Overall, then, the common good is served by a system of free and fair elections. Establishing a legitimate government, providing an incentive for governments to be responsive to those they govern, and providing a peaceful mechanism to remove governments that do not deserve to continue to be in power is good for all members of the political community.

Key Terms

Discussion Questions

1. Are Canadian elections free and fair? Should Canada change its electoral system?

2. Should politicians be expected to keep the promises they make in an election campaign? What should happen if they do not?

3. How would you interpret the outcome of the last national, provincial, or local election? Did voters send a message as to the direction that they wanted their government to follow?

4. What criteria have you used, or do you think that you should use, in deciding how to vote? Should you vote for the best leader, the best party, or the best local candidate?

5. Do voters generally make intelligent choices in elections?

Further Reading

Baumgartner, J.C. *Modern presidential electioneering: An organizational and comparative approach.* Westport, CT: Praeger, 2000.

Clarke, H.D., Jenson, J., LeDuc, L., & Pammett, J. *Absent mandate* (3rd ed.). Toronto: Gage, 1996.

Courtney, J.C. *Elections.* Vancouver: UBC Press, 2004.

Duffy, J. *Fights of our lives: Elections, leadership and the making of Canada.* Toronto: HarperCollins, 2002.

Hyde, H. *Promises, promises: Breaking faith in Canadian politics.* Toronto: Penguin, 1997.

Milner, H. *Making every vote count: Reassessing Canada's electoral system.* Peterborough, ON: Broadview Press, 1999.

Pammett. J.H., & Dornan, C. (Eds.). *The Canadian general election of 2004.* Toronto: Dundurn Press, 2005.

Plasser, F., & Plasser, G. *Global political campaigning: A worldwide analysis of campaign professionals and their practices.* Westport, CT: Praeger, 2002.

Chapter 11

INTEREST GROUPS

PHOTO ABOVE: They are gas guzzlers, polluters, and far more prone to flipping and rolling over than cars—but because they meet fuel efficiency and safety regulations set for light trucks more than three decades ago, SUVs are perfectly legal. Automakers and autoworker unions have fiercely resisted attempts to make streets and highways safer by bringing SUVs under the same standards that apply to cars.

CHAPTER OBJECTIVES

After reading this chapter you should be able to:

1. distinguish among different types of interest groups
2. discuss the organization and activities of interest groups
3. examine the influence capabilities of interest groups
4. explain the pluralist and corporatist models of the relationship between interest groups and government

Today it seems as if half the vehicles on the road in North America are either pickup trucks or SUVs—sport utility vehicles. It wasn't always that way. Thirty years ago pickups were working vehicles and SUVs didn't exist. What happened to change this picture was not just the changing tastes of the North American automobile buyer, but also politics.

In the 1970s, North America experienced its first round of rapidly rising fuel prices. This led governments, especially the United States, to set fuel economy standards for vehicles, but they applied only to passenger cars. Trucks, even light trucks like pickups and what would become SUVs, were excluded. The argument was that these were working vehicles and that government should not add unnecessarily to their price by mandating the same fuel efficiency standards that applied to cars. This logic was also extended to safety regulations.

Then automakers created the SUV. The success of Chrysler's 1984 Jeep Cherokee spurred other companies to turn out their own models. SUVs are very profitable for automakers because they are built on existing truck frames, which are also simpler and cheaper to build than passenger car frames. However, SUVs use more gas and are far more prone to flipping and rolling over than cars. Accidents involving SUVs produce a high rate of fatalities, particularly among the passengers of the other vehicle in a collision. Yet SUVs are perfectly legal because they meet the fuel efficiency and safety regulations set for light trucks. Attempts to bring SUVs under the guidelines that apply to cars are met with fierce resistance by automakers, who don't want to see their most profitable lines affected, and autoworker unions, who are happy to see their members making over US$100 000 yearly thanks to the overtime they get building enough SUVs to meet demand.

So a political decision made almost three decades ago to give a break to the tradesmen and farmers, who were then the usual owners of pickups and four-wheel drives, today prevents governments from setting regulations that would make our streets and highways safer. And despite technological advances that can make automobiles more fuel efficient and less polluting, overall motor vehicle fuel efficiency has not improved in North America—in fact, SUVs are a major contributor to the increase in greenhouse gases that cause global climate change. The interest group representing the auto industry has been successful in ensuring that U.S. fuel efficiency standards have not been raised since 1985 and that the SUV loophole remains.

Meanwhile, in Canada the auto industry successfully pressured the Canadian government not to impose fuel efficiency regulations in 1982. In return, it agreed to voluntarily follow the American regulations. Early in 2004, Environment Minister David Anderson demanded that the auto industry move to increase fuel efficiency by 25 percent within six years. The Canadian Vehicle Manufacturers Association (CMVA) claimed that this was too great a challenge and pressured members of Parliament from Ontario, where most of the auto industry is located, to help it resist such policies. David Anderson was dropped from the cabinet in July 2004, and at the time this textbook was written, Stéphane Dion, the new environment minister, had not taken a position on this issue.

This chapter explores interest groups like the CVMA and the ways that they influence the making and implementation of government policies and laws.

POLITICAL CONNECTIONS

Greenpeace. The Canadian Bankers Association. The Canadian Vehicle Manufacturers Association. The Canadian Labour Congress. The Canadian Federation of Students. The Canadian Council of Churches. The Assembly of First Nations. How powerful are such interest groups? Do they help make government responsive to society? Do they help or hinder the achievement of the common good of the political community?

An **interest group** is a group of people who have joined together to pursue common interests. Unlike political parties, whose major objective is to elect members to the legislature and, if possible, form the government, interest groups are generally focused on trying to influence the making and implementation of the laws and policies of a political community. Interest groups are sometimes referred to as pressure groups because they are often involved in applying pressure on political decision-makers and government officials in order to promote their interests.

Many interest groups do not exist exclusively for political purposes. However, in representing the interests of a particular segment of society, interest groups often find political action necessary or desirable to protect or promote the interests of the group (see Box 11-1, Are You a Member of an Interest Group?). For example, the major activities of the Canadian Medical Association include the exchange of medical information and the certification of doctors. However, because the interests of doctors are strongly affected by government policy, the Canadian Medical Association is also active in developing and promoting a variety of policy positions concerning the medical system. The Canadian Automobile Association is well known for the roadside assistance and travel planning that it provides to its motoring members. However, it also involves itself in political action—for example, by urging that the Canadian government establish stricter regulations concerning automobile fuel efficiency.

INTEREST GROUP
A group of people who have joined together to pursue common interests and to try to influence the making and implementation of the laws and policies of a political community.

TYPES OF INTEREST GROUPS

The many thousands of interest groups in modern democracies vary greatly in their characteristics, ability to influence the political process, and the strategies they use to achieve their objectives. One way to make sense of the great variety of groups is to consider the different types of interests and goals that interest groups pursue.

Self-Interest Groups

Many groups have been formed to express specific economic and occupational interests. Groups to promote various business, agricultural, and labour interests were among the first to be established in many countries. Most professions have also developed well-organized interest groups. Other groups

Are You a Member of an Interest Group?

Many people are members of interest groups, even if they did not deliberately join a group to undertake political action.

Sometimes people are not even aware that they are members or supporters of an interest group. For example, at many universities students are required to support the Canadian Federation of Students through their student fees. This organization takes action on such issues as student loans and government financing of post-secondary education. It also supports a variety of national and international causes, such as the anti-globalization protests in Quebec City in 2001 (see the opening vignette in Chapter 1).

Many workers belong to a labour union affiliated with the Canadian Labour Congress, which promotes the interests of workers and the cause of equality. Many small business owners are members of a local branch of the Canadian Chamber of Commerce and/or the Canadian Federation of Independent Business, organizations that regularly lobby government on issues such as taxes. If you are a member of a religious organization, you may be interested in knowing that all major religious organizations have some political involvement. For example, the Canadian Council of Churches, representing the major Christian denominations, has expressed support for the rights of Aboriginal peoples and advocates "just trade" rather than "free trade."

Even if your only organized activity is sports, you may belong to an organization that is involved in political action to try to persuade governments to provide better sports facilities or more assistance to athletes. Women who join the YWCA for its athletic facilities may be surprised to learn that this indirectly makes them members of the National Action Committee on the Status of Women, which has been prominent in pursuing feminist causes.

One final example: the Consumers' Association of Canada claims to speak on behalf of all consumers in Canada, despite its relatively small formal membership. So even if you are not a formal member of an interest group, there may be an interest group that claims to represent you!

Canadian Federation of Students
cfs-fcee.ca

Canadian Ethnocultural Council
www.ethnocultural.ca

SELF-INTEREST GROUP

An interest group whose primary objective is to promote the interests of the interest group and its members.

have been formed to develop, express, and promote the identity, rights, and interests of a particular segment of society—consider the variety of interest groups representing different ethnic groups (for example, the Chinese Canadian National Council). Groups formed to organize recreational activities occasionally undertake political action particularly to gain government assistance: a softball association may try to persuade a city council to improve the condition of ball fields in public parks.

Interest groups whose primary objective is to promote the interests of the group and its members are often referred to as **self-interest groups** (see Table 11-1). However, when pursuing their interests through political action, they usually claim that the policies they hope to obtain will benefit the whole community. Business groups seeking lower taxes will claim that such policies will help to create jobs and prosperity. Ethnic groups may claim that support for maintaining their culture helps Canada to be a more diverse and interesting country. Recreational groups will point to the benefits of better facilities for the health and well-being of the population.

Canadian Council of Chief Executives
ceocouncil.ca

Public Interest Groups

Other groups are less directly connected to the particular interests of a specific part of society or economy, and thus are often referred to as **public interest groups** or citizens' groups (see Table 11-1).

Some groups have been formed to promote a particular perspective on a single issue. For example, pro-choice and pro-life groups are active in promoting their viewpoints on the issue of whether or not abortions should be legal. Mothers Against Drunk Drivers seeks tougher laws concerning drinking and driving.

Other public interest groups have a broader focus in seeking to promote a general perspective and to affect public policy on a variety of issues. For example, the National Citizens Coalition (headed at one time by Stephen Harper) takes a strong free-enterprise perspective, promotes tax cuts, and advocates a reduction of government activity. Democracy Watch terms itself a "citizens' advocacy group" and campaigns for democratic reforms, government accountability, and corporate responsibility. Of course, claims that particular issue positions, general perspectives, or causes are in the interest of the public as a whole are often controversial.

PUBLIC INTEREST GROUP
A group that is concerned with the public interest rather than the particular interests of a specific part of society or economy.

Greenpeace Canada
www.greenpeace.ca

National Citizens Coalition
www.morefreedom.org

Council of Canadians
www.canadians.org

Issue-Oriented Groups

Interest groups are also often analyzed in terms of the extent of their organizational development. Some **issue-oriented groups** spontaneously develop to express the views of people on a particular issue, concern, or grievance (see Table 11-2). For example, in many rural communities, groups have formed from time to time to demand better roads.

Such issue-oriented groups often only have a temporary existence and are not concerned about developing a formal organization. When the issue is

ISSUE-ORIENTED GROUP
An interest group that spontaneously develops to express the views of people on a particular issue, concern, or grievance.

SELF-INTEREST GROUPS	PUBLIC INTEREST GROUPS
Canadian Manufacturers & Exporters	Council of Canadians
Canadian Bankers Association	World Wildlife Fund
Canadian Petroleum Association	Amnesty International
Canadian Vehicle Manufacturers Association	Ontario Public Interest Research Group
Canadian Auto Workers	John Howard Society
Fisheries Council of Canada	Canadian Civil Liberties Association
Canadian Polish Congress	Sierra Club
Canadian Association for the Fifty-Plus	Canadian Nature Federation

TABLE 11-1
SELF-INTEREST AND PUBLIC INTEREST GROUPS

resolved or passions concerning the issue dissipate, such groups often fade away. However, some issue-oriented groups, such as those involved with the abortion issue, have maintained their existence over a considerable length of time, built an organization to carry out the objectives of the group, and developed expertise in promoting their goals.

Institutionalized Interest Groups

Some of the more influential interest groups have developed a formal organization with a stable membership, paid professional staff, access to the government officials who are relevant to their objectives, and regular means to keep their members and the public aware of their activities. Such groups, termed **institutionalized interest groups** (see Table 11-2), typically develop and promote positions on a variety of issues, monitor the activities of government, and develop close working relationships with key government officials. They are regular and long-lasting organizations that, like political parties, are important features of political life (Pross, 1993).

Distinguishing Between Interest Groups and Social Movements

A distinction is usually made between social movements (which will be discussed in Chapter 12) and interest groups, even though these two forms of group activity overlap and cannot always be easily distinguished. Interest groups generally engage in political activity with the goal of influencing government policies. **Social movements** seek major social and political change particularly by acting outside of established political institutions (Martell, 1994). Movements may, like interest groups, seek to change various laws and public policies. However, movements also have broader goals, such as challenging and transforming the values, power relationships, and institutions of society.

The distinction between social movements and interest groups is often not clear because many public interest groups originated in, and are associated

INSTITUTIONALIZED INTEREST GROUP
A group that has developed a formal organization with a stable membership, paid professional staff, access to the government officials who are relevant to its objectives, and regular means to keep its members and the public aware of its activities.

SOCIAL MOVEMENT
A network of groups that seek major social and political change, particularly by acting outside of established political institutions.

TABLE 11-2
ISSUE-ORIENTED AND INSTITUTIONALIZED INTEREST GROUPS

ISSUE-ORIENTED GROUPS	INSTITUTIONALIZED GROUPS
Non-Smokers' Rights Association	Canadian Federation of Agriculture
Mothers Against Drunk Driving	Canadian Bar Association
Campaign Life	Canadian Chamber of Commerce
Canadian Abortion Rights Action League	Canadian Labour Congress
Community Air (opposed Toronto Island Airport link)	Assembly of First Nations
United Students Against Sweatshops	Canadian Federation of Students

with, social movements. There are, for example, many environmental interest groups that focus on influencing public policy concerning a particular set of problems but view themselves as part of a broader environmental movement. The National Action Committee on the Status of Women (NAC) could be viewed as representing the women's movement in Canada, but NAC and its affiliated member organizations also act as interest groups in trying to influence a variety of government policies.

National Action Committee on the Status of Women
nac-cca.ca

MEMBERSHIP IN INTEREST GROUPS

Organized action gives individuals a chance to be influential. That is basically why people join and support interest groups. Modern governments are large and the policy-making process is complex. Few individuals have the contacts and expertise needed to influence decisions. Although your member of Parliament may be willing to listen to your request, and a letter or e-mail to a cabinet minister or the prime minister may result in a computer-generated response, it is highly unlikely that an individual's demands or opinions will affect government decisions. Most individuals are much more likely to influence political decisions through membership in an organization than by trying to influence politicians and government officials themselves.

The Free Rider Problem

Mancur Olson (1965) has questioned whether it is rational for individuals to join and support groups to pursue their political interests. In what he describes as the *free rider problem,* an individual can often enjoy the benefits of the successes of an interest group whether or not that individual is a member or financial supporter. If, for example, an environmental group is successful in a campaign to reduce air pollution, we all take advantage of that action whether or not we supported the group. Rational, calculating individuals may figure that it is to their advantage to let others contribute time and money to the campaign. Of course, if enough people think this way, an interest group will not be able to survive.

The free rider problem is particularly serious for public interest groups because the goals they seek benefit the political community as a whole. Interest groups that seek a benefit for only a small sector of society find it easier to gain and maintain the support of the small number of people who will potentially benefit. For example, the Pulp and Paper Association of Canada may have little difficulty in gaining the support of the few large paper-product corporations in order to fund its efforts to promote the interests of that particular industrial sector. Individual companies can anticipate a direct and substantial impact on their profitability if the organization is successful or not in persuading government to adopt certain policies.

In some cases, the free rider problem is largely irrelevant because membership in an interest group is compulsory. For example, in unionized workplaces, union dues are automatically deducted from paycheques. Likewise, student unions, after obtaining a majority vote of students, have convinced university administrations to require that all students pay union dues. If one wants to practise as a doctor, engineer, or pharmacist, one has to be a member of the appropriate professional association.

Benefits

SELECTIVE INCENTIVE
A particular benefit that is made available to members of an interest group but is not available to the public as a whole.

To some degree, public interest groups can try to avoid the free rider problem by offering some particular benefits (termed **selective incentives**) to their members. Some groups provide a glossy magazine to their members, offer merchandise at reduced rates, and arrange for reduced insurance rates and discounts on car rentals and hotel accommodations. Professional associations provide useful information to their members, arrange conferences, and offer continuing professional education.

Many public interest groups that provide few selective incentives have developed in recent decades, with some attracting very large numbers of members and supporters. People often join or support public interest groups because of the satisfaction that can be achieved by expressing one's values and contributing to the good of the community. Some people also join interest groups for social reasons; that is, because they enjoy interacting and working with like-minded persons. More generally, an increasingly educated population with greater skills and more leisure time is more likely to pursue various causes through political action. Public interest groups are seen by many people as the most effective way to pursue the causes that they believe in. As well, modern communications and transportation technologies have made it easier for groups to organize people around the country and around the world.

Thus, just as many individuals do not join a political party in the hopes of gaining some particular benefit for themselves if their party is elected, so too the lure of individual material benefits does not explain interest group membership. Nevertheless, many public interest groups experience a high turnover in membership and face large swings in membership and financial support as different causes become more popular. Therefore, they often have to devote considerable effort and resources to motivate volunteers and maintain financial solvency.

Encouragement

The development of many interest groups is not only the result of the willingness of individuals to join or support the group. Governments and philanthropic organizations have often provided some financial support and encouragement for the formation and development of interest groups. For example, since the 1960s, Canadian governments have encouraged and helped to finance the development of groups representing segments of the population that were largely unrepresented by well-organized interest groups, including Aboriginals, women, and poor people (Pal, 1993).

Why would governments fund groups representing disadvantaged segments of the population when such groups are often critical of government policies and government's lack of action to deal with their problems? Some governments have hoped to offset the heavy influence that groups representing business and other privileged elements of society are often able to exert on government. This may allow politicians and government officials greater flexibility to act in accordance with their own interests and values.

Particular government departments and agencies may find it useful to have active and vocal interest groups in their policy area so as to assist their struggle with other departments or agencies of government for more funds or new programs. Strong and active environmental groups, for example, may help the Department of the Environment (Environment Canada) convince the rest of government to treat environmental issues more seriously, thus allowing Environment Canada employees to gain the resources and policies they feel are needed for their programs. More recently, as the scope of government has been reduced, government has found it useful and cost-effective to support interest groups that can take on some of the tasks that formerly were carried out by government departments and agencies. Some environmental groups, for example, undertake environmental monitoring, organize clean-ups of streams, and conduct public awareness campaigns to promote pollution prevention.

Sierra Club of Canada
www.sierraclub.ca

Funding and Criticism

It is sometimes thought that interest groups that receive assistance from government will become tame supporters of government. This is not always the case, however. For example, feminist, Aboriginal, and poor people's groups that have received funding from the Canadian government have at times been sharply critical of the policies of the governments that helped fund them. In response, governments have sometimes reduced their funding of groups that are critical of government policies and actions. For example, the Assembly of First Nations (AFN) found that its funding was reduced after it chose a leader who was strongly critical of the government's Aboriginal policies. This, in turn, contributed to the AFN's 2003 election of a new leader, Phil Fontaine, who promised to rebuild good relations with the Canadian government in order to try to secure a substantial increase in funding.

Assembly of First Nations
www.afn.ca

There has been some criticism of government funding of interest groups, particularly by those who feel that some of the groups are too radical. Often ignored in this discussion is the fact that business-oriented interest groups are, in effect, subsidized by government. Businesses can deduct contributions to interest groups and other expenses they incur in trying to influence government in calculating their taxes. In contrast, individuals can only receive a tax credit for contributing to organizations that are deemed to be charitable, which generally excludes organizations that devote significant resources (more than 10 percent of their revenues) to political action.

Faced with criticism of the funding of interest groups, the Canadian government has shifted much of its funding towards indirect assistance, such as paying groups for specific projects, providing assistance for research and participation at public hearings on particular issues, and funding conferences. Such piecemeal support creates uncertainty for groups that are dependent upon government funding, as they have no assurance that they will have the money needed to continue to pay their staff and rent their offices. It also means that their staff has to devote much time to preparing proposals for specific grants.

INTEREST GROUP ORGANIZATION

Most interest groups give the appearance of being democratic organizations. Institutionalized interest groups typically have some regular method for electing their chairperson and board of directors, who oversee the operations of staff members. However, it is often unclear as to whether there is a strong relationship between the members of an interest group and those who act on its behalf. Indeed, some interest groups do not have formal membership. The group's "members" may be simply those who have made a financial contribution in response to an appeal in the mail, subscribed to a magazine produced by the group, volunteered for the group, or expressed an interest in the group's activities (Shaiko, 1999).

Even though some interest groups do not provide a strong vehicle for the voices of their members, there will usually be some shared perspectives between the spokespersons for the group and its members. A group that deviates strongly from the views of its grassroots supporters or members may quickly find that its funds, membership, or magazine subscriptions dwindle, and that it is unable to mobilize volunteers.

Of course, the situation is somewhat different for organizations that have compulsory membership, provide useful services to their members, or, as in the case of cultural, religious, and recreational groups, were not formed to pursue a particular political issue or cause. In these cases, the interest group may be able to retain its members even if the political positions it pursues are not fully in tune with the views of the membership.

INTEREST GROUP ACTIVITY

In analyzing how interest groups go about trying to influence public policy, a distinction may be made between inside and outside strategies (Walker, 1991).

Inside strategies involve interest group leaders developing close contacts with key decision-makers in government and the public service so that influence can be exerted in a quiet fashion. **Outside strategies** involve appealing to the public for support (for example, through the mass media and advertising) and mobilizing members and supporters to put pressure on decision-makers (for example, through petitions, e-mails, and demonstrations).

Inside strategies have the advantage of directly influencing those responsible for developing government policies. They are less likely to stimulate opposition and criticism than outside strategies. However, developing a very close relationship with the government may result in interest group leaders becoming influenced by, and associated with, the policy direction and concerns of the government. Outside strategies, if successful in mobilizing the support of the public, may be useful in pressuring politicians who are worried about their chances for re-election. Outside strategies may also be useful in building and maintaining an active membership-based organization.

Choice of Strategies

Different types of interest groups tend to use different mixtures of strategies. Business and professional associations are more likely to use inside strategies, although they may devote some attention to outside strategies if they find government unsympathetic to their concerns or if other groups mount strong public campaigns against their interests. Unions, public interest groups, issue-oriented groups, and groups that have developed out of social movements are more likely to use outside strategies, although they may find that combining this with inside strategies is useful in persuading government to adopt specific policies (such as in Box 11-2, Campaigning for a Clean Harbour).

The political activities and strategies of interest groups will also be affected by the nature of government. In countries where government policy-making is a rather closed process, groups are more likely to use an inside strategy, if possible, and dramatic forms of protest, if alternatives are impossible. Further, interest groups pursuing inside strategies will, if possible, devote most of their effort to try to influence those with real power. Thus, the targets of interest group persuasion will vary from country to country, depending upon the nature of the governing system. American interest groups, for example, devote considerable effort to trying to influence individual representatives in Congress and members of congressional committees because of the ability of the members of Congress to affect government policies (see Chapter 15). Likewise, while interest groups may try to influence governing institutions at a variety of levels (local, provincial, national, and international), they will naturally devote the most attention to the level of government that most affects their interests.

INSIDE STRATEGIES
Strategies in which interest group leaders develop close contacts with key policy-makers in government and the public service in order to influence public policies.

OUTSIDE STRATEGIES
Strategies in which interest group leaders appeal to the public for support in order to put pressure on decision-makers concerning public policies.

BOX 11-2

Campaigning for a Clean Harbour

Trying to clean up the St. John's harbour has meant dredging up support from far and wide.

The Newfoundland capital is just one of several Canadian cities that continue to dump untreated sewage into their harbours. Not only is raw sewage toxic to marine life, it also interferes with the development of the tourist industry and the enjoyment of the harbour. But in the case of St. John's, the substantial cost of building sewage treatment facilities, estimated at $93 million in 1997, was beyond the capability of the city government.

An arrangement to share the costs among the national, provincial, and local governments was worked out in the early 1980s. However, a dispute between the Canadian and Newfoundland governments in 1982 over an unrelated issue (the control of offshore oil) led to the suspension of plans to build a sewage treatment facility. The St. John's city government was subsequently unable to persuade the senior levels of government to carry out their commitments to provide funding.

In 1991, the Canadian government decided as part of its Green Plan to establish the Atlantic Canada Action Program (ACAP) to encourage community initiatives, particularly those that would deal with the environmental problems of harbours and coastlines. Based on this, the St. John's Harbour ACAP organization was formed by a group of local citizens. It built on a citizens' group, the Friends of St. John's Harbour, and included representatives of the three levels of government. Partial funding for the organization was provided by Environment Canada.

In addition to carrying out scientific research to document the environmental problems of the harbour, the St. John's ACAP decided that it needed to take political action to clean up the harbour. Its approach involved an outside strategy of mobilizing public support and an inside strategy of collaborating with governments to design the appropriate facilities and negotiate suitable financial arrangements. The group raised the issue in federal, provincial, and municipal elections and kept the public informed of the issue. It lobbied governments and gained the support of local businesses, especially the tourist and convention industries, for its goal.

In 1996, pressure from the St. John's ACAP helped persuade the three municipal governments in the St. John's area to commit themselves to the project and begin some preliminary work. It was another four years before the provincial government, worried that the Canadian government would not contribute, was persuaded to commit to sharing the costs of the project. The Canadian government was reluctant to commit to the project, fearing that it would be seen as a special handout to one area of the country. Finally, in 2002 as part of a national infrastructure-building program, the Canadian government agreed to provide one-third of the funding.

Although the experience of the St. John's ACAP suggests that a combined inside/outside strategy is desirable, it has its difficulties. Putting outside pressure on government may result in an antagonistic relationship that may impede efforts to collaborate with government. Interestingly, although the Canadian government (through Environment Canada) was involved with the formation and activities of the St. John's ACAP, the group had a difficult time persuading the Canadian government to act. On the other hand, an inside strategy of collaborating with government may detract from efforts to mobilize the public support that is often needed to convince governments to act. In this case, over time the two dedicated part-time staff members of the St. John's ACAP were able to learn the skills of successful interest group activity. They patiently pursued their goal despite years of frustration (Close & Mintz, 2001).

The results to date? Preliminary work on the harbour cleanup project began in 2003. And in 2007, the primary sewage treatment plant is scheduled to begin operations!

Canadian Interest Groups

Canadian interest groups, particularly institutionalized interest groups, tend to direct much of their activity towards influencing those public servants who are important in developing public policy and the particular cabinet minister whose government department is most relevant to the concerns of the interest. For example, interest groups representing farmers devote much of their efforts to trying to influence those involved in policy development within the department of agriculture and meet regularly with the minister to inform the minister of their concerns and proposals.

By developing close contact with those within government who have the primary responsibility for developing policy, institutionalized interest groups can "get in on the ground floor." It is usually easier to have influence before the government becomes committed to a course of action. At an early stage, an interest group can provide information and research that is useful to policy developers and can supply proposals for consideration. After government has publicly committed itself to a particular course of action, it is harder for an interest group to exert influence, as governments are reluctant to be seen as backing down under pressure.

Overall, there is often a close relationship and close collaboration between the leading institutionalized interest groups and the departments of government that are most relevant to their concerns. Sometimes, government departments formalize this relationship by setting up advisory committees consisting of leading interest group representatives. In other situations, there is an informal expectation that key interest groups will be consulted before major new policies are developed. Canadian members of Parliament do not normally receive the same level of attention from the major Canadian interest groups as senior officials in government departments because of their limited role in developing policy and because proposed laws are rarely rejected by Parliament (see Chapter 15).

Public Support

Most interest groups also pay some attention to gaining support from the public for their concerns and proposals. For issue-oriented groups that have not developed close connections with policy-makers, taking their case to the public may be the only way of effectively influencing public policy. Interest groups often try to build coalitions with other interest groups in order to add weight to their claim to speak on behalf of a large number of people on a particular issue. For example, to bolster its campaign for stronger lobbying and ethics rules, Democracy Watch has built a coalition of thirty-one groups, ranging from the Canadian Labour Congress and the National Action Committee on the Status of Women to the Canadian Friends of Burma.

Democracy Watch
www.dwatch.ca

Using the Legal System

Court Challenges Program of Canada
www.ccppcj.ca

Interest groups often make use of the judicial system to advance their interests. For example, Canadian environmental groups have had some successes in the courts in forcing the Canadian government to undertake environmental assessments of proposed projects that have potentially negative effects on fish habitats. However, using the court system to pursue interests can be costly. The Canadian government has financed the Court Challenges program to assist equality-seeking groups, particularly women's groups and groups representing linguistic minorities, in challenging laws and policies that are viewed as discriminatory under the provisions of the Canadian Charter of Rights and Freedoms. Some other groups have been able to benefit from the services of lawyers who share a belief in their cause.

The use of the legal system to pursue interest group objectives is particularly common in the United States, where laws often contain highly specific obligations for government action and thus provide scope for legal action if the obligations are not fulfilled. In contrast, laws in Canada and elsewhere typically provide considerable discretion to government and administrators in determining when and how to carry out the general objectives contained in the law. For example, most environmental laws enable provincial or national governments in Canada to take action to protect the environment, but do not require that they do so (Boyd, 2003). However, some recent legislation, such as the *Canada Environmental Protection Act*, 1999, does contain mandatory requirements and opens up the possibility that citizens can take legal action if government does not live up to its obligations (Valiante, 2002).

Links Between Interest Groups and Political Parties

Canadian Labour Congress
clc-ctc.ca

Interest groups have often been viewed as a different link between citizens and government than political parties. However, in various countries there are links between interest groups and parties. In some cases, interest groups have been involved in the establishment of a political party. For example, the Canadian Labour Congress played a key role in the establishment of the New Democratic Party. Agricultural interests have played a major role in establishing parties representing agrarian interests in several countries, although such parties have become more broadly based as the farming community declined. The Catholic Church has played a major role in Christian Democratic parties in some countries (see Box 11-3, Religious Interests and Political Parties).

In general, the relationship between interest groups and political parties is often an uneasy one. Although interest groups are, in some cases, an important source of support for a political party, the goals of the two types of organizations often differ. The support of a particular interest group may be detrimental to the attempts of a party to expand its base of popular support

BOX 11-3

Religious Interests and Political Parties

It may seem strange to discuss religious organizations as a political interest group. However, beyond the articulation and promotion of moral values that, like ideologies, have relevance to political thought and action, religious institutions have specific interests.

The Catholic Church, for example, has a strong interest in controlling the education of Catholic children and obtaining state subsidies to provide for this education. It also has lobbied governments for what it views as family-oriented laws that prohibit divorce, abortion, and homosexual behaviour. And, along with other religious organizations, it has sought preferential tax treatment.

Like other major interest groups, the Catholic Church has, in some situations, found it useful to ally itself with a political party. Historically, the Catholic clergy in Quebec supported the Conservative party and opposed the Liberals, who originally favoured removal of the special privileges of the Church. In Italy, the Catholic Church, through groups such as Catholic Action, the Popular Movement, and the Italian Association of Christian Workers, was closely associated with the Democratic Christian Party. This party dominated Italian governments from 1945 until its collapse as a result of patronage scandals that rocked the Italian party system in 1994 (Constantelos, 2001).

The Catholic Church has also supported the Christian Democratic Union in Germany and the allied Christian Social Union, although the relationship between the Church and the Christian Democratic Union (a party that represents both Catholics and Protestants) has not been as close as it was in Italy. In the case of France, the Catholic Church withdrew its support of the Mouvement républicain populaire in the early 1950s when that party moved away from supporting generous state subsidies for Catholic schools and amnesty for those who had collaborated with the Vichy (wartime Nazi puppet) regime in France. With other major parties taking an anti-clerical position, the Church subsequently refrained from active involvement in French party politics (Warner, 2000).

The relationship between a religious organization and a political party can be an uneasy one. To gain broader support, a political party may compromise some of the principles of the religious organization and may be unwilling to submit to control by a religious organization. If the political party and the government controlled by the political party engage in corrupt or immoral practices, this may reflect badly on the religious organization with which they are connected (Warner, 2000)

The Catholic Church is not the only religious group that involves itself in party politics to promote its values and interests. In the United States, various fundamentalist and evangelical groups involved in the Christian Right have allied themselves with the Republican party through groups such as the Christian Coalition and have influenced the Republican platform. Several parties based on ultra-orthodox Judaism often have considerable influence on Israeli governments through their participation in coalition governments.

or to form a coalition with other parties. For example, the close connection between the New Democratic Party and its affiliated unions has been both an element of financial and organizational strength for the party and a potential detriment to its electoral fortunes.

In many cases, however, the relationship between interest groups and political parties is of a more informal nature. Business interests often have an informal relationship with conservative and moderate liberal parties, but this does not generally take the form of the direct involvement of business interest groups in the affairs of a particular party. For example, although individual businesses have been major contributors to Canadian political parties, business interest groups rarely contribute to political parties. Many interest groups want to avoid direct involvement with political parties so that they can maintain or develop good relationships with government leaders regardless of which party happens to be in power.

LOBBYING

LOBBYING
An attempt to influence legislators, executives, or public officials, particularly by a person or firm that specializes in representing clients who seek to gain special benefits from government.

The term **lobbying** arose from the practice of those seeking favours from government to congregate in the lobby of the British House of Commons to make their case to members of Parliament as they left the legislative chamber. In contemporary usage, lobbying refers to efforts to influence not only legislators, but also those involved in the executive and administrative aspects of government.

Lobbying has increasingly become a professionalized activity. In addition to individuals within corporations and interest groups who are employed to lobby government, a number of consulting firms specialize in lobbying on behalf of a variety of clients. In 2002, for example, there were 1440 persons who registered as lobbyists at the national level in Canada. Many of them worked for a lobbying consultant firm (Dyck, 2004).

Many professional lobbyists are persons who have had high-level experience in government as senior administrators, cabinet ministers, or political assistants to cabinet ministers. Their inside knowledge of the workings of government and the thinking of policy-makers, as well as their extensive contacts within government and administration, can make them valuable assets to their clients. However, the revolving door between working in government and working as a lobbyist and the government's hiring of lobbying firms for research and public relations often leads to ethical questions being raised about whether the relationship between government and lobbyists is too close.

For example, Paul Martin has a very close relationship with key people at one lobbying firm, the Earnscliffe Strategy Group. David Herle, a principal partner at Earnscliffe, ran Martin's leadership campaign, headed up the transition team when Martin became prime minister, and managed the 2004 Liberal election campaign. Other lobbyists at Earnscliffe have been appointed to key positions in Martin's government. Earnscliffe regularly receives government contracts to provide advice on how to communicate its positions on various issues and represents major corporations on how to influence government—sometimes on the same issues (CTV News, 2004).

◀ Professional lobbyists' inside knowledge of the workings of government and the thinking of policy-makers, as well as their extensive contacts within government and administration, can make them valuable assets to their clients. However, the revolving door between working in government and working as a lobbyist often leads to questions about whether the relationship is too close, as is the case with the Earnscliffe Strategy Group in Canada. Scott Reid, pictured here, recently left Earnscliff to become a senior strategy advisor in the Prime Minister's Office.

EXERTING INFLUENCE

Interest groups vary in their capabilities to influence public policy. Several factors contribute to the amount of influence that a group can exert:

- The size of the group's membership may affect the willingness of politicians to take the group seriously. However, a well-organized and cohesive smaller group may be better able to exert influence than a disunited large group.

- Financial resources help in maintaining an effective organization, hiring professional lobbyists and political consultants who understand the workings of power and have good contacts with key officials, and conducting research and advertising on behalf of the group's concerns.

- Groups that are able to develop close ties with key government officials are more likely to be influential.

- Groups that are seen by government and the public as having expertise and credibility, such as the Canadian Medical Association and the Canadian Bar Association, have a strong influence potential.

- Groups whose ideas and proposals coincide with the general thinking of government, the media, or the public are more likely to be successful than groups whose ideas are out of favour or controversial.

- The ability to make credible threats about the adverse consequences of failing to act as the group recommends can also be useful.

- Finally, a group is more likely to be influential if it does not face competing interest groups in a particular policy area.

INTEREST GROUPS AND GOVERNMENT: TWO MODELS

The terms *pluralism* and *corporatism* are often used to describe two different patterns of relationships between interest groups and government. One features a competitive relationship among interest groups, while the other involves efforts to create a cooperative relationship between interest groups and government.

Pluralism

In the *pluralist perspective*, liberal democracies provide individuals the freedom to establish and join groups in order to advance their ideals and interests. Using this freedom, a wide variety of groups expressing different interests have developed. The formation of a group expressing a particular interest stimulates the formation of other groups expressing opposing interests. With a wide variety of groups competing to influence government, no one group is dominant. As Robert Dahl argued, "Few groups in the United States who are determined to influence the government—certainly few who are organized, active and persistent—lack the capacity and opportunity to influence some officials somewhere in the political system in order to obtain at least some of their goals" (1963, p. 386).

Although groups are not equal in their ability to influence government, pluralist theory assumes that some resources that are useful in attempting to exert influence—such as information, expertise, money, and the support of large numbers of people—are available to most groups. A further assumption of pluralist theory is that the governing authorities are open to influence from a wide variety of groups. Indeed, those who hold the pluralist perspective typically view politicians as devoted to arranging compromises to satisfy as many groups as possible. If a group feels left out, it will mobilize support to try to modify the policy. Thus, in the pluralist view, the power to affect what government does is widely dispersed, and interest groups play a central role in ensuring that government is responsive to the variety of demands of the people.

CRITICISMS Does pluralism provide a good description of the relationship between interest groups and government in countries such as Canada and the United States? Critics argue that power is not as widely dispersed as pluralist theory claims.

For one thing, some segments of society are less likely to be organized into effective and influential interest groups than are the more privileged segments of society. Although there are a wide variety of interest groups in the advanced democracies, this does not necessarily mean that there is a balanced representation of the range of interests in society. While the privileged elements of society are well organized and influential, the poor, unemployed, and single parents often lack effective interest group representation, despite the importance of government programs to their well-being (Walker, 1991).

Second, many analysts argue that business interests are particularly influential in affecting what government does. Not only do business interests have considerable resources with which to try to exert influence, but also business has a privileged position because of its ability to affect the material well-being of the political community (Lindblom, 1977). Governments view maintaining the confidence of the business community as essential for the creation of jobs and prosperity, which are needed to keep voters happy and to carry out their objectives.

As well, there are often close ties between political and business leaders. For example, former Prime Minister Jean Chrétien used a senior executive of Power Corporation to run two national election campaigns and had a personal tie through his daughter's marriage to a member of the Desmarais family, which controls the corporation. Paul Martin was an executive of Power Corporation and bought Canada Steamship Lines, a leading global freight carrier, from the company, transferring ownership to his sons just before assuming the office of prime minister in 2003. President George W. Bush, Vice-President Cheney, and a number of senior personnel in the Bush administration have close ties to the American oil industry and firms like Haliburton that are involved in the reconstruction of Iraq.

Finally, from a different perspective, some argue that pluralism's description of liberal democracies exaggerates the influence of interest groups on government. Government officials and politicians are more than neutral referees in the competition of interest groups to affect public policy. Government officials and politicians have their own goals and are not simply involved in arranging compromises among competing interest groups or bending to the will of the groups that are able to mount the most pressure at a particular point in time.

Corporatism

The term **corporatism** is often used to describe political systems in which the state actively collaborates with selected major interests to set the direction for the political community, particularly in terms of economic and social policies. Major societal interests are *incorporated* (integrated) into the state in the sense that they are recognized by state officials as representatives of major segments of society.

In particular, "peak" organizations representing major interests such as business and labour have a formal, regular relationship with the state (Chalmers, 1991). State officials guide the development of a consensus among the major interests. The leaders of these interests then persuade those that they represent to accept the agreements that have been reached.

CORPORATISM
A political system in which the state actively collaborates with selected major interests to set the direction for the political community, particularly in terms of economic and social policies.

CATHOLIC ORIGINS The idea of corporatism was developed by the Catholic Church in the late nineteenth century as an alternative to liberalism and Marxism. An authoritarian version of corporatism in which groups were coerced into arrangements dominated by the state (termed **state corporatism**) was adopted by various fascist and other non-democratic regimes in the period between the two world wars.

After World War II, a more open and democratic version of corporatism, often referred to as **neo-corporatism** or societal corporatism, developed, particularly in Western Europe. In this version of corporatism, interest groups are not dominated by the state, involvement by groups is voluntary, and the representation of major interests is seen as supplementing, rather than replacing, liberal democracy.

CORPORATIST COUNTRIES A number of countries, including Japan and many countries in Western Europe, are often described in corporatist terms. However, only in a few countries have regular interactions between government and the leading interest groups consistently resulted in **policy concertation**: wide-ranging agreements on public policy. (Austria is one example.) In other European countries, corporatist arrangements have led to a more limited range of policy agreements (as in the Netherlands, Germany, and Sweden) or a sporadic pattern of agreements (as in Italy, Ireland, and France) (Compston, 2003).

Elsewhere, some traces of corporatism can be found in formal government consultations with leading interest groups and the inclusion of representatives of major interests on government advisory committees. In Quebec, attempts have been made, particularly by Parti Québécois governments, to find a social consensus among labour and business interests.

CHALLENGES TO CORPORATIST PRACTICES The neo-liberal emphasis on the virtues of the free market has led to challenges to corporatist practices in recent decades. For example, British Prime Minister Margaret Thatcher successfully attacked the influence of the unions and abolished corporatist institutions. Even in countries that are viewed as corporatist, there have been difficulties in reaching and implementing a consensus among the major interests. Today, the formation of new interest groups, such as environmental and women's groups, has challenged the monopoly on interest representation often enjoyed by leading business and labour groups.

Generally, corporatism requires that major interests be hierarchically organized such that peak organizations can speak for and make binding commitments on behalf of the segment of society that they represent. As well, the participants in corporatist relationships, such as business, labour, and government, need to have shared goals and mutual trust. These conditions are not fully met in many countries.

STATE CORPORATISM
An authoritarian version of corporatism in which groups were coerced into arrangements dominated by the state.

NEO-CORPORATISM
A version of corporatism in which interest groups are not dominated by the state, involvement by groups is voluntary, and the representation of major interests is seen as supplementing, rather than replacing, liberal democracy.

POLICY CONCERTATION
Wide-ranging agreements on public policy resulting from regular interactions between government and the leading interest groups in a corporatist system.

Is Either Model Ideal?

Thus far, we have been considering pluralism and corporatism as descriptions of the different patterns of relationships between interest groups and the state. We can also consider the desirability of pluralism and corporatism as ideals. Pluralism is often viewed as an elaboration of liberal democracy. In the pluralist ideal, power is dispersed and government is responsive to the demands and opinions of a wide variety of groups in society. Thus, pluralism is seen as avoiding the danger of the majority dominating minorities.

Those who favour the corporatist ideal argue that it can avoid the free-for-all characteristics of a more pluralistic system and reduce the class conflict that has divided many societies. Instead, corporatist institutions can limit conflict among differing interests and encourage the development of a stable, orderly pattern of relationships. Those who favour the corporatist model believe that the state can guide society, through the major interest representatives, towards the common good (Chalmers, 1991).

Corporatist arrangements could be viewed as somewhat undemocratic. Key decisions are made by a small number of people. Members of an interest group are expected to go along with whatever their leaders have worked out. New groups or groups outside the inner group may not be viewed as legitimate participants in the policy process.

Summary and Conclusion

Interest groups are often considered an essential feature of modern liberal democracies. The freedom to organize into groups to express one's views and to try to affect the decisions of the political community is a crucial element of liberal democracy. Interest groups potentially allow people to participate in the political process on a day-to-day basis, not just on the infrequent occasions when elections occur. They convey the views, opinions, and problems of various elements of society to government and to other citizens on a regular basis.

However, interest groups have been criticized as threats to the common good and as undemocratic. Many interest groups seek special privileges for their members or for particular segments of society—privileges that may work against the interests of society as a whole. With a wide variety of groups seeking special privileges, who is concerned about the well-being of the country as a whole? For example, many business groups seek tax breaks or subsidies for their particular sector of the economy. However, if government satisfies these demands, this may mean that the population as a whole will have to pay higher taxes or suffer reduced government services. Similarly, groups that can convince government to protect their products or services from foreign competition or allow the group to limit production (as, for example, with various agricultural products in Canada) can maintain their viability while the general public pays higher prices.

Finally, although all are free in a liberal democracy to form interest groups to represent their interests, some elements of society are better represented than others by interest groups. In general, the well-off elements of society are better represented by interest groups than those who are poor, uneducated, or otherwise disadvantaged. Business groups are often considered to be highly influential in the making of public policy; further, individual business corporations are able to influence the political process through their public affairs staff, by hiring lobbyists, making large contributions to political parties where this is not prohibited, and funding influential policy research institutes.

It would be misleading to think that only the rich and powerful are capable of having an impact on public policy. Groups representing segments of society that have been largely ignored in the past, such as Aboriginals, women, and ethnic minorities, have developed important interest groups. A large number of interest groups representing various public interests and causes have emerged. Such groups have been able to get their message across through the skillful use of their resources and have found sympathetic supporters in the media, universities, and government to carry their message.

The public may see groups based on economic interests as self-interested and view their messages with suspicion, but perceive other groups as promoting just causes that are for the common good of society. Nevertheless, groups representing disadvantaged sectors of society or causes that do not have the support of the privileged often require financial support from government or philanthropic sources and access to coverage by the mass media in order to be heard.

The models of pluralism and corporatism provide useful tools for analyzing the relationships between interest groups and the state. Although these models could be viewed as simplifications and distortions of the complex realities of politics, they alert us to the fact that the role of interest groups varies considerably across different countries and different points in time. As ideals about how politics *should* be organized, both pluralism and corporatism emphasize the importance of interest groups in representing the public.

Pluralism sees individuals as having a variety of interests and voluntarily joining a number of groups to promote their interests. Through a fluid pattern of bargaining and negotiating, compromises can be worked out that satisfy a variety of different interests. By satisfying a wide variety of interests, the common good of the political community is protected. Corporatism emphasizes the importance of economic interests, such as business, labour, and the professions, and advocates the development of a consensus among the major interests, guided by a concern for the common good of the political community. Government, in the corporatist perspective, plays an important role in encouraging the major interests to act in the common good.

Does the development of interest groups make political parties as a means of representing the public irrelevant? Despite the criticisms that are often raised about political parties, they tend to be more likely than interest groups to develop broad platforms of general popular appeal and to have a vision of where the political community should be headed. Interest groups concerned with promoting a particular interest or cause tend to have a narrower vision and are less concerned about developing positions with broad appeal.

Key Terms

Discussion Questions

1. What interest groups are you a member of? Do you think that they reflect your views?

2. Is the distinction between self-interested and public interest groups meaningful?

3. Do you think that the relationship between interest groups and government in Canada is accurately depicted by the pluralist perspective?

4. What are the advantages and disadvantages of corporatism? Do you think that it could work in Canada?

5. Are interest groups a threat to democracy and the common good?

Further Reading

Berry, J.M. *The new liberalism: The rising power of citizen groups.* Washington, D.C.: Brookings Institution Press, 1999.

Grant, W. *Pressure groups and British politics.* Houndmills, Basingstoke, Hampshire, UK: Macmillan, 2000.

Mahood, H.R. *Interest groups in American national politics: An overview.* Upper Saddle River, NJ: Prentice Hall. 2000.

Pal, L.A. *Interests of state: The politics of language, multiculturalism and feminism in Canada.* Montreal: McGill-Queen's University Press. 1993.

Pross, A.P. *Group politics and public policies* (2nd ed.). Toronto: Oxford University Press. 1993.

Schier, S.E. *By invitation only: The rise of exclusive politics in the United States.* Pittsburgh, PA: University of Pittsburgh Press, 2000.

Shaiko, R.G. *Voices and echoes for the environment: Public interest representation in the 1990s and beyond.* New York: Columbia University Press, 1999.

Silver, J. *Thin ice: Money, politics and the demise of an NHL franchise.* Halifax, NS: Fernwood, 1996.

Vickers, J., Appelle, C., & Rankin, P. *Politics as if women mattered: A political analysis of the National Action Committee on the Status of Women.* Toronto: University of Toronto Press. 1993.

Wiarda, H.J. *Corporatism and comparative politics: The other great "ism."* Armonk, NY: M.E. Sharpe, 1996.

Chapter 12

SOCIAL MOVEMENTS, POLITICAL PROTEST, AND CONTENTIOUS POLITICS

PHOTO ABOVE: Lois Gibbs turned political activist extraordinaire when her children fell seriously ill and she realized that the Love Canal toxic dump she lived on top of was to blame.

CHAPTER OBJECTIVES

After reading this chapter you should be able to:

1. discuss why people form political movements
2. explain what political protest is and why people use protest as a political tool
3. discuss why some but not all political protest is democratic
4. examine why protest is an integral and essential part of democratic politics

Lois Gibbs was a housewife who became a political activist when her children fell ill. In 1976, Gibbs learned that the blue-collar subdivision in Niagara Falls, New York where she lived, with her husband and two small children was built on the Love Canal—an unfinished canal that had been used as a chemical disposal site. Over the years, the Hooker Chemical Company, later bought by oil giant Occidental Petroleum, had dumped 20 000 tonnes (over 18 000 kilograms) of highly toxic chemical waste into the never-completed canal. It was covered over and the land was sold to the municipality of Niagara Falls for one dollar.

In 1978, Gibbs's children became very sick. Her son developed epilepsy and her daughter almost died of a rare blood disease. Gibbs went around to her neighbours with a petition, asking them if they were as upset as she was. They were, and soon they had formed the Love Canal Homeowners Association. Over the next two years, Gibbs led the association in legal and political battle against Occidental Petroleum and all three levels of government—city, state, and federal. Although the company and the governments all argued that the toxic wastes under Love Canal did not cause the residents' health problems, the community eventually won a settlement of US$120 million and over eight hundred families were relocated to safe, healthy homes. President Jimmy Carter later declared the Love Canal a national disaster area.

The protest that Lois Gibbs organized and led has left two important legacies. One is the United States Environmental Protection Agency's Superfund, monies used to find and clean up toxic sites throughout the United States. The other is the Center for Health, Environment, and Justice (CHEJ), which Gibbs founded and heads. The CHEJ works with community groups across the United States to protect neighbourhoods from the hazards of toxic wastes.

The Love Canal incident sparked thousands of other grassroots campaigns against toxic sites. By being brave enough to stand up to the powerful and resourceful enough to found and lead successful political protest, Lois Gibbs showed that even ordinary people can wield a lot of political power when they organize and refuse to take no for answer. This is the force that underlies social movement and protest politics, which we examine in this chapter.

THE RIGHT TO DISSENT

Social movements have been prominent political entities since the beginning of the democratic age in the late 1700s. A *social movement* mobilizes large numbers of people to pursue an aim that those who are involved fervently believe will advance the common good. The activity of movements generally takes place outside the formal democratic political channels of elections, political parties, and pressure groups. Nevertheless, some movements work within established political institutions and only move outside established paths occasionally; others concentrate more on political protest.

The term *political protest* might conjure up images of helmeted police and rock-throwing demonstrators, but it can also suggest people picketing peacefully in front of city hall or organizing a petition. **Political protest** takes many forms (Figure 12-1). The most moderate of these methods include petitions, legally approved demonstrations, and voluntary boycotts of certain products or firms. Non-violent direct action—for example, civil disobedience, illegal demonstrations, or peaceful occupation of a building or office—is a stronger form of protest. It involves illegal activities but is not violent, as is best exemplified by **civil disobedience**: deliberate lawbreaking that accepts punishment by state authorities as part of the action.

Very different is protest action that involves violence. Protest has opened the way to fuller political participation for many groups in every democratic political system. But protest politics can sometimes be violent, even emerging as war or terrorism. Sometimes violence is an unintended consequence of a march or boycott, but it can also be used intentionally as a provocation. Assassinations and guerrilla warfare fall into this category, as does **terrorism**.

Seeking Change

Change is the objective of most social movements, regardless of how much or how little they use protest to promote their vision of the common good. Those who form or join movements usually do not work through established

POLITICAL PROTEST
Oppositional political action that takes place outside formal channels, generally seeking to have government make significant changes in its policies.

CIVIL DISOBEDIENCE
Deliberate lawbreaking that accepts punishment by state authorities as part of the action.

TERRORISM
The deliberate use of violence designed to induce fear in a population in order to achieve a political objective.

FIGURE 12-1
THE CONTINUUM OF PROTEST

INSTITUTIONAL	MODERATE PROTEST	DIRECT ACTION	VIOLENCE
Voting	Petitions	Unofficial strikes	Unintentional
Lobbying	Legal demonstrations	Illegal demonstrations	Throw rocks, break windows
Interest groups	Boycotts	Peaceful occupations	Guerrilla warfare
		Civil disobedience	Assassination
			Terrorism

SOURCE: Adapted with modifications from *Citizen Politics* (p. 60), by R.J. Dalton, 2002, New York: Chatham House.

parties or pressure groups because they believe that they will be more successful in achieving major changes if they operate unconstrained by the usual conventions of politics.

Although, as we note later, some movements do not use protest action, protest and social movements are frequently linked in the public mind. Because both are forms of political action that work outside established channels, the perception exists that movements and protest are somehow undemocratic. This is ironic because even though social movements exist in all political systems, they are particularly common in democracies. Citizens of democratic countries can organize freely and petition government for the redress of grievances because democratic governments recognize their citizens' right to lay complaints at their doorstep.

ANALYZING PROTEST

To most people, seeking the common good suggests reasoned deliberation and debate, which are hallmarks of democratic politics. However, democracy did not grow just through the use of reason and polite persuasion. Those who hold power, the elite, are rarely keen to see their power diminished; thus, logic has often needed to be supplemented by more **contentious politics**—that is, protest involving ordinary citizens, often joined by more influential citizens, uniting to confront "elites, authorities, and opponents" (Tarrow, 1999, p. 2).

CONTENTIOUS POLITICS
Protest involving ordinary citizens, often joined by more influential citizens, uniting to confront elites, authorities, and opponents.

All political protest is political action because those who protest want government to do something. Protest is an attempt to influence what government does. This political action is oppositional because those who protest want government to change its policies. This can mean that a government starts to do something it does not do now, stops doing something it now does, or takes action instead of doing nothing. However, oppositional activity can be wide-ranging and does not always include protest. We reserve the label *protest* for political actions with the following characteristics:

1. Actions take place outside of formal channels.
2. They are usually carried out by individuals or groups who are not ordinarily important political actors.
3. Protest politics generally aims to have government make significant changes in the policies it pursues.

We will look at each of these three traits separately.

Politics Outside Formal Channels

Whether in dictatorships or democracies, politics works in set patterns. There are rules you are expected to follow if you want something done. They may not always be formal written rules, but rather norms or unofficial standards. In either case, being politically effective and getting what you want usually requires following those rules and working within channels.

Playing by the rules benefits both governments and the groups and individuals that regularly deal with government. It obviously helps governments because they set the rules. However, keeping within channels also works well for those who deal regularly with government because they master the rules and can use them to their own benefit. But what if going through channels does not produce any results? In that case, there are two options: accept your fate or go outside channels.

When people have an issue that is very important to them, they are not likely to be satisfied with accepting defeat graciously. This is true even when the defeat comes as a result of a democratic process and reflects the will of the majority. Such an outcome is especially likely where the protesters belong to some permanent minority (for example, an ethnic or religious group) that the majority or government has consciously marginalized. Ordinary democracy may not work for those who can never become a majority.

"Unimportant" Actors or Issues

Protest is sometimes called the tool of the marginalized—people without the resources needed to gain political influence. We usually think of political influence as the ability to shape decisions, being able to control large blocks of votes, or having lots of money or particularly valuable information. Having these resources makes an individual or group valuable to government, and governments often accommodate those who are valuable to them. Prospects are bleak for those groups or individuals with scarce resources unless they can find a way to make themselves important to government.

Beginning in the 1960s, political scientists began to see protest itself as a political resource (Lipsky, 1968). Protest disrupts government's routines, making the authorities at least see that something is happening. Although government officials often characterize protest as simple lawlessness, they still know that some part of their community feels strongly enough about some issue to take to the streets. In reality, the marginalized may have little option but to resort to protest. Largely invisible to those in power before they begin to protest, those on the outside frequently find that the rules of the game do not work for them. Once a protest movement has the authorities' attention, however, it can mobilize other resources, such as numbers of voters, and raise its profile.

MARGINALIZATION
Exclusion from the mainstream.

Marginalization does not refer only to the dispossessed and literally disenfranchised. Issues, too, can be marginalized and only appear on the government's agenda after supporters take extraordinary measures. This explains the apparently contradictory phenomenon of the well-educated, middle-class or higher protester (Dalton, 2002), whose activity has been notable from the anti-Vietnam War movement of the 1960s to today's anti-globalization demonstrations. Although these individuals may have other resources that they can use to influence government, these resources may not work for a given issue. Thus, protest is another resource that the politically active can add to their arsenals (Opp, 1989).

Challenges and Benefits of Organizing We should not think, however, that mobilizing a social movement or promoting political protest is the easiest way to enter politics. There is, first, the problem of organizing people to act collectively. Mancur Olson (1965) argues that the rational thing for a person to do is not to join a movement, but rather to wait on the sidelines to see what it accomplishes. These *free riders* share the benefits of the organization's labour without having to do any work or take any risks.

Beyond the matter of getting people to join, movements cannot know how government will respond to their demands. There is no guarantee that time and energy invested in building a movement and organizing protest actions will change the status quo and advance a group's vision of the common good. Nevertheless, over the years, Canadians have seen workers, farmers, women, fishers, Quebec nationalists, Aboriginals, gays and lesbians, and anti-abortion activists use social movements and political protest to put themselves and their causes on the public agenda. Many of these groups became regular parts of the political process, and today governments, whether federal or provincial, generally do not question the right of these groups to have a voice in policy making. Whether events would have turned out this way had the groups not protested is impossible to determine. What we do know is that protest advanced their causes substantially.

Gay and Lesbian Emergence:
Out in Canada (CBC Archives)
archives.cbc.ca/IDD-1-69-599/
life_society/gay_lesbian

Seeking Significant Change

Since protest generally involves those who are not normally involved in politics moving outside normal channels, perhaps even acting illegally, it is unlikely that people will turn to protest without a good reason. Protesters usually believe that there is something terribly wrong that must be righted. Often, at least some of those who protest will have tried to get the changes they want by conventional means, such as voting or contacting government officials. It is usually when the ordinary mechanisms of political pressure have failed that people begin to protest: they see it as their last chance to be heard. This is why protest has been used to gain political rights for the excluded, to try to end wars, and to make absolutely clear the opposition of some part of the citizenry to some government policy. Protest is about changing what government does, and people have organized themselves into movements that seek political change for a very long time.

Riseup.net (contemporary progressive movements)
lists.riseup.net

SOCIAL MOVEMENTS AND POLITICS

Although protest can be the work of individuals,[1] it is most often the work of large movements, made up of "ordinary people (who) try to exert power by

---

[1] The most obvious example is the assassin, but we often see a single protester maintaining a lonely, peaceful vigil outside a government installation. Individual protest also occurs when a citizen writes a letter to the editor, contacts a politician, or calls a hotline to voice opposition to some government action.

contentious means" (Tarrow, 1999, p. 2). Usually called *social movements*, they are driven by a strong purpose and a desire to effect dramatic changes. Movements advocating political change appeared in the early stages of industrialization in Europe some two hundred years ago.

Social movements are politically important because as "large-scale, collective efforts to bring about or resist changes that bear on the lives of many" (Oberschall, 1993, p. 2) they necessarily want things done that only governments can do. Sometimes social movements morph into political parties. Britain's Labour party has its roots in the labour movement and Germany's Green party grew out of that country's environmental movement, drawing on anti-nuclear power, peace, and feminist movements as well. More commonly, social movements assume the role of active, permanent pressure groups. In either case, their political roots are obvious.

Students of movements (Heberle, 1951) tell us that social movements began with the coming of the industrial age in Europe. One of the earliest movements was for the abolition of slavery in Britain in the late 1700s (Coupland, 1964). Another early British movement, the Chartists, pressed for the expansion of democratic rights in the 1830s (Thompson, 1984).[2] Other European movements sought basic democratic rights for ordinary people, especially the emerging industrial working class, but there were also movements for national independence (for example, in Greece and Hungary) and voting rights for women. The real-path breaker in Canada was the labour movement, which dates from the first half of the nineteenth century (Herron, 1996).

Some of these movements, notably those built by workers and nationalists, eventually formed political parties, but others did not. Collectively these are called "old social movements." In the 1950s and 1960s, new social movements began to form. They focused on issues such as the environment, peace and nuclear disarmament, ethnicity, the rights of indigenous peoples, gender, and sexual identity. Again, a few of these, such as some environmental and ethnic movements, have formed political parties, but most have not.

Social movements sometimes resemble parties when they seek legislative representation or even control of government. They also often resemble interest groups in trying to influence government policies. However, movements constitute a distinct form of political organization. Where parties and interest groups are generally centrally directed, social movements tend to be more loosely organized. In fact, they are often networks of smaller, independent organizations that share a common vision, such as securing votes for women or opposing the sale of genetically modified foods. Further, interest groups and parties generally speak with one voice, but movements frequently reflect a wider variety of viewpoints.

---

[2] The Chartist movement was named for the People's Charter, 1838, a six-point resolution that called for giving the vote to all men as part of a package of reforms to democratize British government.

Having a relatively flexible organization is especially characteristic of the new social movements. The old social movements, such as the farmers' movements, the labour movement and some nationalist movements, are distinguished by having relatively strong and centralized formal organizations. This made it both easier and more natural for them to either form political parties or ally with existing parties.

The more flexible structures adopted by the new social movements give them real advantages because a broad framework allows a movement to grow and encompass as many as possible of those who share its broad objectives. However, this very breadth can harm movements by presenting a confused picture of who they are and what they want. For example, some individuals aligned with the anti-abortion (right to life) movement have decided that the most effective form of protest is to attack clinics and even kill the doctors who perform abortions. Although the members of this movement who endorse deadly violence are a minuscule and marginalized minority, their very presence makes it seem that the entire anti-abortion movement espouses violent action.

PROTEST AND POLITICAL CHANGE

People protest because they perceive what Clark, Grayson, and Grayson call "institutional deficiencies"—they think that something is not working right and has to be fixed (1976, p. 3). Often, although not always, people first try to work through channels and then, getting poor results, move to protest. This is not a decision to be taken lightly. They may risk imprisonment and in the end they may still fail to gain any political ground. Nevertheless, political protest has secured some dramatic results and contributed greatly to strengthening democracy, both in Canada and abroad. For example:

- *Women's right to vote.* Until the late 1800s, women everywhere were denied basic political rights. It was only in the twentieth century that political equality between men and women became a generally accepted principle of democratic life. The first step toward equality for women was winning the right to vote. Although we now find it unthinkable that women did not have the same political rights as men, it took Canadian women over fifty years to gain the right to vote in all provinces. Along the way, the proponents of women's suffrage (women's right to vote) lobbied governments and used various forms of protest, such as staging mock parliamentary debates, to demonstrate that they could argue as persuasively and as rationally as men (Cleverdon, 1974).

- *Making farmers' voices heard.* Farmers in Canada in the late nineteenth and early twentieth centuries felt excluded from power and sought to change the political system to better reflect their needs (Lipset, 1950; Macpherson, 1954; Morton, 1950). Unlike the movement for women's suffrage, farmers' movements decided that they needed to form new political parties. Although farmers were then the largest occupational group in the country, they had little influence. Farmers felt that the parties that existed at the time, the Conservatives and Liberals, ignored their views and listened only to the demands of big business. The parties the farmers' movements founded (United Farmers, Progressives, Cooperative Commonwealth Federation [CCF]) or supported (Social Credit) sought to represent the views of not just farmers, but all ordinary working people against the concentrated power of corporate interests. Although none of these parties ever won power federally, several of them governed provinces. Moreover, a number of them created Crown corporations (government-owned enterprises) that brought electricity and telephone service to many parts of rural Canada. One, the CCF, set up the country's first medicare system in Saskatchewan.

Votes for women and more political power for farmers were issues that Canada's political establishment of a century past would not put on the public agenda. For these two marginalized groups to have their demands heard, they had to move outside the usual political channels. The mechanisms of ordinary democracy had served them badly, but political protest benefited them and democracy well.

PROTEST IN DEMOCRACY

There are those who argue that political protest does not have a place in a democracy. People have the right to make their feelings known in elections, to work through their elected representatives, and to pressure government. Obviously, not everyone gets what they want, but that is not cause to go outside fair, well-known rules and procedures. If you fail to get what you want by working through regular democratic processes, it indicates that you are simply too weak or are pursuing goals that seem too radical for the majority. Rather than protest, you should change your objectives and build a broader base.

The crux of this argument is the belief that democratic politics has not contained and can not contain any biases. Although this view underlies our most basic beliefs about democracy, it is not entirely accurate. Besides the two cases we looked at above, there are many instances in which following established democratic procedures did not help the weak and marginalized. This was the case for African Americans who turned to protest to challenge the discriminatory system of **segregation** (see Box 12-1, The Civil Rights Movement).

SEGREGATION
The legal separation of Blacks and Whites, particularly in the Southern United States.

Civil Disobedience

Civil disobedience involves people consciously breaking laws they feel are discriminatory, unjust, and contrary to the spirit of their constitution. The lawbreakers do not resist arrest and accept that they will be tried and convicted.

BOX 12-1
The Civil Rights Movement

The U.S. civil rights movement is one of the most famous examples of how people without power were failed by the democratic process.

Although Abraham Lincoln declared the abolition of slavery of 1863, for the next century African Americans suffered systemic discrimination. Conditions were worst in the southern states where **segregation**, the legal separation of races, was in force. This meant that Black children and White children went to different schools, that Blacks and Whites could not use the same rest rooms or drinking fountains, and that Blacks even had to give up their seats on buses to Whites.

Throughout the first half of the twentieth century, African Americans worked patiently through their country's courts to have segregation legislation declared unconstitutional. Although they had some significant victories, such as *Brown v. Board of Education*, 1954, which declared segregated education unconstitutional, actually getting states to change their laws proved difficult. Despite a constitutional provision adopted in 1870 establishing that the right to vote cannot be denied on account of race or colour, various means such as literacy tests were used to prevent most African Americans from voting.

Clearly, the normal channels of influence were of little use in trying to change discriminatory laws and policies. Protest action by the civil rights movement was needed to pressure governments to treat African Americans fairly.

They then appeal their convictions to a higher court, arguing that the law they broke actually violated the constitution and should have no force. The greatest American proponent of civil disobedience was Dr. Martin Luther King (1929–1968), an African-American Baptist minister who lived in the South.

Sit-ins were one of the most effective tactics used by the civil rights movement. Black students would sit in the section of a restaurant or lunch counter that was reserved for Whites. They would be refused service and told to leave, but they would stay until arrested. Eventually this practice mobilized public opinion in America behind the civil rights movement and legislation outlawing segregation followed.

Had African Americans tried to keep working within the rules, as they had for many years, segregation might have continued much longer. Politicians were hesitant to change the law, fearing that White voters would defeat them at the next election. Taking dramatic action like sit-ins focused the country's attention on the abuses of segregation and hastened that system's demise.

Structures

POLITICAL OPPORTUNITY STRUCTURES (POS)
The openings that political institutions and processes offer to (or withhold from) movements.

What allowed the protests in Canada and the United States to work was the ability of the movements' leaders to use the opportunities offered by their political systems. **Political opportunity structures (POS)** refer to the openings that political institutions and processes offer to or withhold from movements (Kitschelt, 1986; Tarrow, 1999). For example, the farmers' movement in Canada was able to build political parties and win power because our electoral system and system of parliamentary government, as well as the fact that farmers formed a majority of voters in several provinces, made this a workable option. More recently, **secessionists** in Quebec have used the same strategy with some success because the supporters of Quebec's independence could unite behind a single separatist party and gain control of the Quebec government. However, because they are less likely to vote as a bloc, women have not developed a specifically women's political party to advance their cause.

SECESSIONIST
A person who favours separation of a territory from an existing state.

Changes in Movements

The cases just sketched demonstrate that movements sometimes change into political parties or pressure groups that are regular actors in the established political system. When this happens we speak of the *demobilization* or *routinization* of a movement. It loses some of its spontaneity and becomes less contentious in its relations with government.

Nevertheless, it may still be appropriate to speak of the movement as a movement, as we do with the women's and environmental movements. Not only may there still be specific groups that remain on the fringes of normal politics (the usual and expected actors, issues, and methods that define most of what a political system does), but a substantial part of a movement's influence lies in its continuing ability to mobilize those who share its goals to pressure government in various ways. Just because a movement now looks more like a party or interest group than a protest organization does not mean that it has forever abandoned the tools of political protest. For example, although many environmental groups now work closely with government, other groups such as Greenpeace continue to engage in protest activity.

Protest, then, can be an essential tool of democracy. However, we should not take this to mean that all protest is necessarily democratic.

PROTEST, VIOLENCE, AND TERRORISM

Violence can enter political protest movements in three different ways (see also Box 12-2, Violence and Politics):

1. *Violence can be a tactic chosen by the protest movement to advance its aims.* Although this is more common in countries that are not democracies and consequently do not allow an open political opposition, even long-established constitutional democracies such as Canada or the United States can harbour groups that feel they must use violence to achieve their goals.
2. *The actions of government can also introduce violence into political protest.* Governments may want protests stopped and may even order the police or military to use force against the protesters. While such tactics are common in non-democratic countries, democratic governments sometimes react in the same way.
3. *Finally, violence can be an unplanned and undesired side effect of protest.* Due to some unpredictable event, either the protestors or the police become aggressive and the two sides clash.

Canadians are generally repelled by political violence. A movement that regularly uses violence, as did the Front de libération du Québec (FLQ), a revolutionary separatist group that kidnapped and murdered a Quebec cabinet minister in 1970 (as discussed later in this chapter), is likely to lose public support. This revulsion also occurs when the police react with excessive force, as happened at the 1997 APEC summit in Vancouver.[3] Canadians, like people in most democratic countries, usually draw the line at premeditated violence.

---

[3] RCMP officers and Vancouver riot police used violence against students who were peacefully protesting the presence of the Indonesian dictator Suharto at a meeting of the Asia–Pacific Economic Cooperation (APEC), being held at the University of British Columbia in 1997. Although there were suspicions that the prime minister's office had ordered the demonstrators to be forcefully dispersed, a later inquiry found no direct links.

BOX 12-2

Violence and Politics

British political scientist Bernard Crick argued that politics, which he termed the political method of rule, is built on negotiation and the reconciliation of differences. As such, it effectively excludes the use of violence as a governing instrument (Crick, 1993).

Nonetheless, we see violence used for political ends every day, both by governments and by groups challenging government's authority. Two questions arise from this: Why do people use violence for political ends? And how we can distinguish political violence from simple criminality?

States may use violence legitimately, either to defend themselves and their citizens or to preserve order. Sometimes, however, dictatorships and other non-democratic governments use violence simply to suppress their opponents and repress dissent. In such cases, violence may be the only instrument that citizens can use to protect themselves against the state or to try to change their government's behaviour. Many would consider this a legitimate use of political violence.

Violence becomes political when it is used to influence, defend, or overthrow government. That seems clear, even if no government would ever say that any use of violence against it was anything but criminal. However, revolutionaries committed to toppling a government often resort to ordinary criminal methods such as robbery or kidnapping to finance their operations or simply to display their strength. In these cases, the line between political and criminal action seems to disappear. A further complication arises when peaceful protest turns violent unexpectedly, or when violent elements, even criminal ones, use ordinary protest as a cover for their illegitimate intentions.

POLITICAL VIOLENCE
The use of physical force that has a political objective.

Political violence can be defined as the use of physical force that has a political objective. What particularly sets terrorism apart from other forms of political violence, such as war, rebellion, coup d'état, and revolution, is its conscious targeting of the innocent (see Box 12-3, Terrorism Today). Terrorists use this tactic to sow fear among the population, either simply to demonstrate their power or in the hope that citizens will pressure their governments to meet the terrorists' demands.

Those who defend the use of terror by those fighting against an illegitimate or immoral regime usually assert that when fighting the strong, the weak must use any instrument that advances their cause, including not just violence but the use of violence against any target. This is the logic of total war. It is not surprising, therefore, that terrorists also contend there are no innocent victims. Everyone who is not on the terrorists' side, fully supporting their cause, is an enemy—and in total war, whatever can be done to defeat the enemy must be done.

BOX 12-3
Terrorism Today

Even before al-Qaeda's terrorist attacks on the United States on September 11, 2001, democracies were acquainted with terrorism. For example:

- North Americans have witnessed terrorist attacks by those who bomb abortion clinics, the right-wing extremists who blew up the Murrah Building in Oklahoma City in 1995, and Theodore Kaczynski (a.k.a. the Unabomber), who sent package bombs to unwitting victims.
- In Ireland and Britain, the Irish Republican Army (IRA) and its various factions have long used violence in their quest to bring Northern Ireland (Ulster) into the Irish Republic. The same applies to Spain, where the ETA (*Euzkadi Ta Askatasuna*, Basque Homeland and Freedom) has waged a decades-long armed struggle to separate the Basque provinces from Spain.
- In the 1970s and 1980s, Germany faced serious episodes of terror by the Baader–Meinhoff Gang (a.k.a. the Red Army Faction), while Italy suffered terrorist attacks from both the Red Brigades on the extreme left and fascists on the extreme right.
- Continuing into the twenty-first century, Israelis live perpetually with terror, as organizations such as Hamas and Hezbollah have turned to suicide bombers as a regular political tool to press for rights for Palestinians. These tactics provoke strong responses from the Israelis, leaving the Palestinians themselves in a state of insecurity that approximates terror.

Terrorism is not only a form of violence used by groups fighting against established states.* Some states also use terror against their own citizens. Campaigns of ethnic cleansing, systematic attempts to remove all people of a particular ethnicity from a region, often by killing them (for example, as carried out in Rwanda and Yugoslavia in the 1990s), qualify as terror.

Police states and totalitarian regimes often resort to indiscriminate arrests, torture, and even murder to intimidate the population they govern. In many Latin American countries, particularly in the 1980s, "death squads" associated with repressive governments terrorized the population. As well, states sometimes sponsor terrorism to achieve international objectives. For example, Libyan intelligence agents were involved in the bombing of Pan-Am Flight 103 over Lockerbie, Scotland in 1988, killing all on board (Coombes, 2003)—presumably as retaliation for an American attack against Libya's leader.

Terrorism is not unknown in Canada. Between 1963 and 1970, members of the Front de libération du Québec (FLQ) planted bombs, held up banks, and caused at least five deaths by bombs and gunfire. In October 1970, the FLQ kidnapped James Cross, the British trade commissioner in Montreal, and Pierre Laporte, labour minister in the Quebec government. Although Cross was released, Laporte was murdered by the terrorists. But Canada's worst terrorist attack occurred on June 22, 1985, when bombs were planted by terrorists on board Air India Flight 182 before it left Vancouver. The bombing was apparently in retaliation for the Indian government's attack on the Golden Temple at Amritsar, the holiest Sikh shrine. The bombs exploded while the 747 was over the North Atlantic and killed all three hundred and twenty-nine passengers and crew, the great majority of whom were Canadians.

Why is terror used to achieve political objectives? Is it because people see the stakes as being so high that the most extreme measures are justified? Or do those committed to some cause see the odds so stacked against them that only terror will let them be heard? Whatever the cause, terrorism is an ever-present concern.

*The designation of actions as terrorism is often highly controversial. For example, the Russian government condemns Chechen separatists who have bombed buildings and taken hostages as terrorists. Supporters of the Chechen rebels view the Russian government and military as terrorists for their brutal suppression of the breakaway Chechen Republic.

SOCIAL MOVEMENTS AND POLITICAL PROTEST IN CANADA

Canada has been called "the peaceable kingdom," a country characterized by "peace, order and good government" in the words of the *British North America Act*, 1867. However, we should not believe that Canada has had no important episodes of movement politics and political protest in its history, nor that Canadians are dramatically less likely to turn to protest than are the citizens of other democracies. The evidence, in fact, points the other way (Table 12-1).

As in all democratic countries, people in Canada have had to move outside the bounds of official politics to claim their rights. Although there have been many instances of protest politics in Canada, we shall look at just four cases:

- the Rebellions of 1837–38
- the Newfoundland Fisherman's Protective Union
- Quebec nationalism
- Aboriginal rights

The Rebellions of 1837–38

The colonies that became the provinces of Quebec and Ontario—Lower Canada and Upper Canada, respectively—enjoyed only a limited measure of democracy during their five decades of existence (1791–1841). Male citizens (and in Lower Canada, women) who met a property qualification could elect representatives to their colonial legislative assemblies, but the colonial governors were appointed by Britain and did not have to heed the wishes of the people. In fact, both colonies eventually fell under the control of **oligarchic** factions.

In Lower Canada, the oligarchy was called the Chateau Clique; in Upper Canada, it was known as the Family Compact. These two groups of wealthy elites repeatedly ignored popular demands for schools, roads, hospitals, and

OLIGARCHY
Rule by or control by the rich or an economic elite.

TABLE 12-1
THE FREQUENCY OF PROTEST: SELECTED DEMOCRATIC COUNTRIES

COUNTRY	ACTION			
	SIGN PETITION	JOIN BOYCOTT	ATTEND DEMONSTRATION	OCCUPY BUILDING
Canada	71.1%	19.8%	14.6%	2.9%
U.S.A.	68.6%	17.4%	18.2%	1.8%
France	49.1%	11.9%	29.5%	7.5%
Britain	66.0%	10.8%	12.1%	2.5%
Sweden	65.9%	19.6%	22.7%	0.4%

SOURCE: *Compiled from 1981, 1990, and 1995 surveys (combined data set), by World Values Survey, retrieved on July 21, 2004, from www.worldvaluessurvey.org/services/index.html.*

especially calls for responsible government, which would make the governor follow the policies approved by the elected members of the legislatures.[4]

Discontent simmered for several years and finally reached a boiling point in late 1837. Each colony developed its own movement, with its own leadership. Joseph-Louis Papineau, a *seigneur* (upper class landowner) was the leader in Lower Canada. In Upper Canada, the leader was William Lyon Mackenzie, a journalist and the first mayor of Toronto. Both chafed under oligarchic rule and eventually turned to insurrection. However, the British military forces were too much for the patriots, as the rebels called themselves (*les patriotes* in Lower Canada), and the rebellions were crushed.

We cannot say that the patriots lost, however. Just ten years after the revolts had failed, responsible government came to Canada. The colonies of Canada (comprising Lower and Upper Canada, which were joined under one administration in 1841) and Nova Scotia gained control over their internal affairs in 1848. These events show us how seriously nineteenth-century Canadians took the principles of democracy.

Newfoundland's Fishermen's Protective Union

In the early twentieth century, when farmers in Western Canada were forming political movements to protect their rights, a similar process was taking place among Newfoundland fishermen. Newfoundland was not a part of Canada at the time, and had already twice rejected union with the dominion to the west. Nevertheless, what happened has since become part of Canada's political history.

William Ford Coaker formed the Fishermen's Protective Union (FPU) in 1908 and quickly set about organizing the men who worked the waters of the island's many bays. Like its Western counterparts, the FPU sought both benefits specifically for fishermen and reforms that would benefit society as a whole. Like the farmers' movements, Coaker's organization devoted a lot of energy to forming cooperatives.[5]

The FPU entered politics in the 1913 Newfoundland elections and wound up holding the balance of power among three parties. However, the FPU was never able to take power or to consolidate a permanent place in Newfoundland's political life. By the mid-1920s its effective life had ended.

Quebec Nationalism

As an ideology, nationalism has existed in Quebec for nearly two and a half centuries. Yet it has only spurred movement politics on a few occasions. The

---

[4] As well as elected legislatures, both Lower and Upper Canada also had appointed Legislative Councils, rather like today's Senate. These were controlled by the elites of each colony.

[5] Brief introductions to Coaker and the FPU can be found in Rowe (1980, pp. 356–362) and Major (2001, pp. 359–363).

first of these was in the 1830s and led to the rebellion in Lower Canada. Later, during both the First and Second World Wars, there were substantial anti-conscription protests in Quebec, opposing a draft of men for military service. The strongest, longest-lasting, and most influential movement to grow from Quebec nationalism, however, is the separatist or independence movement, which still exists today.

QUIET REVOLUTION
The changes in Quebec that began in 1960, based on the view that Quebec should become a modern, secular, technological society, led by an activist Quebec government that could promote a Québécois identity and place greater control of governing and the economy in the hands of Quebeckers.

Although we can trace contemporary Quebec nationalism to the **Quiet Revolution** that began in 1960, separatism only emerged as a significant force in Quebec politics with the formation of the Parti Québécois (PQ)[6] in 1968. The new party received over 20 percent of the vote in the first two elections in which it ran (1970 and 1973), but that support translated into less than 10 percent of the seats in Quebec's National Assembly. However, in 1976, running on a platform that de-emphasized the independence question, the PQ won power. Since then, the Parti Québécois has been either the government or the official opposition in Quebec.

Under the PQ's leadership, Quebec's nationalist movement brings together unions, women's groups, and nationalist organizations such as la Societé Saint-Jean Baptiste. The movement's principal objective is achieving sovereignty–association, which would see an independent Quebec forming a very close economic and political relationship with Canada. The PQ has organized two referendums on the issue of sovereignty–association. The first, in 1980, lost badly, receiving only 40 percent of the votes; the second, in 1995, nearly won, carrying 49.6 percent of the votes. In recent years, the independence issue has become less important and the PQ lost control of the Quebec government in 2003 with the election of the Liberals under Jean Charest. However, the Bloc Québécois, the party that supports Quebec independence in Canada's Parliament, won fifty-four of Quebec's seventy-five seats in the 2004 election. The movement backing independence remains in place and continues to be dedicated to its objectives.

Aboriginal Rights

For much of the country's history, Canada's Aboriginal peoples have been ignored as political actors. North American Indians, Inuit, and Métis simply did not count in politics—indeed, many did not have the right to vote until 1960. At least partly as a result of their exclusion from politics, indigenous Canadians have suffered severe poverty and social and cultural marginalization.

However, beginning in the 1960s and 1970s, indigenous people in Canada began to demand their rights. In doing so, they sought not only their

---

[6] Two smaller secessionist parties, the Rassemblement pour l'indépendance nationale (RIN) and the Ralliement national (RN), merged with the Mouvement souveraineté-association (MSA) in 1968 to form the Parti Québécois.

rights as citizens (including freedom from discrimination and the right to a fair trial), but also special rights that earlier governments had ceded their ancestors in treaties between the British Crown and various Native nations. Even those groups that had never signed a treaty began to press for Aboriginal rights. These might include unrestricted rights to hunt, fish, or cut timber; exemptions from certain taxes; and regaining lands improperly taken from Aboriginal communities over the years.

In recent years Canada's indigenous people, of whom there are over 975 000, have made significant gains in negotiations over land claims and have seen Aboriginal rights enshrined in the constitution. Yet it has been violent confrontations between Aboriginal communities and federal or provincial authorities that most captured public attention. Two of these were especially important:

- *Oka*. In 1990, plans by the town of Oka in Quebec to expand a golf course involved expropriating land that held a local Mohawk cemetery. An armed stand-off between Quebec Provincial Police and the Mohawk Warriors' Society eventually left a police officer dead and saw the army called in to keep the peace.

- *Burnt Church*. In 1999, a confrontation at Burnt Church, New Brunswick, brought Native and non-Native fishermen into conflict. A month before this episode, a Supreme Court decision held that treaties from the 1760s exempted Natives in the Maritimes and Eastern Quebec from current fisheries regulations. Non-Aboriginal fishermen objected, fearing that uncontrolled fishing would destroy the resource. The two sides clashed violently at Burnt Church, leading to the destruction of much of the Natives' gear and the burning of three fish-processing plants.

The Oka Crisis (CBC Archives)
archives.cbc.ca/IDD-1-71-99/
conflict_war/oka/xxx

While political protest has included violence in Canada's past, such as the Rebellions of 1837–38, it is relatively rare and we are quick to forget how easily it can happen. Ted Robert Gurr's Frustration–Aggression hypothesis (Gurr, 1967) directly addressed the question of what triggers violent protest. Gurr argued that where levels of frustration are high within a population, these feelings can readily find violent expression. This certainly seems to be what occurred at both Oka and Burnt Church. However, this theory does little to explain why people sometimes direct their energies into social movements or ordinary political action.

Why Canadian Social Movements Take the Political Forms They Do

Canada is basically a peaceful country, in part because of the country's political opportunity structure (POS), which has resulted in some of the country's most politically important movements forming political parties. Leon

Epstein's (1964) analysis suggests that the combination of the federal system and parliamentary government accounts for this.

The federal system plays a role simply by creating provinces that are sufficiently socially homogeneous (Macpherson, 1954) that a social movement based on a single class or group, such as grain growers in Saskatchewan and Alberta or francophones in Quebec, could command enough votes to win an election. This makes changing itself into a party a plausible way for a movement to get the power needed to secure its objectives.

Also contributing to the success of Canadian movements-turned-parties is another feature of this country's constitution: parliamentary government. If a party wins a majority of the seats in the legislature, it forms the government. (Because of the nature of the electoral system, this can be achieved with less than a majority of the popular vote.) As the government, it controls both the executive and the legislature. Its legislative proposals are almost certain to pass and its program will be enacted. (The situation is somewhat different if it does not win a majority of seats in the legislature.) In contrast, in an American state it would be necessary to capture three separate elections to gain the same degree of control: the governorship, the state house of representatives and the state senate.

Thus, two very basic parts of Canada's constitutional make-up, federalism and parliamentary government, have influenced how social movements in this country have pursued their political objectives. However, not all movements have wanted to become parties. In some cases, including those that are too specialized (anti-smoking) or too internally diverse (women and Aboriginals), forming a party is not a viable option. In these cases, taking the institutional form of an interest group is a better choice.

Permeability

Although many factors combine to determine a movement's political success, there is one concept that affords a good, rough guideline to its chances: the permeability (Gamson, 1975) of the political system.

Permeability refers to how easily interests and actors can enter the political system and stand a reasonable chance of using politics to secure their aims. In general, the political opportunity structure of a democracy is relatively permeable. It offers both numerous opportunities for people to express their views to government and real possibilities that the authorities will consider those views seriously and act to implement them. However, no political system, no matter how democratic, is perfectly permeable. Moreover, no government treats all groups and interests exactly alike; rather, it favours some over others. As we noted earlier, it is precisely for this reason that people form movements and turn to protest.

The political opportunity structures that matter here start with, but then stretch beyond, the confines of formal governmental institutions. People must believe that they have the right to organize themselves to seek action from government. At least as important, they must believe that government has a responsibility to listen to them. Last, they must trust that the political system as a whole, not just the government of the day, is fair and open enough to be persuaded by the arguments the movement makes. These circumstances do not generally apply to non-democratic countries (see Box 12-4, Political Protest in China).

BOX 12-4

Political Protest in China

Canadian social movements are influenced by the political opportunity structures offered to them by a relatively permeable Canadian political system. Other movements in other countries obviously work within different structures with different levels of permeability.

In the late 1980s, for example, Mikhail Gorbachev began opening up the political system of the Soviet Union. This inspired university students in the People's Republic of China (PRC) to press their own government to move toward democracy. The Chinese government had already taken some steps to relax its hold on the economy, so there was reason to hope for a positive response. However, the Communist party's control of the political system made working through official channels impossible. Protest was the logical alternative.

On April 15, 1989, students began a series of demonstrations in Tiananmen Square, the main public plaza in Beijing, the PRC's capital. Soon, urban workers joined them and eventually over one million people were involved in the protest. As the demonstrations continued into May, the government declared martial law. When this also proved ineffective, the government called in troops from outside the capital. On the night of June 4, 1989,

soldiers cleared the square. Sporadic fighting continued for a short time, leaving an estimated 2500 civilians dead.

The Chinese government manifested a high level of impermeability. Not only did it offer few opportunities to advance dissenting views through regular state institutions, it eventually resorted to deadly force to assert its authority. Protest does not always work, and protest in a dictatorship is always fraught with peril.

Civil disobedience against military might in Tiananmen Square.

TRANSNATIONAL POLITICAL PROTEST

Zapatistas in Cyberspace
www.eco.texas.edu/faculty/
Cleaver/zapsincyberwebsites.html

Social movements and political protest have often migrated across borders. Nineteenth-century examples of transnational movements include the anti-slavery and labour movements. Later, the student movement of the 1960s and the women's rights movement of the 1970s were also international in scope. As well, protestors in one country, such as the Zapatistas in Mexico, increasingly seek support for their cause from sympathizers around the world. But, ironically, it is the anti-globalization movement that best exemplifies globalized political protest. It is only with the arrival of globalization in the 1990s that social movements and political protest have become truly transnational, turning into worldwide phenomena instead of an array of related national movements.

Peoples' Global Action
www.nadir.org/nadir/initiativ/agp/
en/index.htm

The anti-globalization movement has focused on some specific elements of globalization, particularly international finance and its effects on the world's economy. This has led the movement to target meetings of the World Trade Organization (WTO) and other forums promoting increased economic integration, such as the G8 summits of the leaders of the major industrialized countries, meetings of the International Monetary Fund and World Bank, and the European Union summits, for its protests. Since the movement's first major operation in 1998, in which it brought to the public's view a hitherto secret draft of a proposed Multilateral Agreement on Investment (Clarke & Barlow, 1997), the movement has moved more fully into contentious direct actions. Following the protests in Seattle in 1999 there have been several big demonstrations every year (Table 12-2), most of them involving clashes with police.[7] One, in Genoa, Italy, saw three demonstrators killed, several hundred injured, and charges of torture levelled against the Italian police.

**TABLE 12-2
PARTICIPATION IN ANTI-GLOBALIZATION PROTEST ACTIONS**

Note: Estimates of the number of demonstrators varies widely.

PLACE	DATE	ESTIMATED NUMBER OF PARTICIPANTS
Seattle	September 1999	100 000
Washington	April 2000	10 000
Prague, Czech Republic	September 2000	12 000
Quebec City	April 2001	30 000
Genoa, Italy	September 2001	100 000
Barcelona, Spain	March 2002	250 000
Miami	November 2003	10 000

SOURCE: *Compiled by authors from press estimates, 1999–2003.*

[7] The largest global protest demonstrations, however, have been held to protest the invasion of Iraq, attracting over ten million demonstrators worldwide in March 2003, including one million or more in London, Rome, Madrid, and Barcelona.

The anti-globalization movement is particularly adept at making use of modern communications technology. Of special importance is its use of e-mail and the Web (Lee, 2003). These instruments, themselves part of the phenomenon of globalization, allow the anti-globalization movement to organize effectively without needing complex permanent structures. However, this flexibility also brings costs to the movement. Because there really is no central core institution, any group can adhere to the movement and participate in its demonstrations.

As a result, violent anti-capitalist groups, who wish to destroy the entire capitalist system, mix with far less confrontational anti-globalizers, who focus on what they see as the unfair system of international trade rules. The anti-capitalist and anarchist groups, a small minority within the anti-globalization movement but the part most likely to seek violent confrontations with the authorities, give the entire movement a far more radical appearance than many of its members desire.

Summary and Conclusion

Political protest attempts to influence the policy choices governments make. It can be the best, or only, political tool available to the excluded. Even in democracies, normal channels can prove ineffective for the weak and marginalized. Similarly, people choose social movements to mobilize in support of some objective instead of working through political parties or interest groups because they believe that parties and groups will not accord their cause high enough priority. Social movements and political protest are thus alternative ways to seek the common good that are likely inevitable in a democratic society.

Yet protest always poses difficult questions for democratic citizens. On the one hand, most of us play by the established rules of politics most of the time. We believe that these rules are generally fair or, if they are not, that they can be changed by normally available methods. On the other hand, we know full well that some of our fellow citizens are not able to make those rules work for them. We may or may not endorse their aims, but we may be perplexed by the fact that our democratic rules make effective political action impossible for some people. We

can never resolve our dilemma. The best we can do is to be aware of it and acknowledge that we are witnessing a perennial problem of democratic politics.

Very few members of a democratic society are able to accept using terror or even employing violence as a regular instrument for political ends. At times we may sympathize with guerrilla rebels in distant lands who wage wars to overthrow brutal dictators. Where reasonable channels of political expression exist, though, it is hard to justify the use of force. It is even harder for citizens of Canada or other well-functioning democracies to countenance the use of terror as a means of protest. While terror unfortunately may have a place in war (although we should question whether the use of indiscriminate killing of civilians and the use of chemical, biological, and nuclear weapons is ever justified), we are loath to grant it status as a legitimate instrument of politics. Likewise, we find it troubling that some democratic states have supported and provided assistance to governments, security forces, or rebels who use terrorist tactics.

Key Terms

Discussion Questions

1. Have you ever been involved in a political protest? In what circumstances do you think that you would get involved in protest activity? Would you engage in civil disobedience?

2. Have social movements contributed to the development of Canadian democracy?

3. Is terrorism ever justified? Are terrorists irrational?

4. What are political opportunity structures and why are they important in understanding political protest?

5. Why do you think political violence has had a relatively limited role in Canadian protest politics?

Further Reading

Carroll, W. (Ed). *Organizing dissent: Contemporary social movements in theory and practice* (2nd ed.) Toronto: Garamond Press, 1997.

Clark, S., 1959. *Movements of social protest in Canada: 1640–1840.* Toronto: University of Toronto Press.

Irvin, C. *Militant nationalism.* Minneapolis, MN: University of Minnesota Press, 1999.

Keck, M., & Sikkink, K. *Activists without borders.* Ithaca, NY: Cornell University Press, 1998.

Smith, J., & Johnston, H. (Eds.). *Globalization and resistance: Transnational dimensions of social movements.* Lanham, MD: Rowman & Littlefield, 2002.

Snow, D., Soule, S., & Kreisi, H. (Eds.). *The Blackwell companion to social movements.* Malden, MA: Blackwell Publishers, 2004.

Zakuta, L. *A social movement becalmed: A study of change in the CCF.* Toronto: University of Toronto Press, 1964.

THE CONSTITUTION, RIGHTS AND FREEDOMS, AND THE RULE OF LAW

PHOTO ABOVE: When Kevin Bourassa and Joe Varnell exchanged wedding vows in Toronto's Metropolitan Community Church in 2001, attendees included Ontario's NDP leader and journalists from around the world. Outside, protesters wore devil masks.

CHAPTER OBJECTIVES

After reading this chapter you should be able to:

1. explain the importance of a constitution and constitutional government
2. describe the major characteristics of the Canadian constitution
3. outline the provisions of the Canadian Charter of Rights and Freedoms
4. discuss the political importance of the courts
5. explain the meaning of the rule of law

When Kevin Bourassa and Joe Varnell exchanged wedding vows in Toronto's Metropolitan Community Church on January 14, 2001, Ontario's NDP leader attended, along with journalists from around the world. Governor General Adrienne Clarkson sent a congratulatory telegram. Outside, protestors wore devil masks.

The Ontario government of the time refused to register the couple's wedding licence and a legal battle over same-sex marriage ensued. Within a few years, courts in Ontario, Quebec, British Columbia (2003), and Nova Scotia and the Yukon (2004) ruled that the traditional legal definition of marriage—a union of one man and one woman—was discriminatory and violated the equality rights provisions of the Charter of Rights and Freedoms in Canada's constitution. Bourassa and Varnell's marriage was officially registered on June 11, 2003, and since then many gays and lesbians have been legally married. However, Alberta Premier Ralph Klein indicated that, if necessary, he would use the "notwithstanding clause," a clause in the Charter that allows the passing of legislation that infringes on rights, in order to prevent the legalization of same-sex marriages in Alberta.

Although in 1999 the Liberals had supported a Reform party motion upholding the traditional definition of marriage, following the provincial court decisions Prime Minister Jean Chrétien decided to introduce legislation to define marriage as involving two persons. Calgary's Catholic bishop said that Chrétien risked burning in hell, and the Pope reminded Catholic politicians of their obligation to vote according to their faith. On becoming prime minister, Paul Martin tried to downplay the issue, hoping that a

decision could be delayed until after an election. However, toward the end of the 2004 election campaign, Martin, facing a possible Liberal defeat, decided to use the issue to attack the Conservatives.

The Conservatives, Martin argued, would use the notwithstanding clause in the Charter to take away people's rights. Conservative leader Stephen Harper said that he opposed same-sex marriage and would allow a free vote in the House of Commons to decide the issue. But while he avoided the question of whether the notwithstanding clause should be used to protect a ban on same-sex marriages from court challenges, other Conservatives were more forthright. MP Randy White proclaimed, "To heck with the courts... the politicians make the laws"(Hume, 2004).

The issue of same-sex marriage raises questions not only about how marriage should be defined, but also about how rights should be protected. Should the courts or legislative bodies have the final say in determining how general constitutional rights such as equality rights should be applied to particular issues? In this chapter, we focus on the Canadian constitution, including the Charter of Rights and Freedoms and its controversial notwithstanding clause.

WHAT IS A CONSTITUTION?

In 1988, abortion was in effect legalized in Canada by a Supreme Court of Canada interpretation of the Charter of Rights and Freedoms, an important element of the country's constitution since 1982. The court struck down a law that had made abortion a criminal offence unless a hospital committee certified that continuation of the pregnancy would endanger the woman's life or health. In the court's view, the abortion law violated the right to "life, liberty and security of the person" that is protected in the Charter. A subsequent attempt to pass a new law specifying conditions under which abortion would be allowed failed to be approved by Parliament.

The abortion decision, very much like the same-sex marriage developments we read about in this chapter's opening vignette, is a striking example of the role of a constitution. A **constitution** establishes the fundamental rules and principles by which a state is governed. It determines which institutions have the authority to make laws and governing decisions. It indicates what procedures need to be followed in selecting the government and in passing laws, and what rights and freedoms are guaranteed to the population. As well, constitutional documents often contain a general statement of the values and goals of the political community.

A constitution is generally considered to be the supreme or basic law of a country. Governments are expected to follow its provisions, and the laws that they pass are expected to conform to the provisions of the constitution. However, non-democratic governments, and occasionally democratic ones, sometimes ignore their constitution when it suits their purposes. Although most countries have some form of constitution, many do not have a **constitutional government**. A constitutional government is one that consistently acts in accordance with the rules and principles established in the constitution.

"Unwritten" Constitutions

The United Kingdom, which could be considered the first country to adopt a constitutional government, is sometimes described as having an unwritten constitution. Much of the British constitution consists of **constitutional conventions**—fundamental principles that are consistently followed, even though they are not contained in a legal document and not enforceable in the courts. For example, by convention, the British monarch will always give the assent needed for a bill (proposed law) to become a law if a majority in Parliament has passed it. The British constitution is not entirely unwritten, as there have been a number of important laws passed by the British Parliament concerning various aspects of the system of government. There is, however, no single constitutional document or clearly defined set of constitutional documents that could be defined as the British constitution. Thus it is better described as an uncodified, rather than an unwritten, constitution.

CONSTITUTION
The fundamental rules and principles by which a state is governed.

CONSTITUTIONAL GOVERNMENT
A government that consistently acts in accordance with the rules and principles established in its constitution.

CONSTITUTIONAL CONVENTION
A fundamental principle that is consistently followed even though it is not contained in a legal document and not enforceable in the courts.

In addition, **parliamentary supremacy** (also termed parliamentary sovereignty) is a basic principle of the British system of governing, meaning that Parliament is the supreme law-making body. Thus, a majority in Parliament can change the constitution through an act of Parliament. The British constitution does not limit the power of a government that has majority support in Parliament. In reality, however, basic constitutional principles are deeply entrenched in the British political culture and thus are generally respected by the government.

PARLIAMENTARY SUPREMACY
A basic principle of the British system of governing, recognizing Parliament as the supreme law-making body.

Formal Constitutions

The United States (1787) and France (1789) pioneered the use of a formal, written, codified constitution. Almost all countries today have a formal constitution or set of constitutional documents that establishes the major constitutional provisions. Generally, a codified constitution is considered to be the basic or supreme law of the country. Laws and governmental actions are expected to be consistent with the higher law of the constitution. Special procedures usually have to be followed if the codified constitution is to be changed.

Constitution Finder
confinder.richmond.edu

The distinction between a written, codified constitution and an unwritten, uncodified constitution should not be exaggerated. Formal constitutional documents typically do not provide a comprehensive set of provisions concerning how a country is to be governed. Various laws, conventions, customs, and judicial interpretations are also an important part of any constitution.

The Canadian Constitution

The core element of the Canadian constitution is the *Constitution Act, 1867* (originally known as the *British North America Act*), an act of the Parliament of the United Kingdom that established Canada by uniting the colonies of Canada (Ontario and Quebec), Nova Scotia, and New Brunswick. Over the years, there have been a number of amendments to the *Constitution Act* (see Figure 13-1). Of particular importance is the *Constitution Act, 1982,* which made the constitution a fully Canadian document. The *Constitution Act, 1982* made it clear that the formal constitution is the supreme law of Canada, and specifically indicated which documents are to be considered part of the codified constitution.

CONSTITUTION ACT, 1867
An act of the Parliament of the United Kingdom that established Canada by uniting the colonies of Canada (Ontario and Quebec), Nova Scotia, and New Brunswick, and set out the framework for governing.

CONSTITUTION ACT, 1982
The act that made the constitution fully Canadian and added the Charter of Rights and Freedoms to the constitution.

Beyond the formal, codified constitution, there are a variety of ordinary legislative acts, such as the *Supreme Court Act* and the *Canada Elections Act,* that might be considered constitutional because of their fundamental importance. Much of the actual workings of the system of government are established through constitutional conventions, many of which were inherited from Britain, rather than through formal constitutional documents. As well, judicial bodies have played a major role in interpreting the constitution and thus, in effect, added to the bare bones of the formal constitutional documents.

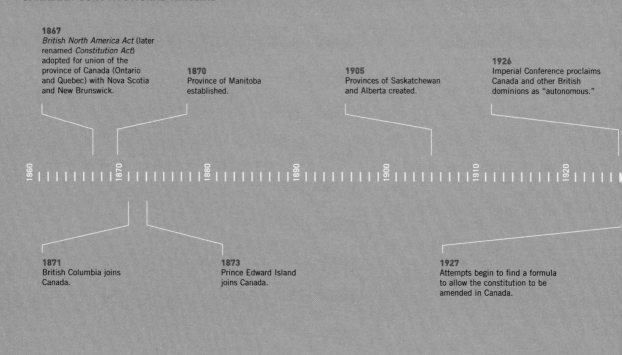

FIGURE 13-1
CANADIAN CONSTITUTIONAL TIMELINE

1867
British North America Act (later renamed *Constitution Act*) adopted for union of the province of Canada (Ontario and Quebec) with Nova Scotia and New Brunswick.

1870
Province of Manitoba established.

1905
Provinces of Saskatchewan and Alberta created.

1926
Imperial Conference proclaims Canada and other British dominions as "autonomous."

1871
British Columbia joins Canada.

1873
Prince Edward Island joins Canada.

1927
Attempts begin to find a formula to allow the constitution to be amended in Canada.

AMENDING THE CONSTITUTION

Constitutional amendments (changes) are needed from time to time because of changing circumstances and the changing values of a country's citizens. Experiences with the constitution may also lead to a desire to improve it.

Special Procedures

Typically, formal constitutional documents can only be amended through special procedures to ensure that there is a broad consensus in support of the changes and that the basic features of governing are not arbitrarily changed to benefit those in positions of political power. For example, amendments to the American constitution require a two-thirds majority in each of the Houses of Congress and ratification by three-quarters of the state legislatures. Only twenty-six amendments to the American constitution have been passed in over two hundred years. Likewise, many countries require votes by large majorities in their legislative bodies, final ratification after a general election, or ratification by a referendum.

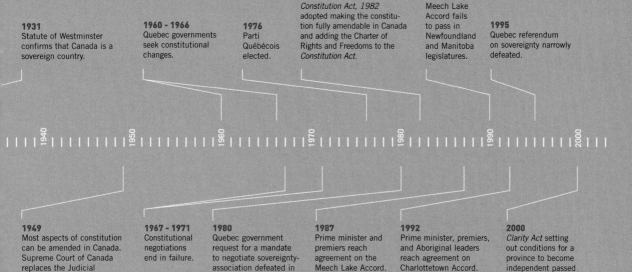

1931
Statute of Westminster confirms that Canada is a sovereign country.

1960 - 1966
Quebec governments seek constitutional changes.

1976
Parti Québécois elected.

1982
Constitution Act, 1982 adopted making the constitution fully amendable in Canada and adding the Charter of Rights and Freedoms to the *Constitution Act*.

1990
Meech Lake Accord fails to pass in Newfoundland and Manitoba legislatures.

1995
Quebec referendum on sovereignty narrowly defeated.

1949
Most aspects of constitution can be amended in Canada. Supreme Court of Canada replaces the Judicial Committee of the British Privy Council as the highest court of appeal.

1967 - 1971
Constitutional negotiations end in failure.

1980
Quebec government request for a mandate to negotiate sovereignty-association defeated in a Quebec referendum.

1987
Prime minister and premiers reach agreement on the Meech Lake Accord.

1992
Prime minister, premiers, and Aboriginal leaders reach agreement on Charlottetown Accord. Accord defeated in a national referendum.

2000
Clarity Act setting out conditions for a province to become independent passed by Parliament.

Amending Canada's Constitution

Some aspects of the Canadian constitution can be changed without any procedural difficulties. The unwritten aspects of the Canadian constitution—conventions and judicial interpretations—typically evolve over time. Ordinary laws that are of constitutional significance can be changed by the adoption of a new law by a simple majority in Parliament or a provincial legislature. The *Constitution Act*, in contrast, is difficult to change.

A few provisions of the *Constitution Act*, such as the offices of the monarch, governor general, and lieutenant-governors, and the composition of the Supreme Court of Canada, are only amendable by the resolution of a majority in Parliament[1] and in all of the provincial legislatures. Most of the *Constitution Act* (including the law-making authority of Parliament and

---

[1] A majority in each of the chambers of Parliament (that is, the House of Commons and the Senate) is needed to amend the constitution. However, if the Senate does not pass the resolution for the amendment, after one hundred and eighty days the House of Commons can repass the resolution, in which case the approval of the Senate is not needed for the amendment.

provincial legislatures) can be changed with the agreement of a majority in Parliament and at least two-thirds of the provincial legislatures, provided that those legislatures represent provinces containing at least one-half of the population of all the provinces.[2]

Major amendments to the formal constitution have proven difficult to achieve, as witnessed by the failures of the **Meech Lake Accord** and the **Charlottetown Accord** (see Box 13-1, The Politics of Canadian Constitutional Change). Instead, modifications to the system of government have been achieved at times without changing the formal constitution.

RIGHTS AND FREEDOMS

Nearly all constitutions contain provisions establishing the rights and freedoms of individuals, with some constitutions also establishing certain group rights. In the United States, for example, the Bill of Rights has been part of the constitution since 1791. As a result, American governments are prohibited from passing laws that infringe upon those rights.

Protecting Rights in Canada

The original Canadian constitution, the *Constitution Act, 1867*, did not explicitly protect rights and freedoms, other than the right to use English or French in Parliament, the Quebec legislature, and certain courts, as well as the rights of denominational schools to receive public funding in some provinces. Instead, following British practice, it was assumed that Parliament and provincial legislatures would not infringe upon traditional liberties and that judicial bodies would interpret laws in a manner consistent with those liberties.

Although the tradition of respecting rights and freedoms was generally followed, there had been important exceptions, such as the treatment of Aboriginal peoples and the incarceration of Canadian citizens of Japanese descent during World War II. In the 1960s, the Canadian government and many provincial governments adopted Bills of Rights, although these did not have the weight of a constitutional provision. In 1982, the **Charter of Rights and Freedoms** was added to Canada's formal written constitution (see Box 13-2, The Canadian Charter of Rights and Freedoms: Basic Provisions). The Charter is superior to ordinary legislation, explicitly allows the courts to

MEECH LAKE ACCORD
A 1987 package of constitutional changes that was not passed. It contained controversial provisions, including the recognition of Quebec as a distinct society.

CHARLOTTETOWN ACCORD
A package of constitutional changes, including recognition of the inherent right of Aboriginals to self-government and major changes to the Senate to provide for equal representation by each province regardless of population size. It was defeated in a referendum in 1992.

Canadian Civil Liberties Association
www.ccla.org

CHARTER OF RIGHTS AND FREEDOMS
Part of the *Constitution Act, 1982*, the Charter is superior to ordinary legislation, explicitly allows the courts to invalidate legislation, and applies to the actions of all governments and organizations under the direct control of government.

---

[2]Although this is still the procedure in the *Constitution Act*, the Canadian Parliament passed legislation in 1996 requiring that proposed constitutional changes introduced into the Canadian Parliament must also have the support of Ontario, Quebec, British Columbia, the Prairies (in effect, Alberta plus either Saskatchewan or Manitoba), and Atlantic Canada (at least two provinces containing at least one-half of the region's population). Although there is no requirement that constitutional changes be approved in a referendum, there is now an expectation that substantial constitutional changes will be submitted to the public.

BOX 13-1

The Politics of Canadian Constitutional Change

The constitution has often been a flashpoint for political controversy in Canada.

Starting in 1927, national and provincial leaders met on and off in an attempt to reach agreement on a formula for amending the constitution in Canada. The formula that was finally adopted in 1982 was reached only after a bitter set of negotiations between the Canadian and provincial governments.

In addition to disagreements over the choice of an amending formula, there have been serious disagreements over the content of the constitution. Beginning in the early 1960s, Quebec governments sought constitutional changes to give them greater power to lead the social and economic development of Quebec. Other provincial governments, including Alberta and Newfoundland, have sought greater powers over their natural resources, as well as a stronger voice for the less populated provinces in Parliament through changes to the Senate.

The *Constitution Act, 1982* was put into effect over the objections of the Quebec government and many Aboriginal leaders. Quebec provincial politicians claimed that constitutional convention necessitated the agreement of all provincial legislatures for constitutional changes that affected the powers of the provinces. As well, the Quebec government was disappointed that promises of constitutional changes to enhance the position of Quebec were not fulfilled. Aboriginal leaders argued that treaties that had been signed with the British Crown were being transferred to Canada without their agreement.

Although challenges to the Constitution Act, 1982 in the courts proved unsuccessful, Quebec governments have questioned the legitimacy of Canada's written constitution. To try to resolve this issue, Prime Minister Brian Mulroney and all ten premiers agreed on a package of constitutional changes in 1987, termed the **Meech Lake Accord**. However, there was widespread opposition to the accord among English-speaking Canadians, particularly to the proposal that Quebec be recognized in the constitution as a distinct society. Aboriginal Canadians were disappointed that the Meech Lake Accord did not include recognition of their inherent right to self-government. The accord, which required the agreement of all legislatures, failed to pass in the Manitoba and Newfoundland legislatures and thus died in 1990.

A second package of constitutional changes, the **Charlottetown Accord**, was agreed to by the prime minister, ten premiers, two territorial leaders, and leaders of the four major Aboriginal organizations in 1992. Its centrepiece was the recognition of the inherent right of Aboriginals to self-government. It also proposed major changes to the Senate to provide for equal representation by each province regardless of population size, and recognition of a variety of characteristics of Canada, including a somewhat more specific definition of Quebec's distinctiveness than presented in the Meech Lake Accord.

The Charlottetown Accord was defeated in a national referendum by a vote of 55 percent to 45 percent. The majority of English-speaking Canadians felt that it gave too much to Quebec, the majority of French-speaking Quebeckers felt that it gave too little to Quebec, and the majority of Aboriginals felt that the self-government provisions were too limited.

Canadian Charter of Rights and
Freedoms
laws.justice.gc.ca/en/charter

invalidate legislation, and applies to the actions of all governments and organizations under the direct control of government.[3]

BOX 13-2

The Canadian Charter of Rights and Freedoms: Basic Provisions

The basic provisions of the Canadian Charter of Rights and Freedoms include the following:

- *Fundamental freedoms* (Section 2) protect freedom of conscience and religion, and freedom of opinion and expression, including freedom of the media, freedom of peaceful assembly, and freedom of association.

- *Democratic rights* (Sections 3 to 5) include the right of all citizens to vote and hold elected office. The maximum term of Parliament and provincial legislatures is limited to five years.

- *Mobility rights* (Section 6) include the right to move and to pursue a livelihood in any province. However, provinces are allowed to adopt policies that give preference to their own residents for such matters as employment if the province has a below-average rate of employment

- A variety of *legal rights* (Sections 7 to 14) include the right to life, liberty, and security of the person, the right to be secure against unreasonable search or arbitrary detention, the right to a trial within a reasonable period of time, the right to be presumed innocent until proven guilty, and the right not to be subject to any cruel and unusual punishment.

- The *equality rights* clause (Section 15) provides that every person is equal under the law and has the right to the equal protection and equal benefit of the law without discrimination on such grounds as race, origin, colour, religion, sex, age, or mental or physical disability. However, *affirmative action* laws or programs designed to help disadvantaged individuals or groups are permitted.

- *Language rights* (Sections 16 to 23) include the declaration that English and French are the official languages of Canada and New Brunswick and are given equal status in the operations of the Canadian and New Brunswick governments. Canadian citizens whose mother tongue is either English or French have the right to have their children educated in their own language where numbers warrant, although in Quebec this right only applies to parents who received their schooling in Canada.

- Although not part of the Charter, the *Constitution Act* (1982) also recognizes *Aboriginal rights* and rights that Aboriginal peoples have obtained through treaties and land claims agreements.

---

[3] Human rights codes adopted by provincial and national governments provide for various human rights, including protection against various forms of discrimination by private employers and other organizations and individuals. These codes, however, are not part of the constitution.

Positive Rights Not Included

Some countries go beyond protecting individual freedoms and guaranteeing the right to participate in political life. Many European countries include **positive rights** in their constitutions—rights to services or benefits such as the right to education, health care, and employment. Such rights, however, are not generally enforceable through the legal system, but rather are statements of goals and principles that are implemented through the ordinary processes of governing (Glendon, 1995). Although positive rights are not included in the Charter, Canada, along with the majority of countries of the world, has signed the International Covenant on Economic, Social, and Cultural Rights, which includes a commitment to a variety of positive rights.

POSITIVE RIGHT
A right to services or benefits such as the right to education, health care, and employment.

International Covenant on Economic, Social, and Cultural Rights
www.unhchr.ch/html/menu3/b/a_cescr.htm

"Reasonable" Limits

Rights and freedoms are not absolute. For example, freedom of expression is an important right, but it does not give a person the right to yell "Fire!" in a crowded theatre when there is no fire. The **reasonable limits clause** of the Canadian Charter allows for reasonable limits to be placed on rights and freedoms, provided that the limits can be "demonstrably justified in a free and democratic society"(Section 1).

The Supreme Court of Canada, for example, has upheld laws prohibiting hate literature and pornography as reasonable limits on freedom of expression. The Supreme Court also upheld a provision in the Canadian election law that limits the amount of money any person or group other than a registered party or candidate may spend on advertising during an election to support a candidate or highlight an issue. On the other hand, a law banning tobacco advertising was struck down by the Supreme Court, which did not view it as a "demonstrably justified" limit on freedom of expression.

REASONABLE LIMITS CLAUSE
A provision of the Canadian Charter of Rights and Freedoms that allows for "reasonable limits" to be placed on rights and freedoms provided that the limits can be "demonstrably justified in a free and democratic society."

Overriding the Charter: The Notwithstanding Clause

Section 33 of the Charter of Rights and Freedoms allows Parliament or a provincial legislature to override some rights by the use of the **notwithstanding clause** (see Table 13-1). This involves a legislative body explicitly declaring that a particular law shall operate *notwithstanding* the provisions of the Charter. Such a declaration is only effective for five years, although it can be re-enacted as often as is desired. Box 13-3, The Use of the Notwithstanding Clause, provides an example of how the notwithstanding clause has been used.

NOTWITHSTANDING CLAUSE
A provision in the Charter of Rights and Freedoms that allows a legislative body to explicitly declare that a particular law (related to some parts of the Charter) shall operrate *notwithstanding* the provisions of the Charter. Such a declaration is only effective for five years, although it can be re-enacted as often as is desired.

JUDICIAL REVIEW

In some countries with codified constitutions, the courts have the authority to strike down legislation or governmental actions that the courts deem to be

TABLE 13-1
THE CHARTER AND THE NOTWITHSTANDING CLAUSE

PROVISIONS THAT CANNOT BE OVERRIDDEN	NOTWITHSTANDING CLAUSE APPLIES TO
Democratic rights	Fundamental freedoms
Mobility rights	Legal rights
Language rights	Equality rights
Male–female equality rights	

BOX 13-3

The Use of the Notwithstanding Clause

The notwithstanding clause in Canada's Charter of Rights and Freedoms has stirred much controversy. Some view it as an unfortunate compromise between the supporters and opponents of the Charter that makes some rights vulnerable to the whims of the governing party in Parliament or a provincial legislature and to the pressure of public opinion. Others argue that the clause allows flexibility and protects the democratic principle by ensuring that responsibility for some political decisions ultimately lies with the elected representatives of the people (Petter, 1990).

The notwithstanding clause has been very rarely invoked. Considerable attention was given to its use to protect the French character of Quebec. The Supreme Court of Canada struck down the provision in Quebec's Charter of the French Language (Bill 101) that required most public signs in that province to be exclusively in French. The Quebec government then invoked the notwithstanding clause and passed a sign law permitting only French on signs outside stores while allowing French and English on signs inside stores. However, the Quebec government did not renew its use of the notwithstanding clause when the five-year limit ran out. Instead, it passed a new law, presumably more consistent with the Charter, that required that French be given a prominent position on signs in Quebec.

The requirement that legislation must explicitly state that the Charter is being overridden makes it politically risky for a government to use the notwithstanding clause. Opponents of a government's use of the clause may accuse the government of trampling on individual rights. However, as we saw in the opening vignette, there have been demands for the use of the notwithstanding clause to circumvent court rulings on morally charged issues such as homosexual rights and same-sex marriage.

JUDICIAL REVIEW
The authority of the courts to strike down legislation or governmental actions that the courts deem to be in violation of the constitution.

in violation of the constitution. For example, although the power of **judicial review** is not explicitly stated in the American constitution, the courts have assumed this power since 1803.

In a number of European countries, including Germany and Austria, judicial review is carried out by a special constitutional court rather than by the regular court system. Many countries, however, do not provide for judicial review, or only have a weak version of it (Lane & Ersson, 2000). Rather than determining whether legislation is constitutional, the courts in many countries may interpret laws in ways that emphasize individual rights and procedural fairness.

Judicial Activism

Even in countries where judicial review is available, there is considerable variation in the degree to which the judiciary is active in invalidating legislation and government actions that are inconsistent with the constitution. The United States is often viewed as the best example of **judicial activism**. For example, since the 1950s the American Supreme Court has had a major impact on American politics by overturning state laws that provided for racial segregation and ordering the busing of children from one neighbourhood to another to try to achieve racial integration in public schools.

In Canada, the courts have always had some ability to invalidate the laws passed by Parliament and provincial legislatures if the laws exceed the authority granted by the constitution to that level of government. The authority to invalidate legislation was expanded by the Charter of Rights and Freedoms in 1982. Since then, the courts have exhibited a degree of judicial activism by invalidating some laws and regulations. For example, the Supreme Court ruled that the unemployment insurance law discriminated against men by providing maternity leave but not paternity leave. Parliament subsequently passed legislation to provide for paternity leave. The courts have also struck down various laws that discriminate against homosexuals by interpreting the equality rights provision in the Charter so as to prohibit discrimination on the basis of sexual orientation.

As discussed in Box 13-4, Is Judicial Activism Desirable?, there has been considerable controversy about the role of judicial activism in Canada's courts.

JUDICIAL ACTIVISM
The term used when the judiciary is active in invalidating legislation and government actions that are inconsistent with the constitution.

THE RULE OF LAW

Closely connected to the idea of constitutional government is the concept of the *rule of law*. The idea is that we should be subject to *known, predictable,* and *impartial* rules of conduct, rather than to the arbitrary orders of particular individuals.

An important aspect of the rule of law is that both the rulers and the ruled are subject to the law. It also carries with it the idea that the state should not be able to use its coercive powers against an individual unless that person has violated a specific, known law, as judged by an impartial institution (that is, an institution that is not influenced by the government). Further, the rule of law includes the idea that the laws should only be made by known and accepted procedures.

Generally, in liberal democracies the principle of the rule of law is well established, although, as with all principles, some exceptions do occur. Security forces in many countries have violated the law in order to deal with

Human Rights Watch
www.hrw.org

BOX 13-4

Is Judicial Activism Desirable?

Some commentators have argued that the expansion of judicial review has made Canadian courts too powerful. Instead of the elected representatives of the people making decisions about controversial issues, appointed judges who are unaccountable are, in effect, making important decisions concerning issues such as abortion, same-sex marriage, and the legalization of the medical use of marijuana. Because governments have been very reluctant to use the Charter's notwithstanding clause, there is no check on what some view as the excessive activism of the courts (Morton, 2003)

Other commentators argue that by using the Charter, the courts have helped to protect the rights of minorities. When it adopted the Charter of Rights and Freedoms, Canada established itself as a true constitutional democracy in which an independent judiciary sets limits to the power of government (Potter, 2003). The courts are more likely to protect the rights of unpopular minorities than elected officials, who may be pressured by majority opinion.

In assessing each argument, it should be noted that the courts have been more active at some points in time and more deferential to the wishes of legislative bodies at other points in time, depending on the issues involved and the judges who are hearing the cases. As well, governments and legislative bodies have sometimes preferred to leave some controversial moral issues to the courts to decide, as in the case of abortion law.

The courts generally only consider the validity of laws and regulations when faced with a particular case. Given the costs of pursuing cases through the court system, many laws and government actions are not reviewed by the courts. Governments can refer a proposed law to the Supreme Court for an advisory opinion (as the Canadian government did concerning same-sex marriages) although this use of the courts is not very common. Nevertheless, governments will usually try to ensure that new legislation is "Charter proof" to avoid the possibility that it will be struck down when a case comes before the courts.

those that they consider threats to national security. To deal with terrorism, governments have, on occasion, suspended or ignored rights and freedoms (see Box 13-5, Terrorism and the Rule of Law).

Overall, the rule of law does *not* simply mean that everyone should obey the law, and that laws should be enforced. Dictators can pass laws or decrees that give them absolute powers and then punish people for disobeying the arbitrary laws they have established. But this does not constitute the rule of law. Instead, the rule of law exists where there are limits on the powers of government and those who act in the name of the state, laws are not arbitrary and unfair, and procedures are followed to ensure that every person accused of violating a law is given a fair and impartial hearing.

THE INDEPENDENCE OF THE JUDICIARY

To ensure that the rule of law is upheld, we expect the courts to be independent of government and other influences. Where there is no independent court system, governments and their agents can intimidate the population,

BOX 13-5

Terrorism and the Rule of Law

Terrorism and the rule of law: several hundred foreigners have been held for very lengthy periods of time at Guantanamo Bay, a U.S. military base leased from Cuba, without being charged. Allegations of ill treatment and torture of prisoners later surfaced.

In the wake of the 9/11 attacks on the United States in 2001, the governments of a number of democratic countries took strong measures to deal with terrorism. Some measures violated long-established legal principles, as the following examples show.

Canada adopted anti-terrorism legislation in 2001 that permits arrests on the basis of suspicion of future wrongdoing. Individuals can be held for seventy-two hours without a charge being laid and could be imprisoned for up to twelve months if they do not abide by certain restrictive conditions. The broad definition of terrorism under the law could result in persons who engage in disruptive acts of civil disobedience being charged with terrorism rather than less serious offences. Those called before an investigative hearing can be compelled to testify—a change from the traditional right to silence. Lawyers may be required to report in secret to government authorities if they believe that their clients are engaged in suspicious transactions, contrary to the principle of lawyer–client confiden-

tiality. The legislation allows broad powers to the government to determine what groups or individuals are terrorist, and makes it a serious offence to give money, financial, or other related services to such groups or individuals. It allows government to intercept private communication without judicial authorization and to use secret evidence in court.

The United Kingdom opted out of its commitments under its *Human Rights Act* in order to allow the indefinite detention without charge of foreign nationals suspected of having an association with terrorists.

The United States has gone further in its "war against terrorism." Several hundred foreigners, including juveniles, have been held for very lengthy periods of time at Guantanamo Bay, a U.S. military base leased from Cuba, without being charged. As well, they were denied access to their families and to legal counsel. Prisoners have been subjected to ill treatment and some "enemy combatants" have been transported to foreign countries, where allegedly they have been tortured. Under a military order signed by President Bush, anyone who is not an American citizen can be tried in a military court and, potentially, be executed in secrecy without recourse to the due process of law. In one case, an American citizen was arrested in Chicago in 2002 and held in solitary confinement in a military jail without charges being filed, access to legal counsel, or the right to challenge his detention (Hentoff, 2003). This action would seem to violate *habeas corpus*, one of the oldest legal rights, as well as the American constitution.

We are left to consider the following questions: Does the war on terrorism and the need to defend democracy against those who would destroy it justify extraordinary measures? Or does ignoring the rule of law and international human rights provisions bring mature democracies down to the level of dictatorships and terrorists?

and the principle that all persons should be treated fairly and equally by the law is likely to be undermined.

To ensure the independence of the judiciary, judges in Canada and many other constitutional democracies are given a high level of job security, such that in most cases they cannot be removed from their position by the government. For federally appointed judges in Canada, removal can only occur through the agreement of a majority in both Houses of Parliament, who will only take this action after the Canadian Judicial Council, which is composed of the chief justices and associate chief justices of Canada's superior courts, conducts an inquiry.

In addition, it is considered improper for politicians to try to influence judge, for example, by calling a judge to discuss a case. Judges are expected to refrain from political activity once appointed to the bench. In a number of continental European countries, judges receive specialized professional training that helps them to maintain their neutrality.

Selection Process

Although judges are supposed to be completely non-political and non-partisan once appointed, the selection of judges is often in the hands of political leaders. For example, the Canadian prime minister recommends the appointment of the justices of the Supreme Court of Canada and the chief justices of the provincial Supreme Courts. The Canadian justice minister appoints other federally appointed judges. A provincial cabinet minister, the attorney general, appoints judges to the lower provincial courts. The appointment of judges usually follows consultation with the bar association or law societies, although no public hearings or legislative investigation occurs. At the time that this textbook went to press, there were indications that a system in which a parliamentary committee would review nominees for Supreme Court appointments would soon be adopted.

Generally, the appointment of judges, particularly at the Supreme Court level, will tend to reflect the perspective of the prime minister. Some provincial premiers have argued that the appointment of Supreme Court judges on the recommendation of the Canadian prime minister jeopardizes the ability of the Supreme Court of Canada to fairly adjudicate disputes between the Canadian government and provincial governments.

In the United States, the president's nominees for the Supreme Court must face hearings conducted by the Senate Judiciary Committee before the Senate decides whether to confirm the nomination. Some of these hearings have involved extensive investigations into the lives and beliefs of the nominees. Presidents choose nominees based on their ideological orientations, and the Senate has rejected nominees whose views differ substantially from that of the Senate majority. In some American states, judges are elected by voters rather than appointed, and are subject to re-election at regular intervals.

While this provides for some democratic accountability of judges, it may reduce their willingness to act fairly and impartially when the public is incensed about a particular crime or issue.

Summary and Conclusion

The basic legal framework for governing is provided by the constitution. Ideally, constitutions reflect a fundamental consensus among citizens about how they should be governed. Where the constitution is widely accepted, the power of those in governing positions becomes legitimate authority as long as constitutional rules are followed.

In Canada, particularly since the early 1960s, there has been considerable conflict over attempts to reshape the *Constitution Act*. In part, this reflects the different views of the nature of Canada held by many English-speaking Canadians, French-speaking Quebeckers, and Aboriginals. At times, the disagreements have been strong enough to threaten the break-up of the country. However, while disagreements over constitutional change have often been intense, there are many aspects of the constitution that do reflect a broad consensus of the Canadian population.

The Charter of Rights and Freedoms has been a very popular aspect of the Canadian constitution since its adoption in 1982. Indeed, it has been argued that the Charter has helped to build a sense of Canadian identity based on our common possession of rights (Cairns, 1992). Nevertheless, conservatives with particular moral concerns have called for the use of the notwithstanding clause to circumvent some of the liberal rulings of the Supreme Court. As well, conservatives have been critical of the judicial activism of the courts (Morton & Knopff, 2000).

The idea that all people throughout the world should be guaranteed a variety of human rights, including civil rights (such as freedom of expression), political rights (such as the right to take part in governing), and positive rights (such as the right to an adequate standard of living), has become increasingly accepted in Canada and elsewhere. However, despite various international human rights agreements, abuses of human rights are still prevalent in many countries. Even Canada was found by a 1998 United Nations Committee to be negligent in its protection of economic and social rights through cutbacks in its social programs, by the dismal conditions on Aboriginal reserves, and by the increasing number of homeless people.

The protection of rights may be considered as desirable for the promotion of the common good. A free society in which people do not fear arbitrary action by government and have the right to participate in political life will be more likely to foster the good of all than a society controlled by an authoritarian government. Establishing rights to education, housing, employment, social security, and a clean environment may also work to the benefit of the community as a whole. However, this raises the question of how such positive rights should be provided if they are to be more than rhetorical promises.

Some commentators argue that too much emphasis is placed on individual rights, particularly in the United States and Canada, without a corresponding concern for the responsibility of individuals to each other and to their community. For example, it can be argued that the right to vote carries with it a responsibility to make an informed judgment about what is good for the community when voting. Similarly, the freedom of the media should be used to provide fair and honest reporting to the public.

Others argue that if freedoms are only granted to those who act "responsibly," then the freedoms may be so limited as to be meaningless. The point of political freedoms is to allow a diversity of opinions to be expressed so that through discussion the best course of action can emerge. Developing a sense of responsibility in all citizens is undoubtedly desirable, but it is best achieved through encouragement and education rather than by legal requirements.

Critics of our "rights culture" also argue that by focusing attention on individual rights, discussion about the common good may be neglected. Going to court to pursue one's rights is not only expensive, and thus more available to the wealthier elements of society, but also detracts from the democratic political activity of trying to convince others that a particular course of action is for the common good. Taking legal action can be a useful way to get government, public agencies, or private businesses to live up to their responsibilities. However, frivolous lawsuits can be costly to society as a whole.

The provision of law is a basic and essential function of government. Laws are necessary if we are to enjoy freedom. Without laws, some people would use fear and intimidation to limit the freedom of others. Our freedoms can also be limited if government and its agencies do not feel bound by the rule of law. Preventing the abuse of power by government and its agencies is not an easy task given the power resources available to governments. However, the great powers that governments possess make it important that government and its officials as well as the general population be equally subject to known, predictable, and impartial laws.

The courts are important not only in ensuring that people accused of violating the law receive a fair trial, but also in interpreting and, in some countries, reviewing laws and government actions. To ensure that the judicial system works for the common good and protects the rights of individuals and minorities, the judiciary needs to be independent of government, impartial, and fair. The process of selecting judges is very important because in order to maintain their independence and neutrality, judges are not held accountable for their decisions.

Since of the addition of the Charter of Rights and Freedoms to the constitution, the courts have become increasingly important in Canada in making important political decisions. While few would doubt that the courts are generally effective in protecting individual rights, questions do arise from time to time about whether the courts are a suitable vehicle for pursuing the common good.

Key Terms

Discussion Questions

1. Should efforts be made to overcome the opposition of Quebec governments to the adoption of the *Constitution Act, 1982*? Should Quebec be recognized in the constitution as a distinct society?

2. Should positive rights be added to the Canadian Charter of Rights and Freedoms?

3. Should the notwithstanding clause be eliminated from the Canadian constitution?

4. Should the rule of law be suspended in times of emergency?

5. How should judges be chosen? Is judicial activism desirable?

Further Reading

Coyne, D. (1992). *Roll of the dice*. Toronto: James Lorimer.

Knopff, R., & Morton, F.L. (1992). *Charter politics*. Scarborough, ON: Nelson Canada.

Mandel, M. (1989). *The charter of rights and the legalization of politics in Canada* (Rev. ed.). Toronto: Wall and Thompson.

McRoberts, K. (1997). *Misconceiving Canada: The struggle for national unity*. Toronto: Oxford University Press.

Russell, P. (1993). *Constitutional odyssey* (2nd ed.). Toronto: University of Toronto Press.

Webber, J. (1994). *Reimagining Canada: Language, culture, community, and the Canadian constitution*. Montreal: McGill–Queen's University Press.

Chapter 14

MULTIPLE GOVERNMENTS: UNITARY, FEDERAL, AND CONFEDERAL SYSTEMS

PHOTO ABOVE: Ex-radio journalist Joey Smallwood made passionate political speeches about the benefits that Newfoundlanders would reap by joining the Canadian Confederation. On April 1, 1949, the once independent Dominion of Newfoundland became Canada's newest province.

CHAPTER OBJECTIVES

After reading this chapter you should be able to:

1. explain unitary, federal, and confederal systems
2. assess each type of governing system
3. define the meaning of devolution and discuss how it has been applied
4. outline the basic features of the European Union
5. discuss the nature of local government

On April 1, 1949, the once independent Dominion of Newfoundland became Canada's newest province. In the previous years bitter controversy had raged over whether to join the Canadian federation. Joey Smallwood, familiar to radio audiences across Newfoundland from his days as a journalist, made passionate political speeches about the benefits that people would reap by joining a wealthy country. But Newfoundland nationalists, along with the Catholic Church and the elites of society, fought for an independent Newfoundland.

However, Newfoundlanders had suffered greatly during the Depression of the 1930s. In the outport fishing communities, Smallwood's message of hope for a better future had great appeal. After an inconclusive referendum in which three options were provided, a second referendum in 1948 resulted in 52 percent of Newfoundlanders voting to join Canada.

To this day, many Newfoundlanders argue about whether the right choice was made in 1948. As premier until 1971, Smallwood continually pointed to the large number of new schools, new roads, and new money that had been brought to this underdeveloped region. With Canadian government assistance, Newfoundland was overcoming its traditional poverty.

Others noted that the cod fishery, the mainstay of Newfoundland's economy, was neglected and mismanaged by the Canadian government until it had to be closed. Tens of thousands left to find employment elsewhere. The great wealth of natural resources that the province brought to Canada—iron ore, hydro-electric power, oil, and nickel—provided little net benefit to the provincial government, which continues to rely heavily on money from Ottawa. By contrast, Iceland, a comparable small country, has developed and prospered in the past half-century.

Newfoundlanders are not alone in grumbling about the workings of the Canadian federal system. Nova Scotia and New Brunswick joined Canada in 1867 over the objections of much of the population and angrily watched as central Canada prospered while the economy of the Maritimes declined. Westerners have often felt ignored by the Canadian government, which they view as oriented to the interests of the industrial heartland of Ontario and Quebec. Although the federal system allows provincial governments to control many aspects of life in their province, those in smaller provinces often feel that they do not have sufficient power to affect the decisions of the Canadian government.

Despite its problems, the Canadian federal system is often held up as a model that allows unity to coexist with diversity. People in such troubled countries as Sri Lanka, Afghanistan, and Iraq often look to Canada's federal system as a desirable model of governing. In this chapter, we examine the federal system, the unitary system that is used in the majority of countries, and the confederal system that is becoming more important in our globalizing world.

GOVERNING SYSTEMS

Virtually every country has more than one government. In addition to the central government, often termed the national government, there are usually a variety of local governments. Many countries also have regional governments or regional administrative units. This raises several important questions:

- How do governments within a country relate to one another?
- Is the central government the supreme authority, or is authority shared between central and regional governments?
- Do different governments within a country cooperate for the common good of the country, or are the relations between governments characterized by conflict and power struggles?

To understand the relations among governments within a country, it is important to make a distinction between unitary systems and federal systems. In a unitary system, sovereign authority rests with the central government. In a federal system, sovereign authority is divided or shared between the central government, often termed the federal government, and regional governments, such as provincial and state governments.

UNITARY SYSTEM
A system of governing in which sovereign authority rests with the central government; regional and local governments are subordinate.

UNITARY SYSTEMS

Many countries have **unitary systems** of government (see Table 14-1 for examples). The relationship among different governments is hierarchical,

TABLE 14-1
UNITARY, FEDERAL, AND CONFEDERAL SYSTEMS

UNITARY	FEDERAL	CONFEDERAL
Bangladesh	Argentina	Caribbean Community
Bolivia	Australia	Commonwealth of Independent States
Chile	Austria	European Union
Czech Republic	Belgium	Organization of African Unity
Denmark	Brazil	
Finland	Canada	
France	Germany	
Greece	India	
Hungary	Malaysia	
Ireland	Mexico	
Japan	Nigeria	
Netherlands	Russia	
New Zealand	Switzerland	
South Korea	United States	
Poland		
Sweden		
Turkey		
United Kingdom		

with regional and local governments subordinate to the central government. Even though the central government typically delegates some powers to other levels of government or to regional and local administrative authorities, the central government is superior to other governments.

Unitary systems generally provide uniformity across the country in terms of common laws and policies. However, the central government may make some adjustments in its laws and policies for the circumstances of different parts of the country. As well, it may rely on regional or local authorities to carry out some of its policies.

Regional Powers

The governments of a number of countries with unitary systems have granted some legislative (law making) as well as administrative responsibilities to one or more regional bodies—a process termed **devolution**. In Spain and France, for example, regional governments with elected assemblies have been established in each of the regions of the country. In the case of Spain, seventeen autonomous communities have powers equivalent to that of regional governments in some federal systems. In recent years the United Kingdom has established regional governments and legislatures for the distinctive regions of Scotland, Wales, and Northern Ireland, though not for England, which has a dominant position in the U.K. Parliament. These governments are able to legislate on such matters as health, education, law and order, and transportation. However, the powers of these governments concerning taxation are very limited in the case of Scotland and non-existent in the case of Wales and Northern Ireland.

Devolution does not involve establishing regional government with a degree of sovereignty. The Parliament of the United Kingdom could revoke the devolution of powers regardless of the wishes of the regional legislature. For example, the Parliament of the United Kingdom suspended the Parliament of Northern Ireland in 1972 because of the conflicts in that territory. Nevertheless, many see Scotland as becoming increasingly self-governing within the United

DEVOLUTION
A system of governing in which the central government grants some legislative (law making) as well as administrative responsibilities to one or more regional bodies.

◀ The Parliament of the United Kingdom suspended the Parliament of Northern Ireland in 1972 because of religious and political conflicts in that territory.

Kingdom, and it is unlikely that the British government would try to take away the powers that have been granted to the Scottish Parliament.

Generally, there has been a tendency in recent decades for central governments in unitary systems to devolve powers to regional authorities. In part, devolution has allowed for greater responsiveness to the needs, cultures, and circumstances of different parts of the country and for greater participation of citizens in governing. As well, devolution is often a response to nationalist movements seeking self-government or independence.

FEDERAL SYSTEMS

In *federal systems*, regional governments, such as the provincial governments in Canada and the state governments in the United States, are not subordinate to the central (national or federal) government. The national and provincial governments each derive their authority from the constitution. Provincial governments cannot be abolished by the national government, nor can the national government be abolished by provincial governments. Constitutional changes, particularly those that affect the powers of the two levels of government, require the agreement of both levels of government.

Early Systems

The first modern federal system was established in the United States in 1789 when the thirteen former colonies that had fought for their independence from Britain agreed, somewhat reluctantly, to unite, but feared being dominated by a strong central government. Subsequently, a variety of other countries (listed in Table 14-1) adopted federal systems.

In many cases, federal systems were established as a way of creating or holding together large countries. Federal systems have often been adopted in countries with sharp language or cultural divisions. By providing different regions of a country with an element of self-government, conflicts among different cultural groups living in different parts of the country can potentially be reduced.

Canada adopted a federal system because the idea of uniting the British North American colonies that was proposed in the 1860s met with considerable opposition in both Quebec and the Maritimes, where many people feared being dominated by the central government. Maritimers wanted to retain the legislatures that they had developed. Quebeckers, fearful of the consequences of becoming a minority in the new country, wanted to retain control over their own culture.

Division of Powers in Federal Systems

Federal systems typically involve a division of powers between national and provincial governments, with the constitution giving some responsibilities to the national government and other responsibilities to provincial governments (see Table 14-2). However, it is virtually impossible to divide legislative authority neatly between the national and provincial governments, and thus there is inevitably some overlap in the responsibilities of each level of government.

In what is often termed **classical federalism**, the federal and provincial governments each concern themselves with their own areas of constitutional authority without infringing upon the areas of authority of the other level of government. Thus, classical federalism, which in Canada lasted from the mid-1890s until 1939, with the exception of the period around the First World War, involves a low level of interaction among governments.

Contemporary federal systems typically feature a substantial amount of sharing of powers and financial resources between the two levels of government. As the activities of governments expanded, particularly during and after World War II, the need to coordinate the policies of the central and provincial governments became more important.

The Canadian System

The federal system in Canada and elsewhere in the past half century is often described as **cooperative federalism**. The two levels of government are jointly involved in developing and administering many government services. In

Canadian Network of Federalism Studies
www.rcef-cnfs.net/home.php

CLASSICAL FEDERALISM
A version of federalism in which the federal and provincial governments each concern themselves with their own areas of constitutional authority without infringing upon the areas of authority of the other level of government.

COOPERATIVE FEDERALISM
A federal system in which the two levels of government are jointly involved in developing and administering many government services.

TABLE 14-2
THE CONSTITUTIONAL DIVISION OF POWERS IN CANADA

AREAS OF LAW-MAKING THAT ARE THE EXCLUSIVE RESPONSIBILITY OF THE PARLIAMENT OF CANADA	AREAS OF LAW-MAKING THAT ARE THE RESPONSIBILITY OF THE PROVINCIAL LEGISLATURES	AREAS IN WHICH BOTH PARLIAMENT AND PROVINCIAL LEGISLATURES HAVE LAW-MAKING AUTHORITY
Regulation of trade and commerce (interprovincial and international)	Management of public lands	Agriculture
Unemployment insurance	Hospitals	Immigration
Postal service	Municipal institutions	Public pensions
Defence	Education	
Fisheries	Most "local works and undertakings"	
Currency	Laws concerning property rights and the relations among individuals	
Banking	Administration of justice within a province	
Indian affairs	"Generally all Matters of a merely local or private nature in the Province"	
Criminal law		
Marriage and divorce		
The "peace, order, and good Government of Canada"		
Foreign affairs		

addition, the Canadian government contributes to the financing of many programs that are the constitutional responsibility of provincial governments (see Box 14-1, Health, Education, and Social Programs in Canada).

Despite the substantial level of cooperation among the two levels of government, the Canadian federal system features considerable conflict between national and provincial governments. A number of provincial governments have resented the "interference" of the national government in areas of

BOX 14-1

Health, Education, and Social Programs in Canada

The Canadian constitution places the responsibility for education, health care, and most social programs in the hands of the provincial level of government, but the federal government has been involved in all of these programs to varying extents.

Through the Canada Health Transfer and the Canada Social Transfer, the Canadian government provides some of the money needed by provincial governments, on an equal per capita basis, to fund post-secondary education, medical and hospital insurance (medicare), and social assistance (welfare).

In the case of health care funding, the Canadian government requires that provincial governments adhere to five basic principles in order to receive the federal government's contribution to the cost of the program. The provinces must ensure that:

- all persons are covered
- all basic services are covered
- health care is publicly administered
- persons moving from one province to another are covered
- all persons have reasonable access to insured services without cost

Provinces that do not adhere to the principles may have the Canadian government's contribution reduced.

In the case of social assistance, provincial governments cannot impose minimum residency requirements. Within these qualifications, provincial governments are free to spend the money they receive from the Canadian government as they see fit.

The Canadian government, however, often is interested in becoming directly involved and gaining the political credit for its spending, even though its contribution to the costs of these programs is much smaller than that of provincial governments. In the area of post-secondary education, for example, the Canadian government has become directly involved—despite the objections of some provincial governments—in such areas as research funding and the Millennium Scholarships.

In the health care field, the Canadian government has earmarked new federal health care spending for new programs, new equipment, and new technologies. Although provincial governments have been demanding substantially more money from the Canadian government for health care, some provincial governments are unhappy that additional money often comes with stipulations as to how it should be spent.

As the costs of providing important services continues to escalate, conflicts over the sharing of costs and control of the programs will likely continue to be an major feature of politics in Canada.

provincial authority and have wanted increased powers for provincial governments along with a larger share of tax revenues. Cooperative federalism is not really all that cooperative!

Attempts to coordinate the activities of the two levels of government often involve difficult negotiations between the Canadian and provincial governments. Unlike many federal countries, Canada has developed few formal mechanisms to facilitate the coordination of the two levels of government. Although officials and cabinet ministers from the two levels of government do meet quite frequently to try to coordinate their policies, the development of intergovernmental decision-making organizations has been rather limited. There has, nevertheless, been an increasing level of collaboration among Canadian governments in recent years (Simeon & Cameron, 2002). For example, to a considerable extent environmental policy is the product of a consensus among provincial, territorial, and Canadian ministers of the environment and their officials since the adoption of the Canadawide Accord on Environmental Harmonization in 1998.

Centre for Research and Information on Canada
www.cric.ca/en_html/guide/federalism/federalism.html

Regional Representation

In many federal countries, regional interests are represented in a chamber of the national Parliament and thus coordination can be worked out, at least in part, at the national level. In the case of Germany, for example, the *länder* governments are represented in the upper chamber (Bundesrat) of Germany's Parliament by their premier ("First Minister") and some cabinet ministers. The Bundesrat can prevent the passage of laws that affect the länder (Watts, 1999). By contrast, the Canadian Senate, although intended to represent regional interests, does not provide an effective voice for the provincial governments because it consists of appointees of present and past prime ministers.

Differences in Federal Systems

There are considerable differences among federal systems in the extent to which governing is decentralized. In some federal systems, the national government can be considered the major government, with considerable control over government finances and with the ability to take a leading role in a wide variety of policy areas. The Canadian federal system, on the other hand, features strong provincial governments whose decisions have a major impact on the lives of citizens.

Federalism and Multi-Level Governance
www.unc.edu/depts/europe/conferences/mlg

The extent to which a federal system is centralized or decentralized is affected not only by the provisions concerning the division of powers in the constitution, but also by various political, social, and economic factors. For example, despite being established as a quite decentralized federal system, the central government has come to play a leading role in American politics, although state governments continue to have important powers. Many

Institute of Intergovernmental
Relations
www.iigr.ca/iigr.php

Americans look to the central government to solve economic and social problems. The international role of the United States helps to enhance the power and prestige of the central government.

The Canadian federal system, in contrast to the United States, initially concentrated considerable power in the hands of the Canadian government. Over time, a number of provincial governments have been assertive in using their powers, which were enhanced by judicial decisions in the late nineteenth and early twentieth centuries, and in resisting attempts by the central government to get involved in matters under provincial jurisdiction. In recent decades, the threat of Quebec independence has helped to move the Canadian federal system further towards decentralization. As well, resource-rich provinces such as Alberta, along with the large and powerful province of Ontario, have at times created strong pressures in favour of decentralization. The poorer provinces that are more dependent upon the central government for assistance have tended to be less amenable to decentralization, which they fear may weaken the Canadian government's ability to assist them.

In some federal systems, as well as in some unitary systems, the relationships between central and regional governments are asymmetrical. That is, some regional governments have a greater degree of self-government than other regional governments. This is the case, for example, in India, Russia, Malaysia, and Belgium (Watts, 1999). In Canada, the question of whether Quebec should be recognized as a distinct society, which could provide a justification for greater powers than the other provinces, has been very controversial.

For many English-speaking Canadians, the principle of the equality of the provinces is fundamental. Each provincial government should have the same powers and Quebec should not have any form of special status. Many French-speaking Quebeckers, on the other hand, view the Quebec government as representing one of the major founding peoples of Canada and support the desire of the Quebec government to lead the social and economic development of the province. Because many Canadians outside of Quebec prefer a strong central government, while many French-speaking Quebeckers prefer a strong provincial government, some Quebec governments have suggested that the Quebec government have a wider range of powers than that of other provincial governments. Although proposed constitutional changes to recognize Quebec as distinct have been defeated, there are in practice some asymmetrical aspects to the Canadian federal system. For example, Quebec has its own public pension plan, which is similar to the Canadian Pension Plan but controlled by the Quebec government.

Finally, although federalism usually involves a division of authority between the central government and a number of regional governments, federalism can also involve linguistic, ethnic, or religious communities having a degree of self-government. For example, the federal system in Belgium involves three communities (corresponding to the Dutch-, French-, and German-speaking groups) that have responsibility for linguistic and cultural matters, as well as three regional governments. In Canada, the gradual movement towards Aboriginal self-government could result in a "third order" of government, with substantial authority based on membership in particular Aboriginal communities. Such governments might not be confined to Aboriginal lands, but could have some ability to provide education and social services to Aboriginals living in cities.

ASSESSING UNITARY AND FEDERAL SYSTEMS
Benefits of the Unitary System

There are several reasons why a unitary system might be the best way to provide for the common good. In a unitary system:

- The governing authorities may be more likely to work for the common good of the whole country, as there are no strong provincial governments promoting the particular interests of their region.
- National unity may be promoted because greater attention is likely to be given to national issues and problems. In a federal system, provincial governments may find it politically advantageous to highlight and exaggerate regional grievances so that they can be perceived by voters as defenders of their province.
- The central government can be more easily held accountable by citizens—it cannot easily shift blame for problems to other governments.
- People will be more likely to have the same level of government services available in all regions. Uniform standards for education, health care, and environmental quality are likely to be adopted. In a federal system, provincial governments competing to attract investment may lower environmental standards or offer subsidies and tax breaks to companies. Unless adequate **equalization payments** are provided, people in poorer provinces will receive a lower level of services from their provincial government than people in the richer provinces (see Box 14-2, Equalization Payments). Thus, the sense of everyone being equal citizens may be weaker in a federal than in a unitary system.
- Greater efficiencies in governing are possible. With a central government in control, policies can be consistently directed towards certain objectives without different governments' pursuing different and possibly inconsistent goals. Costly duplication of services by different governments may be avoided. Total administrative costs will likely be lower if many of the activities of government are centralized.
- People are unlikely to find barriers when transferring professional qualifications from one area of the country to another or in conducting business in different parts of the country.

EQUALIZATION PAYMENT
A payment made by the federal government to try to ensure that different provincial governments are able to provide an equivalent level of services to their populations without resorting to excessive levels of taxation.

BOX 14-2

Equalization Payments

Most federal systems other than the United States provide some form of **equalization payment** to try to ensure that different regional governments are able to provide an equivalent level of services to their populations without resorting to excessive levels of taxation.

The Canadian government, for example, provides equalization payments to the governments of the poorer provinces (as of 2004, all provinces except Alberta and Ontario) to give them the same financial capability (ability to raise money through taxes) as an "average" province (see Figure 14-1). Nevertheless, this may be insufficient to provide equivalent services in provinces where needs are greater or the costs of providing services are higher.

The government of Newfoundland and Labrador, for example, has often pointed out that the cost of providing services to a geographically dispersed small population is higher than in central Canada, while the need for government services is greater because of the province's high unemployment rate and lower level of economic development. Furthermore, the determination of the average financial capability is currently based on an average of only five provinces and excludes the rich province of Alberta; therefore, it does not bring the poorer provinces fully up to the national average. The equalization formula has also been criticized because increases in provincial government royalties resulting from resource development lead to a substantial reduction in equalization payments. The governments of the poorer provinces argue that they do not gain the full benefits of their natural resources.

FIGURE 14-1

EQUALIZATION PAYMENTS PER CAPITA, 2004–05

Note: Payments are estimates based on projections concerning provincial government revenues.

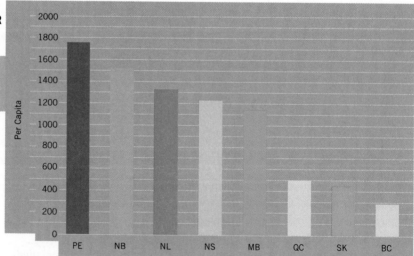

Source: Adapted from *Transfer Payments to Provinces: Equalization Program,* by the Department of Finance (Canada), 2004, retrieved July 13, 2004, from www.fin.gc.ca/fedprov/eqpe.html. Reproduced with the permission of the Minister of Public Works and Government Services Canada, 2004.

Benefits of the Federal System

Federal systems also have a variety of positive features:

- Provincial governments may be more sensitive to the needs and desires of people in particular areas of the country. The flexibility of a federal system enables provincial governments to adopt policies that reflect the circumstances of their region.
- Less populated and remote areas of the country might be ignored in a unitary system, but can find a voice in their own provincial government.
- Citizens may find it easier to participate in the policy-making process in their own province than in the processes of a distant central government.
- A federal system allows for greater diversity than a unitary state. Minorities that are concentrated within a particular province can use their provincial government to develop their culture. For example, the French language and culture in Canada has been preserved and developed in part because of the powers of the Quebec government. In this case, a group that is a minority in the country as a whole constitutes a large majority in a particular province, and thus is able to achieve a degree of self-government.
- Conflicts between cultural groups can be reduced through the adoption of a federal system. For example, Belgium, faced with continuing tensions between the Dutch-speaking Flemish community and the French-speaking community in Flanders, gradually moved away from a unitary system and in 1993 adopted a federal system. Similarly, a number of countries that have experienced severe ethnic, linguistic, and religious conflicts (for example, Sri Lanka) are considering the adoption of a federal system.
- A federal system helps to limit the concentration of power. Consistent with the ideal of liberal democracy, a federal system places constitutional limits on the powers of each government. Competition between central and provincial governments may serve to check the power of each level of government.
- A federal system can allow for experimentation with different policies and approaches by different governments. For example, the government of Saskatchewan initiated the system of free medical care that was subsequently adopted by other provinces and then turned into a nation-wide program, funded, in part, by the Canadian government (see the opening vignette for Chapter 17). Because of the array of forces opposed to public health care (doctors, private insurance companies, conservative governments), medicare might not have been adopted across the country without the successful example set by a determined provincial government.

Change

In the past, it was often thought that as countries modernized, they would tend to move in the direction of centralization. Federal systems would, in practice, become more like unitary systems. Regional differences would decline as transportation and communication links tied a country closer together. The increased mobility of people would make ties to a particular place of residence less important. A strong central government would be needed to manage the national economy effectively. However, the trend in recent decades has generally been in the opposite direction. In both unitary and federal systems there has been a tendency to disperse authority from the central government to regional and local governments (Hooghe & Marks, 2001).

Impact of Globalization

Some analysts have suggested that globalization encourages decentralization (Courchene, 1992). In a more globalized economy, the ability of central government to manage the national economy is reduced. Regions and important cities can develop international and global links.

In Canada, the North American Free Trade Agreement has to some extent increased economic links between Canadian provinces and neighbouring American states at the expense of economic links across Canada. The development of the European Union (discussed below) is often viewed as encouraging the development of regionalism in a number of countries, leading to political pressures for decentralization.

Thus, globalization and international agreements may make central governments less relevant. Alternatively, however, people may look to the central government to shield them from the effects of globalization or to provide them with the resources needed to adapt to globalization.

CONFEDERAL SYSTEMS

Independent states generally retain their sovereignty when they interact with each other on the international stage. In some cases, however, sovereign states have agreed to delegate some of their authority to a joint government with limited authority, while retaining their identity as sovereign states. In this arrangement, known as a **confederal system**, the confederal government only has those powers that have been delegated to it by the governments of the sovereign states.[1]

Unlike a federal system, in which both central and regional governments exercise authority over individuals, in a pure confederal system only the member states directly interact with their populations. The confederal

CONFEDERAL SYSTEM
A system of governing in which sovereign states have agreed to delegate some of their authority to a joint government with limited authority while retaining their identity as sovereign states.

---

[1] Although the formation of Canada in 1867 is often described as Confederation, Canada has never had a confederal system.

governing bodies act on agreements made by the governments of all of the member states and rely on the member states to implement the agreements.

Confederal systems are not very common. Switzerland, until 1848, was a confederation of cantons. After the War of Independence, the independent American states initially set up a confederal system but within a few years converted it into a federal system (1789). The southern states in the U.S. that tried to secede during the American Civil War (1861–65) set up the Confederacy.

In modern times, the European Union (discussed below) is the most prominent example of a confederal arrangement. The Caribbean Community (Caricom), consisting of fifteen member countries and five associate members, could also be considered a confederal system. The twelve-member Commonwealth of Independent States established after the dissolution of the Soviet Union is based on the confederal model, although it is potentially an instrument for the re-establishment of Russian dominance in the region. In 2002, fifty-three African countries launched the African Union, modelled on the European Union and replacing the more limited Organization of African Unity.

The European Union

The **European Union** (EU), which now provides quite a high level of integration among most European countries, began in 1951 as a six-member common market for the coal and steel industries. It now includes most European countries (twenty-four in 2004).

Over time, a more comprehensive single market involving the free flow of goods, services, persons, and capital among the member countries was established. Common policies in a variety of areas such as agriculture, culture, the

EUROPEAN UNION (EU)
A confederal system composed of twenty-four European countries (as of 2004); it involves a common market enabling the free flow of goods, labour, and capital among the member countries, and a variety of common policies.

◀ The European Union, which includes 24 countries, is an example of a confederal arrangement.

environment, energy, and transportation have been adopted. The EU also encourages cooperation among member countries in developing common foreign and defence policies and in combating terrorism and drug trafficking. The EU provides substantial assistance to its poorer member countries to assist in their development. In 2002, a common currency (the euro) was adopted, replacing national currencies in twelve countries. For those countries that have adopted the euro, the European Central Bank has considerable control over their fiscal policies, including the level of government deficits that they are allowed. Generally, the EU has considerable responsibility for economic policy while the member states continue to have primary responsibility for social policy.

The major institutions of the EU are:

- *The European Council.* At this twice-yearly meeting of the presidents or prime ministers of the member states, general policy guidelines for the EU are defined.
- *The European Commission.* Appointed by the governments of the member states subject to acceptance by the EU Parliament, the Commission initiates legislative proposals, oversees the implementation of common EU policies (either by the civil service of the EU or member states), and acts as guardian of the EU treaties. Members of this Commission are expected to act independently of the government of the state that selected them.
- *The Council of the European Union* (also known as the Council of Ministers). The major decision-making body of the EU, the Council is composed of ministers from each of the member countries. Different ministers sit on the Council, depending upon the policy area being considered.
- *The European Parliament.* Voters in the EU countries directly elect the European Parliament. Originally it was only a consultative body, but it now has joint legislative and budgetary powers with the Council of the EU. It can censure the Commission and conduct independent inquiries.
- *The Court of Justice of the European Union.* Composed of one independent judge from each member state, the Court interprets the rules of the EU.

CONFEDERAL OR FEDERAL? The EU is basically a confederal system. The member states are largely responsible for implementing and administering EU laws and regulations, and the EU lacks the financial capabilities of central governments in a federal system (Watts, 2003). Few people identify themselves as European rather than, say, French or Greek or German.

However, the EU does have some elements of federalism. Unlike a pure confederal system, decisions of the EU institutions do not generally require the agreement of all member states. The European Parliament represents individual voters rather than the governments of the EU members and has gradually become more significant. The ability of the Court of Justice of the EU to make decisions based on European law that are binding on the member countries can also be considered a federal element (Watts, 2003).

Thus, although the organizations of the EU do not have the same level of authority as the central governments of federal countries such as Canada and the United States, the EU is much more than a loose alliance or an agreement on specific matters among sovereign states. Unlike the North American Free Trade Agreement, the EU has established significant governing bodies and the EU participates in international affairs.

Some European leaders, such as German Foreign Minister Joschka Fischer, have advocated converting the EU into a fully federal system. Others, such as French President Jacques Chirac, favour strengthening the organizations of the EU, but stop short of advocating a European super state. Public support for the EU is limited, however, and there is considerable reluctance in many countries (for example, the United Kingdom) toward transferring more sovereignty from their own state to the EU. The EU also faces considerable challenges as it becomes more culturally diverse, a result of its recent expansion to include many of the poorer countries of Eastern Europe and potentially Turkey.

LOCAL GOVERNMENTS

Local governments are very important. They are responsible for many essential basic services such as water, sewage treatment, garbage disposal, road maintenance, public transportation, fire and police protection, land development and zoning, parks, and recreational facilities. Some local governments have responsibilities for administering welfare and other public services. Local governments are also usually involved in promoting economic development for their community.

United Cities and Local Governments
www.iula.org

Local governments often only have whatever authority the central government—or, in the case of federal systems, provincial governments—decide to delegate to them. Thus, despite their importance, local governments are generally subordinate to higher levels of government. However, a few countries (for example, Germany, India, and Switzerland) do provide constitutional protection for the powers of local governments (Watts, 1999). Likewise, in the United States, many state constitutions provide some protection for the powers of municipal governments, with the larger cities often provided with some form of "home rule" that protects their powers and structures from being changed without their consent (Sancton, 2002).

The Canadian Version

In Canada, local governments are the responsibility of provincial governments. Although local governments make important decisions affecting their communities, they generally have to carry out their activities in accordance with the rules and regulations adopted by their provincial government. Indeed, provincial governments can alter the boundaries of municipal governments as they see fit. For example, in 1998, the government of Ontario decided to amalgamate the five municipalities of the metropolitan Toronto area despite opposition from local political leaders and a majority of voters in a referendum.

Local governments are dependent upon the higher levels of government for much of their revenue. They typically raise money through property taxes and various fees, but these sources of revenue are often inadequate to provide for municipal services. This problem has worsened in recent times as provincial and national governments have downloaded some programs onto municipal governments without providing sufficient financing. The Federation of Canadian Municipalities claims that there is a $60 billion gap between the cost of municipal programs and what municipal governments can afford (CBC News, 2004). During the 2004 Canadian election campaign, Prime Minister Paul Martin promised to give cities a share of the Canadian government's gasoline tax revenues—provided that the money was spent on priorities established by the Canadian government.

As cities have grown, demands have developed to give city governments greater political and financial power. Former Toronto Mayor Mel Lastman argued that Toronto, with a greater population than all of the Atlantic provinces plus two of the Prairie provinces combined, should be given provincial government status. David Miller, elected mayor of Toronto in 2003, argues that urban issues need to be given greater prominence on the Canadian government's agenda. In conjunction with the mayors of other large cities, Miller has proposed a "new deal" involving direct agreements between cities and the Canadian government to deal with issues such as immigration and public transit. Not surprisingly, provincial governments oppose proposals that would substantially reduce their power and revenues.

Complex Governing Authorities

There are often complex sets of governing authorities at the local level. Schools are generally run by elected school boards that may be responsible for all the schools in a city or in a region of a province. Likewise, there may be library boards, police boards, community centre boards, health boards, hospital boards, transit authorities, conservation authorities, parks boards, public utilities commissions, and water and sewage authorities. Such agencies, boards, and commissions are often independent of the municipal government and may service a broader geographical area than a municipal government. In some provinces and in the United States, there is a two-tier system of local government with county, regional, or metropolitan governments existing above the level of municipal governments (Tindal & Tindal,

2000).

In Canada, unlike many other countries, local politics and government do not generally involve political parties. Civic parties have developed in Montreal and Vancouver, and the NDP has at times involved itself in the politics of some cities. The general lack of involvement by national and provincial parties may help to ensure that local politics focuses on local issues rather than being a continuation of the competition among parties at the higher levels. On the other hand, voters may have difficulty knowing what candidates stand for. This is particularly a problem in cities where there are many names on the ballot and a large number of positions to be filled.

In some cases, the independence of each member of local councils may make concerted and consistent action difficult to achieve. In other cases, there may be little public debate and discussion because of the lack of an organized opposition. The city manager, an appointed official, may have great influence over part-time elected councillors, or council may simply reflect the interests of the local business community or the property developers who are often involved in financing the election campaigns of councillors (Tindal & Tindal, 2000).

Summary and Conclusion

Almost all countries have multiple governments. The existence of multiple governments adds complexity to political life and makes an understanding of the relationships among governments essential for an understanding of the governing process. In a unitary system, sovereignty rests primarily with a central government; in a federal system, sovereignty is divided between the central government and regional governments; and in a confederal system, sovereignty rests primarily with the member states.

Unitary systems feature a hierarchical relationship among governments with the central government superior to other governments, although some distinctive parts of the country may be granted a significant level of autonomy. Federal systems feature a substantial level of self-government for provinces or their equivalent and, generally, a shared involvement in a number of policy areas between the central and provincial governments. Each citizen is directly affected by both national and provincial governments, and citizens elect both a national and a provincial government. Confederal systems result when sovereign states join together to establish a central governing agency with somewhat limited powers delegated from the member states. In addition to "higher" governments, there are a variety of local governments that provide important services to their communities

The existence of multiple governments has important political implications. For federal systems, in particular, political conflict between national and provincial governments can sometimes overshadow other bases of political disagreements. Coordination and cooperation among different governments within a country is an important requirement for effective governing. However, power struggles between national and provincial governments, as well as their different interests and values, can make cooperation difficult to achieve. This has often been the case in Canada, where the conflicting views of prime ministers and premiers have been highly publicized.

Canada's prime ministers have often argued that the central government is best suited to pursue the common good of the country as a whole. Provincial governments are depicted as promoting particular interests. If provincial governments obtain too much power, it will undermine national unity and the pursuit of national interests. However, in a diverse country where many people identify with their local, provincial, and cultural communities as well as the national community, should the common good of the country override the common good of the communities within the country?

If Canada is viewed as one nation, then the answer to former Prime Minister Pierre Trudeau's rhetorical question, "Who speaks for Canada?", is, the Canadian government. The implication drawn is that the Canadian government should have the power to determine all matters of national concern. But if Canada is viewed as a "community of communities," as was suggested by former Prime Minister Joe Clark, then both national and provincial governments together, along with Aboriginal governments, can claim to speak for Canada. This perspective suggests that many decisions with national implications should be made jointly by national and provincial (and perhaps Aboriginal) governments.

The increasing importance of international and global institutions suggests that the issues of cooperation and coordination that arise in federal systems will be of great significance in the future in all countries. Globalization will likely lead to more complex patterns of governing, in which a variety of levels of governance affect our lives. Globalization may not simply mean the development of institutions above the level of the state, but may also lead to a greater significance for urban and regional governments. Acting to ensure that many levels of government work towards the common good will be a difficult challenge.

Key Terms

Classical federalism 315

Confederal system 322

Cooperative federalism 315

Devolution 313

Equalization payment 319

European Union (EU) 323

Unitary system 312

Discussion Questions

1. What are the advantages and disadvantages of a federal system?

2. Why has the Canadian federal system tended to become more decentralized?

3. Do you think that the Canadian government should continue to set conditions for provincial health care systems?

4. Do you think that Canada should adopt a confederal system as a way of resolving tensions between Quebec and the rest of Canada?

5. Do you think that local governments should have greater authority?

Further Reading

Bakvis, H., & Skogstad, G. (Eds.). *Canadian federalism: Performance, effectiveness, and legitimacy.* Don Mills, ON: Oxford University Press, 2002.

McCormick, J. *Understanding the European Union: A concise introduction* (2nd ed.). Houndmills, Basingstoke, Hampshire, UK: Palgrave, 2002.

Rocher, F., & Smith, M. (Eds.) *New trends in Canadian federalism* (2nd ed.). Peterborough, ON: Broadview Press, 2003.

Tindal, C. R., & Tindal, S.N. *Local government in Canada* (5th ed.). Scarborough, ON: Nelson Canada, 2000.

Watts, R.L. *Comparing federal systems* (2nd ed.). Montreal: McGill–Queen's University Press, 1999.

Westmacott, M., & Mellon, H. (Eds.). *Challenges to Canadian federalism.* Scarborough, ON: Prentice-Hall Canada, 1998.

Chapter 15

PARLIAMENTARY AND PRESIDENTIAL SYSTEMS

PHOTO ABOVE: Days after Federal Finance Minister John Crosbie (left) delivered an unpopular budget in the House of Commons in December 1979, the budget was defeated and the minority PC government of Joe Clark was forced to resign.

1. outline the basic differences between parliamentary and presidential systems of government
2. describe how the prime minister and cabinet are chosen in Canada
3. define the meaning of majority, minority, and coalition governments
4. explain the significance of party discipline in a parliamentary system
5. discuss the relationship between the president and Congress in the United States
6. evaluate the strengths and weaknesses of parliamentary and presidential systems

John Crosbie wore sealskin mukluks to the House of Commons on December 11, 1979. Though it is traditional that the finance minister wear new shoes when presenting the government's budget, the fall-out from that particular budget was so dismal that Crosbie's choice may not be duplicated any time soon.

The PCs had been elected in 1979 with 136 seats, just less than half the 282 seats in the House of Commons. Clark formed a minority government (a government based on a party that does not control a majority of House of Commons seats). The PC budget included an unpopular eighteen-cents-per-gallon (four-cents-per-litre) increase in the tax on gasoline, which Finance Minister Crosbie described as "short-term pain for long-term gain." But with Liberal leader Pierre Trudeau having announced his retirement, and the small Créditiste party, whose support was sufficient to give the PCs a majority, fearful of being wiped out in an election, Clark felt that he didn't have to worry about all of the other parties ganging up to defeat him. The PCs could govern as if they had a majority and not bother negotiating with the other parties for support. In particular, the PCs refused to consider the Créditiste demand that a tax credit be given to lower-income earners to offset the gasoline tax increase. The leaderless Liberals, gathering at a pre-Christmas party, decided to capitalize on the situation and try to defeat the PCs.

When a vote of non-confidence on the budget was called, Clark thought he had enough support and did not try to delay it. But with fewer PC votes than expected (External Affairs Minister Flora MacDonald was caught in Europe, desperately trying to find a flight home) and the Créditistes abstaining, the Liberals and New Democrats were able to defeat the budget. An election was called and Pierre Trudeau came back from retirement to lead the Liberals to an easy victory in February 1980.

Minority governments are sometimes seen as inevitably unstable and unproductive. This is not necessarily the case, however. In the 1960s, Liberal Prime Minister Lester Pearson led two minority governments that were highly productive. With the support of the NDP, the Liberals were able to pass legislation establishing medicare, the Canada Pension Plan, and the new Canadian flag. Unlike a majority government situation when one party has a majority of seats, the prime minister and cabinet usually get their way, and power is highly concentrated, in a minority government situation the governing party has to take into account the wishes of other parties and reach suitable compromises.

Some see minority governments as undesirable because they can give considerable power to small parties. However, small parties in minority governments are often unwilling to see the governing party defeated—they lose their bargaining power if a majority government is elected. Problems arise if the governing party thinks it can win a majority in a new election and thus sees no need to listen to other parties, or if differences among the parties are too great to allow compromises to be made.

In this chapter, we will examine the parliamentary system, which functions quite differently depending upon whether or not the governing party has a majority. The American presidential system, which is also discussed in this chapter, is different again, but like a minority government in the parliamentary system, the presidential system often requires that politician's achieve their objectives through negotiations and compromise.

ORGANIZING GOVERNMENTS

There are two basic patterns of organizing the institutions of government:

- parliamentary systems
- presidential systems

Most long-established democratic countries—including Canada, the United Kingdom, the other countries of the British Commonwealth, most Western European countries, and Japan—have parliamentary systems of government, while the United States has a presidential system. Many of the newer democratic countries have some form of presidential system, including most of the countries of Latin America and Africa, many of the former communist countries, and some Asian countries (Derbyshire & Derbyshire, 1996). Several countries, including France and Russia, have a mixture of parliamentary and presidential systems.

To understand the differences between parliamentary and presidential systems of government, we need to note that there are three basic types of activities involved in governing:

1. **Legislative activities,** which involve making general laws.
2. **Executive activities,** which involve implementing and administering laws and policies, and making specific decisions to put into effect the general laws.
3. **Judicial activities,** which involve resolving disagreements about how to interpret the laws, and determining if laws have been violated.

In **parliamentary systems** there is a close relationship between the legislative and executive branches of government. The authority of the political executive (the prime minister and cabinet) is based on their ability to maintain the support of the elected legislative body. If that support is withdrawn, the executive cannot remain in office.

Presidential systems, in contrast, are characterized by a separation of power between the legislative and executive branches. The president (the head of the executive branch) and Congress (the legislative branch) each derive their authority from being elected by the people. The president does not depend upon Congress to remain in office. Nor can the president dissolve Congress in the hope that a new election will result in a Congress that is more willing to support the executive. Another basic difference between the two systems of governing is that in presidential systems, the president is both the official head of state and the head of the executive branch of government. In parliamentary systems, different people hold the offices of head of state and head of government.

THE PARLIAMENTARY SYSTEM

The **head of state** is an important but largely ceremonial position in a parliamentary system of government. The head of state carries out a variety of

LEGISLATIVE ACTIVITIES
Activities that involve making general laws.

EXECUTIVE ACTIVITIES
Activities that involve implementing and administering laws and policies, and making specific decisions to put into effect the general laws.

JUDICIAL ACTIVITIES
Activities that involve resolving disagreements about how to interpret the laws, and determining if laws have been violated.

PARLIAMENTARY SYSTEM
A system of governing in which there is a close relationship between the legislative and executive branches of government. The authority of the executive (the prime minister and cabinet) is based on their ability to maintain the support of Parliament.

PRESIDENTIAL SYSTEM
A system of governing characterized by a separation of power between the legislative and executive branches. The president and Congress each derive their authority from being elected by the people. The president is both head of government and head of state.

HEAD OF STATE
A largely ceremonial position as the official representative of the state. In a parliamentary system, the head of state is expected to be "above" politics and thus is not usually involved in making governing decisions.

official functions, but is expected to be "above" politics and thus is not usually involved in making governing decisions (see Box 15-1, Should Canada Have Its Own Head of State?). Having a non-political head of state can provide a symbol of unity for a country. The head of state will not be tarnished by government incompetence or scandal because the head of state is not involved in politics and governing. In times of political crisis, the head of state has the legitimacy to appoint a new government.

Canada's Monarchy

In formal terms, Canada is a constitutional monarchy: our governments act in the name of the Crown. However, the largely ceremonial duties and responsibilities of the monarch, Queen Elizabeth II, have been delegated to the **governor general** at the national level and the **lieutenant-governors** at the provincial level. The governor general and lieutenant-governors are appointed by the monarch on the recommendation of the Canadian prime minister for a five-year term. The monarch and the monarch's representatives, filling the role of head of state, are expected to be non-political and thus are not significant in the processes of governing except in unusual circumstances.

The governor general has the important responsibility of ensuring that there is a government (prime minister and cabinet) in place at all times. Usually, the choice of prime minister is merely a formality: The governor

Commonwealth Parliamentary Association
www.cpahq.org

GOVERNOR GENERAL
The person who carries out the largely ceremonial duties and responsibilities of the monarch in Canada. The governor general is appointed for a five-year term on the recommendation of the prime minister.

LIEUTENANT-GOVERNOR
The person who carries out the largely ceremonial duties and responsibilities of the monarch at the provincial level in Canada. The lieutenant-governor is appointed for a five-year term on the recommendation of the prime minister.

BOX 15-1
Should Canada Have Its Own Head of State?

Canada's use of the British monarch in her role as Queen of Canada as head of state emphasizes Canada's historic ties to Britain and continuing membership in the Commonwealth, of which the Queen is the ceremonial head. However, for a significant proportion of Canada's population, the use of a foreign monarch as the formal head of state is an outdated relic of the colonial past.

The issue of the monarchy has occasionally generated political debate, as for example in 2002, when Foreign Affairs Minister John Manley suggested that Canada should have an elected head of state. Generally, though, other constitutional issues

have tended to overshadow differences of opinion concerning the monarchy. In contrast, in Australia there has been serious discussion about replacing the British monarch with an Australian head of state. However, despite popular support for replacing the monarch, disagreements about how to choose an Australian head of state have thus far prevented this change from occurring.

All parliamentary systems separate the position of head of state from that of head of government. However, the head of state does not need to be a monarch; many parliamentary systems have an elected or appointed president as head of state.

About Government
www.gc.ca/howgoc/howind_e.html

general is expected to choose the leader of the party that has the support of the House of Commons (the elected chamber of Parliament). In the event of the death, retirement, or resignation of the prime minister, the governing party will recommend a replacement. The governor general must also approve all legislation, a variety of appointments, and various executive decisions, such as the ratification of treaties and a declaration of war. However, in these matters, the governor general always acts on the advice of the prime minister and cabinet. Only if the prime minister and cabinet were ignoring the constitution or lacked the support of the House of Commons would the governor general be justified in acting independently. Lieutenant-governors have essentially the same powers and responsibilities at the provincial level.

The Prime Minister and Cabinet

HEAD OF GOVERNMENT
The person who heads the executive side of government. In Canada's parliamentary system, the prime minister is the head of government.

The **head of government**, the prime minister, is not directly elected by voters. Rather, the prime minister is the leader of the party that is able to maintain control of the House of Commons.[1] Normally, the prime minister is a member of the House of Commons. In a **majority government** situation (that is, where the prime minister's party has a majority of the members of the House of Commons), the prime minister chooses the cabinet from among his or her party's members of Parliament and the support of the House is assured.

MAJORITY GOVERNMENT
The government formed when the prime minister's party has a majority of the members of the House of Commons; thus, a single party forms the government.

Usually all of the cabinet ministers have been elected to the House of Commons except for one minister chosen from the Senate. If no party has a majority of members of the House of Commons, then two or more parties may join together in a *coalition government* to govern. In this case, the cabinet positions will be divided among the members of the parties involved in the coalition government. Although this is common in many European parliamentary systems, it has never occurred at the national level in Canada, with the exception of a wartime coalition government established in 1917. At the provincial level, there have been a small number of coalition governments.

MINORITY GOVERNMENT
A single party governs, but that party that does not have a majority of members in the House of Commons; thus, a minority government needs to gain the support of one or more other parties to pass legislation and to stay in office.

On a number of occasions, a **minority government** (one that is based on a party that does not have a majority of members in the House of Commons) has been formed. In this situation, the prime minister is usually but not necessarily the leader of the party with the most members of the Commons. For example, the Liberal party formed a minority government in 2004 as a result of winning 135 of the 308 seats in the House of Commons. As with a majority government, the prime minister chooses a cabinet from among his or her party members of Parliament. However, in a minority government situation, the governing party has to bargain and compromise with other parties in the Commons to stay in office and pass legislation. This support may be on an issue-by-issue basis or be part of a general agreement or understanding

---

[1] In some parliamentary systems (for example, Germany), the head of government is elected by the members of Parliament.

between the governing party and one or more of the other parties. For example, the minority Progressive Conservative government elected in Nova Scotia in 2003 has had to modify its policy proposals to gain the support of either the New Democratic party or the Liberal party in order to pass legislation. The Liberal minority that governed Ontario from 1985 to 1987 had a formal agreement with the NDP in which the NDP agreed to support the government for two years in exchange for the passage of some legislation that the New Democrats wanted. During this period, the Liberals governed Ontario even though the opposition PCs had more legislative seats than any other party.

POWERS   The prime minister and cabinet are responsible for the executive powers of government. This includes the conduct of relations with provincial and foreign governments, the issuing of a large number of regulations, the making of a substantial number of important appointments, and oversight of the administrative apparatus of government. More generally, the prime minister and cabinet provide leadership within government, set priorities, and oversee the development of new laws and the spending and taxing proposals of the government. The prime minister and cabinet also play a key role in the legislative process. Almost all of the legislation that is passed by the Canadian Parliament is proposed to Parliament by the cabinet. Parliament has to approve proposals for raising and spending money by government, but such proposals can only be made by the cabinet.

CONFIDENCE   The prime minister and cabinet hold their positions only as long as they maintain the confidence of the majority of members of the House of Commons (see Figure 15-1). If the majority of members of the House of Commons pass a motion of non-confidence in the government, or if a major proposal made by the cabinet, such as a budget proposal, is defeated by a majority in the House of Commons, the prime minister must either request that the governor general call an election or resign.[2] If a prime minister resigns without an election being called, the cabinet no longer exists and the governor general has to appoint a new prime minister to form a government.

The parliamentary system is often termed **responsible government** in the sense that the prime minister and cabinet are responsible to the House of Commons, which can theoretically force them from office. In practice, it is highly unlikely that the House of Commons would force a government from office if it has a majority of seats in the House of Commons. However, regardless of whether the governing party has a majority or a minority of seats, there is an expectation that the prime minister and cabinet will defend

RESPONSIBLE GOVERNMENT
The parliamentary convention that the prime minister and cabinet are responsible to the House of Commons, which can theoretically force them from office.

---

[2] In the parliamentary system of Germany, the Bundestag (the equivalent of the House of Commons) can only vote non-confidence in the government if the majority of elected representatives are able to agree on a different person to serve as chancellor (the equivalent of prime minister). This provision, termed a "constructive vote of confidence," makes it less likely that the government will be forced out of office.

FIGURE 15-1

A SIMPLIFIED DEPICTION OF THE CANADIAN PARLIAMENTARY SYSTEM

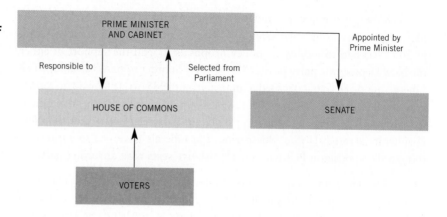

Parliament

Most, but not all, countries have two separate chambers or houses involved in the legislative process. Generally, this is a carry-over from the non-democratic past when a body representing privileged interests was seen as necessary to check the power of a body representing the people. In most federal systems, the second or upper chamber represents the interests of provinces or states.

The Parliament of Canada consists of two chambers: the House of Commons and the Senate. Provincial legislatures have only a single chamber of elected representatives.

HOUSE OF COMMONS   The Canadian **House of Commons** is the elected chamber of Parliament, with each member representing a particular geographical constituency. Representation is by population, with constituency boundaries drawn so that, in most cases, each member of the House of Commons represents approximately the same number of people. However, there are constitutional guarantees to maintain a minimum level of representation from the smaller provinces and territories. Thus, even though Ontario and Quebec have the majority of seats in the House of Commons, there is a slight overrepresentation, in terms of population, of the smaller provinces and territories.

On the surface, the House of Commons controls the executive because the prime minister and cabinet have to maintain the confidence (support) of the House of Commons. But in reality it is the prime minister and cabinet who normally control the House of Commons. *Party discipline* is the basic operating principle of the House of Commons (see Box 15-2, Should Party Discipline Be Relaxed?). That is, members of each party normally vote in accordance with the position that the party has adopted in **caucus** (a closed-door meeting of the party's members of Parliament). The prime minister and cabinet are usually

The Parliament of Canada
www.parl.gc.ca

HOUSE OF COMMONS
The elected chamber of Parliament, with each member of the House representing a particular geographical constituency.

CAUCUS
A closed-door meeting of a party's members of Parliament.

BOX 15-2
Should Party Discipline Be Relaxed?

Party discipline has generally been tighter in Canada than in other countries such as the United Kingdom, where strict party discipline is only maintained for votes of non-confidence, votes on the government's budget, and votes on certain issues deemed to be crucial to the government's program.

In the United Kingdom, unlike Canada, it is not unusual for legislative proposals coming from cabinet to be defeated in the House of Commons. Votes in the British House of Commons are designated according to three classifications: one-line votes, in which MPs, including cabinet ministers, are free from party discipline; two-line votes, in which party members are encouraged and cabinet ministers are expected to vote in accordance with their party's position; and three-line votes, in which party discipline is imposed on all members.

In Canada, there have only been a few free votes in which party discipline is withdrawn—usually on controversial moral issues such as capital punishment and abortion—so that members can follow their consciences.

The tightness of party discipline in Canada has often been criticized. Party discipline reduces the significance of ordinary members of Parliament, who are expected to toe the party line. Members may be expected to vote against the wishes or interests of their constituents. Provincial and regional interests may not be adequately represented in Parliament because parties and their leaders may be concerned about the dominant interests of the country as a whole.

There are, however, some positive features to party discipline. Party discipline helps to ensure that the positions taken by different parties are clear. This makes it easier for voters to choose among competing parties and to hold the governing party accountable for its actions. As well, it means that individual members of Parliament are less subject to pressure from lobbyists and special interests. Further, it means that the government can focus on doing what it considers to be for the common good of the whole country without having to contend with individual members of Parliament seeking special benefits for their constituency in return for their voting support.

A number of party leaders have promised to loosen party discipline, but have been reluctant to do so after becoming prime minister. Nevertheless, in recent years, there has been an increasing number of votes in which some party members have not supported the position of their party. This was particularly evident between 2000 and 2003 as a result of feuding within the governing Liberal party between the supporters of Prime Minister Jean Chrétien and would-be Prime Minister Paul Martin.

In his campaign for the leadership of the Liberal party, Paul Martin promised to eliminate what he termed the "democratic deficit" by increasing the role and independence of members of Parliament. In a plan announced March 4, 2004, Martin proposed the adoption of the British system of classifying votes, with the intention that only a few matters would be subject to a three-line vote. If implemented, this could give members of Parliament who are not in the cabinet a greater ability to influence ordinary legislative proposals. But at the time this book was written, it was not known whether the loosening of party discipline would occur in the minority government situation that resulted from the 2004 election.

able to convince their party's members in the House of Commons to support them and their legislative proposals. Thus, as long as a party elected a majority of members to the House of Commons, the prime minister and cabinet do not have to worry about losing the confidence of the House of Commons. Party discipline ensures that the political executive will remain in power.

Private Members Ordinary members of the House of Commons who are not in the cabinet (termed **private members**) have generally played a limited role in the governing process. Very few bills proposed by private members are passed by Parliament. Nevertheless, ordinary members of Parliament are, at times, successful in proposing minor modifications in legislation proposed by the cabinet.

Committees **House of Commons committees**, composed of government and opposition party members in proportion to their party's strength in the House, provide detailed examination of proposed legislation, and often suggest modifications to the legislation. At times they investigate or hold public hearings on particular policy issues, thus making some contribution to the development of new policies.

Opposition The House of Commons is particularly important in providing a public forum for the criticism and defence of the actions of the executive and its legislative proposals. The party with the second-highest number of seats is designated as the **official opposition** and leads off the questioning or criticism of government every day that the House is sitting. Other parties that have at least twelve seats in the House of Commons have official party status, which, along with other privileges, gives parties a budget for hiring research and support staff.

Various opportunities are provided for the opposition members to propose **non-confidence motions** in the government. Although non-confidence motions are usually unsuccessful, the establishment of a legitimate role for opposition provides a check on the great power exercised by the prime minister and the cabinet. Sometimes the opposition can persuade the government to change its policies and proposals, particularly if it can mobilize public opinion to its side.

Although the House of Commons provides a forum for debating proposed legislation, the governing party often uses motions of closure and time allocation to cut off or limit debate in the House of Commons, sometimes in response to filibustering—the term for delaying tactics by the opposition. For example, the Liberal government of Jean Chrétien used closure to end debate on anti-terrorism legislation in 2001 and on ratification of the Kyoto Protocol on global climate change in 2002. The increasing use of motions to limit debate by governments, both national and provincial, has been criticized by many political observers.

PRIVATE MEMBERS
Ordinary members of the House of Commons who are not in the cabinet.

HOUSE OF COMMONS COMMITTEES
Committees composed of government and opposition party members in proportion to their party's strength in the House of Commons; they provide detailed examination of proposed legislation, and often suggest modifications to the proposed legislation.

OFFICIAL OPPOSITION
The party with the second-highest number of seats in the House of Commons is designated as the official opposition and leads off the questioning or criticism of government every day that the House is sitting.

NON-CONFIDENCE MOTION
A motion put forward by the opposition members in a legislature expressing a lack of confidence in the government. If passed, the prime minister is expected either to resign or request that an election be held.

THE SENATE   Canada's **Senate**, the other chamber of Parliament, was established, in part, to provide for a body of "sober second thought" to check the democratic tendencies of the House of Commons. Legislation needs the approval of the Senate as well as the House of Commons (see Box 15-3, Is the Canadian Senate Important?). In contrast, the British House of Lords, the equivalent of the Canadian Senate, can only delay legislation passed by the House of Commons.

The Senate was also designed to provide equal regional representation to offset the representation by population in the House of Commons. There are twenty-four senators from each of Ontario, Quebec, the Maritimes (ten each from Nova Scotia and New Brunswick; four from Prince Edward Island), and the West (six each from Manitoba, Saskatchewan, Alberta, and British Columbia), plus six from Newfoundland and Labrador and one from each territory. However, since senators are not elected by provincial voters nor appointed by their provincial legislature or provincial government, it is questionable whether senators "represent," in a meaningful way, the province for which they are appointed.

Appointments   Senators are appointed by the prime minister and hold their positions until age seventy-five. A senator can only be removed from office for failing to attend two consecutive sessions of Parliament, becoming bankrupt, or being convicted of treason, a felony, or other "infamous crime." Most senators are appointed because of their loyalty to the party and the prime minister that is in power. When former hockey star Frank Mahovlich was appointed to the Senate, he told reporters, "I guess it's because I kept my mouth shut and didn't cause any trouble. I'm not familiar with the Senate and policies" (quoted in Bercuson & Cooper, 1998).

Because prime ministers appoint mostly party loyalists to the Senate, when another party is elected it will typically find that the outgoing party continues to control the Senate. For example, despite losing the 1993 Canadian election, the PC party continued to hold the majority in the Senate for several years. As senators reached retirement age, Liberal Prime Minister Chrétien filled Senate vacancies with his party's supporters.

There have been many proposals in Canada for changing or even abolishing the Senate. The ability of an appointed body to reject legislation passed by an elected, representative body is often viewed as a relic of the non-democratic past. It has also been argued that in a federal system, the Senate should represent provincial interests.

The Triple-E Senate   A significant development in efforts to make the Senate more relevant has been the movement for a **"Triple-E"** Senate (one that is *elected*, *effective*, and based on an *equal* number of representatives from each province). A Triple-E Senate would give a stronger voice to the smaller provinces.

SENATE (CANADIAN)
The upper chamber of Parliament, appointed on the recommendation of the prime minister. Senators hold their position until age seventy-five.

The United Kingdom Parliament: An Introduction to Parliament
www.parliament.uk/works/index.cfm

TRIPLE-E SENATE
A proposed reform that would make Canada's Senate elected, effective, and based on an equal number of representatives from each province.

BOX 15-3

Is the Canadian Senate Important?

Because the prime minister and cabinet are not expected to maintain the support of the Senate and the Senate does not hold non-confidence votes, the Senate, unlike the House of Commons, cannot force the resignation of the government.

However, the Senate does have the right to reject legislation that has been passed by the House of Commons, thereby potentially frustrating the government's plans. Senators have generally avoided obstructing the will of the majority in the House of Commons. Nevertheless, during the years that Progressive Conservative Brian Mulroney was prime minister (1984 to 1993), the Liberal majority in the Senate engaged in confrontation with the PC majority in the House on a number of important issues.

The Senate refused, for example, to pass the Canada–U.S. Free Trade Agreement until the Mulroney government won the 1988 election. It twice rejected legislation to extend the length of patent protection for prescription drugs before finally relenting. It opposed the imposition of the Goods and Services Tax (GST) until Prime Minister Mulroney invoked an obscure constitutional provision to appoint an additional eight senators. Angered by limitations on debate on the GST, Liberal senators tried to disrupt Senate proceedings by playing kazoos, inviting the media onto the floor of the Senate, and rushing the speaker's chair until a compromise allowing more time for debate was reached.

The Senate has continued to be somewhat more active even after the Liberal Party regained control of both the House of Commons and the Senate. In 2003, for example, the Senate rejected a bill passed by the House of Commons concerning stricter penalties for cruelty to animals.

The Senate has also been active in investigating a number of issues, including poverty, the mass media, science policy, free trade, terrorism, and aging. Some of these reports have been of high quality because of the time available to senators, the less intensely partisan nature of discussion in the Senate, and the competence and experience of many senators. Nevertheless, the Senate is still, to some extent, a comfortable retirement home for politicians and loyal party workers.

An elected Senate with equal representation from each province would probably quite frequently be controlled by a different party than the House of Commons. Being elected, senators would be reluctant to back off from a confrontation with the House of Commons. Thus, there would be a need for negotiation and compromise between the governing party and the Senate to avoid a deadlock in Parliament.

What is the likelihood of the Triple-E proposal being adopted? Changing the number of representatives from each province to create a Triple-E Senate would involve the difficult process of constitutional amendment. It is unlikely that Quebec and Ontario would agree to the reduction in their power that would result from the election of an equal number of representatives from each province in an effective Senate. As well, it is likely that various groups, such as women and Aboriginals, would insist on guaranteed representation in a reconstituted Senate.

THE PRESIDENTIAL SYSTEM

The presidential system of government was developed in the United States. The founders of the U.S., having for years clashed with the powerful British-appointed royal governor of each colony, were concerned about concentrating powers in the hands of a single person. Concentration of power, they felt, would threaten individual liberty—a key value for the revolutionaries. However, many of the founders of the U.S. also recognized the need for strong leadership, and thus they devised a system in which the president, although the dominant figure in the executive branch, was to be checked and balanced by the powers of other branches of government.

As a result, the American system of government features a separation of powers. There are three branches of government:

1. legislative, represented by **Congress**
2. executive, headed by the president
3. judicial, particularly the Supreme Court

These branches are independent of each other and relatively equal in power. The legislative and executive branches need to cooperate with each other to get things done, but each branch has its own mandate so that it can check the power of the other branches.

CONGRESS
The legislative branch of the American government.

The President

The American president is both head of state and head of government. That is, the president carries out the ceremonial duties associated with the head of state, but also heads up the executive branch of government. As chief executive, the president commands the armed forces, exercises considerable control over foreign policy, helps to shape domestic policy, and exercises some control over the public service. The president appoints a variety of senior officials and Supreme Court and other federal judges. However, to check the power of the president, these appointments must be approved by the Senate (the upper chamber of Congress).

Subject to Senate ratification, the president appoints cabinet secretaries, who serve the president and report to Congress. Cabinet secretaries head up the various departments of government and are thus somewhat similar to cabinet ministers in a parliamentary system. However, unlike the cabinet in a parliamentary system, the American cabinet as a whole is not a key decision-making body. Some presidents have avoided regular cabinet meetings, and the president does not necessarily follow the advice of cabinet. Although some individual cabinet secretaries are important advisors to the president, much of the advice given to the president comes from the White House staff—usually individuals with strong personal loyalties to the president.

The American President
www.whitehouse.gov

The president appoints the top officials in the public service, can issue executive orders concerning how laws and policies are to be carried out, and has a number of executive agencies to keep tabs on different aspects of government activity.

CONGRESS'S OVERSEEING ROLE Congress exercises oversight of the activities of the public service because of its powers to investigate government activity. Public servants are frequently called to testify before Congressional committees. Both Congress and the president take an active role in determining the government's spending plans (unlike the system in Canada, where parliamentary approval is normally a formality). Permanent public servants (that is, those who are not political appointees) often work closely with Congressional committees and interest group representatives, thus limiting the power of the president and the president's staff to control the workings of the public service.

THE VICE-PRESIDENT The vice-president is handpicked by a candidate for the presidency to serve as a running mate in a presidential election, typically selected to provide balance in the sense of appealing to different regions and to persons with a somewhat different ideological perspective than the president. The vice-president has the constitutional right to preside over the Senate, although only occasionally does so, and can only vote in case of a tie. Otherwise, the major constitutional role of the vice-president is to be available to take over the presidency in case the president dies or is unable to continue in office (see Box 15-4, The Significance of the Vice-President). Depending on the president, some special tasks may be assigned to the vice-president.

PRESIDENTIAL SELECTION AND TERM The president, along with a vice-presidential running mate, is elected by the American people. Although voters in the United States choose among the competing presidential candidates, technically they are voting for members of the *electoral college* committed to casting their ballot for a particular presidential candidate. A majority of electoral college votes is needed to elect a president (see Chapter 10). In the unlikely event that no candidate has a majority of electoral college votes, the president would be elected by the House of Representatives, the lower house of Congress, with each state casting a single vote

The president has a fixed term in office of four years and can be elected to a maximum of two terms. Unlike the prime minister in a parliamentary system, the president holds office even if the president lacks the support of Congress. The president and other top officials can only be removed from office if convicted of "treason, bribery or other high crimes and misdemeanours." This is a difficult and lengthy process. The House of Representatives has to pass articles of impeachment stating the offence. Then, after holding a trial, a two-thirds majority in the Senate has to find the pres-

The Significance of the Vice-President

The office of vice-president has not attracted the most flattering commendations:

- "The most insignificant office that ever the invention of man contrived." (President John Adams, 1735–1826)
- "It's not worth a pitcher of warm spit; it doesn't amount to a hill of beans." (Vice-President John Nance Garner, 1868–1967)
- "About as useful as a cow's fifth teat." (President Lyndon B. Johnson, 1908–1973)
- "The only thing the job calls for is waiting: waiting for the president to die or be impeached; waiting for the Senate to wind up in a tie so the vice-president can break it. That's all the vice-presidency is about: waiting. Everything else is make-work." (Lynn Cheney, wife of Vice-President Richard Cheney, in 1988)

But is the insignificance of the vice-president exaggerated? Since Walter Mondale was vice-president during Jimmy Carter's administration in the late 1970s, vice-presidents have provided advice to the president and been included in top-secret briefings (O'Connor & Sabato, 1995). Many observers of the administration of George W. Bush have suggested that Vice-President Richard (Dick) Cheney has a major influence on government policies. In this case, a president with no national political experience and very limited knowledge of world affairs appears to have relied heavily on a more experienced vice-president. Unlike other vice-presidents in recent decades, however, Cheney, because of his age and health, is unlikely to be a candidate for president.

Thus, although the significance of the vice-president depends primarily upon the wishes of the president, the vice-presidency has evolved into an important executive institution.

ident guilty. No president has ever been removed by this process. Richard Nixon resigned before he could be impeached for participating in the cover-up of illegal activities. Bill Clinton was impeached for lying to a grand jury and obstructing justice, but survived a trial in the Senate.

The American Congress

The American Congress is a legislative body composed of two separate bodies:

- The **House of Representatives,** which is elected every two years from districts of approximately equal population size.
- The **Senate,** which is composed of persons elected for six-year terms on a two per state basis.

The president does not have the power to dissolve Congress and thus may have to live with a Congress that has a different perspective (see Figure 15-2). Because the president does not need the support of Congress to remain in office, Congress can feel free to reject legislative or budgetary proposals from

HOUSE OF REPRESENTATIVES
The lower chamber of the American Congress, elected for a two-year term from districts of approximately equal population size.

SENATE (AMERICAN)
The upper chamber of Congress. Two Senators are elected by voters in each state for a six-year term.

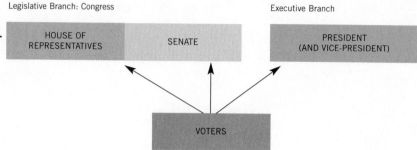

VETO
The ability to prevent the enactment of a measure, such as the authority of the president of the U.S. to veto laws passed by Congress (although this veto can be overridden by a two-thirds majority in each House of Congress).

the president, knowing that it will not lead to a new election. To protect the independence of Congress, the president and the cabinet secretaries are not allowed to be members of Congress.

Although the executive branch prepares many of the legislative proposals that Congress considers, Congress is very active in modifying or rejecting the executive's proposals. Members of the American Congress have sizable staffs who are often involved in drafting and modifying legislative proposals. Congress is therefore active not only in approving legislation, but also in the development of legislation. As a check on the legislative power of Congress, the president has the authority to **veto** any law passed by Congress, and does so quite often. Congress can override the presidential veto, but this requires a two-thirds majority in each body of Congress, and thus is quite rare.

PARTY DISCIPLINE Party discipline in the American Congress is not particularly tight. Individual members of Congress frequently vote as they see fit, or in the interests of the constituency they represent, rather than as members of a party team. This means that the president may not be able to get Congress to support his policies even when the president's party controls Congress. For example, after being elected in 1992, President Bill Clinton, a Democrat, was unable to persuade Congress to vote for legislation establishing a universal medical care system, even though the Democratic party had a majority in the House of Representatives and the Senate for his first two years in office.

Conversely, a president faced with a Congress with a majority of opposing party members has some ability to influence individual members of Congress regardless of their party affiliation. For example, in the early 1980s, Republican President Ronald Reagan was able to get much of his program adopted despite the control of Congress by the Democratic party. Reagan persuaded some conservative-minded Democrats of the virtues of his proposals. As well, by making his case directly to the American public, he created a favourable climate of opinion for his proposals, thus putting pressure on members of Congress to pass his proposals.

Although party discipline is not as tight in the United States as in most parliamentary systems, it should not be concluded that parties are irrelevant. The parties in Congress have become somewhat more cohesive in the past couple of decades as the Democrats have become more consistently liberal or centrist and the Republicans more conservative. Party members do tend to vote with their party. This can create difficulties that may result in **gridlock,** particularly when the president is of a different party than the party that has a majority in one or both houses of Congress, or if there is a strong ideological difference between the president and the majority in Congress (see Box 15-5, Gridlock).

GRIDLOCK
A term used to describe the situation in American politics that can occur when Congress is not controlled by the president's party and disagreement between the executive and legislative branches stalls the process of governing.

BOX 15-5

Gridlock

The American system of government occasionally suffers from **gridlock** when it is difficult to get things done because of tension between the executive and legislative branches. For example in 1995, Democratic President Clinton and a Congress dominated by right-wing Republicans were unable to agree on the government's budget. For over two weeks in December, the American government was shut down, public servants were laid off, and major decisions were deferred until after the November 1996 elections (Hauss & Smith, 2000).

However, in 1998 Clinton was able to get the Republican-controlled Congress to approve the major elements of his budget by emphasizing some popular measures—such as making money available to hire more teachers—and threatening to shut down the government and blame the Republicans during that year's Congressional elections. In return for the support of the Republicans, Clinton's budget was designed so that Republicans could claim credit for increases in military spending, more money for the tough anti-drug programs they advocated, and tax cuts.

Because Congress has in recent decades often been controlled by a different party than that of the president, the possibility of gridlock has become quite common. The ability of the president and Congressional leaders to negotiate acceptable compromises is necessary to make the system work.

COMMITTEES   A final major feature of the American Congress is the importance of congressional committees. It is in the committees of the House and Senate that legislative proposals are usually most thoroughly debated, modified, or eliminated. The chairs of these powerful committees are chosen by the majority party in each House; the chair is usually the party member who has served on that Committee the longest. The committee chairs are often quite independent-minded and thus do not feel the need to always adhere to their party's positions.

In general, the passage of legislation in the American system is a very difficult process. There are a large number of obstacles to overcome in order to pass legislation. Presidents have to use all of their persuasive capabilities and negotiating skills in order to get their proposals accepted. As former President George Bush Sr. said, perhaps with some exaggeration, it was easier to deal with Iraqi dictator Saddam Hussein than with the American Congress.

Unlike the fusion of executive and legislative power characteristic of parliamentary systems, the American presidential system divides power so as to try to ensure that no one individual or institution is too powerful. Although the president can be very powerful—for example, in making the decision to

▶ American presidents have found ways to avoid the constitutional provision that only Congress has the authority to declare war.

send troops to intervene in foreign countries without necessarily gaining the approval of Congress—the president often has to bargain and deal with an independent-minded Congress. Thus, some political scientists have suggested that it would be more accurate to describe the American system of government as presidential–congressional rather than presidential.

Other Presidential Systems

The presidential system adopted by other countries often functions quite differently than the American presidential system. There is considerable variation in the rules (such as how the president is chosen, how many terms the president can serve, and whether cabinet and other appointments have to be approved by Congress) and in the powers of the president. Just as important, presidential systems in practice often work in quite different ways, depending on the extent to which Congress or the equivalent is independent-minded, and the extent to which political parties are united and disciplined.

EVALUATING PARLIAMENTARY AND PRESIDENTIAL SYSTEMS

Is a parliamentary system better than a presidential system? Evaluating these two basic systems is not an easy task. The quality of each system varies from country to country, depending upon such factors as the nature of the party system and the political culture, as well as the specific way that the parliamentary or presidential system functions. Each system has both positive and negative features. Some Americans have urged the adoption of some parliamentary features to improve their governing process, while some Canadians have looked to the American system for ideas about how to reform the workings of Canada's parliamentary system (Cutler, 1980; Gibbins, 1982).

Accountability

A parliamentary system of government tends to facilitate the accountability of government, particularly if one party forms a majority government. Voters can make a simple choice as to whether or not they want the governing party to remain in office depending on their general satisfaction or dissatisfaction with the performance of the government. As well, because the prime minister and cabinet actively participate in the House of Commons, the public has the opportunity to assess the performance of the government through the ongoing debate between government and the opposition in the House. By contrast, with authority split between the executive and the legislative branches in a presidential system, each branch can try to shift blame to the other for any problems. The president and cabinet do not sit in Congress and are not accountable to Congress.

Leadership

Those who prefer a presidential system often view it as providing strong leadership. The president clearly leads the executive branch of government and is secure in office. As well, the president can claim to speak for the people as the president has been elected by citizens in the country as a whole. As head of state, a president can usually count on the respect and support of the people. However, since most presidential systems limit the president to one or two terms in office, a president may be relatively powerless (a "lame duck") in the final years in office as important political forces await the election of a new president. As well, in the final term of office, there is no incentive for the president to be responsive to the wishes of the electorate.

In a parliamentary system, the prime minister and cabinet are capable of decisive action in a majority government situation because of their domination of the legislative branch. However, the dominance of the prime minister and cabinet may mean that different viewpoints and interests are ignored in reaching decisions. In contrast, passing new legislation is often a difficult and lengthy process of bargaining and compromise in the American presidential system. On the positive side, the separation of powers helps to make each branch of government more vigorous and may encourage greater deliberation and openness (Zvesper, 1999).

Government Strength and Flexibility

In some countries, the parliamentary system is associated with weak and unstable governments. In multiparty systems, coalition or minority governments are common. Bargaining and negotiating among parties is required to gain majority support for legislative proposals. Coalition governments can be considered to be more representative and more deliberative than majority governments because various viewpoints have to be considered in drafting policies. However, in some situations (for example, the parliamentary systems of France prior to 1958 and Italy until fairly recently) building stable coalitions has been difficult and many governments were short-lived.

Parliamentary systems can be more flexible than presidential systems (Linz, 1994). A government that is unable to retain the confidence of the majority in the House of Commons can be removed from office. Likewise, prime ministers that lose the support of their party or caucus can be forced or pressured to step down. For example, British Prime Minister Margaret Thatcher was removed by her party's caucus, and Canadian Prime Minister Jean Chrétien was pressured to retire, particularly by Paul Martin's supporters in the Liberal Party. The fixed terms of office in presidential systems make it difficult to resolve impasses between the executive and legislative branches or to remove a president who has lost support. Congress cannot be dissolved and a new election held to resolve an impasse.

Representativeness

The American presidential system tends to be more representative of different interests than a parliamentary system with a majority government. Members of Congress have greater independence to represent the population and interests of their district or state. By contrast, the party discipline characteristic of parliamentary systems limits the ability of members of the House of Commons to represent their constituents.

Degree of Democracy

The presidential system could also be viewed as somewhat more democratic than the parliamentary system as the president is elected by the people. However, it can be questioned whether concentrating executive power in one person is truly democratic. Although prime ministers have become increasingly powerful in relation to cabinet, the cabinet is still an important decision-making body in parliamentary systems. In contrast to a system in which the president dominates the executive branch, the prime minister usually works with the cabinet in reaching decisions.

Openness

The presidential system tends to be more open than the parliamentary system. Rather than having policy choices made in the secrecy of cabinet, legislation is often thoroughly discussed and modified in Congress and its committees. Policy differences between Congress and the president are often publicly aired. This transparency may facilitate greater public participation in the policy-making process. However, it also makes the American political system more susceptible to influence by interest groups that may be able to prevent laws for the common good from being passed.

Experience

The American presidential system often features "outsiders" being elected as president. Former military leaders and popular personalities may be able to appeal to the public at large even though they have little connection to a particular party. Although this may bring a fresh perspective to national politics, it means that the president may have very limited experience in national politics and government (neither Bill Clinton nor George W. Bush had experience in national politics before becoming president). This difference should not be exaggerated, though, as some Canadian prime ministers (for example, Brian Mulroney in 1984) have come to office with little or no experience as an elected politician. However, unlike parliamentary systems, where potential prime ministers can gain experience and knowledge by serving as leaders of opposition parties, presidential systems offer no formal role for losing presidential candidates.[3] Likewise, although a president has a much larger talent pool to draw from in choosing cabinet secretaries, cabinet ministers in parliamentary systems are more likely to have extensive political experience.

National Interest

A major problem with the American system is the general difficulty in adopting a coherent set of policies that reflect the national interest. Bargaining and compromise are at the core of American politics, such that a president and the president's advisors often have difficulty enacting their vision. Further, because members of Congress are focused on their district or state, they may be able to use their independence to block nationally desirable policies that have negative local implications. Powerful interests are often able to block measures through their influence on individual members of Congress. The oil industry, for example, has been able to prevent the adoption of a national energy policy, particular through its influence on members of Congress from oil-producing states.

MIXED PARLIAMENTARY/PRESIDENTIAL SYSTEMS

A number of countries, including France, Russia, Finland, Sri Lanka, and Portugal, have adopted systems of governing that are a mixture of parliamentary and presidential systems (often referred to as semi-presidential).[4] Such **mixed parliamentary/presidential systems** feature a dual executive in which both the president and the prime minister possess political authority (Linz, 1994).

MIXED PARLIAMENTARY/ PRESIDENTIAL SYSTEM
A governmental system that features a dual executive in which both the president and the prime minister possess political authority.

The French System

In France, the president is elected for a fixed five-year (formerly seven-year) term and cannot be removed from office during that time. The president appoints the prime minister, usually a leading figure in the majority party or coalition of parties in the elected Assembly. The president, with advice from the prime minister, appoints the members of the Council of Ministers (cabinet), as well as top public, military, and judicial officials. As in the American presidential system, ministers do not sit in the Assembly. The Assembly, elected for a maximum five-year term, can censure the prime minister and cabinet

---

[3] One exception is Nicaragua, where the runner-up in the presidential election automatically receives a seat in the National Assembly.

[4] Switzerland has a unique system that can be considered neither parliamentary nor presidential. The government of Switzerland is headed by a collegial seven-person executive (Federal Council), representing the major political parties, elected by the Swiss Assembly for a fixed four-year term of office. The Assembly also chooses a president and vice-president from among the Federal Council for a one-year term.

and force them to resign, but cannot censure the president or force a presidential election. However, unlike the American presidential system, the French president can dissolve the Assembly and have a new Assembly election conducted.

The French president has considerable powers to pass decrees on foreign and economic policy that do not require parliamentary approval. As well, the president can call national referendums, determine when the National Assembly meets and what its agenda will be, assume emergency powers, and propose constitutional amendments.

The French system was set up with the intention of making the president a very powerful figure. The president is dominant in French government, making the key policy decisions, while the Assembly is very limited in power and authority (Kesselman, Krieger, & Joseph, 1996). However, if the president does not have the support of a majority in the National Assembly and is unable to gain a majority through new elections, the president's power is substantially reduced. From 1986 to 1988 and 1993 to 1995, the Socialist President François Mitterand shared power with the conservative parties that controlled the Assembly, a situation termed **cohabitation**. Likewise, from 1997 to 2002, President Jacques Chirac, a conservative, shared power with the Socialist Prime Minister Lionel Jospin. In these situations, the prime minister could be considered, in effect, as the head of the government, with the system essentially parliamentary in its characteristics (Lijphart, 1994).

COHABITATION
The sharing of power between the French president and the National Assembly that occurs when the Assembly is controlled by a party opposed to the president.

The Russian System

Russia also has a mixed parliamentary/presidential system in which the president, elected for a fixed four-year term, has considerable power to rule by decree and is responsible for appointing the cabinet. The president's nomination of a prime minister has to be approved by Parliament. If his choice is rejected three times by Parliament, Parliament is dissolved and a parliamentary election results. Although the Russian Parliament has featured lively debates—including fistfights among members!—it is limited in power and cannot force the prime minister and cabinet out of office.

Evaluation of Mixed Systems

Do mixed systems combine the best features of the parliamentary and presidential systems? Or is the dual executive a recipe for instability? France, which changed in 1958 from a parliamentary system to a mixed system after decades of political instability, is typically viewed as a success story, even though its government has functioned in quite different ways depending upon whether or not the president controls the majority in the Assembly. The French system has been criticized for giving the president excessive power at times. However, at other times, the cohabitation arrangement that has forced presidents to share power with a prime minister and Assembly of a different political persuasion seems to have functioned reasonably well. On the other hand, the mixed system in Germany from 1919 to 1933 created serious problems and contributed to the coming to power of Adolf Hitler and the Nazi party (Linz, 1994).

Summary and Conclusion

Parliamentary systems are often described as having a fusion (close interrelationship) of legislative and executive powers. Despite the label *parliamentary system*, very considerable power rests with the prime minister and cabinet, particularly in a majority government situation. Nevertheless, they are expected to be responsible to the House of Commons for their actions.

The term *presidential system* can also be misleading. The president does control the executive branch of government and serves as both head of state and head of government. However, the separation of powers allows each of the three branches of government to check the powers of the other branches. At times, the president has tended to dominate the political system. At other times, Congress has asserted its powers and reduced the capabilities of the president. Generally, power is more diffused in a presiden-

tial system than in a parliamentary system (Smith, 2000). The sharing of powers between the president and Congress usually makes compromises necessary for each to achieve its objectives.

When one party controls a majority of legislative seats, a parliamentary system facilitates decisive action by the government. There are fewer checks against a domineering government than in the American presidential system. The American presidential system tends to be somewhat more democratic and representative than most parliamentary systems because of weaker party discipline in Congress and the direct election of the president. However, the fusion of powers in a parliamentary system facilitates the accountability of the government to the people and can make it easier for the government to act for the good of the country as a whole.

Key Terms

Discussion Questions

1. Does the parliamentary system tend to give too much power to the prime minister?

2. Should party discipline in Parliament be loosened?

3. Should the Canadian Senate be maintained, changed, or abolished?

4. Should Canada replace the monarchy with an elected head of state?

5. Do you think that it would be best for a new democracy to adopt a parliamentary, presidential, or mixed system?

Further Reading

Cohen, R.E. *Washington at work: Back rooms and clean air* (2nd ed.). Needham Heights, MA: Allyn and Bacon, 1995.

Docherty, D.C. *Mr. Smith goes to Ottawa: Life in the House of Commons.* Vancouver: UBC Press, 1997.

Fisher, L. *The politics of shared power: Congress and the executive* (3rd ed.). Washington, D.C.: Congressional Quarterly Press, 1993.

Franks, C.E.S. *The Parliament of Canada.* Toronto: University of Toronto Press. 1987.

Lijphart, A. (Ed.). *Parliamentary versus presidential government.* Oxford: Oxford University Press, 1992.

Lijphart, A. *Patterns of democracy: Government forms and performance in thirty-six countries.* New Haven: Yale University Press, 1999.

Chapter 16

GOVERNMENT AND ADMINISTRATION

PHOTO ABOVE: Unlike average applicants, Iraq's former ambassador to the United States Mohammed Al-Mashat and his wife were fast-tracked through Canada's bureaucracy for landed immigrant status within a month. Ministers in the governing Progressive Conservative party blamed senior officials for not notifying them about this controversial immigrant, and thus avoided taking responsibility for the decision.

CHAPTER OBJECTIVES

After reading this chapter you should be able to:

1. discuss the power of the prime minister
2. outline the organization and operation of the cabinet
3. discuss the bureaucratic form of organization
4. examine the traditional relationship between government and administration
5. evaluate the new public management

In the run-up to the 1991 Gulf War, Mohammed Al-Mashat, Iraq's ambassador to the United States, was a familiar face on North American television as he defended Iraq's recent invasion of Kuwait. When U.S.-led Allied forces invaded Iraq in early 1991, Al-Mashat was recalled to Baghdad. Two and a half months later, he and his wife came to Canada as ordinary landed immigrants. In contrast to the lengthy wait normally faced by those who apply for landed immigrant status, Al-Mashat's application had been processed within a month. Indeed, the Canadian Security Intelligence Service had reviewed his case in a single day.

When Al-Mashat's new Canadian status became public, the opposition parties went ballistic and the media devoted extensive coverage to the affair. Ministers in Progressive Conservative Prime Minister Brian Mulroney's cabinet were quick to claim that they had not been informed by their officials and aides about Al-Mashat's entry to Canada. Instead, they pointed fingers at Raymond Chrétien, a senior official in the Department of External Affairs, and David Daubney, the chief of staff (top political aide) to External Affairs Minister Joe Clark, for allegedly failing to inform them.

Not surprisingly, the opposition Liberals focused their attacks on Daubney, a former PC MP, rather than Chrétien, a twenty-five-year veteran of the foreign service who just happened to be the nephew of Liberal leader Jean Chrétien. Hearings into the incident were held by a committee of the House of Commons, which allowed some questioning of ministers. However, members of the governing party that controlled the committee ended the hearings quickly, and gave little opportunity for Daubney and Chrétien to defend themselves.

Traditionally, in Canada's parliamentary system, the cabinet is expected to take responsibility for what goes on in government. This does not mean, as opposition parties sometimes claim, that cabinet ministers should resign if any wrongdoing occurs in the departments they head. However, they should admit that mistakes have been made, investigate how the problem occurred, and report back to Parliament on how the problem has been rectified.

Public servants are responsible to cabinet ministers and traditionally operate outside of the political spotlight to avoid being seen as partisan. Because they are expected to avoid criticizing their political bosses and required to keep many matters confidential, they cannot easily defend their actions in a public hearing or in the media. Instead of being defended by their superiors, in the Al-Mashat case public servants became the scapegoats.

In this chapter we look at the organization and processes of governing in Canada, although the issues discussed are generally applicable to other democratic countries. Many political scientists and other observers of politics have been concerned with the tendency for power to become concentrated in the hands of the prime minister and a small inner circle connected to the prime minister. Some (Savoie, 2003) see criticism of public servants by cabinet ministers, as in the Al-Mashat case, as part of government efforts to change the nature of the public service so as to reduce its influence or even move toward privatization of public services.*

*This vignette is based on Sutherland (1991).

GOVERNMENT ORGANIZATION

Governments have become large and complex organizations in the past half-century, responsible for developing a large number of laws and regulations, administering a wide array of programs, and providing grants, subsidies, and tax breaks for a variety of purposes. A large number of people are employed by government, although, as Table 16-1 indicates, there has been a decline in the number of government employees, particularly when measured against the increasing size of the population.

There are several important issues to consider regarding government organization:

Government of Canada
www.gc.ca

- Is this machinery of governing efficient and effective?
- Is the governing executive effectively held accountable for its actions?
- Are there adequate controls on the administration?
- Should government be run more like a business?

THE POLITICAL EXECUTIVE

EXECUTIVE DOMINANCE
A descriptive term applied to the Canadian parliamentary system because it places considerable power in the hands of the prime minister and cabinet through their ability to control the House of Commons.

The prime minister and cabinet (the political executive) are at the centre of the governing process at the national level in Canada. Although the prime minister and cabinet are expected to be responsible and accountable to Parliament for their actions, in reality the prime minister and cabinet normally control the dominant party in the House of Commons. Thus, the Canadian parliamentary system can be described as a system of **executive dominance**, as it places considerable power in the hands of the prime minister and cabinet, particularly in a majority government situation.

TABLE 16-1
GOVERNMENT EMPLOYEES IN CANADA

Note: Panel A includes the military; Panel B excludes the military.

PANEL A: EMPLOYEES PER 1000 PEOPLE	1992	1999	2003
Federal government	14.5	10.8	11.6
Total government sector	96.1	82.5	83.4

PANEL B: TOTAL NUMBER OF EMPLOYEES, 2003	
Federal	258 000
Provincial	222 500
Local	255 500

SOURCES: *Adapted from the Statistics Canada website (2004b), Employment and average weekly earnings (including overtime), public administration and all industries, www.statcan.ca/english/Pgdb/govt19a.htm, retrieved July 17, 2004; and Number of employees, federal, provincial and territorial governments Canada, 1992, 1999, 2003, www.statcan.ca/english/freepub/68-213-SIE/2004000/tables/table1.htm, retrieved July 17, 2004.*

The Prime Minister

The prime minister is the leading figure within the cabinet. The prime minister determines who will be appointed to the cabinet and what their responsibilities will be. At any time, the prime minister may change the responsibilities of any cabinet minister or demand a cabinet minister's resignation. The prime minister is also responsible for organizing the cabinet, and thus determines what **cabinet committees** there will be and who will sit on those committees. The prime minister chairs cabinet meetings, sets the agenda for those meetings, and, since votes are not held in the cabinet, determines the consensus of the cabinet.

In addition to playing a leading role in cabinet, prime ministers are party leaders. They take on responsibility for their party's election campaigns and play a leading role in defending the government in the House of Commons. The mass media and the public pay far more attention to the prime minister than to any other political figure. Prime ministers make a substantial number of prestigious appointments and thus can reward loyal supporters. Although modern prime ministers do not run a particular department of government,[1] prime ministers normally play a leading role in representing the country in international meetings, in federal–provincial relations, and in constitutional negotiations.

The **Privy Council Office (PCO)**, an administrative structure that is directly responsible to the prime minister, has a central role in organizing the cabinet and trying to coordinate and direct the activities of government. It is also very important in providing policy advice to the prime minister. The **Prime Minister's Office (PMO)**, comprising mainly loyal party supporters, does not only provide secretarial support such as scheduling appointments and handling correspondence, but also is involved in maintaining the prime minister's power and popularity by providing partisan advice, writing speeches, managing the media, making recommendations concerning patronage appointments, and dealing with party matters (Dyck, 2004). Together, the PCO and PMO provide the prime minister with a dedicated source of advice and a capability to direct and coordinate the activities of government.

POWER   Some analysts suggest that Canada has developed a **prime ministerial government** in which the prime minister has become the equivalent of the American president in the sense of being the chief executive, rather than occupying the traditional position as "first among equals" in the cabinet. (See Box 16-1, The Concentration of Governing Power in Canada.) Indeed, the prime minister can be considered more powerful than the president in the sense that Canada does not have the equivalent of a strong and independent Congress

CABINET COMMITTEE
A committee of cabinet ministers appointed by the prime minister.

PRIVY COUNCIL OFFICE (PCO)
A central agency, directly responsible to the Canadian prime minister, that has a key role in coordinating and directing the activities of government and in providing policy advice to the prime minister.

PRIME MINISTER'S OFFICE (PMO)
The office that provides support and political advice to the prime minister.

PRIME MINISTERIAL GOVERNMENT
The view that the prime minister has become the equivalent of the American president in the sense of being the chief executive, rather than the traditional position as "first among equals" in the cabinet.

[1] Some premiers, particularly in the smaller provinces, do take responsibility for a particular department.

The Concentration of Governing Power in Canada

Donald Savoie, Professor of Public Administration and Economic Development at the Université de Moncton, makes the case, based on interviews with top governmental and administrative officials, that central agencies such as the Privy Council Office now have a pre-eminent position within government and allow the prime minister to exercise considerable control over government.

Savoie writes (1999):

Power in the federal government has shifted away from line ministers and their departments towards the centre, and also, within the centre itself, power has shifted to the prime minister and his senior advisers at both the political and public service levels

and away from Cabinet and Cabinet Committees.... Cabinet has now joined Parliament as an institution being bypassed.... The Canadian prime minister has little in the way of institutional check, at least inside government, to inhibit his ability to have his way.

Given Savoie's arguments, Canadians might well wonder whether Canada has evolved into what journalist Jeffrey Simpson (2001) terms a "friendly dictatorship." Is it undesirable for power to be concentrated in the hands of the prime minister? Is it an exaggeration to view the prime minister as an elected dictator?

to check the power of the prime minister (Smith, 1971). Similar arguments have been made that Britain and some other parliamentary systems based on the British model have moved from cabinet government to prime ministerial government (Weller, 1985). Continental European parliamentary systems are less likely to feature prime ministerial dominance (Lane & Ersson, 2000), in part because governments typically involve a coalition of parties.

Despite the powers of the Canadian prime minister, some cabinet ministers are also very important in government policy-making because of the departments that they control and because of their popularity within the party or the country. For example, through most of the decade that Jean Chrétien was prime minister, he had to contend with the considerable power wielded by his popular rival, Paul Martin, who held the important position of finance minister. On the other hand, when Paul Martin took over from Jean Chrétien as Liberal party leader and prime minister, he filled most of his cabinet positions with his own supporters. Sheila Copps, who challenged Martin for the Liberal leadership, was removed from the cabinet and lost the Liberal nomination in her constituency when Martin supported a rival candidate.

Generally, prime ministers have been able to maintain the support of their party and their party caucus. However, as noted in Chapter 15, the political careers of British Prime Minister Margaret Thatcher and Canadian Prime Minister Jean Chrétien were ended by their failure to maintain this support.

◀ Former British Prime Minister Margaret Thatcher's political career was ended by her failure to maintain the support of her party and her party caucus.

The power of a prime minister may also be limited by the pressures of globalization, the influences of powerful economic and social forces, and, in decentralized federal systems, by the power of provincial governments.

The Cabinet

Canadian prime ministers devote considerable attention to ensuring that their cabinets are geographically representative. There is always at least one cabinet minister from each province (except occasionally Prince Edward Island), with more cabinet ministers from the provinces with greater populations. The proportion of French-Canadians in the cabinet has generally been roughly in proportion to their share of Canada's population. There is also an expectation that French-Canadians outside Quebec and English-speaking Quebeckers will each have their own representative in the cabinet.

Consider the cabinet appointed by Prime Minister Martin on July 20, 2004. The thirty eight cabinet ministers included sixteen from Ontario, seven from Quebec (plus the prime minister), five from British Columbia, two from each of Nova Scotia and New Brunswick, and one from each of Newfoundland and Labrador, Prince Edward Island, Manitoba, Saskatchewan, Alberta, and the Territories. Although all provinces are represented in the cabinet, some Albertans and Quebeckers felt that the cabinet did not adequately represent them. Concerns were also raised about the proportion of ministers from Ontario in the cabinet.

Before 1957, cabinets were exclusively composed of males of British, Irish, or French ancestry. In recent times, prime ministers have made an effort to try to appoint more women and persons of different ethnic and racial backgrounds to the cabinet. Nevertheless, the cabinet, like Parliament, is not fully representative of the diversity of Canadian society. For example, the cabinet appointed in July 2004 only included nine women.

DEPARTMENTS The activities of government are divided among a number of departments and agencies. There are about two dozen departments, each headed by a cabinet minister. (Examples include Agriculture and Agri-Food, Environment, Finance, Industry, Justice, Foreign Affairs, Health, National Defence, and Natural Resources.) Other cabinet ministers, termed **ministers of state**, are given responsibilities for policy areas such as sport, public health, multiculturalism, and families and caregivers, but have no department to oversee.

Because each department is concerned with a particular policy area and the particular set of interests associated with that policy area, there is often some tension among the different departments. For example, the Agriculture Department has had a more favourable view of the use of certain pesticides than the Department of the Environment. Further, each department will typically seek more money and employees for its programs, while the Department of Finance and the Treasury Board, a cabinet committee responsible for the government's expenditures, will normally try to limit spending.

MODERN CABINETS   The cabinet has traditionally been viewed as a collective decision-making body. Because each member of the cabinet is expected to maintain **cabinet solidarity** (that is, to fully support and defend the decisions and actions that cabinet takes), there is an expectation that the cabinet as a whole will discuss and deliberate on the key governing decisions. In reality, however, modern cabinets are too large and have too little time to fully consider all of the decisions that government makes.

Over time, cabinets have grown in size because of the expansion of government activities and expectations that the cabinet will be representative of different segments of society. Many individual cabinet ministers are busy overseeing the activities of their department and the development of new policies related to their department, as well as carrying out myriad political activities to support the governing party and maintain their own popularity. Thus, they generally have little time to involve themselves in considering all of the issues before the cabinet.

Because of the large size of modern cabinets, decision-making has sometimes devolved to a smaller, select group of cabinet ministers. In Britain, for example, a cabinet of twenty-two members (as of 2004) is responsible for decision-making while a much larger ministry deals with matters in various government departments but rarely meets as a decision-making body.

Canadian prime ministers have used various means to deal with the large size of cabinets. Many decisions in the government of Brian Mulroney were made in the Priorities and Planning Committee of the cabinet, chaired by the prime minister. Jean Chrétien abolished the Priorities and Planning Committee and instead created a two-tier cabinet system in which a number

MINISTERS OF STATE
Cabinet ministers who are not responsible for a particular government department.

CABINET SOLIDARITY
The convention in a parliamentary system that each member of the cabinet is expected to fully support and defend the decisions and actions that the cabinet takes.

of **secretaries of state** had a limited role in cabinet. Paul Martin did away with the two-tier system. After restoring the Priorities and Planning Committee in December 2003, he disbanded it in July 2004. Instead, Martin has established eight cabinet committees, with the Domestic Affairs and Global Affairs Committees as well as the Treasury Board and an Expenditure Review sub-committee at the centre of the cabinet decision-making process. As a result of being reduced to a minority government in 2004, the Operations Committee of the cabinet, which is responsible for implementation of the government's agenda and day-to-day strategy in the House of Commons, is also likely to be important.

COORDINATION Although many individual cabinet ministers are responsible for overseeing a department of government, in recent decades considerable attention has been devoted to trying to coordinate the diverse activities of government. Dealing with problems effectively often requires coordination among a variety of different government departments. The concern for coordination has stimulated the development and expansion of **central agencies** that attempt to provide direction and coordination to government.

As noted earlier, the Privy Council Office plays a major role in coordinating the activities of cabinet and the public service. The Prime Minister's Office is concerned with providing partisan advice, particularly to ensure that government actions are directed with an eye towards re-election of the governing party. The **Department of Finance** is influential throughout government because of its responsibility for assessing the potential impact of government actions on the economy and developing the government's budget. The **Treasury Board**, a cabinet committee with its own staff, plays a central role because of its responsibility for the expenditures and management practices of government.

In general, proposals coming from an individual department are assessed by the central agencies. Cabinet committees will then discuss the proposal presented by the department, keeping in mind the assessments offered by the central agencies. The cabinet as a whole often ratifies the decision with little or no debate unless the decision is highly controversial or would have an impact on the political fortunes of the government.

HOUSE OF COMMONS The prime minister and cabinet are accountable for their actions in governing through their responsibility to the House of Commons. Because the prime minister and cabinet hold their positions only as long as they have the support of the majority of members of the House of Commons, there is an expectation that the cabinet as a group will defend, explain, and take responsibility for the actions of the government in Parliament. In a majority government situation, where the governing party has a majority of seats in the House of Commons, it is highly unlikely that the House of Commons would pass a motion of non-confidence in the government or defeat important legislative and financial proposals presented by the cabinet.

SECRETARIES OF STATE
Junior ministers in Prime Minister Jean Chrétien's two-tier cabinet system.

Institute on Governance
www.iog.ca

CENTRAL AGENCY
An organization that tries to provide direction and coordination to the executive side of government. In Canada, the key central agencies are the Privy Council Office, the Prime Minister's Office, the Treasury Board, and the Department of Finance.

DEPARTMENT OF FINANCE
The government department responsible for preparing the government's budget and analyzing the interaction of the government's financial activities and the country's economy.

TREASURY BOARD
A cabinet committee with its own staff that plays a central role in governing because of its responsibility for the expenditures and management practices of government.

Nevertheless, the rules of the House of Commons provide opportunities for the opposition parties to raise questions and criticisms about the actions and performance of the government. In particular, the daily Question Period provides for lively, if not always informative, exchanges between the opposition and governing parties.

INDIVIDUAL RESPONSIBILITY In addition to the **collective responsibility** of the cabinet to the House of Commons, there is an expectation that individual cabinet ministers will take responsibility for the activities of the department that they administer. If there are serious problems within a department, opposition party members typically call for the minister to resign from the cabinet. However, cabinet ministers in Canada have not resigned for the errors of the officials in the departments they administer. Instead, cabinet ministers are more likely to promise to look into a problem (see Box 16-2, Ministerial Responsibility and Cabinet Resignations).

SECRECY The accountability of the government is also limited because of **cabinet secrecy**. The cabinet meets behind closed doors, cabinet documents normally remain secret for thirty years, and the advice given to the cabinet is not usually released publicly. Cabinet secrecy helps to maintain cabinet solidarity and ensure that the cabinet is seen as a united team, regardless of the disagreements that undoubtedly exist among individual cabinet ministers. Cabinet discussions can be full and frank because participants know that word of disagreement will not get out to the media or opposition parties. As well, it helps to shield public servants who advise the cabinet from public criticism (public servants, being politically neutral, do not normally respond to criticisms). On the other hand, the principle of cabinet secrecy can be used to avoid releasing research conducted by the government that would aid in public discussion of an issue and assist the opposition parties and the public in holding the government accountable for its actions.

In recent times, the *Access to Information Act* has allowed journalists, interest groups, opposition parties, and concerned citizens the ability to obtain information that had previously remained secret. Although such laws have made government more transparent, various types of information can be withheld from the public, and officials have frequently been slow to respond to requests for information. The 2000 Report of the Information Commissioner, for example, stated that the Canadian government had a penchant for secrecy that undermined the democratic process and failed to live up to the spirit of its access to information legislation. The Commissioner also alleged that his staff members had been threatened by the PMO. In overturning the government's attempt to keep some documents secret, Madam Justice Eleanor Dawson ruled that limitations to access to information should be "limited and specific" so that "citizens can participate meaningfully in the democratic process" and ensure "that politicians and bureaucrats remain accountable to citizens" (quoted in Sallot, 2004).

COLLECTIVE RESPONSIBILITY
The convention that the cabinet as a group will defend, explain, and take responsibility for the actions of the government in Parliament.

CABINET SECRECY
The convention that the cabinet meets behind closed doors, cabinet documents normally remain secret for a lengthy period of time, and the advice given to the cabinet is not usually released publicly.

Access to Information and Privacy
canada.justice.gc.ca/en/ps/atip

BOX 16-2

Ministerial Responsibility and Cabinet Resignations

In many cases, it would be unfair to expect cabinet ministers to resign because of problems in their department as the minister cannot be expected to know everything that is going on in a large department. However, there are times when lack of knowledge may be an excuse to avoid responsibility.

One would expect ministers to insist that their top officials inform them of important problems in their department's activities; otherwise, they are evading their responsibilities. Sometimes, though, it is possible that officials deliberately keep their minister in the dark to allow the minister to avoid responsibility.

The quick granting of landed immigrant status to Mohammed Al-Mashat, discussed at the start of this chapter, was one incident in which officials involved were publicly blamed, fairly or unfairly, by cabinet ministers for failing to notify them of the issue. But it is not the only case, as the following examples show:

- In 1992, Canadian soldiers involved in peacekeeping operations in Somalia tortured and killed a sixteen-year-old boy who had broken into the Canadian base to steal supplies. Defence Minister Kim Campbell complained that she had not been informed by the military. A Commission of Inquiry found

that the military had attempted to cover up the incident and the head of the military resigned. However, important questions about whether and why the minister was not informed were left unanswered when the government cut short the investigation.

- In 2002, Defence Minister Art Eggleton was accused of misleading Parliament by claiming that he had not been made aware that Canadian troops in Afghanistan had handed prisoners over to the Americans. In this case, military officials indicated that they had briefed him three times about this matter. He was not removed from the cabinet for this incident. However, Eggleton was later dismissed from the cabinet after an untendered $36 500 contract awarded to a former girlfriend for writing a fourteen-page report became publicized.

Although the opposition parties and the media are diligent in bringing to public attention wrongdoings within government, it is ultimately up to the public in an election to decide if the government has not lived up to its responsibilities

ADMINISTRATION

In the **traditional administrative model**,[2] there is a clear division of the roles and responsibilities of government and administration (Savoie, 2003). Public servants within each department of government provide unbiased, expert advice to the minister in charge of the department. The minister considers this advice in light of political considerations and takes a recommendation to the full cabinet for discussion and approval in keeping with the overall direction being pursued by the government.

TRADITIONAL ADMINISTRATIVE MODEL
A model of government organization that involves a clear division of the roles and responsibilities of government and administration, with public servants within each department of government providing unbiased, expert advice to the minister in charge of the department.

---

[2] The discussion of this model is based on Savoie (2003).

A proposed law or spending plan is then taken to Parliament for debate and approval. Public servants carry out approved programs and laws under the direction of the cabinet minister, with top administrators providing instructions and directions through a chain of command to those carrying out specific duties. In this model, public servants have considerable importance, but operate anonymously, with politicians taking credit or blame for the actions of the government (Borins, 2002; Savoie, 2003).

It is often difficult, however, to distinguish between what is political and what is non-political. Like any model, the traditional administrative model is a simplification of a complex reality. And, as we will see, the nature of the relationship between the executive and the administration has been moving away from the traditional model.

Bureaucratic Organization

BUREAUCRACY
The permanent employees of government.

Connected to the traditional administrative model is the development of a professional public service often referred to as the **bureaucracy** (a term that literally means "rule by offices"). In the view of German sociologist Max Weber, bureaucratic organizations are a key characteristic of modern societies, reflecting the capitalist system's concern with efficiency and the modern political system's concern for legal–rational forms of rule. A pure bureaucratic organization is one in which people are hired and promoted on the basis of their qualifications and merit, work is organized in terms of specialized positions (offices), detailed rules and procedures are followed by all members of the organization, and there is a hierarchical chain of command so that those at the top can direct and supervise large numbers of people.

Although Weber viewed bureaucratic organizations as efficient, their adherence to rules and regulations can make bureaucratic organizations inflexible and impersonal. Weber also thought that the powerful bureaucratic organizations controlled by senior officials would dominate the governments of modern societies and limit the applicability of the democratic ideal of rule by the people (Heywood, 2002).

Public Service Commission of Canada
www.psc-cfp.gc.ca

GOVERNMENT BUREAUCRACY Canadian governments, like the governments of most other developed countries, have adopted a bureaucratic model of organization for the administration. The government bureaucracy is expected to be a highly competent but politically neutral organization that will work with the political executive of any government that happens to be elected. In the early twentieth century, the adoption of the merit principle instead of political patronage as the basis for hiring Canadian government employees helped to create a professional public service devoted to the public interest.

PATRONAGE
Hiring government employees or awarding government contracts based on party or personal ties to the governing party.

Patronage (hiring based on party or personal ties to the governing party) makes it difficult to hire and retain competent people, creates problems if government employees are expected to engage in partisan (party) work, and discriminates against those who did not support the governing party. Patronage also often results in administration by inexperienced persons, as a change in government will lead to a new set of government employees.

Staffing the public service strictly on the basis of merit, however, can have the effect of making the public service unrepresentative of the characteristics of the society as a whole. An emphasis on formal qualifications such as a university degree and scores on public service examinations may result in hiring practices that favour people from some parts of society rather than others. In Canada, efforts began in the 1960s to increase the relatively small proportion of French-speaking persons in the public service in order to create a public service that could operate in both official languages and would increase French Quebeckers' attachment to the Canadian government.

Beginning in the 1980s, the government expanded its efforts to create a more **representative bureaucracy** by establishing targets for hiring and promoting more women, Aboriginals, visible minorities, and disabled people in the public service. As Table 16-2 indicates, **employment equity** programs have had considerable success in creating a more diverse public service. Although there have been criticisms that such programs are contrary to the merit principle, those hired and promoted still have to meet basic standards of competence.

PROTECTION Canadian public servants enjoy protection against being fired for political reasons. This leaves them free to provide advice that is based on their knowledge, experience, and understanding without fear of being fired for having views that are contrary to those of the governing party. Only **deputy ministers,** who are appointed by the prime minister in consultation with the clerk of the Privy Council, the senior public servant, do not enjoy job security, as they are expected to provide political as well as managerial advice to cabinet ministers. In contrast, many of the higher-level public service positions in the United States are considered political in nature, and thus occupants can be replaced when a new president is elected.

In recent times, members of the political staff of cabinet ministers have been able to move into senior public service positions, thus raising questions about whether this interferes with the non-partisanship of the bureaucracy (Savoie, 2003). As well, when one governing party has been in power for a

REPRESENTATIVE BUREAUCRACY
A bureaucracy that reflects the characteristics of society, particularly by trying to ensure that all levels of the public service have a proportion of women and various minority groups similar to that of the population as a whole.

EMPLOYMENT EQUITY
Measures taken to increase the proportion of persons from disadvantaged groups in the workplace (including senior positions).

DEPUTY MINISTER
The executive head of a department of government, appointed by the prime minister in consultation with the clerk of the Privy Council.

TABLE 16-2
EMPLOYMENT EQUITY IN THE CANADIAN PUBLIC SERVICE

YEAR	% WOMEN	% WOMEN EXECUTIVE	% WOMEN SCIENTIFIC/ PROFESSIONAL	% ABORIGINAL PEOPLES	% PERSONS WITH DISABILITIES	% PERSONS IN VISIBLE MINORITY GROUPS
1993	46.1	17.6	28.3	2.0	3.1	3.8
2003	52.8	33.8	40.3	3.9	5.6	7.4

SOURCE: *Extracted from Employment Equity in the Federal Public Service, 2002–2003 (Table 1 and Statistical Highlights), by the Treasury Board Secretariat, retrieved July 17, 2004, from www.tbs-sct.gc.ca/report/empequi/2003/ee05_e.asp#Tables.*

long period of time, senior public servants can become very closely associated with the government and committed to its policies. If another party is elected to govern, it may distrust the advice given by public servants and believe that they will be resistant to the new directions being pursued by the government.

Controls on the Administration

Weber's argument that bureaucratic organizations are a powerful force in modern governments is echoed by those who claim that political power has shifted from the executive to the bureaucracy. Cabinet ministers are often dependent upon public servants for information and policy advice. Instead of the executive giving direction to the public service, some suggest that senior public servants have a considerable ability to influence cabinet ministers.

Given the size and political importance of the administration, an important issue is how to ensure that the administration operates in the public interest and is responsible for its actions. In theory, cabinet ministers oversee the operations of their department and, in a parliamentary system, take responsibility for their department in the House of Commons. Because the opposition parties will publicize deficiencies that they see in the operations of government, there is an incentive for cabinet ministers to try to ensure that their department will not act in ways that are politically embarrassing. However, given the wide scope of governing activities, cabinet ministers have difficulty overseeing all of the actions of their department. As well, the opposition parties in the House of Commons will tend to focus on a few potential scandals, rather than examine the more mundane details of government operations.

ADDITIONAL CONTROLS   There are some additional controls over the administration. Of particular importance are the financial controls on the spending of government departments. The detailed spending plans of each department (termed the **Estimates**) are examined by the Treasury Board and approved by the cabinet and then submitted each year to Parliament for formal approval. An officer of Parliament, the **auditor general**, examines government spending to ensure that it conforms to the purposes for which the money was granted by Parliament, that the money was spent efficiently, and that government is getting value for the money spent (see Box 16-3, The Auditor General's Report).

Although the auditor general cannot order the government to act, the annual report of the auditor general brings publicity to inefficiency and waste within government. The Public Accounts Committee of the House of Commons uses the auditor general's report for further examination of government spending practices. In recent years, a Commissioner of the Environment and Sustainable Development, with responsibility for examining the Canadian government's environmental performance, has been attached to the auditor general's office and issues an annual report.

Auditor General
www.oag-bvg.gc.ca

ESTIMATES
The detailed annual spending plans of each department of government; they must be approved by Parliament.

AUDITOR GENERAL
An independent officer of Parliament who examines government spending to ensure that it conforms to the purposes for which the money was granted by Parliament, that the money was spent efficiently, and that government is getting value for the money spent.

The Auditor General's Report

The auditor general's report usually contains some headline-grabbing examples of government waste and mismanagement. A report of the auditor general released in February 2004 brought great attention to the "sponsorship scandal" that subsequently dominated Canadian politics for months and created difficulties for the government of Paul Martin, which had come to office just before the report's release.

In her report, Auditor General Sheila Fraser was strongly critical of a $250 million program to promote national unity by increasing the visibility of the Canadian government through the sponsorship of various events. More than $100 million had gone to advertising agencies with connections to the Liberal party. In a number of cases, the report alleged, these agencies had provided little of value. Further, according to the auditor general, "just about every rule" had been broken by those involved in the program, which had not been subject to the usual financial controls.

Supporters of the program claimed that the need to defeat Quebec separatism justified going outside the normal rules and procedures. A special Parliamentary committee established to investigate the scandal heard conflicting testimony as to whether public servants or cabinet ministers were responsible for the problems with the sponsorship program. The former public works minister, whose department was responsible for the program, told the committee that he did not control what happened in his department and therefore was not responsible for the outcome.

Partisan disputes prevented the committee from issuing recommendations. The slower processes of a judicial inquiry and criminal investigations and trials may be more effective in shedding light on the issue.

The office of auditor general has been widely praised for its diligence in bringing problems of financial management and waste within government to public attention. This does not necessarily mean, however, that government spending is generally out of control. Given that there is a large number of programs in which government is involved, it is unfortunate, but perhaps inevitable, that some financial mismanagement and waste will occur.

The analysis of whether government is getting value for the money it spends on various programs often involves controversial political judgment calls. For example, although a previous auditor general criticized the money spent on the Hibernia oil development offshore of Newfoundland as an expensive "make-work" project, others would see it as helping regional development and ultimately providing substantial revenues to the Canadian government.

A number of democratic countries have adopted the institution of **ombudsman**, pioneered in Sweden in 1809, to investigate citizens' complaints concerning the administration. All Canadian provinces except Prince Edward Island have an ombudsman or citizens' representative who is an independent officer of the legislature. There is no ombudsman for the Canadian government, but there are officers of Parliament who deal with complaints on specific topics (human rights, official language rights, the rights of penitentiary

OMBUDSMAN
An independent officer of the legislature who investigates citizens' complaints concerning the government's administration.

inmates, the rights of members of the armed forces, privacy rights, and information rights). An ombudsman or officer of Parliament cannot force a change in the actions of the administration, but he or she can discuss the complaints with government officials and generate publicity for justified complaints that have not been settled.

Crown Corporations and Regulatory Agencies

Many of the controls placed on the administration only apply to the departments of government and the public servants who work for those departments. Governments also attempt to achieve their objectives through state-owned corporations, termed **Crown corporations** in Canada, that operate somewhat like private-sector business corporations, and through regulatory agencies.

Examples of Crown corporations include the Canadian Broadcasting Corporation (CBC), the Bank of Canada, and Canada Post. Generally, Crown corporations are more independent of political control and responsibility than are government departments. In some cases this independence has been established so that the Crown corporation can effectively compete in the marketplace. In other cases, such as the CBC, it is important that the Crown corporation's operations be seen as non-partisan and non-political.

Usually the cabinet appoints a board of directors to oversee the Crown corporation, along with a president who manages it. Employees of Crown corporations are not usually public servants and the cabinet does not take responsibility for the actions of Crown corporations.

There are also a number of **regulatory agencies** (independent agencies of government involved primarily in regulating the activities of private business) that operate at arm's length from government so that their decisions will be viewed as fair and impartial. One example is the Canadian Radio-television and Telecommunications Commission (CRTC), which allocates broadcasting licences and sets performance criteria.

PUBLIC INTEREST Despite establishing Crown corporations and regulatory agencies with the intention that they should be independent of government, many of the members of the boards of directors and commissioners are associated with the governing party. Thus, their appointments might be viewed as patronage-based. Some appointees to regulatory agencies have been associated with the companies being regulated, leading to allegations that the public interest is not being served. For example, before they took office both Françoise Bertrand, CRTC chair from 1997 to 2000, and Charles Dalfen, the current chair, had been paid consultants for major corporations that are regulated by the CRTC.

Although the independence of the Crown corporations from direct government control may increase their efficiency (they can, for example, hire and

CROWN CORPORATION In Canada, a state-owned corporation that operates independently from direct governmental control.

REGULATORY AGENCY An independent agency of government involved primarily in regulating the activities of private business.

fire employees more easily), it may also create situations where their actions may not be in the public interest or may be embarrassing to the government. For example, some years ago Atomic Energy of Canada, Ltd., was found to be paying millions of dollars in bribes to persuade officials of dictatorial governments to buy Canadian nuclear power reactors. Likewise, there was considerable public criticism when it was discovered that the Federal Business Development Bank (subsequently renamed the Business Development Bank) was providing loans to strip clubs in Ontario and Quebec.

On the other hand, direct political interference with Crown corporations or regulatory agencies is often considered improper. Former Prime Minister Jean Chrétien, for example, was criticized for calling the president of the Business Development Bank concerning a loan for a hotel in his constituency. (The hotel was owned by a friend and allegations were made that the loan may have indirectly benefited Chrétien.)

THE NEW PUBLIC MANAGEMENT

The government bureaucracy has come under considerable criticism in recent decades for several reasons:

- Bureaucratic organization is often viewed as slow-moving, rigid, and inflexible rather than efficient.

"We can keep dumping in this river for now... it'll take the government at least five years to legislate a ban."

- The commitment of public servants to the public interest is sometimes questioned.
- Users of government services sometimes receive insufficient attention and respect.

PUBLIC CHOICE THEORY
A theory based on the assumption that individuals always pursue their own self-interest.

In particular, **public choice theory**, based on the assumption that individuals always pursue their own self-interest, has been used to argue that public servants seek to expand the programs and expenditures of government so as to enhance their own position, privileges, and power. The effect, compounded by the efforts of government to try to satisfy the demands of interest groups, is that government has become much larger than necessary. This, in the view of many public choice theorists, has stifled the growth of the more dynamic and efficient private sector.

Thinking about government administration has also been influenced by the popular book *Reinventing Government,* which argues that governing should involve "steering" rather than "rowing." In other words, the development of policy, which is the proper role of governing, should be separated from the delivery of services, which should be contracted out to private business as much as possible (Osborne & Gaebler, 1993).

Generally, then, concerns about administrative inefficiencies, the stifling of entrepreneurial initiatives by government "red tape," and excessive rules and regulations have led many governments to undertake major reforms of their administrative structures and practices.

Adopting Business Practices

NEW PUBLIC MANAGEMENT
The adoption of contemporary business practices in the administration of government.

The adoption of contemporary business practices is a major feature of **new public management,** an idea that has influenced changes to government administration in many countries. In part, this new administrative management style includes devising business plans for each unit of government, establishing performance indicators for public servants, and treating people as customers of government services.

Instead of the hierarchical chain of command characteristic of bureaucratic organizations, a more flexible, results-oriented, modern business management style is preferred. Generally, the new public management can be summed up by the slogan, "Let the managers manage." In other words, the public service managers should be given the authority to provide services without being tied by a variety of rules and regulations. Further, because the new public management concept suggests that public service managers should focus on delivering services rather than being involved in developing policies, governments have increasingly called upon the political staff of cabinet ministers, outside consultants, research institutes, and interest groups for policy advice.

Alternative Service Delivery

Another important aspect of the new public management is the development of new methods of delivering government programs, termed **alternative service delivery**. One form of alternative service delivery in Canada involves the establishment of service agencies that have considerable autonomy from the normal departmental structures and rules. Examples include the Passport Office, the Canada Revenue Agency, the Canadian Food Inspection Agency, and Parks Canada. In some cases, these agencies are expected to be self-financing.

Another form of alternative service delivery involves establishing partnerships with business (sometimes referred to as public–private partnerships), other levels of government, and voluntary organizations to deliver services. For example, the Career Edge internship program involves a partnership of the Canadian government with the YMCA and private businesses (Zussman, 2002). Alternative service delivery can also involve contracting out government activities to private business or to groups of former public servants. This approach is particularly common in the United States, where private businesses have been contracted not only by a number of cities to manage

ALTERNATIVE SERVICE DELIVERY
New methods of delivering government programs, such as the establishment of service agencies that have considerable autonomy from the normal departmental structures and rules, and establishing partnerships with business, other levels of government, and voluntary organizations to deliver services.

"Wouldn't it be great if government no longer ran the parks?"

garbage collection and road maintenance, but also by state and national governments to run prisons and carry out a variety of military functions.

Effects on Administration

New public management has had a significant effect on government administration in Canada. However, unlike a number of other countries, including New Zealand, Australia, and the United Kingdom (as discussed in Box 16-4, Changing Administration in the United Kingdom), the Canadian government has not thoroughly and consistently applied the tenets of the new public management (Aucoin, 2002).

Senior public servants continue to have an important influence on the development and implementation of policies, although with increased oversight by the central agencies. Various forms of alternative service delivery

BOX 16-4

Changing Administration in the United Kingdom

The influential British television series *Yes Minister* featured a particularly negative depiction of the relationship between cabinet ministers and senior public servants. This coincided with the real-world perspective of Margaret Thatcher, Conservative prime minister from 1979 to 1990. Thatcher viewed the public service as a serious obstacle to implementing her free-market ideological vision.

In *Yes Minister*, a savvy senior public servant manipulated a hapless, inexperienced cabinet minister. The minister was dependent on the public servant, who really ran the department and made sure any of the minister's proposals for changes that might be inconsistent with the department's interests were not acted upon (Savoie, 2003).

During the Thatcher years, the government, facing serious economic problems, instituted major changes in the traditional British administration. Many state-owned enterprises were privatized, regulation of private business was reduced, the expenditures of

government departments were scrutinized, and public service staff numbers were substantially reduced.

Thatcher's reforms included the establishment of one hundred and thirty eight independent executive agencies that employed about three-quarters of the public service. These agencies, headed by a chief executive officer, are provided with performance targets by a cabinet minister, but are given a considerable level of autonomy to achieve the targets. A Citizen's Charter requires that departments and agencies establish standards for their services and publicly disclose if these standards were being met. Finally, a system of market testing allows private companies to compete against government agencies and departments for contracts to provide various public services (Borins, 2002).

As for *Yes Minister*—the program ended in the 1980s, a relic of a bygone era in the British civil service, but Margaret Thatcher made sure the show's writer was awarded with a knighthood!

have removed some government services from bureaucratic controls, but the public service is still an important part of government's operations.

Problems with New Public Management

A key problem with the efforts to make government more business-like is that there are inherent differences between government and business. Business is concerned with making a profit; government should be concerned with the common good, even if this means undertaking activities that are costly. The objectives of government are more complex than the simple bottom line of profitability that drives business activity. Indeed, a focus on profitability may conflict with the interests of the public.

The idea that the public service should be primarily involved in managing programs rather than developing policies is also controversial. Based on its experience in administering programs, the public service is able to provide useful advice in developing new policies and modifying existing ones. Further, a knowledgeable, professional public service protected by a high level of job security may be more likely to provide honest, forthright advice than consulting firms and partisan advisors who may tend to tell ministers what they want to hear (Savoie, 2003).

Finally, the idea that much of the work of the public service should be done by autonomous agencies, each responsible for a particular program, has been questioned. In looking at Britain and New Zealand, analysts have found that adopting this approach can make it more difficult for governments to deal with complex problems that require coordination among a variety of departments and agencies (Aucoin, 2002).

Summary and Conclusion

Considerable power is placed in the hands of the political executive. Although the executive in a parliamentary system must retain the support of the elected legislature, this is largely a formality in a majority government situation. Parliamentary systems feature collective decision-making by the prime minister and cabinet, with cabinet ministers often chosen to be representative of some of the important segments of society. Power has, however, tended to drift from the cabinet as a whole to the prime minister and a small group of aides, officials, and ministers at the centre. Critics argue that this concentration of power is inconsistent with democratic principles.

Because of the great power exercised by the prime minister and other members of the executive, it is important that the government be held accountable for its actions in order to ensure that government is acting for the common good. Although the prime minister and cabinet are responsible to the House of Commons for the actions of the government, cabinet secrecy, the strength of party discipline, and the large number of activities government engages in can limit the ability of the House of Commons to hold the government accountable. Access to information legislation, however, has made government more transparent and thus facilitated scrutiny and criticism of government actions.

Theoretically, the administration in Canada is under the direction and control of the cabinet, which in turn is responsible to the House of Commons. In reality, however, cabinet ministers may be dependent on senior public servants for advice and may provide only limited oversight over the administration of programs in their department. Nevertheless, the increased control exercised by the central agencies limits the autonomy of the officials in each department of government.

The idea that the government bureaucracy is efficient and dedicated to the public interest has been challenged by those who contend that public servants pursue their own interests by seeking to expand the activities of government. The public service has also been criticized as being too rule-bound, slow to act, and prone to act in established ways. Attempts have been made to adopt a more business-like approach to administration through the techniques of the new public management. Providing greater autonomy and flexibility for administrative managers may be useful in reducing inefficiency and cutting red tape. However, it may also reduce the accountability of administration to government and Parliament.

Despite the criticisms that are often levelled at the bureaucracy, a strong, professional public service is important in the effort to pursue the common good of a political community. Good public administration involves not only the efficient delivery of services, but also the provision of quality advice to government. Even though there are now a variety of sources of advice that are used by government in developing its policies, the assessment of that advice and the coordination of the variety of governmental programs is necessary for good governing (Aucoin, 2002).

More generally, there has been a growing tendency for policy-making and administration to move away from the direct control of the executive and administrative aspects of national governments. This tendency involves upward shifts to international bodies such as the World Trade Organization and the North American Free Trade Agreement, downward shifts to regional and local bodies, and horizontal shifts to the courts and a variety of autonomous agencies, public–private partnerships, and private contractors (Van Kersbergen & Van Waarden, 2004). Assuming that these shifts continue, developing mechanisms of accountability so that the common good is protected will be an important but difficult challenge.

Key Terms

Discussion Questions

1. Does Canada have a "prime ministerial government"? If so, is this desirable or undesirable?

2. Is it important that the cabinet and bureaucracy be representative of the diversity of society?

3. Why do people tend to have an overly negative view of government bureaucracy?

4. Should government be more business-like?

5. Should many of the services provided by the public administration be contracted out to private business?

Further Reading

Blakeney, A., & Borins, S. *Political management in Canada: Conversations on statecraft* (2nd ed.). Toronto: University of Toronto Press, 1998

Dunn, C. (Ed.). *The handbook of Canadian public administration.* Don Mills, ON: Oxford University Press, 2002.

Inwood, G.J. *Understanding Canadian public administration: An introduction to theory and practice* (2nd ed.). Toronto: Pearson Prentice Hall, 2004

Osborne, D., & Gaebler, T. *Reinventing government: How the entrepreneurial spirit is transforming the public sector.* Reading: Addison-Wesley, 1992.

Robertson, G. *Memoirs of a very civil servant: Mackenzie King to Pierre Trudeau.* Toronto: University of Toronto Press, 2002.

Savoie, D.J. *Breaking the bargain: Public servants, ministers and parliament.* Toronto: University of Toronto Press, 2003.

Savoie, D.J. *Governing from the centre: The concentration of power in Canadian politics.* Toronto: University of Toronto Press, 1999.

Weller, P. *First among equals: Prime ministers in Westminster systems.* Sydney: George Allen & Unwin, 1985.

Chapter 17

PUBLIC POLICY

Tommy Douglas, the man who fought to get Canada a free public medical care plan, would have lost a leg as a boy had it not been for the compassion of a visiting doctor.

CHAPTER OBJECTIVES

After reading this chapter you should be able to:

1. describe the stages of the policy process
2. discuss the models of policy making
3. outline the factors that influence policy

As a young boy growing up in the first decades of the twentieth century, Tommy Douglas was diagnosed with osteomyelitis in his right leg. Because his family was not wealthy and could not pay for proper treatment, he would have lost his leg if not for the compassion of a visiting doctor. This inspired Douglas's lifelong fight for a free, public medical care plan that would cover all Canadians, rich or poor.

As the Co-operative Commonwealth Federation (CCF) premier of Saskatchewan, Douglas instituted universal hospital insurance in 1946. His government brought in a public medical care insurance system in 1962, despite opposition from the North American medical profession that culminated in a strike by doctors. Later, as leader of the New Democratic Party (NDP), Douglas campaigned for a national medicare system. With the support of the NDP, the Liberal minority government of Lester Pearson agreed in 1966 to provide federal funding for provinces that established medicare programs under federal guidelines, despite the opposition of some provincial governments. Douglas's dream was fulfilled in 1971, when all the provinces had joined the program and all residents of Canada were covered by medicare.

The medicare system has become a symbol of national pride and identity for many Canadians. Medicare is seen as the leading example of how Canada is a more caring and egalitarian society than the United States, where about one-sixth of the population is not covered by medical insurance plans and thus has trouble paying for costly medical treatment. Although many Americans are dissatisfied with their medical system, attempts to move towards universal health care coverage in the U.S. have been resisted by the powerful health insurance industry's campaign against "socialized medicine." Reform proposals developed by Hillary Rodham Clinton and put forward by Democratic President Bill Clinton failed to come to a vote in Congress despite his party's majority in that body.

This chapter introduces the study of public policy by examining the process of policy making and the factors that affect the policy decisions that are made. This helps us to understand why certain policies are adopted and why different countries often have different policies, as we have seen in the example of health care. The study of public policy, an important subfield of political science, also involves an evaluation of different policies and therefore can be useful to those involved in government and other aspects of political life.

GOVERNMENT PROBLEM-SOLVING

Making public policy is a key aspect of governing. *Public policy* has been defined as "a course of action or inaction chosen by public authorities to address a given problem or interrelated set of problems" (Pal, 1992, p. 2). A public policy generally involves a series of decisions or actions to try to achieve a particular objective.

Although policies may be intended to deal with a problem, we should not assume that they will be successful in achieving their objective. For example, many cities have dealt with the problem of traffic congestion by building freeways. Building freeways, however, encourages people to become more dependent on cars, often leads to greater automobile usage, and may eventually result in increasing congestion.

In some cases, government may deliberately choose inaction to avoid controversy. For example, Canadian governments have often been reluctant to deal with difficult moral issues such as abortion and homosexual rights, preferring to let the courts deal with such issues by utilizing the Charter of Rights and Freedoms.

THE POLICY PROCESS

The policy process is often analyzed in terms of a sequence of steps. We will discuss the process in terms of six steps (Howlett & Ramesh, 1995):

1. agenda setting
2. policy formulation
3. decision making
4. policy legitimation
5. policy implementation
6. policy evaluation

Agenda Setting

In any sizable political community, innumerable problems and concerns could potentially become a subject for public policy. However, only a small number of problems can be dealt with at any time. **Agenda setting** refers to the process by which potential problems come to the attention of policy-makers.

It is important to examine agenda setting to understand why certain issues come to the attention of policy-makers. There are a variety of potential influences on agenda setting, including political parties, interest groups, social movements, and the mass media. Crises, particularly crises emphasized by the mass media, can also affect the level of attention given to different problems. For example, the deaths caused by contaminated drinking water at

AGENDA SETTING
The process by which potential problems come to the attention of policy-makers.

Walkerton, Ontario, in 2000 turned the problem of water safety into a major political issue.

Not all issues on the government's policy agenda originate from the demands of various groups and individuals in society. Various departments and agencies of government may initiate the policy process by raising issues that the public may not necessarily view as serious problems. Individual politicians may act as **policy entrepreneurs** by trying to promote a particular issue or cause to advance their political career. In such cases of "inside initiation," efforts may be made by the department, agency, or individual politician to persuade the public, as well as the government as a whole, that a particular problem should be given priority in the policy process (Hessing & Howlett, 1997).

POLICY ENTREPRENEUR
Someone who is ready to push a pet policy proposal whenever an opportunity arises.

PUBLIC VERSUS GOVERNMENT AGENDA A distinction is sometimes made between the issues that are considered important by the public—the public agenda—and the issues that are considered important by the government—the governmental agenda. There is usually some relationship between the public agenda and the governmental agenda as political leaders want to be seen as dealing with issues that are deemed important by the public. Governments make extensive use of public opinion polling to keep track of public concerns.

However, the relationship between the two agendas is not always a close one. Governments often place a high priority on issues that are of little concern to the public at large—such as constitutional issues in Canada. Political leaders may give high priority to problems that can be easily labelled and have solutions that can work to their political advantage. Complex problems with no easy and uncontroversial solution may be ignored or downplayed.

Furthermore, politicians may give symbolic recognition to a problem or concern of the public without developing a substantial policy. For example, some political leaders have viewed the provision of subsidized child care as a low-priority issue. Although they claim that they fully support such a policy, governments have said for many years that they are "studying" the issue.

Policy Formulation

The **policy formulation** stage of the policy process involves developing and evaluating different courses of action to deal with a problem (Adolini & Blake, 2001). A variety of individuals and groups are typically involved at this point. Inside government, public servants in policy-oriented positions often play a leading role in developing possible policy options. Governments also often commission outside experts such as consultants, pollsters, and academics to help in the formulation of policy. Reports of Parliamentary Committees sometimes provide recommendations that are useful in policy formulation.

POLICY FORMULATION
Developing and evaluating different courses of action to deal with a problem.

C.D. Howe Institute
www.cdhowe.org

Fraser Institute
www.fraserinstitute.ca

Interest groups concerned about a particular policy area typically provide policy advice and interact with government policy-makers. Think-tanks (policy research organizations such as the C.D. Howe Institute and the Fraser Institute) often provide analyses of problems and policy recommendations.

It is important to note that different governmental and nongovernmental actors are involved in different policy formulation areas. For example, the Department of Agriculture and the Canadian Federation of Agriculture play an important role in the development of agricultural policies, but have little significance in the formulation of banking or defence policy.

OPENING THE PROCESS The policy formulation process in advanced democracies has generally moved towards the involvement of a larger number of participants. Rather than a tight and closed relationship between a government agency and a small number of leading interest groups (a relationship sometimes referred to as "iron triangles" in the United States and "subgovernments" in Canada), analysts often talk about a **policy network**. A policy network is a collection of governmental and nongovernmental actors that participate in the development of policies in particular policy fields.[1] The membership in the policy network may change from issue to issue, and no one set of actors or interests is in complete control of the policy area (Heclo, 1978). The extent to which governmental actors play a leading or dominant role in policy formulation and the extent to which a variety of different interests have a significant role in policy formulation vary considerably from policy area to policy area and from one country to another (Howlett & Ramesh, 1995). As noted in Chapter 11, countries with corporatist relations between government and key interests have a more controlled process of policy formulation than countries characterized by pluralism.

POLICY NETWORK
The governmental and non-governmental actors that participate in the development of policies in a particular policy field.

DEFINING THE PROBLEM The problem that needs solving has to be defined before policies are developed, and the way the problem is defined is very important. Different definitions of a problem can lead to very different types of policies. For example, the issue of poverty may be defined in terms of inequalities in income and wealth, the unwillingness of those on welfare to seek work, insufficient growth in the economy, lax moral standards that result in single mothers raising children, inadequate educational and training opportunities, deficiencies in social programs, or low minimum wages. These differing views of poverty lead to different views about what should be done about the problem.

Canadian Council on Social Development
www.ccsd.ca

Canadian Policy Research Network
www.cprn.org

Problems may be defined, sometimes in competing ways, at the agenda-setting stage. However, those involved in formulation may modify or transform the way the problem is defined as they develop policy options.

---

[1] A distinction is often made between a *policy network*, consisting of those actors who have a direct (usually economic) interest or involvement in a policy area, and a broader *policy community*, which also includes all groups and individuals who have a more general interest in a policy area. The assumption is that members of the policy network will tend to be more influential in policy formulation than other members of the policy community (Hessing & Howlett, 1997).

The formulation of policies often involves the development of different options to deal with the problem being addressed. Those developing policy then have to analyze the pros and cons of the different options. A key tool is assessing policy proposals is **cost–benefit analysis** (see Box 17-1, Sizing Things Up: Cost-Benefit Analysis).

POLICY INSTRUMENTS In formulating policy, government must consider a variety of different policy instruments (for example, taxes, subsidies, and regulations) in order to assess which instrument or set of instruments will be most likely to achieve the desired results. For example, in dealing with the problem of industrial pollution, a government may establish regulations that limit the amount of discharge allowed, provide subsidies to help companies pay for pollution control equipment, levy a tax on each unit of harmful emission that is released, or encourage industry to adopt voluntary guidelines on emission reductions. The use of regulations has been the major approach used by Canadian governments to deal with pollution, although in recent times voluntary guidelines have increasingly been used. Emission taxes have been a more important policy instrument in some European countries than in North America. Another, newer policy instrument, adopted for some pollutants in the United States, is the use of tradeable emission permits. Permits to emit a certain quantity of pollutants are issued by government, but industrial facilities that do not use the full amount of their permits can trade or sell their unused allotment. Pollution is reduced by issuing a smaller number of permits to each facility each year. This instrument is viewed as a cost-effective method of dealing with pollution as each company can calculate whether it is financially better to adopt pollution-reducing measures or buy permits from other companies.

The choice of policy instrument is affected by the nature of the problem that the policy is seeking to address. Some types of policy instruments are more effective in dealing with certain types of problems. As well, the choice of instruments may be affected by the ideological perspective of those in governing positions and in the electorate. Neo-liberals are more likely to favour instruments that provide the least government intervention and distortion of the free market. Social democrats are more likely to favour strict regulation of business activity. In addition, the choice of instruments may be affected by the ability of different interest groups to influence government. Business interests are more likely to favour voluntary guidelines, while environmental groups are more likely to favour strict government regulations and emission taxes to deal with pollution problems.

Decision Making

The decision-making stage involves choosing among a small number of different options or deciding to postpone the adoption of any policy. In

Public Policy Forum
www.ppforum.ca

COST–BENEFIT ANALYSIS
An economic technique that determines whether, and to what extent, the benefits of a policy exceed the costs.

BOX 17-1

Sizing Things Up: Cost–Benefit Analysis

Cost–benefit analysis is a useful tool that provides a means of comparing differing policy options and helps to ensure that a particular policy actually has a net benefit.

Cost–benefit analysis is an economic technique that determines whether, and to what extent, the benefits of a policy exceed the costs. Because it involves putting a monetary value on all of the consequences of the policy there are limitations to the approach. Assigning a monetary value to all costs and benefits can be difficult or arbitrary. If, for example, the policy option being considered involves allowing forest companies to cut trees in an area of natural beauty, how does one value natural beauty? Is it something more than the number of tourist dollars that might be lost? Likewise, in deciding on a new highway speed-limit policy, what value does one put on the lives that might be saved by a lower speed limit? Is it something more than the expected lifetime earnings of the victims?

Cost–benefit analysis is not as simple and straightforward as it seems. It is often very difficult to predict the consequences of a policy. For example, rent control is designed to ensure that housing is affordable, but it may have the unintended effect of reducing apartment construction and increasing the conversion of rental units into individually owned condos. If insufficient rental units are then available, people looking to rent may have to pay large bribes to landlords in order to find accommodation.

Another complication of cost–benefit analysis is that the costs or benefits of a policy often fall unevenly among different groups of people. Consolidating waste disposal in one location may bring cost savings that benefit the political community as a whole—but for the people who live next to the dump, the negative impact may far outweigh the benefits.

Cost–benefit analysis is sometimes criticized for ignoring the ethical dimension of policy making. Is it always right to take a particular course of action just because the calculation indicates that the benefits outweigh the costs? Should financial considerations be the only measure of what is the best policy option?

Finally, although cost–benefit analysis can apparently analyze policy options in a rational or scientific way while avoiding political considerations, this is often a false hope. Different analysts using different assumptions often come up with widely differing assessments of costs and benefits. For example, in discussions of whether or not Canada should ratify the Kyoto Protocol to reduce greenhouse gas emissions related to global climate change, there were massive differences in assessments of the costs and benefits of that policy. Not surprisingly, analyses commissioned by environmental groups determined that there would be net benefits if Canada reduced greenhouse gas emissions, while analyses conducted by petroleum producers determined that there would be massive costs to the Canadian economy. Similarly, policy analysts working for the government in Alberta, where limitations on greenhouse gas emissions would have the most negative economic effect, calculated that the costs would be much greater than did the policy analysts working for the Canadian government.

Although cost–benefit analysis can be a useful tool in policy making, its limitations clearly must be kept in mind as options are discussed and evaluated.

parliamentary systems, policy decisions are generally made at the executive level—particularly by the prime minister and cabinet or a cabinet committee.

Traditionally, the advice of senior public servants strongly influenced the decision-making process. However, as noted in Chapter 16, outside consultants have increasingly been used as an alternative source of policy advice. The political effects of different courses of action, such as the effects on the government's popularity, relationships with other governments, and overall goals, as well as on power relationships within the governing party, are important factors in the minds of government decision-makers and their political advisors. Pressure from interest groups and the opinions of the public also have an influence on decision making.

Policy Legitimation

Although the prime minister and cabinet have a key role in making policy decisions, such decisions have to be approved by Parliament if they involve new or amended legislation, or spending or raising money. This approval not only fulfills important legal requirements, but also can be a form of **policy legitimation** (that is, it adds legitimacy to the policy).

Discussion of a proposed policy in a legislature may help to increase awareness of the policy, and the public may be reassured that there has been an airing of different views before the policy was adopted. As well, the process of parliamentary approval sometimes results in changes, usually of a minor nature, in the legislation needed to put the policy into effect. This may have the effect of appeasing some groups who are opposed to the legislation.

POLICY LEGITIMATION
Gaining acceptance of a policy proposal; for example, through formal approval by a legislative body.

Policy Implementation

Policy implementation is a very important part of the policy process, but it is sometimes overlooked. The passage of a law or regulation to deal with a problem does not necessarily mean that the action is carried out. Typically, programs need to be designed; money, staff, and expertise must be provided; and the legislation needs to be interpreted.

Bureaucratic discretion is often necessary because of the complex, technical nature of policies. Rather than simply applying the words of a law or regulation, bureaucrats may need to apply specialized knowledge to figure out the most appropriate means to achieve the general objective. To help with implementation, bureaucrats may strike compromises and work with the groups affected. For example, regulators often reach agreements with industries being regulated to allow the industry time to adjust its operations to comply with a new regulation.

The implementation of policies does not only involve senior bureaucrats under the supervision of a cabinet minister designing a program and providing instructions to public servants to carry it out. To be effective, those

POLICY IMPLEMENTATION
Taking measures to put a policy into effect, such as developing rules and regulations and establishing an administrative structure.

responsible for carrying out a policy have to be motivated to carry out the policy. Issuing commands and having subordinates carry them out may work in the military, but often does not work when those providing government services are professionals who believe that they should use their own judgment. For example, a government policy intended to increase the literacy and numeracy of students is only likely to succeed if teachers are committed to the policy.

ENFORCEMENT   Enforcement is an important aspect of the implementation of many policies. Although some policies offer encouragement to act in a certain way or provide for voluntary compliance, effective policies often require enforcement of their provisions. For example, it would be naive to expect an industry to voluntarily reduce its emissions of pollutants simply because the government asks it to if such reductions are costly.

However, strict enforcement is sometimes undesirable or unworkable. Strict enforcement of pollution regulations may result in a major industry closing down because the costs of compliance are too high. Thus, government officials are often willing to give considerable leeway to companies that claim difficulty in meeting emission standards.

As well, enforcement of a policy may involve difficult and costly monitoring. For example, monitoring fish catches to ensure that quotas are not being exceeded is often difficult and evasion is common. Further, where a law is widely violated (for example, the law prohibiting the possession of cannabis), some police forces may decide that their limited resources are better spent on other offences.

Finally, policy implementation may be difficult if the cooperation and coordination of other levels of government needs to be obtained. For example, the Canadian government has at times faced difficulties in implementing its national health care policy because provincial governments are responsible for the health care system.

Overall, then, policy implementation is not simply a matter of administration—that is, of putting a policy into effect. There can be a considerable difference between the policy as envisioned by decision-makers and the policy that is actually put into effect. The implementation stage thus involves a combination of administrative and political decisions.

Policy Evaluation

POLICY EVALUATION
Determining the extent to which a policy is achieving its objectives and how it can be made more effective.

The evaluation of policy is important, but it is an area of the policy process that may receive little or no attention, for a variety of reasons. **Policy evaluation** involves determining the extent to which a policy is achieving its objectives and how it can be made more effective. Such evaluation can potentially lead to policy change, whether by scrapping an unsuccessful policy or by making modifications to improve a policy's effectiveness.

Policy evaluation is important because few policies are completely successful in solving the problems for which they were designed. However, governments are generally not systematic in carrying out such evaluation. Not only is the evaluation of policy often difficult, but governments may be reluctant to fully evaluate policies that they have become politically committed to for fear that the evaluation will reflect badly on them or because they do not want to reopen a controversial issue. Senior public servants may have a tendency to defend the programs that they are responsible for and be reluctant to conduct thorough evaluations that could lead to reductions in the budgets and staff associated with the programs they administer.

WHO DOES IT?   Some evaluation is performed by those involved in carrying out programs, the auditor general, the public and interest groups, and government agencies or other groups through the statistics they gather. Some laws require that government undertake a review of the law: in the case of the *Canadian Environmental Assessment Act*, the review must be done after five years. Health care agreements between the national and provincial governments require that each government issue a report on the quality of health care in its jurisdiction according to a standard set of indicators.

Various interest groups conduct evaluations of the successes and failures of government policies. For example, to make their case clearly to the public, some environmental groups issue report cards on government environmental performance. Businesses and business-oriented think-tanks typically evaluate policies in terms of their effects on business profitability and competitiveness. Some international agencies provide a comparative analysis of the performances of different countries in various policy areas.

Policy evaluation is not simply a technical procedure. It can also be highly political as different groups evaluate policy from their particular perspective or for their particular purposes. The business-supported Conference Board of Canada is likely to come to a different evaluation of policies than the union-backed Canadian Centre for Policy Alternatives.

Conference Board of Canada
www.conferenceboard.ca

Canadian Centre for Policy Alternatives
www.policyalternatives.ca

The Policy Cycle

The policy process is often described as a **policy cycle** (see Figure 17-1). This assumes that policies are continually undergoing modification in response to evaluations of the policies. Evaluations of existing policies may have an agenda-setting effect. Unsuccessful programs will likely lead to demands for change and place a particular problem back on the public and/or governmental agenda. This can potentially make the policy process a continuous, cyclical process.

However, the depiction of the policy process as a smooth, continuous cycle can be misleading. Policy evaluations that would, ideally, lead to policy changes are not always done. Unsuccessful programs have to compete with

POLICY CYCLE

The analysis of the policy process as a continuous cycle of stages, with policies continually undergoing modification in response to evaluations of the policy.

FIGURE 17-1
THE POLICY CYCLE

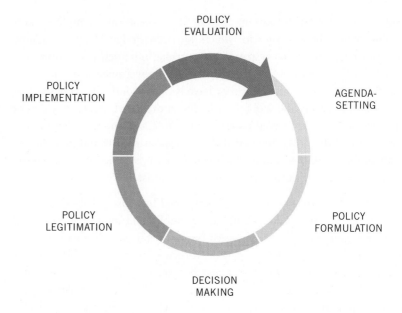

other policy problems for attention at the agenda-setting stage. If action is taken on a problem, the general public may believe that the problem has been resolved, thereby reducing demands for further actions. Nevertheless, the policy process is dynamic and never-ending. New policy actors, new data and arguments, new ways of looking at problems, new expectations, changing circumstances, and new solutions mean that the policy process is a continuous one, with recurring debate over what should be done (Kraft, 2004).

IS POLICY MAKING A RATIONAL PROCESS?

Analysts of public policy often focus on three competing models of how policy is made:

1. the rational–comprehensive model
2. the incremental model
3. the streams and windows model

Related to these models are differing views about how policy should be made, as discussed next.

Rational–Comprehensive Model

According to the **rational–comprehensive model**, policy-makers establish clear goals to deal with a problem, examine all the alternatives for dealing with the problem in terms of measuring the consequences (costs and benefits) of each alternative, and choose the best alternative (the one that maximizes the attainment of the goals at the lowest cost). This alternative is implement-

RATIONAL–COMPREHENSIVE MODEL OF POLICY MAKING
A policy-making model that views policy-makers as establishing clear goals to deal with a problem, examining all the alternatives for dealing with the problem in terms of measuring the consequences, and choosing the best alternative, which is implemented, then monitored and evaluated to assess whether the goals have been achieved, and changed if necessary.

ed, then monitored and evaluated to assess whether the goals have been achieved, and changed if necessary (Anderson, 1979). Even if this model does not perfectly describe the actual policy-making process, governments have devoted considerable efforts to try to create a more rational policy process.

Critics, however, argue that the rational policy-making model is unrealistic, and that attempts to apply this model have often been unsuccessful. Governments often have ambiguous or conflicting goals. Policy-makers do not have the information they need for fully rational decision making, and the information that is available is often biased in favour of the interests that are supplying the information. Governing decisions are often made in a hurry, or even in an atmosphere of crisis, because governments tend to react to problems rather than anticipating them. Because policy-makers lack the resources, time, information, and capabilities to fully examine all possible options and their potential effects, they will likely choose the first acceptable policy alternative that is presented to them—one that looks like it will work and meet their goals—rather than the best possible solution to a problem (Simon, 1957).

Incremental Model

The **incremental model of policy making** suggests that the policy process usually involves making minor changes from existing practices. Rather than searching for the best solution to a problem, decision-makers tend to "muddle through" (Lindblom, 1959), trying to cope with problems through a limited response. Policy-makers typically only examine a small number of fairly similar alternatives based on past experience, and do not try to evaluate all of the possible consequences of each alternative. Rather, by making only minor adjustments to existing policies, policy-makers can rely on past experience to assess the policy options being considered (Doyle & Kellow, 1995).

Because policy making typically involves reaching compromises among a variety of views and interests, both inside and outside of government, policy-makers tend to avoid the risks involved in taking a new policy direction. Instead, they hope to accommodate different interests by making small adjustments to existing policies.

IS INCREMENTAL POLICY-MAKING DESIRABLE? Generally, analysts and commentators have assumed that the rational model is a desirable, if perhaps unrealistic, ideal. However, Charles Lindblom (1959) has argued that incremental policy making is desirable because policy-makers typically operate under conditions of uncertainty regarding the consequences of different policies. Small changes can be more easily corrected than major changes, and policy modifications can build on past experiences. An incremental decision-making process is also more likely to allow a political consensus to develop because it is easier to reach agreement among conflicting

Institute for Research on Public Policy
www.irpp.org

INCREMENTAL MODEL OF POLICY MAKING
A policy-making model that suggests the policy process usually involves making minor changes from existing practices.

groups about minor changes, rather than about changes that are of great magnitude.

Incremental decision making may be undesirable when problems are serious enough to necessitate decisive actions. Marginal adjustments to existing policies may not be enough to deal effectively with such problems (Doyle & Kellow, 1995). Furthermore, incremental policy making may result in a piecemeal rather than a coordinated strategy to deal with sets of problems. For example, environmental policies that make adjustments to specific policies concerning air, water, and soil pollution tend to be less effective than an integrated approach to pollution control that examines how to reduce the total burden of pollution on the environment. Likewise, dealing with the problem of poverty by making incremental changes to specific policies and programs, such as minimum wage laws, employment insurance, social assistance, and subsidized housing, may be less effective than adopting a more comprehensive or innovative approach.

An incremental decision-making process may also tend to work in the interests of the most powerful and organized in society rather than the under-privileged. Thus, it has been criticized as a conservative approach that does not challenge those who benefit from the existing ways of doing things.

Streams and Windows Model

STREAMS AND WINDOWS
MODEL OF POLICY MAKING
A policy-making model that
views the policy process as
fluid, with changes in the identification of problems, policy
proposals, and political circumstances creating windows of
opportunity in which policy
entrepreneurs may successfully
push their pet proposals.

In the **streams and windows model** developed by John Kingdon, policy making is depicted as a fluid process, rather than a process involving an overall plan or a series of limited steps. Policy, problem, and politics streams move independently of each other. The problem stream involves the processes by which "various problems come to capture the attention of people in and around government." The policy stream refers to the proposals that a variety of individuals and groups interested in a policy area are continually developing. The politics stream includes the campaigns of interest groups and political parties, election outcomes and changes in government, and shifts in the national mood and public opinion. At times, the streams meet, resulting in "windows of opportunity" in which policy entrepreneurs—whether interest group leaders, academics, journalists, politicians, or bureaucrats—can successfully push their pet proposals (Kingdon, 1995, p. 87).

Consider the following examples. In the early 1990s the need to change the health care system in the United States became identified as a major problem. The election of a Democratic Congress and president favourable to change seemed to create a window of opportunity for health care reform. However, the other stream, policy, did not meet up with the problem and politics streams. Various proposals for reform were floated, but there was no consensus among those pushing for reform as to which policy proposal was best (Kingdon, 1995). The potential opportunity was missed. Even though the problems of health care remained, elections brought to power conservatives who opposed increased government involvement in the health care system. In Canada, on the other hand, concern about the problem of access to medical care, the election of a Liberal minority government supported by the NDP, and a consensus among those favouring reform that a universal, public medicare system was best (based on the positive experience of the system adopted in Saskatchewan, along with the recommendations of a Royal Commission) combined to overcome opposition in 1966. (For a further discussion of health care issues, see Box 17-2, Health Policy).

Policy making might be best understood in terms of a mixture of the three models. Some policies result from a lengthy and rather comprehensive process of examining and assessing various alternatives. Many government actions involve only minor adjustments to existing policies and programs. Occasionally, however, major shifts in public policy occur. Sometimes these shifts occur with a change of government, particularly when a party with a different ideological perspective comes to power (for example, the Common Sense Revolution instituted by Mike Harris's Progressive Conservative government in Ontario in the 1990s). At other times, a perceived crisis may lead to major changes in policy direction, as when Jean Chrétien's Liberal government slashed government spending in 1995 to deal with the government's budget deficit, a critical issue in the view of the financial community.

Because of the constraints of party discipline and cabinet solidarity, policy entrepreneurs may not be as prevalent within the Canadian governing system as they are in the United States. Nevertheless, the difficulties of coordinating the differing interests of the departments and agencies of government and the complexities resulting from the federal system mean that the policy process in Canada does not often follow a straightforward, predictable pattern.

WHAT AFFECTS POLICY?

We have thus far been considering public policy in terms of how policy is made. But we also need to consider what affects public policy, so that we can understand, for example, why some types of policies are preferred by policymakers, and why different countries tend to adopt different types of policies.

Five major types of factors affect policies (Adolini & Blake, 2001):

1. cultural
2. economic
3. political
4. governing system
5. external

Culture

Although most citizens in the advanced democracies expect governments to provide a variety of services and deal with a variety of problems (Dalton,

BOX 17-2

Health Policy

"Now, I know it's not going to be easy adjusting to these cuts in your health care at first . . . but you'll thank me 30 years from now."

Canada's medicare system is less comprehensive than those of some other advanced democracies in that a variety of services, including prescription drugs, home care, glasses, and dental work, are not generally covered by public health insurance. On the other hand, unlike a number of other countries, Canada has no user fees for covered medical and hospital services, and a separate private insurance system is not allowed for covered services. In sum, Canada, like most other countries, has a mixture of public and private components to its health care system; it is the elements of the mixture that differ from country to country.

How effective and efficient are different health care systems? The American system, in which millions of people do not have adequate access to medical care, does not perform particularly well when compared to the more universal access provided by other wealthy countries. The United States has the highest infant mortality rate and the lowest life expectancy of comparable countries.

Surprisingly, however, total per capita spending on health care in the United States is substantially higher than in other countries (see Table 17-1). To some extent, this is a result of higher administrative costs involved in the largely private provision of health insurance and delivery of services.

Before we gloat about the superiority of the Canadian health care system, we should note that all is not well. The costs of the health care system have been rising quite rapidly to the point that health care has become the largest expense of provincial governments. With projections that health care costs will continue to rise faster than government revenues, provincial governments will likely have to limit or reduce spending on other important items like education and roads to fund health care, even with new money for health care provided by the Canadian government. There are also shortages of general practitioners and long waiting times for diagnostic services and operations.

This situation raises many questions. Should the medicare system be further expanded to provide more comprehensive coverage, as the Romanow Commission on the Future of Health Care in Canada suggested in 2002, even if this means higher taxes? (For example, Canada's premiers in July 2004 asked the Canadian government to provide a comprehensive system of pharmacare—free prescription drugs—at an estimated cost of seven to twelve billion dollars per year.) Should user fees be instituted to discourage excessive use of the health care system? Should greater emphasis be placed on health promotion (for example, through more encouragement of healthy lifestyles) and less emphasis on expensive treatments? Would replacing fee-for-service payment of doctors with salaries or with a fixed annual payment for each listed patient reduce health care costs? Would a team approach to providing primary care, involving doctors, nurses, pharmacists, nutritionists and other health care professionals in clinics, reduce costs and provide better care? Would allowing competitive private provision of health care encourage hospitals to become more efficient, or would it reduce the quality of care?

As with other areas of public policy, difficult choices must often be considered to determine the best course of action.

TABLE 17-1
HEALTH CARE SPENDING, PUBLIC AND PRIVATE

	% PUBLIC SPENDING 1997–2000	% PRIVATE SPENDING 1997–2000	TOTAL SPENDING AS A PROPORTION OF GDP (2001)
Australia	72.4%	27.6%	9.5%
Belgium	71.2%	28.8%	8.9%
Canada	72.0%	28.0%	9.5%
Denmark	82.1%	17.9%	8.4%
France	76.0%	24.0%	9.6%
Germany	75.1%	24.9%	10.8%
Italy	73.7%	26.3%	8.4%
Japan	76.7%	23.3%	8.0%
Netherlands	67.5%	32.5%	8.9%
Spain	69.9%	30.1%	7.5%
Sweden	77.3%	22.7%	8.7%
Switzerland	55.6%	44.4%	11.0%
United Kingdom	81.0%	19.0%	7.6%
United States	46.5%	53.5%	13.9%
Middle-income countries	51.8%	48.2%	5.9%
Low-income countries	27.1%	72.9%	4.3%

SOURCE: *Extracted from HNP Statistics, by the World Bank Group (n.d.), retrieved July 17, 2004, from http://devdata.worldbank.org/hnpstats/AAgselection.asp.*SOURCE:

2002), there are substantial differences in the political cultures of different countries that can affect the ways that policy problems are dealt with. For example, there is variation among different political cultures in terms of the proportion of people that think that government should have a responsibility for particular policy areas. In particular, Americans are less likely than persons in most other advanced democracies to feel that government should be responsible for providing health care (as we read in the opening vignette), ensuring a decent living standard for the elderly or unemployed, and stimulating job creation (Dalton, 2002).

Economy

Economic conditions clearly affect public policy. Generally, prosperity is associated with an expansion of government activities: the governments of the richer countries are able to provide much more extensive and better quality programs than poorer countries. However, the extent of government activity is also affected by other factors. Despite its wealth, the United States devotes less of its **gross national product (GNP)** to government services than do most other, less wealthy advanced democracies (Adolino & Blake, 2001).

GROSS NATIONAL PRODUCT
The market value of goods and services produced in a country, including the value of exports less the value of imports.

Politics

Among the political factors that influence public policy is the importance of social democratic parties in a country's party system. Countries where social democratic or labour parties play a major role in the legislature and government are more likely to develop an extensive welfare state (Castles,

▶ The governments of richer countries are able to provide more extensive and better quality programs than those offered in poorer countries.

1982). This does not necessarily mean that social democratic governments spend money like drunken sailors while conservative governments are Scrooge-like misers. In Canada in the 1990s, provincial governments across the political spectrum, from NDP and Liberal to Progressive Conservative, engaged in substantial spending cutbacks. And while some social democratic governments avoided budget deficits (for example, the NDP in Saskatchewan), some of their conservative counterparts (for example, the PCs in Saskatchewan and Ontario) accumulated massive debts through their tax-cutting policies.

Governing System

The governing system of a country can also have an effect on the general nature of public policy. Some research has found that government spending on social welfare tends to be lower in federal systems than in unitary systems because of the difficulties involved in reaching agreement on new policies where a number of governments are involved (Cameron, 1978). Likewise, the separation of powers and the difficulty in passing legislation in the American presidential system of government may have contributed to the lower level of total government activity in that country. However, if countries with unitary and parliamentary systems (for example, the United Kingdom) tended to be faster to adopt welfare state policies in the past because of the ease with which new policies can be adopted, such countries can also move faster in the opposite direction in response to changing ideological thinking or financial circumstances (Adolini & Blake, 2001). In other words, the governing structure may affect how fast changes in public policy occur.

External Factors

Finally, external factors, such as international agreements, play an increasingly important role in limiting the range of policy options that can be considered. International environmental agreements, for example, require that governments phase out the use of ozone-depleting chemicals and prohibit trade in products made from endangered species.

Trade agreements are particularly controversial because people hold different ideological views about free trade (see Box 17-3, Turtles and Trade). From the neo-liberal perspective, trade agreements are for the common good of the world as a whole. They allow the poorer countries to have access to the markets of the richer countries and thus assist the poorer countries in developing their economies—as well as giving businesses in the richer countries access to new markets.

Those who are critical of the neo-liberal perspective argue that trade agreements limit the ability of governments to regulate business for the common good (for example, by making it more difficult to adopt environmental regulations or by restricting the import of goods produced in sweatshops). As well, by protecting the rights of corporations, some trade agreements can make it difficult for governments to use public provision of services as a policy instrument if such services are already provided by private business.

Turtles and Trade

Protesters dressed up as sea turtles were an incongruous sight at the 1999 anti-globalization demonstrations that shut down a meeting of the World Trade Organization (WTO) in Seattle. But the flamboyant costumes were a vivid symbol of protesters' concern for an endangered species.

The WTO oversees a set of agreements that create legally binding rules and obligations on most of the countries of the world to achieve the objective of global free trade. The rules prevent countries from discriminating against the goods and services of other member countries. Dispute settlement panels can penalize offending countries for non-compliance with the rules.

In 1997, India, Malaysia, Pakistan, and Thailand took a complaint to the WTO concerning an American law banning the import of shrimp caught by trawlers that did not use devices to prevent harm to sea turtles, an endangered species. A dispute settlement panel of the WTO upheld the complaint, ruling that the American law resulted in a discriminatory trade practice that worked to the advantage of American fishers.*

The North American Free Trade Agreement, involving Canada, the United States, and Mexico, goes further by allowing businesses to sue the governments of any of the three countries if they adopt trade-restrictive policies that cause them to lose business opportunities or future profitability. For example, Ohio-based S.D. Myers Corporation, a hazardous waste disposal firm, successfully sued the Canadian government to compensate it for the Canadian policy banning the export of PCBs, a potentially toxic chemical. By banning the export of PCBs, the Canadian government reduced the potential profits that S.D. Myers would obtain by processing Canadian PCBs at its American plant. Likewise, the Vancouver-based Methanex Corporation sued the American government for nearly one billion dollars because California banned the fuel additive MTBE, which is made from methanol that Methanex produces. California claimed that MTBE contaminates groundwater and soil through leaking storage tanks.

The cases of sea turtles and toxic chemicals illustrate an important issue: how trade agreements can make it more difficult for governments to adopt such policies as strict environmental measures if they are deemed to be undue limitations on trade.

*The original ruling stated that "like goods" (similar foreign or domestic products) have to be treated the same, regardless of whether or not the good was produced in an environmentally friendly manner. An appeal panel upheld the original ruling on the grounds that the United States had discriminated against Asian countries by providing only Caribbean countries with assistance to deal with the problem.

Summary and Conclusion

The policies adopted by governments are typically the result of a complex process involving a variety of different political actors. Interest groups, social movements, political parties, think-tanks, and journalists seek to influence the choice of issues that will be the subject of policy making, as well as trying to affect how policy-makers think about those issues.

The prime minister and cabinet are important in setting the priorities and overall direction of the government. However, the development of specific laws and policies is generally the responsibility of public servants in the administration, often working with those in major institutionalized interest groups. Once the cabinet has decided on a particular policy, discussion of proposed legislation, along with minor modifications of the details, will occur in Parliament.

A very important part of the policy process is its implementation, which involves the administrative aspect of government. Laws and policies are of little importance unless they are actually carried out, and the method by which they are carried out can modify the original intention of the law or policy. Finally, assessments of the effectiveness of the policy may be carried out by a variety of groups within and outside government. However, changes to policies often only occur when strong political pressure is mounted.

Policy making is not simply a matter of problem solving, or trying to determine the best policy to achieve the common good. Rather, it is a matter of choice in which resources are limited and the goals and objectives of those interested or involved in policy making differ and cannot easily be weighed against each other. Most public policies have an effect on the distribution of well-being in society—the benefits and costs of a policy may not be evenly shared. For example, since pollution is often worse in poor communities, restrictions on pollutants may be of greater benefit to the health of underprivileged persons. The imposition of a heavy tax on gasoline to reduce pollution will have a greater effect on commuters than on users of public transportation.

In other words, the policy process is a *political* process in which different goals, interests, and values are involved (Simeon, 1976). Because the policy process is a political process, the distribution of power in a society and the dominant ideological perspectives will likely affect which problems are addressed, how problems are defined, and what policies are adopted and implemented. The policies that are adopted and implemented do not necessarily reflect the common good, but rather tend to reflect the political interests of the government, the values and ideologies of those involved in the policy process, and the ability of various groups and individuals to exert influence.

Key Terms

Agenda setting 378

Cost–benefit analysis 381

Gross national product (GNP) 392

Incremental model of policy making 387

Policy cycle 385

Policy entrepreneur 379

Policy evaluation 384

Policy formulation 379

Policy implementation 383

Policy legitimation 383

Policy network 380

Rational–comprehensive model of policy making 386

Streams and windows model of policy making 388

Discussion Questions

1. Can the best public policies be chosen scientifically?

2. Which model of policy making is the most realistic? Which would be the most desirable?

3. Are major changes needed in Canada's health care system?

4. Is greater public participation in the policy process desirable?

5. Should trade agreements contain provisions allowing corporations to sue governments that adopt policies that limit their profitability?

Further Reading

Adolini, J.R., & Blake, C.H. *Comparing policies: Issues and choices in six industrialized countries.* Washington, DC: CQ Press, 2001.

Brooks, S. *Public policy in Canada* (3rd ed.). Toronto: Oxford University Press, 1998.

Boyd, D.R. *Unnatural law: Rethinking Canadian environmental law and policy.* Vancouver: UBC Press, 2003.

Heidenheimer, A.J., Heclo, H., & Adams, C.T. (1990). *Comparative public policy: The politics of social choice in Europe and America* (3rd ed.). New York: St. Martin's Press.

Johnson, A.F., & Stritch, A. (1997). *Canadian public policy: Globalization and political parties.* Toronto: Copp Clark.

Maioni, A. "Health care in the new millennium." In H. Bakvis & G. Skogstad (Eds.), *Canadian federalism: Performance, effectiveness, and legitimacy* (pp. 87–104). Don Mills, ON: Oxford University Press, 2002.

Pal, L.A. *Beyond policy analysis: Public issue management in turbulent times.* Toronto: ITP Nelson, 1997.

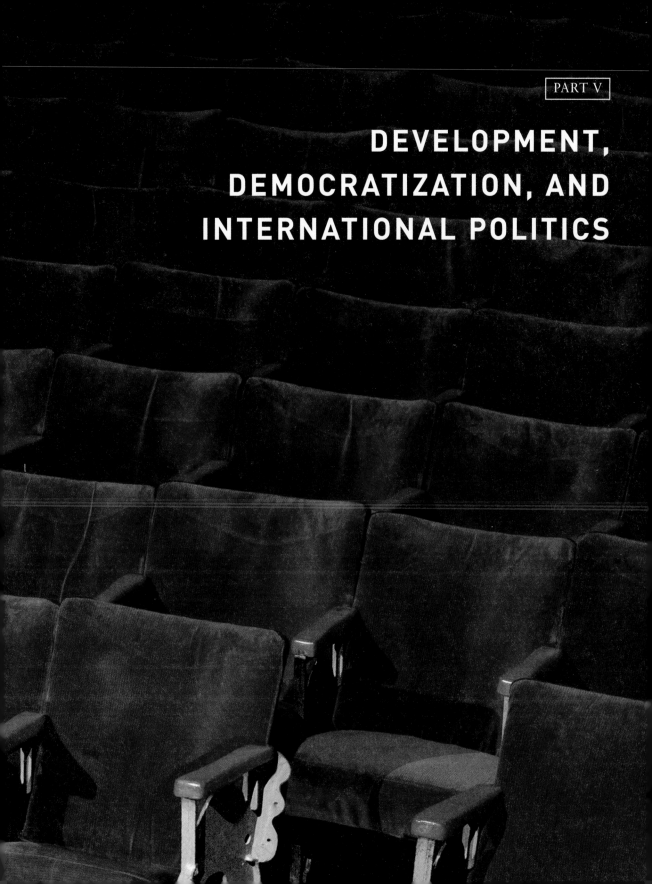

PART V

DEVELOPMENT, DEMOCRATIZATION, AND INTERNATIONAL POLITICS

Chapter 18

POLITICS AND GOVERNMENT IN THE WORLD'S POORER COUNTRIES

PHOTO ABOVE: The clients of the Grameen Bank in Bangladesh are among the world's poorest people—and the bank's pride and joy. Muhammad Yunus, an economist, believed the country needed a bank that would extend credit to Bangladesh's millions of landless men and women, thereby letting them create their own jobs and look after their families better.

CHAPTER OBJECTIVES

After reading this chapter you should be able to:

1. identify the terms that are used to depict the poorer countries
2. outline the extent of global inequality
3. discuss the meaning of development and the different development strategies
4. evaluate Canada's foreign aid policies
5. examine the political problems of the Third World

The clients of the Grameen Bank in Bangladesh are among the world's poorest people—and the bank's pride and joy. Ordinary commercial banks would not touch them because they have no collateral to pledge. The difference is that Dr. Muhammad Yunus, the University of Chittigong economist behind the creation of the Grameen, believed the country needed a bank that would extend credit to Bangladesh's millions of landless men and women, thereby letting them create their own jobs and look after their families better. The bank, whose name means rural in Bangala, the language of Bangladesh, was founded in 1983 and has now lent to more than three million borrowers.

The Grameen Bank believes that credit for self-employment is a basic human right. It makes small loans that are limited to about US$400 for business start-ups and US$650 for home building (Bangladesh has a per capita annual income of US$500, so the sums are not trivial). To help assure repayment and the proper use of loans, the bank organizes its customers to use peer pressure. The result has been a default rate of less than one-half of one percent and an on-time repayment record of 98 percent.

Perhaps the most striking thing about the Grameen Bank is its clientele: 94 percent of its customers are women. The bank makes women its priority for three reasons. First, they are the poorest members of society and therefore the least likely to get help from a regular credit institution. Second, when extra cash comes into a home, women are more likely to use the money for the family's good, whereas men tend to spend it on themselves. Finally, it is not uncommon for a man to desert his family, leaving a woman as the sole breadwinner.

The Grameen Bank has become a model for economic developers in other countries. It is not a silver bullet that will solve all the problems of underdevelopment, just a partial response to one set of the many problems of poor countries. However, by showing that mixing a lot of local initiative with creative thinking produces better lives for many people, the Grameen Bank has an importance that stretches far beyond Bangladesh to all the world's poor countries.

To many Canadians, "development" means giving a poor country a standard of living that approaches Canada's, complete with personal computers and a car for everyone. In the very poor, extremely underdeveloped countries of the Third World, that kind of development, which has long been the goal of foreign aid programs, can leave the poorest untouched. Even the most entrepreneurial and energetic of the poor find it almost impossible to get ahead under conventional development projects. That is why the Grameen Bank is so important.*

*For information about the Grameen Bank, see Wood and Sharit (1997), Yunus (1999), and the bank's web site at www.grameen-info.org/.

THE DEVELOPMENT GAP

Less than one-sixth of the people in the world live in high-income countries like Canada and the United States. The remaining five-sixths have a per capita income less than half that of Canada (see Table 18-1). Canadian governments have trouble funding all of the services that people need, so the situation is obviously worse in the majority of countries where the money per person available to fund education, health care, roads, and other important services is far less than that of Canada. This is a world, after all, in which the average income of the twenty richest countries is thirty-seven times that of the twenty poorest countries (World Bank, 2003). Is it meaningful to talk about achieving the common good in the poorest countries? Should Canadians be concerned about the problem of global inequality? How can poor countries develop?

Over the years, social scientists have applied a variety of names to the poor countries of the world. Among them have been **Third World**, developing, less developed, **underdeveloped**, and the **South** (terms discussed in Box 18-1, Evolution of the Term "Third World"). Political science inclines toward the use of Third World (Green & Luehrmann, 2003; Handelman, 2003), but uses all terms noted above. Whatever name is used, however, it is the mix of the economic and social characteristics of poor states, on the one hand, and how their political systems function, on the other, that has drawn the attention of political scientists, policy-makers, and large segments of the politically informed public in the wealthy (or developed) countries of what some call the **North**.

WHAT IS DEVELOPMENT?

Terms such as "**developing countries**," "less developed countries," or "underdeveloped countries" are often used to describe Third World countries, but they raise several questions: What exactly is meant by "development"? In what ways are poorer countries "less developed" than the richer countries? Are the poorer countries in the process of "developing," and does that mean that they will become similar to the richer "developed" countries?

THIRD WORLD
Less developed countries.

UNDERDEVELOPED COUNTRIES
A term often used to describe Third World countries.

SOUTH
Less developed, poorer countries.

NORTH
The rich, developed countries.

DEVELOPING COUNTRIES
Countries that have not reached the same level of development as the richer, advanced countries.

TABLE 18-1
THE WEALTH OF THE WORLD

INCOME GROUP	ANNUAL INCOME RANGE	% WORLD'S WEALTH	% WORLD'S POPULATION
Canada	US $21 500	2.1%	0.5%
High	> US $9 206	81.0%	15.6%
Upper Middle	US $2 975–9 205	8.2%	7.1%
Lower Middle	US $745–2 974	8.5%	36.3%
Low	< US $745	3.4%	41.0%

SOURCE: *Adapted from World Development Report, by the World Bank (2003), Washington: The World Bank.*

BOX 18-1
Evolution of the Term "Third World"

A host of names has developed over the years to refer to the world's poorest countries.

The Third World was political scientists' first choice. That name dates from the late 1940s, when it was introduced to distinguish what was then a small number of independent countries in Africa, Asia, and Latin America from the blocs linked to the two great powers of the day: the United States and the Soviet Union. The United States and its allies among the wealthier industrialized countries (for example, Canada and Britain) formed the First World and the Soviet Union and its allies (for example, Bulgaria and Mongolia) were termed the Second World. Other countries constituted the "Third World."

Although many of these countries later banded together to form the Non-Aligned Movement, the Third World soon came to symbolize poverty and political instability far more than symbolizing an independent line in foreign policy.

The South is another label political scientists have used. This emphasizes the fact that most poor countries lie in the tropics, to the south of the rich states of the northern hemisphere. Of course, the name is not literally accurate, because the southern hemisphere includes developed countries such as Australia and New Zealand. Nevertheless, the title does direct our attention to the realities of the global geography of wealth and power.

Underdeveloped, developing, and *less developed* are variations on a final theme used to categorize the poor states of the world. The focus here is the low levels of economic well-being that characterize the countries in this group. Nevertheless, there is the implicit assumption that development is possible and that some day all the world's countries will do a better job of meeting their citizens' needs.

These countries tend to be new democracies, if they are democratic at all. The nations that broadly fit this description include all of Latin America and the Caribbean; all of Africa; the entire Middle East, except for Israel; and all of Asia, except Japan, Singapore, Taiwan (Republic of China), and South Korea. Interestingly, the last three states were also classed as Third World countries until the 1980s. Now they are often labelled *newly industrialized countries* to indicate that they are no longer poor, underdeveloped countries.

The less developed countries are often compared to the more developed countries in terms of per capita **gross domestic product (GDP)** (that is, the amount of goods and services produced) and in terms of average incomes (see Table 18-1). Such measures are available for nearly all countries and give us a sense of the economic disparities between rich and poor countries. If countries increase their GDP, we can say that economic growth is occurring. Economic growth, however, does not always result in **development** that is good for the country as a whole. For example, economic growth does not necessarily lead to a reduction of poverty. Indeed, in some cases, increased poverty has accompanied increased growth (United Nations Development Programme [UNDP], 2003). Because of the great inequalities in wealth and power in many less developed countries, new sources of wealth can end up in the pockets of the rich. New oil wells, pipelines, mines, factories, stores and

GROSS DOMESTIC PRODUCT (GDP)

The market value of goods and services produced in a country, excluding transactions with other countries.

DEVELOPMENT

A condition that involves the satisfaction of the basic needs of all of the people as well as the means for them to live fulfilling and productive lives based on the creation of a more diversified, sophisticated, and sustainable economy.

Development Versus Growth

Imagine living in a country whose economy is based on mining diamonds.

If we mine and sell more diamonds, the economy will *grow* in terms of gross domestic product. But the country has not necessarily developed. Increased diamond mining might simply result in the mine owners' buying more imported luxury items or investing their profits in other countries. However, processing the diamonds into expensive jewellery or using the profits from diamond mining to develop new industries would lead to a more broadly based economy that would not rely so heavily on one commodity. It would also encourage people to develop more skills.

Generally, if most of the profits from increased mining activity remained in the country to buy locally produced goods and services, the economic *development* of the country would get a boost. Likewise, if government used increased tax revenues to improve roads, schools, and health care, there would be a stronger foundation for future development.

dams may result in the dislocation of peasant farmers, urban workers and indigenous peoples, reducing their ability to eke out a living. The distinction between growth and development is discussed further in Box 18-2, Development Versus Growth.

Development may be thought of in terms of three goals:

United Nations Development Programme
www.undp.org

1. It should involve the satisfaction of the basic needs of all of the people, such as food, housing, clothing, and clean water, as well as the means to live fulfilling and productive lives, such as education, health care, employment, and security against severe hardships. For example, the United Nations Development Programme has set as major objectives the elimination of extreme poverty, currently defined as subsisting on less than US$1 per day (UNDP, 2002), and improving the status of women. Improving the status of women, particularly by ensuring that young women receive an education, tends to result in a healthier population, a reduction in the rate of population growth, and a more skilled workforce.

2. It should involve the creation of a more diversified and sophisticated economy. This second goal involves industrialization, that is, moving from a economy based on the production of commodities such as food and unprocessed natural resources to one based on manufacturing products such as cars, ships, and computers. As well, it involves developing the scientific, technological, and managerial capabilities needed to compete with the developed countries. Further, it requires moving from being a supplier of low-cost labour to multinational corporations based in the rich countries to developing local entrepreneurial capabilities and the banking, legal, and other services needed to support locally based businesses.

3. The development needs to be environmentally sustainable. Economic growth has often been achieved by an unrestrained exploitation of natural

resources. Indiscriminate logging and fishing may bring short-term economic growth and profits, but are destructive to long-term development. Indeed, one of the major dilemmas of development is that industrialization and increased wealth often create a heavy burden on the environment. Although the rich countries use a high proportion of the world's resources and are responsible for a substantial proportion of pollutants, increases in the wealth in heavily populated Third World countries have the potential to place great stresses on the environment of not only the Third World countries but the world as a whole. For example, the shift from bicycles to cars as a major means of transportation is creating serious problems of congestion and air pollution in many Third World cities and also contributing to the problems of global climate change. From an environmental perspective, Third World economic growth that leads to the consumption levels of the richer countries would be disastrous. Both richer and poorer countries need to develop in a more sustainable fashion.

Center for Global Development
www.cgdev.org

Measuring Development

Rather than simply measuring the wealth of a country, the United Nations Development Programme uses an index that is based on literacy and education, life expectancy, and per capita GDP to get a broader picture of how well specific countries are doing in their pursuit of development (see Table 18-2). On the so-called **Human Development Index (HDI)**, rankings do not always correspond exactly to GDP.

Cuba, for instance, ranks 38 places higher on HDI than it does on GDP, indicating that it produces very good human development results for its level of economic activity. At the other extreme, Equatorial Guinea, a small African state, has HDI levels 78 places below its income rank. Equatorial Guinea produces and exports oil, so it has a high national income that has yet to translate into benefits for its people.[1]

The good news is that, however it is measured, development has clearly occurred in parts of the Third World. Compared to 1960, life expectancy has increased substantially, literacy rates and enrollment in education at all levels have jumped, and women in particular have made great gains (UNDP, 1995). The percentage of those living in extreme poverty has fallen from 30 percent in 1990 to 23 percent today (UNDP, 2003). Before we celebrate, however, we should know that these global figures hide disturbing facts.

First, even though a smaller percentage of the world's population qualifies as "extremely poor," over 1 billion people still fall into that category. Further, some parts of the world—most notably Sub-Saharan Africa—are doing far worse than others and have even lost ground in the last twenty-five

HUMAN DEVELOPMENT INDEX (HDI)
An annual index for most countries, calculated by the United Nations Development Programme and based on literacy and education, life expectancy, and per capita GDP.

---

[1] HDI says nothing about a country's political system. Both Cuba and Equatorial Guinea are dictatorships. The difference in their HDIs shows clearly that not all dictatorships are the same.

TABLE 18-2
HUMAN DEVELOPMENT INDEX, SELECTED COUNTRIES, 2003

Note: Gross Domestic Product per capita is calculated in terms of purchasing power parity.

HDI RANK	COUNTRY	GDP PER CAPITA (US$)	% CHILDREN UNDERWEIGHT	% ADULT LITERACY	LIFE EXPECTANCY (YEARS)
7	United States	34 320	1%	100%	77.1
8	Canada	27 130	—	100%	79.3
9	Japan	25 130	—	100%	81.6
52	Cuba	5 259	4%	96.8%	76.5
55	Mexico	8 430	8%	91.4%	73.4
65	Brazil	7 360	6%	87.3%	68.1
75	Ukraine	4 350	3%	99.6%	69.7
104	China (PRC)	4 020	10%	85.8%	71.0
112	Indonesia	2 940	26%	87.3%	66.8
116	Equatorial Guinea	15 073	N/A	84.2%	49.0
120	Egypt	3 520	4%	56.1%	68.8
127	India	2 840	47%	58.0%	63.9
144	Pakistan	1 890	38%	44.0%	61.0
150	Haiti	1 860	17%	50.8%	49.5
152	Nigeria	850	27%	65.4%	51.5
167	Congo (Dem. Rep.)	680	31%	62.7%	41.8
169	Ethiopia	810	47%	58.0%	63.9
175	Sierra Leone	470	27%	36.0%	34.2

SOURCE: *Adapted from Human Development Report, 2003, by the United Nations Development Programme, 2003, New York: Oxford University Press.*

years. The rapid growth of the Chinese and Indian economies over the last decade has reduced poverty there. Since these two countries make up three-eighths of the world's population, improvements in those countries will cause global poverty figures to drop, even though poverty has worsened throughout Africa. Statistics reveal, but they also conceal.

Clearly, individual countries have made great strides. Forty years ago the countries of Southeast and East Asia were extremely poor, with a short life expectancy and high levels of illiteracy and infant mortality. From China to Thailand, however, conditions are much improved. In fact, aside from North Korea, the region's experience demonstrates that development is not just possible, but that countries can make great strides in a generation.

However, just as there are development success stories, there are also failures. The most dramatic cases of failed development are found in sub-Saharan Africa, followed by the Middle East and parts of Latin America. Yet even in most of these cases living standards have improved, and there were periods when they showed remarkable gains before falling back. Box 18-3, Three Development Scenarios, presents some cases of successful and failed development.

BOX 18-3

Three Development Scenarios

The Third World presents us with cases of failed development and reversed development as well as successful development:

1. *Failed development*. When the Belgian Congo became independent in 1960, Belgium had not prepared its colony for independence, so there were few well-educated Congolese to exercise power. The new country plunged into civil war, with the Americans backing one faction and the Soviets another. The eventual winner of the conflict was Joseph Mobutu. Later he changed his name to Mobutu Sese Seko and the country's name to Zaire. From 1965 to 1997 he exercised dictatorial rule, becoming Africa's most corrupt leader. Things did not improve for the Congolese after Laurent Kabila ousted Mobutu and renamed the country the Democratic Republic of the Congo. It soon was swept up in warfare, and in 2001 Kabila was assassinated. His son then seized power and still rules.

    A peace deal concluded among warring Congolese factions and their foreign backers in July 2003 has brought a minimum of stability to the country, but rebuilding will take a long time. The fifty-five million inhabitants have annual per capita incomes of only US$80, but their land is rich in natural resources. The Congolese, however, will not benefit from their gold, silver, and oil, until they get political stability and honest rulers.

2. *Reversed development*. Early in the twentieth century, Argentina had a per capita income similar to Canada's. By 2003, it was less than 30 percent of ours. Argentina is a big country, with thirty-eight million well-educated people. It has significant natu-ral resources (agricultural and mineral), a once-large but now declining manufacturing base, and modern service industries. However, between 1930 and 1983 the country was almost always ruled by dictatorships, all of which pursued bad policies. Since 1983 the country has been democratic, but this has not solved its problems. In December 2001, Argentina's economy nearly collapsed and sparked a political crisis that saw five presidents governing within three months. Argentina should be rich, but it needs more stable democratic politics, as well as a sound and sustainable economic program, to achieve this.

3. *Successful development*. South Korea (officially, the Republic of Korea) is a developed country today. It is not a large country, but has a population of thirty-eight million. At its founding in 1946, the country's prospects were poor. Formerly a Japanese colony, Korea was divided into a communist north (the Korean Democratic Republic) and a non-communist south. Over the next four decades, while North Korea stagnated, South Korea prospered by using a form of government-managed capitalism (Wade 1990). It currently has a sophisticated economy based principally on manufacturing. South Korean firms like Samsung and Hyundai are household names in Canada. Until 1988 South Korea was ruled by a series of dictatorships, most of them military. It is now such a sufficiently stable democracy that it was able to weather a severe economic crisis from 1997 to 1998 without incident.

▶ Argentina should be rich, but it needs more stable democratic politics, as well as a sound and sustainable economic program, to achieve this.

HOW CAN COUNTRIES DEVELOP?

There is no simple solution to the problem of development. Those who have examined the issue often differ sharply on the causes of underdevelopment and on the best approach to achieve development. We will focus on the free-market approach, dependency theory, import substitution industrialization, and export-led industrialization.

The Free Market

Since at least the 1950s, the dominant model (often referred to as a paradigm) in discussions about development has emphasized the free market. The advice that the Third World gets from international agencies such as the International Monetary Fund and the World Bank, as well as from many economists, typically is based on the assumption that government involvement in the economy is undesirable. The *free-market capitalist economic system*, free trade, and unrestricted foreign investment, it is argued, will lead to prosperity.

Free-market approaches to development have come in two packages that offer broadly similar advice: modernization theory and the Washington Consensus.

MODERNIZATION THEORY Modernization theory was important from about 1950 to 1975. This theory viewed the traditional values, practices, and institutions of Third World countries as the basic cause of underdevelopment. More bluntly, the implication was that poor countries were "backward." To develop, poor countries had to change their cultural outlooks, social

MODERNIZATION THEORY
A development model that views the traditional values, practices, and institutions of Third World countries as the basic cause of underdevelopment. To develop, poor countries should change their cultural outlook, social structure, economic organization, and political system based on the model of the advanced Western societies.

structure, economic organization, and political system. The rich Western societies, such as the United States, were the model that Third World countries should copy. This was not as difficult as it might seem because modernization theorists argued that the right economic policies would set everything else moving. Once governments had taken the first steps, their role would be much reduced.

The prescription called for bringing in the most modern firms from abroad, the ones with the newest technology and best management. They would open a plant in a developing country, hire locals, and show other businesses the best way to do things. These local businesses would adopt the practices of the foreign firm and further diffuse the ideas of the developed world through society. Before long, a new middle class and a modern working class would emerge, free from the biases of their old society. These modern sectors would challenge the old elites, come to control government, and build a democracy. Unfortunately, things did not work like that. Foreign firms spun off fewer benefits than expected to their hosts, so the modern, democratic middle and working classes did not grow much. Thus, the old elites retained power and democracy gained little ground. Overall, the economy did improve, but not as much as modernization's promoters had promised.

THE WASHINGTON CONSENSUS The free-market prescription got a second chance in the early 1980s and is still important today. Between 1973 and 1980, world oil prices skyrocketed. This began a chain of events that resulted in many Third World countries' accumulating huge debts with foreign lenders. Because interest rates were also rising throughout that period and sales of Third World exports to the First World were slumping, many countries found themselves unable to meet their debt payments. To solve this problem and ensure that the debtor countries kept paying, the wealthy countries, led by the United States and the two most important **international financial institutions** (IFIs)—the World Bank (WB) and the International Monetary Fund (IMF), put together a series of policies that became known as the **Washington Consensus**.

At the heart of the Washington Consensus are calls for countries to generate more revenue for debt repayment by cutting government expenditures to balance their budgets, selling off government-owned enterprises (privatization), and fully opening their countries to foreign goods and investments. These prescriptions form the heart of **structural adjustment programs** (SAPs). SAPs are administered by international financial institutions that offer governments loans at very favourable interest rates ("soft loans") if their countries enact the programs endorsed by the Washington Consensus. Were a country to refuse to agree to a SAP, it could easily find that it had no access at all to international credit because private banks will not lend to clients, even sovereign states, that have proven unwilling or unable to pay their debts. Without such loans, countries might be unable to import such necessary items

International Monetary Fund
www.imf.org

World Bank
www.worldbank.org

INTERNATIONAL FINANCIAL INSTITUTION (IFI)
An organization that has some ability to affect the global economic system; for example, the International Monetary Fund and the World Bank.

WASHINGTON CONSENSUS
A series of policies put together by the International Monetary Fund and the World Bank that encourage developing countries to generate more revenue for debt repayment by cutting government expenditures to balance their budgets, selling off government-owned enterprises (privatization), and fully opening their countries to foreign goods and investments.

STRUCTURAL ADJUSTMENT PROGRAM (SAP)
A program administered by international financial institutions, which offer loans at very favourable interest rates to governments facing problems paying their debt if they adopt the programs espoused by the Washington Consensus.

as light bulbs or spare parts for cars and trucks, since exporters want to be paid in a major international currency, particularly US dollars.

The first great wave of SAPs in the early 1980s gave little heed to the social consequences of the economic policies that were proposed. These days, SAPs give more attention to the plight of the poor. Their main thrust, however, remains unchanged, even though the programs have had limited success in actually producing development. This has led some to conclude that the SAPs and the Washington Consensus are more about protecting the wealthy countries of the North (for example, by ensuring that countries do not default on their loans, which could cause a collapse in the global banking system) than actually developing the South. Although the World Bank and the International Monetary Fund have a mandate to assist the poorer countries, control of these organizations rests primarily with persons appointed by the governments of the rich countries.

SUCCESS?   Overall, free-market approaches have not been dramatically more successful than others in achieving development. Indeed, no country in the world has ever developed using a *purely* free-market framework. Governments have always taken an active role in shaping the economies of successful developing countries.

Dependency Theory

DEPENDENCY THEORY
A development model that views underdevelopment as a result of unequal power relations between the centre (dominant capitalist countries) and the periphery (poor, dependent countries).

Dependency theory (Cardoso & Falletto, 1979; Frank, 1979) argues that underdevelopment results from unequal power relations between the dominant capitalist countries ("the centre") and the poor, dependent countries ("the periphery").[2]

In particular, Andre Gunder Frank argues that underdevelopment was a result of colonization of the periphery by the European powers. Over time, the centre developed at the expense of the periphery, which became underdeveloped (Frank, 1972). The periphery provides the raw materials and cheap labour needed to keep the capitalist system based in the rich centre profitable. However, the dependence of the periphery on the centre for markets in which to sell its goods and for capital to keep its economy running ensures that the periphery remains underdeveloped.

Dependency theorists also often claim that the centre supports non-democratic governments in the periphery because these are more likely to keep the system of dependency in place. In particular, non-democratic governments have often been based on local business elites that benefit from their connections to the corporations based in the rich countries.

---

[2] The centre is also referred to by dependency theorists as *the core* or *metropolitan countries* and the periphery as *satellites*.

A DIFFERENT FOCUS Dependency theory differs from most conventional theories that see the causes of underdevelopment and poverty in the culture and politics of Third World countries or view the Third World as simply at an earlier stage of development than the First World. Instead, it views the nature of the global economic and political system as preventing the development of the periphery. Because the richer countries of the North are more powerful, North–South relations tend to benefit the North.

CRITICISMS Dependency theory has often been criticized for not offering practical solutions to the problem of development. Some dependency theorists suggest that underdeveloped countries drop out of the global capitalist system (perhaps after a revolutionary overthrow of the local capitalist-oriented state) and focus on becoming self-reliant. As well, some dependency theorists have suggested that peripheral countries work together to create an alternative to the global capitalist system.

However, countries that isolate themselves from the global economic system (for example, North Korea) generally pay a heavy economic price. The People's Republic of China undertook determined measures to become self-sufficient but eventually abandoned this strategy and has become a major exporting country and a member of the World Trade Organization. The creation of an alternative to the global capitalist system appears unlikely, particularly since the collapse of communism.

Two Practical Approaches: ISI and ELI

One practical approach to the problem of achieving development grew out of work done in the 1940s by the United Nations Economic Commission on Latin America (ECLA), which also developed the centre–periphery distinction that dependency analysts use. ECLA theorists used the terms to denote that the centre had diversified economies, sound financial systems, and stable democratic governments, all of which peripheral countries usually lacked. To bring about change, they offered a recipe known as import substitution industrialization.

IMPORT SUBSTITUTION INDUSTRIALIZATION Import substitution industrialization (ISI) called for creating an industrial sector that would make many of the products that a country was importing. Locally produced goods would then have a market as a substitute for imported goods. **Tariffs** (taxes on imports) would protect the domestic industries from foreign competition while they grew. Once grown, they would have transformed their countries by creating a new class of industrialists, a larger middle class, and modern working class. This policy worked in Canada and the United States in the nineteenth century, so it seemed likely to work in the Third World in the twentieth.

IMPORT SUBSTITUTION INDUSTRIALIZATION (ISI)
An economic development model that involves creating an industrial sector by placing tariffs on imported industrial products.

TARIFF
A tax on imports.

For a while, ISI produced good results in countries such as Mexico, Brazil, and Argentina. However, after about thirty years it failed because of problems that may have been inherent in the policy. Many countries following this policy did build new industries, but these industries never flourished. They kept making expensive goods of poor quality. If governments talked about reducing tariffs to make these firms become more efficient, their owners warned of foreign takeovers, while their workers staged demonstrations to protect their jobs. Governments got the message and backed down.

**EXPORT-LED INDUSTRIALIZA-
TION (ELI)**

A model of economic development that features a capitalist system in which government and the biggest businesses work very closely together to develop export industries. Government influences investments, provides incentives for exports, and can decide which firms get to export products and which do not.

ASIAN MODEL

The economic model of export-led industrialization associated with a number of Asian countries.

Association of Southeast Asian States
www.aseansec.org

EXPORT-LED INDUSTRIALIZATION   Another practical approach to development is **export-led industrialization** (ELI), which is now often known as the **Asian model** because Asian countries have used it most effectively. It is only slightly newer than ISI, but has had a longer run of success, only encountering difficulties after about fifty very good years.

Sometimes called "the governed economy" (Wade, 1990), this model builds export industries. It features a capitalist system in which government and the biggest businesses work closely together. Government influences investments, provides incentives for exports, and can even decide which firms get to export products and which do not. Like ISI, some aspects of the domestic market are typically protected from foreign competition. Conditions are often placed on the involvement of foreign companies, such as requiring that partnerships be created with local companies, technological knowledge be transferred, and some of the profits remain in the country. As well, by keeping the value of their currency artificially low and by paying workers very low wages (often maintained by suppressing unions and not enforcing labour laws), the newly industrialized countries can sell goods at very low prices (Martin & Schumann, 1997).

The objective of this model is to build the strongest economy possible in the shortest time possible. Japan had to do this twice: in the nineteenth century when it first industrialized, and then when it rebuilt after World War II. South Korea and Taiwan (the Republic of China) followed Japan's lead. The latter two countries created their own variants of the Asian model to develop rapidly and better defend themselves against their communist neighbours (North Korea and the People's Republic of China, respectively) when U.S. economic assistance was reduced in the 1970s. Other countries that have followed this path more or less successfully include the Asian "tigers": Singapore, Malaysia, Thailand, Indonesia, and more recently and spectacularly, the People's Republic of China.

The Asian Model has two striking features:

1. *It works with non-democratic governments as well as democratic ones.* South Korea, Taiwan, and Indonesia were all dictatorships when they began their spectacular development, although they now have demo-

◀ Export-led industrialization was particularly successful in Asian countries such as Taiwan. Reasons for this success include the support of the U.S., which provided them with billions of dollars in aid and, prior to the 1990s, offered them favourable trading terms as part of a strategy of building a defence against communist countries.

cratic governments. Similarly, although Japan and Singapore are formally democracies, each is governed by a party that seldom loses elections.

2. *It has worked best in Asia.* Some commentators feel this success reflects cultural factors (called Asian values), including a strong work ethic, family and moral values, thrift, discipline, and an emphasis on social cohesion rather than individualism. Others point to the fact that the Asian countries that grew strong and prosperous using this model were particularly adept at using government to lead the way to development, both by managing their economies and by emphasizing education. Finally, some commentators hold that the Asian model has not spread because the international trade rules now in place discriminate against countries that would use government to build their economies. Indeed, export-led industrialization was particularly successful in Japan, Taiwan, and South Korea, in part because the United States provided them with billions of dollars in aid and, prior to the 1990s, offered them favourable trading terms as part of a strategy of building a defence against communist countries.

BOTH APPROACHES HAVE WORKED The two practical approaches, ISI and ELI, have each worked well for a while, in a few places. This suggests that specific policies, even broad approaches to development, may work better in some places and at some times than in others. Intuitively, this makes sense: Canada did not follow exactly the same path to development as the

United States or Britain, yet all became developed democracies. Nevertheless, there is still a tendency to search for the magic bullet that solves everyone's economic and even political problems.

DEVELOPMENT ASSISTANCE AND TRADING RELATIONSHIPS

International Development Studies
Network
www.idsnet.org

Less developed countries often need considerable help from the richer countries if they are to supply the basic needs of their populations. They also need access to the knowledge and technology of the richer countries if they are to compete successfully in global markets. Various charitable organizations provide humanitarian assistance and supply volunteers to assist in development projects. However, it is the governments of the richer countries that have the financial resources to provide substantial development assistance to the poorer countries.

OFFICIAL DEVELOPMENT ASSISTANCE (ODA)
Aid to the poorer countries given by the governments of the richer countries.

Canada's foreign aid to poor countries (referred to in government circles as **Official Development Assistance** or ODA) is sometimes purely altruistic, as in the case of disaster relief or humanitarian assistance. Often, however, wealthy countries use ODA to secure multiple objectives. In the case of Canada, it seems that the most important objective is helping Canadian businesses. In particular, over two-thirds of Canadian aid is "tied" (World Bank, 2004), meaning that the money has to be spent in Canada, on Canadian goods and services, even if these are more expensive or less suited to the needs of the developing countries.

Canada gives less aid than many Canadians think it does. In 1969, former Canadian Prime Minister Lester Pearson proposed that the wealthy countries dedicate 0.7 percent of their GDP to foreign aid. This goal has been accepted by the richer countries and adopted by the United Nations. However, only a few countries have met or exceeded this goal. Canadian governments have continued to be committed to that goal, but in reality, assistance as a proportion of GDP has been declining until recently. In 2004, Canada's ODA was about 0.26 percent of GDP.

Economic Discrimination

Seen from the perspective of the South, the reluctance of the North to send more aid is only part of the problem. Perhaps even more serious is the reluctance of the rich countries to fully open their markets to the Third World and to accept fair global trading rules.

Canada and its wealthy colleagues in the G-8 (the world's six largest economies, plus Canada and Russia)[3] and the Organization for Economic

---

[3] Originally (1975), the organization was the G-6: the United States, Great Britain, the Federal Republic of Germany, Japan, and France. Canada joined in 1976. Russia received partial membership in 1994 and full membership in 1998. Were the G-8 to include the world's eight largest economies, Russia would have to be dropped in favour of the People's Republic of China, the sixth-biggest economy in the world, and Canada might have to yield its seat to Spain.

Cooperation and Development (thirty countries with a commitment to capitalist economics and democratic politics) talk about free trade and levelling the international economic playing field. But when it comes to trading with poor countries, the richer countries find ways to discriminate against the products that poor countries produce more cheaply, mostly foodstuffs and textiles, in order to protect their own producers. As well, the richer countries heavily subsidize the production of many exports, which then have a major competitive advantage over Third World products. However, we insist that Third World countries must not protect their producers from our products. We can do this because we are stronger and the poorer countries need to trade with us so desperately that they often accept an unfair deal.

Trade Pacts

There is an increasing number of trade agreements involving both rich and poor countries. A substantial majority of the world's countries (one hundred and forty-seven in August 2004) are now members of the World Trade Organization (WTO), an international organization dealing with the rules of trade between countries and the only international organization concerned with economics that does not assign member countries votes based on the size of their economies. There are also a variety of regional free-trade agreements such as the North American Free Trade Agreement (involving Canada, the United States, and Mexico), as well as bilateral agreements such as the Canada–Chile Free Trade Agreement.

Free-trade agreements establish binding rules of trade and set up impartial panels to settle trade disputes. In theory, this is in the interests of weaker countries as the arbitrary power of stronger countries can be constrained by the rules. The products of the poor countries can potentially gain access to the large, rich markets of the world's developed countries without facing discriminatory tariffs and quotas. However, many poor countries argue that the rules of trade agreements are biased towards the interests of the richer countries and do not provide for fair trade relations. For example, agriculture is the major economic activity in many less developed countries, with a large proportion of the population often engaged in farming. However, agriculture in the less developed countries faces severe challenges that the WTO, whose task is to facilitate international trade, has had trouble addressing.

The rich countries provide US$1 billion a day in subsidies to their own farmers. Agricultural products are then exported at a very low price, making it very difficult for farmers in the less developed countries to sell their products. Indeed, it has been estimated that the rich, developed countries spend six times more on subsidizing their own agricultural production than they spend in development assistance to the poor countries (Oxfam, 2003).

In a major meeting at Doha, Qatar, in 2001, the WTO launched a round of trade negotiations aimed at phasing out agricultural export subsidies and eliminating most tariffs. However, at a September 2003 WTO meeting in Cancún, Mexico, talks to achieve these objectives broke down. The rich countries wanted new trading rules on international investment, competition, and government purchasing policies that would benefit the multinational corporations based in the rich countries.

A group of twenty-two developing countries, led by Brazil, China, and India, viewed the reductions in agricultural subsidies proposed by the European Union and the United States as too limited and walked out. Some saw the formation of a bloc of developing countries that insisted on better trading rules as an important shift in the power relations between the developed and developing countries. Others worried that the developed countries would close their markets to those poor countries that would not accept their rules. Because the poor countries are dependent on access to the markets of the rich countries, they are vulnerable to pressure to accept rules that may be more beneficial to the rich countries. In any event, WTO members reached a framework agreement in July 2004 that included a 20 percent cut in agricultural subsidies and laid the foundation for an eventual full-scale treaty to cut subsidies and import tariffs.

POLITICS IN THE THIRD WORLD

Most Third World countries used to be colonies of European countries. Few have been able to develop effective democratic systems since achieving their independence. Politics in most of these states has often been characterized by instability, military rule, violence, and corruption. These characteristics have contributed to the problems of development.

In the last quarter of the twentieth century, many less developed countries embraced democratic government as part of what has been called the "third wave of democracy" (Huntington, 1991).[4] To date, though, only a minority of countries have succeeded in forming strong, stable democracies (termed

---

[4] Samuel Huntington identifies three great historic waves in which countries became democratic. The first wave began in the late eighteenth century and lasted until the 1920s. It was focused in what are now the world's historic democracies: for example, the United States, Canada, the United Kingdom, and much of Western Europe. A second wave, associated with decolonization, began immediately after World War II and crested in the early 1960s. The latest wave started in 1974 with the fall of dictatorships in Portugal and Greece. It achieved perhaps it greatest success with the fall of the Soviet Bloc between 1989 and 1991. It continues today. Waves of democracy are treated in greater depth in Chapter 19.

consolidated democracies). We shall consider the process of democratization in greater detail in Chapter 19.

In one sense, politics in the Third World is no different from politics in Canada or anywhere else. People want to control the state, to make rules that they think are good, and to enforce those rules as they think best. However, Third World politics diverges from politics in consolidated democracies, like Canada, in three important ways:

1. Liberal democracies have been rare in the Third World.
2. Third World countries have weak governmental institutions.
3. Violence plays a much bigger part in Third World politics than in developed, consolidated democracies today.

Few Liberal Democracies

Liberal democracies are constitutional political systems in which the government has to obey the law, just as any citizen does. In such systems, all citizens are assured that their rights and freedoms are recognized and protected, and they have a voice in how their government is run. Although these principles are well established in Canada and in most other First World countries, this has only rarely been the case in the Third World.

If we had looked at the governments of the Third World in 1980, we would have found only a handful of liberal democracies, including India in Asia, Botswana in Africa, Costa Rica in Latin America, and Jamaica and Barbados in the Caribbean. There were also countries that were semi-democracies or marginal cases, such as Singapore and Sri Lanka, but most Third World countries of the South would not have been considered democratic.

Over the last quarter-century, many countries have made transitions to democracy such that the majority of countries, North and South, can now be classified as democratic. **Authoritarian government** (another name for non-democratic states) failed and were replaced by systems in which governments are elected. In some cases, the failure resulted from the authoritarian government's mismanagement, in others from the breakdown of communism, which left some Third World dictatorships without patrons. A few transitions were the result of external pressure from the United States and the international financial institutions. Most of the transitions were completed by the early 1990s.

However, it takes more than dismantling an authoritarian state and holding elections to build a strong, stable democracy. The transition to democracy has been difficult for many countries. A number of countries have the form but not the substance of democracy. In particular, there are often very few institutional limits on the executive's power. Once elected, a president or prime minister often has the power to govern without restraint until the next election.

CONSOLIDATED DEMOCRACIES Countries with democratic governments that are stable and well accepted by both ordinary citizens and political elites, and which face little danger of being overthrown.

Organization of American States **www.oas.org**

AUTHORITARIAN GOVERNMENT A non-democratic system of government.

PERSONALISTIC LEADER
A political leader whose claim
to rule is based on some presumed inherent qualities of the
person himself or, far less commonly, herself. It also implies a
government in which all important decisions are made by the
leader, according to the leader's
wishes, and in which it is the
leader who determines who gets
what, when, and how.

Weak Institutions

Strong, **personalistic leaders** have historically dominated politics in many
poor countries. Almost always men, they are called *caudillos* in Latin
America, *big men* in Africa, and *bosses* just about everywhere. The concentration of power in the hands of one leader can be a problem anywhere, even
in the United States (Schlesinger, 1973), Britain (Weir & Beetham, 1999), and
Canada (Simpson, 2001). Consolidated democracies, however, generally have
counterweights to executive power that seldom exist in new democracies.

These counterweights include political institutions inside and outside of
government, such as legislatures, courts, the public service, the media, organized interests, political parties, and the diverse set of groups outside of government known as civil society. To function properly, democracies need to
have both sets of institutions working well. Having many strong political
institutions lessens the risk that one person, group, or organization will
become too powerful in two different ways. A multiplicity of robust institutions disperses power among many centres, each having some ability to
counter the actions of the others. As well, having several powerful institutions in the same political system gives citizens more chances to present their
views to government.

Almost all countries have at least one strong governmental institution: the
executive. In Canada, the executive refers to the prime minister or premier,
the cabinet, and the entire public service. In much of the Third World, however, the president or prime minister monopolizes executive power. As a
result, there is little accountability and corruption is a very serious problem
in some less developed countries as described in Box 18-4, Political
Corruption: Nicaragua.

The Role of Force and Violence

Violence has always characterized politics in the developing world (as it did
in the developed countries in the past). Even countries that now have long
histories of democratic rule, such as Costa Rica, experienced many coups,
revolutions, and insurgencies in the past. Other democracies, like Jamaica,
still have a lot of political violence, especially during election campaigns. And
the non-democratic countries face even graver challenges, as violence is often
a standard instrument of rule.

The most obvious contemporary instances of political violence and its
devastating effects on a country are found in a number of sub-Saharan
African states. In the continent's east, Rwanda and Burundi have been
wracked by ethnic warfare that spilled over their borders and affected neighbouring states. Governments in the West African states of Sierra Leone and
Liberia have collapsed, leaving their citizens to be plundered and murdered
by marauding armed bands. Development is obviously impossible in these

Political Corruption: Nicaragua

Alberto Aleman was elected president of the Central American country of Nicaragua in 1996, six years after entering public life as mayor of the capital, Managua. In 1990, Aleman had declared his personal wealth at US$30 000, good for a country where the per capita income was US$500 per year, but not exorbitant. When he left the presidency in 2001, the media estimated his wealth at US$250 million.

Investigations that begun after Aleman stepped down unearthed evidence that made the quarter-billion dollar figure believable. The former president was charged with embezzling over US$100 million directly from government accounts while in office. He had even used a government credit card to pay for his engagement party and honeymoon (Close & Deonandan, 2004).

Aleman is just one example of a corrupt leader, but he stood out from most Third World strong men in two ways. Instead of seizing power in a coup or by a rigged vote, he actually won an open election. Equally important, although he seldom gave his opponents a break, Aleman did not resort to violence to get his way.

settings. Why, though, has violence been so common throughout the Third World?

In part, it is another consequence of weak political institutions that cannot protect the public's interests. It is also a sign that politics has been a winner-take-all game, with no place left for opponents. Exacerbating both of these is a failure of legitimacy. The people do not trust government because government excludes many interests and concentrates control in the hands of the already powerful. Governments then use force to keep their opponents at bay, and those opponents use force to try to change the government. Although this oversimplifies the situation, it does give us a sense of the dynamics that produce political violence in the Third World.

CHANGING TIMES Nevertheless, there are signs that the military is assuming a less prominent political role throughout the Third World than it did in the past. Consequently there are fewer *coups d'état* (forcible seizures of power by the armed forces or occasionally the police). Militaries in poor countries have long been politicized; that is, they have regularly taken clear political stances and often seized government to run it themselves. They have done this because they have the guns, but also because they are commonly the best organized institution in a country, with the highest concentration of technically skilled, well-trained personnel. Accordingly, when civilian politicians have been corrupt or incompetent, or have gone against the military's wishes, the soldiers would step in and take over (see Box 18-5, Military Coups).

Through the 1980s, it seemed that there was no general solution to the problem of politically active militaries. However, the wave of **democratic transitions** that began then has coincided with a sharp fall in the frequency of

COUP D'ÉTAT
A forcible seizure of power by the armed forces or occasionally the police.

DEMOCRATIC TRANSITION
A process of change involving abandoning authoritarian government for democratic rule.

BOX 18-5

Military Coups

Military takeovers of government do not just happen. Numerous studies of coups and how they work will help us to understand this phenomenon (Farcau, 1994; Fitch, 1977; Luttwak, 1969).

- First, the army will almost certainly be involved because, of all the armed services, it has the resources that are best suited to toppling a government: armed troops, tanks, and other armour. The air force is useful for strafing buildings and opposing troops, while the navy can shell shorelines and block harbours, but the army secures the area.

- Second, although some coups have been led by sergeants and field marshals, many coups are led by majors and colonels because they are in direct command of large numbers of soldiers.

- Third, coups work or fail based on whether key figures oppose or support the movement. For example, an attempted coup failed in Spain in 1981 because the king opposed it publicly, which caused military commanders to fall in line behind him.

- Fourth, successful coups capture not only government leaders, but also the communications media. When a coup succeeds, it often forms a governing committee or junta, (the Spanish word meaning simply "board" or "committee"). The junta contains all the key players in coups.

- Finally, some coups are bloodless, because they are essentially unopposed, but others can spur civil wars or lead to cruel dictatorships.

coups. This may reflect a heightened democratic consciousness among soldiers, but there are several other explanations to consider.

One explanation is that citizens in many countries have become dissatisfied with military governments. This is especially true of four southern South American countries (Argentina, Brazil, Chile, and Uruguay) that saw very brutal and very long-lasting military regimes in the late twentieth century. Another is that militaries around the world have themselves become disenchanted with their nearly uniform failure as governors. Militaries can impose order and throw out inept rulers, but with only a handful of exceptions, they have not presided over extended periods of development. Finally, the international community is no longer tolerant of military governments. The international financial institutions now are very reluctant to make loans to military regimes and often demand that civilian governments cut military budgets as a condition for receiving money from one of these organizations.

The military will always be a political actor and there will likely always be some military regimes. However, current trends suggest that there will be many fewer governments run by generals than in the past.

HISTORICAL PERSPECTIVE We are left to consider why the political conditions just described apply to the Third World. The fact that today's wealthy democracies have pasts as unsavoury and unpromising as what we

"The president says that if we export more oil, we can buy more weapons so that our country will be stronger."

find in the contemporary developing world tells us that improvement is possible. We too often forget that the process of democratization—in its social and economic manifestations of less rigid class barriers and a more equal distribution of wealth as well as its political form—has been under way for over two hundred years in the historic democracies of northwestern Europe and North America. To expect Africa, Asia, and Latin America to cover the same distance in a decade or even a generation is unrealistic. Nevertheless, ever more countries are offering their citizens increasingly accountable, honest, and efficient government. This signifies progress towards building a state that is able to pursue the common good.

We must recognize, however, that poverty makes good government difficult to achieve. In poor countries, controlling the state may offer the surest road to wealth. Where that is the case, keeping the power to govern may seem too important for a government to risk by submitting to elections, allowing a free press, and encouraging citizens to organize freely and press their demands on government. Such conditions also work against building strong state institutions other than the presidency and the security forces because strong organizations can become independent and work toward the common good instead of the ruler's interests. In addition, poor countries often have difficulty in establishing an honest, efficient, and knowledgeable staff for government and its agencies. Because government may not be able to pay adequate salaries, public servants may look to other sources of income, such as soliciting bribes or holding multiple jobs, to make a decent living.

Foreign Intervention

The political problems that many Third World countries face are not simply of their own making. To a considerable extent, they are a product of a history of domination and exploitation.[5]

The control and colonization of most of the world by the European powers often left Third World countries ill-prepared for governing after they achieved their independence. In a number of cases, the boundaries of the new countries made little sense as they combined groups of people of different ancestries, cultures, languages, and religions. To make matters worse, the imperial powers frequently stimulated ethnic divisions within the territories that they controlled as part of a divide-and-rule strategy. In other cases, the descendants of the European colonists tried to maintain their economic and political power after independence against the challenges of indigenous peoples.

POST-INDEPENDENCE Further, although most of the Third World was able to achieve independence in the decades following World War II, this did not end foreign intervention in their affairs. Some imperial powers have continued to intervene in the affairs of their foreign colonies. During the Cold War, the Western and Soviet blocs struggled to gain the support of Third World governments. This involved not only providing economic and military aid to their supporters, but also assisting in the overthrow of governments, supporting repressive governments, revolutionary movements, and terrorist groups, and, in some cases, encouraging wars among Third World countries.

The end of the Cold War reduced the use of these negative forms of foreign intervention that disrupted the political development of Third World countries. However, concerns about international terrorism, the rise of militant **Islamism**, security of oil supplies, and the international trade in illegal drugs have resulted in continuing intervention of powerful countries in the politics of the Third World.

OTHER FORMS OF POLITICAL INTERVENTION There are also three other forms of political intervention that have become important in recent times:

ISLAMISM
The perspective often associated with those seeking to purge "degenerate" foreign elements from Muslim society and base governing on Islamic-inspired regulations of life.

---

[5] We should be careful to note that domination and exploitation have not only been associated with Western powers. Imperialism, colonization, slavery, forced religious conversion, and the massacre of conquered peoples have been carried out at various times by the powerful, whether Western or non-Western.

1. humanitarian intervention in failed states
2. democracy strengthening and promotion
3. politically conditioned aid

The first primarily involves international organizations like the United Nations; the second is carried out primarily by individual countries, mostly the United States, although the United Kingdom and some other countries are also active; and international financial institutions and governmental development assistance agencies are responsible for the last.

Failed states are those that no longer have the capacity to maintain order. This is not a new phenomenon, but we have only recently given it a name. Examples of failed states in recent years include Sierra Leone, Liberia, Somalia, and Haiti. In all of these cases troops from several countries were dispatched under United Nations authority to try to restore order. One hundred years ago, either the disorder in a country whose government had ceased functioning would have been ignored or, more likely, a powerful state like Britain, France, or the United States would have taken over.

North–South Institute
www.nsi-ins.ca

Neither democratic strengthening nor political conditions for aid require sending troops. Both, though, make a country change its policies to conform to standards set by outsiders. In democratic strengthening, discussed further in Chapter 19, a foreign government or a non-governmental organization (NGO) contracted by a foreign government offers assistance to a recipient country to make parts of its political system more democratic. Usually the advice offered reflects the practices and interests of the government paying for the program. Although the recipient does not have to follow that advice, its government knows that keeping good relations with the donor demands enacting at least some of the proposed reforms. The world's leading promoter of democratic strengthening is far and away the United States (Carothers, 1999). Canada does rather less of this kind of work, generally limiting its involvement to assistance with the technical aspects of elections.

Aid is politically conditioned when countries have to adopt specific economic policies, usually involving reduced government spending and greater openness to foreign investment and foreign products, in order to receive financial assistance from the World Bank or International Monetary Fund. Being able to withhold funds from countries in need gives these institutions the leverage to get their favoured policies enacted because without these loans a poor country will usually be unable to buy even such basic foreign-produced goods as glass or paper. In the early twentieth century, great powers often imposed economic policies on weaker states over which they exercised military control. Now international financial institutions and donor countries use the promise of economic assistance to secure the same end. In either case, the weaker party cedes to the stronger.

Summary and Conclusion

Although there have been improvements in living standards throughout much of the Third World, particularly in the newly industrialized countries of East Asia, differences between the richest and the poorest countries continue to increase. About one-fifth of the world's population still lives in extreme poverty (UNDP, 2003). Feeding growing populations, creating employment, and providing housing and other services to those who have flocked to the slums of congested cities provide difficult challenges for many countries.

The problems of the world's poorest states are everyone's problems. A world of great wealth for some and grinding poverty for others is, potentially, a very unstable place. Political violence in Third World countries is not only local in nature, but can involve or affect people in all countries. Poverty, unemployment, or violence in underdeveloped countries leads to migration, legal or illegal, to the richer countries. Environmental problems, such as the destruction of rainforests to achieve rapid economic growth, affect the ecosystems of the world as a whole.

We do not fully understand how countries can successfully develop. There does not seem to be a single, universally applicable route to solving the economic and political problems of underdevelopment. We know that some policies have worked for a while but that none has fully delivered on its promises. Adopting the free-market policies of the United States and other rich Western countries has not generally been highly successful. In the past, the adoption of the state socialist approach of the Soviet Union failed. Although a number of Asian countries have achieved high rates of economic growth through export-led industrialization, it is unclear whether this approach can be replicated successfully elsewhere or, indeed, if successes of some Asian countries can be maintained. Despite improvements in the living standards of the Third World other than Africa, only Japan and the city-state of Singapore have succeeded in fully entering the ranks of the wealthy developed countries.

Development is a political and social issue as well as an economic issue, and thus abstract theoretical economic theories need to be qualified by an understanding of the political, social, and cultural realities of particular underdeveloped countries. Political problems such as corruption, wars, instability, ineffective government administration, and inadequacies in the regulation of economic activity create serious obstacles to development. Political institutions, both governmental and non-governmental, need to be strengthened and reformed to involve the people in the process of development, to hold government accountable for its actions, and to ensure that sound policies are designed and implemented. The development of Third World countries can also be promoted by pressuring various international institutions to provide fairer opportunities for countries that are weak and poor. Social and cultural changes such as improving the status of women and encouraging the involvement of local communities in the development process can be very helpful.

Overall, the poorer countries face difficult problems in trying to achieve the common good of their citizens. With limited wealth, it can be difficult to meet even the most basic needs of the population. Governments often lack the resources needed for effective governing. The substantial inequalities that exist in many poor countries mean that the wealthy can often wield substantial political power, which may hinder needed reforms. Further, underdeveloped countries face not only internal problems, but also problems resulting from global inequities in power. The poorer countries have faced domination and exploitation by the powerful wealthy countries, whether by imperialism or by the global economic system that is supported by the international financial institutions. Various forms of assistance to the poorer countries are often insufficient to overcome the challenges that they face.

In sum, if we want to achieve the common good of humanity, addressing global imbalances in economic and political power as well as providing meaningful assistance to developing countries is necessary. A key problem is that governments and citizens typically are concerned primarily with the good of their own country.

Key Terms

Discussion Questions

1. Why is global inequality so severe?
2. What should a poor country do to develop?
3. Why have some countries in the Third World prospered while others remain poor?
4. Should wealthy countries provide greater assistance to poor countries?
5. Should developed countries help less developed countries to become consolidated democracies?

Further Reading

Bill, J.A., & Springborg, R. *Politics in the Middle East.* Upper Saddle River, NJ: Pearson, Allyn & Bacon, Longman, 2000.

Chazan, N., Lewis, P., Mortimer, R., Rothchild, D., & Stedman, S.J. (Eds.). *Politics and society in contemporary Africa.* Boulder, CO: Lynne Rienner Publishers, 1999.

De Rivero, O. *The myth of development: The non-viable economies of the 21st century.* London, Zed Books, 2001.

Huntington, S. *Political order in changing societies.* Boston: MIT Press, 1968.

North–South Institute. *Canadian development report.* Ottawa: North-South Institute, [annual].

Seligson, M., & Passe-Smith, J. (Eds.). *Development and underdevelopment: The political economy of global inequality.* Boulder, CO: Lynne Rienner Publishers, 1998.

Sen, A. *Development as freedom.* New York: Knopf, 1999.

Thomas, C. *In search of security: The Third World in international relations.* Boulder, CO: Lynne Rienner Publishers, 1987.

Vanden, H., & Prevost, G. (Eds.). *Politics of Latin America: The power game.* New York: Oxford University Press, 2002.

Wang, J.C.F. *Comparative Asian politics: Power, policy and change.* Upper Saddle River, NJ: Prentice Hall, 1998.

United Nations Development Programme. *Human development report.* New York: Oxford University Press, [annual].

Wilber, C., & Jameson, K. (Eds.). *The political economy of development and underdevelopment.* New York: McGraw Hill, 1996.

World Bank. *World development report.* Washington: The World Bank, [annual].

Chapter 19

NON-DEMOCRATIC SYSTEMS AND THE TRANSITION TO DEMOCRACY

PHOTO ABOVE: The power went out in Mexico, forcing a halt to the vote count just as an opposition candidate seemed to be winning the country's 1988 presidential election. But the lights went on in the Mexican electoral reform movement.

CHAPTER OBJECTIVES

After reading this chapter you should be able to:

1. distinguish among the various forms of authoritarian governments

2. understand what a democratic transition is

3. explain what democratic consolidation means and how it is different from a democratic transition

4. discuss what democracy promotion is and what its strengths and weaknesses are

5. outline what it takes to build and maintain a democratic political system

When the power went out, forcing a halt to the vote count just as an opposition candidate seemed to be winning the country's presidential election, the lights went on in the Mexican electoral reform movement. It was the scandal-ridden 1988 election, and the maxim of "the one who counts wins" was being applied just as it had been since 1929. But two innovations were about to help turn the Mexican system on its ear: an independent national electoral authority and groups of citizen electoral observers.

The government party, the PRI (Institutional Revolutionary Party)* used to arrange the elections and count the votes in Mexico. The PRI went beyond "innovative" counting to assure itself victory by excluding opponents from voters' lists, buying votes, and stuffing ballot boxes. But in 1990, Mexico's national electoral authority, the IFE (Federal Electoral Institute) was founded. It was further strengthened by reforms in 1993 and 1996 (Schedler, 2000). Where earlier electoral authorities had operated only during elections and had little independence from the governing party, the IFE is an autonomous institution that operates on a permanent basis, just like Elections Canada.

The IFE's first big test came in 1997, when the PRI lost its majority in Mexico's lower house for the first time ever. Then, in 2000, Mexicans voted in the first non-PRI president in over seventy years. When the PRI regained much of its legislative strength in 2003, the IFE's reputation guaranteed that the results were accepted without question.

The other part of Mexico's success story involves the citizens who serve as independent electoral observers. As their name implies, electoral observers watch the campaign, witness the voting and vote counting, and report any violations of a country's electoral laws that they encounter. The presence of these observers, who are organized by national or local civic organizations, seems to give voters confidence that the rules will be applied fairly. They work in many countries where free and competitive elections have only recently begun to be held. In 2000, out of a total population of 100 million, about 80 000 Mexicans (excluding party poll watchers) acted as election observers (Polisource, 2003). This is proof of a strong commitment to making democracy work.

Where there are robust electoral institutions and citizens who care enough about democracy not just to vote but even to dedicate their time to assuring that elections are properly run, elections can serve the proper democratic function. Democracy doesn't just happen. It must be built.

---

*The PRI was called the PNR (National Revolutionary Party) from 1928 to 1938 and then the PRM (Party of the Mexican Revolution) from 1938 to 1946, but through these name changes it has been the same organization.

DEMOCRATIC GOVERNMENT

Democracy is a relatively new form of government. As we saw in Chapter 4, the Athenians experimented with democratic rule about 2500 years ago, but from then until the late eighteenth century it was missing in action.

The idea of letting the people govern themselves grew during the nineteenth century, and by the end of the twentieth century most of the world's population lived in states that have at least some plausible claim to being called democratic (see Table 19-1). All of these countries have:

- leaders chosen in competitive multi-party and multi-candidate elections
- an opposition with a real chance to win
- a system where no adult citizen is precluded from voting by reason of sex, race, religion, or wealth (Freedom House, 1999)

In fact, Table 19-1 underlines that it really was during the last century that democracy established itself: if in 1900 there were no countries that we today would consider democratic (because none allowed women to vote), by 2000 there were one hundred and twenty democracies.

National Democratic Institute
www.ndi.org

But a number of questions immediately arise. Why has this form of political organization taken so long to reach a majority of the world's people? Even more puzzling, why are there countries that still are not democratic? And what claim can a non-democratic government make to pursuing the common good? Answering these questions requires that we examine some of the non-democratic systems that have existed and give special attention to what has been called the **Third Wave of Democracy** (Huntington 1991), the dramatic extension of democracy to many countries in the late twentieth century.

THIRD WAVE OF DEMOCRACY
The broad move to democratic government that began in 1974 and that still continues.

The Waves of Democracy

Huntington (1991) argues that democracy has not spread throughout the world at a steady pace. Rather, it has expanded in large and long-lasting waves, the first two of which (1810 to 1926 and 1942 to 1962) spawned reverse waves in which the number of democracies shrank. The latest or Third Wave of democracy began in 1974, with the fall of dictatorships in Portugal and Greece. It gathered momentum throughout Latin America in the

TABLE 19-1
THE GROWTH OF DEMOCRACY IN THE TWENTIETH CENTURY

	NUMBER OF DEMOCRACIES	POPULATION (MILLIONS)
1900	0 (0%)	0 (0)
1950	22 (14.3%)	743.2 (31.0%)
2000	120 (62.5%)	3439.4 (58.2%)

SOURCE: *Democracy's Century: A Survey of Political Change in the 20th Century*, by Freedom House, 1999, retrieved August 20, 2004, from www.freedomhouse.org/reports/century.html.

1980s and reached a crescendo between 1989 and 1991 as communism failed in the Soviet Union and its allies.

We refer to this process of change as *democratic transition*, which means simply abandoning authoritarian government (another name for non-democratic systems) for democratic rule. Since the early 1990s, the number of transitions has declined, as the world's remaining authoritarian states—forty-nine in 2003, ruling 35 percent of the world's people, according to Freedom House (2003)[1]—grow fewer in number but perhaps more resistant to change.

Consolidation Phase

DEMOCRATIC CONSOLIDATION
The situation when a country's commitment to democracy is strong and sure, such that democracy is likely to persist.

Once a country has opted for democracy it embarks on the path of **democratic consolidation**. The concept of democratic consolidation is intuitively easy to grasp because it describes a situation when a country's commitment to democracy is strong and sure, and when citizens can use governmental processes to extend democracy and tailor it to their needs. However, democratic consolidation is hard to measure. We have no problem deciding when a country has thrown off a dictatorship or lost its democracy. However, it is far harder to be able to say with certainty that democracy is well entrenched in a country. Further on in this chapter, we explain why it sometimes can be difficult to decide that a country has a consolidated democracy.

NON-DEMOCRATIC SYSTEMS

Because democracy is relatively new, for most of human history people have lived within non-democratic systems. All such systems, whether from another era or in today's world, are often grouped under a single label: *authoritarian*. This term was originally employed by Juan Linz (1964) to refer only to those non-democratic governments that, unlike totalitarian states, did not attempt to control all facets of public life in a country. Using it now to describe any political system that is not democratic leaves us unable to distinguish a state that is murderously despotic from one that gains and keeps power through electoral fraud, corruption, and legal manoeuvres to hobble the opposition.

Our first step, then, is to unpack the concept of authoritarian government in order to view its component parts. Although some of the specific political systems no longer exist, many can still be found today. And far more importantly, the anti-democratic values that underlaid these systems have never

---

[1] Freedom House categorizes countries according to their levels of political rights and civil liberties. Canada, for example, is among the countries with the highest levels of freedom. It is scored *Free* and shares this rating with the United States, Chile, Botswana, and India. In contrast, countries like Honduras, Tanzania, and Russia are scored *Partly Free*. It is the category of countries that are *Not Free* that we take as being authoritarian governments. Among these forty-nine countries we find Pakistan, Afghanistan, Belarus, the People's Republic of China, Saudi Arabia, and North Korea.

ceased to exist.[2] Specifically, we look at six types of authoritarian systems to grasp the variety of patterns of anti-democratic government:

- totalitarian states
- absolute monarchies
- personal dictatorships
- party dictatorships
- military dictatorships
- theocratic dictatorships

Totalitarian Systems

All dictatorships share a common trait: a high level of concentration of political power. Ordinary citizens do not even have the right to select their governors, let alone participate more actively in making the laws that govern them. The distinguishing characteristic of a *totalitarian* dictatorship is that it seeks to control all aspects of life within a country (see Box 19-1, Totalitarianism Versus Authoritarianism). Benito Mussolini, the founder of Italian fascism, neatly summed up the nature of totalitarianism with the slogan, "All within the state, nothing outside the state, nothing against the state!"

Such complete domination was probably always a tyrant's dream but before the twentieth century it was impossible. During the last hundred years, however, advances in transportation and especially communications have made it possible to achieve an approximation of total control. Carl Friederich and Zbigniew Brzezinski (1956) identified six traits that characterized the totalitarian dictatorships of the first part of the twentieth century. All had:

1. an official ideology
2. a single mass party usually led by one man, the dictator, and made up of no more than 10 percent of the population
3. a police state that used terror to control the population
4. a nearly complete monopoly by the party over all means of mass communication
5. a similarly complete monopoly by the party over all means of armed combat
6. an economy planned and controlled by the party

MOST IMPORTANT PRACTITIONERS The most important practitioners of totalitarian rule were the various fascist and communist movements that

---

[2] A good place to start investigating ideas opposed to democracy is David Spitz (1965).

Totalitarianism Versus Authoritarianism

Jeane Kirkpatrick, an American political scientist who served as her country's ambassador to the United Nations, argued in a famous article that authoritarian and totalitarian dictatorships were intrinsically different (Kirkpatrick, 1979).

Authoritarian governments, which she labelled traditional autocracies (one of many synonyms for non-democratic government), were less entrenched, wrought fewer changes in their countries, and could be reformed from within. Totalitarian regimes (revolutionary autocracies in Kirkpatrick's parlance), turned their countries upside down and were incapable of changing their ways. Was she right?

As is so often the case in political science, it is necessary to conclude that she was partly right and partly wrong. The collapse of Eastern European communism a scant ten years after Kirkpatrick's article appeared, followed just two years later by the disappearance of the Soviet Union, suggests that totalitarianism was not impervious to internal pressures. It was, in fact, attempts to reform communism by Soviet leader Mikhail Gorbachev that set the process of change in the Soviet Union in motion.

However, some old-style totalitarian states still exist among the handful of communist systems that remain. Of these, North Korea comes closest to the totalitarian mould, followed by Cuba, while Vietnam and China have moved further away from the old model, especially its economic aspects.

reached their highest point between 1920 and 1970. Although they were different in many ways, both communism and fascism sought to unite all the people of a country in a common project commanded by an individual leader and a single political party.

Leading the totalitarian states were very powerful, unchecked rulers, dictators such as Benito Mussolini in Italy, Adolf Hitler in Germany, Joseph Stalin in the old Soviet Union, and Mao Zedong in the People's Republic of China. All were able to mobilize their populations and harness them to the needs of the state. As well, totalitarians ruled by force and violence. Leading great projects that were supposed to transform society, even remake human nature, totalitarians brooked no interference and wasted no time negotiating with those who opposed them. In this respect they acted as dictators have always acted. It was their ability to monitor and control the lives of their citizens that made the totalitarians distinctive.

Yet all the totalitarians failed. World War II put an end to Mussolini and Hitler, and while communism in the Soviet Union and China lived on after Stalin and Mao, later rulers generally reduced repression and relaxed to a limited degree their control over their people. The Soviet Union joined the ranks of failed totalitarian regimes when it ceased to exist in December 1991.

PATHOLOGICAL TYRANTS It is not only big, powerful states that have flirted with totalitarianism. Perhaps the most shockingly bloodthirsty totalitarian of our age was Pol Pot, who terrorized Cambodia from 1975 to 1979 (Kiernan, 2002). He and his Khmer Rouge turned the Southeast Asian country into a killing field, murdering 1.5 million of its roughly 8 million inhabitants.

Pathological tyrants are neither new nor especially uncommon, however. Nineteenth-century Paraguay produced José Gaspar Rodríguez de Francia, who styled himself *El Supremo* and shut his country off from the rest of the world for almost thirty years (White, 1978). More recently, the tiny African country of Equatorial Guinea had the misfortune to fall under the control of Francisco Macias, who brutalized and impoverished his nation while persecuting educated individuals (Decalo, 1988).

CASTRO Finally, our survey of totalitarian rulers points to Cuba's Fidel Castro, who has ruled since 1959 and is the world's longest-serving head of state. Although Castro has looked out for the welfare of his people, his regime conforms perfectly to Friedrich and Brzezinski's definition.[3]

EMERGENCE FROM A VACUUM We should note here that totalitarian states, whether ruled by madmen or shrewd dictators, grow out of periods of turmoil and societal chaos. It is as if the vacuum caused by breakdown opens the way to those who would exercise total control over their people. This suggests that societies that are able to function are poor targets for totalitarians.

Absolute Monarchies

Historically, most people have been ruled by monarchs. Some contemporary monarchies, like the British, Dutch, or Spanish, are constitutional, meaning that the monarch is subject to the law, like everyone else, and has very limited powers. The monarch is the symbolic leader of his or her country rather than having an active role in governing. However, some monarchies, such as Saudi Arabia's, are labelled absolute because the monarch has unlimited power. This was the sort of system that the French Revolution toppled in 1789. In fact, much of today's thinking about democratic government was first conceived to serve as an antidote to absolutism.

In absolute monarchies, political activity is severely constrained. Political parties are often prohibited, and there are no elections since government positions are filled by royal appointment. If there is a representative assembly it is more likely to be a council of nobles than an elected body that speaks for

[3] Some might argue that the nearly permanent presence of thousands of Canadian and European tourists in Cuba suggests that Castro's is not a totalitarian regime. However, both Hitler and Mussolini welcomed travellers, too, and, more to the point, although Castro lets visitors in, he does not let Cubans out.

the people. There is usually strict censorship and the liberties of those outside
the ruling circle are radically circumscribed.

Given those characteristics, it will not be a great surprise to learn that in
the twentieth century absolute monarchies were often victims of revolution.
This fate befell the Russian empire in 1917, the Ethiopian empire in 1974,
and the Iranian empire in 1979. However, in none of these cases was the
ensuing regime democratic. Rather, absolutism gave way to other forms of
dictatorship. It may be that making political activity illegal forces those who
want change into clandestine revolutionary movements. If successful, they
may use their tight, disciplined organizational structure to control the state.

Four Kinds of Dictatorships

There has never been a true democratic dictatorship because all dictatorships
vest power in the hands of a ruler who is not accountable to the mass of the
public. Dictatorships, like totalitarian regimes, often claim that they work on
behalf of the great majority of their citizens. However, these governments
would not put their hold on power to the test of an open and honest election.
Dictatorships can be built around one person or around an institution, such
as a party, the military, or a religious elite. In short, there are four kinds of
dictatorships: personal, party, military, and theocratic.

PERSONAL DICTATORSHIP
An undemocratic government
dominated by a single individual. Saddam Hussein's Iraq was
a classic example of this kind
of system.

PERSONAL DICTATORSHIPS Personal dictatorships are less easy to find
now, at the start of the twenty-first century, than they would have been even
two or three decades ago. They are distinguished by being dominated by a
single leader who rules far more according to personal preferences than by
following the law. Historically, personal dictators have always been men, but
there is no reason to suppose that women could not fill the role. The great
danger in this form of government is that, as in all dictatorships, there are no
institutional constraints on the leader, who leaves power only when he dies
or is driven out by armed force.

PARTY DICTATORSHIP
An undemocratic political system that is controlled by one
party. The most familiar examples are found in communist
political systems.

PARTY DICTATORSHIPS Party dictatorships are different in that political
life is controlled by a single party rather than a lone individual. In the most
unambiguous cases, only one party has the legal right to exist, or, if others do
exist, only one party is legally able to exercise power. Communist states have
provided the best-known party dictatorships, but they are not the only ones.
Besides the obvious instances of Mussolini's Italy and Hitler's Germany,
Portugal and Spain also had one-party dictatorships for extended periods in
the twentieth century. One-party states were also very common in Africa
from independence, usually in the 1960s, to the early 1990s. Rulers of these
African states generally justified their turn to one-party rule in terms of unifying the nation. They argued that the best way to build a strong nation out
of the many tribes that often coexisted uncomfortably within the borders of
their countries was to channel all political action through one party.

Although this is a logical premise, in practice, eliminating other parties led to dictatorship. Throughout history, most dictatorships of this sort have met violent ends, but since the 1970s more of them are negotiating the conditions of their demise with other political forces.

MILITARY DICTATORSHIPS In **military dictatorships**, the military obviously provides the rulers (Fitch, 1998; Janowitz, 1977). These systems are established in the wake of a military seizure of power, usually called a *coup d'état*. Sometimes military dictatorships are run by committees of a country's armed forces, known as military juntas. Most military regimes start with a junta but many them are quickly dominated by a single leader. When this happens the resulting government takes on some of the traits of a personal dictatorship, distinguishing itself mostly through giving the military special benefits. Unlike other dictatorships, however, military governments often leave power of their own volition. It is quite common for the military to oust a civilian government, rule for a few years, and then arrange elections for a new civilian government. Although the military frequently imposes restrictions on who may compete for power, the transition is at least peaceful.

MILITARY DICTATORSHIP
An undemocratic government run by the military.

"The people of this country are going to catch on to this thing called democracy... and if they don't we'll make them!"

THEOCRATIC DICTATORSHIP
Undemocratic state run by religious elites. The best contemporary example is Iran.

THEOCRATIC DICTATORSHIP A **theocratic dictatorship** is run by religious elites (theocracy is government in the name of God or by priests). Iran is the best current example of a theocratic state, although it is now substantially less dictatorial than it was at its founding in 1979 (see Box 19-2, Theocracy in Iran). Until overthrown in 2001 by U.S.-led forces that included Canada, the Taliban government in Afghanistan was the most extreme theocratic dictatorship of modern times. Basing its governing philosophy on

BOX 19-2

Theocracy in Iran

Iran's 70 million people have had very little experience with democracy. Only under the Mossadegh government, which ruled for only a few short days in 1953, was there a respite from authoritarianism.

Although the 1979 Iranian Revolution held out the promise of greater freedom after overthrowing the increasingly repressive and autocratic monarchy headed by the Shah, it soon instituted a theocratic system, an Islamic Republic, headed by the religious leader Ayatollah Ruhollah Khomeini. Best known in the West for its uncompromising application of law based on religious doctrine, Iran's political system has also relied on the country's armed forces, the Revolutionary Guards, to use force to assure compliance.

By 1997, however, there were signs that Iranians had had enough of strictly enforced religious principles. They elected Muhammad Khatami, a moderate cleric committed to reform, president of Iran. The reformers were fought at every turn by conservatives who supported a theocratic dictatorship, but the forces of change and moderation made significant gains. The Majlis (legislative) elections of 2000 produced a pro-reform majority and Khatami himself was re-elected in 2001 with a huge majority. A moderation of the radically religious regime seemed in the offing. However, although Khatami and his allies in Majlis had popular support, they were not Iran's ultimate authority. That power

rested in the hands of a religious leader, Ayatollah Ali Khameni, Iran's "Supreme Leader." The Supreme Leader is chosen by an elected, seventy-member Council of Experts, all of whom currently are clerics. Among his other roles, the Supreme Leader is commander-in-chief of the armed forces and the police, head of the state television and radio company, and the country's top jurist.

In 2003, university students led Iranians to the streets in a call for freedom and democracy. Their demonstrations were broken up not just by the police, but also by vigilantes who used clubs and chains. Then, in the run-up to legislative elections in 2003, the Guardian Council (a twelve-member chamber, half of whom are appointed by the Supreme Leader and half by the Majlis, with absolute veto powers) struck four thousand reformist candidates from the lists. The remaining reformers boycotted the vote. The conservative candidates, approved by the Guardian Council, won in a landslide.

In an authoritarian state, it is common and usually legal for elites to disregard the public's wishes. Such systems also use force with impunity when challenged by their citizens. That in cases like Iran the authorities believe that they are acting morally, indeed in accordance with the will of God, may only serve to strengthen their resolve and make movement toward more rights for more people even harder.

◀ Until overthrown in 2001 by U.S.-led forces that included Canada, the Taliban government in Afghanistan was the most extreme theocratic dictatorship of modern times.

a radical reading of the Koran, the Taliban was infamous for eliminating virtually all rights for women. Both the Iranian and Taliban regimes emerged when a preceding secular authoritarian state was overthrown.

Although Islam is the faith underlying today's theocracies, it is important to recall that other religions have been the basis for theocratic rule. North America produced one in the seventeenth-century Massachusetts Bay Colony, which was founded and run by the Puritans, a Protestant sect. As with any religious dictators, the Puritans declared that no one had the right to sin and were zealous in their pursuit of those who violated the colony's rigid moral codes (Parrington, 1987). Immigration and the establishment of religious tolerance in neighbouring colonies ended the Puritans' experiment. Thus, dictatorships based on religion can evolve into more democratic political systems.

Final Thoughts on Authoritarian Government

All the different kinds of non-democratic government that we now label authoritarian share two characteristics:

1. All of them give the right to determine what constitutes the common good to a restricted number of people. Thus, in authoritarian systems the common good is less what is good for everyone than what the rulers believe is good. (Skeptics will say that the same thing happens in democracies, because elites set the agenda there as well.)
2. In general, authoritarian governments are more likely to use coercion as a normal governing instrument than are democratic ones. There are good reasons for this. A government that is unelected and unaccountable does not fear the judgment of its citizens. Therefore, it does not need to

Rights and Democracy: International
Centre for Human Rights and
Democratic Development
www.ichrdd.ca

convince them that a given line of action is good for the country; it is enough to declare it so and punish those who object. In a democracy, persuasion and consultation are government's best and most useful tools. In an authoritarian state, although a government there can try to persuade its people, coercion is easier and more effective, at least in the short term.

We can sum up the differences between democratic and authoritarian governments in this way: Democracy aims to be rule *by* the people. Authoritarianism aims only to rule the people.

DEMOCRATIC TRANSITIONS

Any country that is now democratic has an undemocratic past. Even Canada and the United States, which along with Australia and New Zealand are the only countries never to have known authoritarian rule since they became independent, have all undeniably become far more democratic over the years, for example by eventually extending the right to vote to all citizens (see Box 19-3, Expanding Democracy in Canada).

BOX 19-3

Expanding Democracy in Canada

It is easy to take Canadian democracy for granted and assume that it has always been a part of this country's political life. Although it is true that Canada is one of the few countries in the world never to have suffered under a dictatorship, democracy, as it exists today, took time to develop. We can find evidence of this by looking at restrictions on the franchise, the right to vote (Elections Canada, 1997).

Until early in the twentieth century, Canada had a property franchise. This meant that those who did not own property worth a certain value or have an income of a specified level were unable to vote. Until the 1940s, some provinces restricted the rights of people of certain non-European ethnic backgrounds, especially Asians, even though the individuals were Canadian citizens. Women were denied the vote federally until 1918, and some

Aboriginals were not enfranchised until 1960. (For more details, see Chapter 4, especially Figure 4-1.)

More than voting rights have been extended. Before the 1960s, official bilingualism had a limited reach. It was only in that same decade that laws were adopted promoting and protecting women's rights. Aboriginal rights only arrived on the national agenda in the 1970s, and gay and lesbian rights did not become an important issue until the 1980s and 1990s.

Canada is not alone in expanding democratic rights slowly. All of the world's historic democracies have done the same. This should make us question whether we are right to expect countries just completing their transitions to democracy to offer the same array of rights and freedoms, and to have a similar roster of institutions that we find in Canada, Britain, or the United States.

Political science has always been interested in how political systems become democratic in the first instance and how they become even more democratic as their democracies mature. However, the democratic transitions of the 1970s and 1980s made political scientists take a fresh look at how democracies arise.

Democracy's Revival

Until the Portuguese revolution of April 25, 1974, the twentieth century had produced more cases of democracies failing and falling into authoritarian rule than vice versa.[4] Not only did the Depression of the 1930s take its toll, but also the flood of new states that accompanied decolonization from the late 1940s to the early 1960s produced only a handful of long-lasting democracies.[5] Then, in 1973, two of Latin America's most well established democracies, Chile and Uruguay, crumbled before military coups. In fact, the failure of democracies was so common that a number of political scientists collaborated to write a book entitled *The Breakdown of Democratic Regimes* (Linz & Stepan, 1978).

As far as democracy's prospects went, then, a sombre panorama confronted the world in the early 1970s. States that had suffered under non-democratic regimes for a long time, such as the Soviet Union, showed no signs of being able to shake them. The new states of Africa and Asia proved, on the whole, unable to sustain democratic rule for any more than brief periods. Although the historic heartlands of democracy—northwestern Europe, North America, Australia, New Zealand, Japan, and India—were in no danger,[6] it would have taken a brave political scientist to have predicted in the early 1970s that most of the world's countries would enjoy some form of democratic rule by century's end. Yet that is precisely what happened.

SHRUGGING OFF CHAINS   The first movement came from southern Europe as first Portugal, then Greece, and finally Spain shrugged off the chains of dictatorship between 1974 and 1978. Next, the venue shifted to Latin America, where throughout the 1980s military dictatorships gave way to electoral democracies. In Asia, both South Korea and the Republic of China (Taiwan) joined the democratic procession. Even in Africa, a bastion of dictatorships of all sorts since the end of colonial rule in the 1960s, countries began to abandon authoritarian ways.

---

[4] We must note, however, that many of the failed democracies collapsed only after having been invaded by Nazi Germany during World War II.

[5] Before 1974, only India, Botswana, and Sri Lanka had managed to maintain democratic government continuously since independence.

[6] Even in the historic, well-established democracies, some authors spoke of a "crisis of democracy" (Huntington, Crozier, & Watanuki, 1975).

The big story, however, was the fall of communism in Europe,[7] first in the former satellites at the end of the 1980s and then in the Soviet Union itself, which ceased to exist at the end of 1991. Although some dictatorships have yielded to democratic rules since the early 1990s, most notably Indonesia in 1998, the great Third Wave of democratic change seems to have drawn to a momentary close. There are still some very important countries that are not democracies—the People's Republic of China, Cuba, Iran, Syria, and Saudi Arabia—and, as we shall see later in this chapter, there are countries that have reverted to less democratic ways. Nevertheless, the world is far more democratic early in the twenty-first century than it was forty or fifty years earlier. In fact, it is fair to describe the last quarter of the twentieth century as the era of democratic transitions.

At the start of this chapter, we defined democratic transitions as the move from an authoritarian government of any kind to a democracy. While that is a handy definition, it leaves two questions unanswered. First, why did the old regimes fail? They were, after all, authoritarians who had once repressed dissidents without a second thought. Second, how did the transitions occur—was there a recipe for democratic transition?

The Failure of Authoritarianism

It is sometimes hard for people who know only democratic politics to imagine an authoritarian system failing. After all, these governments worry about neither losing elections nor keeping their citizens happy. A substantial number of them had been working smoothly for many years. There are two obvious explanations for why the clock should run out on so many nondemocratic states at the same time: inability to manage an increasingly complex economy, and pressures, domestic and international, to open closed political systems. Looking at a few examples will explain how and why this occurred.

Managing the national economy well is important for any government, but for many years it was not seen as having any relation to democracy. In fact, commentators often asked if democracy harmed a country's economic health by putting political concerns ahead of purely economic ones or even suggested that rapid economic growth and development were incompatible with democratic government (Bhardwaj & Vijaykrishnan, 1998; Leftwich, 1996; Organski, 1967).[8]

---

[7] This also marked the fall of communism in Mongolia, which was closely allied to the Soviet Union.

[8] Those who argue that democracy impedes economic development assert that development demands sacrifices and that democracies are not very good at forcing people to make sacrifices. There is now a growing body of research to suggest that this argument is ill founded (Remmer, 1996).

By the 1980s, however, several forces pushed toward democracy. First, growing globalization demanded more open economies that could not be controlled by authoritarian governments. Thus, governments had to choose between being shut out of the global economy or adopting policies that were better managed by democracies.

Second, most authoritarian states were failing to produce good economic results by that date. Even though some authoritarian governments had presided over rapid growth in the past, by the last quarter of the twentieth century many, though not all, were facing economic hardship.

Finally, many international economic organizations were demanding democratic political systems either as a condition for entry, as with the European Union, or as a qualification for continued eligibility for loans to reconstruct battered economies, which was the case with international financial institutions such as the International Monetary Fund.

EXTERNAL PRESSURE   External pressure for political change came not just from international lenders. During the Cold War between the West and the Soviet Bloc, the world's democracies would accept any government that was anti-communist, but the West began to push other countries to get on the democratic track as signs of reform emerged in the Soviet Union in the late 1980s. For example, in 1988 Chile's military dictatorship organized a plebiscite to see if the public wished to extend the government's mandate or preferred returning to the democracy they had lost in 1973. The United States government, which had once supported the dictatorship, changed sides and began to work on behalf of those seeking a return to democracy, principally in the form of financial aid to assure "a level playing field" (Sater, 1990; Sigmund, 1993).

Despite this dramatic shift in outlook and behaviour, there are still instances where democracies, such as Canada or the United States, support authoritarian governments for strategic reasons related to fighting international terrorism. What is important is that such cases are less common than before.

Bringing About Democratic Transition

Political science has charted two routes that people can take to bring about a democratic transition in their countries. One stresses the role of elites working from the top down (Di Palma, 1990). These are called **pacted transitions** because they are produced by pacts or agreements among elites that permit the establishment of democratic government. This form of transition was the norm in Latin American and Southern Europe.

The other route for democratic transition stresses the role of mobilized citizens forming a movement to overthrow authoritarian rule and build democracy. This was the route that was generally followed in the formerly communist-ruled countries of Eastern and Central Europe (Bunce, 2003).

PACTED TRANSITION
A democratic transition that occurs when pacts or agreements among the elites of formerly undemocratic states permit the establishment of democratic government.

Once the elites have agreed to proceed to democracy or the mass of citizens have proceeded there regardless of the wishes of the governing elite, democratic transitions are mostly about elections. The central event in a transition is the **transitional election**, which marks the official beginning of a democratic regime. It is their character as cornerstones for an entirely new system that gives these elections such importance and makes it imperative to get them right.

Elections raise technical concerns, such as the matters of assuring a quick and honest count of the vote, guaranteeing all serious candidates some minimum of media time so voters can find out about them, and ensuring that the people who run the polling stations are non-partisan and are trained to do their jobs. Once this initial election has been held, the transition is over.

In essence, democracy is equated with holding elections, a notion that can be traced back to Joseph Schumpeter (1950). Obviously, these elections have to be fair and open, and are often observed by foreign organizations to assess whether the vote was really free and the results represented the people's will (Montgomery 2000). However, even with these provisions, treating elections as the principal condition a country must meet to be called a democracy is problematic. First, elections exist outside democracies. This is true historically and it also applies even today to dictatorships that stage sham elections. Second, there are other parts of a political system that are equally essential to building a democracy, including the institutions that administer justice and a political culture that encourages effective participation.

CONSTRAINED DEMOCRACY   A system featuring free and competitive elections can coexist with a very thin and constrained example of democracy. Even after broadening the concept of transition to include a democratic constitution and institutions such as a representative legislature, transition is still bones with no flesh. The institutions that form democracy's skeleton are there but the outcomes and practices that are democracy's muscle are not yet evident. As with any **procedural definition of democracy**, concentrating on institutions can lead to ignoring the results those institutions produce.

Instead of focusing on the transitional election, the transition to democracy may be thought of as consisting of a series of steps (Carothers, 2002):

1. An opening when an authoritarian regimes shows weakness.
2. A breakthrough when the authoritarian regime collapses.
3. The transitional election, which is the first experience with democratic politics.
4. Consolidation when democracy becomes widely accepted within the country.

DEMOCRATIC CONSOLIDATION

There is no doubt that some democratic systems are so securely anchored and deeply embedded in their societies that it is scarcely possible to think of any

---

TRANSITIONAL ELECTION
An election that marks the official beginning of a democratic regime.

Institute for Democracy and Electoral Assistance
www.idea.int

PROCEDURAL DEFINITION OF DEMOCRACY
A definition of democracy in terms of procedures and institutions (such as elections) rather than outcomes.

other form of government existing. At least equally important, consolidated democracies can extend democracy's reach by, for example, increasing opportunities for participation by the people in decision making. Canada fits this description, as does the United Kingdom and many others. That knowledge, however, does not make the concept easy to define precisely; and it is even harder to measure accurately. However, if consolidation is the endpoint of any democratic transition, having a sure grasp on the concept is critical (see Box 19-4, Democratic Consolidation).

Green and Luehrmann (2003) offer a useful framework for thinking about consolidation. They suggest adding another phase to the sequence of democratic change mentioned earlier. Specifically, these political scientists

BOX 19-4

Democratic Consolidation

Democratic consolidation is a complex phenomenon.

To be able to study it effectively and understand its workings correctly, we look for indicators—something that we treat as reflecting or revealing the presence of what we want to study. Perhaps the best indicator of democratic consolidation is persistence. A country that has maintained over a substantial time a series of the characteristics that most people agree are necessary for democracy would be deemed consolidated.

There are two problems here, however—deciding how long is long enough, and deciding what goes into the list of essential characteristics. We can propose any number of them: for example, the absence of a significant oppositional force opposed to democracy, or high popular support for democratic institutions as reflected in public opinion polls. However, there will always be debate about the appropriateness of the criteria that we use to measure democracy, as well as concerns about how hard it might be to collect the data we would need. Not all democratic countries produce the kind of information that we want.

This has led political scientists to propose an electoral turnover guideline. Thus, a democracy would be deemed consolidated when the governing party lost an election and turned over power to an opponent. This has the virtues of being easy to understand and having readily available data on which to make a decision. If it were thought that one turnover was insufficient, making the rule two changes of governing party is easy to do.

Unfortunately, reality is occasionally too complicated for this rule. For example, Botswana, generally considered the most robust democracy in Africa, has been governed by the Botswana Democratic Party since independence in 1966. And we know that in Canada, provincial political parties can have very long uninterrupted runs in office, like the Ontario Conservatives' forty-two-year stretch from 1943 to 1985, but we do not believe that this imperils any province's claim to being democratic. So, while the electoral turnover rule is a good preliminary indicator of democratic consolidation, we must apply it carefully and be attentive to idiosyncrasies that could lead us to make erroneous conclusions.

believe that transition is a two-step process that is complete only when "all politically significant groups agree to abide by the procedural rules of the game (and)... no politically significant groups are trying to overthrow the democratic regime" (p. 309). This implies that democracy is broadly accepted as not just a good way of conducting public affairs, but as the only legitimate and acceptable way to govern. Once a country has reached this point, its citizens will defend the democratic system even when their government faces grave economic or political problems. There are no solutions outside democratic institutions and values in a consolidated democracy.

Yet even adding this helpful step leaves two important questions. The first of these is whether all transitions produce consolidated democracies. In other words, is consolidation the automatic and guaranteed outcome of a democratic transition? The second question is the logical counterpart of the first: Can a transition stop somewhere short of full democracy? For example, a country may have free and fair elections and all significant political actors may accept that elections are the only conceivable way to gain power. Once in power, though, a government may pack the civil service and courts with its followers or amend laws to make corruption harder to punish or try to rig the system to give it and its supporters permanent legal advantages. These systems show enough signs of democracy that we would hesitate to call them authoritarian—indeed, somewhat similar systems existed in Canada and the United States in the nineteenth and early twentieth centuries—but the system still seems to fall short of what we instinctively believe that a consolidated democracy should be.

If this were only a question of semantics or deciding which country goes into which pigeonhole, it would be unimportant. Unfortunately, there are numerous cases of democratic transitions stalling and leaving countries with political systems that have important non-democratic traits. Political science has to take this reality into account if it is to help people understand the political world around them.

Partial or Imperfect Democracy

By one set of standards, limited or imperfect democracies should not be counted as consolidated democracies. There are too many points of divergence between our views of what a democracy should do and how some supposedly democratic governments behave. However, if the country is more democratic than it was before, giving people more freedom and equality, and if the institutional and procedural arrangements it has in place look set to last for some years, then it should either join the ranks of consolidated democracies or political scientists should change how they think about democratic consolidation. The latter view has come to predominate and has led to the classification of several varieties of imperfect democracies.

◀ Thin democracy? In Guatemala, democracy depends on the backing of the military.

THIN DEMOCRACY   Countries where the democratic transition stalled before taking full effect constitute one class of imperfect democracy. Ronaldo Munck (1997) uses the term "thin democracy" to characterize democracy in Argentina in the 1990s. Although the country seemed to have put a long history of military dictatorships behind it, Munck feared that democracy still did not penetrate all areas of the country's political life. Gill, Rocamora, and Wilson (1993) talk about "low-intensity democracies" whose existence depends on the real but extra-official backing of the military. Guatemala has exemplified this kind of system since abandoning direct military rule in 1986.

DELEGATIVE DEMOCRACY   A second class of imperfect democracy is made up of countries where democratic achievements have been reversed, although not entirely obliterated. Guillermo O'Donnell (1994), an Argentine-born political scientist who now lives in the United States, coined the phrase "delegative democracy" to fit one set of these cases.

These delegative democracies have competitive elections, wide-ranging political opposition, free media, and functioning legislatures and courts. What they do not have is any serious control over their president or prime minister between elections. They are governed by a boss who has as free a hand as the boss dares to use.

In particular, when faced with a crisis, leaders in a delegative democracy will typically assume great powers to deal with the crisis. Although the same can occur in consolidated democracies, in a delegative democracy the leader is likely to continue to wield the added powers even after the crisis has passed. Delegative democracies in effect adapt the pattern of one-person, unaccountable rule found in authoritarian states to the requirements of a democratic constitution.

The Failure to Consolidate Democracy

Governments do not always seek to extend or perfect democracy. They may be unwilling to go beyond a limited form of democracy either to retain power or because extending and consolidating democracy could bring the government into conflict with powerful interests who prefer a less democratic government to a more democratic one, leading government to "undo democracy" (Box 19-5, Undoing Democracy). Indeed, both motives could be at work. What this suggests is that the sequence of events leading from the first tremors of a dictatorship to having an unshakably solid democracy is less certain than observers and analysts once thought.

Democracy Promotion and Democratic Strengthening

To maximize the chances that a country embarking on a democratic transition actually emerges as a consolidated democracy, a number of already consolidated, stable democracies have added a democracy promotion or

BOX 19-5

Undoing Democracy

Governments can consciously work to make democracy more imperfect.*

They do this by removing some of the impediments that democracy puts in the way of easy administration, thus letting them rule with less accountability and fewer restraints. It may seem odd that a democratically elected government should want to limit democracy, but there is a logic at work here. Governing is hard work and democracy makes it even harder. In a democracy the government should be honest and transparent, and even encourage citizens to take a hand in running things. Worst of all, in democracies governments have no job security. Ungrateful electors can turn them out in any election.

In poor countries with weak economies, where government is often the best road to riches, loss of power is a daunting possibility. So too, however, are accountability and having to tolerate a free and active opposition and media that believe they

should investigate what government does. It is no surprise, then, that a government may feel compelled to remove the constraints that democracy puts on its operations. With a little luck, and perhaps more than a little money, a government can simply ignore the rules. In some cases, however, it may believe that it has to change those rules.

There is one bit of good news, though. Whereas in the past governments that felt hemmed in by democracy simply abolished it and established dictatorships, today they seem more inclined just to weaken it so that it does not work as intended. They probably do so because many foreign aid agencies and international organizations will not deal with dictatorships. Whatever the reason, leaving at least the outward forms of democracy in place leaves a foundation on which some future government that is actually committed to democracy can build.

*This argument is developed more fully by David Close (2004).

democratic strengthening element to their foreign policies. In this endeavour they have been joined by some non-governmental organizations (NGOs) and several international organizations. The work has been underway since the early 1980s and shows little sign of stopping.

Thomas Carothers, one of the world's leading experts on democracy promotion, argues that there is a "democracy template" (Table 19-2) that embodies the "core strategy" of democratic strengthening (1999, pp. 86–88).[9] Translated into practice, this means focusing on the electoral process, state institutions, and civil society. The United States is the most active proponent of democracy promotion, followed by Germany, the United Kingdom, the Scandinavian states, the Netherlands, and Canada.

Among the countries that are important sources of economic aid, only Japan does not have a significant democracy promotion program (Perlin, 2003). Overall, these states, plus international organizations like the United Nations Development Programme and the World Bank, and non-

National Endowment for Democracy
www.ned.org

United Nations Development Program
www.undp.org

TABLE 19-2
THE DEMOCRACY TEMPLATE

SECTOR	SECTOR GOAL	TYPE OF AID
Electoral process	Free and fair elections	Electoral aid
	Strong national political parties	Political party building
State institutions	Democratic constitution	Constitutional assistance
	Independent effective judiciary and other law-oriented institutions	Rule-of-law aid
	Competent, representative legislature	Legislative strengthening
	Responsive local government	Local government development
	Prodemocratic military	Civil-military relations
Civil society	Active advocacy non-governmental organizations (NGOs)	NGO building
	Politically educated citizenry	Civic education
	Strong independent media	Media strengthening
	Strong independent unions	Union building

SOURCE: *T. Carothers, Aiding Democracy Abroad: The Learning Curve (Washington, D.C.: Carnegie Endowment for International Peace), p.88.*

---

[9] Perlin offers a slightly different and somewhat broader list of what he calls "the objectives of political aid" (2003, p. 9): good governance; human rights; democratization; and civil society.

governmental organizations such as George Soros's Open Society Foundation, dedicate about US$3 billion to democracy promotion every year. Is this money well spent?

According to Carothers (2002), at least in the case of the United States, funds for democracy promotion are not well spent. He believes that democracy promotion has fallen prey to a one-size-fits-all outlook that counts on all countries' following the same steps and using the same institutions as they move toward democracy. Going beyond Carothers's critique, the very concept of democracy promotion raises difficult questions. Although it seems obvious that external aid to countries that are building democratic institutions and outlooks is welcome and useful, it seems equally obvious that democracy will take different forms in different countries. Canada has different governmental institutions, political values, and processes than does the United States. If two of the oldest and surest democracies in the world can go about being democracies in quite different ways, why should new and struggling governments not be allowed to seek their own paths? Similarly, it is useful to ask if democracy promoters give new democracies enough time to get their institutions right and to allow a democratic political culture to mature.

A DEMOCRATIC FUTURE?

Currently, all forms of dictatorship and other examples of non-democratic rule are in at least momentary decline. Does this mean that all the world's countries will have at least openly elected governments, the minimal requirement for democracy, in the near future? At least one analyst thinks so.

Francis Fukuyama, a political scientist who worked as an analyst for the United States' Department of State (foreign affairs), argued in 1989 that liberal democracy had proven its superiority and would soon be universally accepted (Fukuyama, 1989, 1992). He based his conclusion on an analysis of key trends, notably globalization and the crisis of European communism, that were becoming evident.

Fukuyama's thesis sparked lively debate. Some argued that the norms of liberal democracy clash with Asian values, which place greater weight on duty and on the family rather than freedom and the individual. Others felt that Fukuyama was too quick to declare the liberal version of democracy the winner, believing that a democracy that emphasized substantive outputs that contributed to the material well-being of the citizenry over procedural inputs still was still a viable option.

But it was likely the terrorist attacks on the United States on September 11, 2001, that most grievously undermined the hope that all of the world's peoples would soon live under democracies. Not only did some people prefer a theocracy, or at least reject liberal democratic values that they associated with the West, but they were ready to take extreme measures to make their preferences clear.

Summary and Conclusion

Canadians generally hope that democracy becomes the most widespread form of government in the world. Democracy is often viewed as the best way to seek to enshrine the common good because only democracy is committed to giving every man and woman a voice in saying how they should be governed and by whom. Thus, as more countries develop democratic political systems, more people will contribute to defining the common good and the policies that governments enact will be more likely to work toward the common good of their countries.

Nevertheless, it is doubtless too soon to talk about democracy as a universal aspect of politics. A wiser approach would be to lower our sights a little. Doing so will show us that a greater proportion of Earth's population lives under democracy in this first decade of the twenty-first century than ever before in human history. That should please all democrats, even if nothing less than universal democracy will satisfy them.

Key Terms

Democratic consolidation 428

Military dictatorship 433

Pacted transition 439

Party dictatorship 432

Personal dictatorship 432

Procedural definition of democracy 440

Theocratic dictatorship 434

Third Wave of Democracy 427

Transitional election 440

Discussion Questions

1. Do you think that most countries will become democratic in the next few decades?
2. What obstacles stand in the way of the democratic transition and consolidation processes?
3. Is totalitarianism likely to reappear as a significant type of political system?
4. Should the promotion of democracy be a leading feature of Canada's foreign policy? Should Canada provide aid only to democratic countries or those moving towards democracy?

Further Reading

Brooker, P. *Non-democratic regimes: Theory, government and politics*. New York: St. Martin's Press, 2000.

Collier, D. (Ed.). *The new authoritarianism in Latin America*. Princeton: Princeton University Press, 1979.

Diamond, L. *Developing democracy: Toward consolidation*. Baltimore, MD: Johns Hopkins University Press, 1999.

Diamond, L., & Plattner, M. (Eds.). *The global divergence of democracies*. Baltimore, MD: Johns Hopkins University Press, 2001.

Gregor, A.J. *Contemporary radical ideologies: Totalitarian thought in the twentieth century*. New York: Random House, 1968.

Journal of Democracy, 1990–.

O'Donnell, G. *Counterpoints: Selected essays in authoritarianism and democratization*. Notre Dame, IN: Notre Dame University Press, 1999.

O'Donnell, G. "Democracy, law, and comparative politics." *Studies in Comparative International Development, 36*(1), 7–36 [2001].

O'Donnell, G., Schmitter, P., & Whitehead, L. (Eds.). *Transitions from authoritarian rule*. Baltimore, MD: Johns Hopkins University Press, 1986.

Pinkney, R. *Democracy in the Third World*. Boulder, CO: Lynne Rienner, 2003.

Przeworski, A., with P. Bardhan, et al., *Sustainable democracy*. New York: Cambridge University Press, 1995.

Reuschmeyer, D., Stephens, E., & Stephens, J. *Capitalist development and democracy*. Chicago: University of Chicago Press, 1992.

Signs read: "TAKE A STAND FOR NEWFOUNDLAND", "for the World!", "DE MASIADO", "F.F.A.W. SUPPORTS Tobin", "Conserve Fish Stocks For ALL", "Brian For Hanging Tough", "THIS IS A WORLD Fishery NOT A SPANISH ONE."

Chapter 20

POLITICS AND GOVERNANCE AT THE GLOBAL LEVEL

PHOTO ABOVE: The international conflict known as the turbot war broke out in March 1995. The Canadian coast guard seized the Spanish trawler *Estai* on the Grand Banks off Newfoundland, accusing it of contravening measures to conserve fish stocks.

CHAPTER OBJECTIVES

After reading this chapter, you should be able to:

1. discuss the differences between national politics and international politics
2. explain the differences between the realist and the liberal–internationalist approach to the study of international politics
3. apply the realist and the liberal–internationalist approaches to contemporary issues
4. assess the chances of international peace and the possibilities of order and governance at the international level

The international conflict known as the turbot war broke out on March 9, 1995, when the Canadian coast guard seized a Spanish trawler, the *Estai*, on the Grand Banks off Newfoundland, accusing it of contravening measures to conserve fish stocks. The Grand Banks used to be one of the richest and most popular fishing grounds in the world. By the 1970s, it became clear that unless rigorous fisheries conservation measures were adopted, its fish stocks would collapse. On January 1, 1977, Canada declared a 200-mile (320-kilometre) exclusive economic zone and imposed strict controls on fishing inside the zone. However, about 10 percent of the Grand Banks, known as the Nose and Tail, are beyond Canada's limit.

In 1979, the conservation of the fish stocks outside the 200-mile limit became the responsibility of an international organization, the Northwest Atlantic Fisheries Organization (NAFO). In February 1995, it announced its allocation decision for the total allowable catch (TAC) for turbot for 1995, with a breakdown for Canada, the European Union (EU), and other countries that left the EU dissatisfied. The EU unilaterally set itself a higher quota.

In part because of NAFO's inability to enforce its own quotas and conservation measures, Canada decided to act in defence of its interests. In May 1994, following the collapse of the cod stocks and the consequent adoption of a moratorium, the Canadian government decided to search, and if necessary seize, any foreign vessels using flags of convenience suspected of fishing in violation of conservation measures. Following the EU decision to set its own quota for turbot, the Canadian government reacted by suggesting a turbot fishing moratorium of sixty days and, at the same time, added Spain and Portugal to the list of states whose ships could be searched and seized.

But the EU refused to impose the moratorium. On March 9, 1995, the Canadian government seized the *Estai* in international waters and accused it of fishing with nets smaller than those permitted under conservation measures and of purposely misreporting its fish landings. The Spanish government brought a case against Canada before the International Court of Justice (ICJ) in The Hague, accusing it of piracy. Eventually, Canada dropped its charges and the ICJ decided not to act on Spain's request.

The turbot war exemplifies the predicament in which states find themselves in international politics, namely whether to entrust the defence of their interests to a weak international legal regime administered by international organizations with very limited enforcement abilities or rely on themselves, which might at times require the use of force. This chapter examines politics at the international level, first pointing out the major differences between national and international politics and then illustrating the differences between the two main approaches to the study of international politics, namely the realist and the liberal–internationalist approaches.

INTERNATIONAL POLITICS AND GOVERNANCE

There is a major difference between national politics (politics within one state) and international politics (politics at the world level). States are entities composed of a population, a government, and a territory. They are sovereign, meaning that their governments have the final authority to make and enforce rules on the population living within their territorial boundaries. The world as a whole does not have such a central authority. There is, in other words, no world government; states live in an **anarchic** world.

All this means that the organization of authority within the world is horizontal rather than vertical (that is, hierarchical), as within a state. The world has as many authorities as there are sovereign states—about two hundred. But the fact that the world is anarchic does not mean that there are no rules in relations among states. Rules do exist. They are based on customary practices that have been codified into law. They are also the result of agreements negotiated and signed by states directly (international treaties) or negotiated and agreed upon within the framework of international governmental organizations, which are associations of sovereign states, created to facilitate cooperation among them in specific issue areas. International rules also derive from interpretations of existing international law provided by the courts.

Because the world is anarchic, though, there is no certain mechanism to enforce international rules. An individual that breaks the law within a state will, more often than not, be apprehended by police, be tried in a court of law, and, if found guilty, be punished. A state that chooses to ignore international rules either because it interprets them in a different way than other states, or simply because it is in its interest to do so will, more often than not, escape punishment. Individuals cannot claim that certain rules do not apply to them or refuse to appear in court if summoned. A state can refuse to be bound by some rules by choosing not to be part of the treaty establishing them. A state may also refuse to submit to a court when accused of violating international law. The International Court of Justice (ICJ), which has the task of settling disputes among states in accordance with international law, has no compulsory jurisdiction. This means that the ICJ cannot summon a state to appear before its fifteen judges who sit in The Hague in the Netherlands unless that state voluntarily agrees to recognize the jurisdiction of the court and submit itself to its judgment.

So although the world does not have a supranational government, it can be said to have **international governance**, which can be defined as the process whereby a number of different actors compete and cooperate in sharing the task of providing a certain degree of order and predictability to international relations.

All scholars of international relations agree in defining the world as anarchic (that is, lacking a central authority). They also agree in recognizing that anarchy notwithstanding, a certain degree of governance exists. When it

ANARCHY
A situation in which there is no central authority.

International Court of Justice
www.icj-cij.org

INTERNATIONAL GOVERNANCE
The process whereby a number of different actors compete and cooperate in sharing the task of providing a certain degree of order and predictability to international relations.

comes to assessing the significance of anarchy, identifying its consequences, and making policy suggestions however, scholars divide themselves into a number of different schools. Each one starts from different assumptions, adopts a different theoretical approach, and ends up making different policy recommendations. This chapter focuses on the two major schools—realism and liberal–internationalism.[1]

REALISM

The realist school assumes that since the world is anarchic, states find themselves in the same predicament as that of individuals in the state of nature imagined by English philosopher Thomas Hobbes (1588–1679). According to Hobbes, life in the state of nature is "solitary, poor, nasty, brutish, and short" (1651/1968, p. 186). Individuals have to fend for themselves in this competitive and dangerous environment.

REALISM also assumes that the main objective of states is their own survival, understood as the defence of their territorial borders and the protection of their population from external threats. This objective is the core of what is usually called the **national interest**, which realists view as the form of the common good that governments pursue when conducting foreign policy—that is, when acting in relation to other states or actors outside their national territories.

For realists, the pursuit of the national interest is a central and constant feature of the foreign policy of any state, regardless of changes of governments or political leaders. So, at least in regard to national security policy, realists regard each state as a unitary actor that makes decisions as if it were a single person, even if decisions are made by different individuals and institutions acting on behalf of the state.

If states can rely only on themselves for their security, it follows that they must seek to preserve and accumulate their power. Power, the ability of a state to get its way in the international arena when its interests or preferences clash with those of other states, derives from a variety of resources or capabilities. These may be tangible and measurable, such as economic and military resources, or intangible and unquantifiable, such as ideological and cultural resources. The first type of resources or capabilities provide what is referred to as hard power; the second is referred to as soft power. Both are important.

Since all states are sovereign, they are equal from a legal point of view. Equal in law, however, does not mean equal in fact. Some states have more

REALISM
The view that because the international system based on sovereign states is anarchic, security is the major preoccupation of states. Peace depends on deterrence, and the possibility of international governance is limited because of the importance of state sovereignty.

NATIONAL INTEREST
The goals that a state pursues to maximize what is perceived to be in its best interest.

---

[1] There are also important feminist, Marxist, and constructivist perspectives on international relations. See, for example, Enloe(1989), Sylvester (1994), Wallerstein (1974–1980), and Wendt (1999).

power than others. This means, as first pointed out by the Greek historian Thucydides some two thousand four hundred years ago, that "the strong do what they have the power to do and the weak accept what they have to accept" (quoted in Goldstein, 1994, p. 48). According to the realist school,[2] a world divided into sovereign states constitutes an **international system**. How power is distributed among states affects the way the system works, that is, how states relate to one another in it (see Box 20-1, Power Distribution at the Pub).

INTERNATIONAL SYSTEM
The relationship among states and international governmental organizations.

BOX 20-1
Power Distribution at the Pub

A university class—a group of students and their lecturer—can be regarded as a type of system. Its components or units are individuals, and when they move out of their normal environment, say to adjourn at the end of class to a local pub, the distribution of power among them will change.

When the class meets in a classroom, power is concentrated in one individual, the lecturer, while the students are in a subordinate position. When they continue their discussion over a drink at the pub, their behaviour will change. Most likely it will be much less formal and predictable than in the classroom.

In a classroom, the lecturer will speak most of the time and occasionally call upon students who signal their desire to speak. While some students will be listening attentively, others will be letting their minds wander. In the pub, the lecturer will no

longer shape the interaction between himself or herself and the students and among the students themselves. Some students might continue debating the topic that occupied them in class, but they will be more willing to express their views and will not ask formal permission from the lecturer to intervene in the conversation. Others will strike up side conversations, maybe on a different topic.

It is because the distribution of power among them has changed that the behaviour of the components of the system changes. Outside the classroom, power is no longer concentrated in one individual, the lecturer, but is equally distributed among all components of the system—students and lecturer. In the pub, the lecturer no longer has any authority over students and consequently their behaviour is no longer constrained in the same way as in the classroom.

---

[2] To be more precise, one should make a distinction between two trends within the realist school. Traditional realism looked at the behaviour of states in the international system the way Hobbes speculated about the behaviour of individuals in a state of nature. The most representative work of this phase is Morgenthau (1948). A more recent group of realists, usually called neo-realists, have concentrated on examining the dynamics of different types of international systems and their impact on the behaviour of states. The most representative work is Waltz (1979).

The modern international system dates from the Treaty of Westphalia of 1648, and so it is sometimes referred to as the Westphalian system. The treaty put an end to the so-called wars of religion that had devastated Europe since the Protestant Reformation of 1517. Even more importantly, it recognized and incorporated the concept of state sovereignty, which had been developed by the French jurist Jean Bodin (1503–1596). Since then, states have been the major units of the system and the concept of sovereignty has been the main principle regulating their interactions. The distribution of power among the states in the system has changed, and with it the system and the behaviour of states in it.

We recognize different types of international systems based on how power is distributed among states. Because each concentration of power is called a **pole**, we talk about multipolar, bipolar, and unipolar international systems (see Figure 20-1).

POLE

A concentration of power in the international system. It could be a state or an alliance.

FIGURE 20-1

TYPES OF INTERNATIONAL SYSTEMS

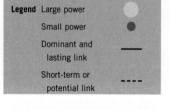

Legend	Large power	
	Small power	
	Dominant and lasting link	
	Short-term or potential link	----

Unipolarity

One superpower has a dominant or hegemonic position in the system.

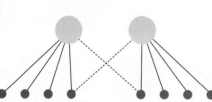

Bipolarity

Two superpowers have a number of allies or satellites (made up of lesser powers). This was the type of international system during the Cold War.

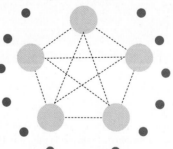

Multipolarity

Four or more great powers compete and cooperate with one another to make sure that none of them emerges as a superpower. Smaller powers do not play a significant role.

SOURCE: Adapted from *International Politics on the World Stage* (9th ed.) (p. 65), by J.T. Rourke, 2003, Boston: McGraw-Hill.

Multipolarity

From the Treaty of Westphalia until the beginning of the twentieth century, the international system was **multipolar**, meaning that it contained four or more major poles.

A multipolar system pushes states to maintain what is called a **balance of power**—that is, to behave in such a way as to prevent the emergence of a dominant power. On the one hand, a state must try to increase its power in order to guarantee its security. On the other hand, it must be careful not to be perceived by other states as representing a threat to them because in such a case it would eventually face a confrontation with them. States thus face what is called a **security dilemma**: they need power to feel secure, but the accumulation of power might undermine rather than increase their security if it leads other states to feel in danger and form an alliance to meet the perceived threat.

Power, in fact, can be augmented not only through an increase in capabilities, but also through the formation of alliances. Indeed, in a multipolar system, the formation of alliances plays a key role in the maintenance of a balance of power (see Box 20-2, Anatomy of an Alliance).

MULTIPOLAR SYSTEM
An international system containing four or more major powers.

BALANCE OF POWER
A situation in which no state is dominant in the global system.

SECURITY DILEMMA
The dilemma that arises when states need power to feel secure, but their accumulation of power might undermine rather than increase their security if it leads other states to feel in danger and form an alliance to meet the perceived threat.

Bipolarity

Occasionally, the distribution of power in the system changes. This may occur when some states are unable to continue producing the power resources and capabilities needed to sustain their position in the international system, or when there are changes in technology such as the development of the nuclear bomb. At the end of World War II, the international system

BOX 20-2
Anatomy of an Alliance

Alliances in the realist perspective are not based on friendship or a commonality of ideology or views but on interest. Alliances are formed, in other words, whenever needed to meet a common threat. There are two main characteristics of alliances:

1. To be effective as a mechanism to balance power, they must not be permanent but be able to shift according to needs.

2. If war becomes necessary to prevent one state from becoming dominant, alliances ensure that the defeated state is not eliminated from the map, but simply cut to size and reinstated in the system. This is, for instance, how European powers dealt with France after they had defeated Napoleon at the beginning of the nineteenth century.

BIPOLARITY

A system in which two super-powers compete with one another. The other states in the system fall within the sphere of influence of one or the other of the two superpowers.

became **bipolar**. The United States and the Soviet Union emerged as rival superpowers, so called because of their formidable nuclear arsenals, which no other country could match.

Their rivalry might have been compounded by the differences in their economic and political regimes—the U.S. was a liberal democracy with a free-market economy whereas the Soviets had a communist dictatorship with a command economy (an economy under the total control of the state). Realists, however, argue that in a bipolar system, the two superpowers were bound to compete with one another. The other states in the system will fall within the sphere of influence of one or the other of the two superpowers, and thus two opposing blocs will be formed. Some states might be able to remain non-aligned, but competition between the two superpowers and their respective blocs will be the dominant issue in a bipolar system and overshadow all others. Each superpower will try to keep the other in check, and at the same time try to increase its own power. They will also try to recruit new members to their respective bloc, while trying to prevent others from joining the rival one.

In the past, the rivalries between Sparta and Athens in the ancient Greek city-state system and between Rome and Carthage ended in a direct military

▶ At the end of World War II, the international system became bipolar. The U.S. and the Soviet Union emerged as rival super-powers: no other country could match their formidable arsenals. With the economic collapse of the Soviet Union, the U.S. became the sole superpower and the system transformed from bipolar to unipolar.

confrontation and the defeat or even destruction of one of the two rivals. This was not the case with the confrontation between the Americans and the Soviets, which is why the period between 1946 and 1989 is known as the Cold War. Realists would argue that the reason why the two superpowers did not clash militarily was the presence of nuclear weapons. As Robert Oppenheimer, one of the scientists who worked on the development of the atomic bomb in the U.S. put it, the two superpowers were like two scorpions in a bottle—if one attacked the other, it must do so at the price of its own destruction (Oppenheimer, 1953, p. 529). While avoiding direct military confrontation, however, the two superpowers did fight each other by proxy. Military confrontation took place between two of their client states or even within one state they were both trying to bring to their respective bloc, in the form of a civil war.

Unipolarity

The economic collapse of the Soviet Union and its subsequent political disintegration at the beginning of the 1990s left the U.S. as sole superpower and transformed the system from bipolar in **unipolar**. Given its overwhelming military superiority, there is no other entity capable of keeping the U.S. in check.

UNIPOLARITY
An international system with a single superpower.

On the one hand, the sole superpower (called by some a hyperpower) has the ability to act unilaterally (that is, without the consent of its allies or international organizations) to suppress any perceived threat to its status. On the other hand, it has an incentive to build as vast a consensus as possible around its choices. This leads the dominant power (sometimes referred to as a hegemon) to exercise power through authority and persuasion rather than solely through coercion. The repeated use of coercion might solve problems in the short run, but in the longer run it will invite the formation of a countervailing bloc, and thus erode its position in the system as well as its security. It seems highly unlikely that France, Germany, Russia, and China, for instance, will be able to form a lasting coalition capable of rivalling the U.S. in the short term. Yet their collective attempt to hold the U.S. back from intervening in Iraq in the winter of 2002–03 provides an example of how a countervailing bloc might originate.

The Limits of International Cooperation

Realists recognize that during and since the twentieth century, **international governmental organizations** (IGOs) have come to play an increasingly more visible role in the international system. They also recognize that IGOs can, and often do, constrain the action of states.

INTERNATIONAL GOVERNMENTAL ORGANIZATION (IGO)
An association of states created to facilitate cooperation among them.

Iraq, for instance, did not get away with its invasion and forced annexation of Kuwait in August 1990. Acting through its Security Council, the

UNITED NATIONS (UN)
An international governmental organization representing almost all of the world's states.

United Nations (see Box 20-3, The United Nations), the most visible and ambitious among IGOs, immediately called for Iraq's withdrawal (Resolution 660 of August 2, 1990). Since Iraq ignored this and subsequent resolutions, the Security Council, through Resolution 678 of November 29, 1990, called for its ousting through the use of military force. Based on this resolution a number of countries led by the U.S. assembled a military coalition, defeated Iraq in the 1991 Gulf War, and forced it to withdraw from Kuwait. What happened to Iraq, however, could not happen to any of the five permanent members of the Security Council, without whose vote no resolution could be approved. It would also be unlikely to happen to any state that is a close ally of any of the permanent five.

United Nations
www.un.org

Realists also underline the fact that the UN is not a supranational body. Its members are sovereign states and the respect of state sovereignty is one of the core principles on which the UN is based. The UN, in the realist view, is simply a multilateral political arena that states have set up and in which they pursue their national interests, as they do in bilateral relations. The big powers, in other words, enjoy as privileged a position within the UN as they do outside.

International Monetary Fund
www.imf.org

FROM STRENGTH TO STRENGTH Realists point out that IGOs have been usually set up through the initiative of big powers. Their institutional structure and the way they work reflect the distribution of power in the international system—or at least the distribution that existed when they were founded. This means that the strong powers occupy a key position and play a key role in the functioning of the organization. Thus, for example, the so-called Big Five, victors in World War II (the U.S., the Soviet Union, Great Britain, China, and France), gave themselves a permanent seat on the UN Security Council as well as the ability to block any of its resolutions through a veto. In the International Monetary Fund, each country has a number of votes proportional to the reserve funds it has contributed, which means that the U.S. has 371 743 votes, corresponding to 17.14 percent of the total number of votes, while the microstate of Palau has 281 votes, corresponding to 0.01 percent.

According to the realists, IGOs are best regarded as tools that big powers create in order to help them fulfill their responsibilities for the maintenance of international order. The role of IGOs is primarily to help foster international consensus, and thus provide legitimacy for such an order that inevitably reflects more closely the interests and preferences of the big powers than those of other states in the system.[3]

---

[3] The radical (or Marxist) school affirms the same thing. The difference between realists and radicals is the following: the former describe the existing order and accept it as an inescapable feature of how international politics works; the latter denounce it as inequitable and oppressive and would like to change it.

The United Nations

The name United Nations was first used during the Second World War in the so-called Declaration by United Nations of January 1, 1942, when representatives of twenty-six countries pledged their willingness to continue fighting together against the Axis powers (Germany, Japan, Italy and their allies).

In 1945, representatives of fifty countries met in San Francisco at the United Nations Conference on International Organization to draw up the United Nations Charter. The Charter, which is the international treaty that set up the UN, was signed on June 26, 1945 and its ratification completed by October 24, 1945. The forerunner and model on which the United Nations was based was the League of Nations, an organization conceived in similar circumstances during the First World War, and established in 1919 to promote international cooperation and to achieve peace and security.

The principal organs of the UN are:

- *The General Assembly*, which seats the permanent diplomatic representatives of all UN member countries (191 as of August 2004). The General Assembly can debate any topic that falls within the provisions of the Charter. Each member has one vote. Its decisions, called General Assembly Resolutions, have no legally binding force for member states. They simply carry the weight of world opinion on major international issues, as well as the moral authority of the world community.

- *The Security Council*, which is the body responsible for peace and security issues. It is supposed to identify aggressors and situations that represent a threat to peace and decide on enforcement measures. It has fifteen members, five of which are permanent (the U.S., Russia, China, Britain, and France). The other ten rotating members are selected for a two-year period. A Security Council resolution needs nine votes, including all those of the five permanent members, to be approved. This means that any of the permanent five can block a resolution, and with it the activity of the Security Council. Security Council resolutions are binding on all UN members, but this does not mean that they can always be enforced. In case of non-compliance on the part of the state to which the resolution is addressed, in fact, enforcement depends on the willingness of other UN members to heed the provisions of the resolution, which might also mean readiness to put some of their military forces at the disposal of the UN.

- *The Secretariat*, the administrative organ of the organization. It has some 8000 international civil servants headed by the secretary-general, who is elected for a five-year renewable term by the General Assembly and the Security Council.

IGOs, once formed, might pose some constraints also for the big powers, but such constraints are largely self-imposed. Even the U.S. in the current unipolar system prefers to act either with the approval of the UN or at least with the political support of a coalition of allies. Realists, however, focus on the fact that when states perceive that a certain action is necessary for their own security, they will act—if they have the power to do so—with or without UN approval, as the U.S. did in the spring of 2003 in Iraq.

These cases might be infrequent but, according to realists, they prove that in the final analysis, states are the main players in the system, not least because they have a monopoly on the use of force. The UN might authorize the use of force or coercion (whether in the form of economic sanctions or military intervention) against one of its members, but the UN has no ability to enforce its own resolutions and depends on the willingness of other member states to do so. States, therefore, work with IGOs when it is in their interest to do so, but cannot, and do not, delegate responsibility for their own security to the UN or any other IGOs.

War and Peace in the International System

Realists view competition and rivalry as the normal, unchangeable mode of interaction among states. So, to maintain peace, the problem is not how to eliminate competition and rivalry and replace them with cooperation and friendship. The problem is how to curb competition and rivalry so that it does not lead to war. The answer is to make war too costly an option for a would-be aggressor to choose. It follows that peace can only be attained through strength. Wolves cannot be turned into lambs, but they can be deterred from attacking if it is clear to them that they cannot possibly prevail.

COLD WAR What keeps peace in a multipolar system is the timely shifting of alliances to counter would-be aggressors. The balance of terror, also known as the doctrine of mutual assured destruction (MAD), kept peace during the Cold War, or to be more precise, prevented a direct military confrontation between the U.S. and the Soviets. The two contenders had accumulated such vast arsenals of nuclear weapons that neither of them had an incentive to launch an attack since the initiator could not hope to survive a retaliatory strike from the adversary. War would mean mutual assured destruction, no matter who initiated it.

The knowledge that peace rested only on the balance of terror or MAD led the two states to sign the 1972 Anti-Ballistic Missile (ABM) Treaty, which purposely limited to two (later reduced to one) the number of strategic defence systems each country could deploy. Since ABM systems were supposed to neutralize incoming missiles while still in the air, it was thought that their deployment would destabilize the balance of terror and hence increase the probabilities of a nuclear exchange. The superpower that would succeed first in protecting all of its territory with such systems might in fact be tempted to launch an initial strike in the hope of being able to withstand the retaliatory one and escape from the exchange relatively unscathed. The signing of the treaty was an implicit acknowledgment that the maintenance of peace did not depend on the simple desire for it—because in this case the two superpowers could have agreed to disarm completely. Peace rested instead on tying one's hands or, to put it differently, resisting any temptation one might have to resort to war by eliminating all advantages one might derive from an attack.

MAINTAINING PEACE IN A UNIPOLAR SYSTEM It is more difficult to analyze how peace can be maintained in a unipolar system since such a system has been around only for about a decade, and hence there are few data on which to base any conclusion. It would appear, however, that in a unipolar system, the sole superpower confronts a rather difficult task. On the one hand, it has primary responsibility for the maintenance of stability and order in the international system. On the other hand, any initiative the superpower takes for this purpose risks being perceived by other actors as nothing but the blatant pursuit of its national interests.

The UN, for instance, could not undertake any military operation with respect to threats to the peace, breaches of the peace, or acts of aggression (the so-called Chapter 7 operations) if it could not rely on the willingness of the U.S. to provide its military forces for such operations. This means, however, that all executions of UN mandates under Chapter 7 of the UN Charter have the U.S. at their centre. As the U.S. also desires to retain command and control of its own troops in such operations, the impression is inevitably given that these interventions are not the dutiful execution of a UN mandate but American wars.

The 1950–53 Korean War and the 1991 Gulf War are often thought of as American wars and not as UN-mandated interventions. When the UN mandate is recognized, the suggestion is often made that the U.S. coerced and cajoled the members of the UN Security Council to obtain its authorization in order to legitimize an intervention it was ready to undertake also unilaterally.

Things are even worse, of course, when the sole superpower takes initiatives without an explicit UN authorization—as was the case in 2003, when the United States and some of its allies invaded Iraq. The provisional conclusion seems to be that in a unipolar system peace depends not only on the willingness of the superpower to intervene to maintain stability and order, but also on its ability to forge consensus around such order and the actions it undertakes to maintain it. Without willing partners and eager followers, **hegemony** deteriorates into domination and a dominant power invites the formation of countervailing alliances, which leads to turbulence and war.

The Realist School and the Limits of Governance

Realists are skeptical about the possibility of international governance. They regard it at best as limited and based on the willingness and ability of big powers to take the lead in shaping and providing it. There are two reasons for such skepticism:

1. Realists focus primarily on the issue of security, which is the central concern of sovereign states, and so unlikely to be completely delegated to any IGO, the UN included.

HEGEMONY
The ability of a dominant power to exert influence, primarily through authority, leadership, and persuading others to accept a particular view of the world.

2. States are unlikely to forgo their sovereignty. Hence, the international system might change in terms of its distribution of power among states, but is unlikely to change in terms of its organization of authority. The system, in other words, is likely to remain anarchic.

For realists, governance therefore means the ability of bigger powers (whether many, two, or one) to develop rules and institutions, which, while conferring privileges on them, also enjoy a minimum of legitimacy among lesser powers in the international system. For realists, in other words, governance means at best the benign rule of hegemons.

LIBERAL–INTERNATIONALISM

The liberal–internationalist school has a less drastic view of the consequences of international anarchy and is more optimistic about the possibilities of governance. **Liberal–internationalism** differs from realism in a number of ways (see also Table 20-1):

LIBERAL–INTERNATIONALISM
The view that increased cultural and social connections as well as economic interdependence are leading to the emergence of a global civil society which values cooperation, the rule of law, and peace, and that international governance is spreading both functionally and geographically.

INTERNATIONAL NON-GOVERNMENTAL ORGANIZATIONS (INGO)
An international organization that is not controlled by governments.

- It tends to look at security as one of the many issues in international relations. States interact in many different issue areas—economic, social, and cultural. Each of these issue areas affects the others and none is dominant all the time. Hence, the issue of national security, although important, cannot be examined in isolation.
- While states might still be the most important actors in international relations, they are not the only ones. Liberal–internationalists believe that other actors, such as IGOs, **international non-governmental organizations** (INGOs; examples include Greenpeace and Amnesty International, to mention only two among the most well-known),[4] specific state institutions such as parliaments and bureaucracies, and even individuals, play an important role.
- Liberal–internationalism does not regard states as unitary actors but as a network of different actors—individuals, societal groups, and governmental institutions—each with different interests, priorities, and preferences. They interact with similar actors across national borders on so many different issue areas that there is no overarching issue capable of relegating all the others to the margins. Unlike realists, liberal–internationalists do not believe that there is a consistent national interest. There are instead many different, shifting, and competing national interests. Even if everyone might agree on the need to defend one's state from external threats, disagreements will inevitably occur concerning the means that should be used to defend oneself from such threats. How a

---

[4] INGOs are distinguished from IGOs because they are set up and controlled by individuals and/or groups drawn from the population of at least two states and not by national governments.

state behaves on the international scene, therefore, is always the result of a bargaining process among competing domestic groups and institutions.

- Liberal–internationalists believe that individuals, groups, and institutions learn from their experiences and mistakes, and hence are capable of modifying their behaviour accordingly.

AN INTERNATIONAL SOCIETY IN THE MAKING

Liberal–internationalists agree with realists that the world is made up of sovereign states and that there is no authority above them. They disagree, however, on the question of how significant anarchy is for the behaviour of the system and those who take part in it. According to them, the principle of sovereignty, which has traditionally regulated interstate relations, is constantly evolving.

The idea has recently gained ground, for instance, that sovereign states have a responsibility to protect their own citizens from avoidable catastrophes as well as to guarantee their enjoyment of human rights. When states are unwilling or unable to do so, that responsibility must be borne by the international community as a whole. Thus, under certain circumstances, it is appropriate for a state, a coalition of states, or an IGO, to take action—including military action—against another state in order to protect its people.[5] This is of course an important limitation on state sovereignty. The intervention by a number of countries against the republic of Yugoslavia in the spring of 1999, for instance, was justified precisely with the argument that intervention was necessary to protect the rights of the Albanian minority in the province of Kosovo.

	REALISM	LIBERAL–INTERNATIONALISM
Key Actors	States	States, IGOs, INGOs, groups, individuals
View of the state	Unitary actor, power seeking, moved by national interest	Network of different actors, competing national interests
View of the international system	Anarchic	Interdependence of actors International society
Views on peace	Attainable through strength, deterrence, balance of power	Attainable through law
Views on possibility of international governance	Weak; provided by hegemonic powers	Strong; governance is spreading fast

TABLE 20-1

MAJOR DIFFERENCES BETWEEN REALISM AND LIBERAL–INTERNATIONALISM

[5] See International Commission on Intervention and State Sovereignty (2001).

INTERDEPENDENCE Liberal–internationalists also point out that the range of international interactions is so vast and its reach so deep that all participants in the system are interdependent, that is, each is affected by the actions of others. The interdependence of participants, the fact that all of them face an increasing number of common challenges, such as environmental degradation, population explosion, and climate change, and the shrinking of the time–space dimensions due to technological advances in communication and travel, have slowly led, according to liberal–internationalists, to the development of a common identity, a sense of "we-ness" on planet Earth.

For all these reasons, liberal–internationalists think that the international system is not simply a structure constraining the behaviour of its units, but an evolving process. Its structure does constrain the behaviour of its units, but the latter—states, groups and individuals—are constantly modifying the system through their own ideas and actions. The increasing number and relevance of INGOs, moreover, is evidence of the rapid emergence of a vibrant, global, civil society, which will eventually give birth to a global and democratic political society. Thus, for liberal–internationalists the world is more than a system of independent sovereign states. It is also an **international society** in the making.

INTERNATIONAL SOCIETY
The idea that the increasing number and importance of international non-governmental organizations marks the development of a global society.

Why States Cooperate

Liberal–internationalists point out that, although there are occasional exceptions, states usually comply with international law even in the absence of a central authority capable of enforcing it. They do so for two reasons:

1. States wish to do what is considered right and moral, and do not wish to lose prestige in the eyes of international public opinion.
2. Even more importantly, states have learned over time that it is in their interest to abide by international law because it is preferable to live in an ordered and predictable world.

Order and predictability allow states not to have to worry too much about the behaviour of other states, since it can be assumed that it will fall within predictable parameters: those allowed by the law.

JOINING INTERNATIONAL GOVERNMENTAL ORGANIZATIONS It is precisely this desire to reduce uncertainty in interstate relations that has pushed states to set up and join an increasing number of IGOs. Although IGOs do not enforce rules on other states, they are useful because they provide a context in which it is easier for states to cooperate with one another. That is, they can help to find a mutually satisfying adjustment in situations of conflicting interests or preferences.

Membership in IGOs does not weaken state sovereignty; it simply provides a different context in which to exercise it. More precisely, the context provided by IGOs reduces the costs of negotiating agreements by providing clear rules, better information, and opportunities for compromises and side-payments through issue linkages. It also improves the chances of compliance since the costs of defection, in terms of reputation and credibility, are higher than they would be in a bilateral relationship. This explains why smaller powers like Canada seem to value membership in IGOs more than big powers. Their sovereignty is enhanced because they gain more voice and hence influence, especially when acting in concert, than they would have in bilateral relationships with bigger powers.

This analysis is undoubtedly very convincing for social and economic issue areas (Keohane, 1984). As interdependence has increased, so has the demand for IGOs and the eagerness of states to form them.[6] The proliferation of IGOs reinforces the habit of cooperation, and this, according to liberal–internationalists, augurs well for an increasingly peaceful future.

Important questions to explore in more depth are: What happens in the field of security, which realists regard as central to the concerns of states? Does interstate cooperation within security IGOs work as well as liberal–internationalists argue it does in the economic ones?

The Problem of Security and the Search for Peace

Unlike realists, who think that states can only rely on self-help for their security, liberal–internationalists believe that states can, and should, rely on IGOs and law. For them, state security is better achieved through a collective approach. The principle of **collective security** posits that states set up an international organization and pledge to intervene on behalf of a member whose security is threatened by the aggressive actions of another state.

COLLECTIVE SECURITY
The principle invoked when states set up an international organization and pledge to intervene on behalf of a member whose security is threatened by the aggressive actions of another state.

The UN is, among other things, a system of collective security, as was its predecessor, the League of Nations. The principle of collective security is also consistent with the realist reliance on deterrence to discourage aggression and maintain peace. If states can be certain that aggression will be punished by collective action, then they will refrain from engaging in aggressive behaviour.

For a system of collective security to work, however, one must assume that participating members can always agree on establishing who is the aggressor when two states come to blows. Unfortunately, this is not so since states, much like individuals, are more likely to listen sympathetically to the arguments of friends than those of foes. For collective security to work, one must also assume that participating members are always ready and willing to act against the aggressor. The historical record on this point is not too

---

[6] The value of international traded goods, for instance, has increased from US$20 billion in 1913 to US$53 billion in 1948, US$1972 billion in 1983, and US$7487 billion in the year 2000. The number of IGOs has increased from nine at the beginning of the century, to 53 in 1950 to 111 in 1980 and over 150 by the end of the century.

comforting. When Japan invaded Manchuria and Italy conquered Ethiopia in the 1930s, members of the League of Nations did not make good on their promise to intervene. Thus, the system of collective security effectively collapsed, leading to further aggression by Germany against Czechoslovakia and Poland and in the end to World War II.

Things did not fare any better with the UN Security Council during the Cold War, since the ideological and political rivalry between the U.S. and the Soviet Union effectively paralyzed the Council until the end of the Cold War. Only two acts of international aggression met with a collective response by the UN between 1945 and 1991:

- The intervention against North Korea for its invasion of South Korea in 1950. The UN was able to intervene, moreover, only because at the time, the Soviet Union was boycotting the meetings of the Security Council to protest the fact that Taiwan and not China had a seat at the UN. Had the Soviet Union been present, it would almost surely have vetoed an intervention against its North Korean ally.
- The 1991 intervention against Iraq following its invasion of Kuwait. The end of the Cold War rekindled liberal hopes that the UN could finally fulfill its collective security responsibility, but these hopes did not last very long.

As the debate over what to do with Iraq in the fall of 2002 showed, disagreements among Security Council members resurfaced almost immediately. They were due partly to the ambiguity of the evidence available to decide whether Iraq represented an immediate threat to regional and world peace, and partly to the desire of some permanent members—France and Russia in particular—to try to constrain the range of action of the lone superpower.

THE CASE OF IRAQ Iraq's protracted defiance of the disarmament terms imposed by the UN Security Council Resolution 687 at the end of the 1991 Gulf War was not challenged by either the UN or the U.S. throughout the decade other than by economic sanctions. The terrorist attacks of September 11, 2001, although not related to Iraq, changed policy thinking, at least in Washington. The U.S. administration reconsidered the policy of containment through economic sanctions—which appeared to reinforce the regime of Iraqi dictator Saddam Hussein rather than undermining it—and concluded that the Iraqi question should be be tackled resolutely, militarily if necessary (Pollack, 2002). (See Box 20-4, The U.S. Changes Its Policy on Iraq.)

U.S. Liberal Optimism The rationale for invading Iraq was not, however, entirely based on realist security and geo-strategic considerations.[7] It also

---

[7] Critics of the U.S. invasion of Iraq claimed that the real reason for the invasion related to control of the oil supplies of Iraq and the Persian Gulf region—an important strategic resource.

The U.S. Changes Its Policy on Iraq

A series of developments during the first eight months of 2002 signalled a change in U.S. policy toward Iraq:

- In his State of the Union Address in January, President George W. Bush identified Iraq as forming, with Iran and North Korea, an "axis of evil."
- Next was the updating of the doctrine of "right of self-defense by preemptive action" that was incorporated in the annual President's Report on National Security Strategy to Congress.
- Finally, Vice-President Richard Cheney made the case for pre-emptive military action against Iraq in a speech delivered at the 103rd National Convention of the Veterans of Foreign Wars in Nashville on August 28, 2002.

The official rationale provided by the U.S. administration for its new course of action was that Iraq, instead of complying with UN Security Council Resolution 687, had been busy enhancing its chemical and biological capabilities and developing nuclear weapons. Given Saddam Hussein's past willingness to use chemical weapons against his enemies both at home and abroad, Iraq was perceived as a threat to regional and international security. To those who argued that such a threat did not appear so imminent as to justify pre-emptive military action,

the Bush administration answered that the concept of "imminent threat" needed to be adapted "to the capabilities and objectives of today's adversaries." One could not wait until terrorists or rogue states had obtained weapons of mass destruction (WMD). Prudence called for action before such threats could be unleashed (pre-emptive action).

Another consideration that could not be avowed openly also played an important role. A change of regime in Iraq could provide the U.S. with a new, key ally in this strategically important region at a time when it could no longer rely on Saudi Arabia to continue playing such a role. The toppling of Hussein also looked appealing because, coming soon after the overthrow of the Taliban regime in Afghanistan, it would send a forceful message to other rogue regimes such as those in Iran and Syria. Finally, it did not appear to contain many risks since it would be welcomed, albeit silently, by almost all major governments in the Middle East. Such a rationale could not, however, be used publicly to justify a military intervention. Hence, the Bush administration focused on the claim (not supported by factual evidence) that Iraq had continued to develop and accumulate weapons of mass destruction, and the danger that these weapons could fall into the hands of terrorist groups.

rested on a good dose of "liberal" optimism and idealism.[8] The Bush administration argued that the replacement of Saddam Hussein's dictatorship with a liberal–democratic regime would bring about similar changes in other countries in the region. The administration occasionally also argued that the removal of Saddam Hussein would free the Iraqi people from a brutal dictatorship, which had not hesitated to kill tens of thousands of its own people.

---

[8] The depiction of the Bush administration's rationale as "liberal" may seem peculiar. As discussed in Chapter 6, the Bush administration's foreign policy reflects the neo-conservative perspective. However, the claim to be pursuing the liberation of Iraqis from tyranny and spreading values of liberal democracy rather than pursuing the American national interest is liberal, as the term is used in this chapter, rather than realist.

The humanitarian intervention argument, however, was used rather sparingly, since the Hussein regime had committed its worst atrocities against Kurdish and Shia Muslim groups in 1987–88 and 1991. At the time of the first instance, the United States was lending support to Iraq in its war with Iran and thus reluctant to criticize the actions of Iraq. In the second instance, the United States encouraged the insurrection of the Kurds and Shia Muslims against the Hussein regime, but failed to act when Hussein brutally suppressed these groups.

European Skepticism Bush's decision to confront Saddam Hussein's regime militarily met with considerable skepticism in Europe. Many Western European governments, most notably the French and German governments, were not convinced that Iraq represented an immediate threat to its neighbours, that it was amassing weapons of mass destruction, or that it had any direct links to international terrorism, apart from the financing of Palestinian suicide bombers. They did not consider regime change as a legitimate aim in itself, and did not believe that liberal democracy could sprout in a region devoid of most, if not all, of its prerequisites. Hence, on balance, they thought that a military intervention was likely to make things worse, perhaps provoking the disintegration of Iraq, boosting al-Qaeda's recruitment efforts and lead to a new outbreak of terrorist attacks, worsening the Palestinian–Israeli conflict, and destabilizing the whole region.

Before the issue could be discussed within the European Union, however, German Chancellor Gerhard Schröder chose to play the anti-war card in the electoral campaign for the German parliamentary elections. He announced that Germany would neither take part in, nor pay for (as it had done in the first Gulf war) any "adventure" in Iraq. This decision would not change, even if the UN Security Council were to give its seal of approval to the intervention.

This declaration transformed the Iraqi question, at least in Europe, into a debate on whether or not the U.S., as the sole superpower, should act unilaterally to maintain international security when confronted with a UN stalemate. This dimension came to overshadow the underlying problem, namely how to deal with a dictatorial regime that had defied UN Security Council resolutions for over a decade. This was especially the case after French President Jacques Chirac took the opportunity provided by the German anti-war declaration and decided to become the self-appointed leader of the camp opposing American intervention. Chirac's decision was in part due to a different assessment of the seriousness and imminence of the Iraqi threat, and in part to strategic considerations. France, in other words, used the Iraqi issue and the German anti-war stance as an opportunity to reassert its ambition to shape the external role of the European Union in a way that would constrain the actions of the sole superpower. (See Box 20-5, Countdown to War, for events that followed.)

Countdown to War

European opposition was unlikely to convince Washington to alter its war course with Iraq, but British Prime Minister Tony Blair was able nevertheless to persuade the U.S. to give peaceful means and the UN Security Council one last chance. In return Blair promised political, and at least symbolic military, support in case the Security Council failed to authorize intervention. It was all but over.

Here's how events unfolded:

- On September 12, 2002, in his remarks at the UN General Assembly, President Bush invited the UN to follow up on its numerous resolutions ordering Iraq to disarm, which Saddam Hussein had largely evaded, or risk becoming inconsequential. If the Security Council failed to act, Bush said that the U.S. would fulfill its responsibility to guarantee security and order and act alone.

- On November 8, after some weeks of haggling, especially between the U.S. and France, the Security Council reached a compromise and adopted unanimously Resolution 1441, which set up a new inspection regime, warned Iraq that this was its "final opportunity to comply with its disarmament obligations," and that it would face "serious consequences" were it to continue to violate its obligations. UN weapons inspectors were supposed to inform the Security Council immediately of any reluctance to cooperate on the part of the Iraqi regime, and to submit a report within two months.

Resolution 1441 confirmed agreement on the principle that force should only be used as a last resort, but did not resolve the central question: At what point could one consider that all peaceful means had been exhausted and the time had come to use force? The U.S. assumed that force could be used at any time if the inspectors encountered uncooperative behaviour or immediately after the filing of their report, unless the latter asserted that Iraq had fully met its obligations. Germany and France, backed also by Russia, maintained instead that the use of force would require yet another Security Council resolution explicitly authorizing it.

- Blair again was able to persuade the U.S. to introduce another resolution. At this point, however, France and Russia (along with Germany, which had begun a two-year term as a non-permanent member of the Security Council on January 1, 2003), jointly pledged to block a second resolution and veto it if introduced.

- The U.S. and the U.K. countered by giving Iraq a deadline for compliance with Resolution 1441 or face war.

- On March 19, 2003, American and British forces crossed into Iraq from Kuwait.

Reducing the Likelihood of War:
The Role of Economic Interdependence

Some liberal–internationalists believe that, as a method of solving interstate conflicts, war is losing legitimacy, just as the duel has lost legitimacy as a way of solving interpersonal disputes (Mueller, 1989). This is due not only to changes in sensibilities but also to changes in interests. The high degree of

▶ President George W. Bush and his consolation prize from the Iraq war.

European Union
europa.eu.int

POSTMODERN STATE
A state in which the meaning and practice of sovereignty have been redefined since tools of governance are shared, foreign and domestic policies have become inextricably intertwined, and security is no longer based on control of borders, and deterrence.

economic interdependence that characterizes liberal–democratic states has made war a very costly mechanism to solve disputes. War entails, in fact, economic disruptions, both commercial and financial, and hence costs for most domestic actors.

For example, France and Germany went to war three times in less than a century, but war between the two countries—or any two European countries, for that matter—would be unthinkable today given their high degree of economic interdependence. Indeed, economic interdependence has also led to the building of a network of common political institutions (the countries belonging to the European Union being those who have gone the furthest in this direction), which has made war an even more remote possibility.

Some liberals argue that the European Union represents an example of a **postmodern state**—that is, a state in which the meaning and practice of sovereignty has been redefined since tools of governance are shared, foreign and domestic policies have become inextricably intertwined, and security is no longer based on control of borders, and deterrence (Cooper, 2000). The idea is that the example of the European Union could be replicated in other parts of the world, until the entire world would become a postmodern state.

Given also the traditional liberal idea—whose origins go back to the German philosopher Immanuel Kant (1724–1804)—that states with a liberal democratic government are less likely than states with other types of government to wage war, especially towards one another, liberal–internationalists also believe in the necessity to foster the development of free-market economies and democratic institutions around the world.[9] Such a promotion, however, if not pursued subtly and carefully, might lead, at least in some parts of the world, to resentment and resistance, and thus end up triggering, rather than preventing, disorders and even military hostilities.

The Liberal–Internationalist Promise of Governance

Liberal–internationalists are more optimistic than realists about the possibility of global governance. The world, it is argued, does not resemble Hobbes' mythical state of nature. It also appears to be increasingly acquiring the features of a global civil society, as evidenced by a growing network of connections across national boundaries (Lipschutz, 2000).

These connections, which have traditionally linked organized groups, now involve also single individuals thanks to the World Wide Web. One can see the slow but nevertheless sure emergence of a global consciousness that is increasingly bringing challenges to, and slowly eroding, the traditional primacy of the sovereign states. To be sure, the world does not yet have a central authority—and it might never have one. Yet it exhibits an increasing number of functional areas (for example, international trade) and geographic areas (for example, the European Union) in which the rule of law prevails. Such a trend, moreover, is self-reinforcing, and hence unlikely to ever be reversed.

---

[9] It should be pointed out that whereas liberal–internationalists see liberal–democracy as a carrier of peace, radical Marxist scholars argue exactly the opposite. They believe that the free-market capitalist economy that usually characterizes liberal democracies is exactly what causes conflict and war, both among classes within states and among states within the international system.

Summary and Conclusion

This chapter has examined the difference between national politics and international politics: the fact that the respect of rules at the international level depends more on voluntary compliance on the part of states than on enforcement. It has also examined the differences between the two major approaches to the study of international politics: realism and liberal–internationalism.

Realists argue that the fact that states are sovereign makes the international system anarchic and hence very similar to Hobbes's state of nature. In such a world, security, which is the major preoccupation of states, depends on self-help and hence on power. Peace depends on deterrence, namely making it clear to potential aggressors that the costs of aggression outweigh the potential benefits. Because states are jealous of their sovereignty, the possibilities of international governance are limited.

Liberal–internationalists argue that although the world is still politically organized in states, each of whose governments claims to be the ultimate authority over its territory and population, increased cultural and social connections and economic interdependence are leading to the emergence of a global civil society—one that values cooperation, the rule of law, and peace. A world political federation might never emerge, but international governance is spreading both functionally and geographically.

Overall, international politics raises difficult issues for the pursuit of the common good. Given the problems that the world faces (such as war, global climate change, global inequality, international terrorism, and the protection of basic human rights), it would be desirable if the common good were considered, at least in part, in terms of common good of humanity or of the entire planet.

However, the realist perspective alerts us to the continuing importance of national interests. The common good of humanity can, at best, only be achieved to a limited degree in an anarchic world. In contrast, liberal–internationalists have a more optimistic outlook on achieving the common good. In their view, the development of international organizations and agreements, along with increased interaction among the peoples of the world in areas such as trade and communications and the spread of democracy, make progress towards a more peaceful and prosperous world possible. But international organizations and trade agreements do not necessarily lead to the global common good; they may reflect the interests of the powerful. As well, international governmental organizations are often not particularly democratic. Achieving the global common good, therefore, presents us with difficult challenges.

Key Terms

Discussion Questions

1. What are the major differences between the realist and liberal–internationalist approaches to the study of world politics? What are the implications for policy suggestions?

2. What are the policy options and the dilemmas a state confronts in trying to guarantee its own security?

3. Can the United Nations be considered a world government? How significant is the lack of a central authority in world politics?

4. Is a peaceful world a realistic objective? How might a more peaceful world be achieved?

Further Reading

Baylis, J., Wirts, J., Cohen, E., & Gray, C.S. *Strategy in the contemporary world: An introduction to strategic studies.* Oxford: Oxford University Press, 2002.

Bull, H. *The anarchical society: A study of order in world politics* (2nd ed.). London: Macmillan, 1995.

Guzzini, S. *Realism in international relations and international political economy: The continuing story of a death foretold.* London: Routledge, 1998.

Jackson, R. *The global covenant: Human conduct in a world of states.* Oxford: Oxford University Press, 2000.

Jackson, R., & Sørensen, G. *Introduction to international relations: Theories and approaches* (2nd ed.). Oxford: Oxford University Press, 2003.

Kennedy, P. *The rise and fall of the great powers: Economic change and military conflict from 1500 to 2000.* New York: Vintage Books, 1987

Olson, W.C., & Groom, A.J.R. *International relations then and now: Origins and trends in interpretation.* New York: HarperCollins Academic, 1991.

GLOSSARY

Affirmative action The adoption of programs designed to make the workplace, universities, legislatures, or other institutions more representative of disadvantaged groups and groups that have suffered from discrimination.

Agenda setting The process by which potential problems come to the attention of policy-makers.

Agenda setting effect The effect of the media on what the public thinks are the key issues or political priorities at a particular point in time.

Alternative service delivery New methods of delivering government programs, such as the establishment of service agencies that have considerable autonomy from the normal departmental structures and rules, and establishing partnerships with business, other levels of government, and voluntary organizations to deliver services.

Anarchism An ideology that views the state as the key source of oppression and seeks to replace the state with a system based on voluntary cooperation.

Anarchy A situation in which there is no central authority.

Asian model The economic model of export-led industrialization associated with a number of Asian countries.

Auditor general An independent officer of Parliament who examines government spending to ensure that it conforms to the purposes for which the money was granted by Parliament, that the money was spent efficiently, and that government is getting value for the money spent.

Authoritarian government A non-democratic system of governing.

Authority The right to make decisions. Those who are in positions of political authority have been *authorized* in some way to make decisions on behalf of the political community.

Balance of power A situation in which no state is dominant in the global system.

Binational and multinational states States in which there are two or more significant nationalities.

Bipolarity A system in which two superpowers compete with one another. The other states in the system fall within the sphere of influence of one or the other of the two superpowers.

Brokerage party A party that tries to appeal to a variety of interests and to bridge differences, particularly by promising benefits to a variety of different interests.

Bureaucracy The permanent employees of government. Generally, a bureaucracy is an organization in which people are hired and promoted on the basis of their qualifications and merit, work is organized in terms of specialized positions (offices), detailed rules and procedures are followed by all members of the organizations, and there is a hierarchical chain of command so that those at the top can direct and supervise large numbers of people.

Cabinet committee A committee of cabinet ministers appointed by the prime minister.

Cabinet secrecy The convention that the cabinet meets behind closed doors, cabinet documents normally remain secret for a lengthy period of time, and the advice given to the cabinet is not usually released publicly.

Cabinet solidarity The convention in a parliamentary system that each member of the cabinet is expected to fully support and defend the decisions and actions that the cabinet takes.

Cadre party A party concerned with the task of electing members of the party to legislative bodies, rather than building a strong, centralized, membership-based organization outside of the legislature.

Catch-all party A party that tries to appeal to all segments of the population, particularly by downplaying or abandoning its ideology and emphasizing the qualities of its leaders.

Caucus A closed-door meeting of the party's members of Parliament.

Central agency An organization that tries to provide direction and coordination to the executive side of government. In Canada, the key central agencies are the Privy Council Office, the Prime Minister's Office, the Treasury Board, and the Department of Finance.

Centrally planned state socialist economic system An economic system involving state ownership of almost all enterprises and centralized planning by state officials.

Charismatic authority Authority based on the extraordinary or supernatural qualities of a leader

Charlottetown Accord A package of constitutional changes. including recognition of the inherent right of Aboriginals to self-government and major changes to the Senate to provide for equal representation by each province regardless of population size. It was defeated in a referendum in 1992.

Charter of Rights and Freedoms Part of the *Constitution Act, 1982,* the Charter is superior to ordinary legislation, explicitly allows the courts to invalidate legislation, and applies to the actions of all governments and organizations under the direct control of government.

Christian Right A perspective that seeks to apply conservative or fundamentalist Christian values to politics. The Christian Right focuses on the promotion of traditional family values, which it views as threatened by abortion, homosexuality, divorce, feminism, and a permissive society.

Citizens' juries Groups of randomly selected persons that deliberate about and make recommendations concerning particular issues.

Citizenship The idea that the permanent residents of a particular country should have legal status as members of the state and should have various rights and responsibilities.

Civic nationalism Nationalism based on the shared political values and political history of those who are citizens of a country.

Civil disobedience Deliberate lawbreaking that accepts punishment by state authorities as part of the action.

Civil society The independent groups and organizations that are not controlled by the state.

Class consciousness The extent to which people see themselves as members of a particular social class.

Classical federalism A version of federalism in which the federal and provincial governments each concern themselves with their own areas of constitutional authority without infringing upon the areas of authority of the other level of government.

Classical liberalism A form of liberalism that emphasizes the desirability of limited government and the free marketplace.

Coalition government A form of government in which two or more parties jointly govern, sharing the cabinet positions.

Coercion A form of influence that involves using fear or threats of harmful consequences to achieve an outcome.

Cohabitation A sharing of power between the French president and the National Assembly that occurs when the Assembly is controlled by a party opposed to the president.

Collective responsibility The convention that the cabinet as a group will defend, explain, and take responsibility for the actions of the government in Parliament.

Collective security The principle invoked when states set up an international organization and pledge to intervene on behalf of a member whose security is threatened by the aggressive actions of another state.

Collectivist perspective A perspective that focuses on the interests and well-being of the political community as a whole.

Common good What is good for the political community as a whole as well as for the general welfare of the members of the political community. This term is contentious, as some view the common good in terms of the interests and well-being of the political community as a whole. Others view the common good in terms of the interests and well-being of the individuals in a political community.

Communism A system in which private property has been replaced by collective or communal ownership and in which everyone would be free to take from society what they need. Communism is often associated with communist parties that, based on the ideas of Marx and Lenin, viewed themselves as leading society through socialism to communism.

Comparative advantage The economic principle that wealth is maximized when countries focus on those activities at which they are most efficient, and then trade with other countries for those products and services that they cannot produce as efficiently.

Comparative politics The branch of political science that examines the similarities and differences in the politics and governing of different countries.

Confederal system A system of governing in which sovereign states have agreed to delegate some of their authority to a joint government with limited authority while retaining their identity as sovereign states.

Congress The legislative branch of the American government.

Conservatism An ideology that emphasizes the values of order, stability, respect for authority, and tradition, based on a view that humans are inherently imperfect, with a limited capacity to reason.

Consolidated democracies Countries with democratic governments that are stable and well accepted by both ordinary citizens and political elites, and which face little danger of being overthrown.

Constitution The fundamental rules and principles by which a state is governed.

Constitution Act, 1867 An act of the Parliament of the United Kingdom that established Canada by uniting the colonies of Canada (Ontario and Quebec), Nova Scotia, and New Brunswick, and set out the framework for governing.

Constitution Act, 1982 The act that made the constitution fully Canadian and added the Charter of Rights and Freedoms to the constitution.

Constitutional amendment A change to the constitution.

Constitutional convention A fundamental principle that is consistently followed even though it is not contained in a legal document and not enforceable in the courts.

Constitutional government A government that consistently acts in accordance with the rules and principles established in its constitution.

Contentious politics Protest involving ordinary citizens, often joined by more influential citizens, uniting to confront elites, authorities, and opponents.

Cooperative federalism A federal system in which the two levels of government are jointly involved in developing and administering many government services.

Corporate state A system associated with fascist Italy in which business and labour are closely tied to the state and directed to goals established by the state.

Corporatism A political system in which the state actively collaborates with selected major interests to set the direction for the political community, particularly in terms of economic and social policies.

Cosmopolitan democracy The extension of democracy to global and transnational institutions.

Cost-benefit analysis An economic technique that determines whether, and to what extent, the benefits of a policy exceed the costs.

Coup d'état A forcible seizure of power by the armed forces or occasionally the police.

Crown corporation In Canada, a state-owned corporation that operates independently from direct governmental control.

Culture wars Controversy between those who hold liberal and conservative (religious) values over issues such as abortion, gay and lesbian rights, multiculturalism, school prayers, and the promotion of safe sex.

Deliberative democracy A political system in which decisions are made based on discussion by citizens rather than by elected representatives alone.

Democracy Rule by the people.

Democratic consolidation The situation when a country's commitment to democracy is strong and sure, such that democracy is likely to persist.

Democratic socialism A version of socialism that argues socialism should be achieved by democratic rather than revolutionary means, and that a socialist society should be democratic in nature.

Democratic transition A process of change involving abandoning authoritarian government for democratic rule.

Department of Finance The government department responsible for preparing the government's budget and analyzing the interaction of the government's financial activities and the country's economy.

Dependency theory A development model that views underdevelopment as a result of unequal power relations between the centre (dominant capitalist countries) and the periphery (poor, dependent countries).

Deputy minister The executive head of a department of government, appointed by the prime minister in consultation with the Clerk of the Privy Council.

Developing countries Countries that have not reached the same level of development as the richer, advanced countries.

Development A condition that involves the satisfaction of the basic needs of all of the people as well as the means for them to live fulfilling and productive lives based on the creation of a more diversified, sophisticated, and sustainable economy.

Devolution A system of governing in which the central government grants some legislative (law making) as well as administrative responsibilities to one or more regional bodies.

Direct democracy A system in which citizens make the governing decisions.

Direct membership vote A system of party leadership selection in which all party members can directly choose among the candidates, rather than selecting delegates to choose the leader.

Dominant ideology perspective on the mass media The view that the major media convey the values of the powerful and serve the interests of those who benefit from the status quo.

Electoral college A body that elects the president of the United States based on the votes that the presidential candidates won in each state.

Electoral–professional party A political party whose dominant concern is winning elections and which relies on professional experts to market the party to voters.

Electoral system The system used to translate the votes that people cast into the composition of the legislature and the selection of the government.

Elite media The newspapers and magazines that are read by decision-makers in government, business, and leading social institutions as well as by those highly interested in public affairs.

Elitist perspective The view that power in all communities is concentrated in a small number of hands, particularly in the elites that hold the top positions in the major institutions of the economy, society, and politics.

Empirical analysis Analysis that involves explaining various aspects of politics particularly by using careful observation and comparison to develop generalizations and testable theories.

Employment equity Measures taken to increase the proportion of persons from disadvantaged groups in the workplace (including senior positions).

Enlightenment An intellectual movement that developed in the mid-eighteenth century, emphasizing the power of human reason to understand and improve the world.

Environmentalism A perspective based on the idea that humanity needs to change its relationship to nature. Environmentalism emphasizes the need to create a sustainable society because there are environmental limits to growth.

Equalization payment A payment made by the federal government to try to ensure that different provincial governments are able to provide an equivalent level of services to their populations without resorting to excessive levels of taxation.

Estimates The detailed annual spending plans of each department of government; they must be approved by Parliament.

Ethnic cleansing The forcible removal and in some cases massacre of people whose ethnic group differed from that of the group claiming and controlling an area.

Ethnic nationalism Nationalism based on ancestry and the historic cultural traditions associated with a particular ethnic group.

European Union (EU) A confederal system composed of twenty-four European countries (as of 2004); it involves a common market enabling the free flow of goods, labour, and capital among the member countries, and a variety of common policies.

Executive activities Activities that involve implementing and administering laws and policies, and making specific decisions to put into effect the general laws.

Executive dominance A descriptive term applied to the Canadian parliamentary system because it places considerable power in the hands of the prime minister and cabinet through their ability to control the House of Commons.

Export-led industrialization (ELI) A model of economic development that features a capitalist system in which government and the biggest businesses work very closely together to develop export industries. Government influences investments, provides incentives for exports, and can decide which firms get to export products and which do not.

Extraparliamentary party A political party organization outside of parliament.

Failed state A state that no longer has the capacity to maintain order.

Fascism An ideology that combines an aggressive form of nationalism with a strong belief in the naturalness of inequality and opposition to both liberal democracy and communism.

Federal system A system of governing in which sovereign authority is divided or shared between the central government and regional governments, with each deriving its authority from the constitution.

Feminism A perspective that views society as patriarchal and seeks to achieve full independence and equality for women.

Fiscal conservatism The view that government spending should be reduced, that government debt should be reduced or eliminated, and that government spending should not exceed government revenues.

Framing Selecting and highlighting some facets of events or issues, and making connections among them so as to promote a particular interpretation, evaluation, and/or solution.

Free rider problem A problem with voluntary collective action that results because an individual can enjoy the benefits of group action without contributing.

Free-market capitalist economic system An economic system involving private ownership and control of most businesses. Economic activity is coordinated primarily through market transactions, rather than by the commands of government or other authorities.

Generational effect The effect on attitudes and behaviour of the views of different generations that persist throughout the life cycle.

Genocide The attempt to eliminate a racial or ethnic group.

Gerrymandering The manipulation of the division of the country into constituencies so as to benefit a particular party.

Globalization The processes that are increasing the interconnectedness of the world.

Government The set of institutions that make decisions and oversee the implementation of decisions on behalf of the state.

Governor general The person who carries out the largely ceremonial duties and responsibilities of the monarch. The governor general is appointed for a five-year term on the recommendation of the prime minister.

Gridlock A term used to describe the situation in American politics that can occur when Congress is not controlled by the president's party and disagreement between the executive and legislative branches stalls the process of governing.

Gross domestic product (GDP) The market value of goods and services produced in a country excluding transactions with other countries.

Gross national product (GNP) The market value of goods and services produced in a country, including the value of exports less the value of imports.

Head of government Heads the executive side of government. In Canada's parliamentary system, the prime minister is the head of government.

Head of state A largely ceremonial position as the official representative of the state. In a parliamentary system, the head of state is expected to be "above" politics and thus is not usually involved in making governing decisions.

Hegemony The ability of a dominant power to exert influence, primarily through authority, leadership, and persuading others to accept a particular view of the world.

Historical materialism The view that historical development can be understood in terms of the way society is organized to produce material goods. Marx and Engels applied historical materialism to argue that society progressed through various stages with feudalism being superseded by capitalism, which in turn will be replaced by a socialist system of production.

Holocaust The systematic extermination of six million European Jews by the Nazis during World War II.

House of Commons The elected chamber of Parliament, with each member of the House representing a particular geographical constituency.

House of Commons committees Committees composed of government and opposition party members in proportion to their party's strength in the House of Commons. These committees provide detailed examination of proposed legislation, and often suggest modifications to the proposed legislation.

House of Representatives The lower chamber of the American Congress, elected for a two-year term from districts of approximately equal population size.

Human Development Index (HDI) An annual index for most countries, calculated by the United Nations Development Programme and based on literacy and education, life expectancy, and per capita GDP.

Hypodermic model The view that the messages conveyed by the mass media have a direct effect on the attitudes and behaviour of the public.

Identity politics A perspective in which groups seek recognition and respect for their particular identity. This may include trying to gain particular rights, political power, and autonomy for a particular group.

Import substitution industrialization (ISI) An economic development model that involves creating an industrial sector by placing tariffs on imported industrial products.

Incremental model of policy making A policy-making model that suggests the policy process usually involves making minor changes from existing practices.

Individualist perspective A perspective of the common good that focuses on the well-being of individuals rather than the community as a whole. The community is seen as only the sum of the individuals who live in that community.

Inducement A form of power that involves using rewards or bribes.

Influence A relationship in which one political actor is able to affect the behaviour of other political actors. Within this general category, we can distinguish among three basic types or means of influence: rational persuasion, power, and authority.

Infotainment The merging of information and entertainment in news and public affairs programming of the mass media, particularly television.

Initiative A procedure that gives citizens the right, by obtaining a sizable number of signatures on a petition, to have a proposition that they have drafted put to a vote by the electorate for approval.

Inside strategies Strategies in which interest group leaders develop close contacts with key policy-makers in government and the public service in order to influence public policies.

Institutionalized interest group A group that has developed a formal organization with a stable membership, paid professional staff, access to the government officials who are relevant to its objectives, and regular means to keep its members and the public aware of its activities.

Interest group A group of people who have joined together to pursue common interests and to try to influence the making and implementation of the laws and policies of a political community.

International financial institution (IFI) An organization that has some ability to affect the global economic system; for example, the International Monetary Fund and the World Bank.

International governance The process whereby a number of different actors compete and cooperate in sharing the task of providing a certain degree of order and predictability to international relations.

International governmental organization (IGO) An association of states created to facilitate cooperation among them.

International non-governmental organization (INGO) An international organization that is not controlled by governments.

International relations The branch of political science that studies politics at the international level.

International society The idea that the increasing number and importance of international non-governmental organizations marks the development of a global society.

International system The relationship among states and international governmental organizations.

Iron law of oligarchy A generalization that claims all organizations, even those that appear democratic, inevitably become dominated by a small, cohesive group of leaders.

Islamism The perspective often associated with those seeking to purge "degenerate" foreign elements from Muslim society and base governing on Islamic-inspired regulations of life.

Issue-oriented group An interest group that spontaneously develops to express the views of people on a particular issue, concern, or grievance.

Judicial activism The term used when the judiciary is active in invalidating legislation and government actions that are inconsistent with the constitution.

Judicial activities Activities that involve resolving disagreements about how to interpret the laws, and determining if laws have been violated. In some countries, the courts can also review legislation and the activities of government to determine if they are consistent with the constitution.

Judicial review The authority of the courts to strike down legislation or governmental actions that the courts deem to be in violation of the constitution.

Jurisdiction The state's governing and law-making authority over a particular geographic area and population.

Keynesian economic policies The idea that government can smooth out the ups and downs of the free-market economy by stimulating the economy when private business investment is low, and cooling down the economy when excessive investment is creating inflation.

Laissez-faire system A system in which privately owned businesses, workers, and consumers freely interact in the marketplace without government interference. The role of government is limited to such activities as maintaining order and enforcing contracts.

Left The general ideological position generally associated with criticism of the capitalist system, advocacy of greater social and economic equality, and liberation from traditional institutions and practices.

Legal–rational authority The right to rule based on legal rules and procedures rather than on the personal qualities or characteristics of the rulers.

Legislative activities Activities that involve making general laws.

Legislature A body that is responsible for the formal approval of legislation.

Legitimacy Acceptance by the members of a political community that those in positions of authority have the right to govern.

Leninism The version of Marxism that includes the belief that the capitalist system can only be overthrown through force by means of a tightly disciplined party controlled by an ideologically oriented leadership.

Liberal democracy A political system that combines the liberal ideas of limited government, individual freedom, and the rule of law with the democratic idea of rule by the people.

Liberal feminism A version of feminism that advocates equal legal and political rights and equal opportunities for women.

Liberal–internationalism The view that increased cultural and social connections as well as economic interdependence are leading to the emergence of a global civil society that values cooperation, the rule of law, and peace, and that international governance is spreading both functionally and geographically.

Liberalism An ideological perspective advocating a high level of individual freedom, based on a belief in the inherent dignity and worth of each individual.

Liberation Freeing the human potential that has been stifled by the organization and values of society.

Liberation theology A theological perspective that argues that the poor should not accept their fate, but rather should actively struggle to liberate themselves from oppression of dominant social, political, and economic institutions and ideologies.

Libertarian perspective on the mass media The idea that the mass media should be free from government control and regulation.

Lieutenant-governor The person who carries out the largely ceremonial duties and responsibilities of the monarch at the provincial level. The lieutenant-governor is appointed for a five-year term on the recommendation of the prime minister.

Life cycle effect The effect on attitudes and behaviour of one's age. As a person grows older, his or her attitudes and behaviours may change due to changing circumstances (such as education, marriage, employment, and retirement) related to age.

Limits to growth The environmentalist view that there are limits to the ability of the earth to sustain the growth of production and consumption of goods and to support the growth of the size of the human population.

Lobbying An attempt to influence legislators, executives, or public officials, particularly by a person or firm that specializes in representing clients who seek to gain special benefits from government.

Majoritarian electoral system An electoral system designed to try to ensure that the winning candidate has the support of the majority of voters.

Majority government The government that results when the prime minister's party has a majority of the members of the House of Commons and thus a single party forms the government.

Managed capitalism An economic system that involves close collaboration among all or some of the major actors in the economy (particularly business, labour, and government) rather than emphasizing competition among businesses.

Manipulation A form of power that involves getting people to act in ways that the powerful would prefer, through providing misleading information and other techniques.

Marginalization Exclusion from the mainstream.

Mass media Television, radio, and widely circulated newspapers that tend to reach a large audience that is not strongly differentiated by social characteristics

Mass party A party that draws its support from a regular dues-paying membership and features a strong extraparliamentary party organization.

Meech Lake Accord A 1987 package of constitutional changes that was not passed. It contained controversial provisions, including the recognition of Quebec as a distinct society.

Mercantilist policies Pursuit of the interests of the nation-state through protectionist policies, the granting of monopolies to particular merchants, and the extraction of wealth from colonies.

Military dictatorship An undemocratic government run by the military.

Minimal effects model Through selective attention and selective perception, individuals filter out messages that might cause them to change their attitudes and behaviour. The effect of messages conveyed through the media is primarily to reinforce existing attitudes.

Ministers of state Cabinet ministers who are not responsible for a particular government department.

Minority government A single party governs but that party that does not have a majority of members in the House of Commons; thus, a minority government needs to gain the support of one or more other parties to pass legislation and to stay in office.

Mixed economy An economic system in which the government owns and controls a substantial proportion of business activity or plays a major role in planning and directing the economy; in other words, a mixture of socialist and capitalist economic systems.

Mixed member proportional (MMP) system An electoral system in which voters cast one vote for the party they prefer and one vote for the candidate they prefer. Some legislators are elected to represent particular constituencies based on gaining the most votes in that constituency, while others are elected based on the popular vote received by their party.

Mixed parliamentary/presidential system A governmental system that features a dual executive in which both the president and the prime minister possess political authority

Modernization theory A development model that views the traditional values, practices, and institutions of Third World countries as the basic cause of underdevelopment. To develop, poor countries should change their cultural outlook, social structure, economic organization, and political system based on the model of the advanced Western societies.

Monetarism An economic perspective based on the view that government's role in the economy should be largely restricted to controlling the supply of money.

Multiculturalism The idea that the diverse cultural heritage of a country should be officially recognized and that different groups should be encouraged to retain their language and culture.

Multiparty system A political party system featuring several parties that are significant actors in the competition for political power.

Multipolar system An international system containing four or more major powers.

Nation A group of people who share a sense of common identity.

Nationalism The idea that humanity is naturally divided into nations, each of which has certain distinctive characteristics.

National interest The goals that a state pursues to maximize what is perceived to be in its best interest.

Nation-state A sovereign state based on people who share a sense of being a member of a particular nation or nationality.

Nazism A version of fascism associated with Adolf Hitler, emphasizing racial conflict and the superiority of the "Aryan race."

Neo-conservatism A version of the New Right, based on the view that the West faces a cultural crisis because of the decline of traditional values. Neo-conservatives argue that the United States should exercise global leadership and use its strength to promote the values of democracy, freedom, and the free-market capitalist system worldwide.

Neo-corporatism A version of corporatism in which interest groups are not dominated by the state, involvement by groups is voluntary, and the representation of major interests is seen as supplementing, rather than replacing, liberal democracy.

Neo-fascism A revival of fascism in contemporary times.

Neo-liberalism A modern version of classical liberalism, focusing on the virtues of a laissez-faire system and the problems caused by government action.

New Left A perspective that sees the marginalized in societies (such as ethnic and racial minorities, students, youth, women, the poor, and the unemployed) as oppressed and the potential source of radical change; it emphasizes the need for liberation, promotion of different identities, and the creation of an egalitarian, participatory society.

New public management The adoption of contemporary business practices in the administration of government.

New Right A perspective that combines, in various ways, a vigorous promotion of free-market capitalism and traditional moral and cultural conservative values.

News management The controlling and shaping of the presentation of news in order to affect the public's evaluation of news stories.

New style of citizen politics Changes in political culture related to postmaterialism, the development of a post-industrial, knowledge-based economy, greater access to higher education, and more effective means of mass communications. This new style includes greater activism, the questioning of authority, the development of new political parties and new social movements, the raising of new types of issues, and the development of more liberal social values.

Non-confidence motion A motion put forward by the opposition members in a legislature expressing a lack of confidence in the government. If passed, the prime minister is expected to either resign or to request that an election be held.

Normative analysis Analysis that involves examining ideas about how the community should be governed and what values should be pursued through politics.

North The rich, developed countries.

Notwithstanding clause A provision in the Charter of Rights and Freedoms that allows a legislative body to explicitly declare that a particular law (related to some parts of the Charter) shall operate *notwithstanding* the provisions of the Charter. Such a declaration is only effective for five years, although it can be re-enacted as often as is desired

Official Development Assistance (ODA) Aid to the poorer countries given by the governments of the richer countries.

Official opposition The party with the second-highest number of seats in the House of Commons is designated as the official opposition and leads off the questioning or criticism of government every day that the House is sitting.

Oligarchy Rule by or control by the rich or an economic elite.

Ombudsman An independent officer of the legislature who investigates citizens' complaints concerning the government's administration.

One-party dominant system A party system in which a single party rules for long periods of time and the opposition parties are not likely to gain the support needed to successfully challenge the dominant party for control of the government.

Outside strategies Strategies in which interest group leaders appeal to the public for support in order to put pressure on decision-makers concerning public policies.

Pacted transition A democratic transition that occurs when pacts or agreements among the elites of formerly undemocratic states permit the establishment of democratic government.

Parliamentary party The aspect of a political party composed of the party's representatives in Parliament.

Parliamentary supremacy A basic principle of the British system of governing, recognizing Parliament as the supreme law-making body.

Parliamentary system A system of governing in which there is a close relationship between the legislative and executive branches of government. The authority of the executive (the prime minister and cabinet) is based on their ability to maintain the support of Parliament.

Party caucus A meeting of the party's parliamentary members.

Party convention A meeting of delegates from party constituency associations, the party's legislators, and party officials.

Party dictatorship An undemocratic political system that is controlled by one party. The most familiar examples are found in communist political systems.

Party discipline The expectation that legislators will vote in accordance with the position that the party has adopted in caucus.

Party government A government controlled by members of a particular political party.

Party identification A long-term psychological attachment to a particular political party.

Party system The pattern of competition among political parties.

Patriarchy A system in which power is in the hands of men and in which many aspects of women's lives are controlled by men.

Patronage Hiring government employees or awarding government contracts based on party or personal ties to the governing party.

Pay equity A policy that employers provide equal pay for work of equal value; for example, by raising the pay of persons in occupations that are largely staffed by females to the same pay as persons in comparable occupations that are largely staffed by males.

Permeability The ease with which interests and actors can enter the political system and stand a reasonable chance of using politics to secure their aims.

Personal dictatorship An undemocratic government dominated by a single individual. Saddam Hussein's Iraq was a classic example of this kind of system.

Personalistic leader A political leader whose claim to rule is based on some presumed inherent qualities of the person himself or, far less commonly, herself. It also implies a government in which all important decisions are made by the leader, according to the leader's wishes, and in which it is the leader who determines who gets what, when, and how.

Plebiscitary democracy A form of democracy in which citizens have more control of decisions than in representative democracy through the use of such devices as referendums, initiatives, and recall elections.

Pluralism/pluralist perspective Individuals' freedom to establish and join groups that are not controlled by the government results in a wide variety of groups having an ability to influence the decisions of government, with no group dominant.

Pole A concentration of power in the international system. It could be a state or an alliance.

Policy analysis Analysis that involves evaluating existing policies and suggesting what policies should be adopted to deal with particular problems.

Policy concertation Wide-ranging agreements on public policy resulting from regular interactions between government and the leading interest groups in a corporatist system.

Policy cycle The analysis of the policy process as a continuous cycle of stages, with policies continually undergoing modification in response to evaluations of the policy.

Policy entrepreneur Someone who is ready to push a pet policy proposal whenever an opportunity arises.

Policy evaluation Determining the extent to which a policy is achieving its objectives and how it can be made more effective.

Policy formulation Developing and evaluating different courses of action to deal with a problem.

Policy implementation Taking measures to put a policy into effect, such as developing rules and regulations and establishing an administrative structure.

Policy legitimation Gaining acceptance of a policy proposal; for example, through formal approval by a legislative body.

Policy network The governmental and nongovernmental actors that participate in the development of policies in a particular policy field.

Political agenda The issues that are considered important and given priority in political deliberations.

Political culture The general political values, attitudes, and beliefs that are widely held within a political community.

Political efficacy The attitude that individuals can have an impact on politics and that government is responsive to what people want.

Political ideology A package of interrelated ideas and beliefs about government, society, the economy, and human nature that affect political action. Each ideology provides a different perspective that is used to understand and evaluate how the world actually works.

Political opportunity structures (POS) The openings that political institutions and processes offer to (or withhold from) movements.

Political party An organization that has a central role in the competition for political power and seeks to occupy positions within the executive and legislative bodies of government.

Political philosophy The branch of political science that examines ideas about how the community should be governed and what values should be pursued through politics.

Political protest Oppositional political action that takes place outside formal channels, generally seeking to have government make significant changes in its policies.

Political science The systematic study of politics.

Political socialization The processes by which the values, attitudes, and beliefs of the political culture are transmitted to members of the political community.

Political violence The use of physical force that has a political objective.

Politics Activity related to making and implementing policies and decisions to deal with what are generally considered to be public problems. Generally, the study of politics focuses on government and those who seek to control or influence government and its decisions. However, politics is sometimes defined in a broader way to refer to activity related to decision-making in any organization or institution particularly where power, authority, or conflict are involved.

Polyarchy A political system characterized by competition for power and a citizenry free to contest government decisions.

Populism A perspective that advocates putting power in the hands of the people rather than the elites who control politics and society.

Positive right A right to services or benefits such as the right to education, health care, and employment.

Postmaterialist theory A theory that modern societies are undergoing a fundamental change in value priorities because generations that grew up in the relative security and affluence of the Western world since the Second World War are more likely to give priority to postmaterialist values than to materialist values.

Postmaterialist values Non-materialist values such as freedom of expression, participation, concern about the quality of life, and appreciation of a more beautiful environment.

Postmodern state A state in which the meaning and practice of sovereignty have been redefined since tools of governance are shared, foreign and domestic policies have become inextricably intertwined, and security is no longer based on control of borders, and deterrence.

Power The ability to get people, groups, or states to act against their own desires or interests through coercion, inducements, or manipulation. In this definition, power is a type of influence that can be distinguished from other types of influence, namely rational persuasion and authority. Some political scientists use the term power in a more general way to refer to any situation where one actor is able to affect the actions of another.

Preferential voting An electoral system in which voters rank candidates in order of preference. If no candidate has a majority of first preferences, the candidate with the least votes is dropped and the second preferences of those who voted for that candidate are added to the votes of other candidates. This process continues until one candidate has a majority.

Presidential system A system of governing characterized by a separation of power between the legislative and executive branches. The president and Congress each derive their authority from being elected by the people. The president is both head of government and head of state.

Presidential veto The ability of a president to reject legislation passed by Congress.

Primary election In the United States, a state-run election in which voters select the candidate they want to represent their party in the general election.

Prime ministerial government The view that prime minister has become the equivalent of the American president in the sense of being the chief executive, rather than the traditional position as "first among equals" in the cabinet.

Prime Minister's Office (PMO) The office that provides support and political advice to the prime minister.

Priming The potential capability of the media to affect the criteria by which people judge political events and personalities.

Private members Ordinary members of the House of Commons who are not in the cabinet.

Privy Council Office (PCO) A central agency, directly responsible to the Canadian prime minister, that has a key role in coordinating and directing the activities of government and in providing policy advice to the prime minister.

Procedural definition of democracy A definition of democracy in terms of procedures and institutions (such as elections) rather than outcomes.

Proportional representation (PR) system An electoral system in which the proportion of seats a party receives in the legislature reflects the proportion of votes it obtains.

Public choice theory A theory based on the assumption that individuals always pursue their own self-interest.

Public interest group A group that is concerned with the public interest rather than the particular interests of a specific part of society or economy.

Public policy A course of action or inaction chosen by public authorities to address a given problem or interrelated set of problems.

Quiet Revolution The changes in Quebec that began in 1960, based on the view that Quebec should become a modern, secular, technological society, led by an activist Quebec government that could promote a Québécois identity and place

greater control of governing and the economy in the hands of Quebeckers.

Radical feminism A version of feminism that views society as based fundamentally on the oppression of women, and seeks to liberate women through the fundamental transformation of social institutions, values, and personal relationships.

Rational–comprehensive model of policy making A policy-making model that views policy-makers as establishing clear goals to deal with a problem, examining all the alternatives for dealing with the problem in terms of measuring the consequences, and choosing the best alternative, which is implemented, then monitored and evaluated to assess whether the goals have been achieved, and changed if necessary.

Rational persuasion A form of influence involving use of true information to encourage people to act in accordance with their own interests or values.

Reactionary A conservative who favours a return to the values and institutions of the past.

Realism The view that because the international system based on sovereign states is anarchic, security is the major preoccupation of states. Peace depends on deterrence, and the possibility of international governance is limited because of the importance of state sovereignty.

Reasonable limits clause A provision of the Canadian Charter of Rights and Freedoms that allows for "reasonable limits" to be placed on rights and freedoms provided that the limits can be "demonstrably justified in a free and democratic society."

Recall A procedure that allows citizens to remove representatives from office. By gaining a sufficient number of signatures on a petition, citizens can require that their representative be required to seek re-election before the representative's term is over.

Referendum A vote by citizens on a particular issue or proposed law.

Reform liberalism A version of liberalism that argues government should play a role in assisting the disadvantaged.

Regulatory agency An independent agency of government, involved primarily in regulating the activities of private business.

Representative bureaucracy A bureaucracy that reflects the characteristics of society, particularly by trying to ensure that all levels of the public service have a proportion of women and various minority groups similar to that of the population as a whole.

Representative democracy A form of democracy in which citizens elect representatives to the legislature to make decisions on their behalf.

Responsible government The parliamentary convention that the prime minister and cabinet are responsible to the House of Commons, which can theoretically force them from office.

Right The general ideological position associated with defending the free-market capitalist system, property rights, and traditional moral values.

Rule of law The idea that we should be subject to known, predictable, and impartial rules of conduct, rather than to the arbitrary orders of particular individuals. Both the rulers and the ruled are subject to the law.

Run-off election An election held if no candidate receives a majority of votes; generally, only the top two candidates appear on the ballot to ensure that the winning candidate has a majority of the votes cast.

Secessionist A person who favours separation of a territory from an existing state.

Secretary of state A junior minister in Prime Minister Jean Chrétien's two-tier cabinet system.

Security dilemma The dilemma that arises when states need power to feel secure, but their accumulation of power might undermine rather than increase their security if it leads other states to feel in danger and form an alliance to meet the perceived threat.

Segregation The legal separation of Blacks and Whites, particularly in the Southern United States.

Selective incentive A particular benefit that is made available to members of an interest group but is not available to the public as a whole.

Self-interest group An interest group whose primary objective is to promote the interests of the interest group and its members.

Senate (American) The upper chamber of Congress. Two senators are elected by voters in each state for a six-year term.

Senate (Canadian) The upper chamber of Parliament, appointed on the recommendation of the prime minister. Senators hold their position until age seventy-five.

Single-member plurality (SMP) system An electoral system in which voters in each geographical constituency elect a single representative to the legislature. The candidate with the most votes is elected, regardless of whether or not that candidate received the majority of votes.

Single transferable vote (STV) An electoral system in which voters mark their preferences for candidates in a multimember constituency. Candidates receiving a certain proportion of the vote are declared elected. The second preferences of votes that are surplus to what the winning candidates need are then transferred to candidates who have not reached the quota. The process is continued until all seats in the constituency are filled.

Social class A grouping of people who have a similar position in terms of their position in the economy or a combination of income, education, and social status.

Social Darwinism The use of Darwin's theory of evolution to argue that competition and conflict allow humanity to evolve through the "survival of the fittest."

Social movement A network of groups that seek major social and political change, particularly by acting outside of established political institutions.

Social responsibility perspective on the mass media The view that the media have a responsibility to serve the public interest by providing fair and objective reporting of politics.

Socialism An ideological perspective based on the view that human beings are basically social in nature and that the capitalist system undermines the cooperative and community-oriented nature of humanity. Socialism advocates the establishment of an egalitarian society.

Socialist feminism A version of feminism that views women as oppressed by both the male-dominated character of society and the capitalist system, and argues that the liberation of women is connected to the transformation of capitalism into a more cooperative and egalitarian socialist system.

South Less developed, poorer countries.

Sovereign state A state that has the ability to govern its population and territory without outside interference.

Sovereignty The principle that states have the right to govern their population and territory without outside interference.

State An independent, self-governing political unit that acts through various governing institutions to make rules that are binding on the population within a particular country.

State corporatism An authoritarian version of corporatism in which groups were coerced into arrangements dominated by the state.

Streams and windows model of policy making A policy-making model that views the policy process as fluid, with changes in the identification of problems, policy proposals, and political circumstances creating windows of opportunity in which policy entrepreneurs may successfully push their pet proposals.

Structural adjustment program (SAP) A program administered by international financial institutions (IFAs), which offer loans at very favourable interest rates to governments facing problems paying their debt if they adopt the programs espoused by the Washington Consensus.

Sustainability Maintaining the integrity of ecosystems by ensuring that renewable resources are not being used at a rate that exceeds the ability of ecosystems to regenerate them, developing renewable substitutes to replace the consumption of non-renewable resources, and ensuring that the emission of pollutants does not exceed the ability of the ecosystem to handle them without damage.

Sustainable development Meeting the needs of the present without compromising the ability of future generations to meet their own needs; it involves development to ensure that the needs of the poor are fulfilled and protecting the environment for the well-being of future generations.

Tariff A tax on imports.

Terrorism The deliberate use of violence designed to induce fear in a population in order to achieve a political objective.

Theocratic dictatorship Undemocratic state run by religious elites. The best contemporary example is Iran.

Third Wave of Democracy The broad move to democratic government that began in 1974 and that still continues.

Third World Less developed countries.

Three faces of power The argument that looking at who affects particular decisions is insufficient to analyze power. Power can also involve the ability to keep issues off the political agenda and the ability to affect the dominant values of society.

Totalitarianism The idea that the state should control all aspects of life within a country. Examples of totalitarian regimes include Mussolini's Italy, Hitler's Germany, Stalin's Russia, and Mao Zedong's China.

Traditional administrative model A model of government organization that involves a clear division of the roles and responsibilities of government and administration, with public servants within each department of government providing unbiased, expert advice to the minister in charge of the department.

Traditional authority Authority based on customs that establish the right of certain persons to rule.

Transitional election An election that marks the official beginning of a democratic regime.

Treasury Board A cabinet committee with its own staff that plays a central role in governing because of its responsibility for the expenditures and management practices of government.

Triple-E Senate A proposed reform that would make Canada's Senate elected, effective, and based on an equal number of representatives from each province.

Two-party system A party system in which two major parties contend to control the government. Two-party systems are competitive in the sense that a single party does not govern for a lengthy period of time.

Two-plus party system A party system in which there are two major contenders for power, but other parties also have a significant amount of support, which may at times prevent either of the larger parties from gaining a majority of legislative seats.

Underdeveloped countries A term often used to describe Third World countries

Unipolarity An international system with a single superpower.

Unitary system A system of governing in which sovereign authority rests with the central government; regional and local governments are subordinate.

United Nations (UN) An international governmental organization representing almost all of the world's states.

Veto The ability to prevent the enactment of a measure, such as the authority of the president of the U.S. to veto laws passed by Congress (although this veto can be overridden by a two-thirds majority in each House of Congress).

Washington Consensus A series of policies put together by the International Monetary Fund and the World Bank that encourage developing countries to generate more revenue for debt repayment by cutting government expenditures to balance their budgets, selling off government-owned enterprises (privatization), and fully opening their countries to foreign goods and investments.

Welfare state A term used to describe countries in which government ensures that all people have a minimum standard of living and are provided some protection from hardships resulting from unemployment, sickness, disability, and old age.

REFERENCES

Adams, I. (2001). *Political ideology today* (2nd ed.). Manchester, UK: Manchester University Press.

Adolini, J.R., & Blake, C.H. (2001). *Comparing policies: Issues and choices in six industrialized countries.* Washington, DC: CQ Press.

Almond, G., & Verba, S. (1963). *The civic culture: Political attitudes and democracy in five nations.* Princeton, NJ: Princeton University Press.

Alterman, E. (2003). *What liberal media? The truth about bias and the news.* New York: Basic Books.

Anderson, B. (1983). *Imagined communities.* London: NLB/Verso.

Anderson, J.E. (1979). *Public policy-making* (2nd ed.). New York: Holt, Rinehart & Winston.

Ansolabehere, S., Iyengar, S., Simon, A., & Valentino, N. (1997). Does attack advertising demobilize the electorate? In S. Iyengar & R. Reeves (Eds.), *Do the media govern? Politicians, voters, and reporters in America* (pp. 195–207). Thousand Oaks, CA: Sage Publications.

Atkinson, A.B. (2000). Can welfare states compete in a global economy? In R.V. Ericson, & N. Stehr (Eds.), *Governing modern societies* (pp. 259–275). Toronto: University of Toronto Press.

Aucoin, P. (2002). Beyond the "new" public management reform in Canada: Catching the next wave? In C. Dunn (Ed.), *The Handbook of Canadian public administration* (pp. 37–52). Don Mills, ON: Oxford University Press.

Bachrach, P., & Baratz, M. (1962). The two faces of power. *American Political Science Review, 56,* 947–952.

Baer, D., Curtis, J., & Grabb, E. (2001). Has voluntary association activity declined? Cross-national analysis for fifteen countries. *Canadian Review of Sociology and Anthropology, 38,* 249–272.

Ball, T., & Dagger, R. (2004). *Political ideologies and the democratic ideal* (5th ed.). New York: Pearson Longman.

Ball-Rokeach, S.J., Rokeach, M., & Grube, J.W. (1984). *The great American values test: Influencing behavior and belief through television.* London: Free Press.

Barber, B. *Jihad vs. McWorld: How globalization and tribalism are reshaping the world.* New York: Ballantine, 1995.

Barnard, F.M. (2001). *Democratic legitimacy: Plural values and political power.* Montreal: McGill–Queen's University Press.

Bell, D. (1998). The end of ideology revisited. *Government and Opposition, 23,* 131–150; 321–328.

Bellini, E. (2004). The robustness of authoritarianism in the Middle East: Exceptionalism in comparative perspective. *Comparative Politics, 36*(2), 139–157.

Bercuson, D., & Cooper, B. (1998, August 8). The logic behind an elected Senate. *Globe and Mail,* D2.

Bhardwaj, R., & Vijayakrishnan, K. (1998). *Democracy and development: Allies or adversaries?* Aldershot, UK: Ashgate.

Blais, A., Gidengil, E., Nadeau, R, & Nevitte, N. (2002). *Anatomy of a Liberal victory: Making sense of the vote in the 2000 Canadian election.* Peterborough, ON: Broadview.

Blais, A, Gidengil, E., Nevitte, N., & Nadeau, R. (2004). Where does turnout decline come from? *European Journal of Political Research, 43,* 221–236.

Blais, A., & Massicotte, L. (2002). Electoral systems. In L. LeDuc, R.G. Niemi, & P. Norris (Eds.), *Comparing democracies 2: New challenges in the study of elections and voting* (pp. 40–69). London: Sage.

Blais, A., Massicotte, L., & Dobrzynska, A. (2003). *Why is election turnout higher in some countries than others?* Retrieved May 26, 2004 from www.elections.ca.

Blondel, J. (1968). Party systems and patterns of government in Western democracies. *Canadian Journal of Political Science, 1,* 180–203.

Blondel, J. (1991). Politics. In V. Bogdanor (Ed.), *The Blackwell encylopaedia of political science* (pp. 482–484). Oxford: Blackwell.

Bookchin, M. (1990). *Remaking society: Pathways to a green future.* Boston, MA: South End Press.

Borins, S. (2002) Transformation of the public sector: Canada in comparative perspective. In C. Dunn (Ed.), *The handbook of Canadian public administration* (pp. 3–17). Don Mills, ON: Oxford University Press.

Bosso, C.J. (1989). Setting the agenda: Mass media and the discovery of famine in Ethiopia. In M. Margolis & G.A. Mauser (Eds.), *Manipulating public opinion: Essays on public opinion as a dependent variable* (pp. 153–174). Belmont, CA: Wadsworth.

Boyd, D.R. (2003). *Unnatural law: Rethinking Canadian environmental law and policy.* Vancouver: UBC Press.

Breuilly, J. (1993). *Nationalism and the state* (2nd ed.). Manchester, UK: Manchester University Press.

Brodie, J., & Jenson, J. (1988). *Crisis, challenge and change: Party and class in Canada Revisited*. Ottawa: Carleton University Press.

Brown, W. (1999). Electoral facts. *Electoral Insight, 1*(2), pp. 28–36.

Brownmiller, S. (1975). *Against our will: Men, women and rape*. New York: Simon & Schuster.

Bryson, V. (2003). *Feminist political theory: An introduction* (2nd ed.). Houndmills, Basingstoke, Hampshire, UK: Palgrave Macmillan.

Bunce, V. (2003). Rethinking recent democratization: Lessons from the postcommunist experience. *World Politics, 55*(1), 167–192.

Burke, E. (1955). *Reflections on the revolution in France.* (T.H.D. Mahoney, Ed.). Indianapolis, IL: The Liberal Arts Press. (Original work published in 1790)

Cairns, A.C. (1968). The electoral system and the party system in Canada, 1921–1965. *Canadian Journal of Political Science, 1*(1), 55–80.

Cairns, A.C. (1992). *Charter versus federalism: The dilemmas of constitutional reform*. Montreal: McGill–Queen's University Press, 1992.

Calhoun, C. *Nationalism.* Buckingham, UK: Open University Press, 1997.

Cameron, D. (1978). The expansion of the public economy: A comparative analysis. *American Political Science Review, 72*, 1243–1261.

Canadian Association of University Teachers (2004). *CAUT almanac of post-secondary education in Canada*. CAUT: Ottawa.

Cappella, J.N. & Jamieson, K.H. (1997). *Spiral of cynicism: The press and the public good*. Oxford: Oxford University Press.

Cardoso, F.H., & Falletto, E. (1979). *Dependency and development in Latin America*. Berkeley: University of California Press, 1979.

Carothers, T. (1999). *Aiding democracy abroad*. Washington, DC: Carnegie Endowment for International Peace

Carothers, T. (2002). The end of the transition paradigm. *Journal of Democracy, 13*(1), 5–22.

Carty, R.K. (2002). Canadian political parties as franchise organizations. *Canadian Journal of Political Science, 35*(4), 723–745.

Castles, F.G. (1982). The impact of parties on public expenditure. In F.G. Castles (Ed.), *The impact of parties* (pp. 21–96). London: Sage.

Caul, M.L., & Gray, M.M. (2002). From platform declarations to policy outcomes: Changing party profiles and partisan influence over policy. In R.J. Dalton & M.P. Wattenberg (Eds.), *Parties with partisans: Political change in advanced industrial democracies* (pp. 208–237). Oxford: Oxford University Press.

CBC (2004a, February 3). Chasing the bouncing loonie: Cities vie for a new deal. Retrieved August 18, 2004 from www.cbc.ca/news/background/municipalities.

CBC (2004b). *CBC/Radio Canada pre-election poll*. Retrieved May 26, 2004 from www.cbc.ca/canadavotes/thepolls/democracypoll.html.

Centre for Research and Information on Canada (2002). *Portraits of Canada, 2002*. Retrieved August 18, 2003 from www.cric.ca/pdf/cahiers/cricpapers_dec2002.pdf.

Chalmers, D. (1991). Corporatism and comparative politics. In H. Wiarda (Ed.), *New directions in comparative politics* (pp. 54–82). Boulder, CO: Westview.

Clark, C., & McCarthy, S. (2003, January 24). Copps decries corporate donations. *Globe and Mail*, A4.

Clark, S. D., Grayson, J.P., & Grayson, L. (1976). General introduction: The nature of social movements. In S.D. Clark, J.P. Grayson, & L.M. Grayson (Eds.), *Prophecy and protest: Social movements in twentieth-century Canada* (pp. 1–38). Toronto: Gage.

Clark, W. (2001). *Economic gender equality indicators 2000*. Retrieved July 15, 2004 from www.swc-cfc.gc.ca/pubs/egei2000/egei2000_e.html.

Clarke, H.D., Jenson, J., LeDuc, L., & Pammett, J.H. (1996). *Absent mandate: Canadian electoral politics in an era of restructuring* (3rd ed.). Toronto: Gage Educational Publishing.

Clarke, T., & Barlow, M. (1997). *MAI: The multilateral agreement on investment and the threat to Canadian sovereignty*. Toronto: Stoddart.

Cleverdon, C.L. (1974). *The woman suffrage movement in Canada* (2nd ed.). Toronto: University of Toronto Press.

Close, D. (2004). Undoing democracy in Nicaragua. In D. Close & K. Deonandan (Eds.), *Undoing democracy: The politics of electoral caudillismo* (pp. 1–15). Lanham, MD: Lexington Books.

Close, D., & Deonandan, K. (Eds.) (2004). *Undoing democracy: The politics of electoral caudillismo*. Lanham, MD: Lexington Books

Close, D., & Mintz, E. (2001). *The Atlantic Coastal Action Program (ACAP): A state-sponsored environmental group*. Paper presented at the meeting of the Association of Canadian Studies in the United States, San Antonio, TX.

Code, L. (1988). Feminist theory. In S. Burt, L. Code, & L. Dorney (Eds.), *Changing patterns: Women in Canada*. Toronto: McClelland and Stewart.

Coleman, W.D. (2002). The politics of globalization. In R. Dyck (Ed.), *Studying politics: An introduction to political science* (pp. 389–405). Scarborough, ON: Thomson Nelson.

Compas (2004). *The Global TV election day poll*. Retrieved on August 16, 2004 from www.compas.ca/data/040628-GlobalTVEDayPollPart1-E.pdf.

Compston, H. (2003). Beyond corporatism: A configurational theory of policy concertation. *European Journal of Political Research, 42*, 787–809.

Connolly, W.E. (1974). *The terms of political discourse*. Lexington, MA: D.C. Heath.

Constantelos, J. (2001). Italy: The erosion and demise of party dominance. In C.S. Thomas (Ed.), *Political parties and interest groups: Shaping democratic governance* (pp. 119–138). Boulder, CO: Lynne Riemmer.

Coombes, C. (2003). *Terrorism in the twenty-first century* (3rd ed.). Upper Saddle River, NJ: Prentice-Hall.

Cooper, B. (1994). *Sins of omission: Shaping the news at CBC TV.* Toronto: University of Toronto Press.

Cooper, R. (2000). *The post-modern state and world order.* London: Foreign Policy Centre.

Coupland, R. (1964). *The British anti-slavery movement.* London: Frank Cass

Courchene, T.J. (1992). *Rearrangements: The Courchene papers.* Oakville, ON: Mosaic Press.

Crick, B. (1962). *In defence of politics.* London: Weidenfield and Nicholson.

Crick, B. (1993). *In defence of politics* (4th American ed.). Chicago: University of Chicago Press.

Cross, W., & Young, L. (2002). Policy attitudes of party members in Canada: Evidence of ideological politics. *Canadian Journal of Political Science*, 35(4), 859–880.

Croteau, D. (1998). *Examining the "liberal media" claim: Journalists' views on politics, economic policy, and media coverage.* Retrieved November 15, 2003 from www.fair.org/reports/journalist-survey.html.

Crozier, M, Huntington, S.P., & Watanuki, J. (1975). *The crisis of democracy.* New York: New York University Press.

CTV News (2004). *February 23, 2004 news broadcast.* Retrieved on August 6, 2004 from www.ctv.ca/servlet/ArticleNews/st...VNews/1077485317480_27/hub=CTVNewsAt11.

CTV.ca (2004). *Instant poll suggests Harper wins 2nd debate.* Retrieved on August 16, 2004 from www.ctv.ca/servlet/ArticleNews/story/CTVNews/1087347912382_160?hub=topstories.

Cutler, L.N. (1980). To form a government. *Foreign Affairs*, 59(1), 126–143.

Dahl, R.A. (1963). *Who governs? Democracy and power in an American city.* New Haven, CT: Yale University Press.

Dahl. R.A. (1961). *Who governs? Democracy and power in an American city.* New Haven: Yale University Press.

Dahl, R.A. (1984). *Modern political analysis* (4th ed.). Englewood Cliffs, NJ: Prentice-Hall.

Dahl, R.A. (1998). *On democracy.* New Haven, CT: Yale University Press.

Dalton, R.J. (2000). The decline of party identifications. In R.J. Dalton & M.P. Wattenberg (Eds.), *Parties without partisans: Political change in advanced industrial democracies* (pp. 19–36). Oxford: Oxford University Press.

Dalton, R.J. (2002). *Citizen politics: Public opinion and political parties in advanced industrial democracies* (3rd ed.). New York: Chatham House.

Dalton, R.J., & Wattenburg, M.P. (2000). Partisan change and the democratic process. R.J. Dalton & M.P. Wattenberg (Eds.), *Parties with partisans: Political change in advanced industrial democracies* (pp. 261–285). Oxford: Oxford University Press.

Daly, H.E., & Cobb, J.B. (1994). *For the common good: Redirecting the economy toward community, the environment, and a sustainable future* (2nd ed.). Boston: Beacon Press.

Decalo, S. (1988). *Psychoses of power: African personal dictatorships.* Boulder, CO: Westview Press.

Department of Finance, Canada. (2004). *Transfer payments to provinces: Equalization program.* Retrieved July 13, 2004 from www.fin.gc.ca/fedprov/eqpe.html.

Derbyshire, J.D., & Derbyshire, I. (1996). *Political systems of the world.* Oxford: Helicon.

Devall, B., & Sessions, G. (1998). Deep Ecology. In D. VanDeVeer & C. Pierce (Eds.), *The environmental ethics and policy book: Philosophy, ecology, economics* (2nd ed.) (pp. 221–226). Belmont, CA: Wadsworth.

DeWeil, B. (2000). *Democracy: A history of ideas.* Vancouver: UBC Press.

Di Palma, G. (1990). *To craft democracies.* Berkeley, CA: University of California Press.

Dickerson, M.O., & Flanagan, T. (2002). *An introduction to government and politics: A conceptual approach* (6th ed.). Scarborough, ON: Nelson Thomson.

Dobson, A. (2000). *Green political thought* (3rd ed.). New York: Routledge.

Doyle, T., & Kellow, A. (1995). *Environmental politics and policy making in Australia.* Melbourne: Macmillan.

Dryzek, J. (1997). *The politics of the earth: Environmental discourses.* Oxford: Oxford University Press.

Duverger, M. (1964). *Political parties: Their organization and activity in the modern state* (3rd ed.). London: Methuen.

Dyck, R. (2004). *Canadian politics: Critical approaches* (4th ed.). Scarborough, ON: Nelson Canada.

Eaman, R.A. (1987). *The media society: Basic issues and controversies.* Toronto: Butterworths.

Easton, D. (1953). *The political system: An enquiry into the state of political science.* New York: Knopf.

Eatwell, R. (1995). *Fascism: A history.* New York: Penguin Books.

Ehrenreich, B., & English, D. (1979). *For her own good: 150 years of the experts' advice to women.* New York: Anchor Press.

Ekos (2004). *Federal election poll #4: Final countdown.* Retrieved on August 16, 2004 from www.ekos.com/admin/pressreleases/26june2004backgrounddoc.pdf.

Elections Canada (1997). *A history of the vote in Canada.* Ottawa: Minister of Public Works and Government Services.

Elections Canada (2004a). *Election night results.* Retrieved on August 16, 2004 from enr.elections.ca/MajorCentres_e.aspx.

Elections Canada (2004b). Retrieved July 11, 2004 from www.elections.ca.

Elections Canada (2004c). *Voter turnout at federal elections and referendums 1867–2000*. Retrieved July 12, 2004 from www.elections.ca.

Elkins, D.J. (1993). *Manipulation and consent: How voters and leaders manage complexity*. Vancouver: UBC Press.

Elkins, D.J. (1995). *Beyond sovereignty: Territory and political economy in the twenty-first century*. Toronto: University of Toronto Press.

Elster, J. (1998). *Deliberative democracy*. Cambridge: Cambridge University Press.

Enloe, C. (1989). *Bananas, beaches and bases: Making feminist sense of international relations*. London: Pandora.

Entman, R.M. (2004). *Projections of power: Framing news, public opinion, and U.S. foreign policy*. Chicago: University of Chicago Press.

Epstein, L. (1964). A comparative study of Canadian parties. *American Political Science Review, 58*(1), 46–59.

Farcau, B.W. (1994). *The coup: Tactics in the seizure of power*. Westport, CT: Praeger.

Fitch, J.S. (1977). *The military coup d'etat as a political process*. Baltimore, MD: Johns Hopkins University Press.

Fitch, S. (1998). *The armed forces and democracy in Latin America*. Baltimore, MD: Johns Hopkins University Press.

Foreman, D. (1991). *Confessions of an eco-warrior*. New York: Harmony Books.

Fournier, P. (2002). The uninformed Canadian voter. In J. Everitt & B. O'Neill (Eds.), *Citizen politics: Research and theory in Canadian political behaviour* (pp. 92–109). Don Mills, ON: Oxford University Press.

Frank, A.G. (1972). The development of underdevelopment. In D. Cockcroft, A.G. Frank, & D. Johnson (Eds.), *Dependence and underdevelopment*. New York: Anchor Books.

Frank, A.G. (1979). *Dependent accumulation and underdevelopment*. New York: Monthly Review Press.

Freedman, J. (2001). *Feminism*. Buckingham, UK: Open University Press.

Freedom House (n.d.). Retrieved May 16, 2004 from www.freedomhouse.org.

Freedom House (1999). *Democracy's century: A survey of political change in the 20th century*. Retrieved August 20, 2004 from www.freedomhouse.org/reports/century.html.

Freedom House (2003). *Freedom in the world 2004*. Retrieved August 20, 2004 from www.freedomhouse.org/research/survey2004.htm.

Friedan, B. (1963). *The feminine mystique*. New York: Dell.

Friedan, B. (1998). *It changed my life: Writings on the women's movement*. Cambridge, MA: Harvard University Press.

Friederich, C., & Brzezinski, Z. (1956). *Totalitarian dictatorship and democracy*. Cambridge, MA: Harvard University Press.

Friedman, T. (2000). *The Lexus and the olive tree*. New York: Anchor Books, 2000.

Frum, D. (1996). *What's right: The new conservatism and what it means for Canada*. Toronto: Random House.

Fukuyama, F. (1989). The end of history? *The National Interest, 16*, 3–18.

Fukuyama, F. (1992). *The end of history and the last man*. New York: Free Press.

Gamble, A. (1994). *The free economy and the strong state: The politics of Thatcherism* (2nd ed.). Houndsmills, Basingstoke, Hampshire, UK: Macmillan.

Garrett, G. (1998). *Partisan politics in the global economy*. Cambridge: Cambridge University Press.

Gibbins, R. (1982). *Regionalism: Territorial politics in Canada and the United States*. Toronto: Butterworths.

Giddens, A. (2000). *Runaway world: How globalization is reshaping our lives*. New York: Routledge.

Gidengil, E., & Everitt, J. (2002). Damned if you do, damned if you don't: Television news coverage of female party leaders in the 1993 federal election. In W. Cross (Ed.), *Political Parties, Representation, and Electoral Democracy in Canada,* (pp. 223–237). Don Mills, ON: Oxford University Press.

Gidengil, E., Blais, A., Nadeau, R., & Nevitte, N. (2002). Changes in the party system and anti-party sentiment. In W. Cross (Ed.), *Political parties, representation, and electoral democracy in Canada* (pp. 68–86). Don Mills, ON: Oxford University Press.

Gidengil, E., Blais, A., Nadeau, R, & Nevitte, N. (2003). Women to the left? Gender differences in political beliefs and policy preferences. In M. Tremblay & L. Trimble (Eds.), *Women and electoral politics in Canada* (pp. 140–159). Don Mills, ON: Oxford University Press.

Gill, B., Rocamora, J., & Wilson, R. (Eds.). (1993) *Low intensity democracy*. London: Pluto Press.

Gilligan, C. (1982). *In a different voice*. Cambridge, MA: Harvard University Press.

Glendon, M.A. (1995). Rights in twentieth century constitutions. In A. Etzioni (Ed.), *Rights and the common good: The communitarian perspective* (pp. 27–36). New York: St. Martin's Press.

Goldstein, J. S. (1994). *International relations*. New York: HarperCollins College.

Green, D., & Luehrmann, L. (2003). *Comparative politics of the Third World*. Boulder, CO: Lynne Rienner Publisher.

Gunther, R., & Mughan, A. (2000). The political impact of the media: A reassessment. In R. Gunther & A. Mughan (Eds.), *Democracy and the media: A comparative perspective* (pp. 402–448). Cambridge, UK: Cambridge University Press.

Gurr, T.R. (1966). *Why men revolt*. Princeton: Princeton University Press.

Habermas, J. (1976). *Legitimation crisis* (T. McCarthy, Trans.). Boston: Beacon Press. (Original work published 1973)

Hackett, R.A., & Zhao, Y. (1998). *Sustaining democracy? Journalism and the politics of objectivity*. Toronto: Garamond Press.

Handelman, H. (2003). *The challenge of Third World development*. Upper Saddle River, NJ: Prentice-Hall.

Harris, M. (1991). *Unholy orders: Tragedy at Mount Cashel*. Toronto: Penguin.

Hartz, L. (1964). *The founding of new societies.* Toronto: Longmans.

Hauss, C., & Smith, M. (2000). *Comparative politics: Domestic responses to global challenges: A Canadian perspective.* Scarborough, ON: Nelson Thomson Learning.

Heard, A. (2002). Political culture, socialization, and how we have been taught to think. In R. Dyck (Ed.), *Studying politics: An introduction to political science* (pp. 73–96). Scarborough, ON: Thomson Nelson.

Heberle, R. (1951). *Social movements.* New York: Appleton, Century, Crofts.

Heclo, H. (1978). Issue networks and the executive establishment. In A. King, (Ed.), *The new American political system* (pp. 87–124). Washington, DC: American Enterprise Institute.

Hedley, R.A. (2002). *Running out of control: Dilemmas of globalization.* Bloomfield, CT: Kumarian Press.

Held, D. (2000). The changing contours of political community: Rethinking democracy in the context of globalization. In R.V. Ericson & N. Stehr (Eds.), *Governing modern societies* (pp. 42–59). Toronto: University of Toronto Press.

Hentoff, N. (2003, September 17). Bush accused by Lords of the Bar. *Village Voice.* Retrieved August 17, 2004 from www.villagevoice.com/issues/0339/hentoff.php.

Heritage Foundation (2004). *2004 index of economic freedom.* Retrieved May 11, 2004 from www.heritage.org/research/features/index/countries.html.

Herman, E.S., & Chomsky, N. (2002). *Manufacturing consent* (updated ed.). New York: Pantheon Books.

Herron, C. (1996). *The Canadian labour movement: A brief history.* Toronto; James Lorimer.

Hessing, M., & Howlett, M. (1997). *Canadian natural resource and environmental policy: Political economy and public policy.* Vancouver: UBC Press.

Heywood, A. (2002). *Politics* (2nd ed.). Houndmills, Basingstoke, Hampshire, UK: Palgrave.

Hibbs, D. (1987). *The political economy of industrialized democracies.* Cambridge, MA: Harvard University Press.

Hobbes, T. (1968). *Leviathan.* C.B. Macpherson (Ed.). Harmondsworth, UK: Penguin.

Hooghe, L., & Marks, G. (2001). *Multi-level governance and European integration.* Boulder, CO: Rowman and Littlefield.

Horowitz, G. (1966). Conservatism, liberalism and socialism in Canada: An interpretation. *Canadian Journal of Economics and Political Science, 32*(2), 143–171.

Howlett, M., & Ramesh, M. (1995). *Studying public policy: Policy cycles and policy subsystems.* Toronto: Oxford University Press.

Hume, M. (2004, July 12). For whistle blower, it got personal. *Globe and Mail,* p. A4.

Hunter, J.D. (1991). *Culture wars: The struggle to define America.* New York: Basic Books.

Huntington, S.P. (1991). *The third wave.* Norman, OK: University of Oklahoma Press.

Huntington, S.P. (1993). The clash of civilizations? *Foreign Affairs, 72*(3), 22–49.

Huntington, S.P. (1996). *The clash of civilizations and the remaking of world order.* New York: Simon & Schuster.

Huntington, S.P, Crozier, M., & Watanuki, J. (1975). *The crisis of democracy.* New York: New York University Press.

Inglehart, R.I. (1977). *The silent revolution: Changing values and political styles among Western publics.* Princeton, NJ: Princeton University Press.

Inglehart, R.I. (1990). *Culture shift in advanced industrial society.* Princeton, NJ: Princeton University Press.

Inglehart, R.I., & Norris, P. (2003). *The true clash of civilizations.* Retrieved on August 10, 2004 from www.globalpolicy.org/globaliz/cultural/2003/0304clash.htm.

International Commission on Intervention and State Sovereignty (2001). *The Responsibility to Protect: Report of the International Commission on Intervention and State Sovereignty.* Retrieved August 20, 2004 from www.dfait-maeci.gc.ca/iciss-ciise/pdf/Commission-Report.pdf.

International Institute for Democracy and Electoral Assistance (n.d.). Retrieved February 22, 2004 from www.idea.int/vt/index.cfm.

International Institute for Democracy and Electoral Assistance (n.d.). Retrieved May 16, 2004 from www.idea.int/.

Inter-Parliamentary Union (2004). *Women in national parliaments.* Retrieved June 30, 2004 from www.ipu.org/wne-e/classif.htm.

Ipsos-Reid (2004). *Ipsos-Reid CTV June 16, 2004 poll.* Retrieved August 16, 2004 from www.ipsos-na.com/news/act_hit_cntr.ctm?id-2294&PDF_name=mr040619-1fb.pdf.

Isaac, J.C., Filner, M.F, & Bivins, J.C (1999). American democracy and the New Christian Right: A critique of apolitical liberalism. In I. Shapiro & C. Hacker-Cordon (Eds.), *Democracy's edges* (pp. 222–264). Cambridge: Cambridge University Press.

Iyengar, S., & Kinder, D. (1987). *News that matters.* Chicago: University of Chicago Press.

Janowitz, M. (1977). *Military institutions and coercion in the developing nations.* Chicago: University of Chicago Press.

Jennings, M.K. (1984). The intergenerational transfer of political ideologies in eight Western nations. *European Journal of Political Research 12,* 261–276.

Jennings, M.K., & Niemi, R.G. (1968). The transmission of political values from parent to child. *American Political Science Review, 62,* 169–184.

Jennings, M.K, & Niemi, R.G. (1981). *Generations and politics: A panel study of young adults and their parents.* Princeton, NJ: Princeton University Press.

Kampfner, J. (2003, May 15). The truth about Jessica. *The Guardian Unlimited.* Retrieved August 11, 2004 from www.guardian.co.uk/Iraq/Story/0,2763,956255,00.html.

Katz, R.S., & Mair, P. (1995). Changing models of party organization and party democracy: the emergence of the cartel party. *Party Politics, 1,* 5–28.

Keating, M. (1996). *Nations against the state: The new politics of nationalism in Quebec, Catalonia and Scotland.* Houndmills, Basingstoke, Hampshire, UK: Macmillan.

Kedourie, E. (1994). *Nationalism* (4th ed.). Oxford: Blackwell.

Kent, A. (1996). *Risk and redemption: Surviving the network news wars.* Toronto: Penguin Books Canada.

Keohane, R.O. (1984). *After hegemony: Cooperation and discord in the world political economy.* Princeton, NJ: Princeton University Press.

Kesselman, M, Krieger, J., & Joseph, W.A. (1996). *Comparative politics at the crossroads.* Lexington, MA: D.C. Heath.

Kiernan, B. (2002). *The Pol Pot regime: Race, power, and genocide under the Khmer Rouge.* New Haven: Yale University Press.

Kingdon, J.W. (1995). *Agendas, alternatives and public policies* (2nd ed.). New York: Longman.

Kircheimer, O. (1966). The transformation of West European party systems. In J. LaPalombara & M. Weiner (Eds.), *Political parties and political development* (pp. 177–200). Princeton, NJ: Princeton University Press.

Kirkpatrick, J. (1979). Dictatorships and double standards. *Commentary, 68*(5), 34–45.

Kitschelt, H. (1986). Political opportunity structures and political protest: Anti-nuclear movements in four democracies. *British Journal of Political Science, 16*(1) 57–79.

Klein, N. (2002). *Fences and windows: Dispatches from the front lines of the globalization debate.* Toronto: Vintage Canada.

Korten, D.C. (1996). *When corporations rule the world.* West Hartford, CT: Kumarian Press.

Kraft, M.E. (2004). *Environmental policy and politics* (3rd ed.). New York: Pearson Longman.

Kristol, I. (1978). *Two cheers for capitalism.* New York: Basic Books.

Ladd, E.C. (1999). *The Ladd report.* New York: Free Press.

Lane, J.-E., & Ersson, S. (2000). *The new institutional politics: Performance and outcomes.* London: Routledge.

Lasswell, H. (1936). *Politics: Who gets what, when, how?* New York: McGraw-Hill.

Lau, R., Sigelman, L, Heldman, C, & Babbitt, P. (1999). The effects of negative political advertisements: A meta-analytic assessment. *American Political Science Review, 93*, 851–875.

Law Commission of Canada. *Voting counts: Electoral reform for Canada.* Retrieved May 17, 2004 from www.cc.gc.ca/en/themes/gr/er/er_main.asp.

Lawson, K. (1997). *The human polity: A comparative introduction to political science* (4th ed.). Boston: Houghton Mifflin.

Laxer, J. (1996). *In search of a new left: Canadian politics after the neoconservative assault.* Toronto: Penguin Books Canada.

Laycock, D. (2002). *The new right and democracy in Canada: Understanding Reform and the Canadian Alliance.* Don Mills, ON: Oxford University Press.

Leach, R. (2002). *Political ideology in Britain.* Houndmills, Basingstoke, Hampshire, UK: Palgrave.

Leach, R. (2003). Whither conservatism? The ideas of the British Conservative Party. *Talking Politics, 15*, 2.

Leftwich, A. (1983). *Redefining politics: People, resources and power.* London: Methuen.

Leftwich, A. (Ed.). (1996). *Democracy and development: Theory and practice.* Cambridge: Polity Press.

Lijphart, A. (1994). Presidentialism and majoritarian democracy: Theoretical observations In J.J. Linz & A. Valenzuela (Eds.), *The failure of presidential democracy: Vol. 1. Comparative perspectives* (pp. 91–105). Baltimore, MD: John Hopkins University Press.

Lijphart, A. (1999). *Patterns of democracy: Government forms and performance in thirty-six countries.* New Haven, CT: Yale University Press.

Lindblom, C.E. (1959). The science of muddling through. *Public Administration Review, 19*(2), 79–88.

Lindblom, C.E. (1977). *Politics and markets: The world's political-economic systems.* New York: Basic Books.

Lindblom, C.E. (2001). *The market system: What it is, how it works and what to make of it.* New Haven, CT: Yale University Press.

Linz, J. (1964) An authoritarian regime: Spain. In E. Allardt & Y. Littunen (Eds.), *Cleavages, ideologies, and party systems: Contributions to comparative political sociology. Transactions of the Westermarck Society, 10*, 291–342.

Linz, J. (1994). Presidential or parliamentary democracy: Does it make a difference? In J.J. Linz & A. Valenzuela (Eds.), *The Failure of Presidential Democracy: Vol. 1. Comparative perspectives* (pp. 3–87). Baltimore, MD: John Hopkins University Press.

Linz, J., & Stepan, A. (Eds.). (1978). *The breakdown of democratic regimes.* Baltimore. MD: Johns Hopkins University Press.

Lipschutz, R. (1992). Reconstructing world politics: The emergence of global civil society. *Millennium: Journal of International Studies, 21*, 3.

Lipset, S.M. (1950). *Agrarian socialism.* Berkeley, CA: University of California Press.

Lipset, S.M. (1990). *Continental divide: The values and institutions of the United States and Canada.* New York: Routledge.

Lipsky, R. (1968). Protest as a political resource. *American Political Science Review, 62*(4), 1144–1158.

Lukes, S. (1974). *Power: A radical view.* London: Macmillan.

Luttwak, E. (1969). *Coup d'etat.* New York: Alfred A. Knopf.

Lutz, M.A. (1999). *Economics for the common good: Two centuries of social economic thought in the humanistic tradition.* London: Routledge.

Lyon, V. (1996). Parties and democracy: A critical view. In A.B. Tanguay & A.-G. Gagnon (Eds.), *Canadian parties in transition* (2nd ed.) (pp. 106–134). Scarborough, ON: Nelson Canada.

MacLean, B.K., Bowles, P., & Croci, O. (1999). East Asian crises and regional economic integration. In A. Rugman, & G. Boyd (Eds.), *Deepening integration in the Pacific economies: Corporate alliances, contestable markets and free trade* (pp. 19–54). Cheltenham, UK: Edward Elgar.

Macpherson, C.B. (1954). *Democracy in Alberta*. Toronto: University of Toronto Press.

Macpherson, C.B. (1965). *The real world of democracy*. Toronto: CBC Publications.

Major, K. (2001). *As near to heaven by sea: A history of Newfoundland & Labrador*. Toronto: Penguin

Marletti, C., & Roncarolo, F. (2000). Media influence in the Italian transition from a consensual to a majoritarian democracy. In R. Gunther & A. Mughan (Eds.), *Democracy and the media: A comparative perspective* (pp. 195–240). Cambridge, UK: Cambridge University Press.

Marshall, T.H. (1950). *Citizenship and social class*. Cambridge: Cambridge University Press

Martel, L. (1994). *Ecology and society: An introduction*. Amherst, MA: University of Massachusetts Press.

Martin, H.-P., & Schumann, H. (1997). *The global trap: Globalization and the assault on democracy and prosperity*. Montreal: Black Rose Books.

Marx, K. & Engels, F. (1955). *The communist manifesto*. New York: Appleton-Century-Crofts. (Original work published in 1848)

Marzolini, M (2002, September). *Polling alone: Canadian values and liberalism*. Paper presented to the conference on Securing the New Liberalism, Toronto. Retrieved August 10, 2004 from www.pollara.ca/new/POLLARA_NET.html.

McLean, I. (Ed.) (2003). *Concise Oxford dictionary of politics*. Oxford: Oxford University Press.

McQuail, D. (1994). *Mass communication theory: An introduction* (3rd ed.). London: Sage.

Meadows, D., Meadows, D., & Randers, J. (1992). *Beyond the limits: Global collapse of a sustainable future*. London: Earthscan.

Meadows, D.H., Meadows, D.L. Randers, J., & Behrens, W.H. (1972). *The limits to growth*. New York: Universe Books.

Medcalf, L.J., & Dolbeare, K.M. (1985). *Neopolitics: American political ideas in the 1980s*. Philadelphia, PA: Temple University Press.

Meisel, J., & Mendelsohn, M. (2001). Meteor? Phoenix? Chameleon? The decline and transformation of party in Canada. In H.G. Thorburn & A. Whitehorn (Eds.), *Party politics in Canada* (8th ed.) (pp. 163–178). Toronto: Prentice Hall.

Michels, R. (1962). *Political parties: A sociological study of the oligarchic tendencies of modern democracy* (E. Paul & C. Paul, Trans.) New York: Collier. (Original work published in 1911)

Miljan, L.A., & Cooper, B. (2003). *Hidden agendas: How journalists influence the news*. Vancouver: UBC Press, 2003.

Mill, J.S. (1912). *On liberty. Representative government. The subjection of women. Three essays*. London: Oxford University Press. (*On Liberty* originally published in 1859)

Miller, W.L., & Niemi, R.G. (2002).Voting: Choice, conditioning, and constraint. In L. LeDuc, R.G. Niemi, & P. Norris (Eds.), *Comparing democracies 2: New challenges in the study of elections and voting* (pp. 169–188). London: Sage.

Millett, K. (1985). *Sexual politics*. London: Virago.

Mills, C.W. (1956). *The power elite*. New York: Oxford University Press.

Milner, H. (2001). Civic literacy in comparative context: Why Canadians should be concerned. *Policy Matters, 2*, 3–39.

Milner, H. (2002). *Civic literacy: How informed citizens make democracy work*. Hanover, NH: University Press of New England.

Mintz, E. (1993). Two generations: The political attitudes of high school students and their parents. *International Journal of Canadian Studies,* (special issue), 59–71.

Mishler, W., & Clarke, H.D. (1995). Political participation in Canada. In M.S. Whittington & G. Williams (Eds.), *Canadian politics in the 1990s* (4th ed.) (pp. 129–151). Toronto: Nelson Canada.

Montgomery, T., (Ed.). (2000). *Peacekeeping and democratization in the western hemisphere*. Coral Gables, FL: North–South Center Press, University of Miami.

More, T. (2004). *Utopia*. In T. Ball, & R. Dagger (Eds.), *Ideals and ideologies: A reader* (5th ed.). New York: Pearson Longman. (Original work published in 1516)

Morgan, R. (1977). *Going too far: The personal chronicle of a feminist*. New York: Random House.

Morgenthau, H.J. (1948). *Politics among nations: The struggle for power and peace*. New York: Knopf.

Morton, F.L. (2003). Can judicial supremacy be stopped? *Policy Options, 24*(9), 25–99.

Morton, F.L., & Knopff, R. (2000). *The Charter revolution and the court party*. Peterborough, ON: Broadview Press.

Morton, W.L. (1950). *The Progressive Party in Canada*. Toronto: University of Toronto Press

Mueller, J. (1989). *Retreat from doomsday: The obsolescence of major war*. New York: Basic Books.

Munck, R. (1997). Introduction: A thin democracy. *Latin American Perspectives, 24*(6), 5–21.

Myers, R.A., & Worm, B. (2003). Rapid worldwide depletion of predatory fish communities. *Nature, 423*(6937), 280–283.

Nadeau, R. (2002). Satisfaction with democracy: The Canadian paradox. In N. Nevitte (Ed.), *Value change and governance in Canada* (pp. 37–70). Toronto: University of Toronto Press.

Needler, M.C. (1996). *Identity, interest, and ideology: An introduction to politics*. Westport, CT: Praeger.

Neocleous, M. (1997). *Fascism*. Minneapolis: University of Minnesota Press.

Nevitte, N. (1996). *The decline of deference: Canadian value change in cross-national perspective*. Peterborough, ON: Broadview Press.

Nevitte, N., Blais, A., Gidengil, E, & Nadeau, R. (2000). *Unsteady state: The 1997 Canadian federal election*. Don Mills, ON: Oxford University Press.

Norris, P. (2000). *A virtuous circle: Political communications in postindustrial societies.* Cambridge, UK: Cambridge University Press, 2000.

Norris, P. (2001a). *Digital divide: Civic engagement, information poverty, and the Internet worldwide.* Cambridge, UK: Cambridge University Press.

Norris, P. (2001b). US Campaign 2000: Of pregnant chads, butterfly ballots and partisan vitriol. *Government and Opposition, 36,* 3–26.

Norris, P. (2002). Campaign communications. In L. LeDuc, R.G. Niemi, & P. Norris (Eds.), *Comparing democracies 2: New challenges in the study of elections and voting* (pp. 127–147). London: Sage.

O'Donnell, G. (1994). Delegative democracy, *Journal of Democracy, 5*(1), 55–69.

O'Neill, B. (2002). Sugar and spice? Political culture and the political behaviour of Canadian women. In Everitt, J., & O'Neill, B. (Eds.), *Citizen politics: Research and theory in Canadian political behaviour* (pp. 40–55). Don Mills, ON: Oxford University Press.

Oberschall, A. (1993). *Social movements: Ideologies, interests, and identities.* New Brunswick, NJ: Transaction Publishers.

Observatory on Media and Public Policy (2004). *2004 federal election newspaper content analysis: Cumulative results May 17–June 25, 2004.* Retrieved July 10, 2004 from www.ompp.mcgill.ca/pages/election2004.htm#media.

O'Connor, K., & Sabato, L.J. (1995). *American government: Roots and reform* (2nd ed.). Boston: Allyn and Bacon.

Ohmae, K. (1995). *The end of the nation state: The rise of regional economies.* London: HarperCollins.

Olson, M. (1965). *The logic of collective action: Public goods and the theory of groups.* Cambridge, MA: Harvard University Press.

Opp, K.-D. (1989). *The rationality of political protest.* Boulder, CO: Westview Press.

Oppenheimer, J.R. (1953). Atomic weapons and American policy. *Foreign Affairs, 31*(4), 525–535.

Organski, A.F.K. (1967). *The stages of political development.* New York: Knopf.

Osborne, D., & Gaebler, T. (1992). *Reinventing government: How the entrepreneurial spirit is transforming the public sector.* Reading, MA: Addison-Wesley.

Oxfam (2003). *Running into the sand: Why failure at the Cancun trade talks threatens the world's poorest people.* Retrieved May 9, 2004 from www.oxfam.org.uk/what_we_do/issue/trade/bp53_cancun.pdf.

Pal, L.A. (1992). *Public policy analysis: An introduction* (2nd ed.). Scarborough, ON: Nelson Canada.

Pal, L.A. (1993). *Interests of state: The politics of language, multiculturalism and feminism in Canada.* Montreal: McGill–Queen's University Press.

Pammett, J.H. (2001) The people's verdict. In J.H. Pammett & C. Dornan (Eds.), *The Canadian general election of 2000* (pp. 293–317). Toronto: Dundurn.

Pammett, J.H., & LeDuc, L. (2003). *Explaining the turnout decline in Canadian federal elections: A new survey of non-voters.* Retrieved May 26, 2004 from www.elections.ca.

Panebianco, A. (1988). *Political parties: Organization and power.* Cambridge, UK: Cambridge University Press.

Panitch, L. V. (1995). Elites, classes, and power in Canada. In M.S. Whittington & G. Williams (Eds.), *Canadian Politics in the 1990s* (4th ed.) (pp. 152–175). Toronto: Nelson Canada.

Parrington, V. (1987). *Main currents in American thought* (Vols. 1–2). Norman, OK: University of Oklahoma Press.

Patterson, T.E. (2000). The United States: News in a free-market society. In R. Gunther & A. Mughan (Eds.), *Democracy and the media: A comparative perspective* (pp. 241–265). Cambridge, UK: Cambridge University Press.

Perlin, G. (2003). *International assistance to democratic development: A review.* IRPP Working Paper Series no. 2003-04. Montreal: Institute for Research on Public Policy.

Petter, A. (1990). When rights go wrong. *Policy Options, 11*(3), 33–34.

Pharr, S., Putnam, R.D., & Dalton, R.J. (2000). A quarter century of declining confidence. *Journal of Democracy, 11*(2), 5–25.

Pierson, C. (1996). *The modern state.* London: Routledge.

Polisource (2003). *Background note: Mexico.* Retrieved August 20, 2004 from www.polisource.com/documents/BackgroundNotes/1838pf.shtml.

Pollack, K.M. (2002). *The threatening storm: The case for invading Iraq.* New York.

Porter, J. (1965). *The vertical mosaic.* Toronto: University of Toronto Press.

Postman, N. (1985). *Amusing ourselves to death: Public discourse in an age of show business.* New York: Penguin.

Potter, S.V. (2003). Judging the judiciary: The rule of law in the age of the Charter. *Policy Options, 24*(9), 34–38.

Pross, A.P. (1993). *Group politics and public policies* (2nd ed.). Toronto: Oxford University Press.

Putnam, R. (2000). *Bowling alone: The collapse and revival of American community.* New York: Simon & Schuster.

Qualter, T.J. (1986). *Conflicting political ideas in liberal democracies.* Toronto: Methuen.

Rae, B. (1998). *The three questions: Prosperity and the public good.* Toronto: Penguin Canada.

Ranney, A. (2001). *Governing: An introduction to political science* (8th ed.). Upper Saddle River, NJ: Prentice-Hall.

Reed, R. (1994). *Politically incorrect: The emerging faith factor in American politics.* Nashville, TN: Word Publishing.

Remmer, K. (1996). The sustainability of political democracy: Lessons from South America. *Comparative Political Studies, 29*(6), 611–634.

Resnick, P. (1997). *Twenty-first century democracy.* Montreal: McGill-Queen's University Press.

Robinson, M. J. (1976). Public affairs television and the growth of political malaise: The case of "The Selling of the

Pentagon." *American Political Science Review, 70*(2), 409–432.

Roese, N.J. (2002). Canadians' shrinking trust in government: Causes and consequences. In N. Nevitte (Ed.), *Value Change and Governance in Canada* (pp. 149–163). Toronto: University of Toronto Press.

Roth, D.F., Warwick, P.V, & Paul, D.W. (1989). *Comparative politics: Diverse states in an interdependent world.* New York: Harper and Row.

Rourke, J.T. (2003). *International politics on the world stage* (9th ed.). Boston: McGraw-Hill.

Rousseau, J.-J. (1968). *The social contract* (M. Cranston, Trans.). Harmondsworth, UK: Penguin. (Original work published in 1762).

Rowe, F. (1980). *A History of Newfoundland and Labrador.* Toronto: McGraw Hill Ryerson.

Sabato, L. (1992). *Feeding frenzy: How attack journalism has transformed American politics.* New York: Free Press.

Sallot, J. (2004, March 27). Information commissioner wins access to documents. *Globe and Mail,* A11.

Sancton, A. (2002). Municipalities, cities, and globalization: Implications for Canadian federalism. In H. Bakvis &G. Skogstad (Eds.), *Canadian federalism: Performance, effectiveness, and legitimacy* (pp. 261–277). Don Mills, ON: Oxford University Press.

Sandbrook, R. (2003). Introduction: Envisioning a civilized globalization. In R. Sandbrook (Ed.), *Civilizing globalization: A survival guide.* Albany, NY: State University of New York Press.

Sater, W. (1990). *Chile and the United States: Empires in conflict.* Athens, GA: University of Georgia Press.

Saul, J.R. (1997). *Reflections of a Siamese twin: Canada at the end of the twentieth century.* Toronto: Penguin.

Savoie, D.J. (1999).*Governing from the centre: The concentration of power in Canadian politics.* Toronto: University of Toronto Press.

Savoie, D.J. (2003). *Breaking the bargain. Public servants, ministers and parliament.* Toronto: University of Toronto Press.

Scarrow, S.E. (2000). Parties without members? Party organization in a changing electoral environment. In R. J. Dalton and M.P. Wattenberg (Eds.), *Parties without partisans: Political change in advanced industrial democracies* (pp. 79–101). Oxford, UK: Oxford University Press.

Scarrow, S.E., Webb, P. & Farrell, D.M. (2000). From social integration to electoral contestation: The changing distribution of power within political parties. In R. J. Dalton and M.P. Wattenberg (Eds.), *Parties without partisans: Political change in advanced industrial democracies* (pp. 129–153). Oxford, UK: Oxford University Press, pp. 129–153.

Schedler, A. (2000). The democratic revelation. *Journal of Democracy, 11*(4), 5–19.

Schlesinger, A.E. (1973). *The imperial presidency.* Boston: Houghton Mifflin.

Schumpeter, J. (1943). *Capitalism, socialism and democracy.* New York: Harper & Row.

Schumpeter, J. (1950). *Capitalism, socialism, and democracy.* New York: Harper Row.

Scott, J. (2001). *Power.* Cambridge, UK: Polity Press.

SES Research (2004). *SES–CPAC poll conducted June 21–23, 2004.* Retrieved on August 16, 2000 from www.sesresearch.com/election/SES%20June%2024E.pdf.

Shaiko, R.G. (1999). *Voices and echoes for the environment: Public interest representation in the 1990s and beyond.* New York: Columbia University Press.

Shively, W.P. (2005). *Politics and choice: An introduction to political science* (9th ed.). Boston: McGraw-Hill.

Shub, D. (1966). *Lenin: A biography.* Baltimore, MD: Penguin Books.

Siebert, F., Peterson, T., & Schramm, W. (1956). *Four theories of the press.* Urbana, IL: University of Illinois Press.

Sigmund, P. (1993). *The United States and democracy in Chile.* Baltimore, MD: Johns Hopkins University Press.

Simeon, R. (1976). Studying public policy. *Canadian Journal of Political Science, 9*(3), 548–580.

Simeon, R., & Cameron, D. (2002). Intergovernmental relations and democracy: An oxymoron if there ever was one? In H. Bakvis & G. Skogstad (Eds.), *Canadian federalism: Performance, effectiveness, and legitimacy* (pp. 278–295). Don Mills, ON: Oxford University Press.

Simon, H.A. (1957). *Administrative behavior: A study of decision-making processes in administrative organization.* New York: Macmillan.

Simon, J.L., & Kahn, H. (1984). *The resourceful earth.* New York: Basil Blackwell.

Simpson, J. (2001). *The friendly dictatorship.* Toronto: McClelland & Stewart.

Smith, A. (2004). An inquiry into the nature and causes of the wealth of nations [excerpt]. In T. Ball & R. Dagger (Eds.), *Ideals and ideologies: A reader* (5th ed.) (pp. 104–106). New York: Pearson Education. (Original work published in 1776).

Smith, D. (1971). President and parliament: The transformation of parliamentary government in Canada. In T. Hockin (Ed.), *Apex of power: The prime minister and political leadership in Canada* (pp. 224–241). Scarborough, ON: Prentice-Hall.

Smith, G., & Wales, C. (2002). Citizens' juries and deliberative democracy. In M.P. D'Entrèves, (Ed.), *Democracy as public deliberation: New perspectives* (pp. 157–177). Manchester, UK: Manchester University Press.

Smith, J. (2000). The grass is always greener: Prime ministerial vs. presidential government. In D. Thomas (Ed.), *Canada and the United States: Differences that count* (2nd ed.) (pp. 229–247). Peterborough, ON: Broadview Press.

Sniderman, P.M., Fletcher, J.F., Russell, P.H., & Tetlock, P. (1996). *The clash of rights: Liberty, equality, and legitimacy in pluralist democracy.* New Haven: Yale University Press.

Spitz, D. (1965). *Patterns of anti-democratic thought.* New York: Free Press.

Statistics Canada (n.d.). *Number of employees, federal, provincial and territorial governments Canada, 1992, 1999, 2003.* Retrieved July 17, 2004 from www.statcan.ca/english/freepub/68-213-SIE/2004000/tables/table1.htm.

Statistics Canada (2004a). *Average hourly wages of employees by selected characteristics, profession, and by province.* Retrieved July 15, 2004 from www.statcan.ca/english/Pgdb/labour69g.htm.

Statistics Canada (2004b, June 23 [modified]). *Employment and average weekly earnings (including overtime), public administration and all industries.* Retrieved July 17, 2004 from www.statcan.ca/english/Pgdb/govt19a.htm.

Stephan, A., & Robertson, G.B. (2003). An "Arab" more than a "Muslim" electoral gap. *Journal of Democracy, 14*(3), 30–44.

Stewart, I. (2002). Vanishing points: Three paradoxes of political culture research. In J. Everitt & B. O'Neill (Eds.), *Citizen politics: Research and theory in Canadian political behaviour* (pp. 21–39). Don Mills, ON: Oxford University Press.

Strauss, L. (1945). On classical political philosophy. *Social Research, 12,* 98–117.

Sunderlin, W.D. (2003). *Ideology, social theory, and the environment.* Lanham, MD: Rowman & Littlefield.

Sutherland, S.L. (1991). The Al-Mashat affair: Administrative accountability in parliamentary institutions. *Canadian Public Administration, 34*(4), 573–577.

Sylvester, C. (1994). *Feminist theory and international relations in a postmodern era.* New York: Cambridge University Press.

Taras, D. (1990). *The newsmakers: The media's influence on Canadian politics.* Scarborough, ON: Nelson Canada.

Tarrow, S. (1999). *Power in movement: Social movements and contentious politics* Cambridge: Cambridge University Press.

Tessler, M. (2002). *Do Islamic orientations influence attitudes towards democracy in the Arab world? Evidence from Egypt, Jordan, Morocco, and Algeria.* Retrieved August 21, 2003 from www.worldvaluessurvey.org/Upload/5_TessIslamDem_2.pdf.

Thompson, D. (1984). *The Chartists.* New York: Pantheon.

Thorburn, H.G., & Whitehorn, A. (Eds.) (2001). *Party politics in Canada* (8th ed.). Toronto: Prentice-Hall.

Tindal, C.R., & Tindal, S.N. (2000). *Local government in Canada* (5th ed). Scarborough, ON: Nelson Canada.

Tocqueville, A. (2000). *Democracy in America* (H.C. Mansfield & D. Winthrop, Trans. & Ed.). Chicago: University of Chicago Press. (Original work published in 1835.)

Treasury Board Secretariat (2004, March 8 [modified]). *Employment equity in the federal public service, 2002–2003.* Retrieved July 17, 2004 from www.tbs-sct.gc.ca/report/empequi/2003/ee05_e.asp#Tables.

Turcotte, A. (2001). Fallen heroes: Leaders and voters in the 2000 Canadian federal election. In J.H. Pammett, J.H., & C. Dornan (Eds.), *The Canadian general election of 2000* (pp. 277–292). Toronto: Dundurn.

United Nations Development Programme (1995). Human development report, 1995. New York: Oxford University Press.

United Nations Development Programme (2002). Human development report, 2002. New York: Oxford University Press.

United Nations Development Programme (2003). Human development report, 2003. New York: Oxford University Press. [Available at http://hdr.undp.org/reports/global/2003.]

United Nations Environment Program (n.d.). *Greenhouse gas emission graphics.* Retrieved July 15, 2004 from the UNEP GRID-Arendal website, www.grida.no/db/maps/collection/climate6/canada.htm.

United Nations Global Teaching and Learning Project (n.d.). Retrieved July 11, 2004 from http://cyberschoolbus.un.org/infonation/index.asp.

Valaskakis, K. (2001, April 19). It's about world governance. *Globe and Mail,* A15.

Valiante, M. (2002). Legal foundations of Canadian environmental policy: Underlining our values in a shifting landscape. In D. L. VanNijnatten & R. Boardman (Eds.), *Canadian environmental policy: Context and cases* (2nd ed.) (pp. 3–24). Don Mills, ON: Oxford University Press.

Van Kersbergen, K., & Van Waarden, F. (2004). "Governance" as a bridge between disciplines: Cross-disciplinary inspiration regarding shifts in governance and problems of governability, accountability and legitimacy. *European Journal of Political Research, 43,* 143–171.

Verba, S, Nie, N., & Kim, J.O. (1978). *Participation and political equality.* New York: Cambridge University Press.

Wade, R. (1990). *Governing the market.* Princeton, NJ: Princeton University Press.

Walker, J.L. (1991). *Mobilizing interest groups in America: Patrons, professions, and social movements.* Ann Arbor, MI: The University of Michigan Press.

Wallerstein, I. (1974–1980). *The modern world system* (Vol. 1–2). New York: Academic Press.

Waltz, K. N. (1979). *Theory of international politics,* Reading, MA: Addison-Wesley.

Warner, C.M. (2000). *Confessions of an interest group: The Catholic Church and political parties in Europe.* Princeton, NJ: Princeton University Press.

Warren, M. (2002). Deliberative democracy. In A. Carter, & and G. Stokes (Eds.), *Democratic theory today: Challenges for the 21st century* (pp. 173–202). Cambridge, UK: Polity Press.

Watts, R.L. (1999). *Comparing federal systems* (2nd ed.). Montreal: McGill–Queen's University Press.

Watts, R.L. (2003). Managing interdependence in a federal state. In T.J. Courchene & D.J. Savoie (Eds.), *The art of the state: Governance in a world without frontiers* (pp.

121–151). Montreal: The Institute for Research on Public Policy.

Weale, A. (1992). *The new politics of pollution.* Manchester: Manchester University Press.

Weber, E. (1976). *Peasants into Frenchmen: The modernization of rural France, 1870–1914.* Stanford, CA: Stanford University.

Weber, M (1958). In H.H. Gerth & C.W. Mills (Eds. & Trans.), *Max Weber: Essays in sociology.* New York: Oxford University Press.

Weir, S., & Beetham, D. (1999). *Political power and democratic control in Britain.* London: Routledge.

Weller, P. (1985). *First among equals: Prime ministers in Westminster systems.* Sydney: George Allen & Unwin.

Wendt, A. (1999). *Social theory of international politics.* Cambridge: Cambridge University Press, 1999.

Whitaker, R. (1977). *The government party: Organizing and financing the Liberal party of Canada 1930–58.* Toronto: University of Toronto Press.

Whitaker, R. (1997). Canadian politics at the end of the millennium: Old dreams, new nightmares. In D. Taras, & B. Rasporich (Eds.), *A passion for identity: An introduction to Canadian studies* (3rd ed.) (pp. 119–137). Toronto: ITP Nelson.

Whitaker, R. (2002). The flight from politics. *Inroads, 11,* 187–202.

White, R. (1978). *Paraguay's autonomous revolution: 1810–1840.* Albuquerque: University of New Mexico Press.

Wilensky, H. (1975*). The welfare state and equality: Structural and ideological roots of public expenditure.* Berkeley, CA: University of California Press.

Willets, P. (1978). *The non-aligned movement: The origins of a Third World alliance.* London: Frances Pinter.

Wiseman, N. (2001). The pattern of prairie politics. In H.G. Thorburn & A. Whitehorn (Eds.), *Party politics in Canada* (8th ed.). Toronto: Pearson Education Canada.

Wolin, S.S. (1960). *Politics and vision: Continuity and innovation in Western political thought.* Boston: Little, Brown.

Wolinetz, S.B. (2002). Beyond the catch-all party: Approaches to the study of parties and party organization in contemporary democracies. In R. Gunther, J. R. Montero, & J.J. Linz (Eds.), *Political parties: Old concepts and new challenges* (pp. 136–165). Oxford: Oxford University Press.

Wood, G., & Sharit, I. (1997). *Who needs credit? Poverty and finance in Bangladesh.* London Zed Press.

World Bank (2002). *World development report, 2002.* Retrieved August 5, 2004 from www.worldbank.org/poverty/data/2_8wdi2002.pdf.

World Bank (2003). *World development report, 2003.* Washington: The World Bank.

World Bank (2004). *World development report, 2004.* Washington: The World Bank.

World Bank Group (n.d.). *HNP Statistics.* Retrieved July 17, 2004 from devdata.worldbank.org/hnpstats/AAgselection.asp.

World Commission on Environment and Development (1987). *Our common future.* Oxford: Oxford University Press.

World Values Survey (n.d.). [Combined data set for 1981, 1990, and 1995 surveys.]. Retrieved July 21, 2004 from www.worldvaluessurvey.org/services/index.html.

Yunus, M. (1999). *Banker to the poor: Micro-lending and the battle against world poverty.* New York: Public Affairs Press.

Zussman, D. (2002). Alternative service delivery. In C. Dunn (Ed.), *The handbook of Canadian public administration* (pp. 53–76). Don Mills, ON: Oxford University Press.

Zvesper, J. (1999). The separation of powers in American politics: Why we fail to accentuate the positive. *Government and Opposition, 34*(1), 3–23.

PHOTO CREDITS

INDEX